T0202903

Lecture Notes in Computer Science   14407

The series Lecture Notes in Computer Science (LNCS), including its subseries Lecture Notes in Artificial Intelligence (LNAI) and Lecture Notes in Bioinformatics (LNBI), has established itself as a medium for the publication of new developments in computer science and information technology research, teaching, and education.

LNCS enjoys close cooperation with the computer science R & D community, the series counts many renowned academics among its volume editors and paper authors, and collaborates with prestigious societies. Its mission is to serve this international community by providing an invaluable service, mainly focused on the publication of conference and workshop proceedings and postproceedings. LNCS commenced publication in 1973.

Huimin Lu · Michael Blumenstein ·
Sung-Bae Cho · Cheng-Lin Liu · Yasushi Yagi ·
Tohru Kamiya
Editors

Pattern Recognition

7th Asian Conference, ACPR 2023
Kitakyushu, Japan, November 5–8, 2023
Proceedings, Part II

Springer

Editors
Huimin Lu
Kyushu Institute of Technology
Kitakyushu, Fukuoka, Japan

Michael Blumenstein
The University of Sydney
Sydney, NSW, Australia

Sung-Bae Cho 🆔
Yonsei University
Seoul, Korea (Republic of)

Cheng-Lin Liu
Chinese Academy of Sciences
Beijing, China

Yasushi Yagi
Osaka University
Osaka, Ibaraki, Japan

Tohru Kamiya
Kyushu Institute of Technology
Kitakyushu, Japan

ISSN 0302-9743   ISSN 1611-3349 (electronic)
Lecture Notes in Computer Science
ISBN 978-3-031-47636-5   ISBN 978-3-031-47637-2 (eBook)
https://doi.org/10.1007/978-3-031-47637-2

This Springer imprint is published by the registered company Springer Nature Switzerland AG
The registered company address is: Gewerbestrasse 11, 6330 Cham, Switzerland

Paper in this product is recyclable.

Preface for ACPR 2023 Proceedings

Pattern recognition stands at the core of artificial intelligence and has been evolving significantly in recent years. These proceedings include high-quality original research papers presented at the 7th Asian Conference on Pattern Recognition (ACPR 2023), which was successfully held in Kitakyushu, Japan from November 5th to November 8th, 2023. The conference welcomed participants from all over the world to meet physically in beautiful Kitakyushu to exchange ideas, as we did in our past ACPR series of conferences. The conference was operated in a hybrid format allowing for both on-site and virtual participation. With all your participation and contributions, we believe ACPR 2023 was a special and memorable conference in history!

ACPR 2023 was the 7th conference of its series since it was launched in 2011 in Beijing, followed by ACPR 2013 in Okinawa, Japan, ACPR 2015 in Kuala Lumpur, Malaysia, ACPR 2017 in Nanjing, China, ACPR 2019 in Auckland, New Zealand, and ACPR 2021 in Jeju Island, South Korea. As we know, ACPR was initiated to promote pattern recognition theory, technologies and applications in the Asia-Pacific region. Over the years, it has actually welcomed authors from all over the world.

ACPR 2023 focused on four important areas of pattern recognition: pattern recognition and machine learning, computer vision and robot vision, signal processing, and media processing and interaction, covering various technical aspects.

ACPR 2023 received 164 submissions from 21 countries. The program chairs invited 141 program committee members and additional reviewers. Each paper was single blindly reviewed by at least two reviewers, and most papers received three reviews each. Finally, 93 papers were accepted for presentation in the program, resulting in an acceptance rate of 56.7%.

The technical program of ACPR was scheduled over four days (5–8 November 2023), including two workshops, four keynote speeches, and nine oral sessions.

The keynote speeches were presented by internationally renowned researchers. Tatsuya Harada, from University of Tokyo, Japan, gave a speech titled "Learning to reconstruct deformable 3D objects". Longin Jan Latecki, from Temple University, USA, gave a speech titled "Image retrieval by training different query views to retrieve the same database images". Jingyi Yu, Shanghai Tech University, China, gave a speech titled "Bridging recognition and reconstruction: Generative techniques on digital human, animal, and beyond". Mark Nixon, from University of Southampton, UK, gave a speech titled "Gait Biometrics – from then to now and the deep revolution".

Organizing a large event is a challenging task, requiring intensive teamwork. We would like to thank all members of the organizing committee for their hard work, with guidance from the steering committee. The program chairs, publication chairs, publicity chairs, workshop chairs, tutorial chairs, exhibition/demo chairs, sponsorship chairs, finance chairs, local organizing chairs, and webmaster all led their respective committees and worked together closely to make ACPR 2023 successful. Our special thanks go to the many reviewers, whom we cannot name one by one, for constructive comments to improve the papers. We thank all the authors who submitted their papers, which is the most important part of a scientific conference. Finally, we would like to acknowledge the student volunteers from our local organizers.

We hope this proceedings could be a valuable resource for the researchers and practitioners in the field of pattern recognition.

November 2023

Cheng-Lin Liu
Yasushi Yagi
Tohru Kamiya
Michael Blumenstein
Huimin Lu
Wankou Yang
Sung-Bae Cho

Organization

Steering Committee

Seong-Whan Lee   Korea University, South Korea
Cheng-Lin Liu   Chinese Academy of Sciences, China
Umapada Pal   Indian Statistical Institute, India
Tieniu Tan   Nanjing University, China
Yasushi Yagi   Osaka University, Japan

General Chairs

Cheng-Lin Liu   Chinese Academy of Sciences, China
Yasushi Yagi   Osaka University, Japan
Tohru Kamiya   Kyushu Institute of Technology, Japan

Program Chairs

Michael Blumenstein   University of Sydney, Australia
Huimin Lu   Kyushu Institute of Technology, Japan
Wankou Yang   Southeast University, China
Sung-Bae Cho   Yonsei University, South Korea

Publication Chairs

Yujie Li   Kyushu Institute of Technology, Japan
Xizhao Wang   Shenzhen University, China
Manu Malek   Stevens Institute of Technology, USA

Publicity Chairs

Jihua Zhu   Xi'an Jiaotong University, China
Limei Peng   Kyungpook National University, South Korea
Shinya Takahashi   Fukuoka University, Japan

Workshop Chairs

JooKooi Tan	Kyushu Institute of Technology, Japan
Weihua Ou	Guizhou Normal University, China
Jinjia Zhou	Hosei University, Japan

Tutorial Chairs

Shenglin Mu	Ehime University, Japan
Xing Xu	University of Electronic Science and Technology of China, China
Tohlu Matsushima	Kyushu Institute of Technology, Japan

Exhibition/Demo Chairs

Zongyuan Ge	Monash University, Australia
Yuya Nishida	Kyushu Institute of Technology, Japan
Wendy Flores-Fuentes	Universidad Autónoma de Baja California, Mexico

Sponsorship Chairs

Rushi Lan	Guilin University of Electronic Technology, China
Keiichiro Yonezawa	Kyushu Institute of Technology, Japan
Jože Guna	University of Ljubljana, Slovenia

Finance Chairs

Quan Zhou	Nanjing University of Posts and Telecommunications, China
Ainul Akmar Mokhtar	Universiti Teknologi Petronas, Malaysia
Shota Nakashima	Yamaguchi University, Japan

Local Organizing Chairs

Nobuo Sakai	Kyushu Institute of Technology, Japan
Naoyuki Tsuruta	Fukuoka University, Japan
Xiaoqing Wen	Kyushu Institute of Technology, Japan

Webmaster

Jintong Cai   Southeast University, China

Program Committee Members

Alireza Alaei	Shinya Takahashi
Noriko Takemura	Xing Xu
Yuchao Zheng	Weifeng Liu
Michael Cree	Kaushik Roy
Jingyi Wang	Quan Zhou
Cairong Zhao	Daisuke Miyazaki
Minh Nguyen	Byoungchul Ko
Huimin Lu	Sung-Bae Cho
Jinshi Cui	Yoshito Mekada
Renlong Hang	Kar-Ann Toh
Takayoshi Yamashita	Martin Stommel
Hirotake Yamazoe	Tohru Kamiya
Weiqi Yan	Xiaoqing Wen
Weihua Ou	Xiaoyi Jiang
Umapada Pal	Jihua Zhu
Wankou Yang	Michael Blumenstein
Shuo Yang	Andrew Tzer-Yeu Chen
Koichi Ito	Shohei Nobuhara
Qiguang Miao	Yoshihiko Mochizuki
Yirui Wu	Yasutomo Kawanishi
Jaesik Choi	Jinjia Zhou
Nobuo Sakai	Yusuyuki Sugaya
Songcan Chen	Ikuhisa Mitsugami
Sukalpa Chanda	Yubao Sun
Xin Jin	Dong-Gyu Lee
Masayuki Tanaka	Yuzuko Utsumi
Fumihiko Sakaue	Saumik Bhattacharya
Jaehwa Park	Masaaki Iiyama
Hiroaki Kawashima	Shang-Hong Lai
Hiroshi Tanaka	Shivakumara Palaiahnakote
Wendy Flores-Fuentes	Limei Peng
Yasushi Makihara	Jookooi Tan
Jože Guna	Shenglin Mu
Yanwu Xu	Zongyuan Ge
Guangwei Gao	Ainul Mokhtar
Rushi Lan	Shota Nakashima
Kazuhiro Hotta	Naoyuki Tsuruta

Chunyan Ma
Sung-Ho Bae
Gong Cheng
Sungjoon Choi
Andreas Dengel
Junyu Dong
Bo Du
Jianjiang Feng
Fei Gao
Hitoshi Habe
Tsubasa Hirakawa
Maiya Hori
Yoshihisa Ijiri
Kohei Inoue
Yumi Iwashita
Taeeui Kam
Kunio Kashino
Sangpil Kim
Jinkyu Kim
Hui Kong
Seong-Whan Lee
Namhoon Lee
Xuelong Li
Zhu Li
Zechao Li
Junxia Li
Jia Li
Qingshan Liu
Feng Lu
Jiayi Ma
Brendan Mccane
Tetsuro Morimoto

Hajime Nagahara
Masashi Nishiyama
Naoko Nitta
Kazunori Okada
Srikanta Pal
Partha Pratim Roy
Hong-Bin Shen
Atsushi Shimada
Xiangbo Shu
Heung-Il Suk
Jun Sun
Minhyuk Sung
Tomokazu Takahashi
Kenichiro Tanaka
Ngo Thanh Trung
Christian Wallraven
Qi Wang
Xiushen Wei
Yihong Wu
Haiyuan Wu
Guiyu Xia
Guisong Xia
Yong Xu
Junchi Yan
Keiji Yanai
Xucheng Yin
Xianghua Ying
Kaihua Zhang
Shanshan Zhang
Hao Zhang
Jiang Yu Zheng
Wangmeng Zuo

Contents – Part II

Bridging Distinct Spaces in Graph-Based Machine Learning

Linlin Jia[1]([✉]) [iD], Xiao Ning[2] [iD], Benoit Gaüzère[3] [iD], Paul Honeine[4] [iD],
and Kaspar Riesen[1] [iD]

[1] Institute of Computer Science, University of Bern, Bern 3012, Switzerland
linlin.jia@unibe.ch
[2] State Key Laboratory of Bioelectronics, School of Biological Science
and Medical Engineering, Southeast University, 2 Sipailou, Nanjing 210096,
People's Republic of China
[3] The LITIS Lab, INSA Rouen Normandie, Rouen, France
[4] The LITIS Lab, Université de Rouen Normandie, Rouen, France

Abstract. Graph-based machine learning, encompassing Graph Edit
Distances (GEDs), Graph Kernels, and Graph Neural Networks (GNNs),
offers extensive capabilities and exciting potential. While each model possesses unique strengths for graph challenges, interrelations between their
underlying spaces remain under-explored. In this paper, we introduce a
novel framework for bridging these distinct spaces via GED cost learning. A supervised metric learning approach serves as an instance of this
framework, enabling space alignment through pairwise distances and the
optimization of edit costs. Experiments reveal the framework's potential
for enhancing varied tasks, including regression, classification, and graph
generation, heralding new possibilities in these fields.

Keywords: Graph-based Machine Learning · Graph Spaces
Alignment · Graph Edit Distances (GEDs) · Metric Learning

1 Introduction

Graph structures have emerged as critical tools for tackling complex challenges
across a range of disciplines, including chemoinformatics [1], bioinformatics [2],
social network analysis [3], computer vision [4], and others. In these fields, intricate relationships can be elegantly represented through graphs, allowing a better
understanding and analysis of complex systems. The benefits of graph structures
are amplified when combined with machine learning techniques, paving the way
for a new era of data exploration and knowledge discovery. In particular, graph-
based machine learning techniques such as graph embedding strategies [5], graph
kernels [6,7], and Graph Neural Networks (GNNs) [8] have shown promise in

Supported by Swiss National Science Foundation (SNSF) Project No. 200021_188496.

H. Lu et al. (Eds.): ACPR 2023, LNCS 14407, pp. 1–14, 2023.
https://doi.org/10.1007/978-3-031-47637-2_1

their ability to harness the complexity and interconnectedness of graph structures. Benefiting from distinct designs and the ability to capture specific information, each of these techniques offer their unique strengths and perspectives when addressing graph-related challenges. However, despite the impressive performance of these models, there remains a critical gap in their application. Specifically, these models typically project the graph structure into different spaces, leading to the potential loss of valuable graph properties and operations, which, in turn, results in a disconnect between the graph space and the learning technique employed. On the other hand, as stated in [9], the use of metric distances, such as graph edit distances (GEDs), directly in a graph space is often practically insufficient, as they are seldom computationally tractable. This limit drives researchers to embed graphs into other spaces, which reduces the interpretability of the underlying operations. Moreover, the connections among these spaces themselves remain unrevealed, keeping the underlying theories and potential applications behind the mist.

To bridge this gap and to ensure the preservation of the essential properties and operations of the graph space, the concept of GED can be leveraged [10]. The key to GED's utility lies in its ability to operate directly within the graph space, maintaining the graph's structural integrity while enhancing the interpretability of operations. Additionally, GED allows for the direct construction of new graphs according to specific edit paths [11], further underscoring its applicability and usefulness. The successful application of GED necessitates the appropriate optimization of edit costs, which have a major impact on the computation of GED and its performance. As the values of edit costs may differ depending on the data encoded by the graph and tasks, methods for performing this crucial step are recently trending to a prosperity. Recognizing the need for an improved approach to bridge graph spaces, we take advantage of these methods and turn to a more comprehensive exploration of edit costs.

In this paper, we propose a novel framework designed to overcome the existing challenges of bridging graph spaces. This framework leverages cutting-edge optimization methods to effectively manage edit costs, thereby enhancing the applicability and efficiency of GED. The innovative nature of this framework goes beyond the integration of improved optimization methods. Its true value lies in its ability to serve as a unifying platform that bridges disparate graph spaces, bringing together the strengths of various graph learning models while addressing their shortcomings. This positions our framework as a promising solution that could advance graph-based machine learning, opening up new avenues for exploration and application in numerous fields.

The remainder of this paper is organized as follows: Sect. 2 discusses related work, including current methods for bridging graph spaces and existing approaches to edit cost learning. Section 3 presents our proposed framework, along with a detailed discussion of GEDs and an application of Supervised Metric Learning. Section 4 explores potential applications of the framework, followed by an examination of our experimental results in Sect. 5. Finally, we conclude with a summary of our findings and future work in Sect. 6.

2 Related Work

The study between distinct graph-based spaces keeps attracting the attention of researchers. In this paper we emphasize on spaces induced by GEDs, graph kernels, and GNNs. In [12], the random walk graph kernel is extended by the GEDs, where the latter is used to evaluate global matching information to guide the local similarity evaluation of the kernel. In [13], an approach is proposed to turn an existing dissimilarity measure (e.g. GED) into a similarity measure, thus construct graph kernels directly from GED. In [14], GED is applied to encode the cross information between treelets. In [15], the graph and graph kernel spaces are aligned through GED to conduct a pre-image problem. Meanwhile, GEDs and GNNs are often bounded by the optimization of edit costs or learning and redesign of edit distances [16].

Connections between graph kernels and GNNs have been established in recent work as well. Graph kernels have be applied in GNN settings as convolutional filters, first-layer representation selection, and pre-train strategies [17]. In converse, graph kernels designs inspired by GNNs are proposed as well [18]. Moreover, The equivalent expressiveness of 1-dimensional Weisfeiler-Leman graph isomorphism heuristic (1-WL) and GNNs are theoretically exhibited in [19].

Despite the thriving of the field, each proposed model operates only in specific spaces or with specific machine learning methods. Through the GED cost learning, however, a universal approach can be systematically established, operating on multiple graph-based spaces. Various edit cost choosing approaches have been proposed in the literature. Manual settings are the most straightforward approach, based on the knowledge on a given dataset/task [20]. To challenge these settings and adapt the method to situations without such prior knowledge, one can tune the edit costs by grid search. However, the time complexity of the GED computation and the number of edit costs restrict its usage. Another commonly-used strategy is to fit edit costs with a particular targeted property, generally a prediction target. This problem can be seen as a sub-problem of generalized metric learning, which consists in learning a dissimilarity (or similarity) measure given a training set composed of data instances and associated targeted properties. In contrast to a valid metric, a generalized metric or a pseudometric (e.g. GED), does not strictly adhere to at least one of the following conditions: non-negativity, identity of indiscernibles, symmetry, positive definiteness, and triangle inequality [21]. For the sake of brevity, we use the term "metric" to denote "generalized metric" in this paper.

One set of strategies is based on a probabilistic approach [22]. By providing a probabilistic formulation for the common edition of two graphs, an Expectation-Maximization algorithm is used to derive weights applied to each edit operation. The tuning is then evaluated in an unsupervised manner. However, this approach is computationally too expensive when dealing with general graphs [23]. Another class of strategies optimizes edit costs by maximizing the similarity between the computed mapping and a ground-truth mapping between the vertices of the graphs [24]. This framework thus requires a ground truth mapping, which is not available on most datasets such as the ones in the chemoinformatics domain. To address this shortcoming, multiple supervised strategies are proposed. In [25], the edit costs are optimized by minimizing the difference between the GED and the distances between the prediction targets. While in [26], genetic algorithms are applied to optimize the costs for classification tasks.

3   Proposed Framework

In this section, we propose first a general framework bridging graph-based spaces through Graph Edit Cost Learning (GECL), and then an instance of this framework taking advantage of supervised metric learning. With these details, we validate GECL's innovations in cost learning and graph embedding spaces bridging, highlighting its versatile applications.

3.1   Graph Edit Distances and Edit Costs

To introduce the GECL framework, we first introduce the necessary preliminaries of the graph edit distances (GEDs). The GED between two graphs is defined as the minimal cost associated with an optimal edit path. Given two graphs $G_1 = (V_1, E_1)$ and $G_2 = (V_2, E_2)$, an edit path between them is defined as a sequence of edit operations transforming G_1 into G_2. An edit operation e can correspond to an insertion, removal, or substitution of vertices or edges. Each edit operation is associated with a cost characterizing the distortion induced by this edit operation on the graph. These costs can be encoded by a cost function $c(e)$ that associates a non-negative real value to each edit operation, depending on the elements being transformed. The total cost of an edit path π is the sum of the costs of all edit operations in the path: $c(\pi) = \sum_{e \in \pi} c(e)$. Then, the GED between G_1 and G_2 is defined as the minimum cost associated with any possible edit path: $\mathsf{ged}(G_1, G_2) = \min_{\pi \in \Pi(G_1, G_2)} c(\pi)$, where $\Pi(G_1, G_2)$ denotes the set of all possible edit paths from G_1 to G_2. The computation of the exact GED is a NP-hard problem [21]. In practice, a sub-optimal approximation algorithm is often used and a cost matrix C is often defined for the edit operations. Then the task of GED computation can be formulated as an optimization problem that minimizes the total edit cost:

$$\min_{\pi \in \Pi(G_1, G_2)} \sum_{e \in \pi} C_e. \tag{1}$$

In the case of G_1 and G_2, the cost matrix C is expressed as:

$$C = \begin{bmatrix} C_s & C_{r_{G_1}} \\ C_{i_{G_2}} & 0 \end{bmatrix} \tag{2}$$

where:

- C_s is the $n_1 \times n_2$ substitution cost matrix with elements $C_{s_{ij}} = c_s(v_{i_{G_1}}, v_{j_{G_2}})$, i.e., the cost of substituting node $v_{i_{G_1}}$ in G_1 with node $v_{j_{G_2}}$ in G_2.
- $C_{r_{G_1}}$ is the $n_1 \times n_1$ matrix with diagonal elements $C_{r_{G_{1_{ii}}}} = c_r(v_{i_{G_1}})$, i.e., the cost of removing node $v_{i_{G_1}}$ in G_1; the off-diagonal elements are set to ∞.

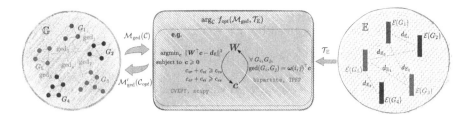

Fig. 1. The GECL Framework.

- $C_{i_{G_2}}$ is the $n_2 \times n_2$ matrix with diagonal elements $C_{i_{G_{2jj}}} = c_i(v_{j_{G_2}})$, i.e., the cost of inserting node $v_{j_{G_2}}$ in G_2, and off-diagonal elements are set to ∞.

Thus, the matrix C represents all possible edit operations and their associated costs, which are utilized in calculating the GED.

3.2 The GECL Framework

The cost matrix C plays an important role in GEDs, actively affecting its computation and performance, thus reshaping the structure of the underlying graph space. Taking advantage of this merit, we propose the GECL framework, and formalize it as follows (See Fig. 1):

We define a space of graphs $\mathbb{G}$ as all possible graphs whose vertex and edge labels are defined by a label alphabet of a domain. Given a dataset $\mathcal{G} \subset \mathbb{G}$ of N graphs such that each graph $G_k = (V_k, E_k)$, for $k = 1, 2, \ldots, N$, we define the set of pairwise GED $\mathcal{M}_{\mathbf{ged}} = \{\mathbf{ged}(G_i, G_j, C_{ij}) \mid i, j \in 1, 2, \ldots, N\}$ as a metric associated with space $\mathbb{G}$. Meanwhile, we define a target measurement $\mathcal{T}_{\mathbb{E}}$ associated with an embedding space $\mathbb{E}$. The GECL framework aims at aligning the two spaces by optimizing a target function f_{opt}. The problem can then be formalized as

$$\arg_{\mathcal{C}} \; f_{opt}(\mathcal{M}_{\mathbf{ged}}, \mathcal{T}_{\mathbb{E}}), \tag{3}$$

where $\mathcal{C} = \{C_{ij} \mid i, j \in 1, 2, \ldots, N\}$ is the set of cost matrices between all pairs of graphs. After optimizing $\mathcal{C}$, the GEDs are recomputed accordingly.

The measurement $\mathcal{T}_{\mathbb{E}}$ and the target function f_{opt} endow the possibility of varied forms. Given $\mathcal{T}_{\mathbb{E}}$ the distances between prediction targets or ground truths, many edit costs optimization strategies fall into this framework, including the ones introduced in Sect. 2 (e.g., [26]). In the next section, we take advantage of a supervised metric learning strategy in [25] and define an instance of the framework.

3.3 GECL Based on Supervised Metric Learning

In many applications, the cost functions are restricted to constants, namely, each type of edit operation is associated to a constant value. Let c_{vs}, c_{vi}, c_{vr}, c_{es}, c_{ei}, $c_{er} \in \mathbb{R}$ be the cost values associated with vertex and edge substitutions, insertions, removals, respectively. The cost associated with edit operations of an edit path represented by π is given by:

$$C(\pi, G_1, G_2) = C_v(\pi, G_1, G_2) + C_e(\pi, G_1, G_2), \qquad (4)$$

where $C_v(\pi, G_1, G_2)$ is the cost associated with vertex operations, namely

$$C_v(\pi, G_1, G_2) = \sum_{\substack{v \in V_2 \\ \pi^{-1}(v) = \varepsilon}} c_{vi} + \sum_{\substack{v \in V_1 \\ \pi(v) = \varepsilon}} c_{vr} + \sum_{\substack{v \in V_1 \\ \pi(v) \neq \varepsilon}} c_{vs}, \qquad (5)$$

and $C_e(\pi, G_1, G_2)$ is the one associated with edge operations, namely

$$C_e(\pi, G_1, G_2) = \sum_{\substack{e=(v_i,v_j) \in E_2| \\ \pi^{-1}(v_i)=\varepsilon \vee \\ \pi^{-1}(v_j)=\varepsilon \vee \\ (\pi^{-1}(v_i),\pi^{-1}(v_j)) \notin E_1}} c_{ei} + \sum_{\substack{e=(v_i,v_j) \in E_1| \\ \pi(v_i)=\varepsilon \vee \\ \pi(v_j)=\varepsilon \vee \\ (\pi(v_i),\pi(v_j)) \notin E_2}} c_{er} + \sum_{\substack{e=(v_i,v_j) \in E_1| \\ \pi(v_i) \neq \varepsilon \wedge \\ \pi(v_j) \neq \varepsilon \wedge \\ (\pi(v_i),\pi(v_j)) \in E_2}} c_{es}. \qquad (6)$$

Let $n_{vs} = |\{v_i \in V_1 \mid \pi(v_i) \neq \varepsilon\}|$ be the number of vertex substitutions, that is, the cardinality of the subset of V_1 being mapped onto V_2. Similarly:

- The number of vertex removals is $n_{vr} = |\{v_i \in V_1 \mid \pi(v_i) = \varepsilon\}|$;
- The number of vertex insertions is $n_{vi} = |\{v_i \in V_2 \mid \pi^{-1}(v_i) = \varepsilon\}|$;
- The number of edge substitutions is $n_{es} = |\{e = (v_i, v_j) \in E_1 \mid \pi(v_i) \neq \varepsilon \wedge \pi(v_j) \neq \varepsilon \wedge (\pi(v_i), \pi(v_j)) \in E_2\}|$;
- The number of vertex removals is $n_{ei} = |\{e = (v_i, v_j) \in E_1 \mid \pi(v_i) = \varepsilon \vee \pi(v_j) = \varepsilon \vee (\pi(v_i), \pi(v_j)) \notin E_2\}|$;
- The number of vertex insertions is $n_{er} = |\{e = (v_i, v_j) \in E_2 \mid \pi^{-1}(v_i) = \varepsilon \vee \pi^{-1}(v_j) = \varepsilon \vee (\pi^{-1}(v_i), \pi^{-1}(v_j)) \notin E_1\}|$.

Then, define $\mathbf{x} = [n_{vi}, n_{vr}, n_{vs}, n_{ei}, n_{er}, n_{es}]^\top \in \mathbb{N}^6$ to represent the count of each edit operation. It is important to note that these values are dependent on both graphs under comparison as well as a specified vertex mapping. In a similar fashion, we create a vector representation $\mathbf{c} = [c_{vi}, c_{vr}, c_{vs}, c_{ei}, c_{er}, c_{es}]^\top \in \mathbb{R}^6$ to represent the costs associated with each edit operation. With these vector representations, we can express the cost associated with an edit path, as defined by (4), in a compact form:

$$C(\pi, G_1, G_2, \mathbf{c}) = \mathbf{x}^\top \mathbf{c}. \qquad (7)$$

The GED between two graphs is consequently defined as:

$$\mathrm{ged}(G_1, G_2, \mathbf{c}) = \min_\pi C(\pi, G_1, G_2, \mathbf{c}). \qquad (8)$$

In this framework, we assume that each graph $G_k \in \mathcal{G}$ maps to a specific element, or "embedding", $f_\mathbb{E}(G_k)$ in an embedding space $\mathbb{E}$. Furthermore, a distance $d_\mathbb{E} : \mathbb{E} \times \mathbb{E} \to \mathbb{R}$ is defined over these embeddings. The core principle of this framework is that the most effective metric in the GED space aligns the most accurately with the distances within the embedded space (i.e., $d_\mathbb{E}$). Guided by this principle of distance preservation, we aim to determine the edit cost vector $\mathbf{c}$ by aligning the GEDs between graphs with the distances between their respective embeddings. It is then ideal to preserve the GED between any two graphs G_i and G_j and the distance between their embeddings (see Fig. 1). That is to say, given a set of N available graphs $G_1, \ldots, G_N$ and their corresponding embeddings $f_{\mathbb{E}_1}, \ldots, f_{\mathbb{E}_N}$, we seek to have

$$\mathbf{ged}(G_i, G_j, \mathbf{c}) \approx d_\mathbb{E}(f_{\mathbb{E}_1}, f_{\mathbb{E}_N}) \qquad \forall\, i, j = 1, 2, \ldots N. \tag{9}$$

Given any pairs of graphs $(G_i, G_j) \in \mathcal{G}$ and a cost vector $\mathbf{c}$, we can define $\mathbf{x}_{i,j} = \omega(G_i, G_j, \mathbf{c})$. Here, $\omega : \mathcal{G} \times \mathcal{G} \times \mathbb{R}_+^6 \to \mathbb{N}^6$ is the function that computes an optimal edit path between G_i and G_j according to $\mathbf{c}$, and the vector $\mathbf{x}_{i,j} \in \mathbb{R}_+^6$ denotes the numbers of edit operations associated with this optimal edit path. Function ω and vector $\mathbf{x}_{i,j}$ can be obtained by any method computing an exact or sub-optimal GED [27]. We further define a matrix $\mathbf{X} \in \mathbb{N}^{N^2 \times 6}$ to gather the numbers of edit operations for each pair of graphs, where $\mathbf{X}_{iN+j,:} = \mathbf{x}_{i,j}^T$. Namely, the $(iN + j)$-th row of $\mathbf{X}$ is $\mathbf{x}_{i,j}^T$. Consequentially, the product $\mathbf{Xc}$ is a $N^2 \times 1$ vector comprising of edit distances between all pairs of graphs computed according to $\mathbf{c}$ and $\mathbf{X}$. Let the vector $\mathbf{d} \in \mathbf{R}^{N^2}$ the differences on embeddings according to $d_\mathbb{E}$, where $\mathbf{d}(iN + j) = d_\mathbb{E}(f_{\mathbb{E}_i}, f_{\mathbb{E}_j})$. With these definitions, the optimization problem can be expressed as

$$\underset{\mathbf{c}}{\arg\min}\ \ \mathcal{L}(\mathbf{Xc}, \mathbf{d}) \qquad \text{subject to } \mathbf{c} > 0, \tag{10}$$

where $\mathcal{L}$ denotes a loss function and the constraint on $\mathbf{c}$ ensures non-negative costs. Besides this constraint, one can also integrate a constraint to satisfy the triangular inequality, or one to ensure that a removal cost is equal to an insertion cost [28].

By defining the loss function $\mathcal{L}$ as the mean square error between computed GEDs and dissimilarities between the embeddings, the optimization problem can be rewritten as:

$$\underset{\mathbf{c}}{\arg\min}\ ||\mathbf{Xc} - \mathbf{d}||_2^2 \qquad \text{subject to } \mathbf{c} > 0. \tag{11}$$

Solving this constrained optimization problem estimates $\mathbf{c}$ which allows to linearly fit GEDs to a specific target embedding space according to the edit paths initially given by ω. However, changes to the edit costs may affect the optimal edit path, and consequently its description in terms of the number of edit operations. This leads to an interdependence between the function ω computing an optimal edit path according to $\mathbf{c}$, and the objective function optimizing $\mathbf{c}$ according to edit paths encoded within $\mathbf{X}$. To address this interdependence, we propose an alternated optimization strategy, summarized in Algorithm 1.1 (See the example shown in Fig. 1). The two main steps of the algorithm are:

- **Estimate c for fixed X** (refer to line 4 in Algorithm 1.1): The given optimization issue is a constrained linear problem, which can also be viewed as

---

Algorithm 1.1 Optimization of constant edit costs according to given embeddings

---

1: $\mathbf{c} \leftarrow \text{random}(6)$
2: $\mathbf{X} \leftarrow [\omega(G_1, G_1, \mathbf{c}) \quad \omega(G_1, G_2, \mathbf{c}) \quad \cdots \quad \omega(G_N, G_N, \mathbf{c})]^\top$
3: **while** not converged **do**
4:    $\mathbf{c} \leftarrow \text{argmin}_{\mathbf{c}} ||\mathbf{Xc} - \mathbf{d}||_2^2, \text{subject to } \mathbf{c} > 0$
5:    $\mathbf{X} \leftarrow [\omega(G_1, G_1, \mathbf{c}) \quad \omega(G_1, G_2, \mathbf{c}) \quad \cdots \quad \omega(G_N, G_N, \mathbf{c})]^\top$
6: **end while**

---

a non-negative least squares problem [29]. This step linearly optimizes the constant costs for a specified set of edit operations between each graph pair, which is done by minimizing the difference between GEDs and the distances between their corresponding embeddings. Several readily available solvers can be used to tackle this problem, such as `CVXPY` [30] and `scipy` [31].

- **Estimate X for fixed c** (refer to line 5 in Algorithm 1.1): As discussed before, the changes made to costs in the preceding step may affect the associated edit path. To account for this, we follow up the cost optimization with a re-calculation of the optimal edit paths in line with the newly computed $\mathbf{c}$ vector which encodes the edit costs. Any method capable of computing GED can accomplish this step. For efficiency, one might opt for an approximated version of GED [27].

These optimization steps are alternately repeated to compute both edit costs and edit operations until the loss value no longer decreases or a iteration number limit is reached. Since the theoretical convergence proof of this optimization scheme has yet not been proposed, we limit the number of iterations to 5 in our implementation, which turns out to be sufficient in the conducted experiments.

The embeddings of the graphs and the distances between them may vary according to the embedded spaces. We consider the following embeddings in the rest of the paper:

- For a target space, the corresponding embeddings are the targets themselves. Since a target space $\mathbb{Y}$ is often a vector space, some off-the-shelf distances on $\mathbb{Y}$ are:
  - The *Euclidean* distance: $d_{\mathbb{Y}}(y_i, y_j) = ||y_i - y_j||_2$.
  - The *Manhattan* distance: $d_{\mathbb{Y}}(y_i, y_j) = ||y_i - y_j||_1$.
  we use the *Euclidean* distance in our experiments.
- For a graph kernel space $\mathcal{H}$, the distance between two elements $\phi(G_i)$ and $\phi(G_j)$ in $\mathcal{H}$ is

$$d_{\mathcal{H}}(\phi(G_i), \phi(G_j)) = \sqrt{k(G_i, G_i) + k(G_j, G_j) - 2k(G_i, G_j)}, \qquad (12)$$

where $k(G_i, G_j)$ is a graph kernel between graphs G_i and G_j.
- For GNNs, we construct the embedding space by extracting the activations before the last layer. As these embeddings are often vectors or tensors, we apply Euclidean and Manhattan distances to them as well.

4   Applications of the Framework

The proposed Graph Edit Cost Learning (GECL) framework promises applications on varied tasks:

Predictions: Leveraging the interrelated spaces in graph structures, GECL can potentially introduce knowledge learned by other machine learning models (e.g., graph kernels, GNNs), thus improving the predictability and accuracy of GED-based prediction models on both regression and classification tasks.

Graph Generation: With the learnt knowledge encoded in the edit costs, GECL can advance the generation of graphs. Specific areas of focus include median graph generation, which benefits from enhanced graph space understandability, and the pre-image problem, which benefits from the connection with the graph kernel space. Furthermore, the generation of Matching-Graphs [11] can be refined through the GECL framework, broadening its application scope.

Graph Matching Problems: GECL opens up new possibilities in addressing graph matching problems by providing a comprehensive view of the graph spaces. It may facilitate the detection and matching of similar patterns across disparate graphs, thereby enhancing the resolution of such problems.

Incorporation of Multi-level Information: the integration of the information at the node and graph level becomes more seamless with the GECL framework. A straightforward strategy would be to set the embedding space as the one of graph-level representations (e.g., vectors).

These potential applications foresee an exciting potential of powering the field of graph-based machine learning by the GECL framework.

5   Experiments

In this section, we exhibit the usage of our framework on two distinct applications: prediction tasks including regression and classification, and a graph pre-image generation task. First, we introduce the datasets used in the experiments.

5.1   Datasets

We conducted experiments[1] on benchmark datasets through multiple fields. Four datasets are evaluated for the regression problem: *Alkane* and *Acyclic* are molecule dataset associated with the boiling point prediction. *Redox* is the newly generated small molecule dataset aiming at predicting the Redox potential, where *Redox* ΔG_{red}^{PBE0} and *Redox* ΔG_{ox}^{PBE0} represent respectively the reduction

---

[1] https://github.com/jajupmochi/ged-cost-learn-framework/tree/master/.

Table 1. Results on each dataset in terms of RMSE for regression and accuracy (in %) for classification, measured on the test sets. The "-" notation indicate that the method is not suitable for the dataset.

Datasets	Random	Expert	Target	Path	Treelet	WLSubtree	GCN	GAT
Alkane	13.4±3.5	10.6±1.6	5.9±0.7	6.4±0.8	5.9±0.7	8.2±1.2	7.4±0.8	8.2±1.0
Acyclic	29.2±4.4	30.4±3.8	15.0±3.6	13.0±3.6	16.8±3.1	14.3±3.6	14.0±3.3	14.6±3.5
Redox ΔG_{red}^{PBE0}	25.3±9.5	36.2±13.3	24.8±7.0	20.1±5.8	19.4±5.5	22.1±6.2	26.1±6.4	21.0±6.0
Redox ΔG_{ox}^{PBE0}	24.4±7.1	40.0±11.5	26.8±10.1	26.4±6.1	25.8±7.8	26.7±6.3	28.5±8.4	26.9±7.8
MAO	80.0±9.9	74.3±10.6	80.0±13.8	81.4±9.7	81.4±10.8	84.3±7.5	84.3±7.5	87.1±10.2
PAH	69.0±11.4	71.0±9.2	68.0±8.1	68.0±7.4	74.0±6.0	71.0±10.9	67.0±11.2	68.0±6.6
MUTAG	80.0±7.1	81.6±6.2	78.9±6.6	82.6±6.2	84.7±5.5	81.1±6.7	80.0±5.8	80.5±5.9
Monoterpens	71.4±3.9	71.7±5.2	70.7±6.3	71.0±5.5	70.0±5.2	72.4±5.3	70.3±6.3	69.7±5.6
PTC_MR	56.3±7.1	56.0±4.4	59.4±4.7	55.7±6.0	55.1±5.8	60.0±3.2	57.4±8.3	54.0±5.4
Letter-high	84.3±8.7	84.3±2.4	91.8±0.9	90.1±2.1	–	–	82.6±1.2	82.6±1.2

and oxidation potential targets[2]. Six datasets associated with classification problems are considered. *MAO, PAH, MUTAG, Monoterpens*, and *PTC_MR* are chemical molecules associated with different classification problems. *Letter-high* involves graphs of highly distorted letter drawings where the task is to classify each graph to the proper letter. These datasets cover unlabeled graphs, graphs with discrete and continuous vertex attributes and edge attributes.

5.2 On Prediction Tasks

To evaluate the predictive power of GED empowered with knowledge of different target spaces, we used a k-nearest-neighbors regression model [32], where k is the number of the neighbors considered to predict a property. The performances are estimated on ten different random splits. For each split, a test set representing 10% of the graphs in the dataset is randomly selected and used to measure the prediction performance. A 5-fold cross-validation (CV) procedure is performed on the remaining 90%. Pairwise distances in the embedded space are computed on the training fold, and then the edit costs are optimized accordingly, and the value of k is optimized through the CV over the candidate values $\{3, 5, 7, 9, 11\}$. The number of iterations to optimize the edit costs is fixed to 5. The GEDs are estimated by the `bipartite` heuristics [27]. Three graph kernels (i.e., path kernel, treelet kernel, and WL-subtree kernel) and two GNNs (i.e., GCN and GAT) are applied to derive embeddings. The proposed optimization procedure is compared to two other edit costs settings: the first is a random set of edit costs; the second is a predefined cost setting given in [27], namely the so-called expert costs with $c_{vi} = c_{vr} = c_{ei} = c_{er} = 3$, $c_{vs} = c_{es} = 1$.

Table 1 shows the average root mean squared errors (RMSE) obtained for each cost settings over the 10 splits, estimated on the test set. The ± sign gives

---

[2] We thank the COBRA lab (Chimie Organique Bioorganique : Réactivité et Analyse) and the ITODYS lab (Le laboratoire Interfaces Traitements Organisation et DYnamique des Systèmes) for providing this dataset.

Table 2. Distances $d_{\mathbb{E}}$ in embedding spaces computed using different methods.

Embedding Spaces	From median set	Random costs	Expert costs	Optimized costs (ours)
Shortest Path (SP)	0.406	0.467	0.451	**0.460**
Structural SP (SSP)	0.413	0.435	0.391	**0.394**

the 95% confidence interval computed over the 10 repetitions. The first four datasets are associated with regression problems, where lower values indicate better results; while the remaining datasets are for classification tasks, with higher values indicating better performance. The best prediction for each dataset over all methods is marked green and bold. As expected, a clear and significant gain in accuracy is obtained by using the proposed framework to introduce knowledge from embedded spaces. Compared with using random and expert costs, the improvements can be up to 57% for regression problems and 17% for classification problems. Five best performances are achieved by treelet kernels, two by WL-subtree kernel, one by path kernel, one by GAT, and two directly on prediction targets. For regression problems, optimizing edit costs through prediction targets can achieve better results than random or expert costs in most cases. When embedded spaces are considered, further precision can be achieved. For classification problems, using prediction targets cannot optimize the edit costs in general. This is due to the fact that the targets (i.e., classes) are symbolic values and even boolean for binary classification. As a result, the corresponding distances have limited values (e.g., only one and zero in the case of binary classification). The only exception is on *Letter-high*, which may due the fact that there are 15 classes on this dataset, thus providing more information for the metric learning. Meanwhile, methods using random and expert costs are beaten by applying embedded spaces on all these data sets in accuracy. This promising result confirms the hypothesis that the edit cost optimized by embedded spaces can capture their underlying information, and thus improve the prediction accuracy while still operating in the graph space.

5.3   Graph Generations: A Pre-image Example

By fixing the embedding space as a kernel space, we align the distances in it and graph space as proposed in Sect. 3.3. The pre-image problem can then be recast as a graph generation problem [21]. We first optimize edit cost constants according to the embedded kernel space, and then we use these optimized edit costs, and take advantage of recent advances where the proposed iterative alternate minimization procedure (IAM) allows generating new graphs [33]. We choose the *Letter-high* dataset to show the potential of our method. Spaces derived from two graph kernels are chosen as the embedded spaces, namely the shortest path kernel and the structure shortest path kernel. The choice is made on the fact that these two graph kernels can tackle continuous vertex attributes. Notice that this specific application is already exhibited in our previous work [15], which serves here as an illustration of the capabilities of our framework.

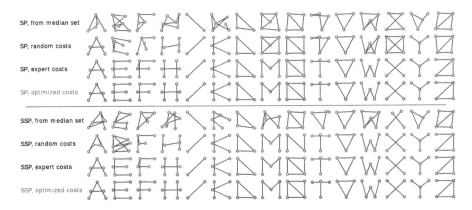

Fig. 2. Pre-images constructed by different algorithms for *Letter-high* with shortest path (SP) and structural shortest path (SSP) kernels.

Table 2 shows the distance $d_\mathbb{E}$ between generated graphs and the "true" median graphs in embedding spaces. "from median set" is a reference method which takes the set median graph from a graph set as the pre-image of its median. Our framework produces smaller or competitive $d_\mathbb{E}$ compared to other methods. Moreover, the advantage of our framework can be evaluated from a more intuitive aspect. Figure 2 presents the pre-images generated as the median graphs for each letter in the *Letter-high* dataset using the aforementioned methods, Vertices are drawn according to coordinates determined by their attributes "x" and "y". In this way, plots of graphs are able to display the letters that they represent, which are possible to be recognized by human eyes. When using the shortest path (SP) kernel (first to fourth rows), it can be seen that when the expert and optimized costs are used, almost all letters are readable, compared to the first two methods, despite that the pre-images of letter F are slightly different (the third and fourth rows). The same conclusion can be derived for the structure shortest path kernel as well (fifth to eighth rows). This analysis indicates that the proposed algorithms are able to generate better pre-images, especially when edit costs are optimized. It provides a "direction" to construct pre-images with respect to the features and structures of graphs. The experiment effectively showcases the capabilities of the GECL framework in handling graph generation tasks.

6   Conclusion and Future Work

In this paper, we proposed the GECL framework which combines the varied graph-based spaces. We showed that this framework has the potential to learn knowledge from embedded spaces by optimizing the edit costs of GEDs. A specific case based on supervised metric learning was proposed as an example to show the power of the framework. Experiments on two different tasks were performed, namely regression and classification predictions and the pre-image problem. Both results showed that the GECL framework outperforms the methods using predefined experts edit costs, bringing promising possibilities to these fields.

In this paper, we only exhibit a special example of the framework. While multiple state-of-the-art metric learning strategies and edit cost learning algorithms can be included in the framework, it would be interesting to tackle their abilities. Furthermore, as described in Sect. 4, exploring the application of the framework in more tasks would be a substantial work to do. Finally, we plan to seek out deeper underlying relationships between different graph-based spaces through a deep study of this framework.

References

1. Trinajstic, N.: Chemical Graph Theory. Routledge, New York (2018)
2. Yi, H.C., You, Z.H., Huang, D.S., Kwoh, C.K.: Graph representation learning in bioinformatics: trends, methods and applications. Brief. Bioinform. **23**(1), bbab340 (2022)
3. Tabassum, S., Pereira, F.S., Fernandes, S., Gama, J.: Social network analysis: an overview. Wiley Interdiscip. Rev. Data Min. Knowl. Discov. **8**(5), e1256 (2018)
4. Jiao, L., et al.: Graph representation learning meets computer vision: a survey. IEEE Trans. Artif. Intell. **4**(1), 2–22 (2022)
5. Goyal, P., Ferrara, E.: Graph embedding techniques, applications, and performance: a survey. Knowl.-Based Syst. **151**, 78–94 (2018)
6. Kriege, N.M., Johansson, F.D., Morris, C.: A survey on graph kernels. Appl. Netw. Sci. **5**(1), 1–42 (2020)
7. Jia, L., Gaüzère, B., Honeine, P.: Graph kernels based on linear patterns: theoretical and experimental comparisons. Expert Syst. Appl. **189**, 116095 (2022)
8. Zhou, J., et al.: Graph neural networks: a review of methods and applications. AI Open **1**, 57–81 (2020)
9. Grattarola, D., Zambon, D., Livi, L., Alippi, C.: Change detection in graph streams by learning graph embeddings on constant-curvature manifolds. IEEE Trans. Neural Netw. Learn. Syst. **31**(6), 1856–1869 (2019)
10. Bunke, H., Allermann, G.: Inexact graph matching for structural pattern recognition. Pattern Recogn. Lett. **1**(4), 245–253 (1983)
11. Fuchs, M., Riesen, K.: A novel way to formalize stable graph cores by using matching-graphs. Pattern Recogn. **131**, 108846 (2022)
12. Neuhaus, Michel, Bunke, Horst: A random walk kernel derived from graph edit distance. In: Yeung, Dit-Yan., Kwok, James T.., Fred, Ana, Roli, Fabio, de Ridder, Dick (eds.) SSPR /SPR 2006. LNCS, vol. 4109, pp. 191–199. Springer, Heidelberg (2006). https://doi.org/10.1007/11815921_20
13. Neuhaus, M., Bunke, H.: Bridging the Gap Between Graph Edit Distance and Kernel Machines, vol. 68. World Scientific, Singapore (2007)
14. Gaüzère, B., Brun, L., Villemin, D.: Graph kernels: crossing information from different patterns using graph edit distance. In: Gimel'farb, G., et al. (eds.) SSPR /SPR 2012. LNCS, vol. 7626, pp. 42–50. Springer, Heidelberg (2012). https://doi.org/10.1007/978-3-642-34166-3_5
15. Jia, L., Gaüzère, B., Honeine, P.: A graph pre-image method based on graph edit distances. In: Proceedings of the IAPR Joint International Workshops on Statistical Techniques in Pattern Recognition (SPR) and Structural and Syntactic Pattern Recognition (S+SSPR), Venice, Italy, 21–22 January 2021

16. Riba, P., Fischer, A., Lladós, J., Fornés, A.: Learning graph edit distance by graph neural networks. Pattern Recogn. **120**, 108132 (2021)

17. Feng, A., You, C., Wang, S., Tassiulas, L.: KerGNNs: interpretable graph neural networks with graph kernels. In: Proceedings of the AAAI Conference on Artificial Intelligence, vol. 36, pp. 6614–6622 (2022)

18. Du, S.S., Hou, K., Salakhutdinov, R.R., Poczos, B., Wang, R., Xu, K.: Graph neural tangent kernel: fusing graph neural networks with graph kernels. In: Advances in Neural Information Processing Systems, vol. 32 (2019)

19. Morris, C., et al.: Weisfeiler and leman go neural: higher-order graph neural networks. In: Proceedings of the AAAI Conference on Artificial Intelligence, vol. 33, pp. 4602–4609 (2019)

20. Riesen, K., Bunke, H.: IAM graph database repository for graph based pattern recognition and machine learning. In: da Vitoria Lobo, N., et al. (eds.) SSPR /SPR 2008. LNCS, vol. 5342, pp. 287–297. Springer, Heidelberg (2008). https://doi.org/10.1007/978-3-540-89689-0_33

21. Jia, L.: Bridging graph and kernel spaces: a pre-image perspective. Ph.D. thesis, Normandie (2021)

22. Neuhaus, M., Bunke, H.: A probabilistic approach to learning costs for graph edit distance. Proc. ICPR **3**(C), 389–393 (2004)

23. Bellet, A., Habrard, A., Sebban, M.: Good edit similarity learning by loss minimization. Mach. Learn. **89**(1–2), 5–35 (2012)

24. Cortés, X., Conte, D., Cardot, H.: Learning edit cost estimation models for graph edit distance. Pattern Recogn. Lett. **125**, 256–263 (2019). https://doi.org/10.1016/j.patrec.2019.05.001

25. Jia, L., Gaüzère, B., Yger, F., Honeine, P.: A metric learning approach to graph edit costs for regression. In: Torsello, A., Rossi, L., Pelillo, M., Biggio, B., Robles-Kelly, A. (eds.) S+SSPR 2021. LNCS, vol. 12644, pp. 238–247. Springer, Cham (2021). https://doi.org/10.1007/978-3-030-73973-7_23

26. Garcia-Hernandez, C., Fernández, A., Serratosa, F.: Learning the edit costs of graph edit distance applied to ligand-based virtual screening. Curr. Top. Med. Chem. **20**(18), 1582–1592 (2020)

27. Abu-Aisheh, Z., et al.: Graph edit distance contest: results and future challenges. Pattern Recogn. Lett. **100**, 96–103 (2017)

28. Riesen, K.: Structural Pattern Recognition with Graph Edit Distance. ACVPR, Springer, Cham (2015). https://doi.org/10.1007/978-3-319-27252-8

29. Lawson, C.L., Hanson, R.J.: Solving Least Squares Problems. SIAM, Philadelphia (1995)

30. Diamond, S., Boyd, S.: CVXPY: a python-embedded modeling language for convex optimization. J. Mach. Learn. Res. **17**(1), 2909–2913 (2016)

31. Virtanen, P., et al.: SciPy 10: fundamental algorithms for scientific computing in python. Nat. Methods **17**(3), 261–272 (2020)

32. Altman, N.S.: An introduction to kernel and nearest-neighbor nonparametric regression. Am. Stat. **46**(3), 175–185 (1992)

33. Boria, N., Bougleux, S., Gaüzère, B., Brun, L.: Generalized median graph via iterative alternate minimizations. In: Conte, D., Ramel, J.-Y., Foggia, P. (eds.) GbRPR 2019. LNCS, vol. 11510, pp. 99–109. Springer, Cham (2019). https://doi.org/10.1007/978-3-030-20081-7_10

A New Contrastive Learning Based Model for Estimating Degree of Multiple Personality Traits Using Social Media Posts

Kunal Biswas[1], Palaiahnakote Shivakumara[2(✉)], Umapada Pal[3], and Ram Sarkar[1]

[1] Jadavpur University, Kolkata, India
`ram.sarkar@jadavpuruniversity.in`
[2] Faculty of Computer Science and Information Technology, University of Malaya,
Kula Lumpur, Malaysia
`shiva@um.edu.my`
[3] Computer Vision and Pattern Recognition Unit, Indian Statistical Institute, Kolkata, India
`umapada@isical.ac.in`

Abstract. Estimating the degree of multiple personality traits in a single image is challenging due to the presence of multiple people, occlusion, poor quality etc. Unlike existing methods which focus on the classification of a single personality using images, this work focuses on estimating different personality traits using a single image. We believe that when the image contains multiple persons and modalities, one can expect multiple emotions and expressions. This work separates given input images into different faces of people, recognized text, meta-text and background information using face segmentation, text recognition and scene detection techniques. Contrastive learning is explored to extract features from each segmented region based on clustering. The proposed work fuses textual and visual features extracted from the image for estimating the degree of multiple personality traits. Experimental results on our benchmark datasets show that the proposed model is effective and outperforms the existing methods.

Keywords: Scene text · Contrastive Learning · Text appearance · Sentiment analysis · Image personality traits

1 Introduction

Personality traits identification is a vital issue in the everyday life of the person such as the results of elections and verdicts of courts [1]. In addition, it can also be used to find leader, assess student performance, interview and selection of students for research or jobs or defense [2]. For all the above applications, it is necessary to estimate the degree of different personality traits in the images. This is because multiple personality traits, like multiple skills, such as agreeableness, openness, and conscientiousness are required to choose suitable candidates especially for hiring software employees and research. At the same time, a few applications may look for particular personality traits irrespective of the degree of personality traits like finance, management, security jobs etc. It is also true

H. Lu et al. (Eds.): ACPR 2023, LNCS 14407, pp. 15–29, 2023.
https://doi.org/10.1007/978-3-031-47637-2_2

that if we look at the facial or posture, pose and background information of the person in the case of images and multiple words in the text lines, one can observe multiple personality traits rather than a single personality trait.

It is illustrated in Fig. 1, where we can see for each image, different personality traits according to textual, facial and background information. For example, (i) Openness: From the image, we can see a creative mask being worn for an ID photo which indicates the openness to experience trait. Also, from the text, the word "*new*" is recognized, which also indicates the openness class, which is the dominant trait. Also, from the dark imagery and the intention of hiding the face, we can infer high traits of neuroticism from the image. (ii) Conscientiousness: The text recognized contains the word "*educate*" which is an indicator of class conscientiousness, which is the dominant trait. We can also infer the trait of agreeableness due to the inference of the words "*reduce poverty*". (iii) Extraversion: The image shows a huge gathering of people all with happy faces and enjoying themselves. This is highly indicative of the trait of extraversion. We can also see that none of the other traits is high in this image. (iv) Agreeableness: The image shows a sympathetic person and the text recognized contains the word "*sorry*" which are both indicative of the trait of agreeableness, which is dominant here. (v) Neuroticism: The image shows a man hiding in dark clothing and the text recognized contains "*madness*". Also, the text infers that a person must not lose their madness which is very indicative of mental instability and the trait neuroticism, which is dominant here.

Therefore, one can infer that for better solutions and decisions, assessing and estimating the degree of multiple personality traits from a single image is vital for many day-to-day situations. For personality traits identification, several methods have been developed in the past using facial information [1], handwritten text information [3], normal text uploaded on social media information [4], and profile information, which provides multimodal information [4]. Most methods aim at detecting single personality traits for the input image or text information. Similarly, if personality traits identification is considered as a classification problem, the methods developed for classification may not perform well for the images containing person, actions and postures etc. [5]. This is due to these models are limited to scene images. This observation has motivated us to introduce multiple personality traits identification in a single image through this work. To the best of our knowledge, this is the first of its kind work.

To localize the content in the image, the proposed work detects text in the images and segments words from the text line. We believe the meaning of text directly represents personality traits like facial information. Therefore, for each word, the proposed method obtains feature vectors. In addition, for the whole input image, the proposed work uses Google Cloud Vision API [6] to obtain labels (text annotations). Besides, if any text, like, the description of the image and profile picture, the proposed work obtains a feature vector. The feature vectors obtained from each word, annotations and description of the images are considered as textual features. To strengthen the feature extraction for personality traits identification, the proposed work segments the whole image into face and background clusters (other than the face and text information in the input image). The features extracted from the image content are called visual features. Finally, the model fuses textual and visual features for estimating multiple personality traits in a single image. Feature extraction from textual and image information is motivated by contrastive learning [7], which has special properties for representing visual and textual features. Then classification is done using an Artificial Neural Network (ANN) model by feeding feature vectors as inputs.

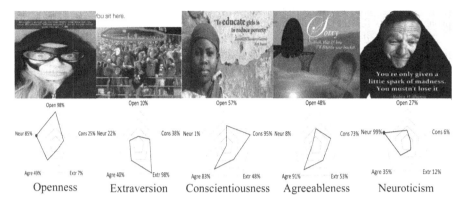

Fig. 1. Sample images with different degrees of personality traits assessments.

The main contributions of the work are as follows: (i) Proposing a new method to estimate multiple personality traits from a single image. (ii) Exploring contrastive learning for feature extraction from visual and textual features is novel here. (iii) The weighted approach for fusing visual and textual features for multiple personality traits estimation is also a novel contribution.

2 Related Work

For personality traits identification/assessment, in the past, many methods have been proposed based on normal text uploaded on social media, handwritten text with a graphological approach, facial information and image-text information. We review some of the methods in this section.

Kumar et al. [8] proposed a language embedding-based model for personality traits assessment using social network activities. The work considers the review or any text which describes personality traits uploaded on social media for personality traits assessment. Anglekar et al. [9] proposed a method based on deep learning for self-assessment, especially for interview preparations. Dickmond et al. [10] explored machine learning for extracting features from curriculum vitae to identify personality traits. It is noted from the above methods that the scope of the models is limited to textual information, and researchers ignored image information for personality traits identification. Therefore, these methods may not be effective for estimating the degree of different personality traits in a single image.

There are methods for personality trait identification using a graphology-based approach, which use handwritten characters to study the behavior of the writer [3, 11, 12]. Although, the models used image information, developed based on an unscientific approach. Therefore, the results of the modes may not be consistent and reliable for estimating the degree of different personality traits in the images.

To improve the performance of personality trait identification, some models used image and textual information [3, 13, 14]. For example, Sun et al. [2] developed a method to evaluate the aptitude and entrance psychological aspects of the students. The approach extracts features from the facial region for assessing personality traits. Beyan et al. [15] extracted non-verbal features from key dynamic images for personality trait identification. The combination of convolutional and long short-term memory models has been proposed for improving performance of the personality traits identification. Xu et al. [16] proposed a model for predicting five personality traits using static facial images and different academic backgrounds. For a given input video frame, Ventura et al. [1] estimated the degree of different personality traits. This model requires a still frame, multiple frames and audio to achieve the best results. Therefore, this model may not perform well for a single image.

Since sentiment analysis is related to personality traits identification, we review the methods of sentiment analysis to show that the methods are not effective for estimating degree of personality traits. For instance, Yu et al. [17] proposed a transformer-based based step to fuse image and text modalities with self-attention layers for sentiment analysis. Thus, estimating the degree of multiple personality traits for a given input image remains challenging. Hence, this work focuses on developing a new model based on segmented local information and contrastive learning for assessing multiple personality traits in the image.

3   Proposed Model

For a given input image, the proposed method segments facial and textual regions and considers other than textual and facial information as background. It is true that each segment provides cues of different personality traits if the image contains multiple people with emotions, expressions and actions. Therefore, this work segments the text using Google Cloud Vision API, face using the Haar cascades algorithm [18]. For the background, the method uses the Google Cloud Vision API for obtaining labels. In the same way, for the detected text and description of the image/profile, this work uses Google Cloud Vision API for obtaining recognition results.

Overall, the Google Cloud Vision API provides recognition results for the text in the image, description of the image, and background scene of the image, which are grouped as textual information, and facial information as visual information. For extracting features from textual and facial information, inspired by the success of contrastive learning for discriminating the objects based on similarity and dissimilarity [6], we explore the same for feature extraction process in this work. The extracted features are fused for estimating multiple degrees of personality traits in the image through five individual neural network regression models. The pipeline of the proposed method can be seen in Fig. 2. For a given input image, the work segments parts for feature extraction are represented as defined in Eq. (1).

$$I_S = T_R + T_A + T_B + I_F \tag{1}$$

where, I_S stands for sample image, T_R stands for text recognized, T_A stands for annotated text, T_B stands for background scene text and I_F stands for facial part. The face is detected using the Haar Cascades algorithm [18], which works based on the sum of the pixel intensities in each region and the differences between the sums. The process is performed in a cascading fashion. The extracted features are then supplied to a machine-learning algorithm for face detection. The detected face and text information is removed from the input image and replaced with a black rectangular patch. This results in a background image as defined in Eq. (2).

$$I_B = I_S - I_F \tag{2}$$

where, I_B is the background image. The background image is fed to the recognizer (Google Cloud Vision API) to determine labels.

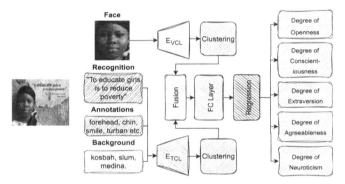

Fig. 2. Block diagram of the proposed method used to estimate the degree of multiple personality traits. The face, text recognition, annotation and background are extracted from the sample image and encoded. Then clustering and fusion steps followed by regression are done to estimate the degree of personalities.

3.1 Contrastive Learning for Textual Feature Extraction

This work considers three types of texts for each sample. Firstly, text recognized from the image is obtained using Google Cloud Vision API [6]. Secondly, image annotations from the sample image are obtained again using [6]. Only the top ten most confident annotations are taken into consideration. Thirdly, background scenes are recognized using ResNet18 [19] which has been trained on the Places dataset [20]. This dataset has 10 million images comprising 400+ unique scene categories. From this model, we choose the top 10 highest confidence scene categories as the background scenes. While assessing the personality traits, the personality trait with the highest degree is known as the dominant personality trait. All texts obtained from the previous step are compiled into a corpus with the text parts as individual documents and the dominant personality trait as the document label.

The text within the corpus is then used to train the representation space. This is done using contrastive learning. A pair of text from the same class labels is taken and fed through a neural network to get a pair of outputs. The similarity score between the pair of outputs from the neural network is calculated using Eq. (3). In another instance a pair of text from two different classes is taken and fed through the same neural network. Again, the similarity score between these outputs is calculated using Eq. (3). Finally, the loss is calculated using Eq. (4). This loss is propagated backwards to the network learns to optimize the loss. This output space of the learned neural network is known as the textual representation space. A pair of texts with different labels repel each other as they are contrastive samples, whereas similar labels attract each other. This is done using NT-Xent loss. This loss uses a similarity function.

$$sim(t_a, t_b) = \frac{t_a^T t_b}{\|t_a\| \|t_b\|} \tag{3}$$

where t_a represents text part a and t_b represents textual part b, t_a^T is the transpose of t_a and $\|t_a\|$ represents the norm of t_a. NT-Xent Loss [6] is given by:

$$L_{a,b} = -\log \frac{e^{sim(t_a, t_b)/\tau}}{\sum_{k=1}^{2N} 1_{[k \neq i]} e^{sim(t_a, t_b)/\tau}} \tag{4}$$

where, $1_{[k \neq i]}$ is an indicator function evaluating to 1 iff $k \neq i$, and $sim(t_a, t_b)$ comes from Eq. (3). Hence minimizing this function in Eq. (4) over all pairs of attractive and repulsive pairs gives us a text representation space. Since there is a variable number of words, and a variable dimensional input to a neural network is not possible, there is a need to fix the number of dimensions. This is performed by clustering the words in the representation space into 10 clusters using K-means clustering. The clusters centroids from the representation space are then considered as the text embeddings. Separate text embeddings for text recognized annotations and background scenes each with 10 centroids are obtained. The value of 10 clusters is determined empirically. This process has been shown in Fig. 3.

$$E_R = TCLR(T_R), E_A = TCLR(T_A), E_B = TCLR(T_B) \tag{5}$$

where, T_R, T_A, and T_B are taken from Eq. (1), and $TCLR()$ is the Textual Contrastive Learning Representation function.

3.2 Contrastive Learning for Visual Feature Extraction

The sample image may contain many facial regions owing to multiple people in the same image. Motivation has been drawn from other visual learning models like [21]. These facial images are labelled according to their dominant personality traits. Now, the visual representation space for facial images is trained using contrastive learning in the same way. Similar to the textual counterpart, two facial images belonging to the same class are considered and supplied to a neural network. The similarity between the outputs is considered and loss is calculated. This loss is propagated back through the network to bring the facial images of same class closer. Facial images of varying classes are used further away with a pair of facial images from different classes. This results in learning visual representation space. Hence this framework can be used for both texts

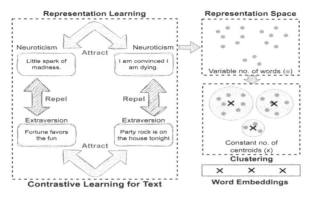

Fig. 3. Block diagram for word embeddings using contrastive learning. The recognized words from same class attract each other whereas, the recognized words from differing class repel each other.

as well as images. The same NT-Xent loss is used for training as shown in Eq. (4). This results in an image embedding for every facial image in the visual representation space. Again, there can be multiple people in a single image resulting in multiple facial image embeddings. To supply this to a neural network, the length of the embedding needs to be fixed. Again, clustering is used in the visual representation space on the facial images. K-means clustering has been used to find two cluster centroids. These are the facial image embeddings. The method has been shown in Fig. 4.

$$E_F = VCLR(I_F) \tag{6}$$

where, I_F is taken from Eq. (1) and $VCLR()$ is the Visual Contrastive Learning Representation function.

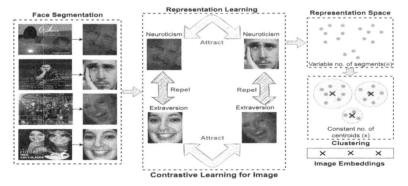

Fig. 4. Block diagram for image embeddings using contrastive learning. The recognized facial images from same class attract each other whereas, the recognized facial images from differing class repel each other.

3.3   Weighted Fusion and Estimating Degree of Personality Traits

In this step, the embeddings obtained in the previous step are fused to obtain the final feature vector F_v. This is performed using a weighted approach. The objective here is to assign the weights so that the features which are more discriminating are given priority. With this motivation, variance has been used as a metric that can evaluate the discriminating power of a feature. The embeddings of text recognized, annotation, background, and facial image are concatenated, and the variance is calculated. The embeddings of all the parts, other than the text recognized, is concatenated and variance is calculated, for calculating for the weightage of text recognized. Then the difference between these two variances is taken and the square root is the weightage of the text recognized and represented by E_R. This calculation has been shown in Eq. (7).

$$W_R = \sqrt{\left[\sigma^2(E_R \oplus E_A \oplus E_B \oplus I_F) - \sigma^2(E_A \oplus E_B \oplus I_F)\right]^2} \tag{7}$$

where, σ^2 is the variance, $\oplus$ stands for concatenation, E_R, E_A, and E_B come from Eq. (5), I_F comes from Eq. (6), and W_R is the weightage of text recognized. Similarly, the weightage of annotations, background scene text and facial image are calculated as follows:

$$W_A = \sqrt{\left[\sigma^2(E_R \oplus E_A \oplus E_B \oplus I_F) - \sigma^2(E_R \oplus E_B \oplus I_F)\right]^2} \tag{8}$$

where, W_A stands for the weightage of annotation. Similarly, W_B, and W_F, which are the weights of background and face respectively, are obtained using Eq. (8). The weightage of text recognition, W_R, is multiplied with the text recognized embedding, E_R to obtain the final weighted text recognition embedding. Similarly, weightage of annotation, W_A, is multiplied with annotation embedding, E_A, weightage of annotation background, W_B, is multiplied with background embedding, E_B, and weightage of facial images, W_F, is multiplied with facial embedding, E_F to obtain the respective final embeddings. These four embeddings are concatenated to obtain the final feature vector as shown in Eq. (9).

$$F_v = W_R \cdot E_R \oplus W_A \cdot E_A \oplus W_B \cdot E_B \oplus W_F \cdot E_F \tag{9}$$

where, F_v is the final feature vector. This process has been shown in Fig. 5.

The final feature vector F_v is supplied to five separate neural networks regression models as shown in Fig. 5 for classification. Each network has four hidden layers with 512, 256, 64, and 16 activation units with the rectified linear unit (ReLU) activation function [22]. The output layer has one unit. The loss function used is Mean Squared Error (MSE) [23] with Adam optimizer [24]. The batch size has been set to 32 with learning rates of 0.001. The training is run for 50 epochs for each neural network separately to obtain the predictions, as shown in Fig. 5.

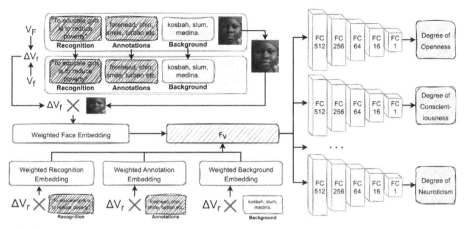

Fig. 5. Weighted fusion technique based on Variance and Estimating degree of personality traits. The representations are multiplied with their weightage and concatenated to form the final feature vector F_V. This F_V is then supplied to FC layers for estimating degrees of personality.

4 Experimental Results

Our dataset includes 5000 Twitter images that are collected from the source given in [25], which provides 559 Twitter user accounts and image posts. For all the collected images, the ground truth is generated via a questionnaire NEO-PI-R [26], which is a standard procedure used for psychological data collection. In the test, responses from the users are recorded for a given multiple questions, and the responses are measured on a Likert scale from 1–5. The weightage has been assigned according to the question. The average of weights is considered the actual label of a personality trait. This calculation results in fine-grained personality trait scores for each individual personality per image. To test the performance of the proposed method on a standard dataset, the PERS Twitter dataset [27] which is a considerably large dataset containing 28434 profile pictures, has been used.

To test the effectiveness of the proposed method, a comparison is done with the following state-of-the-art models. Biswas et al. [4], use a multimodal concept for personality traits identification using Twitter posts. Wu et al. [5], use vision transformers for the classification of images. Further, we also implemented the state-of-the-art method [17] developed for sentiment analysis to show that sentiment analysis method is ineffective for estimating degree of personality traits in the images. The existing methods are fine-tuned with the training sample as the proposed method for experimentation. The same setup is used for all the experiments. The ratio of 70:30 for training and testing is considered for all the experimentation.

For measuring the performance of the method, we use three standard metrics that are (i) Spearman's Correlation Coefficient, (ii) Pearson's correlation, and (iii) Root Mean Square Error (RMSE). Spearman's Correlation Coefficient: Spearman's correlation coefficient is a nonparametric measure of the rank correlation between two variables as defined in Eq. (10). A high value indicates better performance.

$$R_S = 1 - \frac{6\sum_{i=1}^{n}(t_i - p_i)}{n(n^2 - 1)} \qquad (10)$$

where, t_i is the ground truth value, p_i is the predicted value and n is the number of samples. Pearson's correlation coefficient: Pearson's correlation coefficient is the test statistic that measures the statistical relationship, or association, between two continuous variables. It is defined in Eq. (11). A high value indicates better performance.

$$R_P = \frac{n\sum t_i p_i - \sum t_i \sum p_i}{\sqrt{\left[n\sum t_i^2 - (\sum t_i)^2\right]\left[n\sum p_i^2 - (\sum p_i)^2\right]}} \qquad (11)$$

where, n is the number of samples. Root Mean Square Error (RMSE): RMSE shows how far predictions fall from measured true values using the Euclidean distance. It is defined in Eq. (12). A low value indicates better performance.

$$RMSE = \sqrt{\frac{\sum_{i=1}^{n}\|t_i - p_i\|^2}{n}} \qquad (12)$$

where n is the number of samples, t_i is the ground truth value, and p_i is the predicted value.

4.1 Ablation Study

To estimate the degree of multiple personality traits for each image, features, namely, textual, image and weighted fusion are the key components in the proposed model. Therefore, to validate the effectiveness of each component, we have conducted the following experiments. We use (i) Only image features, (ii) Only textual features, (iii) Image along with textual features, (iv) Image features with weighted fusion, and (v) Textual features with weighted fusion, and (vi) Image and textual features with weighted fusion for calculating measures. Table 1 shows that the results of textual features alone are better than image features alone. This shows that textual features provide more rich semantic information than image features. The same conclusions can be drawn from the experimental results shown in (iv) and (v). In the same way, when we combine image and textual features, as reported in (iii), without weighted fusion, which is better than individual features and image features with the weighted fusion. This shows that image and textual features contribute equally to achieving the best results. However, when we combined all images, textual and weighted fusion, which is actually the proposed method, reports the highest results compared to all other experiments. Therefore, one can infer that the key features are effective in coping up with the challenges of multiple personality trait estimations. Note that a " ♦ " in the case of weighted fusion indicates a normal concatenation, whereas, in the case of the features it indicates that the features are omitted. The reported correlations and RMSE are averaged for all the five personality traits scores.

Table 1. Assessing the contribution of each modality using our dataset.

Exp.	Image Features	Textual Features	Weighted Fusion	Rs	Rp	RMSE
(i)	✓	◆	◆	0.19	0.21	1.73
(ii)	◆	✓	◆	0.35	0.42	1.31
(iii)	✓	✓	◆	0.60	0.68	1.23
(iv)	✓	◆	✓	0.20	0.19	1.69
(v)	◆	✓	✓	0.73	0.75	1.18
(vi)	✓	✓	✓	0.81	0.86	1.12

Input images	Text and face	Background scene

Fig. 6. Illustrating segmentation results of the proposed method. Texts are separated by fixing bounding boxes, faces are separated by face detection step and other than a face and text is considered as the background scene.

4.2 Experiments on Segmentation

For evaluating the segmentation step, qualitative results of the proposed method on sample images of different personality traits are shown in Fig. 6, where it is noted that for all three input images, the steps segment text, face and background well. Therefore, we can conclude that the steps are robust to degradation caused by social media.

4.3 Estimating Multiple Personality Traits

Qualitative results of the proposed method for estimating five personality traits for each image are shown in Fig. 7, where it is noted that for all the images of (O, C, E, A, N), the predicted values are almost close to the ground truth. This indicates that our method is capable of estimating multiple personality traits for each image. It is also noted from Fig. 7 that the predicted bold values are still close to the ground truth compared to the score of other personality traits. The dominant score can be used for the classification of single personality traits of each image instead of multiple personality traits. Therefore, the method can be used for estimating multiple personality traits as well as single personality traits. To verify the same conclusions, quantitative results of the proposed and existing methods [4, 5] on our dataset and standard dataset (PERS Twitter) are reported in Table 2 and Table 3, respectively.

The scores of Spearman's and Person's correlation coefficients, and RMSE reported in Table 2 and Table 3 on our and PERS datasets show that our method is better than existing methods in terms of all three measures except the method [4] for one personality

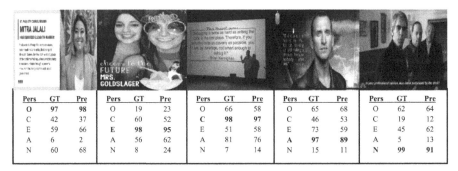

Pers	GT	Pre	Pers	GT	Pre	Pers	GT	Pre	Pers	GT	Pre	Pers	GT	Pre
O	97	98	O	19	23	O	66	58	O	65	68	O	62	64
C	42	37	C	60	52	C	98	97	C	46	53	C	19	12
E	59	66	E	98	95	E	51	58	E	73	59	E	45	62
A	6	2	A	56	62	A	81	76	A	97	89	A	5	13
N	60	68	N	8	24	N	7	14	N	15	11	N	99	91

Fig. 7. Example of the successful result of the proposed method. The bold represents the actual personality traits class if we consider the dominant score as the actual label.

trait. Therefore, it can be concluded that the method estimates multiple personality traits accurately for each image in terms of statistical relationship, monotonic relationship and error. Since the RMSE of the proposed method is lower than the existing methods for almost all personality traits, the predicted score is close to the ground truth. This observation confirms that the proposed method is accurate for multiple personality trait estimations. However, the existing methods report poor results because the method [4] was developed for single personality traits identification, while the method [5] was developed for image classification but not personality traits identification. In the same way, since the method [17] was developed for sentiment analysis, it does not perform well for classification of multiple personality traits in the images. For some personality traits, the method [4] achieves the highest result compared to the proposed and other existing methods [5]. This is because the objective of the method was to estimate single personality traits while the proposed method is to estimate multiple personality traits.

Table 2. Spearman's Correlation Coefficient, Pearson's Correlation Coefficient and RMSE for the proposed and existing methods on our dataset.

Trait	Rp				Rs				RMSE			
	Our	[4]	[27]	[17]	Our	[4]	[5]	[17]	Our	[4]	[5]	[17]
O	**0.68**	0.66	0.34	0.52	0.72	**0.78**	0.48	0.39	**1.14**	1.48	1.74	1.86
C	**0.95**	0.78	0.36	0.43	**0.98**	0.51	0.64	0.44	**1.07**	1.53	1.81	1.59
E	**0.93**	0.81	0.44	0.54	**0.86**	0.81	0.53	0.72	**1.18**	1.71	2.27	2.06
A	**0.65**	0.51	0.28	0.32	**0.98**	0.89	0.49	0.50	**1.16**	1.20	1.97	2.11
N	**0.85**	0.67	0.34	0.46	**0.78**	0.67	0.58	0.63	**1.05**	1.38	1.42	1.55

Sometimes, when the image does not provide sufficient clues for multiple personality traits estimation as shown in sample images in Fig. 8, the method fails to achieve the best results. For example, the third and fifth images from the left-top, where we can see the images lost visual features to define it as an Extraversion (ground truth). The

Table 3. Spearman's Correlation Coefficient, Pearson's Correlation Coefficient and RMSE for the proposed and existing methods on PERS Twitter Dataset.

Trait	Rp				Rs				RMSE			
	Our	[4]	[5]	[17]	Our	[4]	[5]	[17]	Our	[4]	[5]	[17]
O	0.56	**0.62**	0.24	0.31	**0.65**	0.62	0.33	0.36	**1.23**	1.41	1.58	1.59
C	**0.88**	0.64	0.31	0.59	**0.82**	0.59	0.37	0.67	**1.24**	1.38	1.77	1.45
E	**0.65**	0.51	0.28	0.32	**0.72**	0.51	0.27	0.46	**1.18**	1.51	1.61	1.67
A	**0.81**	0.69	0.25	0.21	**0.83**	0.68	0.46	0.24	**1.12**	1.26	1.42	2.16
N	**0.68**	0.54	0.19	0.35	**0.78**	0.65	0.41	0.42	1.28	**1.24**	1.54	1.39

Pers	GT	Pre	Pers	GT	Pre	Pers	GT	Pre	Pers	GT	Pre	Pers	GT	Pre
O	**98**	72	O	19	12	O	49	55	**O**	**96**	**86**	O	41	51
C	56	67	C	80	**89**	**C**	**98**	79	C	89	**86**	C	59	**83**
E	8	24	**E**	**92**	86	E	91	**86**	E	45	66	**E**	**99**	57
A	88	61	A	56	39	A	81	80	A	18	13	A	50	80
N	86	**79**	N	10	56	N	17	8	N	73	84	N	12	32

Fig. 8. Samples where poor results are reported. The bold represents the actual personality traits class if we consider the dominant score as the actual label.

method misclassifies both images as consciousness. In the same way, for the first image, the visual feature indicates Openness, while the textual feature indicates neuroticism and the ground truth indicates Openness. When there is a conflict among the features, the method fails to estimate personality traits correctly. The same conflict can be seen in the second and fourth images, and hence, the method classifies it as Neuroticism. To overcome this problem, we plan to develop an end-to-end transformer, which can cope up with the challenges of degradation and extract minute information. Therefore, there is scope for improvement in the near future.

5   Conclusion and Future Work

In this work, we have proposed a new method for estimating multiple personality traits in a single image rather than a single personality for each image. To extract the local information to study the multiple personality traits, the proposed work segments text, face and background. For each segment, we apply contrastive learning for feature extraction, which extracts textual from text information and visual features from image information. The work also introduces a weighted fusion operation for fusing textual and visual features. The features are fed to five ANN based regression models for estimating five personality traits. Experimental results on our and standard datasets show that the proposed method outperforms the existing methods in terms of statistical relationship, monotonic relationship and mean square error. However, when the image loses clues and conflicts between the visual and textual features, the method performs poorly. We plan to deal with this in the future.

Acknowledgement. The work was supported by Ministry of Higher Education Malaysia via Fundamental Research Grant Scheme with Grant no: FRGS/1/2020/ICT02/UM/02/4. And also, this work was partially supported by Technology Innovation Hub (TIH), Indian Statistical Institute, Kolkata, India.

References

1. Ventura, C., Masip, D., Lapedriza, A.: Interpreting CNN models for apparent personality trait regression. In: Proceedings CVPRW, pp. 55–63 (2017)
2. Sun, X., Huang, J., Zheng, S., Rao, X., Wang, M.: Personality assessment based on multimodal attention network learning with category-based mean square error. IEEE Trans. Image Process. **31**, 2162–2174 (2022)
3. Alamsyah, D., Widhiarsho, W., Hasan, S., et al.: Handwriting analysis for personality trait features identification using CNN. In: Proceedings ICoDSA, pp. 232–238 (2022)
4. Biswas, K., Shivakumara, P., Pal, U., Chakraborti, T., Lu, T., Ayub, M.N.B.: Fuzzy and genetic algorithm-based approach for classification of personality traits oriented social media images. Knowl.-Based Syst. **241**, 108024 (2022)
5. Wu, H., et al.: CVT: introducing convolutions to vision transformers. In: Proceedings ICCV, pp. 22–31 (2021)
6. Google Cloud Vision AI. https://cloud.google.com/vision. Accessed 25 June 2021
7. Chen, T., Kornblith, S., Norouzi, M., Hinton, G.: A simple framework for contrastive learning of visual representations. In: Proceedings ICML, pp. 1597–1607 (2020)
8. Kumar, P.K.N., Gavriova, M.L.: Latent personality traits assessment from social network activity using contextual language embedding. IEEE Trans. Comput. Soc. Syst. **9**(2), 38–649 (2021)
9. Anglekar, S., Chaudhari, U., Chitanvis, A., Shankarmani, R.: A deep learning based self-assessment tool for personality traits and interview preparations. In: Proceedings ICCICT (2021)
10. Dickmond, L., Hameed, V.A., Rana, M.E.: A study of machine learning based approaches to extract personality information from curriculum vitae. In: Proceedings DeSE (2021)
11. Kulsoom, S., Latif, S., Saba, T., Latif, R.: Students' personality assessment using deep learning from university admission statement of purpose. In: Proceedings CDMA (2022)
12. Gahmousse, A., Gattal, A., Djeddi, C., Siddiqi, I.: Handwriting based personality identification using textural features. In: Proceedings ICDABI (2020)
13. Biswas, K., Shivakumara, P., Pal, U., Lu, T., Blumenstein, M., Lladós, J.: Classification of aesthetic natural scene images using statistical and semantic features. Multimedia Tools Appl., 1–26 (2022)
14. Biswas, K., Shivakumara, P., Pal, U., Lu, T.: A new ontology-based multimodal classification system for social media images of personality traits. SIViP **17**(2), 543–551 (2023)
15. Beyan, C., Zunino, A., Shahid, M., Murino, V.: Personality traits classification using deep visual activity-based nonverbal features of key-dynamic images. IEEE Trans. Affect. Comput. **12**(4), 1084–1099 (2019)

16. Xu, J., Tian, W., Lv, G., Liu, S., Fan, Y.: Prediction of the big five personality traits using static facial images of college students with different academic backgrounds. IEEE Access **9**, 76822–76832 (2021)
17. Yu, J., Kai, C., Rui, X.: Hierarchical interactive multimodal transformer for aspect-based multimodal sentiment analysis. IEEE Trans. Affect. Comput. (2022). https://doi.org/10.1109/TAFFC.2022.3171091
18. Viola, P., Jones, M.: Rapid object detection using a boosted cascade of simple features. In: Proceedings CVPR (2021)
19. He, K., Zhang, X., Ren, S., Sun, J.: Deep residual learning for image recognition. In: Proceedings CVPR, pp. 770–778 (2016)
20. Zhou, B., Lapedriza, A., Khosla, A., Oliva, A., Torralba, A.: Places: a 10 million image database for scene recognition. IEEE Trans. Pattern Anal. Mach. Intell. **40**(6), 1452–1464 (2017)
21. Radford, A., et al.: Learning transferable visual models from natural language supervision. In: Proceedings ICML, pp. 8748–8763 (2021)
22. Agarap, A.F.: Deep learning using rectified linear units (ReLU) (2019). arXiv preprint arXiv: 1803.08375
23. Sammut, C., Webb, G.I.: Mean squared error. In: Sammut, C., Webb, G.I. (eds.) Encyclopedia of Machine Learning, p. 653. Springer, Boston (2011). https://doi.org/10.1007/978-0-387-30164-8_528
24. Kingma, D.P., Ba, J.: Adam: a method for stochastic optimization (2014). arXiv preprint arXiv:1412.6980
25. Guntuku, S.C., Lin, W., Carpenter, J., Ng, W.K., Ungar, L.H., Preoţiuc-Pietro, D.: Studying personality through the content of posted and liked images on twitter. In: Proceedings ACM on Web Science Conference, pp. 223–227 (2017)
26. Costa, P.T. Jr.: Revised NEO personality inventory and neo five-factor inventory. Prof. Manual (1992)
27. Zhu, H., Li, L., Zhao, S., Jiang, H.: Evaluating attributed personality traits from scene perception probability. Pattern Recogn. Lett. **116**, 121–126 (2018)

A New Transformer-Based Approach for Text Detection in Shaky and Non-shaky Day-Night Video

Arnab Halder[1], Palaiahnakote Shivakumara[2(✉)], Umapada Pal[1], Tong Lu[3], and Michael Blumenstein[4]

[1] Computer Vision and Pattern Recognition Unit, Indian Statistical Institute, Kolkata, India
umapada@isical.ac.in
[2] Faculty of Computer Science and Information Technology, University of Malaya, Kula Lumpur, Malaysia
shiva@um.edu.my
[3] Nanjing University, Nanjing, China
lutong@nju.edu.cn
[4] University of Technology Sydney, Sydney, Australia
michael.blumenstein@uts.edu.au

Abstract. Text detection in shaky and non-shaky videos is challenging because of variations caused by day and night videos. In addition, moving objects, vehicles, and humans in the video make the text detection problems more challenging in contrast to text detection in normal natural scene images. Motivated by the capacity of the transformer, we propose a new transformer-based approach for detecting text in both shaky and non-shaky day-night videos. To reduce the effect of object movement, poor quality, and other challenges mentioned above, the proposed work explores temporal frames for obtaining activation frames based on similarity and dissimilarity measures. For estimating similarity and dissimilarity, our method extracts luminance, contrast, and structural features. The activation frames are fed to the transformer which comprises an encoder, decoder, and feed-forward network for text detection in shaky and non-shaky day-night video. Since it is the first work, we create our own dataset for experimentation. To show the effectiveness of the proposed method, experiments are conducted on a standard dataset called the ICDAR-2015 video dataset. The results on our dataset and standard dataset show that the proposed model is superior to state-of-the-art methods in terms of recall, precision, and F-measure.

Keywords: Text detection · Transformer · Keyframe selection · Video text detection · Moving text detection

1 Introduction

There is significant progress in text detection, recognition, and spotting in natural scene images but still, it is considered a hot topic for researchers. This is due to several real-world and real-time applications that require text detection and recognition. For example,

automatic driving vehicles, language translation, visual question answering, surveillance, and monitoring applications [1]. It is noted from the literature that most of the
work focuses on natural scene images and video for text detection which is useful for
the applications. However, the above applications do not include real-time applications
like protecting sensitive places and areas day and night automatically without human
intervention. One such application is vehicle movement detection in day and night shaky
and non-shaky videos. The cameras are fixed in this area and have movements sometimes due to wind and storms. At the same time, due to wind and storms, leaves, trees,
and other objects can have movements. As a result, one can have shaky and non-shaky
day-night videos. Although there are several existing methods developed in the past for
addressing challenges like arbitrarily shaped text, low contrast, curved text, and complex
backgrounds, the scope of the methods is limited to day videos/images without shaky
cameras. Therefore, detecting text in such videos is an open challenge and it has not
been addressed so far. This is because the videos are affected by severely poor quality
caused by objects, tree vehicle movements, and low light frames.

(a). Text detection from frames captured by shaky camera.

Fig. 1. (a). Text detection from frames captured by shaky camera. (b) Text detection for the frame
captured by non-shaky camera. (c) Text detection for natural scene images chosen from ICDAR
2015 video.

Night video frame   Day video frame

Proposed model

Existing EAST [2]

(b) Text detection for the frame captured by non-shaky camera.

Proposed model   Existing EAST model [2]

(c). Text detection for natural scene images chosen from ICDAR 2015 video.

Fig. 1. (*continued*)

It is illustrated in Fig. 1(a) and Fig. 1(b), where one can see how quality differs between day and night frames and shaky and non-shaky cameras. It is evident from the results of the existing and proposed method for the sample images shown in Fig. 1(a) and Fig. 1(b). In Fig. 1(a), where the existing method [2], which is a state-of-art method that uses an advanced deep learning model fails to detect text in the night frame and misses text in the day frame, while the proposed model detects text well irrespective day, night, shaky and non-shaky cameras. For the non-shaky camera frame shown in Fig. 1(b), the existing method detects text in night and day frames. For the scene image shown in Fig. 1(c), the existing method detects text properly. However, for all the samples shown in Fig. 1(a)–(c), the proposed model works well. Therefore, one can argue that the existing methods are not capable of handling day-night shaky and non-shaky camera frames.

Hence, in this work, inspired by the capacity of the transformer [3], we propose a new transformer-based approach for detecting text in both shaky and non-shaky day-night videos. It is noted that the temporal frame of the video shares spatio-temporal information of text in the video. It is also true that text in the temporal frames shares common properties, such as contrast, luminance, and structural features. Based on these observations, to reduce the effect of object movement, poor quality, and other challenges mentioned above, the proposed work explores temporal frames for obtaining activation frames based on similarity and dissimilarity measures. The activation frames are fed to the transformer which comprises an encoder, decoder, and feed-forward network for text detection in shaky and non-shaky day-night video. To the best of our knowledge, this is the first work. Therefore, the key contributions are as follows. (i) Exploring temporal information for selecting activation frames that share a high degree of similarity in terms of spatial-temporal information. (ii) Adapting transformer for text detection in day-night shaky and non-shaky video.

2   Related Work

The methods of text detection can be classified broadly into the methods for natural scene images, the methods for videos, and the methods for low light images. These different classes of methods are reviewed here.

2.1   Methods for Text Detection in Natural Scene Images

Wu et al. [1] proposed a context-aware deformable transformer for text detection in scene images. The main objective of the approach is to address the problem of arbitrarily oriented and shaped accurately. The model extracts multi-scale feature perception and fusion operation. Cheng et al. [4] focus on addressing the challenges of setting constant thresholds and degradation of the images. To find a solution, the work proposes an adaptive threshold to analyze the quality of the images through binarization. Zhang et al. [5] explore a segmentation-based model that uses probability maps for handling degradations while the iterative model for predicting missing pixels. Mittal et al. [6] used a combination of handcrafted features and deep learning for solving the problem of the occluded text. For solving the occlusion problem, the approach uses the natural language processing concept. Zhao et al. [7] use center points of the text and the dataset consists of a small number of fully annotated images and a large number of images annotated by weak supervision (annotated center points). Wang et al. [8] develop a model for arbitrarily shaped scene text detection based on fuzzy semantics and separatrix. The ambiguous text instances are detected using fuzzy semantics and the step of separatrix solves the problem of little spacing between the lines. Wang et al. [9] explored a progressive scale expansion network for scene text detection. The approach uses the kernel to extract features in a progressive manner to address the challenges of scene text detection.

In summary, although the methods explore the recent transformer-based models to achieve better results by tackling the above challenges accurately, the same models cannot be employed in videos. The reason is that these methods are not capable of using temporal frames in video. Even if we deploy the methods on extracted individual frames, the models may not be effective because the quality of individual frames varies to a great extent. Therefore, when we supply video captured by shaky and non-shaky cameras day and night, the performance of the methods deteriorates further. Thus, detecting text in day-night images captured by shaky and non-shaky cameras is challenging and it is an open issue.

2.2 Methods for Text Detection in Videos

Banerjee et al. [10] explored an end-to-end model for text watermark detection in the video. The model is capable of detecting captions, scenes, and text watermarks in the video. The approach combines UNet3+ and Fourier contour embedding to reduce the effect of low contrast and complex background. Bennet et al. [11] proposed a deep learning-based model for Telugu text detection in video. The model extracts language-specific features and encodes them with a convolutional neural network to achieve the results. Nandanwar et al. [12] focused on addressing the challenges of text detection in 3D video. The model combines the wavefront concept with deep learning to tackle the problem. In addition, generalized gradient vector flow has been used for dominant point detection before applying the combination of wavefront and deep learning models. Chen et al. [13] used parametric shape regression, propagation, and fusion for text detection in video. The relationship between the intra-frame and inter-frames is used for fine-tuning features that represent text candidates. Chaitra et al. [14] proposed the combination of Yolov5 and TesseractOCR for detecting and recognizing the text in video frames. However, the approach works well for high-quality images because TesseractOCR is sensitive to low-contrast images.

In summary, the approaches use temporal information for improving text detection and recognition performance. However, the scope of the methods is limited to day images but not night videos. Therefore, when the methods are not capable of not handling night video, it is obvious that the models cannot be effective for day-night video captured by shaky and non-shaky cameras.

2.3 Methods for Text Detection in Low Light Images

Xue et al. [15] proposed a model for arbitrarily oriented text detection in low-light scene images. The approach uses maximally stable extremal regions for detecting candidate points, a cloud of line distribution for studying the distribution of detected candidate points, and a convolutional neural network for text detection. Chowdhury et al. [16] used Fractal series expansion to enhance the degraded license plate images to improve text detection performance. To overcome the problems of low light or limited light and night images, the approach explores fractional calculus to smooth the images. Chowdhury et al. [17] explored the U-Net model for enhancing night license plate images. The approach is capable of enhancing both day and night images. The combination of U-Net and convolutional neural networks has been used to achieve the results. Chowdhury et al. [18] proposed an augmentation-based model for text detection in night and day license plate images. The model involves an augmentation module for finding dominant points, fusing color spaces of dominant points, and finally gradient vector flow for removing false positives to improve text detection performance.

In summary, although the approaches consider the challenges of day and night images for improving text detection and recognition performance, the scope of the method is limited to still images but not videos. In addition, the effect of a shaky and non-shaky camera is not considered for enhancement. Overall, it is observed from the review of the models on text detection in natural scene images, video, and low light images that none of the methods consider the challenges caused by shaky and non-shaky cameras. Thus, this work aims to develop a model for text detection in day-night shaky and non-shaky videos.

3 Proposed Model

The aim of the proposed work is to detect text in night-day shaky and non-shaky video and make use of spatio-temporal information to improve the performance of the method. It is true that the number of temporal frames captured per second may not be useful all the time. Therefore, to detect the frames that contribute to detection, this work proposes a step for activation frame selection based on structural features. The selected frames are supplied to a transformer that comprises an encoder and decoder as shown in Fig. 2.

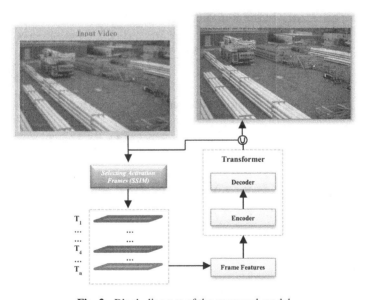

Fig. 2. Block diagram of the proposed model

3.1 Activation Frame Selection

It is observed that the temporal frames in a video share common spatio-temporal information. To extract this observation, the work proposes luminance, contrast, and structural features for activation frame selection. The formal steps for exploiting temporal information are presented below. The similarity score between the frames is estimated and it labels -1, which signifies the most dissimilarity between the reference frame and target frame and the positive 1 indicates the very similar or the same image. The steps and process of activation frame selection are shown in Fig. 3. The measurements can be expressed mathematically,

The Luminance can be denoted by μ which is measured by averaging over all the pixel values for images x and y as defined in Eq. (1).

$$\mu_x = \frac{1}{N}\sum_{i=1}^{N} x_i \; and \; \mu_y = \frac{1}{N}\sum_{i=1}^{N} y_i \tag{1}$$

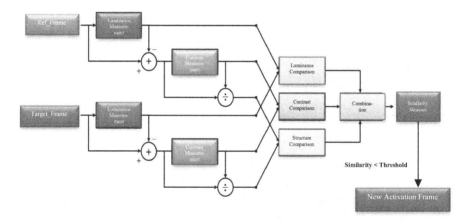

Fig. 3. The steps for activation frame selection

Contrast can be denoted using σ, which is measured by the standard deviation of all pixels for images x and y as defined in Eq. (2).

$$\sigma_x = \left(\frac{1}{N-1}\sum_{i=1}^{N}(x_i - \mu_x)\right)^{\frac{1}{2}} \; and \; \sigma_y = \left(\frac{1}{N-1}\sum_{i=1}^{N}(y_i - \mu_y)\right)^{\frac{1}{2}} \tag{2}$$

The Structure can be defined by dividing the input signal with its standard deviation for both x and y as defined in Eq. (3)

$$s(x) = {(X - \mu_x)}/{\sigma_x} \; and \; s(y) = {(Y - \mu_y)}/{\sigma_y} \tag{3}$$

Now we have to compare these three (luminance, contrast and structure) for both x and y, and the comparison functions can be defined as,

Luminance Comparison can be defined as $l(x, y)$, where x and y are the Reference frame and the target frame of a video as defined in Eq. (4).

$$l(x, y) = \frac{2\mu_x\mu_y + C_1}{\mu_x^2 + \mu_y^2 + C_1} \tag{4}$$

where C_1 is the constant to ensure stability if the denominator becomes 0, it can be defined by,

$$C_1 = (K_1 L)^2 \tag{5}$$

where L is the dynamic range for pixel values. And K_1 constants. if $L = 255$ for 8-bit component frames.

Contrast Comparison can be defined by $c(x, y)$ as defined in Eq. (6).

$$c(x, y) = \frac{2\sigma_x\sigma_y + C_2}{\sigma_x^2 + \sigma_y^2 + C_2} \tag{6}$$

where $C_2 = (K_2 L)^2$ and K_2 is constant. Furthermore, we choose $K_1 = 0.01$ *and* $K_2 = 0.03$. If the range for an image is [0, 1], we set $L = 1$ in order to get the same result, i.e., $C_1 = (K_1)^2$ and $C_2 = (K_2)^2$.

Structure Comparison can be defined for reference frame and target frame or x and y as $s(x, y)$ as defined in Eq. (7).

$$s(x, y) = \frac{2\sigma_{xy} + C_3}{\sigma_x\sigma_y + C_3} \tag{7}$$

where $C_3 = C_2/2$

And, σ_{xy} is defined as shown in Eq. (8).

$$\sigma_{xy} = \frac{1}{N-1} \sum_{i=1}^{N} (x_i - \mu_x)(y_i - \mu_y) \tag{8}$$

So, the SSIM score can be calculated according to Eq. (9).

$$\text{SSIM}(x, y) = \left[l(x, y)\right]^{\alpha} . \left[c(x, y)\right]^{\beta} . \left[s(x, y)\right]^{\gamma} \tag{9}$$

where, $\alpha > 0$, $\beta > 0$, $\gamma > 0$ denote the relative importance for each metric, So, the simplified Equation is defined in (10).

$$SSIM(x, y) = \frac{(2\mu_x\mu_y + C_1)(2\sigma_x\sigma_y + C_2)}{\left(\mu_x^2 + \mu_y^2 + C_1\right)\left(\sigma_x^2 + \sigma_y^2 + C_2\right)} \tag{10}$$

If we assume $\alpha = \beta = \gamma = 1$ and $C_3 = C_2/2$.

Activation Frame Selection is a decision-making process based on *SSIM (Reference Frame, Target Frame)* and a threshold value. Initially, the first frame in the video is considered an activation frame, which is the same as a reference frame. If

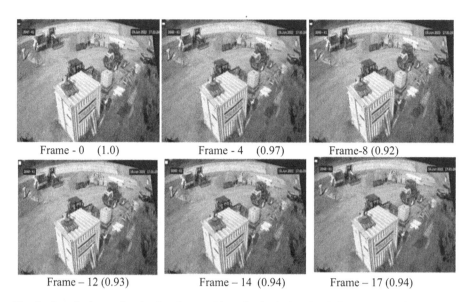

Frame - 0   (1.0)   Frame - 4   (0.97)   Frame-8 (0.92)

Frame – 12 (0.93)   Frame – 14   (0.94)   Frame – 17 (0.94)

Fig. 4. Sample detected activation frames. The value in the bracket indicates the similarity value between the key frame and activation frame.

SSIM (Reference Frame, Target Frame) < Threshold Value, which is calculated empirically that signifies the Target frame is dissimilar from the reference frame. The target frame is set as the activation frame. Else, it remains the same. When the process finds a new activation frame, which passes through the transformer to detect all the identical frames. This process repeats until a new activation frame is found. The effectiveness of the steps can be seen in Fig. 4, where one can see sample activation frames with similarity scores mentioned in the bracket.

3.2   Text Detection

The selected frames obtained by the previous step are supplied to a transformer as shown in Fig. 5, where it can be seen the steps and process for text detection in night-day shaky and non-shaky video. The details of the steps are presented below.

Transformer Backbone: Starting from the initial reference frame, $x_{frame} \in R^{3 \times H_0 \times W_0}$ (with three color channels), We use a CNN backbone to generate a lower-resolution activation map $f \in R^{C \times H \times W}$.

Transformer Encoder: At the first layer, a 1×1 convolution reduces the channel dimension of the high-level activation map to a smaller dimension and creates a new feature map. The encoder architecture is permutation-invariant so, we give a sequence of inputs with a positional encoding with each sequence, and we can get the sequences by collapsing the spatial dimension into one dimension. The encoder layer consists of a multihead-attention module and a feed-forward network.

Transformer Decoder: The Decoder follows the standard architecture of the general transformer decoder, where we transform N embeddings of size d using a multi-headed

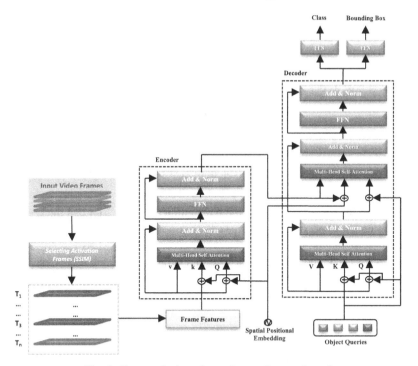

Fig. 5. Proposed adapted transformer for text detection.

self-attention and encoder-decoder attention mechanism, which decodes the N objects in parallel at each decoding layer. All the N Input embeddings also have an additional position or learned positional encodings that we refer to as object queries, and add those to all the attention layers. All the N object queries are transformed into an output embedding by the decoder. Then, they are decoded into the bounding boxes and the classes by the feed-forward network.

Feed Forward Networks (FFNs): The final prediction is computed by a 3-layer perceptron with ReLU activation and a hidden dimension d, and a linear projection layer. The FFN predicts the center coordinates with the height and width of the bounding box, and the linear layer predicts the class label using the softmax activation function.

The effectiveness of the above steps is illustrated in Fig. 1(a)–(c), where one can see the proposed method detects text well in both day-night shaky, non-shaky, and scene video frames. This shows that the proposed method is capable of handling the causes of shaky and non-shaky day and night images without compromising the performance of the on-scene video.

3.3 Loss Function

Text Detection Set Prediction Loss: The transformer infers a fixed-size set of N predictions, in a single pass through the decoder, The main challenge is to score the predicted text position and its size with respect to ground truth. Our goal is to produce an optimal bipartite matching between the predicted and ground truth of the text bounding boxes over the frames and optimize the loss of bounding boxes. Let, y be the ground truth of the text and $\hat{y} = \{\hat{y}\}_{i=1}^{N}$ the set of N predictions. To find a bipartite matching between the ground truth and predicted, we search for permutation of all N elements $\sigma \in G_N$ with the lowest cost as defined in Eq. (11)

$$\sigma = \arg\min \sigma \in G_N \sum_{i}^{N} L_{match}\left(y_i, \hat{y}_{\sigma(i)}\right) \qquad (11)$$

where, $\mathcal{L}_{match}\left(y_i, \hat{y}_{\sigma(i)}\right)$ is the pairwise matching cost between the ground truth y_i and the $\sigma(i)$ indexed prediction $\hat{y}_{\sigma(i)}$.

Bounding Box Loss: The second part of the matching cost is $L_{box}(.)$ that the scores of the bounding boxes. Here we make the box predictions directly. We calculate the loss from a linear combination of the l_1 loss and the generalized IoU loss $L_{iou}(.)$. So, our bounding box loss is defined as mentioned in Eq. (12).

$$L_{box}\left(b_i, \hat{b}_{\sigma(i)}\right) = \lambda_{iou} L_{iou}\left(b_i, \hat{b}_{\sigma(i)}\right) + L_{L1}\left\|b_i, \hat{b}_{\sigma(i)}\right\| \qquad (12)$$

where $\lambda_{iou}, \mathcal{L}_{iou} \in \mathbb{R}$ are the hyperparameters.

4 Experimental Results

4.1 Dataset Creation and Evaluation

For experimentation, we construct our own dataset for evaluating the proposed method. Our dataset consists of 237 videos, of which 51 shaky camera samples and 186 Non-shaky Camera samples. Our dataset includes outlets of industrial areas and factories where materials and goods can be parked in open environments and a huge warehouse. The videos of 1–8 s are captured by a CCTV camera mounted on the roof if it is indoor and poles if it is outdoor scenes. Since videos are captured at different times, situations, and weather conditions, our dataset includes diversified videos, such as videos with low, high quality, degradation, and distortion, and can have any object including humans and vehicles. If it is indoor video, it suffers from poor resolution and quality. If it is outdoor video, it suffers from external factors of weather conditions and the illumination effect of lights. In the case of outdoor video, the presence of trees and leaves makes the problem much more complex. In summary, our created dataset is complex and challenging compared to normal object detection and tracing video.

For the benchmark experimentation, we used the ICDAR-2015 dataset, which was provided by the ICDAR 2015 Robust Reading competition. Google Glasses capture these images without taking care of position, so text in the scene can be in arbitrary orientations. ICDAR 2015 Video [19] consists of 28 videos lasting from 10 s to 1 min in indoor 3 or outdoor scenarios. For measuring the performance of the proposed and existing methods, we use the standard measures as defined in [19], namely, Precision, Recall, and F-Score to evaluate the performance of the proposed and existing methods.

We consider the method [20] which was developed for selecting the frame that contains vital information for comparison with the step of activation frame selection. The motivation behind choosing this method [20] is that the objective of the method is the same as the proposed method. Similarly, for text detection, we consider the well-known existing methods [2, 9, 14] for comparative study in this work because these methods are used widely for text detection in both scene images and videos. Therefore, we consider these methods as baseline methods for text detection. For implementing our model, we use the following system configuration. Total Parms – 41.5M, Trainable Params – 41.3M, Non-trainable Params – 222k. The total implementation is done on the Google Colab Platform, using Tesla T4 GPU, Local System Ram – 4 GB. For all the experiments, we consider a 70:30 ratio for training and testing respectively.

4.2 Ablation Study

In this work, the use of temporal frames is a key step for reducing the effect of day-night shaky and non-shaky cameras. Therefore, to validate the effectiveness of temporal frames, we conducted experiments on our dataset and standard ICDAR 2015 dataset using the proposed and existing methods. It is noted from Table 1 that the proposed and existing methods report better results for those with temporal frames compared to those without temporal frames on both datasets. Therefore, one can conclude that the use of temporal frames is effective in achieving the results. It is also observed from Table 1 that the proposed model performs better than the existing method [2] for both temporal and without temporal frames on both datasets. This indicates that the proposed method is effective for day-night shaky and non-shaky videos while the existing method does not. The reason for the poor performance of the existing method is that the features do not cope with the challenges of shaky and non-shaky day-night videos.

Table 1. Studying effectiveness of temporal and non-temporal frames for text detection

Methods	Our Dataset						ICDAR 2015 Dataset					
	With Temporal			Without Temporal			With Temporal			Without Temporal		
	P	R	F-Score	P	R	F1-Score	P	R	F1-Score	P	R	F1-Score
EAST [2]	56.3	52.4	54.2	54.8	52.6	53.6	55.4	40.0	46.4	51.3	46.2	48.6
Proposed	**82.6**	**79.6**	**81.0**	**78.4**	**76.7**	**77.5**	**80.4**	**77.8**	**79.0**	**66.6**	**69.4**	**67.9**

4.3 Experiments on Active Frame Selection

To evaluate the performance of the proposed activation frame selection step, we calculated the measures for the proposed and existing methods [20] on our dataset. The results reported in Table 2 show that the proposed method is the best compared to the existing method. Therefore, we can conclude that the proposed step of activation frame selection is effective and works well for low- and high-quality images. On the other hand, the existing method [20] shows lower results due to lack of ability in extracting invariant features low and poor-quality images. This makes sense because the existing method [20] was developed for high quality images.

Table 2. Performance of the proposed and existing methods for activation frame selection on our dataset

Methods	P	R	F-Score
TKD [20]	0.73	0.61	0.67
Proposed	0.82	0.80	0.82

4.4 Experiments on Detection

Quantitative results of the proposed and existing methods are reported in Table 3, where it is noted that the proposed method outperforms the existing methods. When we compare the results of existing methods [2, 9, 14], the method [9] is the best one for both the datasets. This is because the methods [2, 14] are too sensitive to low-quality images while the method [9] has some tolerance to cope with the causes of poor quality and degradations. However, when we compare these existing methods with the proposed method, all the existing methods report poor results. Therefore, one can infer that the existing methods do not have the ability to tackle the challenges of shaky and non-shaky video of day and nighttime. On the other hand, the proposed method has the ability to detect text in both day-night shaky and non-shaky videos. The reason for the poor results of the existing method is that the extracted features are not invariant to low-light images.

Table 3. Performance of the proposed and existing methods on text detection

Methods	Our Dataset			ICDAR 2015 Dataset		
	P	R	F1-Score	P	R	F1-Score
EAST [2]	56.3	52.4	54.2	55.4	40.0	46.4
PSENet [9]	82.1	80.1	81.0	78.3	75.7	76.9
YOLOv5s [14]	71.8	62.1	66.5	61.0	46.0	52.44
Proposed	**82.6**	**79.6**	**81.0**	**80.4**	**77.8**	**79.0**

However, sometimes when the videos are affected by severe blur, fog, and snow, the proposed method does not perform well as shown in some sample failure cases in Fig. 6, where it is difficult to read the text with the naked eye and this is beyond the present work. To solve this challenge, our plan is to explore an end-to-end transformer which comprises enhancement models in the future.

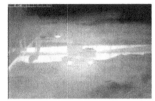

Detections from Foggy, Night and smoky frames

Fig. 6. Limitation of the proposed method.

5 Conclusion and Future Work

We have proposed a new transformer-based approach for text detection in day-night shaky and non-shaky video. To reduce the complexity of the problem, the proposed work exploits the temporal frames for activation frames detection as well as text detection. For activation frame selection, the proposed work extracts low-level features, namely, luminance, contrast, and structure of the characters to estimate the degree of similarity score. In the same way, the detected activation frames are fed to transformers for detecting text in day-night shaky and non-shaky videos. Experimental results on our dataset and ICDAR 2015 standard dataset show that the proposed method outperforms the existing methods. However, the approach does not perform well for the night videos. To overcome this challenge, we plan to explore end-to-end transformers in the future.

Acknowledgement. This work is partly funded by the Ministry of Higher Education of Malaysia for the generous grant Fundamental Research Grant Scheme (FRGS) with code number FRGS/1/2020/ICT02/UM/02/4. Also, this work is partly funded by the Technology Innovation Hub, Indian Statistical Institute, Kolkata, India. This work is also supported by ISI-UTS joint research cluster.

References

1. Wu, Y., Kong, Q., Yong, L., Narducci, F., Wan, S.: CDText: scene text detector based on context-aware deformable transformer. Pattern Recogn. Lett. (2023)
2. Zhou, X., et al.: East: an efficient and accurate scene text detector. In: Proceedings CVPR, pp. 5551–5560 (2017)
3. Raisis, Z,. Younes, G., Zelek, J.: Arbitrary shape text detection using transformers. In: Proceedings ICPR, pp. 3238–3245 (2022)
4. Cheng, P., Zhao, Y., Wang, W.: Detect arbitrarily shaped text via adaptive thresholding and localization quality estimation. IEEE Trans. Circuits Syst. Video Technol. (2023)
5. Zhang, S.X., Zhu, X., Chen, L., Hou, J.B., Yin, X.C.: Arbitrarily shape text detection via segmentation with probability maps. IEEE Trans. Pattern Anal. Mach. Intell., 2736–2750 (2023)
6. Mittal, A., Shivakumara, P., Pal, U., Lu, T., Blumenstein, M.: A new method for detection and prediction of occluded text in natural scene images. Sig. Process. Image Commun. **100**, 1–18 (2022)
7. Zhao, M., Feng, W., Yin, F., Liu, C.L.: Texts as points: scene text detection with points supervision. Pattern Recogn. Lett. **170**, 1–8 (2023)

8. Wang, F., Xu, X., Chen, Y., Li, X.: Fuzzy semantics for arbitrarily shaped scene text detection. IEEE Trans. Image Process. **32**, 1–12 (2023)
9. Wang, W., et al.: Shape robust text detection with progressive scale expansion network. In: Proceedings CVPR, pp. 9336–9345 (2019)
10. Benerjee, A., Shivakumara, P., Acharya, P., Pal, U., Canet, J.L.: TWD: a new deep E2E model for text watermark/caption and scene text detection in video. In: Proceedings ICPR, pp. 1492–1498 (2022)
11. Bannet, M.A., Srividhya, R., Jayachandran, T., Rajmohan, V.: Deep learning-based Telugu video text detection using coding over digital transmission. In: Proceeding ICOEI, pp 1479–1483 (2022)
12. Nandanwar, L., Shivakumara, P., Ramachandra, R., Lu, T., Antonacopoulos, A., Lu, Y.: A new deep wavefront based model for text localization in 3D video. IEEE Trans. Circuits Syst. Video Technol., 3375–3389 (2022)
13. Chen, L., Shi, J., Su, F.: Robust video text detection through parametric shape regression, propagation and fusion. In: Proceedings ICME, pp. 1–6 (2021)
14. Chaitra, Y.L., Dinesh, R., Jeevan, M., Arpitha, M., Aishwarya, V., Akshitha, K.: An impact of YOLOv5 on text detection and recognition system using TesseractOCR in images/video frames. In: Proceedings ICDSIS (2022)
15. Xue, M., et al.: Arbitrarily oriented text detection in low light natural scene images. IEEE Trans. Multimedia, 2706–2720 (2020)
16. Chowdhury, P.N., Shivakumara, P., Jalab, H.A., Ibrahim, R.W., Pal, U., Lu, T.: A new fractal series expansion based enhancement model for license plate recognition. Sing. Process. Image Commun. **89** (2020)
17. Chowdhury, P.N., Shivakumara, P., Ramachandra, R., Pal, U., Lu, T., Blumenstein, M.: A new U-Net based license plate enhancement model in night and day images. In: Palaiahnakote, S., Sanniti di Baja, G., Wang, L., Yan, W. (eds.) Proceedings ACPR, Springer, Cham (2020). https://doi.org/10.1007/978-3-030-41404-7_53
18. Chowdhury, P.N., Shivakumara, P., Pal, U., Lu. T., Blumenstein, M.: A new augmentation-based method for text detection in night and day license plate images. Multimedia Tools Appl. (2020)
19. Karatzas, D., et al.: ICDAR 2015 competition on robust reading. In: Proceedings ICDAR, pp. 1156–1160 (2015)
20. Farhadi, M., Yang, Y.: TKD: temporal knowledge distillation for active perception. In: Proceedings WACV, pp. 953–962 (2020)

MobileViT Based Lightweight Model for Prohibited Item Detection in X-Ray Images

Peng Sun[1,2], Haigang Zhang[1(✉)], Jinfeng Yang[1], and Dong Wei[2]

[1] Shenzhen Polytechnic University, Shenzhen, China
zhg2018@sina.com
[2] University of Science and Technology Liaoning, Anshan, China

Abstract. The application of computer vision technology to detect prohibited items in X-ray security inspection images holds significant practical research value. We have observed that object detection models built upon the Visual Transformer (ViT) architecture outperform those relying on Convolutional Neural Networks (CNNs) when assessed on publicly available datasets. However, the ViT's attention mechanism, while offering a global response, lacks the CNN model's inductive bias, which can hinder its performance, demanding more samples and learning parameters. This drawback is particularly problematic for time-sensitive processes like security inspections. This research paper aims to develop a lightweight prohibited item detection model grounded in the ViT framework, utilizing MobileViT as the underlying network for feature extraction. To enhance the model's sensitivity to small object features, we have established dense connections among various network layers. This design ensures effective integration of both high- and low-level visual features without increasing computational complexity. Additionally, learnable group convolutions are employed to replace traditional convolutions, further reducing model parameters and computational demands. Simulation experiments conducted on the publicly available SIXray dataset validate the effectiveness of the proposed model in this study. The code is publicly accessible at https://github.com/zhg-SZPT/MVray.

Keywords: Object detection · Lightweight model · Visual Transformer · X-ray security inspection

1 Introduction

X-ray security inspections are ubiquitous in airports, railway stations, large event venues, and similar settings, serving to detect any prohibited items that individuals may be carrying in their luggage. The use of computer vision technology for X-ray image analysis has been drawing increasing attention in both industry and academia. In terms of practical application, the intelligent analysis of

This work was supported by the School-level Project of Shenzhen Polytechinc University (No. 6022310006K), Research Projects of Department of Education of Guangdong Province (No. 2020ZDZX3082, 2023ZDZX1081, 2023KCXTD077).

H. Lu et al. (Eds.): ACPR 2023, LNCS 14407, pp. 45–58, 2023.
https://doi.org/10.1007/978-3-031-47637-2_4

X-ray security inspection images falls within the realm of object detection. Such a model is expected to identify both the type and location of a prohibited item. X-ray security inspection images exhibit unique characteristics that often lead to the failure of traditional object detection algorithms. For one, items in the X-ray images are positioned randomly. The penetrative nature of X-rays results in an overlapping effect among different objects. Additionally, prohibited items come in a variety of types and scales, with smaller ones posing the most significant challenge to the model and often leading to detection failures. In light of these technical complexities inherent in the analysis of X-ray security inspection images, traditional machine learning algorithms often fall short. Conversely, deep learning technologies, notably those that involve Convolutional Neural Networks (CNNs), have shown remarkable results in detecting prohibited items in X-ray images [1].

Research into detecting prohibited items in X-ray security inspection images within the deep learning framework primarily encompasses two aspects. On the one hand, there are efforts aimed at developing targeted detection models, taking into account the unique characteristics of X-ray images. For example, [2] implemented more intricate Deep Neural Network (DNN) structures to alleviate the impact of cluttered backgrounds on model performance. Other research, including those conducted by [3,4], focused on addressing the issue of sample imbalance in security inspection datasets to enhance the detection recall rate for prohibited items. The intelligent analysis of X-ray security inspection images also grapples with the challenge of multi-scale object detection. Certain works have managed to maintain the visual features of small-scale objects within the network's high-level semantics through feature fusion and refinement [4,5]. On the other hand, security inspection operations are subject to certain time constraints, necessitating the consideration of the inference speed of visual detection models. A common contention, although not rigorously proven, suggests that increasing the complexity of DNN structures to enhance model feature extraction capability may conflict with the efficiency of inference. In response, some researchers are dedicated to designing lightweight intelligent analysis models for X-ray security inspection images [6,7]. Notably, we have proposed a lightweight object detection framework based on the YOLOv4 algorithm, incorporating MobileNetV3 [8] as the feature extraction backbone [9]. This approach has demonstrated state-of-the-art performance in prohibited item detection within X-ray images.

This paper focuses on the design of lightweight models for prohibited item detection in X-ray images. An effective and practical approach to enhance model inference efficiency is model compression, encompassing techniques like pruning, quantization, lightweight structural design of complex models, and knowledge distillation [10]. Model compression refers to an array of techniques aiming to diminish the size, complexity, and computational demands of a Deep Neural Network (DNN) model, while striving to preserve its performance or impact it minimally. These techniques include weight pruning, quantization, and network architecture search. Lightweight architecture design targets the creation of neural network structures specifically tailored to have fewer parameters, lower computational complexity, and a smaller memory footprint, while still delivering competitive performance. Models such as the MobileNet series [8,11,12] and ShuffleNet [13,14] fall within the category of lightweight CNN models. Distinct from the preceding two strategies, knowledge distillation mimics the teacher-student dynamic, wherein a less complex and smaller "student" model is trained to replicate the behavior of a larger and more complex "teacher" model.

Recently, researchers have attempted to apply the Transformer model, which has proven effective in natural language processing, to the field of computer vision. Vision Transformer (ViT) [15] represents a pioneering application of Transformer attention in the realm of vision, which segments an image into flattened 2D patches and subsequently projects each patch into tokens linearly. ViT model leverages self-attention mechanism for global interaction responses among different patch tokens. Unlike the CNN model, the ViT model emphasizes global feature extraction and lacks inductive bias, therefore demanding more data and learning parameters to ensure optimal model performance. For instance, when compared to the classic lightweight model MobileNetV3 [8], the ViT model boasts 16 times more parameters (85M in ViT-B versus 4.9M in MobileNetV3).

We noticed that MobileViT [16], a lightweight ViT model, integrates the feature extraction capabilities of CNN and ViT and shows impressive performance across multiple visual tasks. This paper employs MobileViT with the YOLO detection head to construct a lightweight detection model for prohibited items in X-ray security inspection images. To enhance model performance, two key improvements have been made. Firstly, we modify the connection mode of the feature extraction blocks in MobileViT to dense connections [17]. This change ensures that the model can achieve cross-scale feature fusion without increasing the computational load, and effectively solve the problem of missed detection for smaller-sized prohibited items. Secondly, the Learning Group Convolution (LGC) [17] is applied into the feature extraction backbone to further reduce the network's learning parameters. The proposed model, tested on the SIXray dataset [18], achieves an mAP of 81.21% with 5.64M learning parameters and 2.72G FLOPs. When compared to CSPDarknet [19], the proposed model reduces the amount of learning parameters and FLOPs by 20.96M and 7.54G, respectively.

2   Related Work

2.1   Vision Transformer

Transformer was first applied to natural language processing (NLP) tasks [20], and ViT [15] is a pure transformer directly applies to the sequences of image patches for image classification tasks. The pure Transformer operation lacks the inductive bias ability of CNN, so on medium or small data sets (ImageNet), the performance of ViT is weaker than that of ResNet model. However, when the ViT model is trained on a larger dataset, its performance surpasses the inductive bias ability of CNN [21]. Currently, in order to further improve the performance of ViT in visual feature extraction, some work combines self-attention and convolution, such as CPVT [22], CvT [23], CeiT [24]. Combining the transformer with convolution can effectively introduce the locality into the conventional transformer. MobileViT [16] is a lightweight version of ViT, which embeds the Transformer block into MobileNet, so that the model has the ability to extract local and global features. MobileViT achieves top-1 accuracy of 78.4% with about 6 million parameters, which is 3.2% more accurate than MobileNetv3 for a similar number of parameters. On the MS-COCO object detection task, MobileViT is 5.7% more accurate than MobileNetv3.

2.2 Prohibited Item Detection in X-Ray Images

From a practical point of view, intelligent analysis of X-ray security inspection images belongs to the task of object detection. In addition to knowing the category of prohibited item, the security inspectors are also very interested in the location information of the prohibited item. Research on prohibited item detection based on computer vision is very common. Mery [25] reviewed the application of computer vision technology in X-ray security inspection image analysis, and pointed out that the object detection technology based on deep learning outperforms traditional algorithms in terms of accuracy and generalization. Deep learning technology in the security field can be divided into three categories according to different needs and application scenarios. They are classification, detection and segmentation [26]. X-ray security package images often suffer from background clutter and target occlusion, compelling researchers to develop more intricate, high-performance network structures [27,28]. However, these complex structures frequently result in slower inference speeds, which could negatively impact security inspection process operations. Consequently, research focused on lightweight object detection models is garnering increased attention within the realm of X-ray security image analysis [9]. The crux of designing a lightweight object detection model lies in avoiding miss-detections, particularly for smaller prohibited items, while simultaneously maintaining a streamlined model structure.

3   MVray Method

In this research, we put forth a novel lightweight object detection model coined as MVray, which is designed explicitly for the analysis of prohibited items in X-ray images. Figure 1 delineates the architectural framework of the MVray model, which employs the MobileViT network [16] as the foundational backbone for feature extraction, and collaboratively interfaces with the YOLO head to execute object detection tasks. The MobileViT network unites the local features extracted by CNN with the global features of the Transformer, thereby amplifying its feature extraction capabilities. While lightweight networks generally falter in detecting smaller objects, to enhance the feature extraction proficiency of our backbone network for X-ray security inspection imagery, we integrate

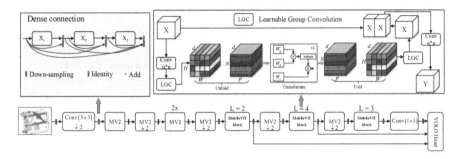

Fig. 1. MVray framework

dense connections within the feature extraction modules [17]. It's notable that
these dense connections linearly aggregate features across diverse scales without
substantially escalating the computational load of the model. Moreover, to prune
redundant features and preserve, or even augment, the lightweight advantage of
the backbone network, we employ the LGC to supersede traditional convolution
operations [17].

3.1 MobileViT Backbone

MobileViT is a potent and streamlined network model, grounded in the
MobileNet architecture, which incorporates a Transformer-based self-attention
mechanism within CNN feature extraction layers. Traditional ViTs necessitate
substantial data and computational power to parallel the performance of CNN
models via a multi-head self-attention mechanism, given that Transformer lacks
the spatial induction bias innate to CNN. The central philosophy behind Mobile-
ViT is to utilize transformers in lieu of convolutions for global representation
learning. As delineated in Fig. 1, Transformer blocks are intricately woven into
the fabric of the MobileViT network.

As shown in Fig. 1, the Transformer block in MobileViT is a plug and play
module. Given an input $X \in R^{C \times H \times W}$, the output Y of Transformer block can
be calculated as

$$Y = LGC_{1 \times 1}\left[X||Transformer\left(LGC_{1 \times 1}\left(X\right)\right)\right] \tag{1}$$

where $Y \in R^{C \times H \times W}$, and C, H and W represent the channels, height, and width
of the input respectively. $||$ represents the concatenation operation, $LGC_{1 \times 1}\left(\cdot\right)$
represents the learnable group convolution operation with 1×1 convolution kernel.

Unlike the traditional Transformer attention mode, the Transformer operation in MobileViT requires fewer learning parameters. The LGC operation
projects the input tensor to a high-dimensional space d $(d > C)$. Then Transformer attention is applied to establish the long-range dependencies, which is
complementary to the local inductive bias of CNN. We unfold X into N non-
overlapping flattened patches $X_U \in R^{d \times P \times N}$, where $P = wh$, and w and h

are the width and height of a patch. So $N = \frac{HW}{p}$. Then the self-attention operations are carried among the flattened patches. The Transformer block in MobileViT does not lose the spatial position information of each visual patch, so it is easy to fold X_U with self-attention to CNN-wise features $X_F \in R^{d \times H \times W}$. Concatenation operator is conducted to achieve feature fusion between the ordinary X and X_F, and another LGC implements channel matching to ensure plug-and-play of Transformer block in MobileViT.

3.2 Dense Connection and Learn-Group-Conv

Prohibited items captured in X-ray security inspection images often display multi-scale characteristics. However, lightweight networks often struggle to achieve satisfactory detection performance, especially for smaller objects. This shortcoming can be attributed to the limited local feature field inherent in the conventional CNN convolution kernel's feature extraction process. Moreover, pooling operations within CNN models tend to diminish the responses of smaller object features within higher-level semantics. One effective and straightforward approach to addressing these challenges is to facilitate feature fusion across various feature layers. This ensures that high-level semantic features incorporate elements of low-level visual details. Importantly, the chosen multi-level feature fusion strategy must maintain computational efficiency, aligning with the lightweight modeling principles underscored in this study. In the MVray model, we integrate dense connection operations [17] into the MobileViT backbone. This incorporation enhances the reusability of shallow features at higher layers, incurring minimal additional computational load on the network. However, it's important to note that dense connections could potentially lead to data redundancy through overly dense connection schemes. To mitigate this issue, the MVray model introduces the LGC module to replace the traditional convolution operation. This substitution results in further parameter reduction within the network, achieving a more lightweight architecture while concurrently addressing data redundancy concerns.

Dense Connection: The traditional CNN is dense because of its progressive design layer by layer. Each layer has to copy the features of earlier layers, which causes a large number of data redundancy. Residual structure design is a popular information fusion strategy used to solve the gradient vanishing problem caused by an increase in the number of hidden layers. ResNets [29], as the representative of residual structure, transfer signal from one layer to the next via identity connections. Unlike residual structure design, the dense connection [17] connects all layers directly with each other. Specifically, in dense connection each feature layer obtains additional inputs from all preceding layers, and then transmits the fusion features to all subsequent layers. We use X_p represents the features on the p layer, and the comparison of residual structure and dense connection is as follows.

$$\begin{aligned} \text{ResnetConnect}: \quad & X_p = F_p\left(X_{p-1}\right) + X_{p-1} \\ \text{DenseConnect}: \quad & X_p = F_p\left(\|\left[X_0, X_1, \cdots, X_{p-1}\right]\right) \end{aligned} \tag{2}$$

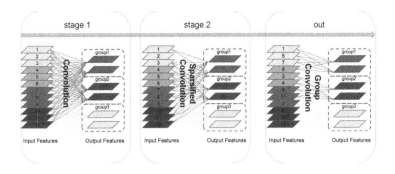

Fig. 2. The diagram of LGC operation with 3 groups.

where $F_p(\cdot)$ represents the composite function composed of convolution operation, batch normalization, and activation function, etc. $\parallel$ is the concatenate operation.

The dense connection strategy integrates concatenation operations to facilitate effective feature fusion, achieving a balance between optimizing feature flow and reducing computational burden. This is accomplished by establishing direct connections between each layer and all of its preceding layers. Such a design minimizes the necessity for feature replication, leading to the accumulation of features from all levels. Consequently, it aids in compensating for potential missing attributes and contributes to improved overall feature representation. Differing from the dense connection mechanism as seen in DenseNet [17], the MVray model employs a distinctive approach to sub-sampling through global average pooling. This enables the model to execute addition-based feature fusion on feature maps of varying resolutions. Importantly, this approach preserves the overarching architectural structure of the model, underscoring its compatibility with the lightweight philosophy emphasized in this research.

Learn-Group-Conv: The *LGC* operation is a robust technique engineered to curtail redundant features in a neural network during the training process, and eliminate the need for pre-established hyperparameters. This operation proves especially beneficial for bolstering the efficiency and precision of models employing dense connections, which could engender feature redundancy. By enabling the model to discern which features are vital and which can be pruned, the *LGC* operation assists in maintaining the model's lightweight nature, whilst still facilitating potent feature extraction. As depicted in Fig. 1, we substitute traditional $1*1$ convolution with the *LGC* operation within the Transformer block.

The *LGC* operation is divided into two stages, as shown in Fig. 2, with the standard convolution on the left and the *LGC* on the middle and right. In the first stage, the input features are segregated into groups, each of which is subjected to a sparse regularization operation to filter out insignificant features. This process involves the addition of a penalty term to the loss function, motivating the network to learn a sparse representation of the input features. The penalty

term is designated as the Group-Lasso of the group convolution filter, pushing
the filter towards zero weights. In the subsequent stage, following the pruning
and fixing of insignificant features, the network undergoes further training. The
surviving features are re-grouped, and the group convolution filters are learned
via backpropagation. The grouping and filter learning occur in unison, ensuring
that each filter can learn the most pertinent input set for the subsequent layers.
Equation (3) replaces the traditional $L1$ regularized group-lasso as a criterion
for filtering non-critical input features.

$$\sum_{g=1}^{G}\sum_{j=1}^{R}\sqrt{\sum_{i=1}^{O/G}\left(F_{i,j}^{g}\right)^2} \tag{3}$$

where G represents the final number of groups, O and R represent the number of
output channels and input channels respectively. F is the weights learned by the
convolution kernel. Each F^g from F^1 to F^G has size $O/G \times R$. $F_{i,j}^{g}$ corresponds
to the weight of the jth input for the ith output within group g. We take the
absolute value, that is $F_{i,j}^{g}$ squares and then takes the square root.

Traditionally, model sparsity is achieved through $L1$ regularization. In this
paper, we leverage group-lasso, which accentuates the afferent features within
the same group, to induce sparsity and ensure that convolution kernels within the
same group utilize the same afferent feature subset. During the training process,
the input feature subset within each group bearing lower weight is progressively
pruned. The significance of the input feature to its corresponding group is determined by aggregating all corresponding weights within the group. To complete
the convolution sparsity operation, input features of marginal importance in the
convolution kernel are set to zero accordingly.

4   Experiment Results

4.1   Experimental Datasets and Implementation Details

We applied the publicly available SIXray dataset [18] to verify the performance
of the proposed MVray algorithm. The SIXray dataset consists of 1,059,231 X-
ray images containing 8,929 prohibited items in 5 categories (Gun, Knife, Pliers,
Scissor and Wrench). The images in the SIXray dataset are all collected in real
life scenarios. We split the training set, the verification set, and the test set in
an 8:1:1 ratio.

All experiments are performed on PyTorch under the Ubuntu 16.04 system
with NVIDIA A100-SXM4-40G GPU. We added the common feature extraction backbone networks to the comparison of model performance. In order to
compare model performance fairly, all the models participating in the comparison experiment adopted the training hyperparameter in Table 1, and carried out
training under the condition of zero pre-training weights.

Table 1. Model training parameters

Name	Parameter
input_shape	(320,320)
Optimizer	adam
Momentum	0.937
Lr_decay_type	cos
Init_lr	1e−3
Batch_size	16
Epoch	300
Num_works	4

4.2 Comparison Results

On the SIXray dataset, our proposed MVray model shows satisfactory performance. Table 2 shows the detection performance of MVray model for 5 types of prohibited items. Overall, the MVray model achieves the mAP value of 81.21% on the SIXray dataset. The AP indicators of individual categories of prohibited items also exceed 70%. The MVray model has the best detection performance for "Gun", achieving the 95.89% AP value.

We make comparison between the proposed MVray model with other lightweight feature backbones, such as MobileNet series [11], GhostNet [30], DenseNet [17], CSPDarknet53 [31] and MobileViT [16]. Table 2 presents the comparison results on SIXray dataset. The proposed MVray model achieves the best prohibited item detection performance with 81.21% mAP, which outperforms the DenseNet model by an absolute gain of 1.94% mAP, the GhostNet model by 9.32% mAP, the MobileNetV3 model by 11.02% mAP, the DenseNet model by 1.94%, and the MobileViT model by 3.96%. CSPDarknet53 is the basic feature extraction backbone for YOLO series models, which achieves the best detection performance with 85.42% mAP. However, CSPDarknet53 backbone network has far more learning parameters than MVray model, as shown in Table 3. For the detection of specific categories of prohibited items, MVray model has an overwhelming advantage in detecting "Scissor" and "Wrench" compared with other models. When detecting "Scissor", the MVray model has improved AP metrics by more than 20% points compared to the MobileNet series models. When detecting the "Wrench", the improvement intensity is about 14% points.

The MVray model aims to achieve a balance between object detection accuracy and efficiency. Therefore, model lightweight and inference efficiency are very important indicators. Table 3 shows the volume and computational efficiency of the model, where the Floating Point Operation (FLOPs), model Parameters (Params) and Frames Per Second (FPS) are taken into consideration. In order to ensure the uniqueness of the differences and achieve the comparison effect, YOLOv4 detection head is selected to make object detection. The proposed MVray model has the same number of learning parameters (5.64M) as Mobile-

Table 2. Comparison results among different feature extraction backbones.

Backbone	AP					mAP
	Gun	Knife	Pliers	Scissor	Wrench	
MobileNetV1	93.75%	75.82%	70.20%	52.07%	57.65%	70.90%
MobileNetV2	92.59%	73.64%	70.60%	52.17%	57.82%	69.36%
MobileNetV3	93.23%	76.08%	69.20%	56.32%	56.10%	70.19%
GhostNet	93.82%	75.38%	70.06%	60.43%	59.76%	71.89%
DenseNet	94.91%	76.64%	78.23%	77.37%	69.18%	79.27%
CSPDarknet53	97.23%	77.55%	84.73%	88.59%	79.00%	85.42%
MobileViT	95.30%	75.83%	77.79%	73.36%	63.98%	77.25%
MVray	95.89%	80.01%	79.67%	78.70%	71.78%	81.21%

ViT model, since neither dense connections nor LGC operations add additional parameters. MobileNetV2 has the least number of learning parameters (3.50M), but its detection performance is 12% mAP lower than the MVray model. MVray model contains 2.72G FLOPs, lower than MobileViT by 0.08G FLOPs. Due to the additional calculation of Transformer attention, the FLOPs index of the MVray model is higher than that of the MobileNet series models. Compared with CSPDarknet with 10.26G FLOPs, the Mvray model has relatively obvious advantages. The comparison of "Model Size" shows the similar results with "Params". The FPS indicator can reflect the inference speed of the model. MVray model achieves 38.84 FPS, which shows that the MVray model can fully meet the timeliness requirements of security inspection.

4.3   Ablation Experiment

This paper proposes the MVray model, which employs two additional operations to enhance the performance of prohibited item detection tasks in X-ray security inspection images, superior to the base MobileViT model. The implementation of a dense connection successfully fuses the visual features across various feature extraction layers, enabling the effective transmission of low-level features into high-level semantics. This crucial enhancement proficiently addresses the issue of missed detection of small targets prevalent in lightweight models. Additionally, the LGC technique further diminishes the model's learning parameters and computational load, while simultaneously minimizing feature redundancy brought about by dense connections. We conducted ablation studies to ascertain the contributions of dense connection and LGC operations, the outcomes of which are demonstrated in Table 4. The integration of dense connection and LGC into the MobileViT model significantly boosted its performance. The inclusion of the dense connection allowed the model to achieve the mAP of 78.79%, marking a 1.54% increase from the base MobileViT model. Furthermore, the introduction of LGC elevated the mAP to 77.90%, an improvement of 0.65% over the base model. When combined, these operations enable the proposed MVray model to reach an impressive mAP of 81.21%, outstripping the MobileViT model by a considerable margin of 3.96% mAP.

In terms of specific prohibited item detection, the incorporation of dense connection and LGC operations significantly enhances the model's performance. Notably, MobileViT achieves the mAP of 63.98% in the detection of the prohibited item of "Wrench". With the introduction of dense connections and LGC operations, the model's performance improved considerably, obtaining 65.58% and 66.65% mAP, respectively. When these two operations were combined, the proposed MVray model displayed a marked improvement. Specifically, in the detection of the "Wrench", the model attains an impressive mAP of 71.78%.

Table 3. Comparison of lightweight indicators.

Backbone	Params	FLOPs	Model Size	FPS	mAP
MobileNetV1	4.23M	1.19G	16.14M	57.28	70.90%
MobileNetV2	3.50M	0.65G	13.37M	46.70	69.36%
MobileNetV3	5.48M	0.46G	20.92M	44.67	70.19%
GhostNet	5.18M	0.30G	19.77M	35.08	71.89%
DenseNet	7.98M	5.88G	30.44M	27.16	79.27%
CSPDarknet	26.6M	10.26G	101.54M	31.76	85.42%
MobileViT	5.64M	2.80G	21.50M	35.98	77.25%
MVray	5.64 M	2.72G	21.50 M	38.84	81.21%

Table 4. Ablation experiment results.

Backbone	AP					mAP
	Gun	Knife	Pliers	Scissor	Wrench	
MobileViT	95.30%	75.83%	77.79%	73.36%	63.98%	77.25%
MobileViT+DC	95.53%	78.65%	76.20%	77.99%	65.58%	78.79%
MobileViT+LGC	95.20%	78.48%	78.09%	71.08%	66.65%	77.90%
MVray	95.89%	80.01%	79.67%	78.70%	71.78%	81.21%

4.4 Visualization

The MVray model proposed herein is capable of identifying the type and location of prohibited items in X-ray security inspection images. This part showcases the MVray model's visual localization performance for detecting the prohibited items. As visualized in Fig. 3 (which can be zoomed in for more precise results), we can draw two primary conclusions. Firstly, compared to other algorithms, the MVray model yields more precise and compact bounding box annotations for prohibited items within X-ray images. Secondly, the MVray model exhibits

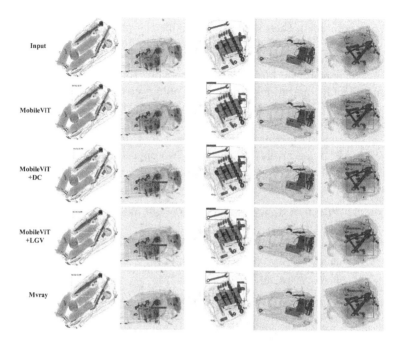

Fig. 3. Visualization results. Zoom in for better results.

a higher degree of confidence in discerning the types of prohibited items. In conclusion, the MVray model's performance in detecting prohibited items in X-ray security inspection images is commendably effective.

5   Conclusion

In this research, we devise a lightweight detection model, named MVray, targeting prohibited item detection in X-ray security inspection images. This model employs the MobileViT paired with a YOLO detection head as its backbone framework for feature extraction. To enhance the detection capabilities for smaller prohibited items, we implement a dense connection operation that effectively amalgamates high-level and low-level features, ensuring the resonance of small target features within high-level semantics. Further, we introduce a learnable group convolution to replace traditional convolution operations, mitigating feature redundancy triggered by dense connections, and thereby solidifying the lightweight characteristic of the model. With only 5.64M learning parameters and 2.72G FLOPs, the proposed MVray model achieves a mean average precision (mAP) of 81.21% on the SIXray dataset.

References

1. Mery, D.: X-ray testing by computer vision. In: Proceedings of the IEEE Conference on Computer Vision and Pattern Recognition Workshops, pp. 360–367 (2013)
2. Liang, T., Lv, B., Zhang, N., Yuan, J., Zhang, Y., Gao, X.: Prohibited items detection in x-ray images based on attention mechanism. J. Phys. Conf. Ser. **1986**(1), 012087 (6pp) (2021)
3. An Chang, Yu., Zhang, S.Z., Zhong, L., Zhang, L.: Detecting prohibited objects with physical size constraint from cluttered x-ray baggage images. Knowl.-Based Syst. **237**, 107916 (2022)
4. Tao, R., et al.: Over-sampling de-occlusion attention network for prohibited items detection in noisy x-ray images. arXiv preprint arXiv:2103.00809 (2021)
5. Zhang, Y., Zhang, H., Zhao, T., Yang, J.: Automatic detection of prohibited items with small size in x-ray images. Optoelectron. Lett. **16**(4), 313–317 (2020)
6. Tao, R., et al.: Towards real-world x-ray security inspection: a high-quality benchmark and lateral inhibition module for prohibited items detection. In: Proceedings of the IEEE/CVF International Conference on Computer Vision, pp. 10923–10932 (2021)
7. Nguyen, H.D., Cai, R., Zhao, H., Kot, A.C., Wen, B.: Towards more efficient security inspection via deep learning: a task-driven x-ray image cropping scheme. Micromachines **13**(4), 565 (2022)
8. Howard, A., et al.: Searching for mobilenetv3. In: Proceedings of the IEEE/CVF International Conference on Computer Vision, pp. 1314–1324 (2019)
9. Ren, Yu., Zhang, H., Sun, H., Ma, G., Ren, J., Yang, J.: LightRay: lightweight network for prohibited items detection in x-ray images during security inspection. Comput. Electr. Eng. **103**, 108283 (2022)
10. Ghosh, S., Srinivasa, S.K.K., Amon, P., Hutter, A., Kaup, A.: Deep network pruning for object detection. In: 2019 IEEE International Conference on Image Processing (ICIP), pp. 3915–3919. IEEE (2019)
11. Howard, A.G., et al.: MobileNets: efficient convolutional neural networks for mobile vision applications. arXiv preprint arXiv:1704.04861 (2017)
12. Sandler, M., Howard, A., Zhu, M., Zhmoginov, A., Chen, L.-C.: MobileNetV 2: Inverted residuals and linear bottlenecks. In: Proceedings of the IEEE Conference on Computer Vision and Pattern Recognition, pp. 4510–4520 (2018)
13. Zhang, X., Zhou, X., Lin, M., Sun, J.: ShuffleNet: an extremely efficient convolutional neural network for mobile devices. In: Proceedings of the IEEE Conference on Computer Vision and Pattern Recognition, pp. 6848–6856 (2018)
14. Ma, N., Zhang, X., Zheng, H.-T., Sun, J.: ShuffleNet V2: practical guidelines for efficient CNN architecture design. In: Ferrari, V., Hebert, M., Sminchisescu, C., Weiss, Y. (eds.) Computer Vision – ECCV 2018. LNCS, vol. 11218, pp. 122–138. Springer, Cham (2018). https://doi.org/10.1007/978-3-030-01264-9_8
15. Dosovitskiy, A., et al.: An image is worth 16x16 words: transformers for image recognition at scale. arXiv preprint arXiv:2010.11929 (2020)
16. Mehta, S., Rastegari, M.: MobileViT: light-weight, general-purpose, and mobile-friendly vision transformer (2022)
17. Huang, G., Liu, Z., Van Der Maaten, L., Weinberger, K.Q.: Densely connected convolutional networks. In: Proceedings of the IEEE Conference on Computer Vision and Pattern Recognition, pp. 4700–4708 (2017)
18. Miao, C., et al.: SIXray: a large-scale security inspection x-ray benchmark for prohibited item discovery in overlapping images. In: Proceedings of the IEEE/CVF Conference on Computer Vision and Pattern Recognition, pp. 2119–2128 (2019)

19. Bochkovskiy, A., Wang, C.-Y., Liao, H.-Y.M.: YOLOv4: optimal speed and accuracy of object detection (2020)
20. Devlin, J., Chang, M.W., Lee, K., Toutanova, K.: BERT: pre-training of deep bidirectional transformers for language understanding. In: Proceedings of NAACL-HLT, vol. 1, p. 2 (2019)
21. Han, K., et al.: A survey on vision transformer. IEEE Trans. Pattern Anal. Mach. Intell. **45**(1), 87–110 (2022)
22. Chu, X., et al.: Conditional positional encodings for vision transformers. arXiv preprint arXiv:2102.10882 (2021)
23. Wu, H., et al.: CVT: introducing convolutions to vision transformers. In: Proceedings of the IEEE/CVF International Conference on Computer Vision, pp. 22–31 (2021)
24. Yuan, K., Guo, S., Liu, Z., Zhou, A., Yu, F., Wu, W.: Incorporating convolution designs into visual transformers. In: Proceedings of the IEEE/CVF International Conference on Computer Vision, pp. 579–588 (2021)
25. Mery, D., Svec, E., Arias, M., Riffo, V., Saavedra, J.M., Banerjee, S.: Modern computer vision techniques for x-ray testing in baggage inspection. IEEE Trans. Syst. Man Cybernet. Syst. **47**(4), 682–692 (2016)
26. Akcay, S., Breckon, T.: Towards automatic threat detection: a survey of advances of deep learning within x-ray security imaging. Pattern Recogn. **122**, 108245 (2022)
27. Aydin, I., Karakose, M., Akin, E.: A new approach for baggage inspection by using deep convolutional neural networks. In: 2018 International Conference on Artificial Intelligence and Data Processing (IDAP), pp. 1–6. IEEE (2018)
28. Gaus, Y.F.A., Bhowmik, N., Akçay, S., Guillén-Garcia, P.M., Barker, J.W., Breckon, T.P.: Evaluation of a dual convolutional neural network architecture for object-wise anomaly detection in cluttered x-ray security imagery. In: 2019 International Joint Conference on Neural Networks (IJCNN), pp. 1–8. IEEE (2019)
29. He, K., Zhang, X., Ren, S., Sun, J.: Deep residual learning for image recognition. In: Proceedings of the IEEE Conference on Computer Vision and Pattern Recognition, pp. 770–778 (2016)
30. Han, K., Wang, Y., Tian, Q., Guo, J., Xu, C., Xu, C.: GhostNet: more features from cheap operations. In: Proceedings of the IEEE/CVF Conference on Computer Vision and Pattern Recognition, pp. 1580–1589 (2020)
31. Kim, J.-H., Kim, N., Park, Y.W., Won, C.S.: Object detection and classification based on yolo-v5 with improved maritime dataset. J. Marine Sci. Eng. **10**(3), 377 (2022)

Typical Contract Graph Feature Enhanced Smart Contract Vulnerability Detection

Chi Jiang[1], Yupeng Chen[2], Manhua Shi[1], and Yin Zhang[1,2(✉)]

[1] School of Information and Communication Engineering, University of Electronic Science and Technology of China, Chengdu 610000, China
[2] Shenzhen Institute for Advanced Study, UESTC, University of Electronic Science and Technology of China, Shenzhen 518000, China
zhangyin123@uestc.edu.cn

Abstract. Due to the significant losses caused by vulnerabilities, the security of smart contracts has attracted widespread attention and research. Existing methods for detecting smart contract vulnerabilities can be classified into traditional detection methods and machine learning-based detection methods. Traditional detection methods rely on fixed expert rules, which result in low robustness and inability to identify complex vulnerability patterns. Machine learning-based detection methods have shown better performance than traditional detection methods. However, some mainstream methods have not fully explored the relationship between contract types and vulnerabilities. In this paper, we attempt to construct typical contract graphs using clustering methods to further extract the type features of smart contracts. We concatenate the type features with the overall semantic syntax features of smart contracts, achieving data enhancement of smart contract features. We evaluate our method on an Ethereum smart contract dataset, and our method achieves an accuracy of 89.28% and a recall rate of 89.08% for detecting reentrancy and timestamp vulnerabilities.

Keywords: Blockchain · Smart Contract · Vulnerability Detection · Feature enhancement · Graph Neural Networks

1 Introduction

Blockchain is a distributed ledger technology that enables information exchange, value transfer, and collaborative governance on decentralized networks. Due to its decentralized, tamper-evident, and traceable nature, blockchain technology is widely used in various fields such as finance, logistics, and entertainment. Smart contracts are a special type of computer program that runs on the blockchain and automatically executes the contents of the contract. However, there are security risks and design flaws in smart contracts that can lead to incorrect contract execution or exploitation by attackers, resulting in serious consequences. The significant property loss events [1] have intensified society's questioning of the security of blockchain technology and also prompted the development of research

ⓒ The Author(s), under exclusive license to Springer Nature Switzerland AG 2023
H. Lu et al. (Eds.): ACPR 2023, LNCS 14407, pp. 59–73, 2023.
https://doi.org/10.1007/978-3-031-47637-2_5

on the security of smart contracts. Due to the tamper-evident nature of smart contracts, it is extremely difficult to make changes to smart contracts deployed on the blockchain. Therefore, it is crucial to detect vulnerabilities in the contract before deployment.

Currently, there are various detection schemes for vulnerabilities in smart contracts. Traditional detection methods use code analysis to detect vulnerabilities, and many vulnerability detection tools have been developed by developers, such as Osiris [2], Oyente [3], Mythril [4] based on symbolic execution, Smartcheck [5] based on program analysis, and Contract Fuzzer [6] based on fuzz testing. Although these tools can effectively detect vulnerabilities in smart contracts, they all rely on rules formulated by experts, which are only artificial summaries of known vulnerability patterns and cannot cover some complex patterns. Therefore, traditional detection methods have significant limitations for diverse smart contract vulnerability situations.

With the rapid development of machine learning technology, researchers have begun to apply machine learning methods to solve problems in their respective fields. Many researchers have also proposed machine learning methods for vulnerability detection in smart contracts. Gogineni et al. [7] use AWD-LSTM to implement multi-classification of smart contracts based on smart contract opcodes. Zhuang et al. [8] convert smart contract source code into graphs to extract syntax and semantic features of smart contracts and use graph neural networks (GNN) to detect contract vulnerabilities. Liu et al. [9] propose to combine GNN with expert knowledge to detect vulnerabilities in smart contracts. Nguyen et al. [10] represent the source code as a heterogeneous contract graph consisting of control flow graphs and call graphs containing different types of nodes and connections, and use a multi-path heterogeneous graph attention network to more accurately capture the semantic of the code in smart contracts. However, the current machine learning-based contract vulnerability detection methods have not fully explored the relationship between the types of contract and vulnerabilities, and vulnerability detection methods using graph structures often require normalization of graphs, which causes some information of the contract to be lost.

To address the limitations of existing methods, we propose a smart contract vulnerability detection method based on typical contract graph (TCG) enhancement. This method, based on extracting the overall semantic syntax features of the contract using GNN, uses unsupervised clustering methods to cluster contracts with similar functional types to obtain TCG. Then, we use GCN and self-attention mechanism to extract features from TCG that include the type information of the contract. Next, we concatenate the type features of the contract with the overall semantic syntax features of the contract to achieve data enhancement. Finally, we classify contracts based on the concatenated features.

The main contributions of this paper are as follows:

– We propose to mine the functional category features of smart contract implementation based on unsupervised clustering method. By clustering similar functional category smart contracts, we obtain typical contract graphs (TCGs), which can contribute to the improvement of the detection performance of smart contract vulnerabilities.

- We use GCN and self-attention mechanism to learn the differences and connections between smart contracts of different types in TCGs. By concatenating type features of smart contract with the overall semantic syntax features of smart contract, we improve the accuracy of vulnerability detection.
- Our method achieves an accuracy of 89.28% in detecting reentrancy and timestamp vulnerabilities through validation on the Ethereum smart contract dataset, representing a 5% improvement compared to the state-of-the-art methods.

The remainder of the paper is organized as follows: Related works are reviewed in Sect. 2. The details of proposed method are presented in Sect. 3. Experimental settings and results to show the effectiveness of our method are presented in Sect. 4. The conclusion is shown in Sect. 5.

2   Related Work

2.1   Smart Contract Vulnerability

Solidity [11] is the mainstream language for Ethereum EVM development. Compared to EVM bytecode, Solidity, as a high-level language, has better readability and writability, but it also leads to the occurrence of smart contract vulnerabilities. Here we introduce two vulnerabilities that we focus on in our research:

Reentrancy, which is officially defined as when contract A interacts with contract B, contract B illegally gains complete control over contract A, causing contract A to fail to end correctly and being repeatedly called by contract B until *gas* is consumed. This is a malicious vulnerability caused by mutual invocation between contracts. If asset transfer operations occur during contract execution, serious economic crimes are likely to occur. Figure 1(a) shows a contract *Bank* with a reentrancy vulnerability, which implements the function of periodic deposits and withdrawals on Ethereum, with functions *save()* and *withdrawal()* respectively implementing deposit and withdrawal functions. For the vulnerability in line 12 of the code, an attacker can construct an attack contract as shown in Fig. 1(b) to implement a malicious withdrawal and steal all user balances.

Timestamp dependence refers to the critical decision-making process in a smart contract being tainted by the timestamp of the current block, making it impossible to execute the predetermined actions without interference. In a smart contract, timestamps are generated locally, and miners have considerable freedom to set the time, as long as it is later than the timestamp of the previous block, to achieve consensus among other nodes. This freedom is fatal for contracts like gambling contracts. Figure 2 shows a smart contract, *Roulette*, with a timestamp vulnerability that performs a simple lottery function by randomly obtaining the contract balance with each 1 ether bet. As mentioned earlier, miners have some autonomy in adjusting timestamps. According to the code on line 9, miners are incentivized to modify the block timestamp to meet the conditions for rewards.

```
1 contract Bank {
2 mapping(address => uint256) public usersinfo;
3     function save() public payable returns (uint256){
4         require(msg.value>0);
5         usersinfo[msg.sender]=usersinfo[msg.sender]+ msg.value;
6         return usersinfo[msg.sender];
7     }
8     function withdrawal() public payable{
9         require(now>saveTime+10)
10        uint amount = usersinfo[msg.sender];
11        if(amount>0) {
12            msg.sender.call.value(amount)("");
13            usersinfo[msg.sender]=0;
14        }
15    }
16    function() external payable{}
17 }
```

```
1 function withdrawal() public {
2     bank.withdrawal();
3 }
4 function() external payable {
5     stack += 1;
6 if (msg.sender.balance >=1 ether && stack < 200){
7     bank.withdrawal();
8     }
9 }
```

(a) A Contract with Reentrancy Vulnerability   (b) Attack Contract

Fig. 1. (a) shows contract *Bank* with reentrancy vulnerability; (b) shows an attack contract against contract (a)

```
1 contract Roulette {
2   uint public pastBlockTime;
3   constructor() {}
4   receive() external payable
5   fallback() external payable {
6       require(msg.value == 1 ether);
7       require(block.timestamp != pastBlockTime);
8       pastBlockTime = block.timestamp;
9       if(block.timestamp % 15 == 0) {
10          payable(msg.sender).transfer(address(this).balance);
11      }
12  }
13 }
```

Fig. 2. A Contract with Timestamp Vulnerability

2.2 Graph Neural Network

Graph Neural Networks (GNN) [12] are a type of neural network model based on graph-structured data, aimed at learning the complex relationships between nodes in a graph. Unlike traditional neural networks, GNNs not only consider the features of nodes themselves but also the topological structure and relationships between nodes, making GNNs more effective in handling graph-structured data. The core idea of GNN is to update the representation of nodes by propagating information in the graph. Figure 3 shows the process by which GNN updates nodes through message passing.

Graph Convolutional Networks (GCN) [13] are currently the most commonly used type of GNN. It is based on the idea of feature extraction and aggregation of local neighborhood information, and uses graph convolution layers to achieve information propagation and aggregation between nodes. In GCN, each node is represented as a vector, and these vectors are passed and updated through a series of graph convolution layers. In each layer, the features of each node are aggregated into the features of its surrounding nodes, thereby achieving information propagation and aggregation. Finally, the features of each node are updated to a new vector, representing its representation in the entire graph structure.

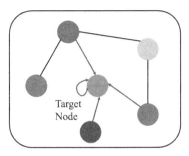

Fig. 3. Node Update

Temporal Message Passing Network (TMP) [8] is a type of GNN for processing dynamic graph data, which consists of a message passing stage and a readout stage. In the message passing stage, TMP sequentially propagates information according to the time order of edges, and finally uses a readout function to aggregate the states of all nodes in the graph to calculate the representation of the entire graph.

2.3 Self-attention Mechanism

The self-attention mechanism [14] is a method that can automatically calculate the correlations between each element in the input. Its core idea is to calculate the similarity between each element in the input based on their representations and to use these similarities as weights for weighted summation. This can adaptively assign a weight to each element, better capturing the dependencies between the elements and allowing the model to focus on the important parts of the input data to obtain effective information.

The self-attention mechanism is mainly composed of three vectors: *Query*, *Key*, and *Value*, which are obtained by multiplying the input data by their respective learnable parameters. When calculating the attention weights, *Query* is used to measure the similarity between each element and all other elements in the input data, while *Key* and *Value* provide representations of each element in the input. To calculate the attention weights, *Query* calculates the dot product with each *Key*, then scales the result by a scaling factor and finally applies the *Softmax* function to obtain the attention weights. These attention weights are used to weight the *Value* of each element in the input data for weighted summation, producing the output of the self-attention mechanism. The calculation process of the self-attention mechanism is shown in the Fig. 4.

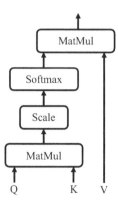

Fig. 4. Self-attention Mechanism

3   Proposed Method

Method Overview. The architecture of our proposed method consists of three stages: (1) semantic syntax feature extraction, which applies GNN to extract semantic and syntax features of the entire smart contract; (2) contract clustering, which clusters contracts of the same type based on identifier matching methods to generate TCGs; and (3) typical contract graph enhancement, which extracts features from the TCGs, concatenates them with the contract semantic syntax features, and achieves data enhancement.

3.1   Semantic Syntax Feature Extraction

We first utilized expert knowledge to extract risky functions in the source code that may contain vulnerabilities, thus eliminating redundant parts of the source code. The work [15] demonstrates that programs can be transformed into graphs that represent the connection relationships using nodes and edges. Based on this, we model the source code of smart contracts in a graphical form, as shown in Fig. 5. While extracting the semantic information of the contract as graph nodes, we preserve the syntax information of the contract through the edges in the graph. Our graph contains three types of nodes: *function nodes*, *variable nodes*, and *callback nodes*. *Function nodes* are used to characterize risky functions that may contain vulnerabilities. *Callback nodes* are used to simulate the triggering mechanism of the contract's callback function. *Variable nodes* complement *function nodes* and represent variables within the contract, such as account balances and bonus pools in reentrancy vulnerabilities, timestamp markers and lottery lucky numbers in timestamp vulnerabilities. These key variables that affect the presence of vulnerabilities will be aggregated into function nodes later. The edge information includes the start node, end node, temporal order, and type of edge. The temporal order indicates the order of this call in the contract execution process, and the edge type is used to distinguish between data flow and control flow.

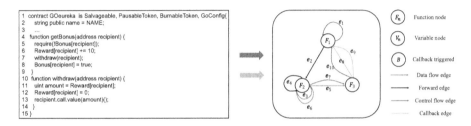

Fig. 5. Graph Modeling of Smart Contract Source Code

After completing the relevant elements in the graph, we use Word2vec to encode variable nodes and function nodes, and use One-hot encoding to encode edge types. Based on the aforementioned work, we apply TMP to aggregate all the features in smart contracts based on the temporal sequence of edges. The model is shown in Fig. 6, where we only list the propagation learning process of the first 7 edges in the contract graph mentioned above.

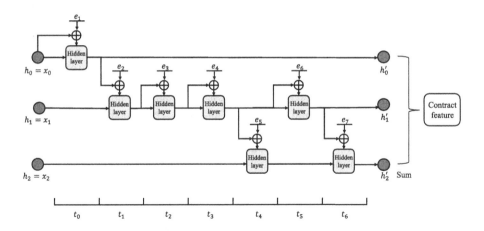

Fig. 6. Generative Model of Semantic Syntax Features

In Fig. 6, x_i represents the feature of each node, e_i represents the category feature of the edge, h_i represents the hidden feature of each node which is initialized with the corresponding node feature at the initial time step. At each time step, messages propagate from the start node to the end node, updating the hidden feature of the end node. Finally, by aggregating (adding) the hidden features of all nodes at the final time step, we obtain the semantic syntax representation of the entire contract.

3.2 Contract Clustering

The emergence of smart contract vulnerabilities is often strongly correlated with the type of smart contract, such as the probability of vulnerabilities appearing in financial or gambling contracts being much higher than that in gaming contracts [16]. In order to extract the type features of contracts, we need to cluster contracts first. We use the code snippet-based identifier sequence matching method [17] to calculate the syntactic similarity between contracts, which is implemented as follows: First, identifiers are generated for each line of code in the code segment to obtain an identifier sequence. Then, by comparing, the longest matching subsequence of identifiers between the code segments is obtained, and the ratio of the length of the matching sequence to the total length of the identifier sequence is calculated to evaluate the syntactic similarity between the two code snippets.

The syntax of smart contracts has been subdivided into 90 types (such as *MappingExpression*, *ModifierDeclaration*, *IfStatement*, *ForStatement*, etc.). We obtain the corresponding abstract syntax tree for the smart contract source code through parsing [18], and then obtain the syntax type of each code line. Afterwards, we use identifiers to label each code line, where each syntax type is assigned a unique hash value. If a code line is labeled with multiple identifiers, its hash value can be obtained by summing the hash values corresponding to each identifier. This process generates a hash sequence for each smart contract. Then, the hash sequences of two contracts are matched, and the matching target is the longest matching subsequence between the two hash sequences, which represents the highest degree of functional overlap between the two contracts. Finally, the syntactic similarity between the two contracts is obtained by calculating the ratio of the length of the longest matching subsequence to the length of the longest hash sequence. The algorithm is shown in Algorithm 1. This method emphasizes the exploration of the overall functional similarity of smart contracts, and is more interpretable compared to the method of directly calculating the similarity of word vectors.

We also calculated the semantic similarity between contracts. First, we vectorized each word in the contract code, then we obtained the contract's vector representation by adding the word vectors along each dimension. Finally, we used the cosine distance between different contract vectors to represent the syntactic similarity between contracts. The semantic syntax similarity between contracts can be represented as a weighted sum of syntactic similarity and semantic similarity:

$$Simi = \alpha \cdot SyntaxSimi + \beta \cdot SemanticSimi \qquad (1)$$

where *SyntaxSimi* and *SemanticSimi* represent syntactic and semantic similarity, respectively, and α and β represent the weights.

After obtaining the *Simi* for all contracts, we set a similarity threshold of 0.7 to determine whether there is a connection between two contracts. Contracts that have a connection tend to belong to the same type. By using the semantic syntax features of the contract as nodes and the connection relationships between

---

Algorithm 1 Syntax Matching

Input: HashList1, 2: hash sequence 1, 2 from contract C_n, C_m
Output: $SyntaxSimi$

 1: **for** $i = 0$ to HashList1.size **do**
 2:    **for** $j = 0$ to HashList2.size **do**
 3:       **if** HashList1.get(i) == HashList2.get(j) **then** $H[i,j] = 1$
 4:       **end if**
 5:    **end for**
 6: **end for**
 7: **for** each $H[n,m]$ **do**
 8:    **repeat**
 9:       **if** $H[n,m] == 1$ **then**
10:         $subseq_t$.add($H[n,m]$)
11:         $n = n + 1$
12:         $m = m + 1$
13:         $remove(H[n,m])$
14:       **end if**
15:    **until** $H[n,m] \neq 1$
16: **end for**
17: **for** each $subseq_t$ **do**
18:    **repeat**
19:       **if** $gap(subseq_t, subseq_{t+1}) < \eta$ **then**
20:         $subseq_t = link(subseq_t, subseq_{t+1})$
21:         $t = t + 1$
22:         $remove(subseq_{t+1}$
23:       **end if**
24:    **until** $gap(subseq_t, subseq_{t+1}) \geq \eta$
25: **end for**
26: $SyntaxSimi = \frac{max\_length\{subseq_1, subseq_2, \ldots, subseq_t\}}{max\_size\{HashList1, HashList2\}}$

---

contracts as edges, we can construct a TCG of contracts that have a connection relationship.

3.3 Typical Contract Graph Enhancement

After processing the first two stages, we can obtain the semantic syntax features of smart contracts and construct TCGs by clustering multiple smart contracts. In this section, we first extract the type features of contracts from the TCG, then concatenate them with the semantic syntax features of the contracts to obtain enhanced features. Based on this, we detect vulnerabilities in contracts. The overall architecture of the model is shown in Fig. 7.

Feature Extraction On TCG. We use $G = \{G_1, G_2, \ldots, G_N\}$ to represent a set of N TCGs. For G_i, $i \in \{1, \ldots, N\}$, we learn the features of its nodes through GCN:

$$\hat{X}_i = GCN(X_i \mid \theta) \tag{2}$$

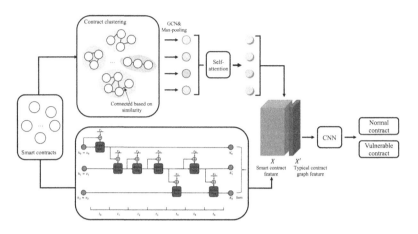

Fig. 7. TCG feature enhanced vulnerability detection model. Firstly, we extract the overall semantic syntax features of the contract using TMP. Based on this, we use unsupervised clustering methods to cluster contracts with similar functional types to obtain TCGs, where the nodes of TCG are represented by the semantic syntax features of the contract. Then, we use GCN and self-attention mechanism to extract features from TCG that include the type information of the contract. Next, we concatenate the type features of the contract with the overall semantic syntax features of the contract to achieve data enhancement. Finally, we use CNN to classify contracts based on the concatenated features.

where X_i represents the initial features of nodes in G_i, θ represents the parameters learned by the model, and $\hat{X}_i$ represents the output node features of the model.

We perform max pooling on $\hat{X}_i = (\hat{x}_1^i, \hat{x}_2^i, \ldots, \hat{x}_M^i)$ to obtain the representation of G_i:

$$g_i = \max_m\{\hat{x}_m^i\}, \quad m = 1, ..., M \tag{3}$$

By performing the above operations on G, we can obtain the representations of N typical contracts $\{g_i\}_{i=1}^N$. Based on the representation of G, we use the cosine function to calculate the vector similarity between different TCGs as attention coefficients:

$$d_{ij} = cos(g_i, g_j) \tag{4}$$

We then normalize it:

$$\alpha_{ij} = Softmax(d_{ij}) \tag{5}$$

α_{ij} is used to represent the importance of G_j to G_i, and we use it to update the representation of G_i:

$$\hat{g}_i = \sigma(\sum_{j=1}^{N} \alpha_{ij} g_i) \tag{6}$$

where σ represents the activation function.

Using attention mechanism here allows the model to focus on contract type features that are more relevant to the current vulnerability detection task and extract useful information.

Data Enhancement. We achieve data enhancement by concatenating the semantic syntax features of contracts with their corresponding TCGs features:

$$\tilde{h}_j = concat(\hat{h}_j, \hat{g}_{n_j}) \quad n_j = 1, ..., N \tag{7}$$

where $\hat{h}_j$ represents the semantic syntax features of the contract, $\hat{g}_{n_j}$ represents the type features of the contract, and the final representation of the contract $\tilde{h}_j$ is obtained by concatenating the two.

Vulnerability Detection. Since smart contract vulnerability detection is basically a binary classification task, i.e., determining whether the contract has vulnerabilities or not, we use CNN as the output classification network of the model. We use the concatenated contract features obtained above as input, and extract the classification information through CNN to output the binary classification results. The loss function of our model is represented as:

$$L = \frac{1}{T} \sum_{j=1}^{T} CE(f(concat(\hat{h}_j, \hat{g}_{n_j}), y_j)) + \lambda r(\Theta) \tag{8}$$

where T represents the number of smart contract samples, $f()$ represents the model used in the task output layer (CNN), y_j represents the label, CE represents the cross-entropy function, $r(\Theta)$ represents the regularization function for the global model parameters and λ represents the regularization parameters.

4   Experiment

In this section, we train our model based on the Ethereum smart contract dataset[1]. Through comparative experiments with baseline methods and ablation experiments, we verify the advantages of our proposed method.

4.1   Experimental Settings

Dataset. The Ethereum smart contract dataset contains 40,932 contracts and approximately 307,396 functions. Since we mainly focus on *reentrancy* and *timestamp* vulnerabilities, all contracts are filtered to ensure the presence of *call.value* and *timestamp* calls. After filtering, the dataset contains 4,871 contracts, as shown in Table 1. In the dataset, smart contracts containing these two types of

---

[1] https://github.com/Messi-Q/Smart-Contract-Dataset.

vulnerabilities are labeled as 1, and those without vulnerability risks are labeled as 0. We divide the dataset into a training set and a test set in a ratio of 7:3.

Baseline. In the experiment, we compare our method with four traditional smart contract detection methods (Mythril [19], SmartCheck [5], Oyente [20], and Securify [21]), as well as two neural network-based machine learning methods (TMP [8], DR-GCN [22]).

Metrics. We compute Accuracy and Recall for comparing our method with previous state-of-art.

Table 1. Data Distribution

Contract Type	Vulnerable Contract		Normal Contract
	Reentrancy	Timestamp	
Amount	2699	2172	4871

4.2 Method Comparison and Analysis

In this subsection, we evaluated the detection performance of our proposed method and other baseline methods on the same dataset to verify the effectiveness of our method. Reference [23] provided several highly recognized and open-source smart contract vulnerability detection systems. We selected four of these systems, Oyente, Mythril, Smartcheck, and Securify, as well as three neural network-based methods, TMP and DR-GCN, as baselines. Since we did not distinguish between types of contract vulnerabilities during model training, we evaluated the performance of the baseline methods that achieved multi-vulnerability detection based on their average indicators for detecting reentrancy and timestamp vulnerabilities.

Table 2. The Results of Comparison Experiment

Methods	Accuracy (%)	Recall (%)
SmartCheck	48.64	36.90
Oyente	60.54	46.58
Mythril	60.81	56.70
Securify	71.89	32.08
TMP	78.12	76.41
DR-GCN	84.29	87.82
Ours	**89.28**	**89.08**

The results of the method comparison experiment are shown in Table 2, indicating that the performance of neural network-based methods is relatively better than that of traditional detection tools. TMP, DR-GCN, and our proposed method can maintain an accuracy of over 0.8. Although the TMP method, DR-GCN, and our method used the same graph-based modeling method for contracts, our method extracted TCGs to achieve better performance, resulting in a 5% increase in accuracy over the best method. This improvement mainly relies on the feature extraction of TCGs to achieve data enhancement of the features, which associates contract vulnerability detection with contract type. Compared to other pre-classification methods for contracts clustering, the method based on identifier sequence matching can uncover the relationship between smart contract types and vulnerabilities.

4.3   Ablation Studies

In order to investigate the impact of our proposed innovations on the model, which includes clustering contracts using identifier sequence matching method and using features extracted from TCGs to perform data enhancement, we conducted ablation experiments. We abbreviate the two innovations as cc (contract clustering) and de (data enhancement), and set up three models as shown in Table 3, where + denotes the existence of the module, and - denotes the absence of the module.

Table 3. Ablation Experiment Setup

Model Setting	Model Description
Ours(cc+ de+)	Prototype model
Ours(cc- de+)	On the basis of the prototype model, the method based on identifier sequence matching is not used to cluster contracts, but only the similarity of contract semantic syntax feature vectors is used to generate the connection relationship between contracts
Ours(cc- de-)	On the basis of the prototype model, the feature data enhancement module is removed, and only the semantic syntax features of the contract are used for classification

The results of the ablation experiments are shown in Table 4. It can be seen that the prototype model ($cc+$ $de+$) exhibits better performance than the other ablated models, and the performance of the model with the identifier sequence matching method removed is better than that of the model with the feature data enhancement module completely removed. Each module that was ablated contributes to the improvement in model performance to some extent.

Table 4. The Results of Ablation Experiment

Model Setting	Accuracy (%)	Recall (%)
Ours(cc+ de+)	**89.28**	**89.08**
Ours(cc- de+)	85.12	85.22
Ours(cc- de-)	81.40	82.90

5 Conclusion

In this paper, we propose an unsupervised smart contract clustering method based on identifier sequence matching, which allows us to cluster functionally similar smart contracts into typical contract graphs without supervision. Based on the typical contract graph, we extract type features of smart contracts as a complement to their semantic syntax features, and achieve contract feature data enhancement by focusing on the smart contract type features that are closely related to vulnerabilities. Experimental results show that our method outperforms traditional smart contract detection methods and some state-of-the-art machine learning methods. We believe that our work provides a good idea for future research on smart contract vulnerability detection by focusing on smart contract types.

Acknowledgments. This research is founded by the National Key R&D Program of China (No. 2020YFB1006002).

References

1. Sayeed, S., Marco-Gisbert, H., Caira, T.: Smart contract: attacks and protections. IEEE Access **8**, 24416–24427 (2020)
2. Torres, C.F., Schütte, J., State, R.: Osiris: Hunting for integer bugs in ethereum smart contracts. In: Proceedings of the 34th Annual Computer Security Applications Conference, pp. 664–676 (2018)
3. Luu, L., Chu, D.H., Olickel, H., Saxena, P., Hobor, A.: Making smart contracts smarter. In: Proceedings of the 2016 ACM SIGSAC Conference on Computer and Communications Security, pp. 254–269 (2016)
4. Mueller, B.: Mythril-reversing and bug hunting framework for the ethereum blockchain (2017)
5. Tikhomirov, S., Voskresenskaya, E., Ivanitskiy, I., Takhaviev, R., Marchenko, E., Alexandrov, Y.: Smartcheck: static analysis of ethereum smart contracts. In: Proceedings of the 1st International Workshop on Emerging Trends in Software Engineering for Blockchain, pp. 9–16 (2018)
6. Jiang, B., Liu, Y., Chan, W.K.: Contractfuzzer: fuzzing smart contracts for vulnerability detection. In: Proceedings of the 33rd ACM/IEEE International Conference on Automated Software Engineering, pp. 259–269 (2018)
7. Gogineni, A.K., Swayamjyoti, S., Sahoo, D., Sahu, K.K., Kishore, R.: Multi-class classification of vulnerabilities in smart contracts using AWD-LSTM, with pre-trained encoder inspired from natural language processing. IOP Sci. Notes **1**(3), 035002 (2020)

8. Zhuang, Y., Liu, Z., Qian, P., Liu, Q., Wang, X., He, Q.: Smart contract vulnerability detection using graph neural network. In: IJCAI, pp. 3283–3290 (2020)
9. Liu, Z., Qian, P., Wang, X., Zhuang, Y., Qiu, L., Wang, X.: Combining graph neural networks with expert knowledge for smart contract vulnerability detection. IEEE Trans. Knowl. Data Eng. (2021)
10. Nguyen, H.H., et al.: Mando: multi-level heterogeneous graph embeddings for fine-grained detection of smart contract vulnerabilities. arXiv preprint arXiv:2208.13252 (2022)
11. Wohrer, M., Zdun, U.: Smart contracts: security patterns in the ethereum ecosystem and solidity. In: 2018 International Workshop on Blockchain Oriented Software Engineering (IWBOSE), pp. 2–8. IEEE (2018)
12. Scarselli, F., Gori, M., Tsoi, A.C., Hagenbuchner, M., Monfardini, G.: The graph neural network model. IEEE Trans. Neural Netw. **20**(1), 61–80 (2008)
13. Kipf, T.N., Welling, M.: Semi-supervised classification with graph convolutional networks. arXiv preprint arXiv:1609.02907 (2016)
14. Vaswani, A., et al.: Attention is all you need. Adv. Neural Inf. Process. Syst. **30** (2017)
15. Allamanis, M., Brockschmidt, M., Khademi, M.: Learning to represent programs with graphs. In: International Conference on Learning Representations
16. Hu, T., et al.: Transaction-based classification and detection approach for ethereum smart contract. Inf. Process. Manag. **58**(2), 102462 (2021)
17. Huang, Y., Kong, Q., Jia, N., Chen, X., Zheng, Z.: Recommending differentiated code to support smart contract update. In: 2019 IEEE/ACM 27th International Conference on Program Comprehension (ICPC), pp. 260–270. IEEE (2019)
18. Neamtiu, I., Foster, J.S., Hicks, M.: Understanding source code evolution using abstract syntax tree matching. In: Proceedings of the 2005 International Workshop on Mining Software Repositories, pp. 1–5 (2005)
19. Feist, J., Grieco, G., Groce, A.: Slither: a static analysis framework for smart contracts. In: 2019 IEEE/ACM 2nd International Workshop on Emerging Trends in Software Engineering for Blockchain (WETSEB), pp. 8–15. IEEE (2019)
20. Liu, C., Liu, H., Cao, Z., Chen, Z., Chen, B., Roscoe, B.: Reguard: finding reentrancy bugs in smart contracts. In: Proceedings of the 40th International Conference on Software Engineering: Companion Proceedings, pp. 65–68 (2018)
21. Tsankov, P., Dan, A., Drachsler-Cohen, D., Gervais, A., Buenzli, F., Vechev, M.: Securify: practical security analysis of smart contracts. In: Proceedings of the 2018 ACM SIGSAC Conference on Computer and Communications Security, pp. 67–82 (2018)
22. Shi, M., Tang, Y., Zhu, X., Wilson, D., Liu, J.: Multi-class imbalanced graph convolutional network learning. In: Proceedings of the Twenty-Ninth International Joint Conference on Artificial Intelligence (IJCAI-20) (2020)
23. Praitheeshan, P., Pan, L., Yu, J., Liu, J., Doss, R.: Security analysis methods on ethereum smart contract vulnerabilities: a survey. arXiv preprint arXiv:1908.08605 (2019)

EfficientSRFace: An Efficient Network with Super-Resolution Enhancement for Accurate Face Detection

Guangtao Wang[1], Jun Li[1(✉)], Jie Xie[1], Jianhua Xu[1], and Bo Yang[2]

[1] School of Computer and Electronic Information, Nanjing Normal University, 210023 Nanjing, China
[2] School of Artificial Intelligence, Nanjing University of Information Science and Technology, 210044 Nanjing, China
{202243023,lijuncst,73049,xujianhua}@njnu.edu.cn, 003402@nuist.edu.cn

Abstract. In face detection, low-resolution faces, such as numerous small faces of a human group in a crowded scene, are common in dense face prediction tasks. They usually contain limited visual clues and make small faces less distinguishable from the other small objects, which poses great challenge to accurate face detection. Although deep convolutional neural network has significantly promoted the research on face detection recently, current deep face detectors rarely take into account low-resolution faces and are still vulnerable to the real-world scenarios where massive amount of low-resolution faces exist. Consequently, they usually achieve degraded performance for low-resolution face detection. In order to alleviate this problem, we develop an efficient detector termed EfficientSRFace by introducing a feature-level super-resolution reconstruction network for enhancing the feature representation capability of the model. This module plays an auxiliary role in the training process, and can be removed during the inference without increasing the inference time. Extensive experiments on public benchmarking datasets, such as FDDB and WIDER Face, show that the embedded image super-resolution module can significantly improve the detection accuracy at the cost of a small amount of additional parameters and computational overhead, while helping our model achieve competitive performance compared with the state-of-the-arts.

Keywords: deep convolutional neural network · low-resolution face detection · feature-level super-resolution reconstruction · feature representation capability

1 Introduction

With the development of deep convolutional neural networks (CNNs), dramatic progress has been made recently in face detection which is one of the most fun-

---

Supported by the Natural Science Foundation of China (NSFC) under grants 62173186 and 62076134.

damental tasks in computer vision [1–3]. With superior representation capability, deep models have achieved unrivaled performance compared with traditional models. In pursuit of high performance, particularly, numerous heavyweight face detectors [4–6] are designed with excessive parameters and complex architecture. e.g., the advanced DSFD detector [7] has 100M+ parameters, costing 300G+ MACs. Although various lightweight designs are used for producing simplified and streamlined networks [8–10], the models trading accuracy for efficiency suffer from degraded performance. Recently, more efforts are devoted to designing efficient network, and the EfficientFace detector [11] has been proposed recently for addressing the compromise between efficiency and accuracy.

Fig. 1. Visualization of detection results achieved by EfficientFace (left) and our EfficientSRFace (right) in two different images. The results demonstrate the advantage of our network against the EfficientFace in the case of dense low-resolution face detection.

However, in real-world scenarios, low-resolution faces account for a large proportion in dense face detection tasks. For example, massive amount of small faces of a human group exist in a crowded scene for a low-quality image. They usually contain limited visual clues, making it difficult to accurately distinguish them from the other small objects and posing great challenge to accurate detection. Although current deep detectors have achieved enormous success, they are still prone to low-resolution face detection accuracy. As shown in Fig. 1, when handling the images including a large amount of densely distributed faces of a large human group with considerable variances, the EfficientFace reveals deteriorating performance without correctly identifying the low-resolution faces (Some small-scale blurred faces in the images are missing in the detection results). To alleviate this problem, we embed a feature-level image super-resolution reconstruction network into EfficientFace, and design a new detection framework termed EfficientSRFace for improving the accuracy of low-resolution face detection. As a simple residual attention network, the newly added reconstruction module can enhance the feature representation capability of our detector at the cost of a small amount of additional parameters and limited computational overhead growth. Notably, the module is only introduced into the training process and is discarded for inference, and thus inference efficiency is not affected.

To summarize, our contributions in this study are twofold as follows:

- In this paper, we develop a new efficient face detection architecture termed EfficientSRFace. Based on the well-established EfficientFace, a feature-level image super-resolution network is introduced, such that the feature representation capability of characterizing low-resolution faces is enhanced.
- Extensive experiments on public benchmarking datasets show that the super-resolution module can significantly improve the detection accuracy at the cost of a small amount of additional parameters and computational consumption, while helping our model achieve competitive performance compared with the state-of-the-arts.

2   Related Work

2.1   Face Detection

With the rapid development of deep networks for general-purpose object detection [12–15], significant progress has been made in face detection. Recently, various heavyweight face detectors have been designed to realize accurate face detection [16–19]. In order to speed up computation and reduce network parameters, Najibi et al. [20] proposed SSH detector by utilizing feature pyramid instead of image pyramid and removing the fully connected layer of the classification network. Tang et al. [2] proposed a new context assisted single shot face detector termed Pyramidbox considering context information. Liu et al. [21] designed HAMBox model which incorporates an online high-quality anchor mining strategy that can compensate mismatched faces with high-quality anchors. In addition, ASFD [22] combines neural structure search techniques with a newly designed loss function. Although the above models have superior performance, they have excessive architectural parameters and incur considerable costs during the training process. Lightweight model design has become the promising line of research in face detection. One representative lightweight model is EXTD [9], which is an iterative network sharing model for multi-stage face detection and significantly reduces the number of model parameters. Despite the success of both heavyweight and lightweight detectors, they still suffer insufficient descriptive ability of capturing low-resolution face, and thus reveal inferior performance when handling low-resolution face detection in real-world scenarios.

2.2 CNNs for Image Super-Resolution

Benefiting from the promise of CNN, major breakthroughs have also been made in the field of super-resolution (SR) reconstruction. Dong et al. [23] proposed a deep learning framework for single image super-resolution named SRCNN. For the first time, convolutional networks were introduced into SR tasks. Later, they improved SRCNN and introduced a compact hourglass CNN structure to realize faster and better SR model [24]. In order to improve the performance of image reconstruction, Kim et al. [25] proposed a deeper network model named VDSR. By cascading small filters in the deep network structure multiple times, the context information can be effectively explored. Wang et al. [26] developed ESRGAN and reduced computational complexity by removing the Batch Normalization (BN) layer and adding a residual structure. Zhang et al. [27] proposed a very deep residual channel attention network, which integrates the attention mechanism into the residual block and forms the residual channel attention module to obtain high-performance reconstructed images. Kong et al. [28] proposed SR pipeline that combined classification and super-resolution on the sub-image level and tackled acceleration via data characteristics. Cong et al. [29] unified pixel-to-pixel transformation and color-to-color transformation coherently in an end-to-end network named CDTNet. Extensive experiments demonstrate that CDTNet achieves a desirable balance between efficiency and effectiveness. In this paper, in order to alleviate the drawback of existing face detectors in low-resolution face detection, an image super-resolution network is embedded into our EfficientFace network to enhance the feature expression ability of the model. To our knowledge, this is the first attempt to incorporate the SR network into efficient face detector to address low-resolution face detection.

3 EfficientSRFace

In this section, we will briefly introduce our proposed EfficientSRFace framework followed by a detailed description of the embedded feature-level super-resolution module. In addition, the loss function of our network will also be discussed.

3.1 Network Architecture

The network architecture of EfficientSRFace is shown in Fig. 2. It adopts the framework of the EfficientFace detector [11] which mainly comprises three key components of SBiFPN, RFE and attention modules. To enhance the expression capability of degraded low-resolution image features and improve the detection accuracy of blurred faces, the feature-level image super-resolution reconstruction module illustrated in dashed box is incorporated into EfficientFace in which EfficientNet-B4 is used as the backbone. Considering that the image super-resolution reconstruction result largely depends on features with sufficient representation capability, the image super-resolution module is added to the feature layer OP_2 of the EfficientFace, since the scale of the feature map at OP_2 is $1/4$ of the original scale after image pre-processing, and encodes abundant visual information to guarantee accurate super-resolution reconstruction.

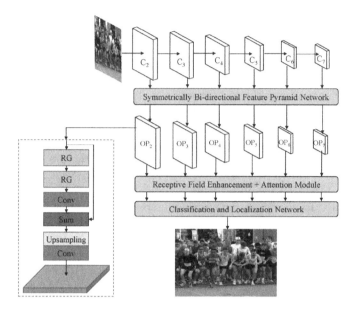

Fig. 2. The network structure of our proposed EfficientSRFace. The introduced Residual Channel Attention Network (RCAN) serving as the super-resolution module is illustrated in a dashed box. To guarantee the reconstruction quality, the module is added to the relatively larger scale feature layer OP_2.

3.2   Image Super-Resolution Enhancement

Although EfficientFace [11] achieves desirable detection accuracy when handling larger scale faces, it reports inferior performance when detecting low-resolution faces in the degraded image. In particular, numerous small faces carry much less visual clues, which makes the detector fail to discriminate them and increases the detection difficulty especially when the degraded images are not clearly captured. Consequently, we introduce Residual Channel Attention Network (RCAN) [27] within our EfficientSRFace, such that we perform feature-level super-resolution on EfficientFace for feature enhancement.

As shown in Fig. 2, Residual Group (RG) component within RCAN is used to increase the depth of the network and extract high-level features. It is also a residual structure which consists of two consecutive residual Channel Attention Blocks (RCABs). RCAB in Fig. 3 aims to combine the input features and the subsequent features prior to channel attention. Thus, it helps to increase the channel-aware weights and benefits the subsequent super-resolution reconstruction. Increasing the number of RGs contributes to further performance gains, whereas inevitably leads to excessive model parameters and computational overhead. This also increases the training difficulty of our network. For efficiency, the number of RGs is set to 2 in our scenario. Afterwards, the input low-level and high-level features resulting from RGs are fused by pixelwise addition strategy to enrich the feature information and help the network to boost the reconstruction quality. Finally, the upsampling strategy is used to increase the scale of features with the upsampling factor within our model set as 4.

It should be noted that the RCAN module only plays a supplementary and auxiliary role during the training process, and it is discarded during reference without affecting detection efficiency within our EfficientSRFace.

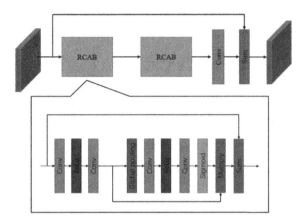

Fig. 3. Network structure of the RG module. It is essentially a residual structure which consists of consecutive Residual Channel Attention Blocks (RCABs). RCABs integrate channel-aware attention mechanism into Residual Blocks (RBs) for accurate super-resolution reconstruction. Although increasing RG modules helps training deeper network and improve SR performance, the number of RGs is set to 2 for efficiency in our case.

3.3 Loss Function

Mathematically, the overall loss function of our EfficientSRFace model is formulated as Eq. (1) which consists of three terms respectively calculating classification loss, regression loss and super-resolution reconstruction loss. Considering that our main focus is accurate detection, we assume the former two terms outweigh the SR loss and utilize the parameter φ to balance the contribution of super-resolution reconstruction to the total loss function.

$$L_{ef} = L_{focal} + L_{smooth} + \varphi L_{sr} \qquad (1)$$

More specifically, taking into account the sample imbalance, focal loss [30] is utilized for the classification loss indicated as:

$$L_{focal} = -\alpha_t(1 - p_t)^\gamma log(p_t) \qquad (2)$$

where $p_t \in [0, 1]$ is the probability estimated for the class with label 1, and α_t is the balancing factor. Besides, γ is the focusing parameter that adjusts the rate at which simple samples are downweighted.

In addition, smooth ℓ_1 is used as the regression loss for accurate face localization as follows:

$$smooth_{\ell_1}(x) = \begin{cases} 0.5x^2 & |y| < 1 \\ |y| - 0.5 & otherwise \end{cases} \tag{3}$$

In terms of super-resolution reconstruction loss, ℓ_1 loss is adopted to measure the difference between the super-resolution reconstructed image and the target image formulated as follows:

$$L_{sr} = \frac{1}{WH} \sum_{i=1}^{W} \sum_{j=1}^{H} |y_{ij} - Y_{ij}| \tag{4}$$

where W and H respectively represent the width and the height of the input image, while y and Y respectively represent the pixel values of the reconstructed and the target image.

4   Experiments

In this section, extensive experiments are conducted to evaluate our proposed EfficientSRFace. Firstly, the public benchmarking datasets and experimental setting will be briefly introduced in our experiments. Next, comprehensive evaluations and comparative studies are also carried out with detailed model analysis.

4.1   Datasets and Evaluation Metrics

We have evaluated our EfficientSRFace network on four public benchmarking datasets for face detection including AFW [31], Pascal Face [32], FDDB [33] and WIDER Face [34]. Known as the most challenging large-scale face detection dataset thus far, WIDER Face comprises 32K+ images with 393K+ annotated faces exhibiting dramatic variances in scales, occlusion and poses. It is split into training (40%), validation (10%) and testing sets (50%). Depending on different difficulty levels, the whole dataset is divided into three subsets, namely Easy, Medium and Hard subsets. For performance measure, Average Precision (AP) and Precision-Recall (PR) curves are used for metrics in different datasets.

4.2   Implementation Details

In implementation, the anchor sizes used in our EfficientSRFace network are empirically set as {16, 32, 64, 128, 256, 512} and their aspect ratios are unanimously 1:1. In terms of the model optimization, AdamW algorithm is used as the optimizer and ReduceLROnPlateau attenuation strategy is employed to adjust the learning rate which is initially set to 10^{-4}. If the loss function stops descending within three epochs, the learning rate will be decreased by 10 times and eventually decay to 10^{-8}. The batch size is set as 4 for network training. The training and inference process are completed on a server equipped with a NVIDIA GTX3090 GPU under PyTorch framework.

Table 1. Comparison of the EfficientFace and our EfficientSRFace detector using different backbone networks.

Backbone	model	Easy	Medium	Hard	Params (M)	MACs (G)
EfficientNet-B0	EfficientFace	91.0%	89.1%	83.6%	3.89	4.80
	EfficientSRFace	92.5%	90.7%	85.8%	3.90	5.17
EfficientNet-B1	EfficientFace	91.9%	90.2%	85.1%	6.54	7.81
	EfficientSRFace	92.7%	90.9%	86.3%	6.56	8.43
EfficientNet-B2	EfficientFace	92.5%	91.0%	86.3%	7.83	10.49
	EfficientSRFace	93.0%	91.7%	87.2%	7.86	11.44
EfficientNet-B3	EfficientFace	93.1%	91.8%	87.1%	11.22	18.28
	EfficientSRFace	93.7%	92.3%	87.6%	11.27	20.06
EfficientNet-B4	EfficientFace	94.4%	93.4%	89.1%	18.75	32.54
	EfficientSRFace	**95.0%**	**93.9%**	**89.9%**	18.84	35.83

4.3 Data Enhancement

In terms of training the image super-resolution reconstruction module, the super-resolution labels are the original images, while the images preprocessed by random blur are delivered to the module. More specifically, in addition to the usual image enhancement methods such as contrast and brightness enhancement, random cropping and horizontal flip, we also leverage random Gaussian blur processing for the input images.

4.4 Results

Comparison of Different Backbones. Table 1 presents the comparison of the EfficientFace and our proposed EfficientSRFace with different backbone networks. It can be observed EfficientSRFace consistently outperforms EfficientFace with different backbones used. In particular, when EfficientNet-B0 is used as the backbone, further performance improvements of 1.5%, 1.6% and 2.2% are reported on the three respective subsets. With the increase in the complexity of the backbone network structure, slightly declined performance gains can be observed. Since EfficientNet-B0 backbone has much less parameters and enjoys more efficient structure, it is prone to insufficient representation capability. In this sense, incorporating the feature-level super-resolution module is beneficial for enhancing the feature expression capability of the backbone, and bring more performance gains compared with our model using other efficient backbones. More importantly, the auxiliary super-resolution module incurs a small amount of additional parameters and slight growth in computational overhead, which suggests it hardly affects the detection efficiency.

In addition to the detection accuracy, we also present the Frame-Per-Second (FPS) values of our EfficientSRFace models for efficiency evaluation. As shown in Fig. 4, although FPS generally exhibits a decreasing trend with the increase of image resolution, our model can still achieve real-time detection speed. For example, our model achieves 28 FPS speed for the image size of 1024×1024 when

EfficientFace-B0 is used as backbone, which fully demonstrates the desirable efficiency of our EfficientSRFace.

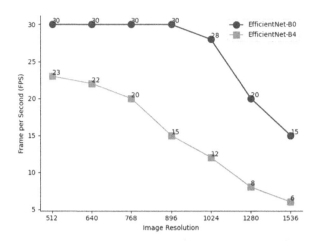

Fig. 4. FPS scores of our models at various scales using different backbones. For each image resolution using specific network backbone, the FPS score is obtained by averaging results of 1000 times.

Parameter Analysis of φ. As shown in Fig. 5, we explore the effects of different weight parameter values of φ on our model performance and compare the results with the EfficientFace (illustrated in dotted line). In this experiment, EfficientNet-B1 is used as the backbone network, and the batch size of model is set to 8. It can be observed that performance improvements to varying extents are reported on Hard subset with different φ values. This demonstrates the substantial advantages of the super-resolution module particularly in the difficult cases including low-resolution face detection. Besides, the highest AP scores of 92.5% (Easy), 91.1% (Medium) and 86.7% (Hard) are reported when φ is set to 0.1, which is consistently superior to EfficientFace achieving 92.4%, 90.9% and 85.3% on the three subsets. Thus, φ is set to the optimal 0.1 in our experiments.

Comparison of EfficientSRFace with State-of-the-Art Detectors. In this part, the proposed EfficientSRFace is compared with state-of-the-art detectors in terms of both accuracy and efficiency on WIDER Face validation set. As shown in Table 2, the competing models involved in our comparative studies include both heavy detectors such as DSFD and lightweight models like YOLOv5 variants and EXTD. In comparison to the heavy detectors, our EfficientSRFace-L using EfficientNet-B4 as the backbone achieves competitive performance with significantly reduced parameters and computational costs. In particular, EfficientSRFace-L reports respective 95.0%, 93.9% and 89.9% AP scores on Easy, Medium, and Hard subsets, which is on par with DSFD achieving 96.6%, 95.7%

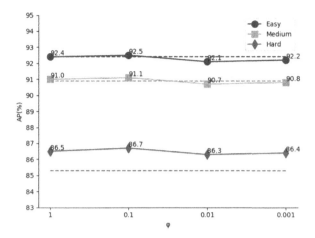

Fig. 5. Influence of different weight parameter values φ on model detection performance, where the dotted line represents that no super resolution module is embedded.

and 90.4% accuracies. However, our model enjoys approximately 6× reduced parameters and costs 10× decreased MACs. Particularly, when EfficientNet-B0 is used as the backbone in our EfficientSRFace detector, EfficientSRFace-S achieves preferable efficiency which is competitive with lightweight YOLOv5n, while outperforming the latter by 5% on Hard set. Benefiting from efficient architecture design of EfficientFace, our model enjoys different variants ranging from extremely efficient model superior to the other lightweight competitors and the relatively larger network comparable to some heavyweight models, and demonstrates the advantages in terms of the compromise between efficiency and accuracy.

Comprehensive Evaluations on the Four Benchmarks. In this section, we will comprehensively compare EfficientSRFace and other advanced detectors in the four public datasets. Figure 7 shows precision-recall (PR) curves obtained by different models on validation set of WIDER Face dataset. Although EfficientSR-Face is still inferior to some advanced heavy detectors, it still achieves competitive performance with promising model efficiency. In addition to WIDER Face dataset, we also evaluate our EfficientSRFace on the other three datasets and carry out more comparative studies. As shown in Table 3, our EfficientSRFace-L achieves respective 99.94% and 98.84% AP scores on AFW and PASCAL Face datasets. In particular, EfficientSRFace consistently beats the other competitors including even heavyweight models like MogFace and RefineFace [35] on AFW. In addition to AP scores, we also present PR curves of different detectors on AFW, PASCAL Face and FDDB datasets as shown in Fig. 6. On FDDB dataset, more specifically, when the number of false positives is 1000, our model reports the true positive rate up to 96.7%, surpassing most face detectors.

Table 2. Comparison of EfficientSRFace and other advanced face detectors. EfficientSRFace-S and EfficientSRFace-L denote our two models with EfficientNet-B0 and EfficientNet-B4 respectively used as the backbones.

Model	Easy	Medium	Hard	Params (M)	MACs (G)
MogFace-E [4]	**97.7%**	**96.9%**	92.01%	85.67	349.14
MogFace [4]	97.0%	96.3%	**93.0%**	85.26	807.92
AInnoFace [5]	97.0%	96.1%	91.8%	88.01	312.45
SRNFace-1400 [6]	96.5%	95.2%	89.6%	53.38	251.94
SRNFace-2100 [6]	96.5%	95.3%	90.2%	53.38	251.94
DSFD [7]	96.6%	95.7%	90.4%	120	345.16
yolov5n-0.5 [8]	90.76%	88.12%	73.82%	0.45	0.73
yolov5n [8]	93.61%	91.52%	80.53%	1.72	2.75
yolov5s [8]	94.33%	92.61%	83.15%	7.06	7.62
yolov5m [8]	95.30%	93.76%	85.28%	21.04	24.09
yolov5l [8]	95.78%	94.30%	86.13%	46.60	55.31
EXTD-32 [9]	89.6%	88.5%	82.5%	0.063	5.29
EXTD-64 [9]	92.1%	91.1%	85.6%	0.16	13.26
EfficientSRFace-S (Ours)	92.5%	90.7%	85.8%	3.90	5.17
EfficientSRFace-L (Ours)	95.0%	93.9%	89.9%	18.84	35.83

Table 3. Comparison of EfficientSRFace and other detectors on the AFW and PAS-CAL Face datasets (AP).

Models	AFW	PASCA Face
RefineFace [35]	99.90%	**99.45%**
FA-RPN [36]	99.53%	99.42%
MogFace [4]	99.85%	99.32%
SFDet [37]	99.85%	98.20%
SRN [6]	99.87%	99.09%
FaceBoxes [38]	98.91%	96.30%
HyperFace-ResNet [39]	99.40%	96.20%
STN [40]	98.35%	94.10%
Ours	**99.94%**	98.84%

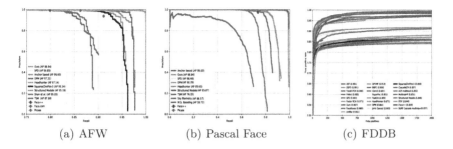

(a) AFW   (b) Pascal Face   (c) FDDB

Fig. 6. Evaluation on common face detection datasets.

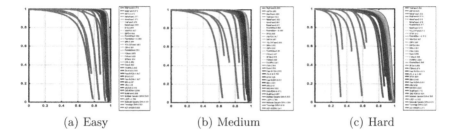

(a) Easy   (b) Medium   (c) Hard

Fig. 7. PR curves of different methods on validation set of WIDER Face dataset.

5   Conclusions

In this paper, we develop an efficient network architecture based on Efficient-Face termed EfficientSRFace to better handle the low-resolution face detection. To this end, we embed a feature-level super-resolution reconstruction module to feature pyramid network for enhancing the feature representation capability of the model. This module plays an auxiliary role in the training process and can be removed during the inference without increasing the inference time. More importantly, this supplementary role incurs a small amount of additional parameters and limited growth in computational overhead without damaging model efficiency. Extensive experiments on public benchmarking datasets demonstrate that the embedded image super-resolution module can significantly improve the detection accuracy at a small cost.

References

1. Vesdapunt, N., Wang, B.: Crface: confidence ranker for model-agnostic face detection refinement. In: Proceedings of the IEEE/CVF Conference on Computer Vision and Pattern Recognition, pp. 1674–1684 (2021)
2. Tang, X., Du, D.K., He, Z., Liu, J.: Pyramidbox: a context-assisted single shot face detector. In: Proceedings of the European Conference on Computer Vision, pp. 797–813 (2018)

3. Ming, X., Wei, F., Zhang, T., Chen, D., Wen, F.: Group sampling for scale invariant face detection. In: Proceedings of the IEEE/CVF Conference on Computer Vision and Pattern Recognition, pp. 3446–3456 (2019)
4. Liu, Y., Wang, F., Deng, J., Zhou, Z., Sun, B., Li, H.: Mogface: towards a deeper appreciation on face detection. In: Proceedings of the IEEE/CVF Conference on Computer Vision and Pattern Recognition, pp. 4093–4102 (2022)
5. Zhang, F., Fan, X., Ai, G., Song, J., Qin, Y., Wu, J.: Accurate face detection for high performance. arXiv preprint arXiv:1905.01585, pp. 1–9 (2019)
6. Chi, C., Zhang, S., Xing, J., Lei, Z., Li, S.Z., Zou, X.: Selective refinement network for high performance face detection. In: Proceedings of the AAAI Conference on Artificial Intelligence, vol. 33, pp. 8231–8238 (2019)
7. Li, J., et al.: DSFD: dual shot face detector. In: Proceedings of the IEEE/CVF Conference on Computer Vision and Pattern Recognition, pp. 5060–5069 (2019)
8. Qi, D., Tan, W., Yao, Q., Liu, J.: Yolo5face: why reinventing a face detector. In: Proceedings of the European Conference on Computer Vision Workshops, pp. 228–244 (2022)
9. Yoo, Y., Han, D., Yun, S.: EXTD: extremely tiny face detector via iterative filter reuse. arXiv preprint arXiv:1906.06579, pp. 1–11 (2019)
10. He, Y., Xu, D., Wu, L., Jian, M., Xiang, S., Pan, C.: LFFD: a light and fast face detector for edge devices. arXiv preprint arXiv:1904.10633, pp. 1–10 (2019)
11. Wang, G., Li, J., Wu, Z., Xu, J., Shen, J., Yang, W.: EfficientFace: An Efficient Deep Network with Feature Enhancement for Accurate Face Detection. Multimedia Systems, pp. 1–15 (2023)
12. Liu, W., et al.: SSD: single shot multibox detector. In: Proceedings of the European Conference on Computer Vision, pp. 21–37 (2016)
13. Redmon, J., Divvala, S., Girshick, R., Farhadi, A.: You only look once: unified, real-time object detection. In: Proceedings of the IEEE/CVF Conference on Computer Vision and Pattern Recognition, pp. 779–788 (2016)
14. Duan, K., Bai, S., Xie, L., Qi, H., Huang, Q., Tian, Q.: Centernet: keypoint triplets for object detection. In: Proceedings of the IEEE/CVF International Conference on Computer Vision, pp. 6569–6578 (2019)
15. Tan, M., Pang, R., Le, Q.V.: Efficientdet: scalable and efficient object detection. In: Proceedings of the IEEE/CVF Conference on Computer Vision and Pattern Recognition, pp. 10781–10790 (2020)
16. Zhang, C., Xu, X., Tu, D.: Face detection using improved faster RCNN. arXiv preprint arXiv:1802.02142, pp. 1–9 (2018)
17. Zhang, S., et al.: Improved selective refinement network for face detection. arXiv preprint arXiv:1901.06651, pp. 1–8 (2019)
18. Zhang, Y., Xu, X., Liu, X.: Robust and high performance face detector. arXiv preprint arXiv:1901.02350, pp. 1–9 (2019)
19. Zhu, Y., Cai, H., Zhang, S., Wang, C., Xiong, Y.: Tinaface: strong but simple baseline for face detection. arXiv preprint arXiv:2011.13183, pp. 1–9 (2020)
20. Najibi, M., Samangouei, P., Chellappa, R., Davis, L.S.: SSH: Single stage headless face detector. In: Proceedings of the IEEE/CVF International Conference on Computer Vision, pp. 4875–4884 (2017)
21. Liu, Y., Tang, X., Han, J., Liu, J., Rui, D., Wu, X.: Hambox: delving into mining high-quality anchors on face detection. In: Proceedings of the IEEE/CVF Conference on Computer Vision and Pattern Recognition, pp. 13043–13051 (2020)
22. Li, J., et al.: ASFD: Automatic and scalable face detector. In: Proceedings of the 29th ACM International Conference on Multimedia, pp. 2139–2147 (2021)

23. Dong, C., Loy, C.C., He, K., Tang, X.: Image super-resolution using deep convolutional networks. IEEE Trans. Pattern Anal. Mach. Intell. **38**(2), 295–307 (2015)
24. Dong, C., Loy, C.C., Tang, X.: Accelerating the super-resolution convolutional neural network. In: Proceedings of the European Conference on Computer Vision, pp. 391–407 (2016)
25. Kim, J., Lee, J.K., Lee, K.M.: Accurate image super-resolution using very deep convolutional networks. In: Proceedings of the IEEE/CVF Conference on Computer Vision and Pattern Recognition, pp. 1646–1654 (2016)
26. Wang, X., et al.: ESRGAN: enhanced super-resolution generative adversarial networks. In: Proceedings of the European Conference on Computer Vision, pp. 36–79 (2018)
27. Zhang, Y., Li, K., Li, K., Wang, L., Zhong, B., Fu, Y.: Image super-resolution using very deep residual channel attention networks. In: Proceedings of the European Conference on Computer Vision, pp. 286–301 (2018)
28. Kong, X., Zhao, H., Qiao, Y., Dong, C.: Classsr: a general framework to accelerate super-resolution networks by data characteristic. In: Proceedings of the IEEE/CVF Conference on Computer Vision and Pattern Recognition, pp. 12016–12025 (2021)
29. Cong, W., et al.: High-resolution image harmonization via collaborative dual transformations. In: Proceedings of the IEEE/CVF Conference on Computer Vision and Pattern Recognition, pp. 18470–18479 (2022)
30. Lin, T.-Y., Goyal, P., Girshick, R., He, K., Dollar, P.: Focal loss for dense object detection. In: Proceedings of the IEEE/CVF International Conference on Computer Vision, pp. 2980–2988 (2017)
31. Zhu, X., Ramanan, D.: Face detection, pose estimation, and landmark localization in the wild. In: Proceedings of the IEEE/CVF Conference on Computer Vision and Pattern Recognition, pp. 2879–2886 (2012)
32. Yan, J., Zhang, X., Lei, Z., Li, S.Z.: Face detection by structural models. Image Vis. Comput. **32**(10), 790–799 (2014)
33. Jain, V., Learned-Miller, E.: FDDB: A Benchmark for Face Detection in Unconstrained Settings. Technical Report, UMass Amherst Technical Report (2010)
34. Yang, S., Luo, P., Loy, C.-C., Tang, X.: Wider face: a face detection benchmark. In: Proceedings of the IEEE/CVF Conference on Computer Vision and Pattern Recognition, pp. 5525–5533 (2016)
35. Zhang, S., Chi, C., Lei, Z., Li, S.Z.: Refineface: refinement neural network for high performance face detection. IEEE Trans. Pattern Anal. Mach. Intell. **43**(11), 4008–4020 (2020)
36. Najibi, M., Singh, B., Davis, L.S.: Fa-rpn: floating region proposals for face detection. In: Proceedings of the IEEE/CVF Conference on Computer Vision and Pattern Recognition, pp. 7723–7732 (2019)
37. Zhang, S., Wen, L., Shi, H., Lei, Z., Lyu, S., Li, S.Z.: Single-shot scale-aware network for real-time face detection. Int. J. Comput. Vision **127**(6), 537–559 (2019)
38. Zhang, S., Zhu, X., Lei, Z., Shi, H., Wang, X., Li, S.Z.: Faceboxes: a CPU real-time face detector with high accuracy. In: 2017 IEEE International Joint Conference on Biometrics, pp. 1–9 (2017)
39. Ranjan, R., Patel, V.M., Chellappa, R.: Hyperface: a deep multi-task learning framework for face detection, landmark localization, pose estimation, and gender recognition. IEEE Trans. Pattern Anal. Mach. Intell. **41**(1), 121–135 (2017)
40. Chen, D., Hua, G., Wen, F., Sun, J.: Supervised transformer network for efficient face detection. In: Proceedings of the European Conference on Computer Vision, pp. 122–138 (2016)

CompTLL-UNet: Compressed Domain Text-Line Localization in Challenging Handwritten Documents Using Deep Feature Learning from JPEG Coefficients

Bulla Rajesh[1,2(✉)] 🆔, Sk Mahafuz Zaman[2], Mohammed Javed[2]🆔, and P. Nagabhushan[2]🆔

[1] Department of CSE, IIIT-SriCity, Chittoor, AP, India
`rajesh.bulla@iiits.in`
[2] Department of IT, IIIT-Allahabad, Prayagraj, UP, India
{`mit2020005,javed,pnagabhushan`}`@iiita.ac.in`

Abstract. Automatic localization of text-lines in handwritten documents is still an open and challenging research problem. Various writing issues such as uneven spacing between the lines, oscillating and touching text, and the presence of skew become much more challenging when the case of complex handwritten document images are considered for segmentation directly in their respective compressed representation. This is because, the conventional way of processing compressed documents is through decompression, but here in this paper, we propose an idea that employs deep feature learning directly from the JPEG compressed coefficients without full decompression to accomplish text-line localization in the JPEG compressed domain. A modified U-Net architecture known as Compressed Text-Line Localization Network (CompTLL-UNet) is designed to accomplish it. The model is trained and tested with JPEG compressed version of benchmark datasets including ICDAR2017 (cBAD) and ICDAR2019 (cBAD), reporting the state-of-the-art performance with reduced storage and computational costs in the JPEG compressed domain.

Keywords: Compressed Domain · Deep Feature Learning · CompTLL-UNet · DCT · Text-Line localization

1 Introduction

Localization of text-lines in the document image is a very crucial pre-processing step towards many significant Document Image Analysis (DIA) applications like word spotting, handwriting recognition, and Optical Character Recognition (OCR) frequently required in many public places like Banks, Postal service and embassies etc. [1]. Specifically, in the case of handwritten documents, the text-lines usually have skew and uneven spacing, and due to which many a time the characters get touching and overlapping, thus making segmentation a challenging problem [2–4]. Apart from these inherent issues, sometimes the contents in

H. Lu et al. (Eds.): ACPR 2023, LNCS 14407, pp. 88–101, 2023.
https://doi.org/10.1007/978-3-031-47637-2_7

the historical handwritten document come up with colossal noise, degraded text, variations of backgrounds, complex layouts, multi-columns, presence of tables, and marginalia, as shown in Fig. 1. Performing segmentation or localization task on such documents further increase the complexity of many challenges [5]. However, the processing of documents directly in compressed form is an important research issue because compressing images before transmission or archival has become the normal trend to save disk space, transmission time and internet bandwidth [6–8]. Therefore, researchers have started looking for technology that can handle or process these compressed images without involving decompression stage that requires more computational overhead [9–11].

In the recent literature [8,12], there are some efforts to process document images directly in the compressed domain and reported less computation time and reduced storage space. Therefore performing text line localization in such complex handwritten documents and that too directly in the compressed domain is going to be advantageous and contributing research problem for all DIA applications. Although analyzing compressed representation is a difficult task, a typical algorithm that is proposed should be able to correctly locate text-lines irrespective of various challenges present in it. Also, the direct processing of compressed data should show a improved performance in terms of reduced computational and storage costs. Therefore, this research paper proposes to tackle the issue of text-line localization and explore text-line segmentation in the case of complex historical handwritten documents directly in the JPEG compressed representation. Unlike the conventional approaches, the proposed method in the present paper applies a partial decompression to extract the JPEG compressed streams of document images, and feeds the input stream directly to the deep learning architectures as shown in Fig. 2.

Fig. 1. Sample complex handwritten document images reproduced from ICDAR2017 dataset

There are three major contributions reported in this research paper:

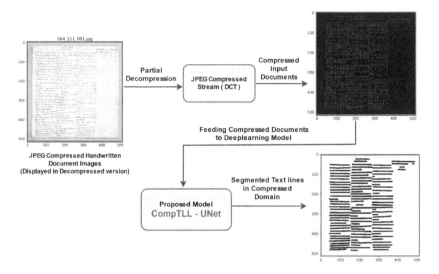

Fig. 2. The flow diagram of the proposed model CompTTL-UNet for localizing the text-lines directly in JPEG compressed document images.

- CompTLL-UNet model for text-line localization in compressed domain.
- Direct feeding of JPEG compressed stream into the CompTTL-UNet model for deep feature learning from compressed data. The mathematical visualization of the processing (in the form of matrix and kernals) of compressed streams and pixel streams has been explained.
- Reduced computational and storage costs in comparison to conventional methods.

The proposed model has been trained and tested on two benchmark datasets, and the results have showed the state-of-the-art accuracy and significant performance in terms of computational cost and storage as explained in detailed in the result section. The rest of the paper is divided into four sections. Section 2 discusses the extraction of JPEG Compressed input stream and feeding to the deep learning model. Section 3 explains the proposed methodology and details of model architecture. Section 4 report the experimental results and analysis, and comparison with existing methods. Section 5 concludes the work with a brief summary and possible future work.

2   Preamble to JPEG Compressed Domain

This section demonstrates the differences between feeding of uncompressed document images and JPEG compressed document images into the deep learning model, and contrasts the challenges associated with JPEG compressed document images against uncompressed document images.

2.1 Uncompressed Document Images

So far, many research problems including feature extraction, segmentation and recognition have been discussed extensively in uncompressed domain and addressed many implementation challenges associated with each problem in the case of uncompressed document images [12,13]. But the challenges with compressed documents are different in comparison to pixel/uncompressed domain, complex to visualize and much more difficult to address [12]. Before looking into the JPEG compressed document images, some common observation available on the uncompressed document images provides background knowledge to understand the JPEG compressed input streams as shown in Fig. 3. The Fig. 3(a) shows the baseline regions of a sample text-lines in an uncompressed document image (064_211_001.jpg) and Fig. 3(b) shows the JPEG compressed representation of Fig. 3(a).

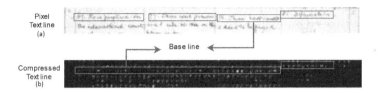

Fig. 3. The visualization of base line regions of text-lines in (a) pixel/uncompressed document and (b) in JPEG compressed document images (064_211_001.jpg).

In the Fig. 3(a), it can be noticed that the text-lines are arranged in four columns with irregular separating spaces and touching of the text with adjacent text-lines. Similarly, in Fig. 3(b) same text-lines which are in the compressed representation not providing any clues of separating space. In order to understand the pixel level details of the same text-lines, a sample pixel values from an 8×8 block of the a text-line is shown in B matrix.

$$B = \begin{bmatrix} 244\ 244\ 244\ 244\ 244\ 244 \\ 244\ 244\ 244\ 244\ 244\ 244 \\ 244\ 244\ 244\ 244\ 244\ 244 \\ 244\ 244\ 244\ 244\ 244\ 244 \\ 244\ 244\ 244\ 244\ 244\ 244 \\ 244\ 244\ 244\ 244\ 244\ 244 \end{bmatrix} \quad K = \frac{1}{9} \begin{bmatrix} 1\ 1\ 1 \\ 1\ 1\ 1 \\ 1\ 1\ 1 \end{bmatrix} \tag{1}$$

In B, it is observed that the pixel values possess high correlation, positive integers and less chaos/variation. Since deep neural networks are well known for processing the regular pixel values with different filters K of sizes 3×3, 5×5, and 7×7, and the networks steadily pool the meaningful features when filters are applied on these pixels at each level in the network. It continue to maintain the pixels correlation it finds as the network goes deep, and eventually learns salient feature representations at every level. However, this process may looks similar in the compressed domain, but that is not the same in the case of JPEG compressed document images because the arrangement of text-line in the compressed representation are resulted from 8×8 DCT transformation without bothering about the positions of the inside text contents, which is explained below.

2.2   JPEG Compressed Document Images

During compression, JPEG algorithm divides the uncompressed image f into 8×8 blocks and transforms each block B using Discrete Cosine Transformation (DCT) as per Eq. (2) and quantization [9], and generates DB (DCT block) and QDB (Quantized DCT block) representations. And further it applies sequence of operations such as DPCM, run-length, and Huffman entropy encodings to compress the contents to its binary form. Since, JPEG compressed images undergo DCT transformation, quantization and subsequent encodings, most of the text contents get overlapped during 8×8 block division and loose some useful visual clues. Some times the text-line get mixed up with adjacent (all sides) text-lines without leaving any separation gap for baseline regions as shown in Fig. 3(b) (green color bounding box). In comparison to the text-line contents in uncompressed documents (a) (red color bounding box), most text-line contents in compressed documents appears in a crooked way as shown for a sample text-line in JPEG compressed domain in Fig. 3. Here, the text-lines in different columns are mixed, and only few minute visual clues are available to analyze. In comparison to pixel block B, the DB and QDB blocks contain very few coefficient values and when a kernal K is applied when fed to deep learning model it process same set of values as shown in DB^* and QDB^* blocks. However it is observed that since these coefficient values are already showing some average spatial behaviour of the block, deep models are optimizing based on the those available values in the DCT stream.

$$F_{uv} = \frac{c_u c_v}{4} \sum_{i=0}^{7} \sum_{j=0}^{7} B(i,j) cos(\frac{(2i+1)u\pi}{16}) cos(\frac{(2j+1)v\pi}{16}) \qquad (2)$$

$$Where, \qquad C_u, C_v = \begin{cases} \frac{1}{\sqrt{2}}, & for\ u,v = 0 \\ 1, & otherwise, \end{cases}$$

$$DB = \begin{bmatrix} 1955 & 0 & 0 & 0 & 0 & 0 & 0 & 0 \\ 0 & 0 & 0 & 0 & 0 & 0 & 0 & 0 \\ -1 & 0 & 0 & 0 & 0 & 0 & 0 & 0 \\ 0 & 0 & 0 & 0 & 0 & 0 & 0 & 0 \\ 0 & 0 & 0 & 0 & 0 & 0 & 0 & 0 \\ 0 & 0 & 0 & 0 & 0 & 0 & 0 & 0 \\ 0 & 0 & 0 & 0 & 0 & 1 & 0 & 0 \\ 0 & 0 & 0 & 0 & 0 & 0 & 0 & 0 \end{bmatrix} \quad DB^* = \begin{bmatrix} 217 & 0 & 0 & 0 & 0 & 0 \\ 0 & 0 & 0 & 0 & 0 & 0 \\ 0 & 0 & 0 & 0 & 0 & 0 \\ 0 & 0 & 0 & 0 & 0 & 0 \\ 0 & 0 & 0 & 0 & 0 & 0 \\ 0 & 0 & 0 & 0 & 0 & 0 \end{bmatrix} \qquad (3)$$

$$QDB = \begin{bmatrix} 122 & 0 & 0 & 0 & 0 & 0 & 0 & 0 \\ 0 & 0 & 0 & 0 & 0 & 0 & 0 & 0 \\ 0 & 0 & 0 & 0 & 0 & 0 & 0 & 0 \\ 0 & 0 & 0 & 0 & 0 & 0 & 0 & 0 \\ 0 & 0 & 0 & 0 & 0 & 0 & 0 & 0 \\ 0 & 0 & 0 & 0 & 0 & 0 & 0 & 0 \\ 0 & 0 & 0 & 0 & 0 & 0 & 0 & 0 \\ 0 & 0 & 0 & 0 & 0 & 0 & 0 & 0 \end{bmatrix} QDB^* = \begin{bmatrix} 13 & 0 & 0 & 0 & 0 & 0 \\ 0 & 0 & 0 & 0 & 0 & 0 \\ 0 & 0 & 0 & 0 & 0 & 0 \\ 0 & 0 & 0 & 0 & 0 & 0 \\ 0 & 0 & 0 & 0 & 0 & 0 \\ 0 & 0 & 0 & 0 & 0 & 0 \end{bmatrix} \tag{4}$$

3   Proposed Methodology

This section explains the proposed methodology and the details of the deep learning architecture to localize the text-line boundaries in challenging handwritten documents directly in JPEG compressed domain.

The sequence of steps in the proposed method are shown in Fig. 2. First the partial decompression (entropy decoding) is applied on JPEG compressed document images to extract the input JPEG compressed streams. This input stream is arranged in quantized representation (QDB) in which except DC most of the AC coefficient values are zero. Then the extracted streams are fed as input to a proposed deep learning model CompTLL-UNet to learn different patterns to localize the baseline regions of text-line boundaries in the JPEG compressed document image.

Since UNet [14] is a popular architecture for segmentation tasks, the proposed architecture in the present paper is designed by modifying the existing UNet [14] architecture. The architecture of UNet is modified in such a way that it can be trained with compressed data and still produce promising accuracy. In the UNet architecture, the successive pooling layers are replaced by up-sampling layers so the successive convolution layer can learn more precise information. It has a large number of feature channels that propagate context information to higher resolution layers. Since the input in the present paper is extracted from compressed streams, the architecture should be redesigned to learn the features from the compressed streams. Based on the experimental study with different parameter settings, the first layer of the UNet model has been modified with 64 channels and employed a stride of 7×7 to observe the DCT patterns at the 1st layer. Average pooling has been applied for down-sampling as most of the DCT coefficients are zero, and less context for preserving the context for successive layers. The average pooling technique has learned more details from the compressed streams and propagates them to the successive consecutive layers.

The model architecture contains 19 convolution layers and 4 layers of convolution transpose. After each layer of convolution, the input stream is normalized with batch normalization and spatial dropout. For every 2 layers of convolution, we have used Max-Pool, ReLU activation, for down sampling the input, and convolution transpose and concatenation are used for up sampling. In the last layer the Sigmoid is used as an activation function. Furthermore, the output image has the same resolution as the input image. In our case, it's 512 × 512 with one channel.

4   Experiments and Analysis

The proposed model has been experimented on two benchmark datasets ICDAR2017 (cBAD) and ICDAR2019. The document images in ICDAR2017 cBAD dataset contains two types of layouts: simple layouts [Track A] and complex layouts [Track B]. The basis of cBAD contains document images from 9 different archives as shown some of them in Fig. 1. There were 216 images in TrackA and 267 images in TrackB with proper annotations. The second dataset is ICDAR2019, which is the extended version of ICDAR2017. In this there are total 1510 images with additional images and more number of additional challenges.

The model has been trained and tested on JPEG compressed version of the ICDAR2017 and ICDAR2019 datasets individually. The datasets are split into two parts where first part contains 90% of images used for training and second part contains 10% of images used for testing. The proposed model has been designed using Keras framework, and trained on Google Colab pro platform with NVIDIA T4 GPU. The compressed input streams are resized into 512 × 512 to feed to deep learning model CompTLL-UNet. The model has been trained and tested on both the datasets. The model has been trained for 50 epochs with a batch size of 5. The performance of proposed model is evaluated by three types of standard and popular [2] metrics Precision, Recall and F-Measure given in Eq. (5), Eq. (6) and Eq. (7).

$$Recall = \frac{TP}{TP + FN} \times 100 \quad (6)$$

$$Precision = \frac{TP}{TP + FP} \times 100 \quad (5)$$

$$F - Measure = 2 \times \frac{Precision \times Recall}{Precision + Recall} \times 100 \quad (7)$$

Since the proposed deep learning model is a segmentation problem we have also evaluated the robustness of the proposed model based on DICE score and IoU as given in Eq. (8) and Eq. (9). Where DICE score is the area overlapped between ground truth and predicted image divided by the number of pixels in two images. And IoU is known as "Intersection over Union", and it specifies an overlapping between ground truth and predicted result.

$$IoU = \frac{TP}{TP + FP + FN} \quad (9)$$

$$DICE = \frac{2TP}{2TP + FP + FN} \quad (8)$$

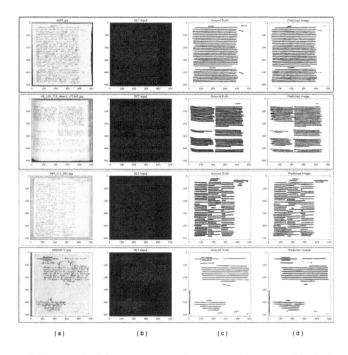

Fig. 4. Some of the sample (a) uncompressed document images with their corresponding (b) JPEG compressed input versions, and (c) the actual ground truths of text-lines, (d) output documents with predicted text-lines locations. First two rows (blue and red colors) are outputs on simple documents and next two rows (green and rose colors) are outputs on complex documents (Color figure online)

The experimental results of the proposed model tested on ICDAR2017 dataset are shown in Fig. 4, where Fig. 4(a) is document image in uncompressed domain and Fig. 4(b) same image with JPEG compressed input stream, Fig. 4(c) is the ground truth along with its predicted output in Fig. 4(d). It can be noticed that the proposed model has localized the text-line regions from both simple (first and second rows) and complex (third and fourth rows) documents, and in the midst of single, multi-columned layouts directly in JPEG compressed domain as shown in Fig. 4. The overall results of model tested on two datasets and evaluated by standard metrics are shown in Table 1. The model has achieved 96.4% dice score and 93.4% IoU on complex images of ICDAR2017 dataset and 96.4% dice score and 93.2% IoU on ICDAR2019 dataset. The overall performance of the proposed model and loss against each epoch are shown in Fig. 5 and Fig. 6 on both Track A and Track B sets. Since input image had some noise, there we performed post processing to improve the dice and IoU scores.

The performance of the proposed model has been compared to different state-of-the-art methods existed both in the pixel domain and compressed domain as tabulated in Table 2. In the table the methods in first 6 rows are in pixel domain and next two rows are in compressed domain. Most of these methods

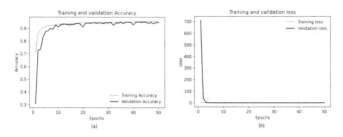

Fig. 5. The (a) accuracy and (b) loss details of the proposed model tested on medium-resolution images (512×512) for Track A (simple documents) images of ICDAR2017

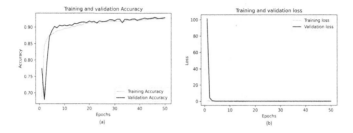

Fig. 6. The (a) accuracy and (b) loss details of the proposed model tested on medium-resolution images (512×512) for Track B (complex documents) images of ICDAR2017

Table 1. Evaluation of the proposed model on CompTLL-UNet ICDAR-cBAD DCT domain

Input	Track	Precision (%)	Recall (%)	F-Measure (%)	Dice Score (%)	IoU (%)
ICDAR2017	Simple layout	96.0	97.0	96.0	97.2	94.0
	Complex layout	95.0	97.0	96.0	96.4	93.4
ICDAR2019	Combined	95.0	96.0	96.0	96.4	93.2

have been tested on simple and less constrained document images. Similarly the performance of the proposed model in terms of DICE score and IoU has been compared with the state-of-the-art result in Table 3. If we observe the results in the Table 2 and in Table 3, it is noticed that the results of the proposed model has outperformed both traditional and deep learning methods both in pixel domain and compressed domain, and showed state-of-the-art performance on challenging handwritten document images in JPEG compressed domain.

In continuation to above experiments, the proposed model has been tested on document images with different scripts such as Telugu, Greek, Hindi, Bangla. The output images are shown in Fig. 7. In the figure, the first column displays text-line in input document with Telugu script, and same document in JPEG compressed representation, and predicted output documents with segmented text-lines. Similarly second column contain document with Greek text-lines.

Table 2. Comparison of the performance of the proposed model with existing methods tested on different handwritten document images in both pixel and compressed domains.

Algorithm	Domain	Dataset	Model Type	Precision (%)	Recall (%)	F-Measure (%)
Kiumarsi et al. [15]	Pixel	ICDAR2013	CC	96.37	96.26	96.32
Renton et al. [2]	Pixel	cBAD	FCN	94.9	88.1	91.3
Barakat et al. [3]	Pixel	IHP	FCN	82.0	78.0	80.0
Mechi et al. [5]	Pixel	cBAD	A-UNet	75.0	85.0	79.0
Gader et al. [16]	Pixel	BADAM	AR2UNet	93.2	94.3	93.7
Demir et al. [17]	Pixel	IHP	GAN	83.0	88.0	85.0
Amarnath et al. [18]	Compressed (Run length)	ICDAR2013	Handcrafted	95.8	89.2	92.4
Rajesh et al. [4]	Compressed (JPEG)	ICDAR2013	Handcrafted	98.40	96.7	97.5
Proposed Method	Compressed (**JPEG**)	cBAD (ICDAR2017)	**CompTLL-UNet** (Deeplearning)	95.5	97.0	96.0
Proposed Method	Compressed (**JPEG**)	cBAD (ICDAR2019)	**CompTLL-UNet** (Deeplearning)	95.0	96.0	96.0

Table 3. Comparing the performance of proposed method with existing state-of-the-art methods in terms of DICE score and IoU.

Model	Input Type	Dataset	DICE Score	IoU
Mechi et al. [5]	Pixel domain	cBAD	–	65.0
Proposed Method	Compressed (ICDAR2017)	cBAD	96.4	93.4
Proposed Method	Compressed (ICDAR2019)	cBAD	96.4	93.2

Third row contain document with Hindi text-lines and fourth contain Bangla text-lines along with their predicted results. Based on these results, it can be understood that the proposed model can be applicable to segment text-lines in document images with different scripts directly in the compressed domain. Since the proposed model has been fed with direct DCT coefficients, we have conducted experiments by analysing the JPEG algorithm manually [19] and noted the computational and storage gain achieved by feeding the JPEG compressed streams. We have observed the computational gain the model achieved based on a batch of 20 images for one complete epoch. The model has gained 20.2% of computational gain in comparison to uncompressed domain. And since the model is fed with direct compressed data we reduce the decompression cost by 73.27%, as shown in the Table 4. Similarly, we have also calculated storage costs with respect to compressed domain by feeding the batch of images and noted the GPU storage costs. In this case the model has shown significant performance with 97.1% reduction in storage. All the details of these experiments are tabulated in Table 4.

In a practical scenario, oftentimes when the same image is transferred to various devices that have different display sizes. Due to such changes, the image resolutions shall be altered, and the original contents in the input image get modified. The contents within the low-resolution images are not as clear as in high-resolution images and may lose many important details when compared to high-resolution images. In order to overcome such practical challenges, the proposed deep learning model CompTLL-UNet has been analyzed with compressed input document images at different resolutions such as high-resolution (1024×1024), medium-resolution (512×512), and low-resolution (250×250).

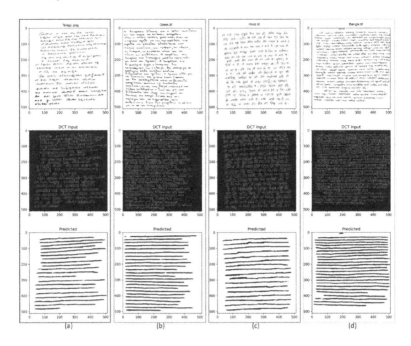

Fig. 7. Segmentation results on various document images containing text-lines in various scripts such as (a) Telugu, (b) Greek, (c) Hindi, (d) Bangla in each column respectively.

Table 4. Evaluation of the proposed model in terms of computational and storage costs with respect to feeding uncompressed document images versus JPEG compressed document images (20 images as batch size of 5)

Complexity Type	Pixel Domain	DCT Domain	% of Reduction
Computational	7.27 s	5.8 s	20.2%
Decompression cost	107 s	28.6 s	73.27%
Storage	22.5MB	0.54	97.1%

The experimental results on the medium-resolution (512×512) are shown in the above section. In order to perform these experiments, we have converted the document images in ICDAR2017 and ICDAR2019 datasets into (1024×1024) and (512×512) resolutions. The experimental results on the compressed version of these high and low-resolution images are tabulated in Table 5. From Table 5, it is noticed that the model has achieved the 97% accuracy when the input resolution is increased, and the model has achieved 95% accuracy when the input resolution is decreased. One point to be noted here is that though the details of the contents in the high-resolution images are greater, the time for training the proposed model with such images is very higher.

Table 5. The experimental results of the proposed model tested on high-resolution (1024 × 1024), medium-resolution (512 × 512) and low-resolution (256 × 256) images extracted from the ICDAR2017 and ICDAR2019 datasets.

Dataset	Layout	Input size	Precision	Recall	F-Measure	Dice Score	IoU
ICDAR2017	Simple	256 × 256	95	96	95	95.8	93.1
	Layout	512 × 512	96	97	96	97.2	94
		1024 × 1024	97	97	97	97.8	94.5
	Complex	256 × 256	95	95	95	95.1	92.6
	Layout	512 × 512	95	97	96	96.4	93.4
		1024 × 1024	96	97	96	97.1	94.2
ICDAR2019	All	256 × 256	95	96	96	94.7	92.8
	Layouts	512 × 512	95	96	96	96.4	93.2
		1024 × 1024	96	97	97	97	94

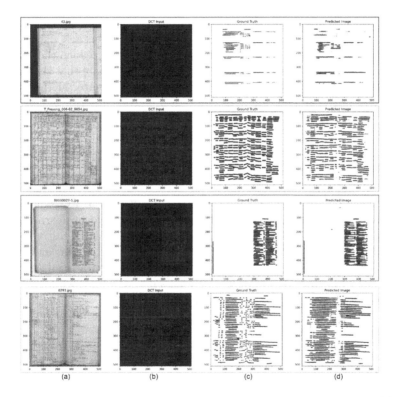

Fig. 8. The experimental results of the proposed model tested on few of the (a) more challenging input document images, where (b) is compressed document images, and (c) is ground truth images and (d) is predicted output images in the compressed domain.

Apart from the above results, there are some more challenging cases where the proposed model is unable to locate the text-line regions in the compressed domain. Some of the cases are shown in Fig. 8. The corresponding compressed input images are shown in Fig. 8(a). It can be noticed that the text-lines in the predicted output images are not as clear as in the ground truth images, as shown in Fig. 8(c) and Fig. 8(d). There are two reasons for this, and one is because the number of samples of such complex document images are less due to that it is unable to learn properly. The second reason is that because of the 8×8 block compressed representation, the adjacent text-lines get overlapped or mixed up into the same DCT block or the text-lines may be overlapped with other additional contents such as vertical/horizontal stripes and background noise as shown in Fig. 8(a). Because of these reasons, the model failed to get the details where contents are completely overlapped as shown in Fig. 8(b). The performance of the model can be increased by adding more number of samples for challenging documents along with some preprocessing to improve the quality of contents in the input documents.

Overall, based on the above results, it can be understood that the proposed CompTLL-UNet model has achieved promising performance in localizing the text-line segments directly in the compressed domain. It has also explained the practical advantages of feeding the compressed data that reduce the computational costs by 20.2% and storage by 89.1%. We also anticipate that the proposed compressed domain model for text-line segmentation is a better method in comparison to the pixel domain methods, and advantageous in terms of storage and computational costs for real-time applications.

5   Conclusion

This paper has discussed a technique for the localization of text-line regions in challenging handwritten document images directly in JPEG domain. The JPEG compressed stream is analyzed through proposed deep learning model CompTLL-UNet to localize the text-line regions. The model is tested on document images with different scripts such as Telugu, Greek, Hindi, and Bengali, and achieved a good performance. We have tested the computational and storage performance by feeding the compressed streams into the proposed model, and it is observed that the model could reduce the computational and storage costs by 20.02% and 97.1%. We anticipate that the proposed method might be helpful in avoiding computational expenses in real-time applications.

References

1. Bisen, T., Javed, M., Kirtania, S., Naghabhushan, P.: DWT-COMPCNN: deep image classification network for high throughput jpeg 2000 compressed documents. In: Pattern Analysis and Applications (2023)
2. Renton, G., Soullard, Y., Chatelain, C., Adam, S., Kermorvant, C., Paquet, T.: Fully convolutional network with dilated convolutions for handwritten text line segmentation. IJDAR **21**(3), 177–186 (2018)
3. Barakat, B., Droby, A., Kassis, M., El-Sana, J.: Text line segmentation for challenging handwritten document images using fully convolutional network. In: ICFHR, pp. 374–379 (2018)

4. Rajesh, B., Javed, M., Nagabhushan, P.: Automatic tracing and extraction of text-line and word segments directly in jpeg compressed document images. IET Image Process. (2020)

5. Mechi, O., Mehri, M., Ingold, R., Ben Amara, N.E.: Text line segmentation in historical document images using an adaptive u-net architecture. In: ICDAR, pp. 369–374 (2019)

6. Javed, M., Nagabhushan, P., Chaudhuri, B.B.: A review on document image analysis techniques directly in the compressed domain. Artif. Intell. Rev. **50**(4), 539–568 (2018)

7. Mukhopadhyay, J.: Image and Video Processing in the Compressed Domain. Chapman and Hall/CRC (2011)

8. Bisen, T., Javed, M., Nagabhushan, P., Watanabe, O.: Segmentation-less extraction of text and non-text regions from jpeg 2000 compressed document images through partial and intelligent decompression. IEEE Access **11**, 20673–20687 (2023)

9. Gueguen, L., Sergeev, A., Kadlec, B., Liu, R., Yosinski, J.: Faster neural networks straight from jpeg. In: ANIPS, pp. 3933–3944 (2018)

10. Ehrlich, M., Davis, L.S.: Deep residual learning in the jpeg transform domain. In: ICCV, pp. 3484–3493 (2019)

11. Rajesh, B., et al.: DCT-COMPCNN: a novel image classification network using jpeg compressed DCT coefficients. In: 2019 IEEE Conference on Information and Communication Technology, pp. 1–6. IEEE (2019)

12. Liu, J., Sun, H., Katto, J.: Semantic segmentation in learned compressed domain. In: 2022 Picture Coding Symposium (PCS), pp. 181–185. IEEE (2022)

13. Chen, L., Sun, H., Zeng, X., Fan, Y.: Learning from the NN-based compressed domain with deep feature reconstruction loss. In: 2022 IEEE International Conference on Visual Communications and Image Processing (VCIP), pp. 1–5 (2022)

14. Ronneberger, O., Fischer, P., Brox, T.: U-net: convolutional networks for biomedical image segmentation. In: Navab, N., Hornegger, J., Wells, W.M., Frangi, A.F. (eds.) MICCAI 2015. LNCS, vol. 9351, pp. 234–241. Springer, Cham (2015). https://doi.org/10.1007/978-3-319-24574-4_28

15. Kiumarsi, E., Alaei, A.: A hybrid method for text line extraction in handwritten document images. In: ICFHR, pp. 241–246 (2018)

16. Ben Aïcha Gader, T., Kacem Echi, A.: Unconstrained handwritten Arabic text-lines segmentation based on ar2u-net. In: ICFHR, pp. 349–354 (2020)

17. Demır, A.A., ÖzŞeker, İ., Özkaya, U.: Text line segmentation in handwritten documents with generative adversarial networks. In: INISTA, pp. 1–5 (2021)

18. Amarnath, R., Nagabhushan, P.: Text line segmentation in compressed representation of handwritten document using tunneling algorithm. IJISAE **6**(4), 251–261 (2018)

19. Zaman, B.R.M.: JPEG-Compression-Algorithm (2022). https://drive.google.com/drive/folders/1fv5wU0bFY0_2nUWyp4x_MtbCN4hFiMd2?usp=sharing. Accessed 10 Aug 2022

Heatmap Overlay Using Neutral Body Model for Visualizing the Measured Gaze Distributions of Observers

Michiko Inoue[✉], Fuyuko Iwasaki, Masashi Nishiyama, and Yoshio Iwai

Graduate School of Engineering, Tottori University, Tottori, Japan
mi.inoue@tottori-u.ac.jp

Abstract. We propose a method for visualizing where an observer's gaze focuses on a subject in a still image using a neutral human body model. Generally, two-dimensional (2D) heatmaps are superimposed on still images to visualize an observer's gaze distribution, which indicates where an observer looks when observing a subject. To investigate gaze distributions, eye-tracking researchers need a method to directly compare the 2D heatmaps because body pose and shape differ among subjects. Thus, a comparison of the gaze distributions using the 2D heatmaps is time-consuming if there is no acceptable method to handle the body pose and shape variations. Instead, our visualization method superimposes a three-dimensional (3D) heatmap representing the gaze distribution on the surface of a neutral human body, which has a fixed pose and shape for all subjects to visualize the locations at which an observer's gaze focuses. Experimental results show that our visualization method allows eye-tracking researchers to compare gaze distributions more directly than the conventional visualization method using 2D heatmaps on still images.

Keywords: Gaze distribution · 3D heatmap · neutral body model · visualization · vertex attention probability

1 Introduction

There are many situations in which people gather together, such as parties and conferences. Eye-tracking researchers in the computer vision and cognitive science fields investigate the gaze distributions of people in these situations, because these gaze distributions indicate the behavior of the observers when they look at the bodies of other people. For example, consider a situation in which some observers judge the aesthetics of subjects attending a ceremonial party. In this situation, the eye-tracking researchers measure the gaze distributions of the observers during this judgement. The researchers then compare the measured gaze distributions of the subjects to determine whether the gaze behaviors of the observers differ. To perform this comparison, it is necessary to visualize the gaze distribution so that the researchers can directly compare the locations on the subjects where the observers focus their attention.

H. Lu et al. (Eds.): ACPR 2023, LNCS 14407, pp. 102–114, 2023.
https://doi.org/10.1007/978-3-031-47637-2_8

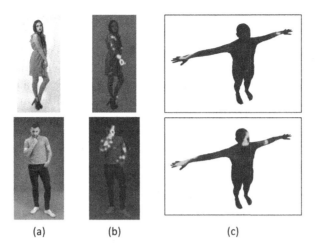

(a)   (b)   (c)

Fig. 1. (a) Measuring and visualizing where an observer's gaze focuses when they look at the subjects in the still images. (b) Superimposing the measured gaze distributions onto the images using 2D heatmaps. (c) Superimposing the distributions on a neutral human body model using 3D heatmaps.

We here consider how to compare whether there are differences in the measured gaze distributions of observers observing an attractive female and male subject. The body poses and shapes of the female and male subject are very different, as shown in the examples in Fig. 1(a). In these examples, the woman has both hands down, and the man has one hand up. Moreover, the woman is slender, and the man is muscular. As these examples illustrate, subjects have various body poses and various body shapes in such situations. Hence, eye-tracking researchers need a visualization method that can directly compare the gaze distributions among subjects, even when they have different body poses and body shapes.

Two-dimensional (2D) heatmaps are often superimposed on still images to visualize where an observer's gaze focuses on a subject. Figure 1(b) shows examples of this visualization. In fact, eye-tracking researchers have commonly used 2D heatmaps to represent gaze distributions [4,6,8]. However, body poses and shapes differ among subjects when this method is used. To compare where the gazes of observers focus in the examples in Fig. 1(b), eye-tracking researchers must pay attention to the different poses of the hands and arms and the different body shapes of the man and woman. Therefore, a visualization that superimposes 2D heatmaps on still images is time-consuming for eye-tracking researchers to analyze them. Other visualization methods [9,10] have been proposed in which 3D heatmaps representing the gaze distributions are superimposed on the surface of artificial objects by aligning the shapes of known objects. It is easier for eye-tracking researchers to directly compare gaze focus on artificial objects with rigid body shapes in various poses. However, applying these methods [9,10] to human subjects is restricting because humans are non-rigid and have various body shapes in different poses.

Here, we propose a visualization method that superimposes 3D heatmaps on the surface of a neutral human body to directly compare the locations of observer gazes when the observers look at subjects in still images. We use a neutral human body model with a body pose and shape that are normalized among subjects. Our visualization method allows eye-tracking researchers to directly compare the gaze distributions on the common 3D surface of the neutral human body model, even if the body poses and shapes of the subjects in still images differ. Figure 1(c) shows examples of 3D heatmaps representing gaze distributions by superimposing them on the 3D surface of the neutral human body model. In our visualization, it is not necessary to consider the differences in the body poses and shapes of the subjects. In addition, the observer gaze distributions can be directly compared by simply looking at the spatially aligned 3D heatmaps superimposed on the surface of the neutral human body model.

2   Our 3D Heatmap-Based Visualization Method

2.1   Overview

In our method, the 3D heatmaps represent which parts of the subject's body the gazes of observers focus. The 3D heatmaps are superimposed on the surface of a neutral human body model. Figure 2 shows an overview of our method. Our method generates images visualizing the measured gaze distributions of the observer using steps S1 to S3 and the neutral human body model connecting these steps.

S1. Computation of the pixel attention probability
   We calculate the probability that the gazes of observers focus on the 2D positions of the pixels in region of the subject in the still image. We call this the pixel attention probability.

S2. Computation of the vertex attention probability
   Using the relationship between the 2D positions of the pixels of the subject region and the 3D positions of the surface of the neutral human model, we calculate the probability that the gazes focus on the vertices of the body model. We call this the vertex attention probability.

S3. 3D heatmap overlay
   We superimpose the 3D heatmap representing the vertex attention probabilities onto the neutral human body model so that eye-tracking researchers can directly compare the gaze distributions among subjects. To do this, we generate an image visualizing each gaze distribution using the 3D heatmap.

Neutral Human Body Model
   We use a neutral human body model with a pre-determined constant body pose and shape parameters to fix the pose and shape of the subjects. The model consists of a set of 3D vertices and the adjacencies between them. Our

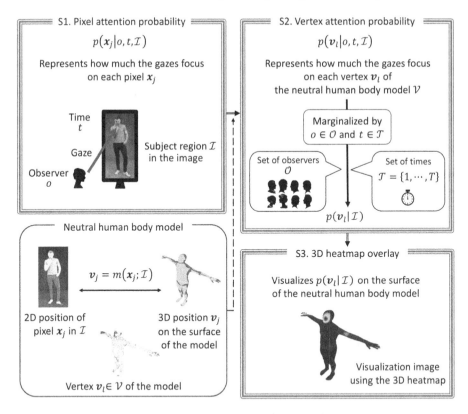

Fig. 2. Overview of our method. When observers look at a certain subject in a still image, we measure where their gazes focus on the subject, and visualize the gaze distribution using the 3D heatmap representing the vertex attention probability.

method transforms the 2D positions of the pixels in the subject region of the still image to the 3D positions on the surface of the neutral human body model.

Here, we discuss the issue of the conventional visualization method using the 2D heatmap representing the pixel attention probability. When body poses and shapes differ among subjects, the alignment of bodies in the subject regions causes gaps among the still images. Therefore, it is difficult to directly compare the pixel attention probability between subjects. Our method reduces the gap between body poses and shapes using neutral human body model with a normalized body pose in a normalized shape to represent the gaze distributions using the 3D heatmaps. Our visualization method enables the vertex attention probability among subjects with various body poses and shapes to be directly compared. In the following, we describe the pixel attention probability in Sect. 2.2, the neutral human body model in Sect. 2.3, the vertex attention probability in Sect. 2.4, and the 3D heatmap for generating the visualization image in Sect. 2.5.

2.2   Pixel Attention Probability

Pixel attention probability indicates how much the measured gazes of the observers focus on each pixel in the subject region of the still image. Suppose that the subject region $\mathcal{I}$ is the set of pixels $\boldsymbol{x}_j$, and the gaze is measured from observer o at pixel $\boldsymbol{x}_t$ in the subject region $\mathcal{I}$ at time t. We denote the probability that the gaze is measured at a pixel $\boldsymbol{x}_j \in \mathcal{I}$ by

$$p(\boldsymbol{x}_j | o, t, \mathcal{I}) \sim \mathcal{N}(\boldsymbol{x}_j | \boldsymbol{x}_t, \boldsymbol{\Sigma}_p), \tag{1}$$

where $\mathcal{N}(\boldsymbol{x}_j | \boldsymbol{x}_t, \boldsymbol{\Sigma}_p)$ is a bivariate normal distribution with mean $\boldsymbol{x}_t$ and covariance matrix $\boldsymbol{\Sigma}_p$. We assume $\boldsymbol{\Sigma}_p = \mathrm{diag}\left(\sigma_p^2, \sigma_p^2\right)$. Here, $p(\boldsymbol{x}_j | o, t, \mathcal{I})$ is assumed to follow a normal distribution. The observer is not only looking at the pixel $\boldsymbol{x}_t$ where the gaze is measured and but also looking at the surrounding pixels. Hence, to approximate this, we use the normal distribution. Pixcel attention probability $p(\boldsymbol{x}_j | o, t, \mathcal{I})$ satisfies the following equation:

$$\sum_{\boldsymbol{x}_j \in \mathcal{I}} p(\boldsymbol{x}_j | o, t, \mathcal{I}) = 1. \tag{2}$$

Note that eye-tracking researchers must handle pixel attention probability carefully because it is difficult to directly compare pixel attention probabilities among subjects because body poses and shapes differ among subject regions in still images, as described in Sect. 1.

2.3   Neutral Human Body Model

Several human body models [2,5,7] have been proposed to represent the human body with various poses and shapes. In these human body models, pose and shape are represented by continuous parameters in function space. We set up the neutral human body model using constant values for the parameters of body pose and shape for all subjects. This model allows us to transform different body poses and shapes into a common body representation for all subjects.

The neutral human body model $\mathcal{V}$ consists of meshes based on a set of vertices $\boldsymbol{v}_l$ and the adjacencies between vertices, as described in [2,5,7]. To indicate how much the gazes focus on a vertex $\boldsymbol{v}_l$, we could simply map pixel attention probability of each pixel $\boldsymbol{x}_j$ in the subject region of a still image to a vertex $\boldsymbol{v}_l$ of the neutral human body model using nearest neighbors. However, the $\boldsymbol{v}_l$ vertices are discrete, and this simple mapping will cause aliasing. For this reason, we use the 3D position $\boldsymbol{v}_j$ that exists continuously on the surface of the neutral human body model.

The method for mapping the 2D position of pixel $\boldsymbol{x}_j \in \mathcal{I}$ in the subject region of a still image to a 3D position $\boldsymbol{v}_j$ on the surface of a neutral human body model is as follows. Specifically, we transform it using function $m()$ as

$$\boldsymbol{v}_j = m(\boldsymbol{x}_j; \mathcal{I}). \tag{3}$$

The function $m()$ first estimates the body pose and shape parameters for each subject in the still image using an existing method, e.g. [1,3,11,12]. Next, the estimated pose and shape parameters are converted to constant values for the neutral human body model. In this transformation, the 2D position of the pixel x_j can be automatically mapped to the 3D position v_j.

2.4   Vertex Attention Probability

We define the vertex attention probability, which represents how much an observer o focuses his/her gaze on a vertex v_l of the neutral human body model $\mathcal{V}$ when looking at the subject region $\mathcal{I}$ at time t as

$$p(v_l|o,t,\mathcal{I}) = \sum_{x_j \in \mathcal{I}} p(v_l|x_j,\mathcal{I})p(x_j|o,t,\mathcal{I}), \qquad (4)$$

where $p(v_l|x_j,\mathcal{I})$ is the probability that the gaze focuses on the 3D vertex v_l of the neutral human body model given the 2D pixel $x_j \in \mathcal{I}$. We transform the 2D position of the pixel x_j on the still image to the 3D position v_j on the neutral human body model surface using Eq. (3) as

$$p(v_l|o,t,\mathcal{I}) = \sum_{x_j \in \mathcal{I}} p(v_l|v_j,\mathcal{I})p(x_j|o,t,\mathcal{I}). \qquad (5)$$

Obtaining this probability using geodetic distances is computationally expensive. Therefore, we make the following assumption to reduce computation time. First, we suppose that the pixel at which the gaze focuses is transformed to 3D position v_j on the neutral human body model. A smaller Euclidean distance from v_j to vertex v_l on the neutral human body model means that the probability that the gaze is measured at that vertex will be higher. Based on this assumption, we express $p(v_l|v_j,\mathcal{I}) \simeq \mathcal{N}(v_l|v_j,\Sigma_v)$ using a normal distribution and calculate the vertex attention probability $p(v_l|o,t,\mathcal{I})$ as

$$p(v_l|o,t,\mathcal{I}) \simeq \sum_{x_j \in \mathcal{I}} \mathcal{N}(v_l|v_j,\Sigma_v)p(x_j|o,t,\mathcal{I}), \qquad (6)$$

where $\mathcal{N}(v_l|v_j,\Sigma_v)$ is a trivariate normal distribution with mean v_j and covariance matrix Σ_v. In our method, the covariance matrix is $\Sigma_v = \mathrm{diag}\left(\sigma_v^2,\sigma_v^2,\sigma_v^2\right)$. Note that $p(v_l|o,t,\mathcal{I})$ satisfies the following equation:

$$\sum_{v_l \in \mathcal{V}} p(v_l|o,t,\mathcal{I}) = 1. \qquad (7)$$

Here, we further enhance the comparison of gaze distributions in eye-tracking research. It is time-consuming to individually check the locations of gaze focus for each observer o and at each time t. We hence marginalize the probabilities using the set of observers $\mathcal{O}$ and set of measurement times $\mathcal{T}$. Given subject region $\mathcal{I}$ in the still image, we calculate the marginal probability that the gazes are measured at the vertex $\boldsymbol{v}_l$ of the neutral human body model as follows:

$$p(\boldsymbol{v}_l|\mathcal{I}) = \sum_{o\in\mathcal{O},t\in\mathcal{T}} p(\boldsymbol{v}_l|o,t,\mathcal{I})p(o)p(t). \tag{8}$$

Let O be the number of elements in set $\mathcal{O}$ and T be the number of elements in set $\mathcal{T}$. Approximating $p(o)$ using the uniform distribution $1/O$ and $p(t)$ using the uniform distribution $1/T$, Eq. (8) is converted to

$$p(\boldsymbol{v}_l|\mathcal{I}) = \frac{1}{OT} \sum_{o\in\mathcal{O},t\in\mathcal{T}} p(\boldsymbol{v}_l|o,t,\mathcal{I}). \tag{9}$$

Note that $p(\boldsymbol{v}_l|\mathcal{I})$ satisfies the following equation:

$$\sum_{\boldsymbol{v}_l\in\mathcal{V}} p(\boldsymbol{v}_l|\mathcal{I}) = 1. \tag{10}$$

We call $p(\boldsymbol{v}_l|\mathcal{I})$ in Eq. (9) the vertex attention probability marginalized by the set of observers $\mathcal{O}$ and set of measurement times $\mathcal{T}$.

2.5   3D Heatmap for Generating the Visualization Image

To visualize the gaze distributions on a neutral body model for direct comparison among subjects, we represent the vertex attention probability $p(\boldsymbol{v}_l|\mathcal{I})$ using a 3D heatmap and overlay it onto the surface of the model. First, we consider a simple, vertex-only heatmap visualization. Figure 3(a) shows examples of the visualization images using the vertex-only heatmap. In the figure, vertices with a higher probability of concentrated gazes are redder in hue, and those with a lower probability of focused gazes are closer to blue. In these visualization images, the front and back vertices of the neutral human body model are both visible, making it difficult to compare the gaze distributions among subjects. Thus, we continuously interpolate the colors representing the high and low probabilities of focused gazes at 3D positions $\boldsymbol{v}_j$ using a mesh on the surface of the neutral human body model. Figure 3(b) shows examples of the visualization images using the 3D mesh heatmap. This heatmap representation prevents the front and back of the neutral human body model from being visible simultaneously, making it easier to directly to compare the gaze distributions among subjects.

3   Experiments

3.1   Visualization Images Generation Conditions

We evaluated the effectiveness of our method using visualization images generated by the following methods.

- Conventional method (M_{2d}): We overlaid the 2D heatmap representing the pixel attention probability described in Sect. 2.2 onto the still image.

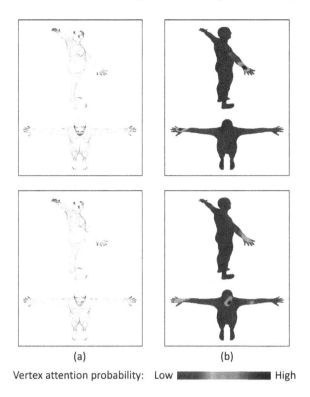

(a)   (b)

Vertex attention probability: Low ▆▆▆▆▆▆▆ High

Fig. 3. Examples of visualization images using 3D heatmaps to represent vertex attention probabilities. (a) Using vertices only. (b) Using a 3D mesh. (Color figure online)

– Our method (M_{3d}): We overlaid the 3D heatmap representing the vertex
  attention probability described in Sect. 2.4 onto the surface of the neutral
  human body model.

Note that the conventional method M_{2d} is equivalent to a visualization of the
measured gaze distributions of observers, such as the methods used in existing
analytical studies [4,6,8].

For our method M_{3d}, we used SMPL [5] to implement the neutral human
body model described in Sect. 2.3. In the neutral human model used in this
experiment, we set the pose and shape parameters of SMPL to their default
values[1]. These default values specify that the body pose is one with arms out-
stretched and legs slightly open, and the body shape is average. The number
of SMPL vertices used was 6890. Adjacency was represented by the meshes of
triangles connecting the three vertices. We used DensePose [3] to estimate the
body pose and shape parameters of SMPL for each subject in the still image for
function $m()$ of Eq. (3), as described in Sect. 2.3.

---

[1] https://smpl.is.tue.mpg.de.

3.2   Gaze Measurement

To obtain measured gaze distributions, we asked several observers the following question Q so that they would evaluate the aesthetics of a subject in still images.

Q: Do you think that the subject's hands are beautiful?

We instructed them to answer "yes" or "no." The number of observers was 24 (12 men and 12 women), and the mean age of the observers was 22.4 ± 1.0 years old.

We first explained question Q to the observers and showed them a randomly selected still image on a display for 7 s. Figure 4(a) shows the still image given to the observers as a stimulus. Subject 1 is a slender woman with her right hand down and left leg slightly shifted forward. Subject 2 is a man with his right hand raised and his legs shoulder-width apart. Subject 3 is a petite woman with her right hand on her hip and her heels together. Figure 4(b) shows the subject regions in the still images.

We measured each observer's gaze using an eye tracker device while displaying the still image. This gaze measurement was repeated until all still images were viewed. The observers were seated 65 cm from the display. We allowed the observers to adjust the chair height so that the eye height was between 110 and 120 cm. We used a 24-inch display with a resolution of 1920 × 1080 pixels and a Gazepoint GP3 HD eye tracker with a 60 Hz sampling rate. The spatial resolution error of the eye tracker device is approximately one degree, as described in the specifications. We displayed the still image at a random position on the display to avoid center bias.

3.3   Visualization Results

Figure 4(c) shows the visualization images generated using the conventional method M_{2d}, which superimposes the 2D heatmaps representing the pixel attention probability on the still images. Because of the variation in the body alignment among subjects, we must consider the differences in the body poses and shapes when comparing the gaze distributions. With these differences in mind, we can infer the following when comparing the results of Fig. 4(c). For subject 1, the observers' gazes focused most often on the right hand, followed by the head. For subject 2, the observers' gazes focused most often on the right hand, followed by the head and left hand. For subject 3, the observers' gazes focused most often on the right and left hands, followed by the head. From these results, we conclude that when question Q is given to observers looking at subjects 1 through 3, the gazes mostly focus on the hands and then on the head.

Figure 4(d) shows the visualization images generated using our method M_{3d}. Our visualization results show that the body poses and shapes of the neutral human body model are the same for all subjects. These 3D heatmaps make the body alignment equal for all subjects so that when analyzing differences in the gaze distributions, eye-tracking researchers only need to compare the same positions on the surface of the model. The gaze distributions for subjects 1

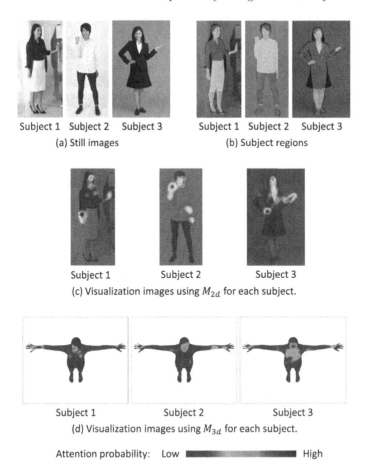

Subject 1 Subject 2 Subject 3   Subject 1 Subject 2 Subject 3
(a) Still images   (b) Subject regions

Subject 1   Subject 2   Subject 3
(c) Visualization images using M_{2d} for each subject.

Subject 1   Subject 2   Subject 3
(d) Visualization images using M_{3d} for each subject.

Attention probability: Low ▬▬▬▬▬▬▬▬ High

Fig. 4. Visualization image results showing the attention probabilities of the measured gaze distributions of observers looking at the still images.

through 3 reveal that the gazes most often focus on the hand, followed by the head. We can reach this conclusion more directly using our method M_{3d} than when using the conventional method M_{2d}.

3.4   Subjective Assessment of the Visualization Images

Conditions of Subjective Assessment

We conducted a subjective assessment to determine whether the visualization images generated by the conventional method M_{2d} or those generated by our method M_{3d} enable the gaze distributions for various subjects to be directly compared. Sixteen eye-tracking researchers participated in the subjective assessment (13 men and three women). These researchers are graduate students studying human and computer vision, including gaze measurement

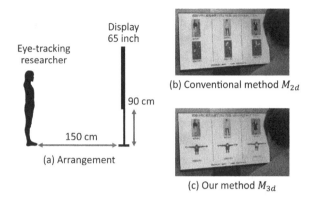

(b) Conventional method M_{2d}

(c) Our method M_{3d}

Fig. 5. Setup of the subjective assessment.

and analysis. Their average age was 23.4 ± 1.5 years old. Figure 5(a) shows the setup of the subjective assessment. The researchers stood upright at a distance of 150 cm horizontally from the display. The size of the display (LG, OLED65E9PJA) was 65 in., and the height from the floor to the display was 90 cm. The researchers compared the results obtained using the conventional method M_{2d} (Fig. 5(b)) with the results obtained using our method M_{3d} (Fig. 5(c)). Visualization images of each method were shown on the display for 60 s each. We randomized the order of displaying the visualization images generated by M_{2d} and M_{3d}. We asked the researchers to choose the visualization images they felt would better directly facilitate the comparison of gaze distributions among the subjects. The researchers replied with one of the following answers: M_{2d}, M_{3d}, or neutral.

Result of the Subjective Assessment

Figure 6 shows the result of the subjective assessment. Five eye-tracking researchers chose the conventional method, two chose neutral, and nine chose our method. Our method M_{3d} obtained the highest results. Some researchers chose the conventional method M_{2d} because they were familiar with the 2D heatmaps on still images, which made it easy to identify the body parts focused on by gaze for each subject. In contrast, some researchers chose our method M_{3d} because the body parts such as the hands, torso, and legs are completely aligned for all subjects, so it is easy to compare the differences in the gaze distributions without having to pay attention to the body poses and shapes. From these results, we confirmed that our method M_{3d} enables eye-tracking researchers to more directly compare differences in the gaze distributions, even when the body poses and shapes are different, than the conventional method M_{2d}.

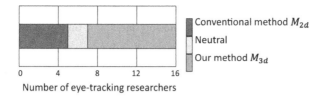

Fig. 6. Result of the subjective assessment comparing visualization images generated using the proposed and conventional methods.

4   Conclusions

We proposed a method of superimposing 3D heatmaps on the surface of a neutral human body model to visualize where the gazes of observers focus when they look at subjects in still images. For the visualization images obtained using our method, we confirmed in a subjective assessment that eye-tracking researchers could directly compare the gaze distributions, even when the body poses and shapes differed among subjects.

In future work, we will expand the evaluation to consider the case in which various shape characteristics, such as the weight, of the subjects in still images change. We also plan to consider the error estimation due to the influence of gender and clothing according to the neutral human body model. Furthermore, we intend to develop a method for calculating the vertex attention probability when there are multiple subjects in a single still image.

Acknowledgment. This work was partially supported by JSPS KAKENHI Grant No. JP23K11145. We would like to thank Mr. Ken Kinoshita for his cooperation in our evaluation and data collection.

References

1. Choutas, V., Müller, L., Huang, C.P., Tang, S., Tzionas, D., Black, M.J.: Accurate 3D body shape regression using metric and semantic attributes. In: Proceedings of the IEEE/CVF Conference on Computer Vision and Pattern Recognition, pp. 2718–2728 (2022)
2. Georgios, P., et al.: Expressive body capture: 3D hands, face, and body from a single image. In: Proceedings of the IEEE/CVF Conference on Computer Vision and Pattern Recognition, pp. 10975–10985 (2019)
3. Güler, R., Neverova, N., Kokkinos, I.: DensePose: dense human pose estimation in the wild. In: Proceedings of the IEEE/CVF Conference on Computer Vision and Pattern Recognition, pp. 7297–7306 (2018)
4. Irvine, K.R., McCarty, K., Pollet, T.V., Cornelissen, K.K., Tovée, M.J., Cornelissen, P.L.: The visual cues that drive the self-assessment of body size: dissociation between fixation patterns and the key areas of the body for accurate judgement. Body Image **29**, 31–46 (2019)
5. Matthew, M., Mahmood, N., Romero, J., Pons-Moll, G., Black, M.: SMPL: a skinned multi-person linear model. ACM Trans. Graph. **34**(6), 1–16 (2015)

6. Nummenmaa, L., Jari, H., Santtila, P., Hyönä, J.: Gender and visibility of sexual cues influence eye movements while viewing faces and bodies. Arch. Sex. Behav. **41**(6), 1439–1451 (2012)
7. Osman, A.A.A., Bolkart, T., Tzionas, D., Black, M.J.: SUPR: a sparse unified part-based human representation. In: Proceedings of European Conference on Computer Vision, pp. 1–18 (2022)
8. Piers, C., Peter, H., Kiviniemi, V., Hannah, G., Martin, T.: Patterns of eye movements when male and female observers judge female attractiveness, body fat and waist-to-hip ratio. Evol. Hum. Behav. **30**(6), 417–428 (2009)
9. Takahashi, R., Suzuki, H., Chew, J., Ohtake, Y., Nagai, Y., Ohtomi, K.: A system for three-dimensional gaze fixation analysis using eye tracking glasses. J. Comput. Des. Eng. **5**(4), 449–457 (2017)
10. Wang, X., Lindlbauer, D., Lessig, C., Maertens, M., Alexa, M.: Measuring the visual salience of 3D printed objects. IEEE Comput. Graphics Appl. **36**(4), 46–55 (2016)
11. Xiu, Y., Yang, J., Tzionas, D., Black, M.J.: ICON: implicit clothed humans obtained from normals. In: Proceedings of the IEEE/CVF Conference on Computer Vision and Pattern Recognition, pp. 13296–13306 (2022)
12. Zhang, H., et al.: PyMAF: 3D human pose and shape regression with pyramidal mesh alignment feedback loop. In: Proceedings of the IEEE/CVF International Conference on Computer Vision, pp. 11446–11456 (2021)

Image Inpainting for Large and Irregular Mask Based on Partial Convolution and Cross Semantic Attention

Yin Wang[✉], Hiroaki Aizawa, and Takio Kurita

Hiroshima University, Hiroshima, Japan
m222775@hiroshima-u.ac.jp

Abstract. Image inpainting is inferring missing pixels in images using known content and surrounding regions. To achieve this task, existing methods have utilized convolutional neural networks and adversarial generative networks. However, these approaches produce blurry and unrealistic completion results when the region of the missing pixels is large and irregular. This is because there is insufficient information to fill the missing region, and the networks fail to utilize known pixel information. Therefore, this study proposes a coarse-to-fine strategy using a pre-trained partial convolution-based encoder-decoder network. Our two-stage image inpainting strategy consists of a coarse inpainting network using partial convolution and a fine inpainting network using cross-attention layers based on an Unsupervised Cross-space Generative Adversarial Network (UCTGAN). In the first stage, the coarse network completes the missing region to feed the clue for inpainting into the following stage. Then, in the second stage, the fine network projects instance images and the coarse clue image into a low-dimensional manifold space and combines low-dimensional spatial features across semantic attention layers. Finally, the generator reconstructs a reconstructed image conditioned on the coarse completion. In the experiments, we qualitatively and quantitatively evaluated generated images in terms of image quality and similarity. As a result, our framework can generate precise completion results for a large and irregular missing region better than the previous methods, such as the methods based on partial convolution or the original UTCGAN.

Keywords: Image inpainting · Deep learning · Convolutional neural network · Partial convolution · Cross semantic attention

1 Introduction

Image inpainting is inferring and filling holes in images using known content and making as few traces of repair as possible. It can be used in many fields, such as object removal, photograph restoration, and diminished reality image editing.

The existing deep-learning-based methods use the content around the missing area of the image to fill the damaged region. Although these methods can achieve

H. Lu et al. (Eds.): ACPR 2023, LNCS 14407, pp. 115–128, 2023.
https://doi.org/10.1007/978-3-031-47637-2_9

good results for small-area holes, it is difficult to get good results for large and irregular holes. Liu, Guilin, et al. [11] proposed to use a partial convolution. By using partial convolution, valid and destroyed invalid pixels are distinguished and treated differently. This technique can solve the problem of irregular mask input, but it is difficult to obtain a clear image when the mask area is too large.

Goodfellow et al. [1]. proposed a generative adversarial network (GAN), which has been widely used in image generation. Several GAN-based image inpainting methods have been proposed [2–5]. However, these methods tend to generate unrealistic results for large missing regions caused by too little reference information when there are too many missing pixels.

Our key idea for solving this issue is inspired by the restoration of paintings by artists. They learn the available content from existing works and combine them with the existing parts of the image to be restored to obtain a more realistic painting. Following this process, we can design a two-stage image inpainting model. The working process of our model is similar to the painting restoration.

Our two-stage image inpainting model aims to solve large and irregular holes and produce semantically consistent inpainted images as much as possible. Stage one is a partial-convolution-based encoder-decoder network. This network is used to infer the possible pixel values of the missing part according to the pixels around the hole to obtain a rough inpainted image. The second stage will match similar pixels from the data set based on the results of the first stage, then extract their features and map the extracted feature maps to a lower-dimensional space, and finally perform feature fusion. At the end of the model, the generator will generate as clear and realistic images as possible based on the fused features, and the discriminator will also evaluate the generated images and give feedback on the results to the generator.

Our model combines partial convolution and traditional GAN-based image inpainting methods to fill holes by referencing both the images in the dataset and the undamaged regions of the images to obtain more realistic and sharp images than either method alone, even if the hole is large and irregular. We have made modifications to the network structure of certain convolutional layers in our model, enabling the first stage to produce a clearer preprocessed image of size 64×64, as illustrated in Table 1. In the second stage, we have also made adjustments to the original UTCGAN model. The discriminator in the original model was quite complex, leading to lengthy training processes. To better suit our model, we simplified the discriminator structure, resulting in faster training. Additionally, we have made corresponding modifications to the loss functions.

2   Related Work

2.1   Image Inpainting

Non-learning Based Image Inpainting. Non-learning image inpainting methods are based on mathematics and physics approaches that mainly use local or non-local information to repair missing parts, and most existing methods mainly repair a pair of images. One of the Non-learning image inpainting methods is the full variational method [6] which considers the smoothness of the image and repairs small missing parts. It is very effective in areas and noise removal. But this method is only suitable for the small missing regions. When the missing region is large, it will produce a blur result when the pixels of the non-damaged area are diffused to the damaged area by this method, and the inpainting result will be poor. The Patch Match [7] is another non-learning image inpainting method that utilizes existing information to search for regions similar to the missing block from the available part of the image to fill the missing region and obtain a better restoration result. However, this method is too dependent on the known part of the image, and if there is no such similar block in the known part, it will not be able to repair the missing area well.

Deep-Learning Based Image Inpainting. In the research of deep learning, especially one of the feedforward neural networks: the convolutional neural network (CNN) in which each artificial neuron only responds to a part of the surrounding units in the coverage area, the CNN has an excellent performance in extensive image processing. In recent years, a CNN-based deep learning network has been proven to capture the abstract information of images at a high level. In the research of texture synthesis and image style transfer, it has been proven that well-trained image features extracted by the CNN network can be used as a part of the objective function so that the image generated by the generative network is more semantically similar to the target image. Coupled with extensive research on generative adversarial networks (GANs) [1], it is demonstrated that adversarial training can enhance the visual quality of images generated by generative networks [3,12–14]. Deep learning-based methods usually initialize the holes with some constant placeholder values, such as the average pixel value of ImageNet [15], and then pass them through a convolutional network. The models based on this method are heavily dependent on the pixel values of the undamaged area of the image, and it is challenging to produce a sharp image when there are too many missing pixels.

2.2 Partial Convolution

For the problem of large holes and irregular masks, Liu, Guilin, et al. [11]. proposed an image inpainting model based on partial convolution. Partial convolution can be regarded as a special case of normalized convolution. The key idea is to separate missing pixels from valid pixels during convolution, so the result only depends on valid pixels.

A partial convolutional layer includes a partial convolution operation and a mask update function. Let $\mathbf{W}$ and b be the convolution filter's weight and bias. $\mathbf{X}$ represents the convolved pixel value (or feature activation value), and $\mathbf{M}$ is the corresponding binary mask, indicating the validity of each pixel/feature value (0 represents missing pixels, 1 represents valid pixels). A partial convolution

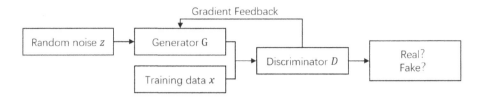

Fig. 1. GAN model

operation can be defined as:

$$x' = \begin{cases} \mathbf{W}^T(\mathbf{X} \odot \mathbf{M})\dfrac{\text{sum}(\mathbf{1})}{\text{sum}(\mathbf{M})} + b, & \text{if sum}(\mathbf{M}) > 0 \\ 0, & \text{otherwise} \end{cases} \tag{1}$$

where $\odot$ denotes element-wise multiplication, $\mathbf{1}$ is an all-ones matrix, and its shape is the same as $\mathbf{M}$. As can be seen from this equation, the results of partial convolutions only depend on valid input values such as $(\mathbf{X}\odot\mathbf{M})$. $\text{sum}(\mathbf{1})/\text{sum}(\mathbf{M})$ is a scaling factor that adjusts the result when the number of valid input values to each convolution varies.

The binary mask is updated after each partial convolutional layer, and if the result of the current convolution has at least one valid input value condition, the corresponding position is valid for the next partial convolutional layer. The mask update function is expressed as:

$$m' = \begin{cases} 1, & \text{if sum}(\mathbf{M}) > 0 \\ 0, & \text{otherwise} \end{cases} \tag{2}$$

As long as the input is an image containing any valid pixels, any mask will eventually be updated to all ones.

2.3   Generative Adversarial Networks

Generative Adversarial Network (GAN) [1] is a method of training generative models proposed by Goodfellow in 2014. Its idea comes from the two-person zero-sum game. In this game, the sum of the interests of two people is zero, and the gain of one is the loss of another one. Different from previous generative models, it guides the training of generative models through a discriminative model. The network consists of generator G and discriminator D. The generator is used to capture the distribution of training data. On the other hand, the discriminator is equivalent to a two-classifier, which is used to judge whether the input data comes from real data or generated data, and the result of the network output represents the probability that the input data comes from real data. The basic structure of the generative confrontation network is shown in Fig. 1.

In the network model, the generator receives a random noise z as input, the discriminator receives real data x or the generated data of the generator as

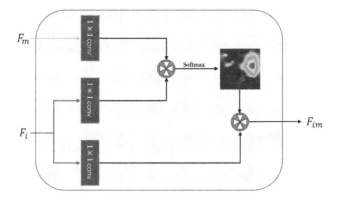

Fig. 2. Cross-semantic attention layer proposed by Zhao, Lei, et al. [16]. The attention map is computed on masked image features and instance image features on the bottleneck layer.

input, the discriminator and the generator are trained at the same time, and the goal of the network is to achieve Nash Equilibrium [21] between generator and discriminator so that the output of the discriminator is $1/2$ constantly, that is, the discriminator can no longer distinguish between real samples and generated samples. The optimization goal of the discriminator is to assign the correct label to the real sample and the generated sample as much as possible; the optimization goal of the generator is to make the generated sample as close as possible to the real sample. The entire network is similar to a two-player minimax game.

GAN is also widely used for image inpainting tasks. Pathak, Deepak, et al. [8] first applied GAN to the field of image inpainting in 2016.

2.4 Cross Semantic Attention

Zhao, Lei, et al. [16] proposed a new cross-semantic attention mechanism in their diverse image inpainting model, its architecture is shown in Fig. 2. The core idea is to project the mask image's features and the instance image's features to two feature spaces through 1×1 convolution and calculate the cross-semantic attention. In other words, the process uses the instance images in the dataset to guide the generation and completion of masked images.

$$F_{im}^n = \frac{1}{M(F)} \sum_{\forall j} exp\left(\left(\overline{F_m^n}\right)^T \left(\overline{F_i^j}\right) d\left(F_i^j\right)\right) \tag{3}$$

Where the F_m is the feature vector of the masked image and F_i is the feature vector of the instance image, finally, the output F_{im} is obtained through a skip connection, and $\overline{F_m^n} = W_f F_m$, $\overline{F_i} = W_k(F_i)$, $d(F_i) = W_d(F_i)$. The equation is normalized by a factor $M(F) = \sum_{\forall j} exp\left(\left(\overline{F_M^n}\right)^T \left(\overline{F_i^j}\right)\right)$. Here j is the index of the enumeration of all possible positions, n is the output position index, W_f, W_k, and W_d are the learned weight matrices. Finally, the output $F_i^O = \Gamma_d F im + F_i$, where Γd is the scale parameter used to balance the weights F_{im} and F_i.

This method is called Unsupervised Cross-space Generative Adversarial Network (UCTGAN).

3   Approach

Our proposed inpainting method consists of two stages. The first stage uses a pertained partial-convolution-based encoder-decoder architecture to obtain a coarse result and use the same loss function as the original paper proposed by Goodfellow et al. [1] in the training process of the first stage. The second stage is a fine inpainting network based on the coarse results of the first stage and guided by the instance images I_i. The training dataset provides the instance image I_i for guidance. The set of all instance images I_i is called instance image space S_i.

3.1   Network Architecture

The model consists of two inpainting networks. The coarse inpainting network is a UNet architecture based on partial convolutions with skip connections. The specific details of the network architecture are shown in Table 1.

The fine inpainting network mainly consists of three modules: conditional encoder module $E1$, manifold projection module $E2$, and generation module G. The first branch is a conditional encoder module $E1$ that acts as a conditional label. The second branch is a projection module $E2$ used to project the instance image space S_i into a lower latent manifold space. Finally, a generation module G calculates those two feature spaces after the cross-semantic attention layer and reconstructs the damaged image. Different from the original UTCGAN [16], we add a pre-trained Encoer-Decoder network before the original model and change the manifold projection discriminator in UTCGAN to a general discriminator.

3.2   Loss Function

Condition Constraint Loss. The results generated by our network need to be as consistent as possible with the original image, which requires the appearance and the perceptual features of the inpainted image to be as consistent as possible with those known pixel regions in the corresponding masked image. Condition Constraint Loss consists of appearance constraint loss $\mathcal{L}_{ccl}^a$ and perceptual constraint loss $\mathcal{L}_{ccl}^f$, which can be defined as:

$$
\begin{aligned}
\mathcal{L}_{ccl} &= \mathcal{L}_{ccl}^a + \mathcal{L}_{ccl}^f \\
&= \mathbb{E}_{I_i \sim p_{\text{data}}}^f \left\| (M \odot U\,(I_i, I_o)) - I_o \right\|_1 \\
&\quad + \mathbb{E}_{I_i \sim p_{\text{data}}} \left\| \varphi\,(M \odot U\,(I_i, I_o)) - \varphi\,(I_o) \right\|_1,
\end{aligned}
\tag{4}
$$

where M is the mask, $U(\cdot)$ represents our model, p_{data} is the distribution of the training dataset, and φ is a pre-trained VGG16 network.

Table 1. First stage is defined as a partial convolutional layer with the specified filter size, stride, and number of filters. PConv1-7 is in the encoder stage, whereas PConv8-14 is in the decoder stage. The BatchNorm column indicates whether PConv is followed by a Batch Normalization layer. The Nonlinearity column shows whether and what nonlinearity layer is used (following the BatchNorm if BatchNorm is used). Skip connections are shown using Concat*, which concatenates the previous nearest neighbor upsampled results with the corresponding results from the encoder stage.

Module Name	Filter Size	# Filters/Channels	Stride/Up Factor	BatchNorm	Nonlinearity
PConv1	5×5	64	2	Y	ReLU
PConv2	3×3	128	2	Y	ReLU
PConv3	3×3	256	2	Y	ReLU
PConv4	3×3	512	2	Y	ReLU
PConv5	3×3	512	2	Y	ReLU
PConv6	3×3	512	2	Y	ReLU
PConv7	3×3	512	2	Y	ReLU
NearestUpSample1		512	2	–	–
Concat1 (w/ PConv6)		512+512		–	–
PConv8	3×3	512	1	Y	LeakyReLU(0.2)
NearestUpSample2		512	2	–	–
Concat2 (w/ PConv5)		512+512		–	–
PConv9	3×3	512	1	Y	LeakyReLU(0.2)
NearestUpSample3		512	2	–	–
Concat3 (w/ PConv4)		512+512		–	–
PConv10	3×3	512	1	Y	LeakyReLU (0.2)
NearestUpSample4		512	2	–	–
Concat4 (w/ PConv3)		512+256		–	–
PConv11	3×3	256	1	Y	LeakyReLU (0.2)
NearestUpSample5		256	2	–	–
Concat5 (w/ PConv2)		256+128		–	–
PConv12	3×3	128	1	Y	LeakyReLU (0.2)
NearestUpSample6		128	2	–	–
Concat6 (w/ PConv1)		128+64		–	–
PConv13	3×3	64	1	Y	LeakyReLU (0.2)
NearestUpSample7		64	2	–	–
Concat7 (w/ Input)		64+3		–	–
PConv14	3×3	3	1	–	–

KL Divergence Loss. The KL divergence loss $\mathcal{L}_{KL}$ can be defined as:

$$\begin{aligned}
\mathcal{L}_{KL} &= \mathcal{L}_{KL}^i + \mathcal{L}_{KL}^m \\
&= KL\left(E_1\left(Z_c \mid I_i\right) \| \mathcal{N}(\mathbf{0}, \mathbf{I})\right) \\
&\quad + KL\left(E_2\left(Z_o \mid I_o\right) \| \mathcal{N}(\mathbf{0}, \mathbf{I})\right),
\end{aligned} \tag{5}$$

where E is converted to a low-dimensional module function, Z_c and Z_o are the normalizations of I_i and I_o (multivariate Gaussian distribution), which is to map the two images to a normal function. This loss balances the model's distribution, which is used to prevent the E module from causing the model to collapse.

Reconstruction Loss. To ensure that the generated image is as close as possible to the ground truth image, Therefore, a reconstruction loss is needed, which is defined as follows:

$$\mathcal{L}_{\text{rec}} = \|I_g - G\left(E_1\left(I_g\right), E_2\left(I_o\right)\right)\|_1, \tag{6}$$

where I_o is the coarse image of first stage, I_g is the ground truth image, E_1 is the projection module, E_2 is the encoder module, and G is a generator.

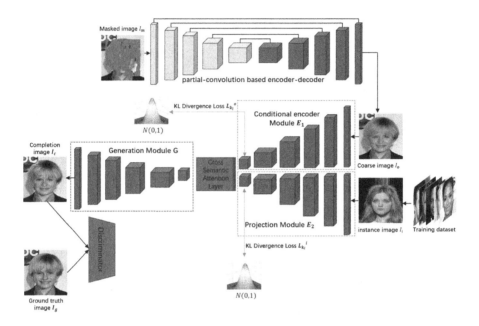

Fig. 3. Overview of our architecture with two stages. The first stage is the coarse restoration network, which is built upon a modified partial convolution model. The second stage is the fine inpainting network, consisting of a conditional encoder module, a projection module, and a generation module.

Adversarial Loss. Our adversarial loss is defined as:

$$\mathcal{L}_{adv} = \min_U \max_D \left(\mathbb{E}_{I_i \sim p_{\text{data}}} \log D\left(I_i\right)\right.$$
$$\left. + \mathbb{E}_{I_i \sim p_{\text{data}}} \log\left(1 - D\left(U\left(I_i, I_o\right)\right)\right)\right), \tag{7}$$

where p_{data} is the distribution of training dataset, D is the discriminator, $U(\cdot)$ represent our model.

Full Objective. The total loss function $\mathcal{L}_{\text{total}}$ of our network consists of four terms as

$$\mathcal{L}_{\text{total}} = \lambda_{\text{rec}} \mathcal{L}_{rec} + \lambda_{ccl}\left(\mathcal{L}_{ccl}^a + \mathcal{L}_{ccl}^f\right)$$
$$+ \lambda_{adv}\mathcal{L}_{adv} + \lambda_{KL}\left(\mathcal{L}_{KL}^i + \mathcal{L}_{KL}^m\right). \tag{8}$$

4 Experiments

4.1 Experimental Setting

We use images of resolution 256×256 with irregular holes [11] with different hole-to-image area ratios: (0.1, 0.2], (0.2, 0.3], (0.3, 0.4], (0.4, 0.5]. We train and test our model on the CelebA-HQ [17], Paris StreetView Dataset [18], and places2 dataset [20]. We use the original train and test split for Paris StreetView Dataset. For CelebA-HQ, we randomly partition into $27K$ images for training and $3K$ images for testing. For the places2 dataset, we selected 4,100 natural scene images from the dataset, 4,000 of which were used as the training dataset and 1,000 as the test dataset. During training, we augment the mask dataset by randomly sampling masks from the mask dataset and then performing random dilation, rotation, and cropping. All masks and images used for training and testing are of size 256×256. We train our networks using Adam Optimizer on a single NVIDIA RTX3090 GPU (24GB) with a batch size of 14.

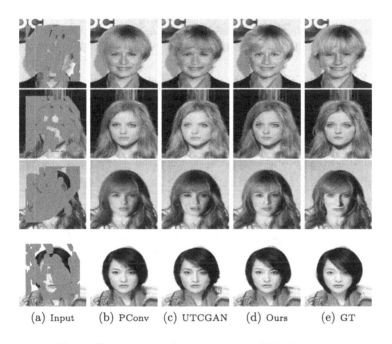

(a) Input   (b) PConv   (c) UTCGAN   (d) Ours   (e) GT

Fig. 4. Comparisons of test results on CelebA dataset

4.2 Qualitative Comparison

We compare our result with the other two methods, partial convolution (PConv) [11] and UCTGAN [16] on CelebA-HQ [17], Paris [18], and Places2 [20] respectively. We show some results with a mask area of 50%, as shown in Fig. 4, 5, and

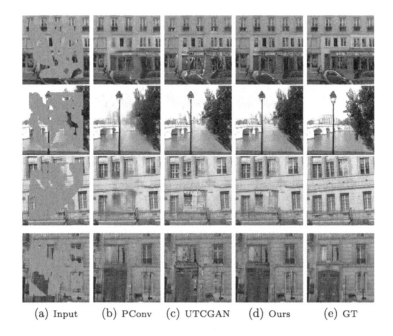

(a) Input   (b) PConv   (c) UTCGAN   (d) Ours   (e) GT

Fig. 5. Comparisons of test results on Paris streetview dataset

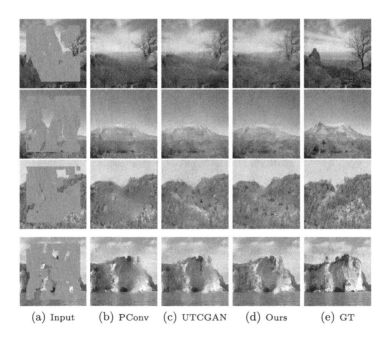

(a) Input   (b) PConv   (c) UTCGAN   (d) Ours   (e) GT

Fig. 6. Comparisons of test results on Places2 dataset

Table 2. Numerical comparisons on CelebA dataset with different mask area ratios. ↓ indicates lower is better while ↑ indicates higher is better.

	PSNR ↑				SSIM ↑				L1 Loss ↓			
Mask	10–20%	20–30%	30–40%	40–50%	10–20%	20–30%	30–40%	40–50%	10–20%	20–30%	30–40%	40–50%
PConv	28.89	26.84	24.92	23.77	0.946	0.889	0.844	0.771	1.25	2.01	2.69	2.37
UTCGAN	28.77	26.32	25.04	23.87	0.933	0.875	0.832	0.783	1.33	2.06	2.44	2.57
Ours	**28.98**	**27.67**	**26.46**	**25.15**	**0.952**	**0.911**	**0.877**	**0.833**	**1.13**	**1.83**	**2.13**	**2.24**

Table 3. Numerical comparisons on Paris streetview dataset with different mask area ratios. ↓ indicates lower is better while ↑ indicates higher is better.

	PSNR ↑				SSIM ↑				L1 Loss ↓			
Mask	10–20%	20–30%	30–40%	40–50%	10–20%	20–30%	30–40%	40–50%	10–20%	20–30%	30–40%	40–50%
PConv	27.23	25.67	24.64	23.77	0.842	0.763	0.712	0.679	1.32	2.23	2.35	2.72
UTCGAN	27.11	26.77	25.39	23.12	0.835	0.811	0.782	0.741	1.43	2.20	2.56	2.83
Ours	**29.53**	**27.56**	**26.21**	**25.67**	**0.854**	**0.911**	**0.878**	**0.792**	**1.12**	**1.86**	**2.21**	**2.44**

Table 4. Numerical comparisons on Placess2 dataset with different mask area ratios. ↓ indicates lower is better while ↑ indicates higher is better.

	PSNR ↑				SSIM ↑				L1 Loss ↓			
Mask	10–20%	20–30%	30–40%	40–50%	10–20%	20–30%	30–40%	40–50%	10–20%	20–30%	30–40%	40–50%
PConv	26.32	24.25	23.44	23.77	0.709	0.632	0.611	0.598	1.57	2.43	2.98	3.45
UTCGAN	26.11	25.72	24.87	23.12	0.835	0.644	0.728	0.645	1.43	2.20	2.56	2.83
Ours	**27.02**	**26.65**	**25.96**	**25.21**	**0.925**	**0.911**	**0.878**	**0.792**	**1.33**	**2.12**	**2.43**	**2.62**

6. It can be seen from the results that partial convolution can only get a rough image, and the details of the image are not handled well. For example, in Fig. 4, partial convolution cannot repair the texture of hair, while our results can clearly see the texture details of the hair. The original UTCGAN model can generate part of the details, but the reconstructed image is still blurred. For example, in Fig. 5, the results of some convolutions cannot see details such as doors and windows. Although UTCGAN can also repair some details of doors and windows, the results still have shadows, and our results can clearly see the details of doors and windows. Our model handles details better, and the inpainting images are relatively sharp.

4.3   Quantitative Comparison

We quantitatively compare our model with PConv [11] and UTCGAN [16] on the CelebA-HQ [17], Paris StreetView Dataset [18], and places2 dataset [20] with different mask area ratios. Table 2, 3, and 4 shows the comparison results of CelebA-HQ, Paris StreetView, and places2, respectively. We use the most commonly used metrics for image inpainting to qualitatively evaluate the results of the model, which are peak signal-to-noise ratio (PSNR), structural similarity (SSIM) [19], and L1 error. We used different hole area ratios to train and test models. From the results, we can see that our model has obtained better results.

As shown in Table 2, when we increased the proportion of the mask, the PSNR and SSIM values from PConv and UTCGAN rapidly decreased, and the L1 error also increased. On the other hand, our proposed method significantly mitigates these degradations, showing that it is able to handle large masks effectively.

4.4 Analysis

Compared with partial convolution [13], the original UTCGAN [16], our proposed model is more semantically consistent with the context. This is because our model uses the instance images in the dataset as a guide to generate corresponding missing region images. Compared with the original UTCGAN, the input of the second stage is a coarsely inpainted image instead of a masked image, and more useful features can be extracted in the feature extraction process of the second-stage refined inpainting network to obtain a clearer inpainting image since our model adds a coarse inpainting network.

Fig. 7. Some failure cases of our model

5 Conclusion

In this paper, we propose a conditional image-to-image translation network to generate semantically reasonable and visually realistic results for image inpainting. Our method finds and learns features of instance images in the dataset to guide the image generation process, which improved image realism and appearance consistency.

The limitation of our model is that it has special requirements for the dataset. The higher the similarity of the dataset, the better our model will perform. This is because our model fills in the missing parts by matching similar images from the dataset and extracting features. When there are no similar images or few similar images in the dataset, it is difficult to get good results. As shown in Fig. 7 is a part of our failure cases, which is due to the lack of similar images in the data set, resulting in poor results.

As for future work, we plan to further improve the clarity and authenticity of the image by changing the discriminator. The specific method is to give more freedom to the area in the center of the mask to reduce the constraints of the original image on the image generation process so that, generates a more realistic image. For the pixels close to the edge of the mask, they are given less freedom to keep them as consistent as possible with the original image to ensure the consistency of the context.

References

1. Goodfellow, I., et al.: Generative adversarial networks. Commun. ACM **63**(11), 139–144 (2020)
2. Yang, C., et al.: High-resolution image inpainting using multi-scale neural patch synthesis. In: Proceedings of the IEEE Conference on Computer Vision and Pattern Recognition (2017)
3. Pathak, D., et al.: Context encoders: feature learning by inpainting. In: Proceedings of the IEEE Conference on Computer Vision and Pattern Recognition (2016)
4. Iizuka, S., Simo-Serra, E., Ishikawa, H.: Globally and locally consistent image completion. ACM Trans. Graph. **36**(4), 1–14 (2017)
5. Demir, U., Unal, G.: Patch-based image inpainting with generative adversarial networks. arXiv preprint arXiv:1803.07422 (2018)
6. Shen, J., Chan, T.F.: Mathematical models for local nontexture inpaintings. SIAM J. Appl. Math. **62**(3), 1019–1043 (2002)
7. Barnes, C., et al.: PatchMatch: a randomized correspondence algorithm for structural image editing. ACM Trans. Graph. **28**(3), 24 (2009)
8. Pathak, D., et al.: Context encoders: feature learning by inpainting. In: Proceedings of the IEEE Conference on Computer Vision and Pattern Recognition (2016)
9. Efros, A.A., Freeman, W.T.: Image quilting for texture synthesis and transfer. In: Proceedings of the 28th Annual Conference on Computer Graphics and Interactive Techniques (2001)
10. Levin, A., Zomet, A., Weiss, Y.: Learning how to inpaint from global image statistics. In: ICCV, vol. 1 (2003)
11. Liu, G., et al.: Image inpainting for irregular holes using partial convolutions. In: Proceedings of the European Conference on Computer Vision (ECCV) (2018)
12. Song, Y., et al.: Spg-net: segmentation prediction and guidance network for image inpainting. arXiv preprint arXiv:1805.03356 (2018)
13. Yu, J., et al.: Free-form image inpainting with gated convolution. In: Proceedings of the IEEE/CVF International Conference on Computer Vision (2019)
14. Liu, H., et al.: Coherent semantic attention for image inpainting. In: Proceedings of the IEEE/CVF International Conference on Computer Vision (2019)
15. Li, Y., et al.: Generative face completion. In: Proceedings of the IEEE Conference on Computer Vision and Pattern Recognition (2017)
16. Zhao, L., et al.: Uctgan: diverse image inpainting based on unsupervised cross-space translation. In: Proceedings of the IEEE/CVF Conference on Computer Vision and Pattern Recognition (2020)

17. Karras, T., et al.: Progressive growing of gans for improved quality, stability, and variation. arXiv preprint arXiv:1710.10196 (2017)
18. Doersch, C., et al.: What makes Paris look like Paris? ACM Trans. Graph. **31**, 4 (2012)
19. Wang, Z., et al.: Image quality assessment: from error visibility to structural similarity. IEEE Trans. Image Process. **13**(4), 600–612 (2004)
20. Zhou, B., et al.: Places: a 10 million image database for scene recognition. IEEE Trans. Pattern Anal. Mach. Intell. **40**(6), 1452–1464 (2017)
21. Girshick, R., et al.: Rich feature hierarchies for accurate object detection and semantic segmentation. In: Proceedings of the IEEE Conference on Computer Vision and Pattern Recognition (2014)

Character Structure Analysis by Adding and Pruning Neural Networks in Handwritten Kanji Recognition

Keiji Gyohten[✉], Hidehiro Ohki, and Toshiya Takami

Faculty of Science and Technology, Oita University, Dannnoharu 700, Oita 870-1192, Japan
gyohten@oita-u.ac.jp

Abstract. In recent years, there has been a growing need for techniques that enable users to explain the basis for decisions made by neural networks in image recognition problems. While many conventional methods have focused on presenting the spatial basis for pattern recognition judgments by identifying the regions in the image that significantly influence the recognition results, our proposed method focuses on presenting a structural basis for recognizing handwritten Kanji characters. This is accomplished by pruning neural networks to acquire detectors for simple patterns that are commonly found in Kanji characters. During the process of sequentially adding these detectors, we also apply pruning to the network connecting the detectors, thereby aiming to precisely acquire simple hierarchical connections among the detectors as a structural recognition process in pattern recognition. We successfully applied this method to simple handwritten Kanji images, and achieved Kanji recognition by combining detectors for simple patterns without significantly affecting the recognition rate.

Keywords: Character Recognition · Deep Learning · Neural Network Pruning · Pattern Detector

1 Introduction

Currently, various studies on deep learning are being conducted worldwide to improve its performance by devising the structure of neural networks and learning from more training data. With such performance improvements, deep learning has been able to penetrate various application fields, and is highly likely to become the foundation of social systems in the near future.

To facilitate the integration of deep learning into diverse social systems, it is imperative that society willingly accept machine-generated judgments. For example, in the medical field [1], a technology that can not only make judgments, but also explain the rationale behind such judgments is needed. The field of deep learning explainability has emerged to address this imperative [2]. Consequently, extensive research efforts have been directed towards the domain of object recognition, with particular emphasis on methodologies that spatially elucidate the regions within an image that significantly influence decision-making processes.

H. Lu et al. (Eds.): ACPR 2023, LNCS 14407, pp. 129–142, 2023.
https://doi.org/10.1007/978-3-031-47637-2_10

On the other hand, techniques that enable machines to provide explanations for their decisions based on the structure of patterns in images have been relatively scarce in the existing research literature. In a typical object recognition application, the recognized objects are composed of complex and hierarchically arranged combinations of different components. For example, a car can be described as a combination of wheels, windows, and a body; decomposing it further reveals that a wheel comprises a tire and rim. The structural representations generated by machines may not always align with human intuition. Nonetheless, empowering machines to explain the rationale behind their decisions by leveraging the pattern is crucial to establishing human confidence in the machine's judgments. To accomplish this goal of structural explanation, it is necessary to not only address the given pattern recognition problem, but also develop methodologies for automatically acquiring the underlying structure of the pattern.

In this study, we proposed an approach to Kanji character recognition that utilizes a neural network to automatically and precisely acquire the underlying structure of patterns, and explain the judgment rationale based on a pattern structure. The motivation for addressing the Kanji recognition problem is that Kanji characters are composed of a limited set of components, which renders them suitable to understand the pattern structure. The proposed method consists of a combination of simple detectors based on a neural network. During the training process, edge pruning techniques are employed within the neural network to acquire detectors that respond to simple patterns present in Kanji characters. Furthermore, by sequentially connecting these detectors and pruning edges within the network of connections among the detectors, we can achieve Kanji character recognition. The sparse connections among the detectors in the final neural network provide a representation of the pattern as a tree structure; this constitutes the foundation for judgments. Through experimentation, we confirmed that the character recognition based on detector connections was feasible without significantly reducing the recognition accuracy. Additionally, we demonstrated the ability to analyze the connection relationships of each detector, thereby allowing us to acquire detectors that respond to multiple Kanji characters in common. Through hierarchical connections of these detectors, we could represent the process of pattern detection as a tree structure.

2   Related Works

2.1   Investigating Explainability in Neural Networks

In recent years, there have been various studies on explainability in deep learning [2]. Many of these methods have been based on approaches that identify important factors that contribute significantly to recognition results. For example, the integrated gradients (IG) method finds the elements by integrating the gradient of the activity value of the output corresponding to the recognition target on a pixel-by-pixel basis [3]. This method provides a pixel-by-pixel representation of which parts of the image contribute significantly to an increase in the activity value of the output corresponding to the recognition target. Local interpretable model-agnostic explanations (LIME) finds which small regions in the input image contribute significantly to the recognition result [4]. This method achieves this by randomly generating a group of small regions with the same features of the image, thus obtaining the activity value of the output corresponding to the recognition target, and expressing the relationship between the two by linear regression. Activation maximization (AM) obtains the input image that mostly activates a certain neuron in a neural network by finding the gradient of its activity value relative to the input image [5, 6]. These methods have received a lot of attention and are at the forefront of explainability in deep learning. Other studies on explainability based on various approaches have also been conducted. Most of these methods represent important elements that contribute significantly to recognition results as units of pixels or regions in an image. Most of them adopt an approach that visually presents the spatial location of the elements in the image.

On the other hand, approaches that explicitly present the structure of recognition targets, such as part-whole relationships, as important elements contributing to the recognition results are not widely observed. In a research effort, based on such an approach, Zhang et al. have achieved highly interesting Kanji character recognition, including zero-shot learning, by utilizing the ideographic description sequence (IDS) dictionary to represent the structure of characters [7]. However, in this method, the structure of the recognition targets must be pre-defined in the dictionary. Generally, it is challenging to pre-define the constituent elements that can represent the part-whole relationships of recognition targets. For example, in the problem of face recognition, assuming that we want to explain a face is recognized based on the fact that it consists of eyes, nose, and mouth, pre-defining the constituent elements of a face and preparing separate recognizers for each of them is not practical. In our research, instead of manually preparing recognizers for the constituent elements of a recognition target, we have attempted to automatically acquire detectors by pruning the edges of a neural network.

2.2 Applying Edge Pruning to Neural Networks

Pruning edges in neural networks, along with quantization, is commonly applied to compress the network size [8]. Various approaches have been attempted to eliminate redundant computations by pruning edges and quantizing the parameters in the network, while preventing degradation of the recognition performance to the extent possible. Our study does not attempt to compress the network size; instead it acquires detectors of simple patterns that commonly exist in the recognition target by means of edge pruning. It is assumed that the performance of a neural network that has been pruned excessively will deteriorate, and distinguishing similar patterns will be difficult. In our study, the neural network that can no longer distinguish similar patterns is used as a detector of patterns that commonly exist in the recognition target.

3 Proposed Method

3.1 Outline

Figure 1 illustrates an outline of the neural network structure employed in the proposed method. Firstly, convolutional neural network (CNN) is utilized to train character images and obtain a character recognition network. After extracting a feature extractor consisting of convolutional layers, pattern detectors composed of dense layers are sequentially added, and the learning process is repeated. During the training, edge pruning is applied to the dense layers to create detectors that capture simple patterns. Moreover, by applying edge pruning to the dense layers, the connectivity of the pattern detectors is simplified. By analyzing this connectivity of the pattern detectors, it becomes possible to acquire the structure of the underlying patterns that form the basis of recognition.

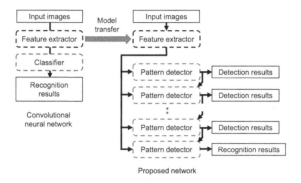

Fig. 1. Outline of the proposed method.

3.2   Obtaining Feature Extractor

First, our method obtains a feature extractor that extracts local features of the input character image. This feature extractor is obtained by transferring the convolution layers from a trained character recognition network based on CNN, which is widely used in pattern recognition. As these filters have a significant impact on character recognition performance, it is necessary to obtain good filters at this stage.

Figure 2 shows the CNN used in this method to obtain the feature extractor. The network is trained using the training data, which consists of binary images of characters as input data and one-hot vectors representing the character types of the input characters as teacher data. Using the training data, the weights in the network are updated to reduce the value of the loss function using an optimization algorithm. The loss function is the categorical cross entropy. During the training process, the weights of the network with the best recognition results for the validation data are used as the final training set. After training, the classifier is discarded and the feature extractor is used as a set of filters to extract the local features of the character images.

3.3   Adding and Pruning Pattern Detectors

Adding Pattern Detectors. Our method adds the 1st pattern detector to the feature extractor obtained in the previous step (see Sect. 3.2), as shown in Fig. 3 and trains the network in the manner described shortly. In the training process, edge pruning is applied to the dense layers in the pattern detector to make it respond to simple patterns in the

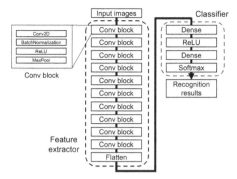

Fig. 2. Convolutional Neural Network for character recognition.

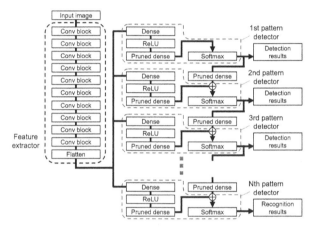

Fig. 3. Adding pattern detectors to the feature extractor.

characters. It may be noted that the weights in the feature extractor are frozen and used in this training process.

After the training of the 1st pattern detector is completed, the 2nd pattern detector shown in Fig. 3 is added and the network is further trained. By adding the 2nd pattern detector, the overall network structure becomes more complex, and a detector that can respond to complex patterns can be obtained. The weights in the 1st pattern detector as well as those in the feature extractor are frozen, and the training with edge pruning described later is applied to the 2nd pattern extractor. By adding pattern detectors sequentially as described above, our method finally obtains the detector that can output the desired Kanji recognition results.

The pruned dense layer within each pattern detector comprises highly sparse edges resulting from the pruning process. As a result, the nodes in the output layer of each pattern detector no longer respond to only one character, but to multiple characters. This signifies that the parameter count representing each pattern detector has been reduced through pruning, thereby enabling it to respond to simple patterns present in multiple characters. The values of these nodes are input to the next pattern detector through the pruned dense layer that connects them. By revealing how pattern detectors are interconnected via the pruned dense layer, it will be possible to explain to the machine the combination of structural patterns present in the input image. Additionally, in the event of a failure in recognizing handwritten Kanji images, it may be possible to explain the cause of recognition failure by observing the output values of each pattern detector and identifying which patterns exhibited weak responses.

Training and Pruning Pattern Detectors. As shown in Fig. 4, the proposed method applies pruning to the dense located just before the output layer of the pattern detector and the dense layer connecting the pattern detectors. The pruning is achieved by fixing the weights of the edges between the nodes in the dense layer to zero. Here, we define sparsity, s_f as the ratio of the number of edges, whose weights are fixed to 0, to the total number of edges in the dense layer. In this method, in the process of training, the weights of the edges in the dense layer are fixed to 0 for edges, whose weights are close to 0. This operation is repeated until s_f reaches a pre-defined value.

This training process is divided into two stages: In Stage 1, training for character recognition with edge pruning, shown in Fig. 4(a), takes place, and in Stage 2, training for a detector that responds to simple patterns, shown in Fig. 4(b), takes place.

In Stage 1, we use the training data described in Sect. 3.2 to update the weights of the dense layer in the pattern detector until the loss function converges. The teacher data in the training data is represented as a one-hot vector. The character type corresponding to the node with the largest value in the output layer is used as the recognition result. In this process, the edge pruning is repeatedly applied to the dense layer just before the output layer of the pattern detector until s_f reaches a pre-specified value.

The training method with edge pruning, as proposed by us, is described below. First, the final value of s_f and the number of sparsity updates I, are determined in advance. Then, using the training data described in Sect. 3.2, the weights in the dense layers are updated until the loss function converges. Then, for the weights within the dense layers, this method fixes the weights whose value is close to 0 to 0 so that s_f can be calculated by the following equation:

$$\text{sparsity} = s_f i / I,$$

where i is the number of updates of the current sparsity. By repeating the above training and pruning I times, s_f within the dense layers becomes the final s_f specified.

In the Stage 2, we aim to obtain detectors that respond to simple patterns using the network obtained after applying edge pruning. The pruning of the dense layers results in a decrease in the network's recognition performance, limiting it to recognizing only simple patterns. In other words, this pruning yields a network that exclusively responds to various simple patterns of kanji characters. We input the character images from the training data into the network and calculate the average values of the nodes in the output layer for each character type. As the pruned network only responds to simple patterns, even when a character image belonging to a particular character type is inputted, multiple nodes in the output layer may exhibit high values. In this approach, as depicted in Fig. 4(b), we apply discriminant analysis [9] to binarize the average values of the nodes in the output layer, thereby determining multiple nodes that respond to character images of a specific character type. Subsequently, we obtain teacher vectors,

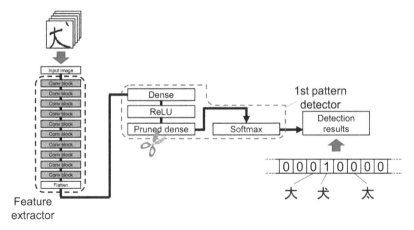

(a)   Training for character region with edge pruning

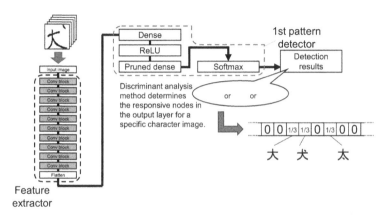

(b)   Training detectors that respond to simple patterns

Fig. 4. Training for pattern detectors.

as shown in Fig. 4(b), where non-responsive nodes have a value of 0, and responsive nodes possess probabilities indicating the correct character type as their element values. Using this training data, we retrain the pruned network to obtain detectors that respond to simple patterns. The loss function used in this stage is also a categorical cross entropy.

Once the training of a detector is complete, the next detector is added, and the same training process is performed. As shown in Fig. 5, the weights within the feature extractor, weights of the learned pattern detectors, and weights of the connections between the pattern detectors are all frozen. Only the weights within the newly added pattern detector and weights of its connections with the previous pattern detector are updated through training. Regarding the weights of the connections with the preceding pattern detector, they are primarily initialized randomly, except for the weights of edges connecting the nodes corresponding to the same character type, which are initialized to 1. This initialization is done to actively utilize the output of the previous pattern detector. By completing the training of the last pattern detector at the stage depicted in Fig. 4(a), we obtain the final character recognition network. Furthermore, as illustrated in Fig. 5, by tracing the sparse connections between detectors from the nodes of the final output layer to the feature extractor, we can understand the simple patterns on which each character is recognized.

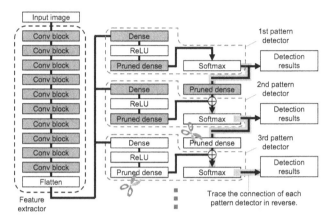

Fig. 5. Adding pattern detectors (gray boxes indicate that weights are frozen).

4 Experimental Results

This section describes the experimental results of the proposed method, which was implemented on a computer with an Intel Xeon E5-1603 v4 2.80 GHz CPU, with 16.0 GB RAM, and an NVIDIA Quadro K620 GPU chip. All the processing was coded in Python. Tensorflow and OpenCV were used to implement the neural network and text image input/output and transformation processes, respectively. The Tensorflow model optimization toolkit was also used for pruning the edges of the neural network. The analysis of the connectivity between pattern detectors was conducted using the anytree library.

The handwritten Japanese character image data set ETL9B was used in this experiment. This set consists of binary images of 201 64 × 63 pixel sized characters for each of the 3036 character types, including Japanese Kanji. In this experiment, 80 types of Kanji learned in the first grade of elementary school, which are relatively simple in structure, were used as the target characters for recognition to confirm whether the basic hierarchical structure within Kanji could be acquired. For each character type, 120, 21, and 60 images were used for training, validation, and test, respectively. For the training images, a random projective transformation was applied to generate 300 character images for each character type. Of the generated images, 270 and 30 were used as training and validation images, respectively. As a result, 390, 51, and 60 images were prepared for training, validation, and test for each character type.

The parameters of the network are shown in Fig. 6. First, as described in Sect. 3.2, we trained the CNN consisting of a feature extractor and a classifier for 1000 epochs using the training images to obtain the model with the best recognition rate for the validation image. The recognition rate of this model for the test image was 97.8%.

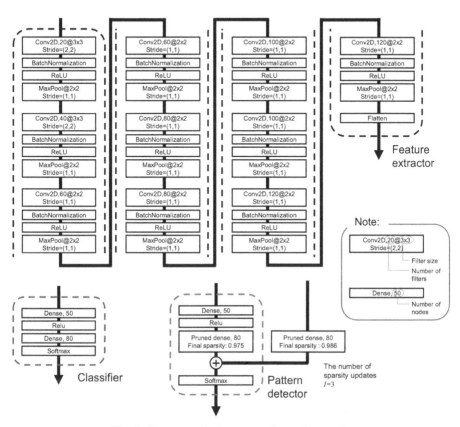

Fig. 6. Parameters in the proposed neural network.

Then, the feature extractor was extracted, and as described in Sect. 3.3, the pattern detectors were sequentially added. By utilizing the learning method described in Sect. 3.3, the weights of the edges in the pruned dense layer within the pattern detector and the one connecting them were acquired while pruning the unnecessary edges. As shown in Fig. 6, the values of final s_f used in the pattern detector were extremely high. This indicates that each node on the output side of the pruned dense layers used in the pattern detectors was connected to at most a few nodes on the input side and, in some cases, might not be connected at all. Therefore, the pruned dense layers used in the pattern detectors were composed of highly sparse edges. During training, early stopping was applied using the validation data to shorten the training time. Figure 7 depicts the recognition rate at the end of character recognition training using edge pruning, where pattern detectors were sequentially added. Despite the pruned dense layers involved in the output of the pattern detector being composed of highly sparse edges, it was observed that by connecting only a few pattern detectors, a performance comparable to a conventional CNN could be achieved. The highest recognition rate was obtained when six pattern detectors were connected, yielding a recognition rate of 98.0%.

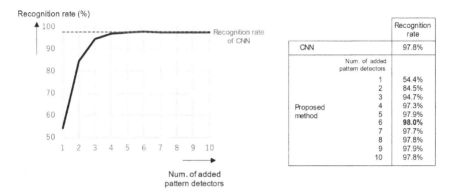

Fig. 7. Recognition rates of the proposed method.

Next, in the network, where the six pattern detectors with the highest recognition rates from Fig. 7 were connected, we examined to which character types the output nodes of each pattern detector's output layer responded. Figure 8 lists the nodes in the output layers of each pattern detector that responded to multiple character types and maintained connections with the output layer of the sixth pattern detector. Clearly, the initially added pattern detector outputted recognition results through a pruned dense layer with highly sparse edge connections, causing many nodes in the output layer to respond to multiple character types. However, as the pattern detectors were sequentially added, it was observed that by utilizing the outputs from the previous pattern detector and the feature extractor, each node in the output layer narrowed down the character types to which it responded. Notably, starting from the fourth pattern detector, each node in the output layer began responding to only one character type. In this validation, we expected some nodes in the output layer of the pattern detector to respond to similar character types. However, as shown in Fig. 8, most of the nodes that responded to multiple character types in the output layer were not responding to character types that appeared very similar. It was unclear whether these were detectors that were mistakenly obtained or if there were indeed common patterns that humans cannot intuitively grasp. Additionally, as mentioned in [4], it was possible that they were also responding to regions that humans did not anticipate. In the future, it will be necessary to combine existing methods, such as activation maximization, as described in Sect. 2.1 to visually present to which parts of characters each node in the output layer of each pattern detector was responding.

1st pattern detector

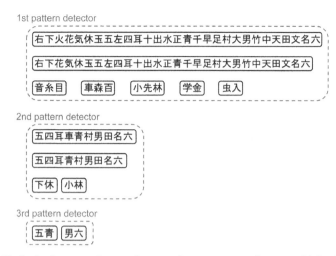

2nd pattern detector

3rd pattern detector

Fig. 8. Nodes in the output layers of pattern detectors responding to multiple characters.

Additionally, the connectivity of the pattern detectors was examined after applying edge pruning to the 6th pattern detector. Several examples are shown in Fig. 9. The solid round rectangles represent nodes in the output layer of the pattern detectors, and the characters inside the rectangles indicate the character types to which the nodes responded in the corresponding character image. The solid round rectangles represent nodes in the output layer of the pattern detector, and the characters in the rectangle indicate that the node responded to character images of that character type. Arrows connecting the nodes represent the remaining edges in the pruned dense layers that connected the pattern detectors. The red round rectangles indicate that when the value of this node increased, the value of the corresponding node in the 6th pattern detector also increased. The blue round rectangles indicate that when the value of this node increased, the value of the corresponding node in the 6th pattern detector decreased. As shown in the upper left tree in Fig. 9, in 51 out of 80 cases, a node responding to a certain character type in the output layer of each pattern detector was serially connected to a node responding to the same character type in the output layer of the sixth pattern detector. Additionally, in the other trees in Fig. 9, where nodes in the output layer of the pattern detectors were interconnected in a more complex manner, it can be observed that this sequential connection was still present. Furthermore, nodes in the output layer of a particular pattern detector tended to suppress nodes that responded to visually similar, but different character types in the output layer of the 6th pattern detector. This hierarchical structure allowed for the acquisition of the similarity relationships among the target character types. Additionally, in Fig. 9, subtrees within the shaded regions of the same color indicate that they shared the same structure. This implies that the nodes indicated by the red arrows contributed to the final recognition results of multiple character types. In other words, acquiring these nodes meant obtaining detectors that responded to simple patterns, which was the goal of this study. Representing these connectivity relationships in a tree structure signifies the description of the underlying patterns governing the decision-making process. However, it should be noted that these considerations are subjective and difficult to evaluate objectively. Future work should explore quantitative evaluation methods.

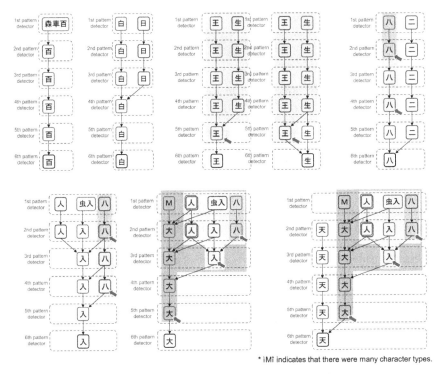

* iMi indicates that there were many character types.

Fig. 9. Obtained connection relationships of pattern detectors.

Figure 10 illustrates examples of node values in the output layer of the pattern detectors for the character images that the proposed method failed to recognize. On the left are the pattern detectors corresponding to the correct character types, while on the right are the pattern detectors corresponding to the misrecognized character types. It can be observed that when the input character was corrupted, nodes corresponding to similar characters also responded and tended to suppress the final output. However, these observations are subjective. In the future, it is necessary to visualize how each node responds to specific patterns using techniques, such as activation maximization. Furthermore, it is essential to establish quantitative measures and conduct more objective evaluations.

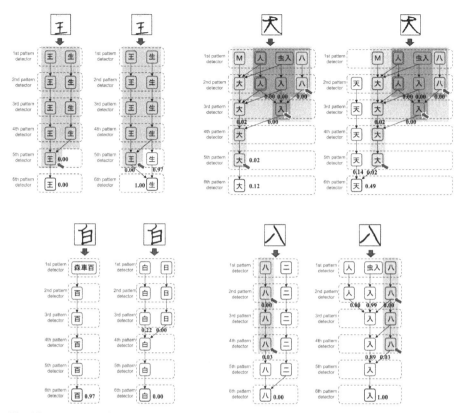

Fig. 10. Examples of node values in the output layers of the pattern detectors for erroneously recognized character images.

5 Conclusions

In this study, we proposed a method to explain the rationale behind judgments based on pattern structure using a neural network for handwritten Kanji character recognition. This approach involved sequentially connecting pattern detectors to feature extractors obtained from a CNN designed for handwritten Kanji character recognition. During the training process, pruning the network enabled each pattern detector to respond to simple patterns shared among similar characters. Furthermore, pruning the network connecting the pattern detectors allowed us to represent the relationships among detectors as tree structures, depicting the foundational patterns for judgments. Through experiments, we confirmed that the proposed method achieved a character recognition performance comparable to that of CNN despite being composed of a sparse neural network. Additionally, we confirmed that the connection relationships among pattern detectors allowed us to understand the relationships among simple patterns shared among similar characters, represented as tree structures.

While we succeeded in acquiring detectors that responded to multiple Kanji characters in common, we were unable to visualize to which patterns in the character images these detectors were responding. In the future, introducing the conventional method described in Sect. 2.1, which visually presents judgment rationale, is necessary. Furthermore, owing to the computational limitations in this study, we froze the weights of the pre-trained feature extractors and pattern detectors, applying learning only to the newly added pattern detectors. Moving forward, we plan to introduce fine-tuning and explore learning methods that tune all the weights within the network.

Acknowledgements. This work was supported by JSPS KAKENHI (Grant Number JP 19K12045).

References

1. Singh, A., Sengupta, S., Lakshminarayanan, V.: Explainable deep learning models in medical image analysis. J. Imaging **6**(6), 52 (2020)
2. Xu, F., Uszkoreit, H., Du, Y., Fan, W., Zhao, D., Zhu, J.: Explainable AI: A brief survey on history, research areas, approaches and challenges. In: Tang, J., Kan, M.-Y., Zhao, D., Li, S., Zan, H. (eds.) NLPCC 2019. LNCS (LNAI), vol. 11839, pp. 563–574. Springer, Cham (2019). https://doi.org/10.1007/978-3-030-32236-6_51
3. Sundararajan, M., Taly, A., Yan, Q.: Axiomatic attribution for deep networks. In: International Conference on Machine Learning, pp. 3319–3328 (2017)
4. Ribeiro, M.T., Singh, S., Guestrin, C.: "Why should I trust you?" Explaining the predictions of any classifier. In: Proceedings of the 22nd ACM SIGKDD International Conference on Knowledge Discovery and Data Mining, pp. 1135–1144 (2016)
5. Erhan, D., Bengio, Y., Courville, A., Vincent, P.: Visualizing higher-layer features of a deep network. Univ. Montreal **1341**(3), 1 (2009)
6. Nguyen, A., Yosinski, J., Clune, J.: Understanding neural networks via feature visualization: a survey. In: Samek, W., Montavon, G., Vedaldi, A., Hansen, L.K., Müller, K.-R. (eds.) Explainable AI: Interpreting, Explaining and Visualizing Deep Learning. LNCS (LNAI), vol. 11700, pp. 55–76. Springer, Cham (2019). https://doi.org/10.1007/978-3-030-28954-6_4
7. Zhang, J., Du, J., Dai, L.: Radical analysis network for learning hierarchies of Chinese characters. Pattern Recogn. **103**, 107305 (2020)
8. Liang, T., Glossner, J., Wang, L., Shi, S., Zhang, X.: Pruning and quantization for deep neural network acceleration: a survey. Neurocomputing **461**, 370–403 (2021)
9. Otsu, N.: A threshold selection method from gray-level histograms. IEEE Trans. Syst. Man Cybernet. **9**(1), 62–66 (1979)

A Few-Shot Approach to Sign Language Recognition: Can Learning One Language Enable Understanding of All?

Ragib Amin Nihal[1](✉)🆔 and Nawara Mahmood Broti[2]🆔

[1] Tokyo Institute of Technology, Tokyo, Japan
ragib@ra.sc.e.titech.ac.jp
[2] Meiji University, Tokyo, Japan

Abstract. Sign language is a unique form of communication in which hand or other body part gestures are used to express oneself. A large proportion of the world's population has speech and hearing impairments and communicates through sign language. Sign language, like verbal language, varies from country to country. Recent researches on automatic recognition focus on specific sign language of a country and require a large dataset. However, a prevalent issue arises when there is plenty of data available for some sign languages, while other sign languages suffer from data scarcity or non-existence of resources. To tackle this issue, our study presents a novel solution by proposing a few-shot learning approach for automatic sign language recognition. This approach involves training the model using data from a single sign language and then leveraging the acquired knowledge to recognize other sign languages, even when limited data is available for those languages. By bridging the gap between limited data availability and accurate recognition of new Sign Languages via employing this few-shot learning technique, our approach contributes to enhancing communication accessibility for the global sign language community. Our experimental results demonstrate promising performance, showcasing the potential of our model in overcoming the challenges of cross-lingual sign language recognition.

Keywords: Sign language · Few shot learning · automatic recognition · multiple sign language

1 Introduction

Sign language (SL) is a distinctive form of communication for hearing and speaking-impaired people that uses hand gestures and non-verbal indicators (such as facial expressions) to convey messages. Rather than using spoken communication and sound patterns, SL users communicate through signs in visual space. Based on a survey by the World Federation of the Deaf, there are more than 300 SLs used by 70 million deaf individuals worldwide [1]. Due to lack of knowledge, most of the hearing population do not understand this language, which raises a barrier for SL users in society. Recently, deep learning-based automatic SL recognition systems are showing promise and may be able to help break down these barriers.

Every country has its unique SL, having its own set of gestures and meanings. However, only a handful of these SL data are publicly available; for the rest, data availability is extremely limited. One of the key reasons is that manually collecting and labeling enough SL samples is expensive and time-consuming. In addition, the data needs to be collected in the presence of SL experts for authenticity. As a result of data scarcity, less-popular SLs do not receive the necessary attention from researchers and remain unexplored.

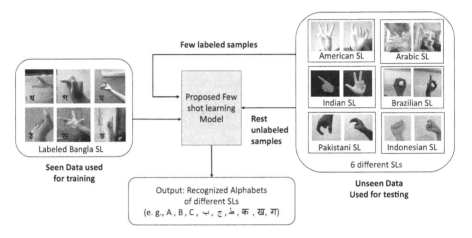

Fig. 1. Overview of the proposed SL recognition system: Bangla SL alphabets are used as training data to train the proposed few-shot learning model; six other countries' SL images are used as test data. The model recognizes alphabets of different SLs from its knowledge from training data and a few labeled samples of other SLs. The few-shot learning approach enables effective recognition of SL alphabets across diverse linguistic contexts, enhancing cross-lingual SL recognition.

SL can be expressed with either motion or static hand gestures. In accordance with how an SL is expressed, the corresponding SL dataset can consist of images or videos. In many researches, traditional Convolutional neural network (CNN) and Recurrent neural network (RNN) based deep learning systems are proven to have extraordinary performance in SL recognition [3–5]. However, the majority of automatic SL recognition systems rely on large-scale data training. Without a large enough dataset, these techniques fail to perform. Recently, some innovative forms of learning is introduced that can learn from very few training data. Few-shot learning is one of them. Few-Shot Learning is a machine learning sub-field that is concerned about categorizing new data when we just have a few supervised training examples [2]. Lately, researchers are applying few-shot learning in automatic SL recognition systems. Wang et al. [6] proposed a metric-based few-shot learning model called Cornerstone Network for Chinese natural

SL recognition. Bohacek et al. [7] introduced an online text-to-video dictionary-based video dataset and a novel approach to training SL recognition models in a few-shot scenario. Shovkoplias et al. [8] utilized video data of hand gestures, as well as Electromyography signal from arm for few-shot learning based SL recognition. Ferreira, et al. [9] proposed a Contrastive Transformer-based model that can learn rich representations from body key points sequences. Hosseini et al. [10] introduced a one-shot learning approach for teaching new Iranian SL signs to a teacher assistant social robot. The performance of image-based few-shot learning in general SL recognition along with cross-lingual SL recognition is yet to be examined. This study tests the viability of learning many regions' static SLs using an image-based few-shot learning approach. As shown in Fig. 1, this work utilizes few-shot learning to learn different SL alphabets from few annotated samples and intends to provide a strong and adaptable tool for properly understanding the hearing and speaking communities. The contributions of the paper are summarized below:

1. **Few-shot Learning for Sign Language Recognition:** The research contributes to the application of few-shot learning techniques in the domain of SL recognition. By training a model on one SL dataset and leveraging the acquired knowledge to recognize signs from other SLs with limited data, the research addresses the data scarcity problem and opens up possibilities for more inclusive and effective SL recognition systems.
2. **Cross-Lingual Sign Language Recognition:** The research explores the potential for cross-lingual SL recognition by training a model on a single SL (Bangla SL) and evaluating its performance on multiple other SLs.
3. **Evaluation of Shot and Way Configurations:** The research conducts extensive experiments with varying shot and way configurations in the few-shot learning setup and selects DenseNet121 as the backbone architecture for feature extraction and Prototypical Networks as the few-shot classification method.

The rest of the paper is organized as follows: In Sect. 2, we discuss the selection and description of our datasets, providing a comprehensive overview of both the seen and unseen class datasets. Section 3 elaborates on the details of our methodology, including the problem statement, framework architecture, and experimental setup. We present the results of our experiments in Sect. 4, showcasing the performance of our model across different shot and way configurations. We then engage in a qualitative discussion in Sect. 5, highlighting the implications and limitations of our work, along with potential future directions. Finally, we conclude in Sect. 6 by summarizing our contributions and the significance of our approach in promoting inclusive communication through cross-lingual SL recognition.

2   Dataset Selection and Description

In the research, the selection of appropriate datasets plays a crucial role in training and evaluating the few-shot learning approach for SL recognition. The chosen datasets should adequately represent the seen and unseen classes, capturing the diversity and variations present in different SLs.

1. Seen Class Dataset:
   The seen class dataset- BdSL [11]- represents the Bangla SL. It is a large dataset of one-handed BdSL alphabet that contains 35,149 images. There are 37 different BdSL sign classes in this dataset, where each class possesses 950–1000 images. The images have versatile backgrounds and a broad range of light contrast, hand size, image scale, and skin tone of hand. The images are captured from more than 350 subjects and various angles. The image size is 64 × 64 pixels. Due to the versatility of this dataset, it is selected as the primary source of labeled support samples for training the few-shot learning model.
2. Unseen Class Datasets:
   The unseen class datasets, UdSL, encompasses six different SLs such as American SL (ASL) [12], Arabic SL (ArSL) [13], Brazilian SL (BrSL) [14], Indian SL (ISL) [15], Pakistani SL (PSL) [16], and Indonesian SL (InSL) [17]. These datasets have completely new SL images and new classes which are not present in the previously described seen class dataset. They represent the target SLs that the few-shot learning model aims to recognize using the knowledge acquired from the BdSL dataset. Each dataset is concisely described in Table 1.

Table 1. Unseen Dataset Description

Dataset	Total image number	Image size	Background	Color	Total class number
ASL	34627	28 × 28	Homogenous	Gray scale	24
ArSL	5832	416 × 416	Versatile	RGB	29
BrSL	4411	200 × 200	Homogenous	RGB	15
ISL	42000	128 × 128	Homogenous	RGB	35
PSL	1549	640 × 480	Homogenous	RGB	38
InSL	520	2000 × 2000	Homogenous	RGB	26

We selected the unseen class datasets considering the diversity of SLs, including variations in hand shapes, gestures, and cultural influences. This promotes the model's ability to generalize to new SLs and improves its overall performance in recognizing signs from different countries.

3   Methodology

3.1   Problem Statement

This research focuses on addressing the challenge of limited data availability for SL recognition systems. Here. *BdSL* represents the seen class, referring to the Bangla SL dataset, and $UdSL$ represents the unseen classes, comprising the $ASL, ArSL, BrSL, ISL, PSL$, and $InSL$ datasets. The goal is to develop a few-shot learning approach that leverages knowledge acquired from the $BdSL$ dataset to accurately recognize signs from the $UdSL$ dataset.

Let $X_s = (x_i, y_i)$ be the seen class dataset, where x_i represents the ith image sample and y_i denotes its corresponding class label from the $BdSL$ dataset. Similarly, let $X_u = (x_j, y_j)$ represent the unseen class dataset, where x_j is the jth image sample and y_j is its class label from the $UdSL$ dataset.

The few-shot learning approach aims to train a model that can generalize knowledge from the seen class dataset (X_s) to effectively recognize signs from the unseen class dataset (X_u). A model is recurrently tested on a collection of N-way K-shot classification tasks, denoted as $D_T = \{T_i\}$, commonly known as episodes, using the standard few-shot learning procedure. To be more precise, each episode has a support set S_i and a query set Q_i split. The support set S_i has N distinct categories, each with K labeled samples, resulting in a total of $N \times K$ examples for training. Each of the N categories in the query-set Q_i has Q unlabeled samples to categorize.

3.2   Overall Framework

In this research, we propose a framework that combines classical training using a CNN architecture with a few-shot learning based network. In the classical training phase, we train a powerful CNN architecture named DenseNet-121 [18]. This model was selected on the basis of our previous research [5,19] that found that DenseNet extracts better features in SL recognition. We trained DenseNet-121 on the seen class dataset- BdSL. This process allows DenseNet-121 to learn discriminative features that capture rich representations of the input data. We optimize the network parameters using a cross-entropy loss across all training classes, which is a widely-used technique in traditional training setups.

The novelty of our research emerges in the second stage, where we introduce a few-shot learning framework. While the DenseNet-121 architecture itself is not a new contribution, the innovative aspect lies in its integration into a few-shot learning context. Specifically, we employ the prototypical network, a well-established approach in few-shot learning, to utilize the learned feature representations from the backbone network. This allows us to effectively recognize signs from unseen classes even when training data is limited.

Once DenseNet-121 is trained, it serves as the backbone network for the subsequent few-shot learning phase. Here, we employ the prototypical network [20], which is designed to handle few-shot learning tasks. In this phase, only a few labeled examples are taken from each unseen class from the unseen class dataset- UdSL. The prototypical network learns to compute class prototypes by averaging the feature embeddings of the support set, which consists of the labeled examples. These prototypes act as representatives of each class.

During testing, we extract feature embeddings of the query examples using the trained DenseNet-121 backbone. The prototypical network then calculates the similarity between the query embeddings and the class prototypes. Based on

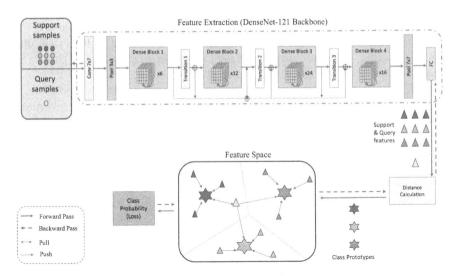

Fig. 2. Proposed Architecture: It incorporates DenseNet-121 as the backbone for feature extraction. The extracted features are used for distance calculation. In the Prototypical Network, class prototypes are calculated by computing the mean of the support samples belonging to each class in the feature space. The distance between the query features and the class prototypes is calculated to determine the class probability for each query sample. The class probabilities are then obtained through the forward pass, followed by the backward pass for training. The model utilizes the pull and push mechanisms to enhance inter-class separability and intra-class compactness, respectively.

these similarities, the query examples are classified into their respective classes. During training, the network undergoes forward and backward passes, where the loss is computed based on the class probabilities and the ground truth labels. The loss is optimized through a combination of pull (attracting query features towards class prototypes of their respective classes) and push (encouraging separation between different class prototypes) operations. This approach allows the network to effectively generalize to unseen classes, even with limited labeled examples. Figure 2 illustrates the architecture of the proposed model.

By combining the strengths of classical training with DenseNet-121 and few-shot learning using the prototypical network, our proposed framework offers a robust and flexible solution for tackling few-shot learning challenges. It harnesses the discriminative power of DenseNet-121 for extracting informative features while leveraging the prototypical network to enable accurate classification with minimal labeled examples. This framework has the potential to benefit various applications in computer vision and pattern recognition domains where few-shot learning scenarios are encountered.

3.3   Experimental Setup

A series of experiments were carried out utilizing multiple shot and way combinations in order to assess the effectiveness of the few-shot learning model to SL recognition. Here, the number of training instances per class is represented by shot, whereas the number of classes in each training episode is represented by way. The studies evaluated our model's capacity to generalize from a single seen SL (BdSL) to identify unseen SLs (ASL, ArSL, BrSL, ISL, PSL, and InSL) with few samples.

The experiments were conducted using a high-performance GPU RTX 2080. The implementation utilized Python programming language and popular deep learning libraries, including PyTorch and Torchvision. A batch size of 512 was used, and Parallel data loading processes were employed to enhance efficiency. The model parameters were optimized using the Stochastic Gradient Descent (SGD) optimizer with a learning rate of 0.1, momentum of 0.9, and weight decay of 5×10^{-4}. The training process spanned 200 epochs. A scheduler was incorporated to adjust the learning rate at specific milestones (150 and 180 epochs) using a gamma value of 0.1.

The model was trained using several shots and ways configurations, such as 1, 3, 5, 10, 20, 30, and 50 shots, as well as 5-way, 10-way, and all-way combinations. Note that, for each training episode, the model was fed with randomly selected shots from the seen class dataset.

3.4   Evaluation Metric

The trained model's performance was evaluated using accuracy as the primary evaluation metric. Accuracy scores were calculated by comparing the model's predictions with the ground truth labels of the unseen class datasets and were recorded for each shot and way configuration, providing a comprehensive assessment of the model's recognition capabilities.

4   Results

The results of the few-shot learning experiments are summarized in the Table 2. The table presents the performance of different SLs (SL) in terms of accuracy for 1, 3, 5, 10, 20, 30, and 50 shots and 5-way, 10-way, and all-way combinations. The accuracy is normalized and reported on a range of 0 to 1, where 1 indicates 100% accuracy and 0 indicates 0% accuracy. Additionally, we plotted the results using line charts to provide a more intuitive representation of the model's performance in Fig. 3. Note that, PSL and InSL datasets did not have enough samples to experiment with 20, 30, and 50 shots.

From the experimental results, we observed that the model's performance improved as the number of shots increased, indicating that more training samples positively impacted its ability to generalize to unseen SLs. This trend was consistent across different numbers of ways (5, 10, and all) and for various SL

Table 2. Accuracy of the proposed model in different SL recognition (Measured on a Scale of 0 to 1.)

SL Name	Way	1-shot	3-shot	5-shot	10-shot	20-shot	30-shot	50-shot
ASL	5 way	0.529	0.661	0.709	0.746	0.768	0.775	0.779
	10 way	0.404	0.543	0.596	0.631	0.657	0.67	0.677
	All way	0.271	0.391	0.434	0.473	0.502	0.51	0.519
ArSL	5 way	0.44	0.54	0.588	0.637	0.673	0.689	0.703
	10 way	0.313	0.407	0.45	0.494	0.528	0.546	0.56
	All way	0.181	0.249	0.279	0.313	0.337	0.35	0.363
BrSL	5 way	0.741	0.861	0.884	0.902	0.917	0.916	0.923
	10 way	0.641	0.787	0.819	0.847	0.862	0.866	0.870
	All way	0.581	0.741	0.780	0.811	0.826	0.828	0.832
ISL	5 way	0.988	0.997	0.998	0.998	0.998	0.999	0.999
	10 way	0.977	0.993	0.996	0.997	0.997	0.997	0.998
	All way	0.943	0.982	0.988	0.992	0.993	0.994	0.994
PSL*	5 way	0.602	0.741	0.786	0.820	–	–	–
	10 way	0.490	0.649	0.684	0.7337	–	–	–
	All way	0.298	0.404	0.436	0.468	–	–	–
InSL*	5 way	0.914	0.959	0.964	0.970	–	–	–
	10 way	0.847	0.913	0.932	0.944	–	–	–
	All way	0.719	0.837	0.863	0.883	–	–	–

*PSL and InSL datasets did not have enough samples to experiment with 20, 30, and 50 shots.

datasets. Notably, the model achieved higher accuracy in the 5-way scenario compared to the 10-way and all-way scenarios, suggesting that distinguishing between fewer classes was relatively easier for the model.

The model performed the best in classifying ISL, with a 5-way, 10-shot accuracy of 0.998 and an all-way, 10-shot accuracy of 0.992. The second and third best performance was achieved in InSL and BrSL classification with 5-way, 10-shot accuracy of 0.97 and 0.902 respectively. In PSL classification, the model achieved an accuracy of 0.820 in the 5-way, 10-shot scenario. In the case of the ASL and ArSL datasets, the model achieved an accuracy of 0.746 and 0.637 respectively in the 5-way, 10-shot scenario. These results demonstrate the model's ability to recognize SLs even with limited training data, indicating the effectiveness of the few-shot learning approach.

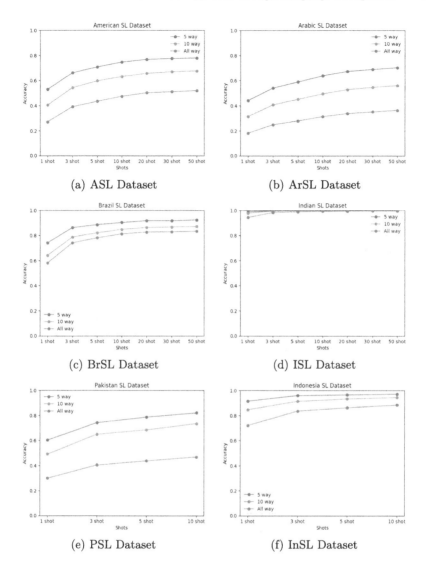

Fig. 3. Performance of the proposed model in different SL datasets

5 Discussion

In this work, we attempted to develop a machine learning model that utilizes few-shot learning in new SL classification from very few training data. From the performance of our proposed model, we have some observations reported as follows.

1. Variations in Datasets: Comparing the performance across different SLs, we observed variations in accuracy. For example, the ISL dataset exhibited consistently high accuracy across different shot and way scenarios, with an accuracy of 0.999 in the 5-way, 50-shot scenario. On the other hand, the ArSL dataset showed relatively lower performance, with a 5-way, 50-shot accuracy of 0.703. This could be attributed to the complexity or diversity of the signs within that particular language. To gain a better understanding of the differences between these two SLs, we performed t-distributed stochastic neighbor embedding (t-SNE) analysis. We plotted the t-SNE visualization of the features extracted from a class in both the ISL and ArSL datasets (Fig. 4). The t-SNE plot provides a visual representation of the similarity and proximity of the feature vectors.

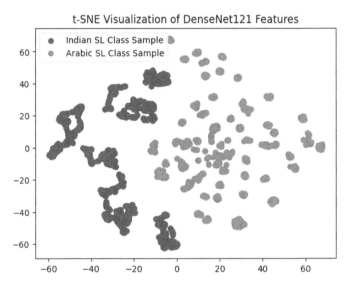

Fig. 4. t-SNE Visualization of Indian SL and Arabic SL features. ISL class features exhibit closer proximity and similarity to each other, indicating a higher degree of intra-class consistency. On the other hand, ArSL class features appear more diverse and spread out in the feature space, suggesting greater inter-class variation.

From the t-SNE plot, it is evident that the features of ISL class samples are more similar and closely clustered with each other, indicating a higher degree of consistency and similarity in the visual patterns of the signs. This cohesion in the feature space can contribute to the model's ability to better discriminate between different ISL signs. On the other hand, the t-SNE plot of the ArSL class features shows more diversity and dispersion among the samples. This suggests that the ArSL signs exhibit greater variability and visual dissimilarity, which can pose challenges for the model in accurately differentiating between them. The scattered nature of the ArSL features indicates the presence of distinct subgroups or variations within the ArSL dataset, making it more difficult for the model to generalize effectively.

2. Convergence Behavior: Another observation from our research is the convergence behavior of the model as we increase the number of shots. We noticed that as the number of shots increased, the model's performance tended to converge to a certain level of accuracy. This convergence behavior indicates that there is a threshold, beyond which providing additional training samples does not significantly improve the model's ability to generalize to unseen SLs.

For example, in the 5-way scenario, we observed that the accuracy of the model gradually improved as the number of shots increased from 1 to 20. However, beyond a certain point, such as 20 or 30 shots, the improvement in accuracy became marginal, and the model's performance stabilized. This suggests that once the model has sufficient exposure to a variety of samples for each class, further increasing the number of shots does not lead to substantial gains in accuracy.

3. Cross-Lingual Sign Language Recognition: The recognition of cross-lingual SLs is a difficult and crucial task in the field of computer vision and machine learning. Individuals with speech and hearing impairments stand to gain significantly from the ability to understand SLs in other languages, as well as communication and inclusivity on a global scale.

The outcomes of our research show how useful this method is for enabling cross-lingual SL recognition. We achieved promising accuracy across various shot and way scenarios by training the model on a single SL dataset and using the learned knowledge to recognize other SLs, even with limited data. However, further research and experimentation are necessary to explore additional techniques and architectures that can improve the accuracy and robustness of the model in diverse SL recognition scenarios.

4. Limitations: Video and action recognition methods must frequently be used for real-world SL recognition. Despite the fact that our study was primarily concerned with image-based recognition using still frames, moving the strategy to video-based recognition would be beneficial for capturing the temporal dynamics and movement patterns that are unique to SL.

The performance of our model heavily relies on the available SL datasets. We used a limited number of SL datasets for testing, which may not fully represent the vast diversity of SLs worldwide. Incorporating a wider range of SLs and dialects would enhance the generalizability and robustness of the model.

6   Conclusion

In this study, we proposed a few-shot learning approach for automatic sign language recognition to address the problem of data scarcity and limited resources. Our proposed approach combines DenseNet-121 architecture and prototypical network to leverage the information from small datasets in accurate recognition of different countries of the world. We trained our proposed model with a large seen dataset (BdSL) and evaluated the model with six different unseen datasets from six different countries. Our approach offers several strengths and contributions that hold significance for both the research community and practical applications. We have showcased the adaptability and versatility of few-shot learning by training on a single sign language dataset and effectively recognizing signs from various other languages. This not only addresses the data scarcity challenge but also paves the way for more inclusive communication for individuals with speech and hearing impairments. Through extensive experimentation, we have demonstrated the effectiveness of our model in recognizing sign languages with limited data availability. Our model achieved impressive performance across various shot and way scenarios, with accuracy ranging from 18.1% to 99.9% on different datasets. These results highlight the potential of our approach in overcoming the data scarcity problem and enabling accurate sign language recognition across multiple languages. Moreover, we observed a converging behavior of the model and noticed that the model performance converges around 20 shots. The findings of our research indicate the significance of this approach for achieving cross-lingual sign language recognition. However, it is important to note that there are still areas for improvement. The proposed system is only verified on alphabet-based static SLs where there are many dynamic word or sentence level SLs that still require being brought under investigation. Future research could focus on developing strategies to handle the nuances of complex signs and gestures, potentially through the integration of temporal information from video data. Additionally, the computational efficiency of our approach could be optimized to facilitate real-time applications, ensuring its practical usability in real-world scenarios. Exploring other advanced deep learning architectures and expanding the range of datasets may lead to better performance and generalization across diverse sign languages. Furthermore, collaborative efforts between experts in SL linguistics and machine learning could lead to the development of more refined and culturally sensitive models for diverse sign languages. We hope that this research will help other researchers learn more about sign language recognition, benefiting hearing and speech-disabled people from all over the world. Further development and exploration of our proposed few-shot learning approach hold promise for improving cross-lingual sign language recognition systems to contribute to a wider sign language community.

References

1. World Federation of the Deaf. https://wfdeaf.org/. Accessed 21 May 2023
2. Wang, Y., Yao, Q., Kwok, J.T., Ni, L.M.: Generalizing from a few examples: a survey on few-shot learning. ACM Comput. Surv. (csur) **53**(3), 1–34 (2020). https://doi.org/10.1145/3386252
3. Oyedotun, O.K., Khashman, A.: Deep learning in vision-based static hand gesture recognition. Neural Comput. Appl. **28**(12), 3941–3951 (2016). https://doi.org/10.1007/s00521-016-2294-8
4. Bantupalli, K., Xie, Y.: American sign language recognition using deep learning and computer vision. In: 2018 IEEE International Conference on Big Data (Big Data), pp. 4896–4899 (2018). https://doi.org/10.1109/BigData.2018.8622141

5. Nihal, R.A., Broti, N.M., Deowan, S.A., Rahman, S.: Design and development of a humanoid robot for sign language interpretation. SN Comput. Sci. **2**(3), 1–17 (2021). https://doi.org/10.1007/s42979-021-00627-3

6. Wang, F., et al.: Cornerstone network with feature extractor: a metric-based few-shot model for Chinese natural sign language. Appl. Intell. **51**(10), 7139–7150 (2021). https://doi.org/10.1007/s10489-020-02170-9

7. Bohacek, M., Hrúz, M.: Learning from what is already out there: few-shot sign language recognition with online dictionaries. In: 2023 IEEE 17th International Conference on Automatic Face and Gesture Recognition (FG), pp. 1–6. IEEE (2023). https://doi.org/10.1109/FG57933.2023.10042544

8. Shovkoplias, G.F., et al.: Improving sign language processing via few-shot machine learning. Sci. Tech. J. Inf. Technol. Mech. Opt. **22**(3), 559–566 (2022)

9. Ferreira, S., Costa, E., Dahia, M., Rocha, J.: A transformer-based contrastive learning approach for few-shot sign language recognition. arXiv preprint arXiv:2204.02803 (2022)

10. Hosseini, S. R., Taheri, A., Alemi, M., Meghdari, A.: One-shot learning from demonstration approach toward a reciprocal sign language-based HRI. Int. J. Social Rob. 1–13 (2021). https://doi.org/10.1007/s12369-021-00818-1

11. Nihal, R. A., Broti, N. M.: BdSL-MNIST, Mendeley Data, V. 1 (2023). https://doi.org/10.17632/6f2wm5p3vf.1

12. Sign Language MNIST. https://www.kaggle.com/datasets/datamunge/sign-language-mnist. Accessed 25 June 2023

13. Arabic Sign Language ArSL dataset. https://www.kaggle.com/datasets/sabribelmadoui/arabic-sign-language-unaugmented-dataset. Accessed 25 June 2023

14. Passos, B.T., Fernandes, A.M.R., Comunello, E.: Brazilian Sign Language Alphabet, Mendeley Data, V. 5 (2020). https://doi.org/10.17632/k4gs3bmx5k.5

15. Indian Sign Language Dataset. https://www.kaggle.com/datasets/vaishnaviasonawane/indian-sign-language-dataset. Accessed 25 June 2023

16. Pakistan Sign Language. https://www.kaggle.com/datasets/hasaniqbal777/pakistan-sign-language. Accessed 25 June 2023

17. Mursita, R.A.: Respon tunarungu terhadap penggunaan sistem bahasa isyarat indonesa (sibi) dan bahasa isyarat indonesia (bisindo) dalam komunikasi. Inklusi **2**(2), 221–232 (2015). https://doi.org/10.14421/ijds.2202

18. Huang, G., Liu, Z., Van Der Maaten, L., Weinberger, K.Q.: Densely connected convolutional networks. In: Proceedings of the IEEE Conference on Computer Vision and Pattern Recognition, pp. 4700–4708 (2017)

19. Nihal, R.A., Rahman, S., Broti, N.M., Deowan, S.A.: Bangla sign alphabet recognition with zero-shot and transfer learning. Pattern Recogn. Lett. **150**, 84–93 (2021). https://doi.org/10.1016/j.patrec.2021.06.020

20. Snell, J., Swersky, K., Zemel, R.: Prototypical networks for few-shot learning. Adv. Neural. Inf. Process. Syst. **30**, 1–11 (2017)

CILF: Causality Inspired Learning Framework for Out-of-Distribution Vehicle Trajectory Prediction

Shengyi Li, Qifan Xue, Yezhuo Zhang, and Xuanpeng Li[✉]

School of Instrument Science and Engineering, Southeast University, Nanjing 211189, China
{li_shengyi,xue_qifan,zhang_yezhuo,li_xuanpeng}@seu.edu.cn

Abstract. Trajectory prediction is critical for autonomous driving vehicles. Most existing methods tend to model the correlation between history trajectory (input) and future trajectory (output). Since correlation is just a superficial description of reality, these methods rely heavily on the i.i.d. assumption and evince a heightened susceptibility to out-of-distribution data. To address this problem, we propose an **Out-of-D**istribution **C**ausal **G**raph (OOD-CG), which explicitly defines the underlying causal structure of the data with three entangled latent features: 1) domain-invariant causal feature (IC), 2) domain-variant causal feature (VC), and 3) domain-variant non-causal feature (VN). While these features are confounded by confounder (C) and domain selector (D). To leverage causal features for prediction, we propose a **C**ausal **I**nspired **L**earning **F**ramework (CILF), which includes three steps: 1) extracting domain-invariant causal feature by means of an invariance loss, 2) extracting domain variant feature by domain contrastive learning, and 3) separating domain-variant causal and non-causal feature by encouraging causal sufficiency. We evaluate the performance of CILF in different vehicle trajectory prediction models on the mainstream datasets NGSIM and INTERACTION. Experiments show promising improvements in CILF on domain generalization.

Keywords: Causal Representation Learning · Out-of-Distribution · Domain Generalization · Vehicle trajectory Prediction

1 Introduction

Trajectory prediction is essential for both the perception and planning modules of autonomous vehicles [12,19] in order to reduce the risk of collisions [13]. Recent trajectory prediction methods are primarily built with deep neural networks, which are trained to model the correlation between history trajectory and future trajectory. The robustness of such correlation is guaranteed by the independent and identically distributed (i.i.d.) assumption. As a result, the model trained on i.i.d. samples often fails to be generalized to out-of-distribution (OOD) samples.

Recently, there has been a growing interest in utilizing causal representation learning [25] to tackle the challenge of out-of-domain generalization [32]. Causal representation learning is based on the Structure Causal Model (SCM) [7,20], a mathematical tool for modeling human metaphysical concepts about causation. Causal representation learning enables the model to discern the underlying causal structure of data by incorporating causal-related prior knowledge into the model.

This paper proposes an Out-of-Distribution Causal Graph (OOD-CG) based on SCM, as shown in Fig. 1. OOD-DG divides the latent features into three categories: 1) Domain-invariant Causal Feature (IC) such as physical laws, driving habits, etc. 2) Domain-variant Causal Feature (VC) such as road traffic flow, traffic scenes, etc. 3) Domain-variant Non-causal Feature (VN) like sensor noise, etc. These features are entangled due to the confounding effects of backdoor confounder (C) and domain selector (D).

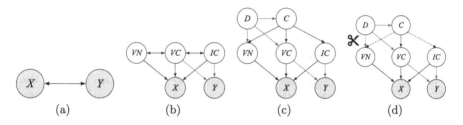

Fig. 1. The step-by-step introduction of OOD-CG. White nodes represent latent features; gray nodes represent observable variables; bidirectional arrows represent correlations; unidirectional arrows represent causal mechanisms; red arrows represent causal mechanisms critical to prediction; and green arrows represent domain effects. (Color figure online)

To leverage causal features for trajectory prediction, we introduce a Causal-Inspired Learning Framework (CILF) based on causal representation learning. CILF includes three parts to block the backdoor paths associated with IC, VC, and VN. First, to block the backdoor path between IC and domain-variant feature V, CILF utilizes invariant risk minimization (IRM) [2] to extract IC and domain contrastive learning [10] to extract V. Then, to block the backdoor path between VC and VN, CILF introduces domain adversarial learning [9] to separate VC and VN.

Our contributions can be summarized as follows:

(1) We propose a theoretical model named OOD-CG, which explicitly elucidates the causal mechanisms and causal structure of the out-of-distribution generalization problem.

(2) Based on causal representation learning, we propose a learning framework called CILF for out-of-distribution vehicle trajectory prediction. CILF contains three steps to block the backdoor connection associated with *IC*, *VC*, and *VN*, allowing the model to employ causal features for prediction.

2   Related Work

Vehicle Trajectory Prediction. Recent works widely employ the sequence-to-sequence (Seq2seq) framework [26] to predict a vehicle's future trajectory based on its history trajectory [1,5,11,27]. Alahi et al. introduce S-LSTM [1], which incorporates a social pooling mechanism to aggregate and encode the social behaviors of surrounding vehicles. Deo et al. propose CS-LSTM [5], which utilizes convolutional operations to enhance the model's performance. Lee et al. introduce a trajectory prediction model called DESIRE [11], which combines conditional variational auto-encoder (CVAE) and GRU to generate multimodal predictions of future trajectories. Tang et al. incorporate an attention mechanism into the Seq2seq framework named MFP [27], a model that can effectively learn motion representations of multiple vehicles across multiple time steps. However, current vehicle trajectory prediction approaches still face the challenge of OOD generalization, posing a serious threat to the safety of autonomous vehicles.

Out-of-Distribution Generalization. Previous methods handle OOD generalization in two paradigms: domain adaptation (DA) and domain generalization (DG) [32]. DA allows the model to access a small portion of unlabeled target domain data during training, thereby reducing the difficulty of the OOD problem to some extent. DA aims to learn an embedding space where source domain samples and target domain samples follow similar distributions via minimizing divergence [8,15], domain adversarial learning [6,28], etc. DG prohibits models from accessing any form of target domain data during training. DG aims to learn knowledge that can be directly transferred to unknown target domains. Relevant literature has proposed a range of solutions, including contrastive learning [17,29], domain adversarial learning [28,31], etc. As for vehicle trajectory prediction, it is difficult to acquire even unlabeled target domain samples. As a result, we follow the paradigm of domain generalization.

Causality Inspired Approaches for Domain Generalization. There has been a growing trend toward utilizing causality inspired methods to address the OOD problem. Some of them suggest using mathematical formulas from causal inference [20], e.g.,front-door adjustment [18] and back-door adjustment [3] formulas, to directly derive the loss function. However, these methods often make strong assumptions (e.g.,restricting the model to be a variational auto-encoder [3]), which decrease the diversity of the model's hypothesis space and limit the applicability of the model. Some approaches instead only make assumptions about the general causal structure of the OOD problem in order to guide the design of network structures [14,16]. We follow this approach in order to enhance the versatility of the proposed model.

3 Theoretical Analysis

3.1 Problem Formulation

We formulated vehicle trajectory prediction as estimating future trajectories $Y_i = \{(x_{i,t}, y_{i,t}) \in \mathbb{R}^2 | t = t_{obs} + 1, ..., t_{pred}\}$ based on the observed history trajectories $X_i = \{(x_{i,t}, y_{i,t}) \in \mathbb{R}^2 | t = 1, 2, ..., t_{obs}\}$ of N visible vehicles in the current scene. In the context of domain generalization, the training dataset is collected from K source domains, denoted as $S \in \{S_1, S_2, ..., S_K\}$, while the test dataset is collected from M target domains, denoted as $T \in \{T_1, T_2, ..., T_M\}$.

3.2 OOD-CG

Figure 1(a). Traditional deep learning is designed to capture statistical correlations between inputs X and outputs Y. Correlations are obviously inadequate to solve the OOD problem. Fortunately, Reichenbach provides us with a strong tool called the common causal principle [23] to decompose these correlations into a set of backdoor features.

Theorem 1. *Common causal principle: if two random variables X and Y are correlated, there must exist another random variable S that has causal relationships with both X and Y. Furthermore, S can completely substitute for the correlations between X and Y, i.e., $X \perp\!\!\!\perp Y | S$.*

Figure 1(b). We divide these backdoor features into three classes: (1) Domain-Invariant Causal Feature (*IC*): Driving habits, physical laws, etc. (2) Domain-Variant Causal Feature (*VC*): Traffic density, traffic scenario, etc. (3) Domain-Variant Non-causal Feature (*VN*): Sensor measurement noise, etc. Bidirectional arrows are used in this step to represent the entanglement between these backdoor features. Previous studies often ignore domain-variant causal feature *VC*, and focus solely on utilizing domain-invariant causal feature *IC* for prediction [3,4,18]. These approaches utilize insufficient causal information for prediction and thus fail to simultaneously improve prediction accuracy in both the source and target domains.

Figure 1(c). According to Theorem 1, we introduce a Confounder (*C*) to summarize all the correlations among *IC*, *VC*, and *VN*. We also introduce a Domain Selector (*D*) to represent domain effects. Since domain label is unavailable during testing, we treat D as an unobservable latent variable consistent with [3,16]. Now we can concretize distribution shifts as differences in feature prior distributions $P(C), P(VC), P(VN)$ and causal mechanism conditional distributions $P(VC|C), P(VN|C)$ between source and target domains.

Figure 1(d). In order to extract domain-invariant causal mechanisms $P(Y|VC)$, $P(Y|IC)$ for prediction, it is necessary to block the backdoor paths connecting these entangled features. To do so, we only need to block the backdoor paths of *IC* and *VN*, which are represented by dashed lines in the figure. Once done, *VC* actually serves as a mediator [7,20] in causal effects from D and C to Y, which can be completely substituted by *VC*. In the next chapter, we introduce a causal-inspired learning framework (CILF) for OOD vehicle trajectory prediction, encouraging models to block the backdoor paths of IC and VN.

4   CILF

Compared to traditional machine learning, deep learning requires searching within an extremely complex hypothesis space. As a result, researchers often introduce inductive bias into deep learning models to reduce search difficulty, allowing models to find some relatively acceptable local optimums within limited training iterations. OOD-CG is proposed to impose such inductive bias theoretically. Guided by OOD-CG, we propose CILF (see Fig. 2) to extract causal features for prediction. First, to block the backdoor connection between IC and V, CILF introduces two kinds of losses: IRM loss to encourage domain-invariant causal feature IC; Domain contrastive loss to encourage domain-variant feature V. Then, to block the backdoor path between VC and VN, CILF introduces domain adversarial learning to train a mask generator able to detect the causal dimensions VC and non-causal dimensions VN of domain-variant feature V.

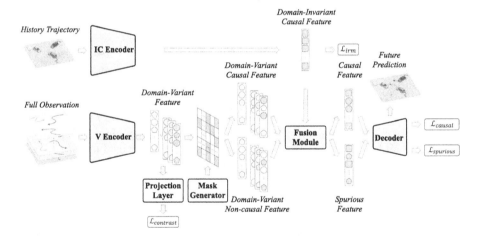

Fig. 2. CILF consists of three parts: (i)IC encoder $\Phi_{ic}(.)$ takes history trajectories of the current vehicle as input. The IRM loss $\mathcal{L}_{irm}$ is utilized to encourage the extracted feature to exhibit domain invariance; (ii)Domain-variant feature encoder $\Phi_v(.)$ takes full observations from each source domain as input, such as history trajectories of neighboring vehicles, map information, etc. The domain contrastive learning loss $\mathcal{L}_{contrast}$ is utilized to encourage the extracted feature to exhibit domain variance; (iii)Mask generator $M(.)$ generates a causally sufficient mask to select the causal dimensions VC and non-causal dimensions VN from V.

4.1   Extract Domain-Invariant Causal Feature

Domain-invariant features are the intersection of feature sets from different domains. The non-causal information within these features exhibits a significant reduction after taking the intersection. As a result, extracting IC can be approximated as extracting the domain-invariant feature. The definition of a domain-invariant encoder is given as follows [2]:

Definition 1. *Domain-invariant feature encoder: An encoder $\Phi(.) : \mathcal{X} \to \mathcal{H}$ is said to be a domain-invariant encoder across all domains $s \in S$ if and only if there exists a decoder $\Theta(.) : \mathcal{H} \to \mathcal{Y}$ that achieves optimum across all domains. This condition can be further formulated as a conditional optimization problem:*

$$\min_{\Phi,\Theta} \Sigma_{s \in S} \mathcal{L}_s(\Theta \circ \Phi),$$

$$\text{subject to } \Theta \in \operatorname*{argmin}_{\bar{\Theta}} \mathcal{L}_s(\bar{\Theta} \circ \Phi), \text{for all } s \in S. \tag{1}$$

However, this is a bi-level optimization problem, which is computationally difficult to solve. In current research, the problem is often relaxed to a gradient regularization penalty based on empirical risk minimization [2]:

$$\min_{\Phi_{IC},\Theta} \frac{1}{|S|} \Sigma_{s \in S} [\mathcal{L}_s(\Theta \circ \Phi_{IC}) + \lambda \|\nabla_\Theta \mathcal{L}_s(\Theta \circ \Phi_{IC})\|^2], \tag{2}$$

$$\mathcal{L}_{irm} = \frac{1}{|S|} \|\nabla_\Theta \mathcal{L}_s(\Theta \circ \Phi_{IC})\|^2, \tag{3}$$

where $\mathcal{L}_{irm}$ denotes the IRM loss, λ denotes the balance parameter.

We separate Φ_{IC} from the backbone to further block the backdoor path of IC, as shown in Fig. 2. Φ_{IC} only accepts the history trajectories of the current vehicle as input, which contains relatively limited domain knowledge.

4.2   Extract Domain-Variant Feature

To extract domain-variant feature, we design $\Phi_v(.)$, which takes full observations from different domains (distinguished by the colors in Fig. 2) as input. Full observations include all the information that an autonomous driving vehicle can observe in a traffic scene (e.g., history trajectories of neighboring vehicles, map information, etc.), which are highly domain-related. $\Phi_v(.)$ is trained using domain contrastive loss [10,14]. In order to calculate this loss, CILF employs dimensional reduction to V through a projection layer $p_i = \beta(V_i)$, where i denotes the domain label. The contrastive loss between a pair of samples p_i and p_j is defined as follows:

$$\mathcal{L}_{contrast} = -\log \frac{\exp(p_i, p_j)/\tau}{\Sigma_k \mathbb{I}_{[k=j \vee S_k \neq S_i]} \exp(\operatorname{sim}(p_i, p_k)/\tau)} \tag{4}$$

where $\mathbb{I}_{[k=j \vee S_k \neq S_i]}$ denotes the indicator function. When sample p_i and p_k are from the same domain, this function equals to 1. τ is the temperature parameter of contrastive learning, $\operatorname{sim}(a,b) = \frac{a^\top b}{\|a\|\|b\|}$ is the cosine similarity.

4.3   Separate Domain-Variant Causal and Non-causal Feature

In Sect. 4.1, we argue that domain-invariant features naturally possess causality as they are the intersection of feature sets from different domains. However, domain-variant features do not naturally carry this causal property. It is necessary to filter out the non-causal dimensions within these features according to causal sufficiency [21,23,24]:

Definition 2. *Causally sufficient feature set: for the prediction task from X to Y, a feature set is considered causally sufficient if and only if it captures all causal effects from X to Y.*

Supervised learning can't guarantee the learned features to be causally sufficient according to Definition 2. Some dimensions may contain more causal information and have a decisive impact on prediction, while other dimensions may have little influence on prediction. CILF introduces a neural network based mask generator $M(.)$ that produces a causally sufficient mask [16] using the Gumbel-SoftMax technique [9]:

$$m = \text{Gumbel} - \text{SoftMax}(M(V), kN), \tag{5}$$

The causally sufficient mask can identify the contribution $k \in (0,1)$ of each dimension in V to prediction. The top kN dimensions with the highest contributions are regarded as domain-variant causal features VC, while the remaining dimensions are considered domain-variant non-causal features VN:

$$VC = V \cdot m, \ VN = V \cdot (1 - m). \tag{6}$$

VC and VN are fused with IC by the fusion module $F(.)$ to form causal features CF and spurious features SF, which are then decoded separately by $\Theta(.)$ to generate future predictions. Prediction losses $\mathcal{L}_{causal}$ and $\mathcal{L}_{spurious}$ can be calculated by RMSE:

$$CF = F(VC, IC) = f_2(f_1(VC, IC) + IC),$$
$$SF = F(VN, IC) = f_2(f_1(VN, IC) + IC), \tag{7}$$

$$\mathcal{L}_{causal} = \text{RMSE}(\Theta(VC), Y),$$
$$\mathcal{L}_{spurious} = \text{RMSE}(\Theta(VN), Y), \tag{8}$$

where f_1 and f_2 are FC layers in fusion module.

Decoder Θ can be trained by minimizing $\mathcal{L}_{causal}$ and $\mathcal{L}_{spurious}$. Mask generator M can be trained by minimizing $\mathcal{L}_{causal}$ while adversarially maximizing $\mathcal{L}_{spurious}$. Overall, the optimization objective can be formulated as follows:

$$\min_{\Phi_{IC}, F, \Theta} \mathcal{L}_{causal} + \mathcal{L}_{spurious} + \lambda \mathcal{L}_{irm} \tag{9}$$

$$\min_{\Phi_v, F, \Theta} \mathcal{L}_{causal} + \mathcal{L}_{spurious} + \alpha \mathcal{L}_{irm} \tag{10}$$

$$\min_{M} \mathcal{L}_{causal} - \mathcal{L}_{spurious} \tag{11}$$

where λ and α are balance parameters.

5   Experiments

This chapter presents quantitative and qualitative domain generalization experiments of the proposed CILF framework on the public vehicle trajectory prediction datasets NGSIM [22] and INTERACTION [30].

5.1   Experiment Design

INTERACTION is a large-scale real-world dataset that includes top-down vehicle trajectory data in three scenarios: intersections, highway ramps (referred to as merging), and roundabouts, collected from multiple locations in America, Asia, and Europe. INTERACTION consists of 11 subsets, categorized into three types of scenarios: roundabouts, highway ramps, and intersections (see Table 1). NGSIM is a collection of vehicle trajectory data derived from video recordings. It includes vehicle trajectory data from three different locations: the US-101 highway, Lankershim Blvd. in Los Angeles, and the I-80 highway in Emeryville. The sampling rate of both datasets is 10 Hz. For each trajectory that lasts 8 s, the model takes the first 3 s as input and predicts the trajectory for the next 5 s.

As shown in Table 1, data volume among different subsets of INTERACTION varies significantly. Subsets 0, 1, and 7 have notably higher data volumes compared to other subsets. To mitigate the potential influence of data volume disparities, we design three contrastive experiments to demonstrate the effectiveness of CILF in addressing the DG problem:

Table 1. INTERACTION Dataset. Data Ratio represents the proportion of data volume in each subset relative to the total data volume.

Subset ID	Sample Location	Scenario	Data Ratio
0	USA	Roundabout	17.9%
1	CHN	Merging	35.2%
2	USA	Intersection	7.9%
3	USA	Intersection	2.6%
4	GER	Roundabout	1.8%
5	USA	Roundabout	5.3%
6	GER	Merging	1.2%
7	USA	Intersection	21.6%
8	USA	Roundabout	3.2%
9	USA	Intersection	2.6%
10	CHN	Roundabout	0.6%

(1) Single-scenario domain generalization: Both training and test datasets come from the same scenario within the INTERACTION. Specifically, the subset with the largest data volume in each scenario is designated as the test set, while the remaining subsets serve as the training set.

(2) Cross-scenario domain generalization: The training and test datasets come from different scenarios within the INTERACTION. Specifically, the three subsets with the largest data volumes (roundabout-0, merging-1, and intersection-7) are selected as training sets, while the remaining subsets are chosen as test sets.

(3) Cross-dataset domain generalization: The INTERACTION is selected as the training set, while the NGSIM is selected as the test set.

We choose three classic vehicle trajectory prediction models as baselines:

S-LSTM [1]: An influential method based on a social pooling model;

CS-LSTM [5]: A model using a convolutional social pooling structure to learn vehicle interactions;

MFP [27]: An advanced model that learns semantic latent variables for trajectory prediction. These baselines are trained under CILF to compare their domain generalization performance.

We employ two commonly used metrics in vehicle trajectory prediction to measure the model's domain generalization performance:

Average Displacement Error (ADE): Average L2 distance between predicted points and groundtruth points across all timesteps.

$$\text{ADE} = \frac{\Sigma_{i=1}^{N} \Sigma_{t=t_{obs}+1}^{t_{pred}} \|\hat{Y}_{i,t} - Y_{i,t}\|}{N},$$ (12)

Final Displacement Error (FDE): L2 distance between predicted points and ground truth points at the final timestep.

$$\text{FDE} = \frac{\Sigma_{i=1}^{N} \|\hat{Y}_{i,t} - Y_{i,t}\|}{N}, t = t_{obs} + 1, ..., t_{pred}.$$ (13)

5.2 Quantitative Experiment and Analysis

Single-Scenario Domain Generalization. Table 2 and Table 3 present the comparison between different models trained under CILF and vanilla conditions in terms of single-scenario domain generalization on the INTERACTION.

CILF achieves both ADE and FDE improvements for all models in both the source and target domains.

In the intersection scenario, as shown in Table 2, for the source domains, CS-LSTM achieves the largest improvement under CILF, with average increments of 7.40% and 5.00% (ADE and FDE). Conversely, S-LSTM shows the lowest improvement, with average increments of 5.86% and 4.00%. As for the target domain, S-LSTM and MFP demonstrate similar improvements, with increments of 1.33%, 1.90% for S-LSTM and 1.40%, 1.33% for MFP.

In the roundabout scenario, as shown in Table 3, for the source domains, MFP achieves the largest improvement under CILF, with average increments

Table 2. ADE and FDE (in meters) results of domain generalization experiment in the intersection scenario. Subset 7 is left for testing, while other subsets of the intersection scenario are used for training.

	S-LSTM		CS-LSTM		MFP	
	ADE	FDE	ADE	FDE	ADE	FDE
Intersection-2	**1.52**/1.59	**4.65**/4.85	**1.53**/1.64	**4.62**/4.86	**1.62**/1.72	**5.05**/5.29
Intersection-3	**1.21**/1.29	**3.48**/3.60	**1.18**/1.28	**3.43**/3.59	**1.25**/1.32	**3.67**/3.83
Intersection-9	**1.20**/1.29	**3.37**/3.53	**1.20**/1.30	**3.36**/3.56	**1.25**/1.34	**3.57**/3.79
Intersection-7	**2.22**/2.25	**6.20**/6.32	**2.34**/2.37	**6.30**/6.47	**2.12**/2.21	**6.02**/6.04

Table 3. ADE and FDE (in meters) results of domain generalization experiment in the roundabout scenario. Subset 0 is left for testing, while other subsets of the roundabout scenario are used for training.

	S-LSTM		CS-LSTM		MFP	
	ADE	FDE	ADE	FDE	ADE	FDE
Roundabout-4	**1.68**/1.75	**4.41**/4.64	**1.62**/1.83	**4.41**/4.81	**1.59**/1.73	**2.86**/3.14
Roundabout-6	**1.03**/1.12	**2.97**/3.09	**1.01**/1.10	**2.86**/3.02	**1.01**/1.14	**2.86**/3.14
Roundabout-10	**1.42**/1.57	**3.60**/3.94	**1.38**/1.51	**3.50**/3.94	**1.30**/1.60	**3.42**/4.05
Roundabout-0	**3.31**/3.34	**9.04**/9.38	**3.24**/3.35	**9.01**/9.09	**3.15**/3.25	**8.80**/8.83

of 12.75% and 9.31% (ADE and FDE). Conversely, S-LSTM shows the lowest improvement, with average increments of 7.20% and 5.82%. As for the target domain, S-LSTM demonstrates the largest improvements, with increments of 3.90% and 3.62%. MFP achieves the lowest improvement, with increments of 3.08% and 2.34%. Obviously, in the roundabout scenario, CILF exhibits larger improvements in both the source and target domains compared to intersection.

Cross-Scenario Domain Generalization. Table 4 presents the comparison between different models trained under CILF and vanilla conditions in terms of cross-scenario domain generalization on the INTERACTION. CILF achieves both ADE and FDE improvements for all models in both the source and target domains. For the source domains, CS-LSTM achieves the largest improvement under CILF, with average increments of 7.54% and 5.95% (ADE and FDE). Conversely, MFP shows the lowest improvement, with average increments of 3.58% and 2.95%. As for the target domain, both three models achieve similar improvements, with increments of 4.73%, 3.53% for S-LSTM; 5.47%, 3.17% for CS-LSTM; and 3.65%, 2.53% for MFP.

Cross-Dataset Domain Generalization. Table 5 presents the comparison between different models trained under CILF and vanilla conditions in terms of cross-dataset domain generalization. CILF achieves both ADE and FDE

166   S. Li et al.

Table 4. ADE and FDE (in meters) results of cross-scenario domain generalization experiment. Subset 0, 1, and 7 are left for training, while other subsets of INTERAC-TION are used for testing.

	S-LSTM		CS-LSTM		MFP	
	ADE	FDE	ADE	FDE	ADE	FDE
Roundabout-0	**1.40**/1.51	**4.33**/4.58	1.36/1.46	4.24/4.46	1.45/1.50	4.47/4.56
Merging-1	**0.83**/0.85	**2.28**/2.33	0.80/0.86	2.24/2.36	0.86/0.89	2.48/2.55
Intersection-7	**1.18**/1.26	**3.60**/3.78	1.14/1.25	3.53/3.83	1.19/1.24	3.70/3.86
Intersection-2	**2.42**/2.52	**7.59**/7.82	2.45/2.55	7.72/7.90	2.42/2.48	7.60/7.72
Intersection-3	**1.63**/1.73	**4.92**/5.23	1.68/1.77	5.13/5.42	1.66/1.71	5.02/5.18
Roundabout-4	**3.32**/3.67	**10.13**11.01	3.42/3.65	10.60/10.76	3.59/3.78	10.71/11.26
Roundabout-5	**1.75**/1.83	**5.16**/5.38	1.72/1.84	5.20/5.36	1.71/1.82	4.97/5.25
Merging-6	**1.19**/1.21	**3.59**/3.63	1.15/1.24	3.54/3.69	1.07/1.14	3.34/3.43
Roundabout-8	**2.07**/2.14	**6.21**/6.34	2.07/2.22	6.21/6.48	2.08/2.13	6.17/6.28
Intersection-9	**1.65**/1.70	**4.90**/5.04	1.66/1,75	4.99/5.19	1.62/1.64	4.86/4.86
Roundabout-10	**2.80**/2.99	**8.64**/8.76	2.84/2.92	8.85/8.75	2.86/2.95	8.50/8.59

improvements for all models in both the source and target domains. For the source domains, CS-LSTM achieves the largest improvement under CILF, with average increments of 7.54% and 5.95% (ADE and FDE). Conversely, MFP shows the lowest improvement, with average increments of 3.58% and 2.95%. For the target domains, S-LSTM achieves the largest improvement under CILF, with average increments of 4.39% and 3.53%. Conversely, MFP shows the lowest improvement, with average increments of 1.12% and 0.64%.

Table 5. ADE and FDE (in meters) results of cross-dataset domain generalization experiment. Subset 0, 1, and 7 of the INTERACTION are left for training, while the NGSIM is used for testing.

	S-LSTM		CS-LSTM		MFP	
	ADE	FDE	ADE	FDE	ADE	FDE
Roundabout-0	**1.40**/1.51	**4.33**/4.58	1.36/1.46	4.24/4.46	1.45/1.50	4.47/4.56
Merging-1	**0.83**/0.85	**2.28**/2.33	0.80/0.86	2.24/2.36	0.86/0.89	2.48/2.55
Intersection-7	**1.18**/1.26	**3.60**/3.78	1.14/1.25	3.53/3.83	1.19/1.24	3.70/3.86
NGSIM	**3.27**/3.42	**8.47**/8.78	3.50/3.60	9.17/9.47	3.54/3.58	9.28/9.38

5.3 Qualitative Experiment and Analysis

This section presents the comparison of predicted trajectories generated by CILF-MFP and Vanilla-MFP in the cross-scenario domain generalization experiment.

Figure 3 illustrates the comparison of predicted trajectories between CILF-MFP and MFP in target domain subset-3 (intersection) and subset-4 (roundabout). The black bold solid lines represent the curb, and the white and gray bold solid lines represent guide lines. The red square denotes the current vehicle, and the blue square represents neighboring vehicles perceived by the current vehicle. The yellow dots represent history trajectories of the current vehicle, while the blue dots represent future trajectories. The red dots represent the predicted future trajectory. The green dots represent the historical and future trajectories of neighboring vehicles.

In both scenarios, CILF-MFP demonstrates remarkable improvement in prediction quality compared to MFP, particularly at the end of the predicted trajectories.

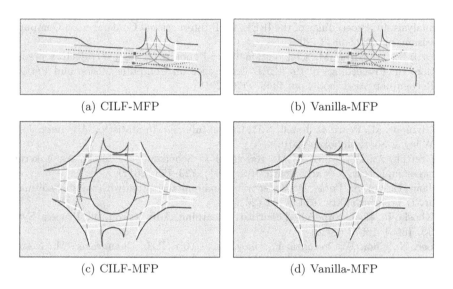

(a) CILF-MFP   (b) Vanilla-MFP

(c) CILF-MFP   (d) Vanilla-MFP

Fig. 3. Contrastive experiments between CILF-MFP and Vanilla-MFP on two target domains. (a) and (b) demonstrate the contrastive experiment on subset-3 (intersection) of INTERACTION, (c) and (d) demonstrate the contrastive experiment on subset-4 (roundabout) of INTERACTION.

6   Conclusion

To improve the generalization ability of vehicle trajectory prediction models, we first analyze the causal structure of OOD generalization and propose OOD-CG, which highlights the limitations of conventional correlation-based learning framework. Then we propose CILF to employ only causal features for prediction by three steps: (a) extracting IC by invariant risk minimization, (b) extracting V by domain contrastive learning, and (c) separating VC and VN by domain adversarial learning. Quantitative and qualitative experiments on several mainstream datasets prove the effectiveness of our model.

References

1. Alahi, A., Goel, K., Ramanathan, V., Robicquet, A., Fei-Fei, L., Savarese, S.: Social lstm: human trajectory prediction in crowded spaces. In: Proceedings of the IEEE Conference on Computer Vision and Pattern Recognition, pp. 961–971 (2016)
2. Arjovsky, M., Bottou, L., Gulrajani, I., Lopez-Paz, D.: Invariant risk minimization. arXiv preprint arXiv:1907.02893 (2019)
3. Bagi, S.S.G., Gharaee, Z., Schulte, O., Crowley, M.: Generative causal representation learning for out-of-distribution motion forecasting. arXiv preprint arXiv:2302.08635 (2023)
4. Chen, G., Li, J., Lu, J., Zhou, J.: Human trajectory prediction via counterfactual analysis. In: Proceedings of the IEEE/CVF International Conference on Computer Vision, pp. 9824–9833 (2021)
5. Deo, N., Trivedi, M.M.: Convolutional social pooling for vehicle trajectory prediction. In: Proceedings of the IEEE Conference on Computer Vision and Pattern Recognition Workshops, pp. 1468–1476 (2018)
6. Ganin, Y., et al.: Domain-adversarial training of neural networks. J. Mach. Learn. Res. **17**(1), 2096–2030 (2016)
7. Glymour, M., Pearl, J., Jewell, N.P.: Causal Inference in Statistics: A Primer. John Wiley & Sons, Hoboken (2016)
8. Gretton, A., Borgwardt, K.M., Rasch, M.J., Schölkopf, B., Smola, A.: A kernel two-sample test. J. Mach. Learn. Res. **13**(1), 723–773 (2012)
9. Jang, E., Gu, S., Poole, B.: Categorical reparameterization with gumbel-softmax. arXiv preprint arXiv:1611.01144 (2016)
10. Khosla, P., et al.: Supervised contrastive learning. Adv. Neural. Inf. Process. Syst. **33**, 18661–18673 (2020)
11. Lee, N., Choi, W., Vernaza, P., Choy, C.B., Torr, P.H., Chandraker, M.: Desire: distant future prediction in dynamic scenes with interacting agents. In: Proceedings of the IEEE Conference on Computer Vision and Pattern Recognition, pp. 336–345 (2017)
12. Lefèvre, S., Vasquez, D., Laugier, C.: A survey on motion prediction and risk assessment for intelligent vehicles. ROBOMECH J. **1**(1), 1–14 (2014). https://doi.org/10.1186/s40648-014-0001-z
13. Li, S., Xue, Q., Shi, D., Li, X., Zhang, W.: Recursive least squares based refinement network for vehicle trajectory prediction. Electronics **11**(12), 1859 (2022)
14. Liu, Y., Cadei, R., Schweizer, J., Bahmani, S., Alahi, A.: Towards robust and adaptive motion forecasting: a causal representation perspective. In: Proceedings of the IEEE/CVF Conference on Computer Vision and Pattern Recognition, pp. 17081–17092 (2022)
15. Long, M., Zhu, H., Wang, J., Jordan, M.I.: Deep transfer learning with joint adaptation networks. In: International Conference on Machine Learning, pp. 2208–2217. PMLR (2017)
16. Lv, F., et al.: Causality inspired representation learning for domain generalization. In: Proceedings of the IEEE/CVF Conference on Computer Vision and Pattern Recognition, pp. 8046–8056 (2022)

17. Motiian, S., Piccirilli, M., Adjeroh, D.A., Doretto, G.: Unified deep supervised domain adaptation and generalization. In: Proceedings of the IEEE International Conference on Computer Vision, pp. 5715–5725 (2017)
18. Nguyen, T., Do, K., Nguyen, D.T., Duong, B., Nguyen, T.: Front-door adjustment via style transfer for out-of-distribution generalisation. arXiv preprint arXiv:2212.03063 (2022)
19. Paden, B., Čáp, M., Yong, S.Z., Yershov, D., Frazzoli, E.: A survey of motion planning and control techniques for self-driving urban vehicles. IEEE Trans. Intell. Veh. 1(1), 33–55 (2016)
20. Pearl, J.: Causality. Cambridge University Press, Cambridge (2009)
21. Peters, J., Janzing, D., Schölkopf, B.: Elements of Causal Inference: Foundations and Learning Algorithms. The MIT Press, Cambridge (2017)
22. Punzo, V., Borzacchiello, M.T., Ciuffo, B.: On the assessment of vehicle trajectory data accuracy and application to the next generation simulation (NGSIM) program data. Transp. Res. Part C: Emerg. Technol. 19(6), 1243–1262 (2011)
23. Reichenbach, H.: The Direction of Time. Dover Publications, Mineola (1956)
24. Schölkopf, B., Janzing, D., Peters, J., Sgouritsa, E., Zhang, K., Mooij, J.: On causal and anticausal learning. arXiv preprint arXiv:1206.6471 (2012)
25. Schölkopf, B., et al.: Toward causal representation learning. Proc. IEEE 109(5), 612–634 (2021)
26. Sutskever, I., Vinyals, O., Le, Q.V.: Sequence to sequence learning with neural networks. Adv. Neural Inf. Process. Syst. 27 (2014)
27. Tang, C., Salakhutdinov, R.R.: Multiple futures prediction. Adv. Neural Inf. Process. Syst. 32 (2019)
28. Tzeng, E., Hoffman, J., Saenko, K., Darrell, T.: Adversarial discriminative domain adaptation. In: Proceedings of the IEEE Conference on Computer Vision and Pattern Recognition, pp. 7167–7176 (2017)
29. Yoon, C., Hamarneh, G., Garbi, R.: Generalizable feature learning in the presence of data bias and domain class imbalance with application to skin lesion classification. In: Shen, D., et al. (eds.) MICCAI 2019. LNCS, vol. 11767, pp. 365–373. Springer, Cham (2019). https://doi.org/10.1007/978-3-030-32251-9_40
30. Zhan, W., et al.: Interaction dataset: an international, adversarial and cooperative motion dataset in interactive driving scenarios with semantic maps. arXiv preprint arXiv:1910.03088 (2019)
31. Zhang, W., Ouyang, W., Li, W., Xu, D.: Collaborative and adversarial network for unsupervised domain adaptation. In: Proceedings of the IEEE Conference on Computer Vision and Pattern Recognition, pp. 3801–3809 (2018)
32. Zhou, K., Liu, Z., Qiao, Y., Xiang, T., Loy, C.C.: Domain generalization: a survey. IEEE Trans. Pattern Anal. Mach. Intell. 45, 4396–4415 (2022)

A Framework for Centrifugal Pump Diagnosis Using Health Sensitivity Ratio Based Feature Selection and KNN

Zahoor Ahmad[1], Niamat Ullah[1], Wasim Zaman[1], Muhammad Farooq Siddique[1], Jaeyoung Kim[2], and Jong-Myon Kim[1,2(✉)]

[1] Department of Electrical, Electronics, and Computer Engineering, University of Ulsan, Ulsan 44610, South Korea
jmkim07@ulsan.ac.kr
[2] PD Technologies Co. Ltd., Ulsan 44610, South Korea

Abstract. A new framework for the fault diagnosis of centrifugal pumps (CP) is presented in this paper. Time domain (TD) features obtained from the vibration signal (VS) of the CP are vulnerable to severe faults and can affect the fault classification accuracy of the classifier. To address this issue, the proposed method selects a healthy reference signal (HRS) and extracts raw statistical features from this signal and the vibration signals of the CP obtained under different operating conditions in the time and frequency domain (FD). The Pearson correlation coefficient is calculated by cross-correlating the time and frequency domain features of the healthy reference signal with the time and frequency domain features extracted from the vibration signal of the CP under different operating conditions. The Pearson correlation coefficient results in a new feature vector, however, some of the coefficients may not be the best to identify the ongoing conditions of the centrifugal pump. To overcome this problem, the proposed method uses a new health sensitivity ratio for the selection of CP health-sensitive features. The health sensitivity ratio (HSR) assesses per-class feature compactness and between-class distance of the features. The selected health-sensitive features are provided to KNN for the identification of centrifugal pump health conditions. The proposed method has achieved a classification accuracy of 97.13%, surpassing that of the conventional methods for CP fault diagnosis.

Keywords: Health Sensitivity Ratio · Fault Diagnosis · Centrifugal Pump

1 Introduction

CPs have become vital to several business operations [1]. Unexpected CP faults may result in longer downtime, financial losses, expensive repairs, and a threat to worker safety [2]. Early fault identification and diagnosis are crucial for extending the functional life of CPs [3].

The amplitude of VS may experience variation due to a mechanical fault (MF) in the CP, which makes VS a valuable tool for diagnosing CP faults [4]. TD features can detect

© The Author(s), under exclusive license to Springer Nature Switzerland AG 2023
H. Lu et al. (Eds.): ACPR 2023, LNCS 14407, pp. 170–179, 2023.
https://doi.org/10.1007/978-3-031-47637-2_13

variations in the VS caused by emerging faults [5]. Nonetheless, due to the variability in fault severity, TD features are considered unsuitable for severe faults [6]. Faults of varying severity can be detected more effectively by the frequency spectrum [7]. FD features are utilized for the fault diagnosis of CP [8]. The VS acquired from the CP under a defective health state is complex and nonstationary, it is known that the spectrum analysis is best suited for stationary signals [9]. The multi-resolution analysis, also known as TFD transformations, is better suited for non-stationary signals. Empirical mode decomposition (EMD), an adaptive decomposition method presented in [10], may be used to analyze non-stationary data. EMD and its variations have been efficiently utilized for the diagnostic purposes of rotating machinery [11]. However, problems of mode mixing and the challenge of extreme interpolation in EMD make it less attractive for VS analysis. Applying wavelet transform (WT) enables the utilization of CP non-stationary transients [12, 13]. Rapur et al. [14] utilized WT the processing of CP VS. The method used two different techniques to extract fault-sensitive features. The first one selects the WT base having maximum energy for feature extraction and the second technique uses the principal component analysis for the base selection and feature extraction. The choice of the fundamental wavelet profoundly influences feature distinctiveness. Opting for the right mother wavelet demands a blend of domain expertise and exhaustive empirical exploration. [15]. To address the above-mentioned problems, a novel fault diagnosis framework for CP has been introduced in this study. In the novel approach, an initial HRS is chosen from which raw statistical features are derived. These features are extracted not only from the HRS signal but also from the VS of the CP acquired across various operational scenarios in both TD and FD. Pearson correlation coefficient is calculated by cross-correlating the TD and FD features of the HRS with the TD and FD features extracted from the VS of the CP under different operating conditions. The Pearson correlation coefficient results in a new feature vector, however, some of the coefficients may not be the best to identify the ongoing conditions of the centrifugal pump.

In intelligence-based fault diagnosis, following feature extraction, the pivotal progression entails feature preprocessing and subsequent classification procedures [16–19]. Nair et al. [20] assessed different feature selection approaches for fault detection in CP's, and principal component analysis (PCA) emerged as the methodology with the most promising results. However, PCA experiences a loss of information. Additionally, PCA does not take inter-class separability into account. Through linear discriminant analysis (LDA) and its variants, low-dimensional and discriminant feature space is produced. This method considers intra-class separation and inter-class compactness [21, 22]. However, the classification accuracy may suffer from the penalty graph illustration of the intra-class segregation. To address this problem, discriminant features based on HSR are selected in this study. The HSR assesses feature compactness in each class and the distance between features of different classes.

The arrangement of this study unfolds across the subsequent segments: In Sect. 2, the experimental testbed used in this study is described. Section 3 elucidates the details of the proposed framework. Section 4 describes the results and discussion. The conclusion and future direction are presented in Sect. 5.

2 Experimental Setup

The VS was collected from a self-developed centrifugal pump testbed presented in Fig. 1. The testbed was equipped with a CP (PMT-4008) powered by a motor of 5.5 kW which is connected to primary and secondary water tanks through steel pipes. In addition, A control panel was established to monitor and adjust the fluid pressure, temperature, and pump performance.

To acquire VS under normal and defective conditions, four accelerometers were employed; with a pair strategically positioned in proximity to the mechanical seal (MS) and impeller, while the other two were close to the pump casing. The data was acquired under four different operating conditions such as normal (NC), impeller fault (IF), MS scratch (MSS), and MS hole (MSH) fault. For each condition VS were collected for 300 s, resulting in the collection of 1200 samples in total. Table 1 provides detailed information on the dataset and fault types observed in this study.

Table 1. Description of the dataset.

Operating Condition	Defect Specification			Samples
	Length	Diameter	Depth	
Normal	–	–	–	300
MSH defect	–	2.8 mm	2.8 mm	300
MSS defect	10 mm	2.5 mm	2.8 mm	300
IF	18 mm	2.5 mm	2.8 mm	300

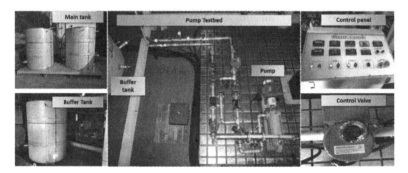

Fig. 1. Experimental testbed for data acquisition.

3 Proposed Framework

The visual representation of our proposed approach's is presented in Fig. 2. Our method consists of the following steps:

Step.1: For cross-correlation analysis HRS selection is of primary importance, therefore, in this step, HRS is selected. For the selection of HRS, the pump was operated at the pump peak effectiveness point (PEP) as shown in Fig. 3, and a total of 20 VS were collected. The PEP is the point in the pump characteristic curve provided by the pump manufacturer at which the CP operates at its highest efficiency. Upon careful examination of the 20 VS obtained from the CP at PEP, the HRS will be the one whose statistical mean aligns closely with the statistical mean of a healthy pump's VS, while simultaneously maintaining the greatest distance from the statistical mean of other classes. Such as MSS, MSH, and IF.

Step.2: TD statistical features such as root amplitude, mean indicator, peak indicator, root mean square, an indicator of skewness, kurtosis indicator, crest indicator, clearance indicator, shape indicator, and impulse indicator are extracted from both the HRS and the VS across various categories. The Pearson correlation coefficient is subsequently computed by cross-correlating the time-domain characteristics of the HRS with the time-domain indicators obtained from the CP's VS under both regular and faulty operating conditions using (1) The Pearson correlation coefficient results in a new feature vector.

$$P_{xy} = \frac{\sum_{i=1}^{n}(x_i - x')(y_i - y')}{\sqrt{\sum_{i=1}^{n}(x_i - x')^2}\sqrt{\sum_{i=1}^{n}(y_i - y')^2}} \tag{1}$$

(1) examines the correlation between features x and y. P_{xy} is the Pearson correlation coefficient calculated between the HRS feature vectors and feature vectors of the CP normal and defective classes.

Step.3: Mean frequency, standard deviation, spectral kurtosis, root variance frequency, and root mean square frequency are derived from both the HRS and the VS of the CP across varying categories in the FD. The computation of the Pearson correlation coefficient involves cross-correlating the FD features of the HRS with the corresponding FD features extracted from the CP's VS, each captured under distinct operational circumstances using (1) The Pearson correlation coefficient is the new feature vector obtained from the preprocessing of the traditional statistical features.

The new features obtained from steps 2 and 3 are combined into one feature vector. The resulting feature vector has a dimension of 16×300, where 16 represents the features and 300 represents per-class samples for each feature.

Step.4: The merged feature feature vector extends into a high-dimensional feature space; however, it's essential to note that not all of these features might be optimal for accurately identifying the conditions of the CP. Therefore, selecting discriminant features is crucial before the classification task. The proposed method uses a new HSR for the selection of CP health-sensitive features. The HSR assesses feature compactness for each class and feature distance for different classes. Following are the steps for the HSR-based feature selections.

1. For each class feature compactness can be obtained by using (2).

$$C_k^S = \frac{1}{N} \sum_{n=1}^{N} C_{n,k},$$
(2)

The $C_{n,k}$ is given in (3),

$$C_{n,k} = \frac{1}{u_n \times (u_n - 1)} \sum_{i,u=1}^{u_n} |y_{s,n,k} - y_{i,n,k}|, i, u = 1, 2, .., u_n, i \neq u.$$
(3)

The CP operating condition and the feature for each health state is represented by N and y, each feature sample is expressed as u in (2) and (3) respectively.

2. calculate mean of the feature in each class $\mu_{N,k}$.
3. calculate distance between each class features B_j^d using (4).

$$B_j^d = \frac{1}{X \times (X - 1)} \sum_{x,i=1}^{X} |\mu_{i,k} - \mu_{x,k}|, x, i = 1, 2, 3, .., X, x \neq i.$$
(4)

4. Calculate the HSR using (5) for each feature.

$$HSR = \frac{B_j^d}{C_k^S}$$
(5)

5. Select health-sensitive (HS) indicators based on the condition in (6).

$$HS_f = \begin{cases} HSR \geq 0.5 \ \text{Sensitive} \\ otherwise \quad \text{less sensitive} \end{cases}$$
(6)

The selected health-sensitive indicators are segregated for the identification of CP health condition using KNN. The KNN classifier is used in this study for the classification task due to its architectural simplicity and low computational cost.

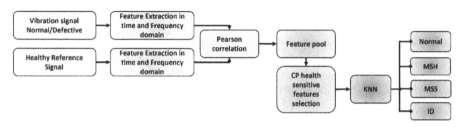

Fig. 2. Graphical flow of the proposed method.

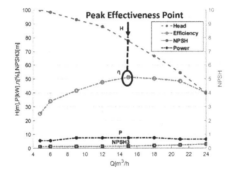

Fig. 3. Peak effectiveness point in the pump characteristic curve.

4   Results and Performance Evaluation

A k-fold cross-validation strategy, where k = 3, is employed to assess the effectiveness of the proposed methodology. To ensure result reliability, experiments were iterated 15 times. In each iteration, 200 samples were randomly selected for training the model per class, with the remaining samples reserved for model testing. Detailed information about the dataset used is provided in Table 1.

The proposed method is compared with both supervised and unsupervised feature processing methods such as Tr-LDA and PCA. For performance comparisons of the model, the true positive rate for each class (TPR-C) and average classification accuracy for each class (ACA-C) are used. (7) and (8) can be used to compute TPR-C and ACA-C.

$$TPR - C = \frac{1}{m} \sum_{l=1}^{k} \left(\frac{(X_{TP}^{l,m})}{X_{TP}^{l,m} + X_{FN}^{l,m}} \right) \times 100(\%) \tag{7}$$

$$ACA - C = \frac{1}{m} \sum_{l=1}^{k} \left(\sum_{m=1}^{L} \frac{X_{TP}^{l,m}}{X_{sanples}} \right) \times 100(\%) \tag{8}$$

In (8) true positive and negatives are represented by X_{TP}, and X_{TN}, False negatives of the classifier is represented by X_{FN}, l signifies the iteration within the k-fold strategy denoted by m, while samples denote the total count of samples within each class for (7) and (8) correspondingly.

A comparative analysis between the proposed method and reference techniques is illustrated in Table 2. As per the table, the proposed method exhibited an improved ACA-C of 97.13%, surpassing Tr-LDA by 7% and PCA by 31.88%. The higher ACA of the proposed approach is due to its unique concept of selecting CP health-sensitive features for classification rather than relying on raw features. Additionally, the performance of the proposed method surpassed that of the reference techniques in terms of TPR-C.

Figure 4(a) supports the high accuracy of the presented approach for CP fault diagnosis, showing that its feature space is more discriminant than the reference methods. However, there is some overlap between the MSH feature and features from other classes, leading to the lower TPR-C of MSH compared to other operating conditions.

Subsequently, a supervised approach Tr-LDA was employed to generate a low-dimensional space by considering the compactness of the inter-class distances and same-class features using the criteria of trace ratio. After applying the step of Tr-LDA provided in [21], an ACA-A of 90% was achieved for our dataset. However, for each class, Tr-LDA exhibited unsatisfactory performance in terms of TPR-C, since it needed to incorporate preprocessing of the features before utilizing the steps of Tr-LDA. Tr-LDA reduced the scatter of the per-class features but failed to distinguish between the features of other classes as evident in Fig. 4(b).

PCA, another reference technique employed in this study, focuses on attaining maximal data variance as a means of dimensionality reduction. Following the procedure outlined in [20], 65.25% classification accuracy is achieved for our dataset. Figure 4(c) demonstrates that PCA was ineffective in feature discrimination before classification. This factor is also responsible for the comparatively lower C-TPR observed in comparison to our approach. The underperformance of PCA was attributed to its failure to consider between-class separability and the challenge of selecting optimal fault-related principal components.

Table 2. C-TPR and ACA-C of the proposed in comparison with existing methods.

Approaches	C-TPR				Classification accuracy (Average)%
	NC	MSH	MSS	ID	
Proposed	100%	92.5%	97.8%	98.1%	97.1%
Tr-LDA	91.0%	92.5%	88.2%	87.6%	90%
PCA	94.0%	54.4%	47.3%	58.4%	65.2%

Based on the fault diagnosis capability of the proposed method for CPs, it can be concluded that the framework is suitable for diagnosing CP faults. The main advantage of the proposed framework lies in its fundamental concept, which involves preprocessing VS and selecting health-sensitive features based on their ability to improve classification accuracy.

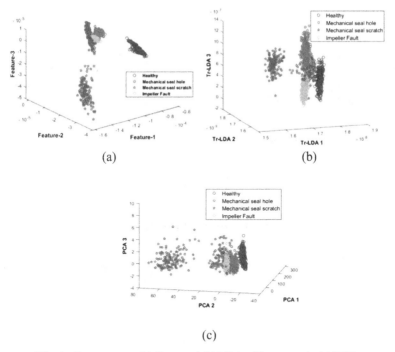

Fig. 4. Feature space (a) Proposed (b) LDA with trace ratio (c) PCA.

5   Conclusion

This paper introduced a systematic approach for diagnosing mechanical faults in centrifugal pumps (CP). The method commenced with the selection of a healthy reference signal. In the subsequent phase, time and frequency domain features are extracted from both the reference signal and vibration signals captured during diverse CP operating conditions. The Pearson correlation coefficient is then computed by cross-correlating the extracted features. All these correlation coefficients are consolidated into a unified feature pool, from which health-sensitive features are discerned using the health sensitivity ratio. In the experimental phase, real-world vibration signals are collected from an industrial CP testbed, encompassing normal, mechanical seal scratch, mechanical seal hole, and impeller defect scenarios. Employing our proposed method on this dataset yields an average accuracy of 97.13% in identifying the CP's ongoing health condition. While this method currently focuses on mechanical faults, future iterations aim to enhance its capability in detecting hydraulic defects like cavitation in CP systems.

Acknowledgements. This research was funded by Ministry of Trade, Industry and Energy (MOTIE) and supported by Korea Evaluation Institute of Industrial Technology (KIET). [RS-2022–00142509, The development of simulation stage and digital twin for Land Based Test Site and hydrogen powered vessel with fuel cell]. This work was also supported by the Technology Infrastructure Program funded by the Ministry of SMEs and Startups (MSS, Korea).

References

1. Ahmad, Z., Rai, A., Maliuk, A.S., Kim, J.M.: Discriminant feature extraction for centrifugal pump fault diagnosis. IEEE Access **8**, 165512–165528 (2020)
2. Prosvirin, A.E., Ahmad, Z., Kim, J.M.: Global and local feature extraction using a convolutional autoencoder and neural networks for diagnosing centrifugal pump mechanical faults. IEEE Access **9**, 65838–65854 (2021)
3. Nguyen, T.K., Ahmad, Z., Kim, J.M.: Leak localization on cylinder tank bottom using acoustic emission. Sensors **23**(1), 27 (2023)
4. Hasan, M.J., Rai, A., Ahmad, Z., Kim, J.M.: A fault diagnosis framework for centrifugal pumps by scalogram-based imaging and deep learning. IEEE Access **9**, 58052–58066 (2021)
5. Dong, L., Chen, Z., Hua, R., Hu, S., Fan, C., Xiao, X.: Research on diagnosis method of centrifugal pump rotor faults based on IPSO-VMD and RVM. Nucl. Eng. Technol. **55**(3), 827–838 (2023)
6. Dai, C., Hu, S., Zhang, Y., Chen, Z., Dong, L.: Cavitation state identification of centrifugal pump based on CEEMD-DRSN. Nucl. Eng. Technol. **55**, 1507–1517 (2023)
7. Chen, L., Wei, L., Wang, Y., Wang, J., Li, W.: Monitoring and predictive maintenance of centrifugal pumps based on smart sensors. Sensors **22**(6), 2106 (2022)
8. Chen, H., Li, S.: Multi-sensor fusion by CWT-PARAFAC-IPSO-SVM for intelligent mechanical fault diagnosis. Sensors **22**(10), 3647 (2022)
9. Ahmad, S., Ahmad, Z., Kim, J.M.: A centrifugal pump fault diagnosis framework based on supervised contrastive learning. Sensors **22**(17), 6448 (2022)
10. Ahmad, Z., Prosvirin, A.E., Kim, J., Kim, J.M.: Multistage centrifugal pump fault diagnosis by selecting fault characteristic modes of vibration and using pearson linear discriminant analysis. IEEE Access **8**, 223030–223040 (2020)
11. Ahmad, Z., Rai, A., Hasan, M.J., Kim, C.H., Kim, J.M.: A novel framework for centrifugal pump fault diagnosis by selecting fault characteristic coefficients of walsh transform and cosine linear discriminant analysis. IEEE Access **9**, 150128–150141 (2021)
12. Kumar, A., Tang, H., Vashishtha, G., Xiang, J.: Noise subtraction and marginal enhanced square envelope spectrum (MESES) for the identification of bearing defects in centrifugal and axial pump. Mech. Syst. Signal Process. **165**, 108366 (2022)
13. Li, G., Chen, L., Liu, J., Fang, X.: Comparative study on deep transfer learning strategies for cross-system and cross-operation-condition building energy systems fault diagnosis. Energy **263**, 125943 (2023)
14. Rapur, J.S., Tiwari, R.: Experimental fault diagnosis for known and unseen operating conditions of centrifugal pumps using MSVM and WPT based analyses. Measurement (Lond) **147**, 106809 (2019)
15. Aguilera, J.J., et al.: A review of common faults in large-scale heat pumps. Renew. Sustain. Energy Rev. **168**, 112826 (2022)
16. Chen, K., Lu, Y., Zhang, R., Wang, H.: The adaptive bearing fault diagnosis based on optimal regulation of generalized SR behaviors in fluctuating-damping induced harmonic oscillator. Mech. Syst. Signal Process. **189**, 110078 (2023)
17. Vrachimis, S., et al.: WaterSafe: a water network benchmark for fault diagnosis research. In: IFAC-PapersOnLine, pp. 655–660. Elsevier B.V. (2022)
18. Saeed, U., Jan, S.U., Lee, Y.D., Koo, I.: Fault diagnosis based on extremely randomized trees in wireless sensor networks. Reliab. Eng. Syst. Saf. **205**, 107284 (2021)
19. Saeed, U., Lee, Y.D., Jan, S.U., Koo, I.: CAFD: Context-aware fault diagnostic scheme towards sensor faults utilizing machine learning. Sensors (Switzerland) **21**(2), 1–15 (2021)
20. Sakthivel, N.R., Nair, B.B., Elangovan, M., Sugumaran, V., Saravanmurugan, S.: Comparison of dimensionality reduction techniques for the fault diagnosis of mono block centrifugal pump using vibration signals. Eng. Sci. Technol. Int. J. **17**(1), 30–38 (2014)

21. Jin, X., Zhao, M., Chow, T.W.S., Pecht, M.: Motor bearing fault diagnosis using trace ratio linear discriminant analysis. IEEE Trans. Ind. Electron. **61**(5), 2441–2451 (2014)
22. Dong, L., Xiao, Q., Jia, Y., Fang, T.: Review of research on intelligent diagnosis of oil transfer pump malfunction. Petroleum. KeAi Communications Co. (2022)

WPT-Base Selection for Bearing Fault Feature Extraction: A Node-Specific Approach Study

Andrei Maliuk[1] and Jong-Myon Kim[1,2]

[1] Department of Electrical, Electronics and Computer Engineering, University of Ulsan, Ulsan 44610, Republic of Korea
jmkim07@ulsan.ac.kr
[2] PD Technologies Co. Ltd., Ulsan 44610, Republic of Korea

Abstract. Wavelet packet transform (WPT) has found extensive use in bearing fault diagnosis for its ability to provide more accurate frequency and time-frequency representations of non-stationary signals. Traditional quantitative methods prioritize unequal node-energy distribution at the desired decomposition level as a criterion for WPT base selection. Decomposition results obtained with WPT-base selected using this approach can be characterized as having one WPT-node with high signal energy which is automatically considered as a component of interest containing information about bearing fault. However, prioritizing one WPT-node at this early stage of fault diagnosis process might not be optimal for all nodes in the WPT-tree decomposition level and might exclude components in other nodes, which may contain features potentially important for fault diagnosis. In this paper, we propose a node-specific approach for WPT-base selection to improve the quality of feature extraction. The new criterion evaluates WPT-bases upon their ability to generate a signal with the highest ratio of energy and entropy of the signal spectrum for a specific node. Using this criterion, the final WPT signal decomposition is constructed using the WPT-nodes produced by the bases with the highest criterion score. This approach ensures the preservation of all meaningful components in each node and their distinction from the noisy background, resulting in a higher quality feature extraction. To evaluate the effectiveness of the proposed method for bearing fault diagnosis, a comparative analysis was conducted using two sets of Paderborn University bearing fault experimental vibration data and the bearing vibration data from the Case Western University benchmark dataset. As a result, the proposed method showed better average performance across three datasets.

Keywords: Bearing Fault Diagnosis · Feature Extraction · Wavelet Packet Transform · Wavelet Packet Base Selection

1 Introduction

Bearings are crucial mechanical components found in various applications, and their faults can cause significant damage, loss of production, and even human casualties [1, 2]. With the availability of high-quality vibration sensors and Machine Learning

© The Author(s), under exclusive license to Springer Nature Switzerland AG 2023
H. Lu et al. (Eds.): ACPR 2023, LNCS 14407, pp. 180–191, 2023.
https://doi.org/10.1007/978-3-031-47637-2_14

(ML) algorithms, data-based fault diagnosis methods are becoming more prevalent. These methods usually involve processing of the signal, extraction of the signal features, feature selection, and ML classification. Deep Learning (DL) can also be used for fault diagnosis, but the issue of explainability remains a challenge. Despite the advantages of DL, traditional ML methods remain a powerful alternative, particularly when data is limited [3].

In machine learning-based fault diagnosis algorithms, the first step is signal processing. Traditionally, Fast Fourier Transform (FFT) has been used, but it has limitations such as poor resolution, inability to capture transient signals, and spectral leakage [4–6]. Short-time Fourier Transform (STFT) solves these issues by sliding a window along the signal and performing FFT on each window to obtain a time-frequency representation. However, STFT has limitations regarding window length selection, which results in a tradeoff between frequency resolution and time resolution [7].

EMD is a time-frequency method that is used for decomposition of the signals into intrinsic mode functions (IMFs) without using a base function. It is particularly useful for non-stationary signals. However, the mode mixing phenomenon can occur when IMFs generated by EMD overlap, making it difficult to interpret and analyze them individually. To overcome this, techniques like EEMD or CEMD have been developed, but they require significant computing time and balancing the number of attempts and decomposition quality [8, 9].

The Wavelet Packet Transform (WPT) offers high time-frequency resolution and sensitivity to transient components by decomposing a signal into various sub-bands with different frequencies using wavelets as decomposition bases. WPT is less adaptive and flexible than EMD, but it is computationally less expensive. The selection of either method depends on the signal and application. Although there are many wavelet base functions available, selecting one remains a vulnerable part of WPT that lacks a general state-of-the-art solution method, creating a need for new solutions to be found.

This paper proposes a method for a novel feature extraction approach by trying to resolve a fundamental drawback of the WPT in comparison with EMD—dependency on the wavelet base. To overcome this limitation and increase the quality of feature extraction using WPT, a new criterion for base wavelet selection is proposed along with the novel node-specific approach for constructing of the representation of the bearing vibration signal. The new criterion evaluates WPT bases based on their ability to generate a signal with the highest ratio of energy and entropy of the signal spectrum for a specific node. The final WPT signal decomposition is constructed using the WPT nodes produced by the bases with the highest criterion score. This approach aims to preserve all meaningful components in each node and distinguish them from the noisy background, resulting in higher-quality feature extraction.

Further this paper is organized as follows: Sect. 2 overviews the datasets used for the validation of proposed method, Sect. 3 provides some technical background on Wavelet Packet Transform, Sect. 4 describes the proposed criterion for WPT base selection and construction of the signal representation, Sect. 5 discusses the fault diagnosis framework used for performance evaluation and Sect. 6 concludes the manuscript.

2 Technical Background

2.1 Wavelet Packet Decomposition

The Wavelet Packet Decomposition or Transform (WPT) decomposes an input signal into a binary tree structure of wavelet packet nodes, which are indexed as (j, n), with corresponding coefficients d_j^n. This allows for analysis of both low and high-frequency spectra, making it useful for characterizing non-stationary bearing fault signals. At the root of the WPT tree, the input signal is located in the node $W(0, 0)$, with $W(1, 0)$ and $W(1, 1)$ representing the low-pass and high-pass filtered branches, respectively, resulting in approximation and detail coefficients d_1^0 and d_1^1. Further decomposition is performed in the same way at every level j. An schematic example of a WPT with j decomposition levels is shown in Fig. 1.

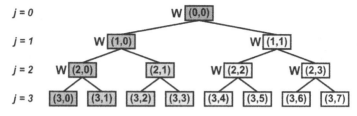

Fig. 1. Wavelet Packet Tree schematic.

The choice of the wavelet base in WPT decomposition is crucial. There are two main families of selection methods: qualitative and quantitative. Qualitative methods focus on properties like symmetry, compact support, orthogonality, regularity and vanishing moment to find the best fitting wavelet. However, relying solely on wavelet properties can be limiting due to the possibility of different wavelets sharing the same properties, making it hard to determine the most suitable one. To address this, researchers have explored shape matching, an alternative qualitative approach that analyzes the geometric shape of wavelets. It aims to find a wavelet base that resembles the shape of the target signal feature, improving signal component extraction. However, despite its benefits, manual shape matching is time-consuming and lacks automation.

Considerable research has been carried out to address the limitations of qualitative methods by exploring quantitative approaches. These approaches utilize various quantitative measures like signal energy, Shannon entropy, cross-correlation, Emlen's modified entropy measure and distribution error criterion to determine the most appropriate wavelet base. In recent times, the criterion based on the ratio of the maximum energy to the Shannon entropy gained significant popularity as one of the leading quantitative methods for selecting the wavelet base. This criterion combines the widely used maximum energy metric and Shannon entropy metric, offering a reliable approach to wavelet base selection. The maximum energy method suggests that the most suitable wavelet base will enable the extraction of the highest possible energy from the analyzed discrete-time signal. The energy E_x of the signal x can be mathematically represented as follows:

$$E_x = \sum_{n=1}^{N} |x_n|^2 \tag{1}$$

It's crucial to acknowledge that signals possessing identical energy levels can exhibit varying frequency distributions. For instance, one signal may have higher energy levels in frequency components important for fault diagnosis, while another signal may have a broad spectrum with uniform energy levels throughout the spectrum, which is not fruitful for fault feature extraction. To quantify the distribution of signal energy among nodes in a wavelet packet decomposition layer, Shannon Entropy H is employed as follows:

$$H = -\sum_{i=1}^{N} p_i \cdot \log_2 p_i \tag{2}$$

Here p_i denotes the probability distribution of the energy among the wavelet coefficients, is presented in the following manner:

$$p_i = \frac{|wt(s, i)|^2}{E_x(s)} \tag{3}$$

where $wt(s, i)$ is a i th wavelet coefficient at the s level.

Then the ratio between energy and Shannon entropy can be expressed as.

$$R(s) = \frac{E_x(s)}{H(s)} \tag{4}$$

The given equation allows for the calculation of the R(s) ratio at the desired level of decomposition for each potential wavelet base. The candidate wavelet which exhibits the highest energy to Shannon entropy value is selected as the basis for decomposing the given signal or set of signals using the WPT method.

3   Proposed Methodology

3.1   Envelope Analysis

The vibration signal from faulty bearings contains high-frequency components resulting from different mechanisms like impact, rubbing, or resonance. These high-frequency elements are frequently concealed by low-frequency components in the signal, which can arise from machine operation, background noise, or measurement noise. To extract these high-frequency components, the Hilbert Transform Envelope Extraction method is employed in the same way as in [6].

3.2 Wavelet Base Evaluation Criterion

The selection of a wavelet basis during the procedure of signal decomposition through Wavelet Packet Transform (WPT) significantly influences the spectral qualities of the resultant coefficients. Each wavelet base possesses distinct qualities that make them better suited for capturing particular types of spectral content or signal features, while others may be less effective in doing so. In the standard WPT procedure, outlined in the Sect. 3, a wavelet base is carefully selected from a poll containing W wavelet bases. Each wavelet base is then applied to decompose a representative subspace of the signal data. The resulting WPT coefficients are subsequently evaluated, and based on this assessment, a final decision is made regarding the most suitable wavelet base for the given signal data.

In contrast, the proposed method endeavors to portray a signal by employing WPT decomposition as a basis, yet it is not constrained to employing only one wavelet base.

In this approach, the signal data is initially decomposed into a specified level, denoted as j, using a poll of W wavelet bases. For each node within the decomposition, ranging from d_j^0 to d_i^n, a score chart is created. This score chart has a length of W, with each element representing the evaluation results of reconstructed coefficients obtained from the WPT decomposition of this node using different wavelet bases. The assessment of these coefficients is based on the evaluation of their spectral content. This evaluation is performed by calculating the relation of the total power of the spectrum to the Shannon entropy of the signal power spectrum. Considering the Shannon entropy of the signal power spectrum H_{ps} is defined as:

$$H_{ps} = -\sum_{i=1}^{N} p_i \log_2(p_i) \tag{5}$$

where N stands for the number of frequency bins in the signal power spectrum and the probability of the signal power being in the i-th frequency bin p_i is defined as:

$$p_i = \frac{P_i}{\sum_{j=1}^{N} P_j} \tag{6}$$

where P_i is the power in the i-th frequency bin.

And the total power of the signal spectrum is computed as:

$$P_{ss} = \sum_{i=1}^{N} P_i \tag{7}$$

So, the final ratio is defined as:

$$R = \frac{P_{ss}}{H_{ps}} = \frac{\sum_{i=1}^{N} P_i}{-\sum_{i=1}^{N} \frac{P_i}{\sum_{j=1}^{N} P_j} \log_2\left(\frac{P_i}{\sum_{j=1}^{N} P_j}\right)} \tag{8}$$

The proposed method utilizes the R-value criterion to assess the reconstructed coefficients and determine the most suitable mother wavelet for representing the signal.

This criterion enables the comparison of spectral content captured by each wavelet and identifies the one that offers the most effective representation. Specifically, the criterion measures the extent to which information in the signal power spectrum is concentrated within specific frequency bands rather than uniformly distributed across the entire spectrum. A preferred wavelet base is one that yields reconstructed coefficients with a higher ratio of signal spectrum total power to its Shannon entropy. This preference indicates a signal with a more predictable and structured spectral composition.

3.3   Signal Representation Using WPT with Node-Specific Bases

Aiming for more efficient feature extraction, the proposed method constructs a representation of the input signal using WPT as a fundament. The node-specific approach for the wavelet base selection uses a rating based on the R-value. Each of the n WPT nodes at decomposition level j has its unique rating of the WPT-bases, where the best base for a particular node has the highest R-value. It means that it is possible to obtain more useful spectral contents for efficient feature extraction from the reconstructed signal of each particular node if it was selected from a WPT tree decomposed using the wavelet base with the highest R-value. Thus, the final representation is obtained when each of the n nodes was selected. This process is illustrated in Fig. 2.

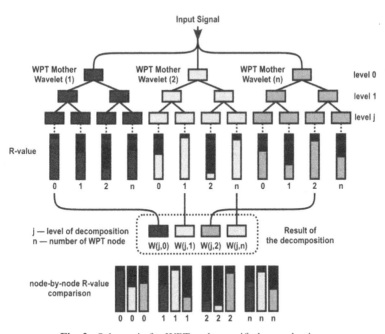

Fig. 2. Schematic for WPT node-specific base selection.

3.4 Statistical Feature Extraction

In order to represent the obtained data in fewer variables, 19 statistical features were extracted from the time and frequency domain of each of the eight reconstructed signals obtained in Sect. 4. Features from each node were concatenated and in the result one second sample of the vibration signal is now represented by 152 features. Table 1 contains the names and formulas for each of these 19 features.

Table 1. Statistical features and their formulas.

Feature	Equation	Feature	Equation
Peak	$X_p = \max_i \lvert x_i \rvert$	5th normalized moment	$HOMn5 = \dfrac{\frac{1}{n}\sum_{i=1}^{N}(x_i-\mu)^5}{\left(\sqrt{\frac{1}{N-1}\sum_{i=1}^{N}(x_i-\mu)^2}\right)^5}$
Root-mean square	$X_{RMS} = \sqrt{\frac{1}{N}\sum_{i=1}^{N} x_i^2}$	6th normalized moment	$HOMn6 = \dfrac{\frac{1}{n}\sum_{i=1}^{N}(x_i-\mu)^6}{\left(\sqrt{\frac{1}{N-1}\sum_{i=1}^{N}(x_i-\mu)^2}\right)^6}$
Kurtosis	$X_{kurtosis} = \frac{1}{N}\left(\dfrac{\sum_{i=1}^{N}(x_i-\mu)^4}{\sigma^4}\right)$	Skewness	$X_{kurtosis} = \frac{1}{N}\left(\dfrac{\sum_{i=1}^{N}(x_i-\mu)^3}{\sigma^3}\right)$
Crest factor	$C_f = \dfrac{X_p}{X_{RMS}}$	Shape factor RMS	$SF_{RMS} = \dfrac{X_{RMS}}{\mu}$
Clearance factor	$L = \dfrac{X_p}{\left((1/N)\sum_{i}^{N}\sqrt{\lvert x_i \rvert}\right)^2}$	Peak-to-peak value	$x_{ptp} = \max\lvert x\rvert - \min\lvert x\rvert$
Impulse factor	$L = \dfrac{\max\{\lvert x_i\rvert\}}{\left((1/N)\sum_{i-1}^{N}\lvert x_i\rvert\right)}$	Energy of signal	$e = \sum_{i=1}^{N} x_i^2$
Shape factor SMR	$SF_{SMR} = \dfrac{X_{SMR}}{\mu}$	Frequency center	$FC = \dfrac{\int_0^\infty fs(f)df}{\int_0^\infty s(f)df}$
Entropy	$H(x) = -\sum_{i=1}^{N} P(x_i)\cdot\log_2 P(x_i)$	RMS frequency	$RMSF = \sqrt{\dfrac{\int_0^\infty f_i^2 s(f_i)df}{\int_0^\infty s(f_i)df}}$
Mean	$\mu = \frac{1}{N}\sum_{i-1}^{N} x_i$	Root variance frequency	$RVF = \sqrt{\dfrac{\int_0^\infty (f_i-FC)^2 s(f_i)df}{\int_0^\infty s(f_i)df}}$
Square mean root	$X_{SMR} = \left(\dfrac{\sum_{i=1}^{N}\sqrt{x_i}}{N}\right)^2$		

4 Experimental Test Bed and Data Collection

The proposed method was evaluated using four bearing-fault datasets to ensure validity and reliability. Three publicly available datasets were obtained from the KAt-DataCenter of Paderborn University (PU) in Germany and Case Western Reserve University (CWRU) [10, 11]. PU datasets are denoted as PUA and PUR for artificial and real bearing faults.

The PU dataset's vibration data was collected using a modular test rig comprising an electric motor (Hanning ElektroWerke GmbH & Co. KG), measuring shaft, a module for bearing installation, flywheel, and motor used for load simulation. The electric motor is a 425 W PMSM controlled by an industrial inverter (KEB Combivert 07F5E 1D-2B0A). Four different experimental conditions used for each bearing are shown in Table 2. Vibration data was obtained using a piezoelectric accelerometer installed on top of the bearing module and sampled at 64 kHz rate. For the current research the signals were downsampled with the factor of eight for faster computations. Each dataset sample represents one second of vibration signal. PU dataset has signals from six healthy bearings with a run-in period of one to 50 h. PUA dataset has 12 bearings with faults inflicted using electric discharge machine, electric engraving, and drilling. Faults have depths of 1–2 mm for EDM trenches and lengths of 1–4 mm for electric engraving. All faults are categorized as Healthy, Outer Ring Fault, and Inner Ring Fault, and their arrangement and codes are demonstrated in Table 3.

Table 2. PU test rig parameters of operation.

No.	Angular velocity [rad/sec]	Torque of the Load [Nm]	Radial Load [N]
0	157.08	0.7	10^3
1	94.25	0.7	10^3
2	157.08	0.1	10^3
3	157.08	0.7	$4 * 10^2$

Table 3. PUA dataset composition.

Bearing type and class	Bearing letter and code
Healthy	[K]: 001-006
Outer Ring Fault	[KA]: 01, 03, 05, 06, 07, 08, 09
Inner Ring Fault	[KI]: 01, 03, 05, 07, 08

The PUR dataset includes 14 bearings with accelerated lifetime faults inflicted by a specially developed machine, imitating natural fault infliction with the extensive radial load. Damages appear as pitting or plastic deformations caused by debris and were categorized into three levels based on the affected area's length on the ring surface.

Bearings were classified as having outer ring fault, inner ring fault, or both. Rolling elements remained intact. PUR dataset arrangement with bearing codes is presented in Table 4.

Table 4. PUR dataset composition.

Bearing type and class	Bearing letter and code
Healthy	[K]: 001-006
Outer Ring Fault	[KA]: 04, 15, 16, 22, 30
Inner Ring Fault	[KI]: 04, 14, 16, 17, 18, 21
Outer + Inner Ring Fault	[KB]: 23, 24, 27

The data obtained from Case Western Reserve University (CWRU) was collected from an experimental setup with a two-horsepower motor, accelerometers, one SKF6205 bearing positioned at the drive end and another installed at the fan end, and a device for measuring rotational force. Vibrations were recorded at 12000 and 48000 samples per second via a 16-channel DAT recorder. Faults were seeded on the following bearing parts: the inner race, the outer race, and the ball using spark erosion tool. The faults ranged in diameter from 0.007 inches to 0.040 inches and were positioned at three o'clock, six o'clock, and 12 o'clock. The data were digitized at a rate of 12000 samples per second and divided into one-second segments, resulting in a dataset with dimensions of 1920 × 12000. The arrangement of CWRU data is shown in Table 5.

Table 5. CWRU dataset composition.

Class names	Bearing identification number
Healthy	97-100
Outer Ring Fault	130-133, 144-147, 156-160, 197-200, 234-237, 246-249, 258-261
Inner Ring Fault	056-059, 105-108, 169-172, 209-212
Ball Damage	048-051, 118-121, 185-188, 222-225

5 Performance Evaluation and Discussion

The proposed method constitutes only a portion of the bearing fault diagnosis framework. However, to evaluate its effectiveness for fault diagnosis through comparative analysis, two complete fault diagnosis frameworks were constructed. The structure of these frameworks is illustrated in Fig. 3. Signal processing and feature extraction stages were established based on the description in Sect. 3. The only discrepancies between the two frameworks lie in the feature engineering stage, specifically in the way the vibration signal is processed after envelope analysis. The framework highlighted in red employs the proposed WPT with node-specific base selection, while the framework highlighted in blue uses the standard WPT. The white elements are identical for both frameworks. To ensure the validity of the comparison, three feature selection approaches were employed. The first approach utilizes the entire feature vector obtained after feature selection, the second approach utilizes Principal Component Analysis to reduce dimensionality by employing a linear combination of original features, and the third approach is a wrapper-based Boruta method that selects features based on their importance score for the Random Forest model. After feature selection, the data is randomly divided, leaving 80% of the data for training and 20% for testing. The 80% chunk is used for training of the k-NN model, and the performance of the trained model is validated using k-fold cross-validation. K-NN model is selected due to its low computational expensiveness and its instance-based nature. It is a non-parametric algorithm that refrains from making any presumptions about the inherent data distribution. Instead, its method of classification involves assessing new instances by contrasting them against the labeled instances present in the training data. Its performance heavily relies on the quality of the features. If the feature space is not well-defined or if irrelevant features are included, the algorithm may not perform well, which means that the quality of the feature set can be fairly assessed by the k-NN performance.

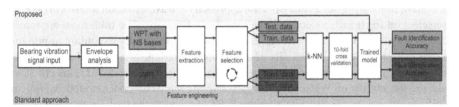

Fig. 3. Bearing fault diagnosis framework for performance comparison.

This bearing diagnosis framework underwent testing on three datasets, and Table 6 presents the accuracy of fault identification for each dataset individually, as well as the average performance across all three datasets. By testing the proposed feature extraction method combined with various feature selection methods, it can be concluded that the suggested approach of WPT node-specific base selection produces signal representations that enhance the performance of fault diagnosis frameworks employing traditional statistical feature extraction and selection techniques, as well as conventional Machine Learning models.

Table 6. Fault identification accuracy comparison.

WPT type	Feature Selection	PU (art) Acc. %	PU (real) Acc. %	CWRU Acc. %	Avg. Acc. % all datasets
Proposed	PCA	90.97	98.43	87.76	**92.39 (+1.09)**
	Boruta 20 features	98.00	99.84	97.14	**98.33 (+1.78)**
	Boruta 10 features	96.61	99.69	96.88	**97.73 (+3.17)**
	Boruta 5 features	96.70	99.68	95.05	**97.14 (+2.96)**
	None	93.40	98.75	94.53	**95.56 (+1.24)**
Standard	PCA	90.02	98.44	85.42	**91.29**
	Boruta 20 features	96.35	100.00	93.29	**96.55**
	Boruta 10 features	96.18	100.00	87.50	**94.56**
	Boruta 5 features	94.96	99.84	87.76	**94.19**
	None	91.84	99.45	91.67	**94.32**

6   Conclusions

The current study proposes a node-specific approach for wavelet packet transform (WPT) base selection for feature selection in bearing fault diagnosis. The traditional approach focuses on a single WPT node with high signal energy, potentially excluding important features present in other nodes. To address this limitation, a criterion based on the energy-entropy ratio of the signal spectrum for each node was introduced. This criterion evaluates the ability of WPT bases to generate signals with concentrated energy in specific frequency bands. By selecting the WPT bases with the highest criterion score, our method ensures the preservation of meaningful components and their distinction from noise. Upon the evaluation using three bearing fault datasets, it was found that on average across three datasets, the proposed method outperforms the traditional approach in fault diagnosis performance.

Our approach provides several benefits, including a comprehensive representation of the signal, explicable diagnostic procedures, and low computational cost. Nevertheless, it's crucial to acknowledge that while our suggested technique has its roots in the Wavelet Packet Transform (WPT), it does not adhere to certain fundamental properties of wavelet decomposition, such as energy conservation and superposition. Thus, it's inappropriate to label it as an advanced WPT technique. Nonetheless, our proposed method remains a valuable tool for feature extraction, leveraging well-founded mathematical principles that underlie the applied signal manipulations, establishing a strong basis for its use. As a result, the extracted features offer valuable information about the signal, which can be applied in various applications including signal processing, classification, and pattern recognition. In conclusion, our node-specific approach improves the accuracy and reliability of bearing fault diagnosis by enhancing feature extraction capabilities. Future work can focus on optimizing the criterion and exploring its applicability to other signal analysis tasks as long as performing more tests with the Deep Learning models.

Acknowledgements. This work was supported by the Technology Innovation Program (20023566, Development and Demonstration of Industrial IoT and AI Based Process Facility Intelligence Support System in Small and Medium Manufacturing Sites) funded by the Ministry of Trade, Industry & Energy (MOTIE, Korea). This work was also supported by the Technology Infrastructure Program funded by the Ministry of SMEs and Startups (MSS, Korea).

References

1. Bazurto, A.J., Quispe, E.C., Mendoza, R.C.: Causes and failures classification of industrial electric motor. In: 2016 IEEE ANDESCON, pp. 1–4. IEEE, Arequipa, Peru (2016)
2. Smith, W.A., Randall, R.B.: Rolling element bearing diagnostics using the Case Western Reserve University data: a benchmark study. Mech. Syst. Signal Process. **64–65**, 100–131 (2015)
3. Chen, L., Xu, G., Tao, T., Wu, Q.: Deep Residual network for identifying bearing fault location and fault severity concurrently. IEEE Access **8**, 168026–168035 (2020)
4. Skora, M., Ewert, P., Kowalski, C.T.: Selected rolling bearing fault diagnostic methods in wheel embedded permanent magnet brushless direct current motors. Energies **12**(21), 4212 (2019)
5. Maliuk, A.S., Prosvirin, A.E., Ahmad, Z., Kim, C.H., Kim, J.M.: Novel bearing fault diagnosis using Gaussian mixture model-based fault band selection. Sensors **21**(19), 6579 (2021)
6. Maliuk, A.S., Ahmad, Z., Kim, J.M.: Hybrid feature selection framework for bearing fault diagnosis based on Wrapper-WPT. Machines **10**(12), 1204 (2022)
7. Pham, M.T., Kim, J.M., Kim, C.H.: Accurate bearing fault diagnosis under variable shaft speed using convolutional neural networks and vibration spectrogram. Appl. Sci. **10**(18), 6385 (2020)
8. Ke, Z., Di, C., Bao, X.: Adaptive suppression of mode mixing in CEEMD based on genetic algorithm for motor bearing fault diagnosis. IEEE Trans. Magn. **58**(2), 1–6 (2022)
9. Lei, Y., Lin, J., He, Z., Zuo, M.J.: A review on empirical mode decomposition in fault diagnosis of rotating machinery. Mech. Syst. Signal Process. **35**(1–2), 108–126 (2013)
10. Lessmeier, C., Kimotho, J.K., Zimmer, D., Sextro, W.: Condition monitoring of bearing damage in electromechanical drive systems by using motor current signals of electric motors: a benchmark data set for data-driven classification, p. 17 (2016)
11. "Welcome to the Case Western Reserve University Bearing Data Center Website|Case School of Engineering|Case Western Reserve University," Case School of Engineering, 10 August 2021. https://engineering.case.edu/bearingdatacenter/welcome. Accessed 20 Oct 2022

A Study on Improving ALBERT with Additive Attention for Text Classification

Zepeng Zhang, Hua Chen$^{(\boxtimes)}$, Jiagui Xiong, Jiayu Hu, and Wenlong Ni

Jiangxi Normal University, Nanchang 330022, Jiangxi, China
{gottenzzp,hua.chen,jiaguixiong,jyhu,wni}@jxnu.edu.cn

Abstract. The Transformer has made significant advances in various fields, but high computational costs and lengthy training times pose challenges for models based on this architecture. To address this issue, we propose an improved ALBERT-based model, which replaces ALBERT's self-attention mechanism with an additive attention mechanism. This modification can reduce computational complexity and enhance the model's flexibility. We compare our proposed model with other Transformer-based models, demonstrating that it achieves a lower parameter count and significantly reduces computational complexity. Through extensive evaluations on diverse datasets, we establish the superior efficiency of our proposed model over alternative ones. With its reduced parameter count, our proposed model emerges as a promising approach to enhance the efficiency and practicality of Transformer-based models. Notably, it enables practical training under resource and time limitations, highlighting its adaptability and versatility in real-world scenarios.

Keywords: Additive attention · ALBERT · Fastformer · NLP · Text classification

1 Introduction

Since the emergence of the Transformer architecture [1], it has garnered significant achievements across multiple domains. Models such as BERT [2], GPT [3–5], built upon this architecture, have become the standard benchmarks for numerous tasks in Natural Language Processing (NLP) and exhibited commendable performance. Before the advent of the Transformer, traditional structures such as Recurrent Neural Networks (RNNs) [6] and Convolutional Neural Networks (CNNs) [7] were widely used in NLP but suffered from issues like information loss and long-term dependencies. In contrast, the Transformer adopts an attention mechanism to concurrently process elements within a sequence, avoiding these issues and enabling better representation learning through pre-training. Besides NLP, researchers are increasingly exploring its applications in other fields, such as Computer Vision. For instance, Vision Transformer (ViT) [8] processes input image blocks as sequential data and has achieved impressive performance in diverse image classification tasks. Similarly, the DETR model [9] leverages the Transformer architecture for object detection tasks, outperforming traditional approaches

H. Lu et al. (Eds.): ACPR 2023, LNCS 14407, pp. 192–202, 2023.
https://doi.org/10.1007/978-3-031-47637-2_15

in accuracy. Additionally, the DALL-E model [10] excels at generating images from textual descriptions, while the Transformer-based Temporal Modeling (TTM) method effectively handles temporal and spatial information in video sequences.

Although models based on the Transformer architecture have achieved impressive results, the dot-product attention in their architecture requires matrix multiplication operations between two matrices $Q^{N \times d}$ and $\left(K^T\right)^{d \times N}$ (where N is the sequence length and d is the feature dimension) for similarity calculations, resulting in a complexity of $O\left(N^2 \cdot d\right)$. This leads to two significant issues: 1. High resource consumption during training; 2. Long training time. Without adequate GPU or TPU resources, it becomes challenging to train an effective model quickly or within limited computing resources, constraining low-resource researchers or companies from pursuing related tasks. To address these problems, researchers have proposed some solutions. For instance, DistBERT [11] employs knowledge distillation to learn from a teacher model, thereby reducing training time. Longformer [12], conversely, enhances the attention mechanism by utilizing local attention, specifically a sliding window mechanism, to compute attention between each word. This approach effectively reduces the time complexity associated with the traditional Transformer's dot-product attention, subsequently shortening the model's training time. While these methods have somewhat expedited training, the resources and time required remain prohibitive for many people.

In this paper, we propose an improved ALBERT [13] based model that replaces ALBERT's self-attention mechanism with an additive attention mechanism. This change achieves a linear reduction in time complexity and significantly reduces the model's parameter count by transitioning from dot product attention to additive attention. We conduct experiments on two text classification datasets to evaluate our model's performance. The results demonstrate that the proposed model outperforms several other models in terms of computational complexity and inference speed. The main contributions of this paper are: 1) proposing an improved ALBERT-based model that incorporates additive attention, reducing computational complexity and enhancing model flexibility; 2) conducting experiments on two text classification datasets, showcasing our model's strong competitiveness.

The rest of this paper is organized as follows: Sect. 2 reviews some related works. Section 3 provides a detailed introduction to our proposed approach. Experiments highlighting the merits of our approach are presented in Sect. 4. Section 5 concludes the paper and discusses future work.

2 Related Work

2.1 Efficient Transformer-Based Models

The Transformer architecture is known for its high time complexity and vast number of parameters, demanding considerable computational resources during training. To address this challenge, several approaches have been proposed to reduce the training time and resource requirements of Transformers. For instance, the Reformer model [14] groups attention scores with similar values into the same bucket, thereby reducing time complexity. Likewise, the Sparse-Transformer [15] divides the input text into fixed-length blocks and limits attention computations to these blocks, effectively diminishing the number of attention operations and further cutting down time complexity. Recently, the BigBird model [16] was introduced to address the computational challenges associated with processing long sequences. By employing a hierarchical block sparse attention mechanism that merges global attention with block-level random attention, BigBird significantly curtails the computational resources needed for processing long sequences.

2.2 ALBERT Model

ALBERT is a variation of BERT that introduces three significant improvements over the original BERT model:

1. ALBERT shares weight parameters across all layers of the model, leading to a reduction in the model's parameter count.
2. ALBERT effectively addresses the interdependency between the word embedding vector's dimension E and the hidden layer size H through factorization. This substantially reduces the model's parameter count, especially when $E \ll H$.
3. The Next Sentence Prediction (NSP) task in BERT has been found ineffective, leading to its removal from the model. Instead, the Sentence-Order Prediction (SOP) loss is used for training, resulting in improved performance in natural language processing tasks.

Benefiting from these improvements, ALBERT retains the same hyperparameter settings as BERT but has substantially fewer parameters—reducing from 108M in BERT to just 12M in ALBERT. Moreover, ALBERT's training speed is 1.7 times faster than that of BERT.

2.3 Self-attention and Additive-Attention Mechanism

The self-attention mechanism is a fundamental computational module of the Transformer architecture, allowing the model to capture contextual dependencies and calculate attention weights for contextual representations. Partitioning the self-attention mechanism into multiple heads enables the model to capture diverse types of contextual relationships. The main equations are shown below:

$$head_i = Attention(Q_i, K_i, V_i) = softmax\left(\frac{QW_i^Q \left(KW_i^K\right)^T}{\sqrt{d}}\right) VW_i^V \qquad (1)$$

$$MultiHead(Q, K, V) = Concat(head_i, \ldots, head_s)W^O \qquad (2)$$

where $W_i^Q, W_i^K, W_i^V \in \mathbb{R}^{d \times d}$ is the learnable parameter matrix and W^O is a fully connected linear matrix. Q, K, V $\in \mathbb{R}^{N \times d}$ is the Query, Key and Value matrix for multiplying the input sequence X with W^Q, W^K, W^V. N is the sequence length and d is the hidden layer dimension.

The Fastformer [17] architecture incorporates the additive attention mechanism as its main computational module, building upon the self-attention mechanism of the Transformer. It first aggregates the query sequences into a global query vector and models their interaction with attention keywords using elementwise products. Next, it employs additive attention to aggregate the keywords into a global keyword vector and model their interaction with attention values. Linear transformations are then applied to learn the context-aware attention values added to the attention queries to generate the final output. This approach reduces the time complexity of attention computation from in the Transformer to linear complexity, significantly accelerating the training speed of the model.

3   Method

The overall framework of the proposed method is illustrated in Fig. 1. The key modification involves replacing the additive attention mechanism with the self-attention mechanism within the ALBERT model. This substitution results in improved computational speed for the whole framework.

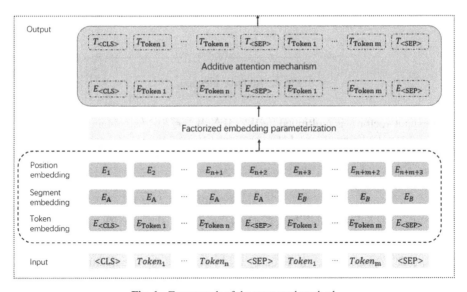

Fig. 1. Framework of the proposed method.

3.1   Overview and Procedure

First, we define the input sequence as $T \in \mathbb{R}^N$, where N represents the number of tokens. Then, we perform word embedding on the sequence to obtain $E \in \mathbb{R}^{N \times ed}$, where N is the length of the input sequence and ed is the word embedding dimension. We also add positional embedding and sentence embedding vectors. Next, the sequence is projected into $E \in \mathbb{R}^{N \times d}$ using factorization in ALBERT, where d represents the hidden layer dimension. Specifically, E is represented as $E = [e_1, e_2, \ldots, e_N]$. Finally, the sequence E is processed using additive attention to compute the interactions between contexts and obtain feature vectors with contextual information. One of the computation graphs for additive attention is shown in Fig. 2.

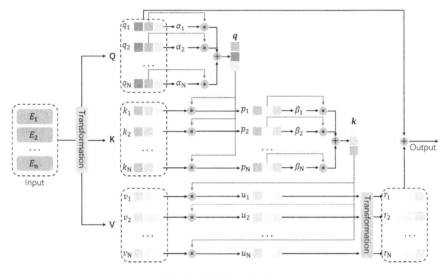

Fig. 2. Additive attention.

The input vector E is multiplied by $W^Q, W^K, W^V \in \mathbb{R}^{d \times d}$ to obtain three matrices Q, K, V. By calculating the global query and key vectors and engaging in additive attention with the value, the final output is obtained. The computation is defined as follows:

$$q = \sum_{i=1}^{N} \alpha_i q_i = \sum_{i=1}^{N} \frac{\exp\left(W_q^T q_i / \sqrt{d}\right)}{\sum_{j=1}^{N} \exp\left(W_q^T q_j / \sqrt{d}\right)} q_i \qquad (3)$$

where $q \in \mathbb{R}^d$ represents the global query vector obtained through additive attention to the q matrix, α_i denotes the attention weight for the i_{th} q vector, and $w_q \in \mathbb{R}^d$ is the learnable parameter vector.

$$k = \sum_{i=1}^{N} \beta_i p_i = \sum_{i=1}^{N} \frac{\exp\left(W_k^T p_i / \sqrt{d}\right)}{\sum_{j=1}^{N} \exp\left(W_k^T p_j / \sqrt{d}\right)} p_i \qquad (4)$$

Since the interaction between the global q vector and each k_i needs to be modeled, $p_i = q * k_i$ is computed through element-wise multiplication. The k matrix, encapsulating the global context, is obtained using the additive attention mechanism. The global $k \in \mathbb{R}^d$ vector is defined as in the equation above, and $w_k \in \mathbb{R}^d$ represents a learnable parameter vector. Similarly, the global key and each value vector are multiplied between elements to compute the vector of key-value interactions $u_i = k * v_i$. The resulting vectors are passed through a linear transformation layer to learn the hidden representations.

3.2 Parameter and Computational Complexity Analysis

In this section, we analyze the computational complexity of our model. In Transformer-based models, the self-attention mechanism is standard, and the complexity of calculating attention weights in self-attention is $O(N^2 \cdot d)$. Conversely, the time and space requirements for learning global query vectors and key vectors in additive attention networks are $O(N \cdot d)$, and the time and space costs of element-wise multiplication are also $O(N \cdot d)$.

In addition, the total number of parameters for additive attention networks and element-wise multiplication is $2hd$, where h is the number of attention heads. At last, we can obtain the parameter size of each layer in our model as $3d^2 + 2hd$ (the sum of the parameters of the two weight matrices W^Q, W^K is $2d^2$; the parameter size of the output transformation matrix is d^2; and adding the $2hd$ mentioned above, the parameter size of each layer is $3d^2 + 2hd$). Moreover, because we use weight sharing for all layers of the model, the total parameter size of our model can also be approximated as $3d^2 + 2hd$, which is fewer parameters compared to the Transformer model that has at least $4d^2$ parameters per layer (encompassing the three weight matrices W^Q, W^K, W^V, the output transformation matrix; excluding bias terms and layer normalization). In conclusion, these analytical results underscore the theoretical efficiency of the method proposed in this paper.

4 Experiments

4.1 Experimental Setup

Our training was conducted on an NVIDIA RTX3090 graphics card, boasting 24 GB of video memory. The system operated on a Windows 10 64-bit platform, with Python version 3.7 and PyTorch version 1.10.1.

We initialized the embedding matrix of our models using Glove [18] word embeddings. This approach allowed us to harness pre-trained word representations, facilitating the capture of intricate semantic relationships within our dataset. To ensure consistent and reliable results across experiments, we set the random seed to 2023. Moreover, each experiment was conducted three times to account for potential variability, with the average performance being reported.

Throughout the training process, we maintained a consistent batch size of 64 for all models. This size indicates the number of training examples processed during each neural network training iteration. For optimization, we chose the AdamW optimizer, renowned for its efficacy in refining deep neural networks. The specific parameters of our hyperparameter settings are detailed in Table 1.

Baselines. We selected four models as our baselines:

Table 1. Hyperparameter setting.

Method	IMDB	Sentiment140
Encoder layer	12	12
Decoder layer	–	–
Window size (Longformer, Bigbird)	8	16
Block length (Bigbird)	4	8
Attention head	12	12
Maximum text length	512	512
Hidden dimension	768	768
Loss	Crossentropy	Crossentropy
Batch size	64	64
Optimizer	AdamW	AdamW
Learning rate	1e−4	1e−4
Epochs	3	3
Dropout	0.1	0.1

Longformer. The Longformer model, a pre-trained language model built on the Transformer architecture, excels in handling lengthy texts. It distinguishes itself from conventional Transformer models by incorporating a novel attention mechanism known as sliding window attention. This mechanism enables the Longformer to sustain high computational efficiency while processing long texts. Furthermore, the Longformer model introduces a new position encoding method called global attention mask. This enables the model to have a more comprehensive understanding of the context in long texts.

Bigbird. The BigBird model is also a pre-trained language model based on the Transformer architecture, which is designed to handle even longer texts than the Longformer model. It introduces a novel sparse attention mechanism that enables the model to focus on a small subset of input tokens during each step while effectively capturing global dependencies across the entire input sequence. Moreover, the BigBird model incorporates a novel position encoding technique known as random attention spans, enhancing its proficiency in handling long texts.

DistilBERT. DistilBERT is an optimized and streamlined version developed from the BERT model. It achieves a more petite model size and faster inference speed through distillation. This approach involves training a compact model to mimic the behavior and knowledge of a larger model. By distilling the essential information from the larger model, DistilBERT retains comparable language understanding capabilities while significantly reducing computational requirements.

ALBERT. ALBERT is based on a simplified version of the BERT model, which addresses the issue of model size and computational efficiency by utilizing parameter sharing and weight matrix factorization techniques. ALBERT maintains the effectiveness of BERT while significantly reducing its size and improving processing speed. This makes it a practical choice for various natural language processing tasks, providing a balance between performance and efficiency.

4.2 Datasets and Evaluation Methodology

To evaluate the performance of our model, we carried out experiments on two text classification datasets: IMDB [19] and Sentiment140 [20]. The IMDB dataset focuses on movie rating prediction, whereas the Sentiment140 dataset is made up of 16,000 English tweets, each categorized as positive, negative, or neutral. This dataset is extensively used for training and evaluating sentiment analysis models. The detailed information of these datasets is showcased in Table 2.

Table 2. Datasets for Text Classification.

Dataset	Train	Val	Test	Avg. len	Class
IMDB	25k	12.5k	12.5k	98.3	2
Sent.140	128.8k	16.1k	16.1k	505.4	2

The reasons for choosing these two datasets are as follows. The IMDB dataset contains short text samples, while the Sentiment140 dataset comprises long text samples. This allows us to evaluate the model's performance on both short and long texts separately.

For text classification, accuracy and the F1 score stand out as pivotal metrics of evaluation. These metrics can be calculated using formulas 5−8, where TP (True Positive) represents correctly predicting positive samples, TN (True Negative) represents correctly predicting negative samples, FP (False Positive) represents incorrectly predicting negative samples as positive, and FN (False Negative) represents incorrectly predicting positive samples as negative. Precision and recall, calculated as

$$Accuracy = \frac{TP + TN}{TP + TN + FP + FN} \tag{5}$$

$$Precision = \frac{TP}{TP + FP} \tag{6}$$

$$Recall = \frac{TP}{TP + FN} \tag{7}$$

The F1-score is computed using accuracy and recall rates, as illustrated in the subsequent formula:

$$F1 = 2\frac{Precision \times Recall}{Precision + Recall} \tag{8}$$

4.3   Comparison of Parameter Numbers and Inference Speed

Table 3 provides a comparison of parameter counts and inference speeds across different models. From the table, it's clear that our model stands out in terms of complexity, parameter counts, and inference speed. Remarkably, our proposed model boasts an impressive 109.7% enhancement in inference speed when pitted against the ALBERT model, eclipsing other models with an acceleration surpassing 222.1%. Furthermore, when juxtaposed with alternative models, our model's complexity remains linear, translating to faster training times and augmented efficiency.

Table 3. The comparison of parameter numbers and inference speed for different models.

Method	Complexity	Parameter numbers	Inference speed
Longformer	$O(N \cdot k \cdot d)$	110M	5.405
Bigbird	$O(N \cdot k \cdot d)$	137M	3.823
DistilBERT	$O\left(N^2 \cdot d\right)$	66M	1.475
ALBERT	$O\left(N^2 \cdot d\right)$	12M	3.520
Our proposed approach	$O(N \cdot d)$	9.5M	1.678

4.4   Experimental Results

Table 4. Experimental results of various models.

Method	IMDB		Sentiment140	
	Accuracy	F1	Accuracy	F1
Longformer	0.850	0.850	0.781	0.781
Bigbird	0.843	0.842	0.783	0.783
DistilBERT	0.847	0.846	0.792	0.792
ALBERT	0.881	0.880	0.839	0.838
Our proposed approach	0.852	0.851	0.825	0.824

As illustrated in Table 4, our proposed approach showcases exemplary performance on both short and long text datasets. Moreover, as indicated in Table 3, our method registers only a slight performance decrement, approximately 1.7%, when compared to ALBERT. Yet, it marks a notable surge of 109.7% in inference speed. These findings underscore the significant benefits of our proposed method, particularly with its incorporation of additive attention, especially in terms of inference speed.

5   Conclusions and Future Work

In this paper, we present an improved ALBERT-based model that replaces ALBERT's self-attention mechanism with additive attention. This additive attention transforms the query matrix into a global query vector. This vector then collaborates with each key vector to generate a global key vector enriched with contextual information. Using the additive attention mechanism, this global key vector interacts with all value vectors, leading to the derivation of the final global attention value. The output from this last attention layer is achieved by melding it with the query matrix using residual concatenation. Our experiments, conducted on two distinct text classification datasets, indicate that our proposed model demands considerably fewer training resources than most Transformer-based counterparts, translating into expedited training durations.

In the future, we plan to pre-train the proposed model to ensure more nuanced context modeling. Additionally, we also envisage integrating a decoder component to fortify tasks related to extended sequence text generation.

References

1. Vaswani, A., et al.: Attention is all you need. In: Advances in Neural Information Processing Systems, vol. 30 (2017)
2. Devlin, J., Chang, M.W., Lee, K., Toutanova, K.: BERT: pre-training of deep bidirectional transformers for language understanding. arXiv preprint arXiv:1810.04805 (2018)
3. Radford, A., Narasimhan, K., Salimans, T., Sutskever, I.: Improving language understanding by generative pre-training (2018)
4. Radford, A., Wu, J., Child, R., Luan, D., Amodei, D., Sutskever, I.: Language models are unsupervised multitask learners. OpenAI Blog **1**(8), 9 (2019)
5. Brown, T.: Language models are few-shot learners. In: Advances in Neural Information Processing Systems, vol. 33, pp. 1877–1901 (2020)
6. Zaremba, W., Sutskever, I., Vinyals, O.: Recurrent neural network regularization. arXiv preprint arXiv:1409.2329 (2014)
7. Kim, Y.: Convolutional neural networks for sentence classification. arXiv preprint arXiv: 1408.5882 (2014)
8. Dosovitskiy, A., et al.: An image is worth 16×16 words: transformers for image recognition at scale. arXiv preprint arXiv:2010.11929 (2020)
9. Carion, Nicolas, Massa, Francisco, Synnaeve, Gabriel, Usunier, Nicolas, Kirillov, Alexander, Zagoruyko, Sergey: End-to-end object detection with transformers. In: Vedaldi, Andrea, Bischof, Horst, Brox, Thomas, Frahm, Jan-Michael. (eds.) ECCV 2020. LNCS, vol. 12346, pp. 213–229. Springer, Cham (2020). https://doi.org/10.1007/978-3-030-58452-8_13
10. Ramesh, A., Dhariwal, P., Nichol, A., Chu, C., Chen, M.: Hierarchical text-conditional image generation with clip latents. arXiv preprint arXiv:2204.06125 (2022)
11. Sanh, V., Debut, L., Chaumond, J., Wolf, T.: DistilBERT, a distilled version of BERT: smaller, faster, cheaper and lighter. arXiv preprint arXiv:1910.01108 (2019)
12. Beltagy, I., Peters, M.E., Cohan, A.: Longformer: the long-document transformer. arXiv preprint arXiv:2004.05150 (2020)
13. Lan, Z., Chen, M., Goodman, S., Gimpel, K., Sharma, P., Soricut, R.: ALBERT: a lite BERT for self-supervised learning of language representations. arXiv preprint arXiv:1909.11942 (2019)

14. Kitaev, N., Kaiser, Ł., Levskaya, A.: Reformer: the efficient transformer. arXiv preprint arXiv: 2001.04451 (2020)
15. Zhao, G., Lin, J., Zhang, Z., Ren, X., Sun, X.: Sparse transformer: concentrated attention through explicit selection (2019)
16. Zaheer, M., et al.: Big bird: transformers for longer sequences. Adv. Neural. Inf. Process. Syst. **33**, 17283–17297 (2020)
17. Wu, C., Wu, F., Qi, T., Huang, Y., Xie, X.: Fastformer: additive attention can be all you need. arXiv preprint arXiv:2108.09084 (2021)
18. Pennington, J., Socher, R., Manning, C.D.: Glove: global vectors for word representation. In: Proceedings of the 2014 Conference on Empirical Methods in Natural Language Processing (EMNLP), pp. 1532–1543, October 2014
19. Maas, A., Daly, R.E., Pham, P.T., Huang, D., Ng, A.Y., Potts, C.: Learning word vectors for sentiment analysis. In: Proceedings of the 49th Annual Meeting of the Association for Computational Linguistics: Human Language Technologies, pp. 142–150 (2011)
20. Go, A., Bhayani, R., Huang, L.: Twitter sentiment classification using distant supervision. CS224N project report, Stanford, 1(12) (2009)

Dual Branch Fusion Network for Pathological Image Classification with Extreme Different Image Size

Shilong Song, Zhengyun Feng, Mingwei Chen, Xinjun Bian, Jiale Chen, Siyang Feng, and Xipeng Pan[✉]

Guilin University of Electronic Technology, Guilin, China
pxp201@guet.edu.cn

Abstract. Pathological image classification is a hot research topic in computer vision. Accurate classification of pathological images plays a vital role in disease diagnosis and prognosis prediction. However, the size of pathological images varies greatly, which brings great challenges to AI-assisted diagnosis. Convolutional Neural Network (CNN) has been widely used in pathological image classification tasks and achieved good results. However, it is difficult for CNN to handle images that are too large in size, it needs to compress excessively large pathological images, which will bring the loss of image information. To address these issues, we proposed a two-branch fusion model, named BiFusionNet, which combines CNN and Graph Neural Network (GNN). In the CNN branch, we employ the Densenet201 network to extract the feature of pathological images. For the GNN branch, we used PNA as the graph neural network, and the pathological images were processed into the graph data structure, and then input into the three-layer graph neural network layer to extract the graph feature. Finally, the convolutional feature and the graph feature were fused to realize a more accurate classification of pathological images. In order to make the two branches complement each other, Focal loss was added to the GNN branch based on Cross Entropy Loss, and the samples, which were difficult to classify, were set to higher weights. Our model achieved the supreme classification performance of 67.03% $\pm$ 2.04% on breast cancer dataset BRACS, and the best classification performance was 97.33% $\pm$ 1.25% in the CRA dataset of rectal cancer.

Keywords: Pathological image classification · H&E stain · Graph neural network · Dual branch fusion

1 Introduction

When we hear about pathological diagnosis, we use tools like microscopes to look at tissue slices of the body to determine the type of cancer. In recent years, digital pathology technology has been widely used. It uses a scanner to capture the entire slide image and stores it as a digital image. Pathological images classification is one of the research hotspots in Computer Vision and Deep Learning. Pathological images are the images of tissue sections taken during medical examination, which usually take pathologists with highly specialized medical knowledge and skills to evaluate it accurately. However, manual evaluation is time-consuming, laborious, and easily affected by subjective factors [1, 2]. Direct classification of pathological images using traditional computer vision methods presents several problems. One significant issue is the large size variability of the images, which can lead to information loss and low classification accuracy when directly compressed. In the previous pathological image analysis, manual features such as fractal features, morphological features, and texture features were generally extracted to classify tumor or normal tissue. But in recent years, with the development of Deep Learning algorithms, CNN has been widely used in pathological image classification tasks and achieved good results. However, due to the CNN has certain restrictions for image size, when the size of the input pathological images is inconsistent, it's challenging to get a good classification effect in images of different sizes, and the compression of large-size images will lead to the severe loss of image information. GNNs have the ability to process input images of different sizes, which mainly benefits from the characteristics of the graph itself. Therefore, GNNs show unique advantages in this challenging problem. Although using the graph method can achieve a performance improvement, the classification results still need to be optimized.

To address these issues, we propose a pathological image classification network based on double-branch fusion. By integrating the respective advantages of CNN and GNN in data representation, the network can effectively address the problems of large-size differences in pathological image classification, so as to improve the classification performance of the model. One branch uses CNN architecture, pathological data of different sizes are processed into images of the same size, but the lost information in the compression process limits the performance of the model; in order to further improve classified performance, another branch uses GNN, pathological images are cut into fixed size image blocks, and every image block is used as a node to construct a graph, this graph maintains the structure of the original pathological image, to a certain extent, it compensates for the information loss by CNN due to image compression. By fusing the two branches, the information is complementary, and more accurate classification results are obtained.

The model was tested on pathological images datasets of breast cancer and colorectal cancer, the results showed that compared with CNN or GNN individually, the two-branch fusion method showed better performance and robustness in solving problems of large-size differences, and it had the potential for practical clinical application. Therefore, the two-branch fusion network proposed in this paper provides a new idea and method for the research and practice in the field of pathological image classification, and also has an important application value.

2 Method

Figure 1 shows the dual-channel hybrid model composed of GNN and CNN proposed in this paper, compared with the single-branch GNN or CNN, the hybrid model has a stronger classification performance. Pathological images of different sizes are compressed and represented as graph data and sent to the network at the same time. Finally, the training and updating of the whole model parameters are completed at two Loss Functions. In this paper, for the GNN layer, PNA is selected as the node information update operation of each layer and the CNN branch uses Densenet201 [3].

In the GNN layer, PNA is used in this paper, and the form of information aggregation is shown in Fig. 2. In the hybrid model in two branches, the GNN branch contains three layers. Since this is a graph-level classification task, in order to extract the graph-level Embedding, the Readout operation is carried out. As shown in Eq. (1), *hi* is each layer GNN output, *Concat* is to concatenate each neural network layer of each graph node in length, average all the nodes' final representation, and finally obtain the image-level representation.

$$Embedding = Mean(Concat\,[hi, i \in \{1, 2, 3\}])   \tag{1}$$

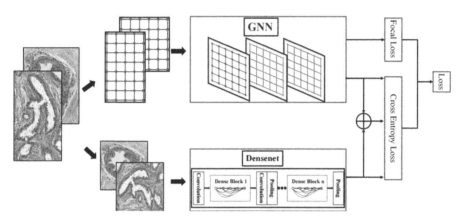

Fig. 1. General block diagram of two-branch fusion model (BiFusionNet).

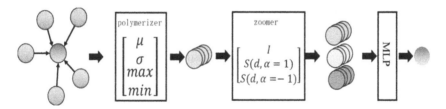

Fig. 2. PNA aggregation neighborhood information diagram.

In the network training, we use Focal loss and Cross Entropy Loss to punish the network and give different weight to the two Loss functions at the same time, as shown in Eq. (2), Floss is Focal loss, and *CEloss* is Cross Entropy Loss. Specifically in network training, in order to make GNN branch pay more attention to the learning of difficult samples, a higher weight is set for difficult samples in Focal loss.

$$Loss = CEloss + \alpha Floss   \tag{2}$$

In the branch of GNN, the construction of graph is very important. In this paper, the construction of complex Cell-tissue-graph [4] is abandoned, and the larger tissue area is selected as the node to represent the variable size pathological images as the graph. This method refers to the practice of Richard J. Chen et al. [5] who represented a full-section pathological image as a 2D point cloud, the ROI diagram of this paper is constructed. In the ROI graph, the pathological images are cut into small non-overlapping image blocks, the size of which is 96 × 96, this size takes into account the situation of small ROI regions. Each image block is regarded as a vertex, the vertex coordinates are the center coordinates of the image blocks, at the same time, the depth feature of the image block is extracted by using the pre-trained depth model on ImageNet as the initial feature of the node. Karen Simonyan et al. [6] in their paper showed that depth models pre-trained on large-scale image datasets can produce good feature representations, and these features can be generalized to other field image tasks. Therefore, these features extracted by the pre-training model used in this paper can represent the original images, and these features also have certain semantic information. Compared with directly using pixel features, it is more conducive to network training and optimization. The edge of the graph adopts the principle of adjacency is the relationship that exists, which connects the image blocks and the neighbor's image blocks in contact with their edges, enabling message passing during forward propagation, as shown in Fig. 3. The near neighbor mode is an 8-near neighbor when the graph is constructed, and the deep feature extraction network uses the pre-training model EfficientNet [7], the initial feature length of the node is 1792. The red dot in the right picture of Fig. 3 corresponds to the graph node, and the black line corresponds to the edge between the nodes.

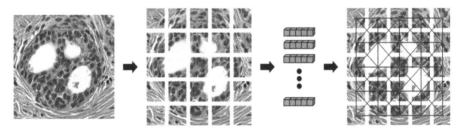

Fig. 3. ROI graph construction.

3   Experiments and Results

3.1   Datasets

The dataset mainly used in this paper is obtained from 325 H&E (hematoxylin, eosin) stained pathological sections from the National Cancer Research Center in Naples, Italy, the slices were digitized to use an Aperio AT2 scanner and their solution is 0.25 μm/pixel. This dataset contains a total of 4549 ROIs [8], multiple different types of ROIs may be derived from the same full-section pathological image (WSI), which is shown in Fig. 4.

The dataset included a total of seven categories, which were normal (N), benign (PB), common ductal hyperplasia (UDH), atypical ductal hyperplasia (ADH), flat epithelial dysplasia (FEA), ductal carcinoma in situ (DCIS), and invasive carcinoma (IC).

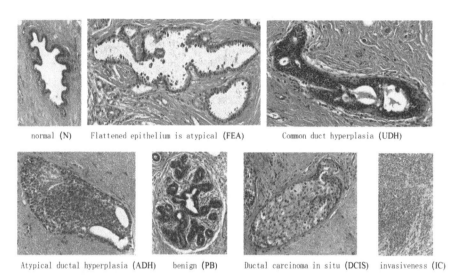

Fig. 4. Breast Cancer ROI example.

In the experiment of this paper, the challenges we face mainly come from the dataset itself, and the ROI mainly comes from the manual sketch, because in the real scene, different ROIs may have different sizes, and some sizes vary greatly, which is the most severe challenge in our experiment; Secondly, the color difference caused by staining and environment during section preparation; In addition, slight differences between classes and significant differences within classes also lead to low classification accuracy. This section presents the differences between the dataset in terms of their dimensions. The final data used in this paper followed the experimental design of HACT-Net [4] and filtered out the ROIs of extreme size. For details, see Table 1 and Fig. 5. In the table, the size of the images is H × W, the unit is megapixels, and the corresponding 95% confidence interval is also calculated. Among all the data, the maximum size of the image is as high as 49.19 megapixels, while the minimum size of the image is as low as 0.055 megapixels, and the ratio of extreme size is as high as 894.644, which is a vast difference; It can also be seen from the boxplot in the table, there are quite a few singular values for the size of each category, which will be a significant obstacle to accurate classification.

When the CNN models classified data, the images need to be reshaped to a fixed size. However, for images like Fig. 6, such operation will not only cause the loss of image information, but also face visual deformation. For example, as shown in Fig. 6, in the dataset, the H/W ratio will be up to 4 times, which will severely compress the image at height when reshaped to a fixed size. But even so, for most of the images, the classification accuracy on CNN is still considerable. In view of this, in the experimental design, CNN is still considered to be included in the design of model.

Table 1. BRACS datasets size statistics.

	train	val	test	all
Number of images	3643	312	566	4521
Size (Megapixel)	2.552 [0.407, 13.78]	2.677 [0.360, 18.348]	1.609 [0.268, 11.403]	2.410 [0.380, 13.80]
Max/Min size ratio	894.644	272.0466	709.124	894.644
Mix size	0.054984	0.108836	0.068493	0.054984
Max size	49.191158	29.608473	48.570084	49.191158

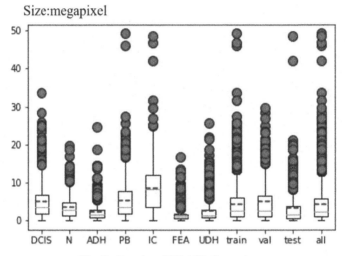

Fig. 5. Boxplot of BRACS dimensions.

3.2   Experimental Setting

In the initial training of the model, for the CNN branch, this experiment uses the model that is pre-trained on ImageNet and fine-tuned on BRACS dataset to initialize the CNN weight. The initial weight is chosen mainly because in the selection of basic model, the model is trained through a large number of experiments, and the model with the highest performance is selected as the CNN branch. While for the GNN branch, we choose the normal random initialization method. We use the Adam as the optimizer of network parameters, the initial learning rate is 10^{-5}, and the learning rate attenuation weight is 5×10^{-3}. For the network parameters, this experiment chooses to update all parameters without freezing some weights. In addition, for the weight of loss function, in weighted summation, Focal loss uses a higher weight of 2.5. At the same time, for Focal loss calculation, this experiment set a higher weight for benign (PB) and common catheter hyperplasia (UDH), while other categories use lower weights. Due to the GPU memory size, the Mini-batch is set to 16, different from the CNN network has a fixed size of data, in the GNN branch, the size of each Mini-batch is different, which mainly depends on

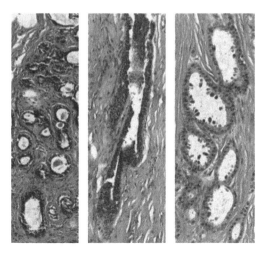

Fig. 6. Strip image example.

the size of the graph loaded currently. To prevent memory overflowing, we need reserve sufficient video memory space.

3.3 Experimental Results and Analysis

We make many experiments in this paper, firstly from the initial selection of the CNN model to GNN certainty, to the final adjustment of hyperparameters. As for the specific problems faced by the classification of pathological images, this paper tries to solve them from two angles. The first is to consider the transformation of pathological images from the perspective of graph representation, so as to ensure that the original spatial information and structure of pathological images are preserved as far as possible when input into the network; Secondly, from the perspective of CNN, most CNN models need the input of a fixed size, so this experiment simply and directly compressed pathological images, as shown in Fig. 7. Although many features are lost, the image itself is a carrier of information redundancy, so the performance achieved by CNN can still match many GNN, even surpass them. It is worth noting that CNN is easy to achieve good performance, but excessive compression also limits the upper limit of CNN, in this experiment, through repeated fine-tuning of CNN, the bottleneck still cannot be overcome. Ablation experiments were also conducted to demonstrate the contribution of each part to the performance, and the model was applied to other datasets to verify the performance of the model further.

Firstly, starting from the selection of the baseline model of CNN, Transformer [9] models are included. After the compression of images directly, they are sent to multiple networks, such as Mae_base, Densenet201, Inception_v4, Vgg19, etc. As shown in Table 2, all models are pre-training models trained on large-scale data, which can easily achieve better performance. However, up to now, there is no standard large-scale graph data, so it is not an excellent choice to load the pre-training model on the graph neural network, and some pre-training models are even worse than the performance of random initialization mode.

Table 2. Comparison of basic models

Model	Accuracy
Mae_base [10]	59.7%
Densenet201 [3]	**61%**
Inception_v4 [11]	57%
Resnet101e [12]	55%
Resnet50 [13]	54%
Vgg19 [6]	56%
Vit_large_patch16_224 [14]	44%
Vit_small_patch16_224 [14]	55%

Then, this paper compares the experimental results with some existing methods. For some methods, this experiment not only reports the results in the original text, but also reproduces some models, as shown in Table 3.

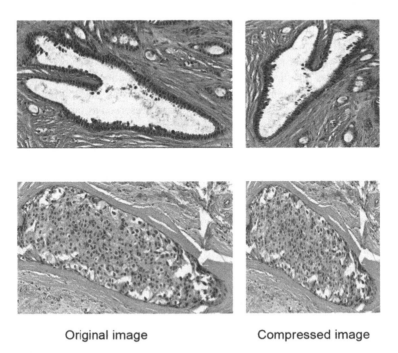

Original image   Compressed image

Fig. 7. Comparison of images before and after compression.

Table 3. Model performance comparison, the results are expressed in percentage, the mean value and standard deviation of F1-Score of each category are calculated, and the mean and standard deviation of the seven categories. src indicates the results of the original report.

Model	N	PB	UDH	ADH	FEA	DCIS	IC	WeightedF1-score
GNN	64.45 ± 4.11	33.09 ± 2.36	23.82 ± 10.49	19.85 ± 9.54	65.95 ± 3.07	50.56 ± 7.54	77.38 ± 2.43	47.85 ± 2.04
CGC-Net (src) [19]	30.83 ± 5.33	31.63 ± 4.66	17.33 ± 3.38	24.50 ± 5.24	58.97 ± 3.56	49.36 ± 3.41	75.30 ± 3.20	43.63 ± 0.51
HACT-Net (src) [8]	61.56 ± 2.15	47.49 ± 2.94	43.60 ± 1.86	40.42 ± 2.55	74.22 ± 1.41	**66.44 ± 2.57**	88.40 ± 0.19	61.53 ± 0.87
HACT-Net	67.14 ± 2.45	42.83 ± 1.71	33.45 ± 3.18	31.72 ± 3.35	68.48 ± 1.46	55.96 ± 4.54	78.93 ± 4.85	54.04 ± 1.61
TransPath (src) [15]	58.5 ± 2.5	43.1 ± 1.8	34.9 ± 5.2	38.3 ± 6.0	66.9 ± 0.8	61.4 ± 1.2	85.0 ± 1.4	56.7 ± 2.0
Ours (without focal loss)	70.97 ± 1.97	48.32 ± 4.43	43.30 ± 2.33	44.96 ± 2.72	76.59 ± 1.13	59.02 ± 1.56	92.08 ± 0.74	62.07 ± 1.50
Ours	**76.76 ± 1.38**	**68.51 ± 5.48**	**50.99 ± 3.15**	40.77 ± 4.58	**83.44 ± 2.38**	56.23 ± 1.35	**93.55 ± 2.00**	**67.03 ± 2.04**

In the above table, the F1-score of each model in each category and the overall weighted F1-score of the model in seven categories are presented. The results are the statistics of the performance of multiple models on the test set after multiple training of the model under the same settings, including the mean and variance. As can be seen from the results of several experiments, this result has achieved the best classification performance in terms of overall performance and has also shown a relatively good F1-score in several categories. In addition, for the model proposed in this paper, a confusion matrix corresponding to classification energy on the BRACS dataset was drawn, as shown in Fig. 8.

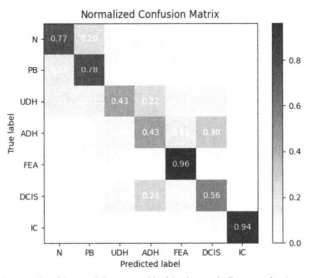

Fig. 8. Confusion matrix of the model proposed in this chapter in 7 categories (row normalization).

In the confusion matrix, the value on the main diagonal represents the accuracy corresponding to the correct category prediction, except the value on the main diagonal, the other values in each row represent the error rate of misclassifying this category into the corresponding category. The darker the color, the greater the accuracy or error rate. As can be seen from the table, the model has the best recognition ability for invasive carcinoma (IC) and flat epithelial atypia (FEA), the classification performance of common ductal hyperplasia (UDH), atypical ductal hyperplasia (ADH) and ductal carcinoma in situ (DCIS) was the worst. Relatively speaking, these categories were easily misclassified into other categories by the model. Unlike invasive cancer and epithelial atypia, the model misclassifies these two categories, but only in one category, so it is better at identifying them.

In the ablation experiment, the model proposed GNN in this paper (without Focal loss) and the model with focal loss were compared, as shown in Table 3. It can be seen from the table that the CNN branch was added on the basis of GNN, and the overall performance of the mold was improved. After adding Focal loss targeted training GNN, the recognition ability of the GNN model for benign (PB) and common catheter hyperplasia (UDH) was improved, so that the overall performance of the model was further improved.

Table 4. Performance comparison on the CRA dataset, src shows the results in the original article.

Model	Accuracy (Mean ± Std)
MobileNet (src) [17]	92.78 ± 2.74
CA-CNN (src) [16]	95.70 ± 3.04
CGC-Net (src) [18]	97.00 ± 1.10
Ours	**97.33 ± 1.25**

As can be seen from Table 4, the model proposed in this paper also achieves optimal performance on the large-size data, that is, it proves that the model can perform well on large-size data and data with large-size differences, and the model can adapt to complex datasets.

4 Discussion

The biggest difference between pathological images and natural images is that pathological images are usually larger in size and stored in pyramid form. This determines that the analysis of a full-section pathological image cannot completely adopt the way of CNN, and the ROI of the analysis of pathological images is also the same. For large-size data, it is easy to think of multi-instance learning [19–21], but multi-instance learning is easy to lose the spatial structure of the data itself. Moreover, according to the results reported by Pati et al., multi-instance learning is not the optimal choice. In the experimental design, this paper tries several schemes. Firstly, influenced by HACT-Net, we tried to imitate such hierarchical representation in the experiment. However, it was also noted in the experiment that such hierarchical representation could make people understand, but there was no corresponding principle to support whether it represented the biological behavior it cared about. In addition, the hierarchical graph construction is greatly affected by the pretest. For example, the accuracy of nuclear segmentation is significantly affected due to the difference in staining color. At the same time, if there are a lot of necrotic areas in the pathological image, the construction of the cell map will be significantly hindered. To obtain accurate nuclear segmentation in the reproduction of HACT-Net, this paper adopted the color normalization method of Vahadane et al. [22] to standardize all images onto one well-stained pathological image, and this staining method was used in all the BRACS experiments in this paper.

The construction method of the graph is an essential part of the graph neural network, which determines what kind of knowledge the network can learn. The construction method of the graph in this paper refers to the ROI diagram of literature [5] and [23]. This method can effectively avoid the problems faced in the construction of cell graphs, and it is also found in the experiment that, this method is not sensitive to color differences, but still retains the operation of image normalization for CNN branches.

5 Conclusions

In this paper, a two-branch network combining CNN and GNN is proposed to solve the problem of low classification accuracy caused by the size difference of pathological images. Specifically, the experiment was conducted on pathological images of breast cancer. First of all, for the input of the GNN branch, this paper effectively transforms the pathological images with size changes into ROI maps. For the CNN branch, color normalization is applied to adjust color distribution after the ROI is compressed to a fixed size. After the model design was determined, the model was trained several times under the same conditions, and the mean value and standard deviation of the model on the test set were compared with the existing methods. To make a fair comparison, this experiment replicates the existing model. The experimental results report the mean and standard deviation of the F1-score for each category, as well as the weighted F1-score for all categories, and also show the recognition performance for each category through the confusion matrix. Secondly, ablation experiments were conducted in this experiment to verify the influence of each component of the model on model performance. Finally, the model was further verified on the colorectal cancer dataset CRA, and the classification performance was also good. In conclusion, the BifusionNet model proposed in this paper effectively improves the classification performance of pathological images with size changes.

References

1. Saltz, J., Gupta, R., Hou, L.: Spatial organization and molecular correlation of tumor-infiltrating lymphocytes using deep learning on pathology images. Cell Rep. **23**(1), 181–193 (2018)
2. Bejnordi, B.E., Veta, M., Van Diest, P.J.: Diagnostic assessment of deep learning algorithms for detection of lymph node metastases in women with breast cancer. JAMA **318**(22), 2199–2210 (2017)
3. Huang, G., Liu, Z., Van der Maaten, L.: Densely connected convolutional networks. In: Proceedings of the IEEE Conference on Computer Vision and Pattern Recognition, pp. 4700–4708 (2017)
4. Pati, P., Jaume, G., Fernandes, LA.: HACT-Net: a hierarchical cell-to-tissue graph neural network for histopathological image classification. arXiv arXiv:2007.00584 (2020)
5. Chen, R.J., et al.: Whole slide images are 2D point clouds: context-aware survival prediction using patch-based graph convolutional networks. In: de Bruijne, M., et al. (eds.) MICCAI 2021. LNCS, vol. 12908, pp. 339–349. Springer, Cham (2021). https://doi.org/10.1007/978-3-030-87237-3_33
6. Simonyan K., Zisserman A.: Very deep convolutional networks for large-scale image recognition. arXiv preprint arXiv:1409.1556 (2014)
7. Tan M., Le Q.: EfficientNet: rethinking model scaling for convolutional neural networks. In: International Conference on Machine Learning, pp. 6105–6114. PMLR (2019)
8. Pati, P., Jaume, G., Foncubierta, A.: Hierarchical graph representations in digital pathology. arXiv arXiv:2102.11057 (2021)
9. Vaswani, A., Shazeer, N., Parmar, N.: Attention is all you need. In: Advances in Neural Information Processing Systems, vol. 30 (2017)

10. He, K., Chen, X., Xie, S.: Masked auto encoders are scalable vision learners. In: Proceedings of the IEEE/CVF Conference on Computer Vision and Pattern Recognition, pp. 16000–16009 (2022)
11. Szegedy, C., Ioffe, S., Vanhoucke, V.: Inception-v4, inception-ResNet and the impact of residual connections on learning. Proc. AAAI Conf. Artif. Intell. **31**, 4278–7284 (2017)
12. Huang, G., Liu, S., Van der Maaten, L.: CondenseNet: an efficient DenseNet using learned group convolutions. In: Proceedings of the IEEE Conference on Computer Vision and Pattern Recognition, pp. 2752–2761 (2018)
13. He, K., Zhang, X., Ren, S.: Deep residual learning for image recognition. In: Proceedings of the IEEE Conference on Computer Vision and Pattern Recognition, pp. 770–778 (2016)
14. Dosovitskiy, A., Beyer, L., Kolesnikov, A.: An image is worth 16×16 word: transformers for image recognition at scale. arXiv arXiv:2010.11929 (2021)
15. Wang, X., et al.: Transpath: Transformer-based self-supervised learning for histopathological image classification. In: de Bruijne, M., et al. (eds.) MICCAI 2021. LNCS, vol. 12908, pp. 186–195. Springer, Cham (2021). https://doi.org/10.1007/978-3-030-87237-3_18
16. Shaban, M., Awan, R., Fraz, M.M.: Context-aware convolutional neural network for grading of colorectal cancer histology images. arXiv arXiv:1907.09478 (2019)
17. Howard, A.G., Zhu, M., Chen, B.: MobileNets: efficient convolutional neural networks for mobile vision applications. arXiv preprint arXiv:1704.04861 (2017)
18. Zhou, Y., Graham, S., Alemi Koohbanani, N.: CGC-Net: cell graph convolutional network for grading of colorectal cancer histology images. In: 2019 IEEE/ CVF International Conference on Computer Vision Workshop (ICCVW), Seoul, South Korea, pp. 388–398. IEEE (2019)
19. Sudharshan, P.J., Petitjean, C., Spanhol, F.: Multiple instance learning for histopathological breast cancer image classification. Exp. Syst. Appl. **117**, 103–111 (2019)
20. Zhao, Y., Yang, F, Fang, Y.: Predicting lymph node metastasis using histopathological images based on multiple instance learning with deep graph convolution. In: 2020 IEEE/CVF Conference on Computer Vision and Pattern Recognition (CVPR), Seattle, WA, USA, pp. 4836–4845. IEEE (2020)
21. Shao, Z., Bian, H., Chen, Y.: TransMIL: transformer based correlated multiple instance learning for whole slide image classification. Adv. Neural. Inf. Process. Syst. **34**, 2136–2147 (2021)
22. Vahadane, A., Peng, T., Sethi, A.: Structure-preserving color normalization and sparse stain separation for histological images. IEEE Trans. Med. Imaging **35**(8), 1962–1971 (2016)
23. Lee, Y., Park, J.H., Oh, S.: Derivation of prognostic contextual histopathological features from whole-slide images of tumours via graph deep learning. Nat. Biomed. Eng., 1–15. https://doi.org/10.1038/s41551-022-00923-0

Synergizing Chest X-ray Image Normalization and Discriminative Feature Selection for Efficient and Automatic COVID-19 Recognition

Salvador Eugenio Ayala-Raggi, Angel Ernesto Picazo-Castillo[✉],
Aldrin Barreto-Flores, and José Francisco Portillo-Robledo

Benemérita Universidad Autónoma de Puebla, Puebla, Mexico
`a.picazo.2505@gmail.com`

Abstract. This paper presents a method for COVID-19 recognition based on the automatic localization and further pose and scale normalization of the region of interest, in this case lungs, in chest radiographs using PCA and weighted K-NN regression. Our proposed technique involves estimating by interpolation the corner positions of the region of interest, and mapping the image within that located region to a standardized fixed size template. The aim is to make all training images from a dataset similar in terms of position, angular pose, scale, and contrast, i.e. to align them. Subsequently, the eigenfaces method is used to obtain a reduced set of principal features of the normalized images. From these PCA-derived features, the ones with the best between class discrimination capability are selected by using the Fisher criterion. Our results show that the combination of our effective lung region alignment technique with the proper selection and weighting of the most discriminant PCA features is enough to achieve maximum accuracies of 95.2% and 97% in the classification of COVID-19 radiographs when traditional classifiers, such as weighted K-NN and MLP respectively, are used. Our results show that in contrast to convolutional neural networks, a simpler technique can be used to obtain similar results for classification.

[CODE: https://github.com/picazo07/LFA.git]

Keywords: K-Nearest Neighbors · Image Classification · Fisher Discriminant Criterion · COVID-19

1 Introduction

COVID-19 is a respiratory disease caused by the SARS-CoV-2 virus. It is primarily transmitted through respiratory droplets and can cause symptoms such as fever, cough, and difficulty breathing. In addition to laboratory tests, chest radiographs are used as a screening tool to evaluate potential signs of pulmonary infection caused by the virus. These images can exhibit characteristic patterns, such as opacities or infiltrates, which can assist doctors in diagnosing and monitoring the disease [6]. Furthermore, various studies have demonstrated the effectiveness of chest radiographs in detecting COVID-19 [1,2,23,27,38].

© The Author(s), under exclusive license to Springer Nature Switzerland AG 2023
H. Lu et al. (Eds.): ACPR 2023, LNCS 14407, pp. 216–229, 2023.
https://doi.org/10.1007/978-3-031-47637-2_17

Currently, there are datasets available that contain labeled radiographs, which can be utilized to train various machine learning algorithms [2]. The construction of these banks has been a collaborative effort involving institutions and medical experts in the field [26,30,33]. However, the challenge lies in the lack of uniformity in the region of interest (lungs) within these images. Some radiographs contain unwanted or irrelevant information for classification, such as additional body parts or objects covering the chest. This can adversely affect the precision metrics of classification algorithms [5,10].

In this work, we aim to demonstrate the hypothesis that aligning the region of interest in both the training images and the test image, such that the anatomical structures within the lungs are positionally consistent across all images, can enable simple and conventional classification methods like K-NN or MLP to achieve better accuracy results, provided that a reliable feature reduction method like PCA is employed in conjunction with a feature selection process based on their discriminatory capability.

To this end, we propose applying two consecutive processes. The first process involves the detection and normalization of the lung region, ensuring that the images within the lung region exhibit the same alignment, location, scale, and improved contrast as much as possible. In the second process, the "Eigenfaces" method (PCA) will be applied to the aligned regions to obtain a reduced set of statistically independent features. Finally, based on the Fisher criterion [35], we propose performing a selection of the features that best discriminate between classes. Using this set of optimal features and a traditional classifier such as K-NN or MLP, the classification accuracy will be measured.

This work comprises seven essential parts. Section 1 introduces the research context, discussing related work and the database. Section 2 outlines the "Lung Finder Algorithm" (LFA) utilized for normalization. Section 3 presents the "Eigenfaces" and Fisher linear discriminant theory, along with our feature weighting approach for normalized image features. Section 4 describes the experimental setup, including the dataset and parameter settings. Section 5 reveals and analyzes the results, demonstrating the performance of our methodology using weighted K-Nearest Neighbors (K-NN) and the Multilayer Perceptron (MLP) [9]. Section 6 delves into result discussion, exploring trends and implications. Lastly, Sect. 7 offers conclusions drawn from the findings and outlines possible future research directions.

1.1 Related Work

Currently, various methodologies have been developed for classification of chest radiographs, as evidenced in previous studies [4,11,13,17,28,31,37]. These methodologies make use of deep learning algorithms or traditional machine learning classifiers [7,8], and have reported high levels of classification accuracy, greater than 96%. However, the architectures employed in these algorithms still face challenges in achieving a reliable classification of COVID-19 [32], as their accuracy decreases when tested with other datasets different from those used for training. This raises the need of exploring new proposals for normalizing and aligning the lungs region before classifying, instead of just facing the problem by training classifiers like CNNs with a large number of different datasets, to cope with the bias imposed by a particular one. Efficient non CNN-based works have been proposed too, as in [3], where a Multilayer Perceptron (MLP) and an architecture based on image involution were used, which proposes kernels similar to CNNs but shares their weights dynamically in all dimensions, thus reducing the number of multiplications necessary for the calculations. The former obtained a maximum classification accuracy of 98.31%. Feature selection has proven to be effective in increasing classification accuracy in other works, as observed in a study on [20] which used support vector machines to recognize the orbit axis of the sensors, as in another study [29] where it was also possible to classify the frequencies of an encephalogram. Furthermore, in a work carried out by Chengzhe et al. [21], the K-NN algorithm was applied successfully. Several studies have shown that image normalization improves classification results. In a study on kidney radiographs [10], the best results were obtained using CNN and image normalization techniques. Also, in another [19] work, different normalization techniques were used on different types of radiographs to improve image classification. It is important to highlight that the results of our work are not intended to devalue CNNs in image classification, but rather to present an alternative option, and to demonstrate that image alignment and a proper feature selection technique can produce results comparable to the most commonly used algorithms. in the state of the art. In the Table 1 we show the comparison of the different pre-processing methods used in some published works [3, 10, 19–21, 29]

Table 1. Comparison of the different preprocessing methods from related works.

Authors	Image Normalization	Features selection	Classifier	Accuracy
Changawala et al., (2021)	Not Used	Not Used	MLP (Involution)	98.31%
Liu et al., (2023)	Not Used	Used	SVM	100%
Park et al., (2015)	Not Used	Used	SVM	93.5%
Lv et al., (2022)	Not Used	Used	KNN	96.14%
Gadermayr et al., (2017)	Used	Not Used	SVM	97%
Kociolek et al., (2020)	Used	Used	SVM	96%
This Work	Used	Used	KNN/MLP	95.2%/97%

1.2   Data Set of Radiographic Images

The database used for this work was "COVID-19 Radiography Database" [4, 31] from kaggle. This data set was selected because it has been used in other similar works [15, 25]. The content of this data set is 6012 images already labeled as pulmonary opacity (other lung diseases), 1345 as viral pneumonia, 10192 as normal, and finally 3616 as COVID-19.

2   Overview of the Lung Finder Algorithm (LFA)

The goal of this algorithm is to locate the lungs in the radiographs, and it consists of a training and testing stage, as shown in Fig. 1. During the training stage, 400 images from the Pneumonia, COVID-19, and Normal classes were randomly selected from the data set. Histogram equalization (HE) [12,24] was applied to all images and regions of interest were manually labeled by placing 4 provisional landmarks easily located by a human user. It was agreed that two of them would be located, one in the middle of the cervical vertebrae just at the upper limit of the lungs, and the other also on the spine but below where the lung region ends. The other two provisional landmarks are forced to the user to place them on a imaginary straight line perpendicular to the spine that intersects it just in the middle of the two previous landmarks. These last two landmarks are located in the left and right sides of lung region. Finally, and by using these 4 provisional positions, we compute 4 final and permanent landmarks at the corners of the rectangular lung region. On the other hand, ten new images randomly rotated and displaced were then generated for each labeled image to increase the data set and have an *augmented dataset*. Next, a dimensionality reduction to this set of 4400 images was applied using the "Eigenfaces" method based on Principal Component Analysis (PCA) [18,39].

During the test stage, and after a contrast improvement (H.E.), a new image is projected to the "Eigenfaces" linear subspace in order to convert it to a compact few dimensions vector which is compared via euclidean distance with each of the 4000 examples contained within the augmented dataset to find k nearest neighbors $k - NN$. The landmarks associated with these k most similar images from the augmented dataset are used to estimate the 4 landmarks of the test image by interpolation. These predicted landmarks are the coordinates of the corners of the lung ROI which can be used to warp the inside region to a standard template of fixed size.

2.1   Coordinates Labeling for the LFA Training Stage

Each of the images selected for this stage requires a manual labeling where the region of interest of the lungs is delimited by a set of coordinates. These points or landmarks become the labels used by a regression weighted K-NN to predict the corner coordinates of the novel image. The coordinates the lung region are shown in Fig. 2, and consist of four points: Q1(x1,y1), Q2(x2,y2), Q3(x3,y3) and Q4(x4,y4). Q1 and Q2 represent the length of the lungs, while Q3 and Q4 represent their width. In total, 400 images were labeled manually.

The labeling process is shown in Fig. 3. First, the Q1 point at the top of the lungs is manually located, using the spine as reference. The Q2 point is then placed at the bottom of the lungs. When the points Q1 and Q2 are placed, a straight line connecting them automatically appears, and at the midpoint of this line a perpendicular line is drawn containing the points Q3 and Q4. These last two points are constrained to be placed by the user only along the perpendicular

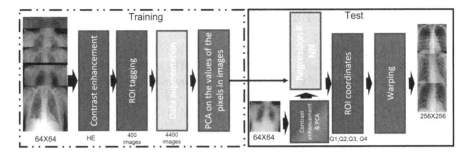

Fig. 1. Lung Finder Algorithm description. During the training phase, 400 images were tagged with their coordinates. PCA was applied to reduce the dimensionality of the images. In the testing phase, an example radiograph is provided as input, and the algorithm extracts the region of interest as the output. During the test phase, the test image is compared with its nearest neighbors to interpolate its coordinates. Finally, the algorithm outputs the extracted region of interest in a new image.

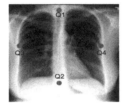

Fig. 2. Example of an array of coordinates Q1, Q2, Q3, and Q4 on a radiograph.

line, and may have a different distance from the midpoint of the Q1Q2 line, due to the fact that the lungs are not symmetrical to each other.

2.2 Data Augmentation

Data augmentation is used in various machine learning tasks, such as image classification, to expand a limited database and avoid overfitting [19,22,34]. In the case of our algorithm, we have used a large dataset [4,31]. However, in order to have a set with ROI coordinates sufficiently varied we decided to generate artificial examples based on a randomly selected set, 400 images extracted from original set. The additional artificial images were generated by producing random translations and rotations of the original images. Ten additional artificial images were created from each of the original 400, resulting in a total of 4400 images. First, it was necessary to define the range of operations on the images. For rotation, we set a range of -10 to $10°$, suggested by [31], and for translation a range from -5 to 5 pixels. These values were calculated by analyzing the coordinates of the 400 manually labeled images. In summary, the LFA training set contains 4400 images where the coordinates of the landmarks are normal distributed. Figure 4 shows an example of artificial images with their corresponding landmarks.

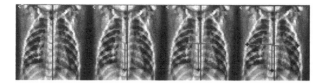

Fig. 3. Sequential placement of the points Q. First Q1 is placed, then Q2 so that Q3 and Q4 appear on the perpendicular line that crosses the midpoint of the line Q1Q2. Finally, Q3 and Q4 are adjusted.

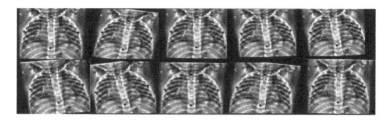

Fig. 4. Example of artificial images during data augmentation, applying translation and rotation operations.

2.3   Estimating the Corner Coordinates of the Lung Region by Regression

As shown in Fig. 1, in the test stage a new image is introduced from which it is desired to obtain its region of interest. Contrast enhancement and feature reduction are automatically applied to the test image by projecting it onto the "Eigenfaces". The weights obtained in this projection are used in the "weighted regression K-NN" algorithm to find the most similar neighbors in the "Eigenfaces" space, using the Euclidean distance. In order to reduce the computational cost, the calculations are performed in a 64×64 resolution.

Once the nearest neighbors have been identified, a regression is performed using the coordinates of the ROIs of these neighbors with the aim of predicting the coordinates of the lungs in the test image. For this, the regression (1) and (2) are used, which are applied to each coordinate, either x or y, of each Q landmark, until completing the entire set of landmarks (Q1, Q2, Q3 and Q4). The regression equations are detailed below

$$x_i = \frac{1}{k} \sum_{i=1}^{k} x_{ni} \tag{1}$$

$$y_i = \frac{1}{k} \sum_{i=1}^{k} y_{ni} \tag{2}$$

2.4 Image Warping

Once the coordinates are obtained through regression, a Warping operation [36] is used to extract the region of interest. In Fig. 5, examples of different test radiographs from the data set are presented along with their automatically estimated ROI coordinates of provisional landmarks (red dots). The calculated coordinates are geometrically transformed to obtain the corners of the ROI (final landmarks depicted as blue dots) that are used in the Warping operation towards a standard fixed size template. On the right side of each image the normalized image resulting from the LFA is shown.

Fig. 5. Two examples of new images with their estimated ROI coordinates used to warp the inside region towards a fixed and normalized template. (Color figure online)

3   Feature Reduction and Selection

After using the LFA on all radiographs in the data set to extract all regions of interest, these new images undergo additional preprocessing before being processed by a classifying algorithm. For our work, we propose the use of [18,39] Eigenfaces as a feature reduction method. In addition, we incorporated a statistical analysis of these features using Fisher's linear discriminant in order to preserve only the most discriminating features and weighing each of them according to their power of discrimination between classes. Together these two methods ensure obtaining a reduced number of discriminant features suitable for efficient classification using traditional classifiers.

3.1   Eigenfaces for Dimensionality Reduction

Eigenfaces [18,39] is based on principal component analysis (PCA) and its objective is to reduce the dimensionality of the images in the [16] dataset. Because each pixel becomes a dimension or feature to be analyzed, processing 256×256 images can be time consuming. On the other hand, a large number of features, in comparison to a smaller number of training examples, could produce missclassification when euclidean distance based approaches as k-NN are used.

The resulting eigenfaces are sorted according to the greater variances of the training set, and can be used to reconstruct every image in the training set as a linear combination of them. Because the greatest amount of variance is concentrated in the first eigenfaces, we can use only a few number of them to efficiently represent all the training images and even novel ones. Thus, every normalized image from the training set can be represented with this compact set of features. Figure 6 shows the Eigenfaces equation, and the matrix Q which columns are the Eigenfaces. The *eigenfaces* method works better and is capable of concentrating more variance in a less number of eigenfaces when training images are more similar. In our case, the normalized images are more similar to each other than the original images from the dataset. For this reason, the number of useful PCA features is necessarily reduced when using the proposed LFA.

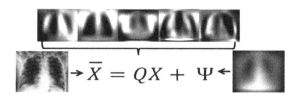

Fig. 6. Reconstructed image (left) is computed as a linear combination of the columns of matrix Q (in the middle) plus the mean image (right)

3.2   Using the Fisher Discriminant to Reduce the Number of Useful Features

Fisher discriminant criterion also known as Fisher ratio FR has been used in Linear Discriminant Analysis for finding a linear projection of features that maximizes the separation between classes. Typically, only one important feature survives this process in two classes problems. However, since the PCA features are to some degree independent, we can use, in a naive fashion, the fisher ratio as a measure of separation between classes for a each feature.

This process is done by evaluating each feature individually, and making sure that the means of the observations in each class are as far apart as possible, while the variances within each class are as small as possible. Using this analysis, it is possible to select a number greater than 2 of those features obtained by the Eigenfaces method that best discriminate the classes in the data set [35]

The FR has been used in works such as the one mentioned in [14], and we denoted it as J. The FR formula is found in Eq. 3 (Fig. 7).

$$J_i = \frac{(\mu_{ic_0} - \mu_{ic_1})^2}{\sigma_{ic_0}^2 + \sigma_{ic_1}^2} \tag{3}$$

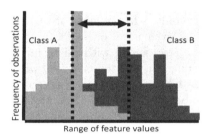 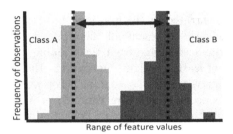

Fig. 7. Example of frequency distributions for each class. The discriminative capability of a feature can be visually assessed by the separation between the means of the histograms. The pair of histograms on the right shows a greater separation, indicating higher discrimination between classes. Conversely, the pair of histograms on the left exhibits lower discrimination.

3.3   The Fisher Ratio as a Weight for Each Feature

We propose to use the FR value as a weigh for each feature, in such a way that those features that possess a greater capacity for discrimination are amplified.

As a first step we standardize all selected features in order to give them a uniform relevance. Then, we calculate $\rho_K = \sqrt{J_K}$ for each feature k. Next, we normalize ρ_K as shown in (4).

$$\varrho_k = \frac{\rho_k}{\sum_{i=1}^{k} \rho_i} \tag{4}$$

Finally, each ϱ_k is used to weigh all the standardized observations for the feature k.

4   Experiments Setup

In this work, the weighted K-NN and MLP algorithms were used for classification. Several experiments were conducted to compare the impact of different image preprocessing and feature enhancement algorithms on classification accuracy. The algorithms used in the training and testing stages included LFA for image normalization and preprocessing, Eigenfaces for dimensionality reduction, FR for selection of the best features, and W for weighting the features based on their discriminative capacity between classes. These two algorithms together aim to improve the discriminative ability of the features across classes. A total of five experiments were conducted for each classifier, which are described in Fig. 8.

A total of 1250 COVID-19 images and 1250 normal images, all of size 256×256 pixels, were used. The region of interest was extracted from these images using the LFA algorithm, forming a bank of normalized images. The images were divided into 2000 training images, with 1000 from each class. For the testing phase, 500 images were selected, with 250 from each class. In the experiments using Eigenfaces-based features, 600 features were used.

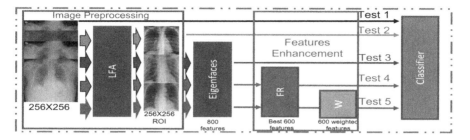

Fig. 8. Graphical representation of the different experiments conducted in image pre-processing. Each arrow represents a sequence of algorithms that may include image preprocessing or feature enhancement. A classification accuracy value is calculated for each arrow.

For the MLP topology, 4 hidden layers with 120 neurons each and a single neuron in the output layer were utilized. The training was conducted for 100 epochs.

5   Experimental Results

Different values were tested for the parameter K in the weighted K-NN, and it was found that the optimal value is 11. On the other hand, experiments were conducted with various topologies and number of epochs in the MLP, but no significant improvements in classification accuracy were observed. The classification accuracy results for all experiments of each classifier are shown in Table 2.

Table 2. Results of the Weighted K-NN and the MLP for the experiments using different preprocessing methods.

Classifier	E1	E2	E3	E4	E5
Weighted K-NN	82.4%	87.8%	88%	91.2%	95.2%
MLP	85%	90.6%	90.8%	93%	97%

Additional tests were conducted in Experiment 5, varying the number of features for both classifiers. However, it was found that 600 is the optimal number of features for both classifiers. Furthermore, Experiment 5 underwent cross-validation to demonstrate the consistency of the proposed set of algorithms in this work. Table 3 displays the results of the 5 tests, along with the average and standard deviation for each classifier.

Table 3. Results of Weighted K-NN and MLP for cross-validation.

Classifier	Test 1	Test 2	Test 3	Test 4	Test 5	Mean	Std
Weighted K-NN	95%	94.8%	95%	94.6%	95.2%	94.92%	0.0022
MLP	97%	96.8%	96.4%	97%	96.8%	96.8%	0.0024

6 Discussion of Results

For both classifiers, the following statements can be made regarding the experiments conducted in image preprocessing:

1. Experiment one, where images have no preprocessing, generally exhibits the worst results.
2. Experiment two demonstrates that image normalization improves results compared to experiment one.
3. In experiment three, where an image representation is projected onto the Eigenfaces space, no notable improvement is observed.
4. Experiment four highlights the importance of feature selection that effectively separates classes using FR, resulting in improved accuracy.
5. Experiment five showcases the effectiveness of our algorithm sequence, which includes image normalization, feature selection, and weighting, yielding the best results.

Additionally, the results demonstrate consistency with minimal variability during cross-validation. Finally, the MLP achieved accuracy results that can compete with other state-of-the-art algorithms for classifying chest X-ray images.

7 Conclusions and Future Work

In this study, we proposed a technique for automatic detection and normalization of the Region of Interest (ROI) in chest radiographs, along with a feature selection method based on Fisher's criterion (FR) using PCA for automatic COVID-19 detection. With the proposed method, a reduced number of highly discriminative features are obtained. The results demonstrate that by utilizing both ROI alignment and feature selection processes, a significant increase in classification accuracy is achieved when using traditional classifiers such as weighted K-NN and MLP. The reported results are reliable as cross-validation techniques were employed to obtain them.

The contributions of this work include a ROI normalization method for lung images and a technique for selecting highly discriminative features using FR. Our approach achieves accuracy values that compete with other state-of-the-art works employing CNN-based techniques.

For future work, the ROI normalization technique can be applied to other databases and for the detection of other lung diseases. Additionally, the feature selection and weighting approaches can be tested to enhance the accuracy of other classification algorithms.

References

1. Alzahrani, S.A., Al-Salamah, M.A., Al-Madani, W.H., Elbarbary, M.A.: Systematic review and meta-analysis for the use of ultrasound versus radiology in diagnosing of pneumonia. Crit. Ultrasound J. **9**(1), 6 (2017)

2. Amatya, Y., Rupp, J., Russell, F.M., Saunders, J., Bales, B., House, D.R.: Diagnostic use of lung ultrasound compared to chest radiograph for suspected pneumonia in a resource-limited setting. Int. J. Emerg. Med. **11**(1), 8 (2018). clinicalTrials.gov/NCT02949141

3. Changawala, V., Sharma, K., Paunwala, M.: Averting from convolutional neural networks for chest X-ray image classification. In: 2021 IEEE International Conference on Signal Processing, Information, Communication and Systems (SPIC-SCON), pp. 14–17 (2021)

4. Chowdhury, M.E.H., et al.: Can AI help in screening viral and COVID-19 pneumonia? IEEE Access **8**, 132665–132676 (2020)

5. Cleophas, T., Zwinderman, A.: Machine Learning in Medicine: Part Two, Machine Learning in Medicine. Springer, Cham (2013). https://doi.org/10.1007/978-94-007-6886-4

6. Daszak, P., Keusch, G.T., Phelan, A.L., Johnson, C.K., Osterholm, M.T.: Infectious disease threats: a rebound to resilience. Health Aff. (Millwood) **40**(2), 204–211 (2021)

7. Do, T.N., Le, V.T., Doan, T.H.: SVM on top of deep networks for COVID-19 detection from chest X-ray images. J. Inf. Commun. Convergence Eng. **20**, 219–225 (2022)

8. El-Kenawy, E.S., et al.: Advanced meta-heuristics, convolutional neural networks, and feature selectors for efficient COVID-19 X-ray chest image classification. IEEE Access **9**, 36019–36037 (2021)

9. Ertel, W., Black, N.: Introduction to Artificial Intelligence. Undergraduate Topics in Computer Science. Springer, Cham (2018). https://doi.org/10.1007/978-3-319-58487-4

10. Gadermayr, M., Cooper, S.S., Klinkhammer, B., Boor, P., Merhof, D.: A quantitative assessment of image normalization for classifying histopathological tissue of the kidney. In: Roth, V., Vetter, T. (eds.) GCPR 2017. LNCS, vol. 10496, pp. 3–13. Springer, Cham (2017). https://doi.org/10.1007/978-3-319-66709-6_1

11. Gazda, M., Plavka, J., Gazda, J., Drotar, P.: Self-supervised deep convolutional neural network for chest X-ray classification. IEEE Access **9**, 151972–151982 (2021)

12. Gonzalez, R., Woods, R.: Digital Image Processing, Global Edition. Pearson Education, New York (2018)

13. Hamza, A., et al.: COVID-19 classification using chest X-ray images based on fusion-assisted deep Bayesian optimization and Grad-CAM visualization. Front. Public Health **10**, 1046296 (2022)

14. Ibis, E.: Sistema de aprendizaje automático para la detección de neumonía. Master's thesis, Benemérita Universidad Autónoma de Puebla, Puebla, México (2022)

15. Islam, N., et al.: Thoracic imaging tests for the diagnosis of COVID-19. Cochrane Database Syst. Rev. **3**(3), CD013639 (2021)

16. Jolliffe, I.: Principal Component Analysis. Springer Series in Statistics. Springer, New York (2002). https://doi.org/10.1007/b98835

17. Khan, A., Khan, S., Saif, M., Batool, A., Sohail, A., Khan, M.: A survey of deep learning techniques for the analysis of COVID-19 and their usability for detecting Omicron. J. Exp. Theor. Artif. Intell. (2022)

18. Kirby, M., Sirovich, L.: Application of the Karhunen-Loeve procedure for the characterization of human faces. IEEE Trans. Pattern Anal. Mach. Intell. **12**(1), 103–108 (1990)
19. Kociolek, M., Strzelecki, M., Obuchowicz, R.: Does image normalization and intensity resolution impact texture classification? Comput. Med. Imaging Graph. **81**, 101716 (2020)
20. Liu, W., Zheng, Y., Zhou, X., Chen, Q.: Axis orbit recognition of the hydropower unit based on feature combination and feature selection. Sensors **23**(6), 2895 (2023)
21. Lv, C., et al.: A classification feature optimization method for remote sensing imagery based on Fisher score and MRMR. Appl. Sci. **12**, 8845 (2022)
22. Mikołajczyk-Bareła, A., Grochowski, M.: Data augmentation for improving deep learning in image classification problem, pp. 117–122 (2018)
23. Moberg, A., Taléus, U., Garvin, P., Fransson, S.G., Falk, M.: Community-acquired pneumonia in primary care: clinical assessment and the usability of chest radiography. Scand. J. Prim. Health Care **34**, 1–7 (2016)
24. Moeslund, T.B.: Introduction to Video and Image Processing: Building Real Systems and Applications. Undergraduate Topics in Computer Science. Springer, London (2012). https://doi.org/10.1007/978-1-4471-2503-7
25. Muljo, H.H., Pardamean, B., Purwandari, K., Cenggoro, T.W.: Improving lung disease detection by joint learning with COVID-19 radiography database. Commun. Math. Biol. Neurosci. **2022**(1), 1–24 (2022)
26. Mustafa Ghaderzadeh, M.A., Asadi, F.: X-ray equipped with artificial intelligence: changing the COVID-19 diagnostic paradigm during the pandemic. Biomed. Res. Int. **2021**, 9942873 (2021)
27. Niederman, M.S.: Community-acquired Pneumonia. Ann. Internal Med. **163**(7), ITC1–ITC16 (2015)
28. Nillmani, et al.: Segmentation-based classification deep learning model embedded with explainable AI for COVID-19 detection in chest X-ray scans. Diagnostics **12**(9), 2132 (2022)
29. Park, S.H., Lee, S.G.: A method of feature extraction on motor imagery EEG using FLD and PCA based on Sub-Band CSP. J. KIISE **42**, 1535–1543 (2015)
30. Qin, C., Yao, D., Shi, Y., Song, Z.: Computer-aided detection in chest radiography based on artificial intelligence: a survey. Biomed. Eng. Online **17**(1), 113 (2018)
31. Rahman, T., et al.: Exploring the effect of image enhancement techniques on COVID-19 detection using chest X-ray images. Comput. Biol. Med. **132**, 104319 (2021)
32. Ridzuan, M., Bawazir, A.A., Navarette, I.G., Almakky, I., Yaqub, M.: Self-supervision and multi-task learning: challenges in fine-grained COVID-19 multiclass classification from chest X-rays (2022)
33. Salvatore, C., et al.: Artificial intelligence applied to chest X-ray for differential diagnosis of COVID-19 Pneumonia. Diagnostics (Basel) **11**(3), 530 (2021)
34. Shorten, C., Khoshgoftaar, T.M.: A survey on image data augmentation for deep learning. J. Big Data **6**(1), 60 (2019)
35. Silva, T.S.: An illustrative introduction to Fisher's linear discriminant (2019). https://sthalles.github.io
36. Szeliski, R.: Computer Vision: Algorithms and Applications, 1st edn. Springer, Heidelberg (2010). https://doi.org/10.1007/978-3-030-34372-9
37. Talaat, A., Yousri, D., Ewees, A., Al-qaness, M.A.A., Damaševičius, R., Elsayed Abd Elaziz, M.: COVID-19 image classification using deep features and fractional-order marine predators algorithm. Sci. Rep. **10**, 15364 (2020)

38. Ticinesi, A., et al.: Lung ultrasound and chest X-ray for detecting pneumonia in an acute geriatric ward. Medicine (Baltimore) **95**(27), e4153 (2016)
39. Turk, M., Pentland, A.: Eigenfaces for recognition. J. Cogn. Neurosci. **3**(1), 71–86 (1991)

A Unified Convolutional Neural Network for Gait Recognition

Sonam Nahar[✉], Sagar Narsingani, and Yash Patel

Pandit Deendayal Energy University, Gandhinagar, Gujarat, India
{sonam.nahar,sagar.nce19,yash.pce19}@sot.pdpu.ac.in

Abstract. Gait recognition stands as a crucial method for distant person identification. Most state-of-the-art gait recognition frameworks consists of two modules: feature extraction and feature matching. The fixed nature of each part in these modules leads to suboptimal performance in challenging conditions as they are mutually independent. This paper presents the integration of those steps into a single framework. Specifically, we design a unified end-to-end convolutional neural network (CNN) for learning the efficient gait representation and gait recognition. Since dynamic areas contain the most informative part of the human gait and are insensitive to changes in various covariate conditions, we feed the gait entropy images as input to CNN model to capture mostly the motion information. The proposed method is evaluated through experiments conducted on the CASIA-B dataset, specifically for cross-view and cross-walking gait recognition. The experimental results strongly indicate the effectiveness of the approach.

Keywords: Gait Recognition · CNN · Cross Walking

1 Introduction

'Gait' is a measure of how a person walks and is used as a behavioral biometric [12]. A gait recognition system can uniquely identify individuals based on their way of walking. In general, gait is considered to be a poorer biometric than the other image-based biometrics such as fingerprint [3], face [15] and iris [13]. This is largely due to the fact that changes in covariate circumstances are more likely to have an impact on gait than other behavioural biometrics. Some of these factors, like the state of one's clothing, how they are carried objects, and the angle at which they are seen, primarily affects how a person appears, while others, like time, surface, and one's shoes, have an impact on gait. Despite this drawback, gait offers a notable advantage over other image-based biometrics in situations like visual surveillance because it doesn't require close proximity to the subject and can operate without interrupting or interfering with the subject's activity.

Today, gait recognition is an active area of research and development in computer vision and biometrics community, with applicationsranging from security and surveillance to healthcare and sports performance analysis [16,18]. Existing vision-based gait recognition techniques mainly fall into two broad categories, namely model based and model free approaches. Model free approaches [1,6] use model information directly extracted from silhouettes, whilst model-based approaches [25,26] fit a model to body and represent gait using the parameters of the model. Model based approaches are more complex and computationally more expensive than model free approaches, and generally require good quality images to correctly extract the model parameters from a gait sequence, which may not be available in a real-world application scenario such as CCTV surveillance in public space. Most of the recent and state of the art research in gait recognition adopt model free approaches since they are computationally less insensitive, more robust to noise, insensitive to the quality of gait sequences, and have a comparable, or better performance when compared to model-based approaches on benchmark datasets [16,18,24]. The work in this paper fall into the model-free category.

Model free gait recognition approaches use silhouettes for human gait representation that can be computed by applying background subtraction on gait sequences. However, these silhouettes are susceptible to variations in the subject's appearance caused by factors such as different carrying styles, clothing and view conditions. To address this issue, several state-of-art gait recognition methods have been proposed, aiming to develop representations that remain unaffected by covariate conditions. Examples of such representations include gait energy image [6], gait entropy image [1], chrono gait image [21], gait flow image [9], frequency domain gait features [10], and more. Despite achieving reasonably satisfactory outcomes in recent years, these gait recognition strategies typically rely on manually designed features and have limited ability to learn intrinsic patterns within the data.

Deep learning has experienced a surge in popularity within various computer vision domains, including image recognition [7], face recognition [20], and human activity recognition [22], due to its remarkable performance. One key advantage of deep learning is its ability to automatically learn features from a large volume of training samples across different layers of a deep neural network. Additionally, it offers a unified framework for both feature learning and classification. Recently, deep learning-based gait recognition methods have emerged as the dominant approach in the field, enabling practical applications [16]. Among the deep architectures, convolutional neural networks (CNNs) have been extensively utilized for gait recognition. CNNs use convolutional layers to extract local features, pooling layers to reduce dimensionality, and fully connected layers to classify images based on learned features. Most existing CNN based gait recognition methods comprise of two steps: feature learning and feature matching [4,17,23]. CNN is used to extract the higher-level features from the gait silhouettes and then a traditional classifier is further used to compare the probe features with the gallery ones in order to identify most similar gait patterns and label them as being from the same subject. However, these frameworks demonstrate subpar performance when faced with demanding tasks such as cross-view or cross-clothing gait recognition on extensive datasets. A potential explanation for this is the sequential approach employed, which leads to a lack of compatibility between the feature learning and classifier training processes.

To better address above problems, it is probably a good choice to adopt an end-to-end framework. A recent study introduced a comprehensive CNN architecture that simultaneously learns gait segmentation and recognition in an end-to-end manner [19]. The segmentation model extracts gait silhouettes, which are subsequently fused using a temporal fusion unit to improve the recognition model's performance. The study also proposes a unified model that trains both segmentation and recognition jointly. While this approach achieved superior results on benchmark datasets, it employs two separate CNN models, which are intricate in terms of architecture. Furthermore, training the CNNs individually and subsequently fine-tuning them in a unified framework is computationally demanding. In this paper, we present the integration of the steps feature learning and feature matching into a single framework. Specifically, we design a unified end-to-end convolutional neural network (CNN) that learns the gait features and perform recognition jointly. View angles, walking with carrying a bag and walking with wearing a coat are used as different covariate conditions for the experiments. We demonstrate the effectiveness of our method in the settings of cross view and cross walking using the large benchmark dataset. Here, cross-view means the test gait sequences are with different view angles from the view point in training sequences. In cross-walking setting, the subjects in test set have walking sequences either with a coat or with a bag, while subjects in the training set are under the normal walking condition. The key contributions of the paper are summarized as follows:

1. We introduce a straightforward CNN model that achieves efficient gait representation and performs gait recognition within a unified framework. The unified model offers two notable advantages: firstly, it significantly simplifies the conventional step-by-step procedures, and secondly, the joint learning of each component yields noticeable performance improvements compared to separate learning approaches.
2. Most of the existing CNN based approaches use gait energy images (GEI) as an input because GEI can efficiently capture both the static (e.g., head, torso) and dynamic parts (e.g., lower parts of legs and arms) of the human silhouette [16]. However, since GEI mainly contain body shape information, they are sensitive to changes in various covariate conditions, and hence is not an appropriate representation to feed in a CNN for learning robust gait features. In our work, we propose to use gait entropy images to be fed as input to our CNN model. Gait entropy image captures the dynamic areas of the human body by measuring the Shannon's entropy [1]. Dynamic areas contain the most informative part of the human gait and are insensitive to changes in various covariate conditions. With gait entropy images as input, our CNN model learns higher level gait features which are invariant to different camera viewpoints, clothing and carrying conditions.

3. We present extensive experimental results for cross-view and cross-walking gait recognition using the CASIA-B benchmark dataset [24].

The rest of the paper is organized as follows: in Sect. 2, related work is reviewed. The proposed gait recognition method is detailed in Sect. 3. Experimental results and conclusion are presented in Sect. 4 and Sect. 5, respectively.

2 Related Work

Typically, model-free gait recognition approaches comprise of two steps: feature extraction and feature matching. The gait features are mainly represented by the silhouettes that are extracted from human walking sequences. The gait energy image (GEI) has been widely used as an effective representation by averaging the pixel values of the silhouettes over the gait period [6]. However, GEI suffers from information loss in gait sequences, which hampers performance when dealing with changes caused by covariate conditions like clothing, carrying variations, and view differences. To address this issue, an entropy-based gait representation is proposed [1,2]. The gait entropy image focuses on dynamic regions and is computed by calculating the pixel-wise entropy of the GEI. Another variant, called Chrono-Gait Image (CGI) is introduced to preserve temporal information by utilizing a multi-channel temporal encoding scheme [21]. Additionally, a gait flow image (GFI) directly emphasizes the dynamic components by averaging the lengths of optical flow observed on the silhouette contour over the gait period [9]. Frequency domain gait features are also proposed [8,10], taking into account the periodic nature of gait. These frequency-based methods learn cross-view projections to normalize gait features, enabling comparison of normalized features from different views and computation of their similarity when comparing two videos.

The latest advancements in gait recognition methods utilizing such gait representations have demonstrated promising outcomes even in the presence of challenging covariate conditions [16,18]. However, these methods rely on manually designed gait features, which possess limited capability to capture the underlying patterns inherent in the data. Moreover, these image-based gait features are transformed into a feature vector, and techniques like linear discriminant analysis (LDA) [6], primal rank support vector machines [5], and multi-view discriminant analysis (MvDA) [11] are employed to extract relevant gait features that remain unaffected by various covariate conditions. Nevertheless, treating each dimension in the feature vector as a separate pixel for subsequent classification/recognition fails to capture the spatial proximity within the gait image, resulting in overfitting issues.

Deep learning-based gait recognition techniques have gained significant prominence in recent times by leveraging their ability to automatically acquire discriminative gait representations. Convolutional neural networks (CNNs) have been predominantly employed due to their capability to capture spatial proximity within images through convolutional operations, resulting in substantial enhancements in recognition accuracy. A noteworthy example is GEI-Net, which directly learns gait representations from gait energy images (GEIs) using CNNs [17]. The authors in [23] proposed a deep CNN-based framework for cross-view and cross-walk gait recognition, where similarities between pairs of GEIs are learned, leading to state-of-the-art performance. Another recent approach called GaitSet treats gait as a set and assumes that the silhouette's appearance contains positional information [4]. It utilizes CNNs to extract temporal information from the gait set. All these methods utilize CNNs for learning gait features, while a separate feature matching module is employed for gait recognition. Typically, direct template matching between gallery and probe features or a K-NN classifier is used for this purpose. However, the fixed nature of the feature learning and feature matching modules results in suboptimal performance under challenging conditions, as they operate independently of each other. To address this limitation, the authors in [19] recently introduced a comprehensive CNN architecture named as GaitNet that simultaneously learns gait segmentation and recognition in an end-to-end manner.

Apart from CNN, various other deep architectures have emerged to address gait recognition challenges [16]. These include deep belief networks (DBN), long short-term memory (LSTM) networks (a type of recurrent neural network), deep autoencoders (DAE), generative adversarial networks (GAN), capsule networks, and hybrid networks that combine multiple architectures. While these methods have demonstrated remarkable performance in demanding scenarios, they often involve complex network structures and necessitate large amounts of labeled data for effective training.

3   Proposed Method

3.1   Generation of Gait Entropy Images

In the given human walking sequence, a silhouette is extracted from each frame utilizing background subtraction [14]. Subsequently, the height of the silhouettes is normalized and aligned at the centre. Gait cycles are then estimated by employing the autocorrelation method described in the [10]. The gait cycle represents the time interval between repetitive walking events, typically commencing when one foot makes contact with the ground. As the walking pattern of an individual is periodic, it is adequate to consider just a single gait cycle from the entire gait sequence.

After obtaining a gait cycle consisting of size-normalized and centre-aligned silhouettes, the next step involves computing a gait entropy image (GEnI). This is achieved by calculating the Shannon entropy for each pixel within the silhouette images throughout the entire gait cycle, as outlined in [1]:

$$GEnI = I(x,y) = \sum_{k=1}^{K} p_k(x,y) \log_2 p_k(x,y), \tag{1}$$

where x and y represent the pixel coordinates, while $p_k(x,y)$ denotes the probability of the pixel having the kth value within a complete gait cycle. For our

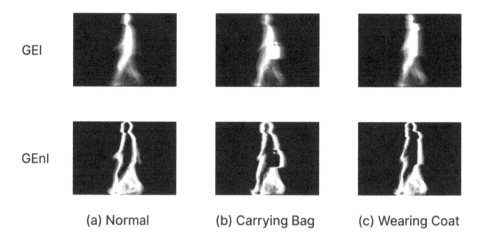

GEI

GEnI

(a) Normal   (b) Carrying Bag   (c) Wearing Coat

Fig. 1. Examples of Gait Energy Images (GEI) and Gait Entropy Images (GEnI) from the CASIA-B dataset [24] with different walking conditions. Columns (a) Normal Walking, (b) Carrying a bag, and (c) Wearing a coat.

specific case, since the silhouettes are binary images, we have $K = 2$. Examples of Gait Entropy Images (GEnIs) and Gait Energy Images (GEIs) extracted from the CASIA-B dataset are depicted in Fig. 1. The GEnIs exhibit higher intensity values in dynamic areas such as the legs and arms, while the static regions like the head and torso demonstrate lower values. This discrepancy arises due to the greater uncertainty and information content of silhouette pixels in the dynamic areas, resulting in higher entropy values. Additionally, the impact of appearance changes caused by carrying a bag or wearing a coat is more pronounced in the GEIs, whereas in the GEnIs, it is substantially diminished and mainly observable in the outer contour of the human body. In our proposed approach, we utilize GEnIs as input to our CNN architecture, allowing our deep model to learn gait features that are invariant to both view and appearance variations which results in effective recognition performance in challenging scenarios.

3.2 Convolutional Neural Network Architecture

Our CNN architecture is comprised of eight layers, with the initial six layers consisting of two sets of convolutions, batch normalization, and pooling layers. The final two layers are fully connected (FC) layers, where the first FC layer contains 1024 units, followed by another FC layer with M number of output units. At each output unit, the SoftMax function is applied. Assuming there are M subjects in the training set, each subject is represented by an integer number ranging from 1 to M.

More precisely, the ith unit in the final layer is ideally designed to output 1 when the input belongs to subject i, while it outputs 0 otherwise. The architecture of our CNN is depicted in Fig. 2. Regularization is implemented using

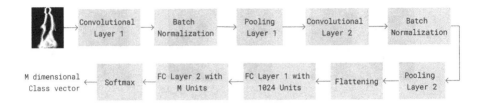

Fig. 2. The CNN Architecture.

dropout, and non-linearity is introduced using the ReLU activation function at every layer except the last layer. To optimize our CNN model, we consider several hyperparameters, including the number of filters, size of filters, number of epochs, dropout rate, and batch size. We determine the optimal values for these hyperparameters through cross-validation. The configuration of each convolutional and pooling layer, along with their corresponding optimal hyperparameters, is presented in Table 1. We employ this configuration for gait feature learning and recognition in an end-to-end manner.

Table 1. CNN Configuration with Optimal Hyperparameters.

Hyperparameters		
Conv Layer 1	# Filters	40
	Size of Filters	3×3
	Stride	2
Max Pooling Layer 1	Size of Filters	2×2
	Stride	2
Conv Layer 2	# Filters	32
	Size of Filters	5×5
	Stride	3
Max Pooling Layer 2	Size of Filters	3×3
	Stride	2
Number of Epochs	100	
Learning Rate	0.001	
Dropout Rate	20%	
Batch Size	64	

Despite being relatively shallow, our CNN architecture effectively learns robust gait representations and achieves good recognition accuracy. This is primarily because gait data, such as silhouettes (e.g., GEnI), do not possess significant complexity in terms of texture information. Therefore, a shallow CNN architecture is sufficient for capturing and encoding gait characteristics. This stands in contrast to other domains like face recognition [20] or activity recognition [22], where deep networks are commonly employed to learn highly discriminative features. Additionally, our preliminary experiments have confirmed that incorporating additional convolutional layers after the existing sets of convolutions, batch normalization, and pooling in our network do not lead to a significant improvement in gait recognition accuracy.

3.3   Training the CNN

Let the training set consist of N gait sequences belonging to M subjects. We start by computing a gait entropy image (GEnI) for each gait sequence, resulting in a set of training GEnIs denoted as $\{I_1, I_2, \ldots, I_N\}$. These GEnIs are accompanied by their corresponding ground truth label vectors $\{y_1, y_2, \ldots, y_N\}$. Each input GEnI, I_i belonging to subject j, is associated with a label denoted by a M-dimensional vector, $y_i = [y_{i1}, y_{i2}, \ldots, y_{iM}]$, where y_{ij} is equal to 1 and the remaining entries are set to 0.

Given an input image I_i and set of weighting parameters w, we define the output z_i of last layer as a function of I_i and w using forward propagation as:

$$z_i = f(I_i, w), \tag{2}$$

where z_i is denoted as a M dimensional vector. We subsequently apply the SoftMax function on every element of z_i and obtain the final class probability vector $\hat{y}_i$ where each jth element in $\hat{y}_i$ is computed using the SoftMax function as follows,

$$\hat{y}_{ij} = \frac{e^{z_{ij}}}{\sum_{j=1}^{M} e^{z_{ij}}}, \quad for \ j = 1, 2, \ldots, M \tag{3}$$

Given a training set: $\{I_1, I_2, \ldots, I_N\}$, we train our CNN network by minimizing the following cross-entropy loss function L using the stochastic gradient descent algorithm:

$$L(w) = \sum_{i=1}^{N} \sum_{j=1}^{M} y_{ij} \log \hat{y}_{ij}. \tag{4}$$

In this training phase, we obtain an optimal set of weighting parameters $\hat{w}$ as:

$$\hat{w} = \arg\min_{w} \ L(w). \tag{5}$$

3.4   Gait Recognition

Given a gait sequence in the test set, we begin by calculating its gait entropy image. This gait entropy image serves as the input to the trained CNN model. At the intermediate layers, the CNN model learns higher-level features, and at the final layer, it performs classification using the SoftMax function. In other words, by utilizing the optimal set of weighting parameters $\hat{w}$, we obtain an M-dimensional class probability vector $\hat{y}_t$ for the test GEnI I_t using the Eq. 2 and 3. The class label or subject ID is determined by selecting the index corresponding to the highest value in $\hat{y}_t$.

4 Experimental Results

4.1 Datasets and Test Protocol

Our experiments utilize the CASIA-B dataset [24]. CASIA-B is a highly utilized and openly accessible gait database, comprising gait sequences of 124 individuals captured from 11 distinct viewpoints spanning from $0°$ to $180°$ (with $18°$ increments). The dataset encompasses three variations of walking conditions namely normal walking (NM), walking with a coat (CL), and walking with a bag (BG), respectively with 6, 2, and 2 gait sequences per subject per view.

To evaluate the effectiveness of our proposed method, we employ the subject-dependent testing protocol. Under this protocol, both the training and testing datasets comprise gait sequences from all subjects in our dataset. For the cross-walking experimental setup, we exclusively utilize four normal walking sequences (NM) of each subject, incorporating each view, for training purposes. Consequently, our training set encompasses a total of 44 gait sequences per subject (11 views multiplied by 4 sequences), resulting in a grand total of $44 * 124 = 5456$ sequences. Conversely, the test set comprises the remaining sequences, including two normal (test subset-NM), two coat (test subset-CL), and two bag (test subset-BG) sequences for each subject and each view. In the case of the cross-view scenario, we assess the test accuracy for each view independently during the cross-walking experiment.

To initiate the training process of the CNN, we begin by computing the gait entropy image (GEnI) for each gait sequence within the training set. These GEnIs have a fixed size of 88×128 pixels. An example of these extracted GEnIs can be observed in Fig. 1. Since our training set is of moderate size, we take precautions to mitigate the risk of overfitting. We accomplish this by employing cross-validation, where we randomly split the training set into a 70% training subset and a 30% validation subset. By selecting hyperparameters that minimize variance error, we aim to identify a set of hyperparameters in which both the training and validation errors are low and their discrepancy is also minimal. Utilizing the training GEnIs and the optimal set of hyperparameters (refer to Table 1), we proceed to train our CNN model as illustrated in Fig. 2, allowing us to learn the weights ($\hat{w}$) of the model. Since our model is trained using GEnIs of normal walking gait sequences captured with different view angles, it learns the reliable gait features invariant to view angles, clothing and carrying conditions. It is important to note that TensorFlow was utilized for training the CNN, and all experiments were conducted on a machine equipped with an 11th Gen Intel (R) Core (TM) i7-1165G7 processor running at a frequency of 2.80 GHz. The machine also featured an SSD with 512 MB storage capacity, 8 GB of RAM, and operated on a 64-bit operating system.

4.2 Results

Rank-1 recognition accuracy is utilized to measure and present our results. Table 2 displays the outcomes for the cross-view scenario across three test subsets. The first row corresponds to the case when the test subset consists of normal walking sequences, while the second and third rows demonstrate the results when the test subsets comprise bag and coat sequences, respectively. In order to incorporate the cross-view setting within the cross-walking scenario, we assess the recognition accuracy for each individual angle, as illustrated in Table 2. The task of cross-view and cross-walking gait recognition is particularly challenging. However, our method has yielded highly promising outcomes on the NM subset. Despite the fact that silhouettes captured from frontal and back viewpoints, such as 0°, 18°, 162°, and 180°, contain limited gait information, our method achieves a remarkable accuracy rate of over 90% on the NM subset. Regarding the BG subset, our method continues to perform well, particularly with test angles of 72°, 90°, 108°, and 126°, as these viewpoints offer the most visible gait information. However, the performance declines for the CL test subset, even for the 90° view, as indicated in Table 2. The reason behind these outcomes is that carrying a bag only impacts a small portion of the gait silhouette, whereas wearing a coat can significantly alter one's appearance. Another potential factor contributing to the performance degradation could be the scarcity of training data. Given the greater appearance variations, the CL subset proves to be more challenging than the NM and BG subsets. Insufficient training data may result in networks being prone to overfitting.

Table 2. Recognition Accuracies in Cross Walking and Cross View Scenarios using CASIA-B dataset. First Row: Results for NM test subset. Second Row: Results for BG test subset. Third Row: Results for CL test subset. Here, the training set contains 4 normal walking sequences of every subject captured with all 18 view angles.

Training Set: NM #1-4 with 0°–180°											
Test Subset	0°	18°	36°	54°	72°	90°	108°	126°	144°	162°	180°	Mean
NM #5-6	91.42	92.59	93.44	95.34	95.57	96.90	95.56	94.77	95.72	93.31	92.49	**94.46**
BG #1-2	27.77	37.12	37.12	46.32	50.76	53.15	51.18	41.48	34.01	33.13	30.10	**40.19**
CL #1-2	14.11	18.13	19.40	22.22	25.28	22.29	22.01	20.72	18.61	17.66	16.15	**19.69**

Table 3 presents the comparison of our proposed method with existing approaches in the literature. These methods were selected as they are the most recent ones evaluated under cross-view and cross-walking scenarios, and their scores were directly obtained from the original papers. For a fair comparison, we also include two traditional methods, namely GEI and GEnI, which utilize gait energy image (GEI) and gait entropy image (GEnI) as features, respectively. These traditional methods perform gait recognition in cross-walking and cross-view scenarios by employing direct template matching (Euclidean distance) between the training and test sets. The available results for cross-walking scenarios involving the BG and CL test sets are limited. However, our proposed method outperforms traditional methods such as GEI and GEnI by significant margins. This highlights the advantage of using learned features from CNN compared to handcrafted features in gait recognition. In the experimental setting where both the training and test sets consist of NM sequences, our method demonstrates superior performance compared to state-of-the-art methods such as CMCC [8] and GEINET [17], and comparable performance with recent deep methods including GaitSet [4], CNN-LB [23], and GaitNet [19]. Moreover, for the bag and coat test sets, our proposed method shows comparable performance. These results underscore the effectiveness of our end-to-end recognition model based on CNN, which outperforms methods that separate feature extraction and recognition into distinct phases.

Table 3. Comparison with state-of-the art gait recognition methods in terms of Rank-1 accuracy (%) using CASIA-B dataset. Here, '-' denotes that results are not reported.

Test		Training (NM #1-4): $0°$ - $180°$											
		$0°$	$18°$	$36°$	$54°$	$72°$	$90°$	$108°$	$126°$	$144°$	$162°$	$180°$	Mean
NM #5-6	GEI	9.14	14.87	15.03	16.07	23.75	22.5	23.91	17.2	12.44	13.49	9.02	16.13
	GEnI	12.45	16.12	13.1	12.38	15.02	23.62	23.21	21.10	15.20	15.57	16.18	16.72
	CMCC [8]	46.3	-	-	52.4	-	48.3	-	56.9	-	-	-	-
	GEINet [17]	45.8	57.6	67.1	66.9	56.3	48.3	58.3	68.4	69.4	59	46.5	58.5
	CNN-LB [23]	79.1	88.4	95.7	92.8	89.1	87	89.3	92.1	94.4	89.4	75.4	88.4
	GaitSet [4]	90.8	97.9	99.4	96.9	93.6	91.7	95	97.8	98.9	96.8	85.8	95
	GaitNet [19]	75.6	91.3	91.2	92.9	92.5	91.0	91.8	93.8	92.9	94.1	81.9	89.9
	Proposed	91.42	92.59	93.44	95.34	95.57	96.90	95.56	94.77	95.72	93.31	92.49	94.46
BG #1-2	GEI	6.44	9.91	11.61	9.32	15.32	12.21	11.65	11.97	8.26	8.94	6.37	10.18
	GEnI	7.64	9.82	7.31	7.08	9.81	13.63	12.37	12.59	7.27	7.26	7.97	9.34
	CMCC [8]	-	-	-	-	-	-	-	-	-	-	-	-
	GEINet [17]	-	-	-	-	-	-	-	-	-	-	-	-
	CNN-LB [23]	64.2	80.6	82.7	76.9	64.8	63.1	68	76.9	82.2	75.4	61.3	72.4
	GaitSet [4]	83.8	91.2	91.8	88.8	83.3	81	84.1	90	92.2	94.4	79	87.2
	GaitNet [19]	-	-	-	-	-	-	-	-	-	-	-	-
	Proposed	27.77	37.12	37.12	46.32	50.76	53.15	51.18	41.48	34.01	33.13	30.10	40.19
CL #1-2	GEI	2.57	4.27	6.23	6.32	6.28	7.01	6.6	6.97	5.18	4.62	2.54	5.33
	GEnI	3.02	5.01	4.61	4.52	6.44	8.24	8.06	8.64	6.36	5.33	4.42	5.88
	CMCC [8]	-	-	-	-	-	-	-	-	-	-	-	-
	GEINet [17]	-	-	-	-	-	-	-	-	-	-	-	-
	CNN-LB [23]	37.7	57.2	66.6	61.1	55.2	54.6	55.2	59.1	58.9	48.8	39.4	54
	GaitSet [4]	61.4	75.4	80.7	77.3	72.1	70.1	71.5	73.5	73.5	68.4	50	70.4
	GaitNet [19]	-	-	-	-	-	-	-	-	-	-	-	-
	Proposed	14.11	18.13	19.40	22.22	25.28	22.29	22.01	20.72	18.61	17.66	16.15	19.69

5   Conclusion

In this paper, we have introduced a unified CNN model that combines gait feature learning and recognition into a single end-to-end network. This model has the capability to automatically discover discriminative representations for gait recognition, ensuring invariance to variations in view angle, clothing, and carrying conditions. By integrating the learning process of each component, our unified model simplifies the traditional step-by-step procedure and yields noticeable performance improvements compared to separate learning approaches. To evaluate the effectiveness of our proposed method, we have conducted extensive experiments using the CASIA-B gait dataset. The experimental results have clearly demonstrated that our method surpasses the performance of state-of-the-art traditional methods and achieves comparable results to recent deep learning-based gait recognition methods in both cross-view and cross-walking scenarios.

References

1. Bashir, K., Xiang, T., Gong, S.: Gait recognition using gait entropy image. In: 3rd International Conference on Imaging for Crime Detection and Prevention, ICDP 2009, pp. 1–6 (2009)
2. Bashir, K., Xiang, T., Gong, S.: Gait recognition without subject cooperation. Pattern Recogn. Lett. **31**(13), 2052–2060 (2010)
3. Cao, K., Jain, A.K.: Automated latent fingerprint recognition. IEEE Trans. Pattern Anal. Mach. Intell. **41**(4), 788–800 (2019)
4. Chao, H., He, Y., Zhang, J., Feng, J.: GaitSet: regarding gait as a set for cross-view gait recognition. CoRR abs/1811.06186 (2018)
5. Chen, X., Xu, J.: Uncooperative gait recognition. Pattern Recogn. **53**(C), 116–129 (2016)
6. Han, J., Bhanu, B.: Individual recognition using gait energy image. IEEE Trans. Pattern Anal. Mach. Intell. **28**(2), 316–322 (2006)
7. Krizhevsky, A., Sutskever, I., Hinton, G.E.: ImageNet classification with deep convolutional neural networks. In: Proceedings of the 25th International Conference on Neural Information Processing Systems, NIPS 2012, vol. 1, pp. 1097–1105. Curran Associates Inc., Red Hook, NY, USA (2012)
8. Kusakunniran, W., Wu, Q., Zhang, J., Li, H., Wang, L.: Recognizing gaits across views through correlated motion co-clustering. IEEE Trans. Image Process. **23**(2), 696–709 (2014)
9. Lam, T., Cheung, K., Liu, J.: Gait flow image: a silhouette-based gait representation for human identification. Pattern Recogn. **44**, 973–987 (2011)
10. Makihara, Y., Sagawa, R., Mukaigawa, Y., Echigo, T., Yagi, Y.: Gait recognition using a view transformation model in the frequency domain. In: Leonardis, A., Bischof, H., Pinz, A. (eds.) ECCV 2006. LNCS, vol. 3953, pp. 151–163. Springer, Heidelberg (2006). https://doi.org/10.1007/11744078_12
11. Mansur, A., Makihara, Y., Muramatsu, D., Yagi, Y.: Cross-view gait recognition using view-dependent discriminative analysis. In: IEEE International Joint Conference on Biometrics, pp. 1–8 (2014)
12. Murray., M.: Gait as a total pattern of movement (1967)

13. Nguyen, K., Fookes, C., Jillela, R., Sridharan, S., Ross, A.: Long range iris recognition: a survey. Pattern Recogn. **72**, 123–143 (2017)
14. Sarkar, S., Phillips, P., Liu, Z., Vega, I., Grother, P., Bowyer, K.: The humanid gait challenge problem: data sets, performance, and analysis. IEEE Trans. Pattern Anal. Mach. Intell. **27**(2), 162–177 (2005)
15. Sepas-Moghaddam, A.: Face recognition: a novel multi-level taxonomy based survey. IET Biometrics **9**, 58–67 (2020)
16. Sepas-Moghaddam, A., Etemad, A.: Deep gait recognition: a survey. IEEE Trans. Pattern Anal. Mach. Intell. **45**(1), 264–284 (2023)
17. Shiraga, K., Makihara, Y., Muramatsu, D., Echigo, T., Yagi, Y.: GEINet: view-invariant gait recognition using a convolutional neural network. In: 2016 International Conference on Biometrics (ICB), pp. 1–8 (2016)
18. Singh, J.P., Jain, S., Arora, S., Singh, U.P.: Vision-based gait recognition: a survey. IEEE Access **6**, 70497–70527 (2018)
19. Song, C., Huang, Y., Huang, Y., Jia, N., Wang, L.: GaitNet: an end-to-end network for gait based human identification. Pattern Recogn. **96**(C), 106988 (2019)
20. Taigman, Y., Yang, M., Ranzato, M., Wolf, L.: DeepFace: closing the gap to human-level performance in face verification. In: 2014 IEEE Conference on Computer Vision and Pattern Recognition, pp. 1701–1708 (2014)
21. Wang, C., Zhang, J., Wang, L., Pu, J., Yuan, X.: Human identification using temporal information preserving gait template. IEEE Trans. Pattern Anal. Mach. Intell. **34**(11), 2164–2176 (2012)
22. Wang, J., Chen, Y., Hao, S., Peng, X., Hu, L.: Deep learning for sensor-based activity recognition: a survey. CoRR abs/1707.03502 (2017)
23. Wu, Z., Huang, Y., Wang, L., Wang, X., Tan, T.: A comprehensive study on cross-view gait based human identification with deep CNNs. IEEE Trans. Pattern Anal. Mach. Intell. **39**(2), 209–226 (2017)
24. Yu, S., Tan, D., Tan, T.: A framework for evaluating the effect of view angle, clothing and carrying condition on gait recognition. In: 18th International Conference on Pattern Recognition, ICPR 2006, vol. 4, pp. 441–444 (2006)
25. Zhang, R., Vogler, C., Metaxas, D.: Human gait recognition at sagittal plane. Image Vis. Comput. **25**(3), 321–330 (2007)
26. Zhao, G., Liu, G., Li, H., Pietikainen, M.: 3D gait recognition using multiple cameras. In: 7th International Conference on Automatic Face and Gesture Recognition, FGR 2006, pp. 529–534 (2006)

A New Lightweight Attention-Based Model for Emotion Recognition on Distorted Social Media Face Images

Ayush Roy[1], Palaiahnakote Shivakumara[2(✉)], Umapada Pal[1], Shivanand S. Gornale[3], and Cheng-Lin Liu[4]

[1] Computer Vision and Pattern Recognition Unit, Indian Statistical Institute, Kolkata, India
umapada@isical.ac.in
[2] Faculty of Computer Science and Information Technology, University of Malaya, Kula Lumpur, Malaysia
shiva@um.edu.my
[3] Department of Computer Science, Rani Channamma University, Belagavi, India
shivanand1971@rcub.ac.in
[4] Institute of Automation of Chinese Academy of Sciences, Beijing, China
liucl@nlpr.ia.ac.cn

Abstract. The recognition of human emotions remains a challenging task for social media images. This is due to distortions created by different social media conflict with the minute changes in facial expression. This study presents a new model called the Global Spectral-Spatial Attention Network (GSSAN), which leverages both local and global information simultaneously. The proposed model comprises a shallow Convolutional Neural Network (CNN) with an MBRes-Next block, which integrates the features extracted from MobileNet, ResNet, and DenseNet for extracting local features. In addition, to strengthen the discriminating power of the features, GSSAN incorporates Fourier features, which provide essential cues for minute changes in the face images. To test the proposed model for emotion recognition using social media images, we conduct experiments on two widely-used datasets: FER-2013 and AffectNet. The same benchmark datasets are uploaded and downloaded to create a distorted social media image dataset to test the proposed model. Experiments on distorted social media images dataset show that the model surpasses the accuracy of SOTA models by 0.69% for FER-2013 and 0.51% for AffectNet social media datasets. The same inference can be drawn from the experiments on standard datasets.

Keywords: Face detection · Facial expressions · Face recognition · Deep learning models · Human emotions recognition

1 Introduction

The use of social media, such as Facebook, Instagram, Twitter, WeChat, and WhatsApp for sharing, communicating, and expressing person views is common. Therefore, developing an automatic Human-Computer Interaction (HCI) system for recognizing facial

H. Lu et al. (Eds.): ACPR 2023, LNCS 14407, pp. 243–257, 2023.
https://doi.org/10.1007/978-3-031-47637-2_19

expressions accurately is challenging [1–3]. This is because when we upload and download images from different social media, the storing mechanism of social media degrades the quality of images. Therefore, the images are called distorted social media images. These artifacts cause minute changes on the facial expression. Thus, achieving accurate and efficient methods for social media images is an open challenge [1–3]. Since emotion recognition is not a new problem, many methods were developed in the past [4–8]. However, most models consider normal facial images for emotion recognition but not social media images. Due to degradations caused by social media, there are chances of an increasing gap between intra-images and decreasing in inter-images. Thus, the existing methods developed so far may not be effective for social media images. The main reason is that most existing models either consider local information or global information but not both for emotion recognition. This observation motivated us to develop a new model for achieving the best results for normal and distorted social media images. In addition, the developed method can fit in the real-time environment.

Sample images of different emotions chosen from the created social media dataset are shown in Fig. 1, where the proposed method recognizes all the classes correctly while the state-of-the-art model [4], which uses a multi-head self-attention mechanism for emotions recognition, misclassifies "Neutral" as "Sad" on FER-2013 dataset and "Fear" as "Surprised" on AffectNet datasets. It is evident that that the existing models are not effective for social media images.

Neutral   Angry   Happy   Sad   Surprised   Disgust   Fear

Social media sample images from FER-2023.

Neutral   Angry   Happy   Sad   Surprised   Disgust   Fear   Contempt

Social media sample images from AffectNet.

Fig. 1. Sample images of the created social media datasets.

Thus, this work aims at developing lightweight models that can fit in real-time environments without compromising accuracy. The proposed lightweight model consists of Global Spectral Spatial Attention Network (GSSN) and shallow convolutional neural network layers. To reduce the effect of degradations caused by social media and to achieve efficiency, the proposed work integrates MobileNext [16], RestNet [17], and DenseNet [18] in a novel way for emotion recognition in this work. MobileNext is a lightweight model, and it performs both spatial convolution and skip connection at high-dimensional data, thus reducing the possibility of information loss and gradient confusion [16]. The Residual block reduces the vanishing gradient problem by identity mapping and also helps in faster training of the module [17]. Each block is connected densely like in DenseNet [18] architectures. The advantages are the reuse of feature maps through dense connections, and the reducing interdependence between layers by reusing feature maps from different layers.

To improve the discriminating power of the feature extraction, GSSN uses features extracted from the frequency domain, which helps us to extract minute changes [9]. These observations inspired us to explore GSSN and shallow CNN (MobileNext, ResNet, and DenseNet) for emotion recognition in this work. Therefore, the key contribution of the proposed work is as follows. (i) Addressing the challenges of normal and distorted social media images is new work. (ii) Exploring GSSAN for extracting global features for emotion recognition. (iii) Proposing shallow CNN layers with the help of MobileNext, ResNet, and DenseNet for extracting local features for emotion recognition. (iv) The way the proposed work integrates the strength of different modules to achieve both accuracy and efficiency is new compared to the state-of-the-art methods.

The rest of the paper is organized as follows. The emotion recognition methods based on machine learning, deep learning and transformers are reviewed in Sect. 2. Section 3 presents the detailed architecture of GSSN and shallow CNN for emotion recognitions. To validate the proposed model, Sect. 4 provides experimental analysis on two standard datasets. Lastly, the findings are summarized in Sect. 5.

2 Related Work

The models of emotion recognition can be broadly classified as machine learning, deep learning, and transformer-based methods. We review the methods of respective categories. Pramerdorfer et al. [6] discussed several methods based on CNN for facial expression recognition. The work discusses the merits and demerits of CNN-based methods for emotion recognition. It is stated that the methods achieve inconsistent results for the same dataset. Fard et al. [3] proposes an adaptive correlation and loss-based method for emotion recognition to decrease the gap between intra-images and to increase the gap between inter-images. To improve the performance of the CNN-based methods, Pham et al. [7] developed a model using a residual masking network for emotion recognition. The approach combines a deep residual network and Unet-like architecture to generate a residual masking network.

Pourmirzaei et al. [11] integrates advantages of images generated by augmentation techniques and training from scratch to improve emotions recognition performance. Therefore, the work introduces hybrid multi-task learning for emotion recognition. Schoneveld et al. [12] explored an audio-visual features-based method for emotion recognition, unlike most methods that use facial features. A recurrent neural network is proposed to extract the temporal dynamics to improve performance. Savchenko et al. [8] proposed a method that is different from other existing methods for emotion recognition based on a single facial expression recognition neural network. This work has been developed for video for emotions recognition. Vignesh et al. [2] stated that CNN-based methods are better than conventional handcrafted features-based methods. Therefore, the authors proposed the combination of CNN and UNet visual geometry group layers for emotion recognition.

Kollias et al. [9] proposed a multi-task learning method for recognizing emotions, affection, and action units. The key advantage of this method is that it performs well for small-sized datasets, small numbers of labels, etc. Pecoraro et al. [3] introduced local multi-head channel self-attention for emotion recognition. It is noted that the self-attention mechanism channel-wise is better than spatial attention. Khaireddin et al. [5] explored VGGNet for emotion recognition. The work adapts the VGGNet and tunes its hyperparameters to improve the performance of the emotions recognition. Wen et al. [10] developed a new model that uses similar appearance and multiple regions in the facial image for emotions recognition. To achieve this, the work explores feature clustering networks, multi-head cross attention network, and attention fusion network.

Leong et al. [13] provided a systematic review of facial expression and body gesture emotion recognition applications to affective computing. In this work, current trends, directions, and limitations are discussed. Liu et al. [14] mentioned that emotion recognition is challenging and low accuracy is reported due to the subjectivity of observers. To find solution to this problem, the authors proposed fine-grained emotional differences based on intra-class correlation and inter-class differences. Verma et al. [15] mentioned that a few methods made an attempt to achieve the best results with minimum expense for emotions recognition. However, the existing methods are insensitive to minute variations in the images. Therefore, one can conclude that achieving the best results without much comuputational burden for both normal and social media images is still considered as an open challenge.

In summary, although robust models were proposed for emotion recognition, the performance of the methods is not satisfactory for the social media images because the methods are not effective for degradations caused by social media. The main reason is that most methods either focus on local features or global features. None of the methods use global and local features effectively for addressing the challenges of normal and social media datasets.

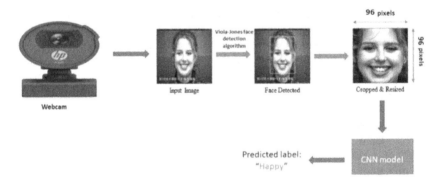

Fig. 2. The overall workflow of the proposed real-time emotion recognition model.

3   Proposed Model

This work aims at developing a new model that can achieve both accuracy and efficiency for emotion recognition using normal and social media face images. The proposed work uses preprocess steps before extracting features as shown in Fig. 2, where for the input image, the face detection method is used to crop the face area and restores it to its original size. The resized image is fed to the proposed model for emotions recognition as shown in Fig. 2.

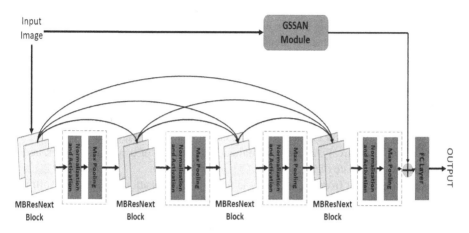

(a). Architecture of the proposed CNN model.

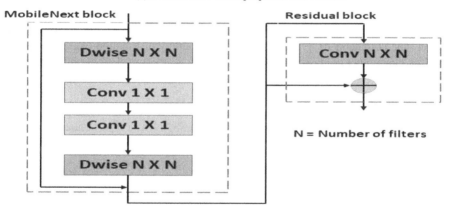

(b). MBResNext module.

Fig. 3. **(a).** Architecture of the proposed CNN model. **(b).** MBResNext module.

3.1 Overview of Proposed Architecture

Figure 3(a) describes the architecture of a convolutional neural network (CNN) model. The input image to the model has dimensions of $96 \times 96 \times 3$, where 3 represents the number of color channels (RGB). The model consists of several convolutional blocks, where each block is composed of an MBResNext block, a Batch Normalization layer, a ReLu activation layer, and a Max Pooling layer (to reduce the dimension by a factor of 2). The MBResNext block (see Fig. 3(b)) is a fusion of the blocks of MobileNext [16] and ResNet [17] architectures. The advantage of using a convolutional block (sandglass-like architecture) from MobileNext is its lightweight computation performs both spatial convolution and skip connection at high-dimensional data, thus reducing the possibility of information loss and gradient confusion. The Residual block reduces the vanishing gradient problem by identity mapping and also helps in faster training of the module. Each block is connected densely like in DenseNet [18] architectures. The advantages are the reuse of feature maps through dense connection, reducing interdependence between layers by reusing feature maps from different layers, providing compact and differentiated input features by shortcut connections of different lengths, and effectively reducing the gradient disappearance problem that is difficult to optimize in deep networks.

The flattened features from the Global Spectral Spatial Attention Network (GSSAN) module and the baseline CNN are added and fed to the Fully Connected (FC) layer. This layer consists of two fully connected layers, each consisting of a dense layer with 256 and 512 units, respectively, a batch normalization layer, a ReLu activation layer, and a dropout layer with a rate of 0.25.

Finally, the output from the FC layer is fed to a classification layer with a softmax activation function, which outputs the probabilities of the input image belonging to different classes.

$$L(y, y') = -\sum_{i=1}^{C} (y_i \log y_i')$$ (1)

The loss function used is described in Eq. 1. Where y is the true probability distribution (one-hot encoded), y' is the predicted probability distribution (softmax output), and C is the number of classes. This is also known as categorical cross-entropy.

3.2 GSSAN Attention Module

The Global Spectral Spatial Attention Network (GSSAN) is a type of attention mechanism used to improve the performance of the CNN model. This attention mechanism

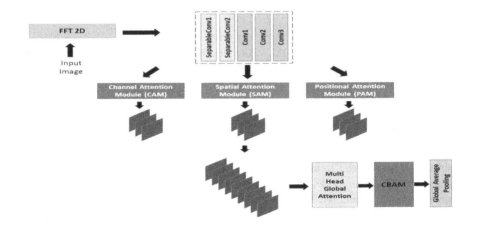

Fig. 4. Block diagram of the GSSAN attention module.

extracts Fast Fourier Transform (FFT) features from the input image, down samples the features using Convolutional layers, and feeds them into the three local attention modules, i.e., Channel Attention Module (CAM) [19], Spatial Attention Module (SAM) [19], and Positional Attention Module (PAM) [20]. These attention modules are extremely potent as local attention mechanisms. The features from these modules are concatenated and passed on to the Multi-head Global Attention [21] to find the intricate relationships of the local features globally. The problem of redundancy with Multi-head Global Attention is avoided here due to the FFT features extracted which have a range of frequency information. The resultant feature map is fed to the CBAM (Convolutional Block Attention Module) [19] to provide more weightage to specific spatial positions and channels. Block diagram of GSSAN is given in Fig. 4.

The feature map from the FFT layer is down-sampled via two layers of Separable Convolutional layers. Separable convolutions consist of first performing a depth-wise spatial convolution (which acts on each input channel separately) followed by a pointwise convolution that mixes the resulting output channels. The depth multiplier argument controls how many output channels are generated per input channel in the depth-wise step. Intuitively, separable convolutions can be understood as a way to factorize a convolution kernel into two smaller kernels, or as an extreme version of an Inception block. Separable Convolutional layers 1 and 2 have filters 4 and 8 respectively, with kernel size of 5 × 5, stride of (2,2), and Gelu activation. These are followed by Convolutional layers 1,2 and 3 with filters of 128, 256, and 128 respectively, kernel size of 5 × 5, and stride of (1,1). Finally, the feature map is flattened using Global average pooling. The flattened feature is added to the flattened features of the main architecture and passed on to the FC layers for final predictions. In summary, the GSSAN module is used to enhance the feature learning process by extracting and concatenating both spatial and spectral features, which helps the model learn facial features more effectively for different emotions.

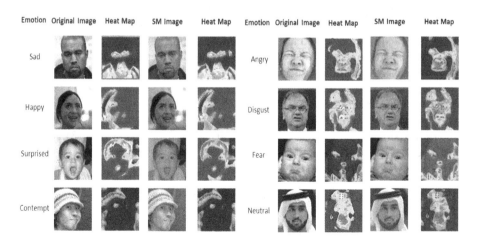

Fig. 5. Visualization of features extracted by the proposed model on AffectNet dataset and the AffectNet Social Media (SM) dataset.

To show the effectiveness of the proposed model, the intermediate results of the heat map are generated for both normal and social media images of the AffectNet dataset as shown in Fig. 5. It is observed from heat maps of normal and social media images that the important cues which are unique for each emotion are highlighted, irrespective of degradations. Therefore, it can be concluded that the proposed model is capable of coping with the challenges of normal and social media images with minimum expense.

4 Experimental Results

To evaluate the proposed method, we consider two well-known datasets, namely, FER-2013 and AffectNet dataset for experimentation. The FER-2013 dataset and the Affect-Net dataset are two challenging datasets for emotion recognition. The FER-2013 dataset contains 35,887 grayscale images of size 48 × 48 pixels, each labeled with one of seven emotion categories: anger, disgust, fear, happiness, sadness, surprise, and neutral. The dataset includes images affected by poor quality, lighting conditions, and facial expressions. Similarly, the AffectNet dataset, on the other hand, is larger and more diverse compared to the FER-2013 dataset, containing over 1 million images with 8 annotated emotion categories: neutral, happiness, sadness, surprise, anger, disgust, fear, and contempt. The dataset includes images of different colors with varying resolutions. Sample images of 8 emotion classes of two standard datasets are shown in Fig. 6, where it can be observed that images of FER-2013 are simple compared to the images of AffectNet. This is because the images of AffectNet contain complex background information and color information, while the FER-2013 dataset does not.

To test the performance of the proposed method on social media images, we use the images of the FER-2013 and AffectNet datasets to upload and download in different social media (Facebook, Twitter, Instagram, WeChat, and WhatsApp). Sample social media images are shown in Fig. 7, where one can notice all the images are degraded and suffered from poor quality, and images lose sharpness and contrast compared to the image shown in Fig. 6. For experimentation, we choose 500 images randomly from each dataset and the 70:30 ratio has been used for training and testing. The reason to choose 500 random images is that we believe that this number includes all the possible distortions created by different social media.

For measuring the performance of the proposed method, we consider the standard metrics as defined in (2)–(5).

Accuracy. It is the ratio of total correctly classified samples to the total number of samples as defined in (2), Precision and Recall measures are defined in (3) and (4), respectively.

$$Accuracy = \frac{TP + TN}{TP + FP + TN + FN} \tag{2}$$

$$P = \frac{TP}{TP + FP} \tag{3}$$

$$R = \frac{TP}{TP + FN} \tag{4}$$

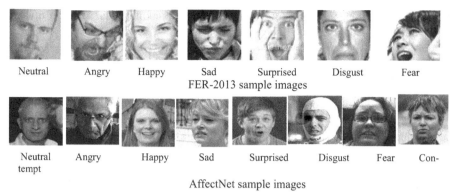

FER-2013 sample images

AffectNet sample images

Fig. 6. Sample images from both the standard datasets.

F1 score. It is the harmonic mean of recall and precision calculated using (5).

$$F = 2 \times \frac{(P \times R)}{(P + R)}$$ (5)

FER-2013-Social media sample images

Fig. 7. Sample images of the created social media datasets.

Implementation. To conduct the experimentations, we trained our emotion recognition model on two standard datasets using popular Python libraries such as Tensor-Flow, Keras, OpenCV, and NumPy. We utilized a 70:30 split for training and testing on both datasets and used the Adam optimizer with a learning rate of 0.001. We trained our overall model for 150 epochs for each dataset to ensure robustness and accuracy. To enable real-time emotion detection, we utilized the Viola-Jones algorithm for face detection, which enabled us to locate the Region of Interest (ROI) for the face. This ROI was then passed to our trained model for the prediction of the corresponding emotional state. The average FPS of the proposed model in real-time testing is 45 ($\pm$5) FPS, which is good for a real-time environment. The existing methods are fine tuned with the samples of both normal and social media image datasets for experimentation. In addition, the same set up and environment has been used for all the experiments.

4.1 Ablation Study

To achieve the best results for emotion recognition using face images, the role of GSSAN for obtaining dominant cues and CNN for feature extraction is vital. Therefore, to validate the contribution of each step, we conducted an ablation study on different experiments listed in Table 1 using FER-2013 original and FER-2013 social media datasets. (i) Calculating measures for emotion recognition by feeding input images directly to the model with normal Convolutional layers without dominant cues obtained by GSSAN. This is to show the contribution of GSSAN to emotion recognition. (ii) Recognizing emotions by replacing Convolutional layers with MBResNext layers. (iii) Recognizing emotions with the addition of Dense connections to connect the MbResNext blocks. (iv) Recognizing emotions using cues obtained by GSSAN and feature extraction by CNN, which is the proposed method. It is observed from Table 1 that the GSSAN and CNN both contribute equally to addressing the challenges of emotion recognition. However, it is noted that GSSAN alone and CNN alone do not achieve the best results as the proposed method. This is because the accuracy increases when we combine both compared to the accuracy of the individual. This shows that the combination of GSSAN and CNN is essential for obtaining the best results. The results of both FER-2013 original and social media datasets, the results of all the experiments on social media are lower than the results of the original dataset. However, the inferences are the same for both the datasets.

Table 1. Ablation study on the FER-2013 dataset and its corresponding social media dataset (in %). Acc denotes Accuracy, and F1 indicates F1-Score.

Experiments	FER-2013				FER-Social media images			
	Acc	P	R	F1	Acc	P	R	F1
(i) Without GSSAN and MBResNext block	63.57	63.34	61.83	62.48	61.16	61.32	60.38	60.85
(ii) Replacing Convolutional layers with MBResNext block	66.19	65.45	77.32	66.37	64.01	63.98	63.46	63.72
(iii) Addition of Dense connections	71.13	72.38	69.83	71.08	68.29	68.74	65.59	67.13
(iv) Proposed (GSSAN + CNN)	76.06	77.06	75.29	76.11	72.87	73.50	71.44	72.45

4.2 Experiments for Emotion Recognition

For testing our method on emotion recognition, qualitative results of the proposed method are shown in Fig. 6, Fig. 7, and Fig. 8, where for all the images in Fig. 6–Fig. 8, the proposed method classifies successfully. The illustration in Fig. 8 shows our method can work in a real-time environment for emotion recognition. Therefore, one can infer that the proposed model is accurate and efficient. For the same images shown in Fig. 6, the existing method [4], LHC-Net wrongly predicts "Disgust" for the "Sad" and "Fear" for "Surprised") on FER-2013 and "Contempt" for "Disgust" on AffectNet. The key reason for the poor results of the existing method is that the models do not use local and global features effectively. In addition, the success of the methods heavily depends on the number of training samples and parameters. It is also noted from the results on social media images that the proposed method classifies all the images in Fig. 7 success- fully while the existing methods [4] misclassify "Surprised" as "Angry" and "Angry" as "Surprised" for the FER-2013 social media dataset, and "Angry" as "Contempt". "Dis- gust" and "Sad" as "Neutral" for the AffectNet social media dataset. The existing model correctly classified these images in their original form but due to the pixel degradation, contrast, and brightness, it fails for the social media ones. Our method considers the FFT features, which are immune to small changes in brightness and contrast of images (only amplitude changes while phase remains constant). This shows that the proposed method is robust to distorted social media images while the existing methods do not. Therefore, the proposed method is generic compared to the state-of-the-art methods.

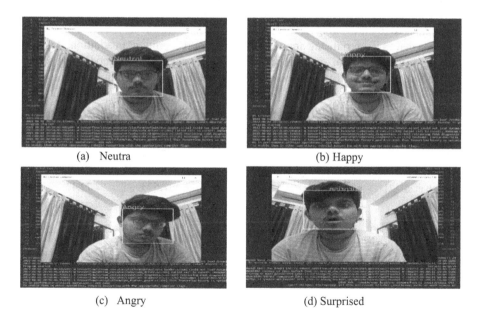

(a)   Neutra   (b) Happy

(c)   Angry   (d) Surprised

Fig. 8. Output of real time emotion detection of the CNN model.

The quantitative results of the proposed and existing methods are reported for FER- 2013 and AffectNet datasets, and distorted social media datasets of FER-2013 and Affect- Net in Tables 2, 3 and 4. The results in Tables 2, 3 and 4 show that the proposed model is the best compared to the existing models. When we look at the accuracy of FER-2013, AffectNet, and respective social media datasets, the accuracy of the proposed model gradually decreases. This indicates that the complexity of the images increases from FER-2013 to social media datasets. This makes sense because AffectNet is complex compared to the FER-2013 dataset. In the same way, social media datasets are much more complex compared to normal FER-2013 and AffectNet datasets. As a result, one can assert that the proposed model demonstrates its capability to handle different complex datasets.

Table 2 presents the accuracy and number of parameters of the proposed and existing methods on the FER-2013 dataset. The proposed method outperforms existing methods in terms of both accuracy and number of parameters, demonstrating its superiority over existing methods. The results of the existing methods reveal that they use a large number of parameters and their extracted features are not robust enough to handle the challenges of intra and inter-class variations for emotion recognition. In contrast, the combination of GSSAN and CNN, as noted from ablation study experiments, extracts robust features that can withstand intra and inter-class variations for emotion recognition. Similar conclusions can be drawn from the results of the proposed and existing methods reported in Table 3 and Table 4 where all the models are trained using the generated social media datasets. The state-of-the-art models are not as accurate as the proposed method.

Overall, the quantitative results show that the proposed method is accurate and efficient compared to the existing methods, and its robustness to handle intra and inter-class variations makes it a promising approach for emotion recognition. In addition, it is also noted from the results on social media datasets that the proposed model has robust degradations created by different social media while the existing methods do not.

Table 2. Evaluating the proposed and existing methods on the FER-2013 dataset (in %).

Accuracy		Efficiency with Accuracy		
Model	Accuracy	Models	Parameters	Accuracy
Vignesh et al. [2]	75.97	ResNet34 [7]	27.6 M	72.42
Ad-corre [3]	72.03	VGG [6]	143.7 M	72.70
Pecoraro et al. [4]	74.42	ResNet152 [7]	60.38 M	73.22
Y et al. [5]	73.28	Inception [6]	23.85 M	71.60
Our model	**76.06**	Our model	**6.06 M**	**76.06**

Table 3. Evaluating the proposed and existing methods on the AffectNet dataset (in %).

Models	[8]	[9]	[10]	[11]	[12]	Proposed
Accuracy	63.03	63.00	62.09	61.72	61.60	**63.51**

Although the proposed method achieves the best results for the FER-2013, Affect-Net and the social media datasets, it sometimes misclassifies, as illustrated in Fig. 9.

Table 4. Evaluating the proposed and existing methods on the social media dataset.

FER-2013 Social Media Dataset				AffectNet Social Media dataset		
Models	[5]	[4]	Proposed	[5]	[4]	Proposed
Accuracy	70.16	72.18	**72.87**	58.93	60.58	**61.09**

Fig. 9. False classification cases of our model. Here, "a -> b" denotes the original ground-truth class is "b" while the classification result of our model is "a".

This is mainly due to the high degree of similarity between the images of inter-classes with minute differences and this indicates that there is a room for improvement in the future. To address this challenge, we plan to develop an end-to-end model that facilitates communication between the dominant cue extraction and robust feature extraction stages. As result, this process helps us to extract invariant features to intra and inter-class variations, thus addressing the limitation of the proposed method.

5 Conclusion and Future Work

The proposed method aims to achieve both high accuracy and efficiency by exploring lightweight models such as the Global Spectral Spatial Attention Network (GSSAN) for extracting dominant cues and shallow convolutional neural network (CNN) layers for feature extraction. The CNN comprises MobileTextNet which integrates MobileNet, ResNet, and DenseNet for extracting fine-tune features. The method fuses the global features extracted from GSSAN and the local features extracted from CNN for recognizing different emotions on two standard datasets and social media datasets. The results on four datasets show that the proposed model is outstanding in terms of accuracy, efficiency and robustness compared to the existing methods. However, when the images of different emotion classes share a high degree of similarity with minute differences, the proposed method does not perform well. To address this limitation, we suggest to develop an end-to-end model with a feedback attention mechanism as a future work.

Acknowledgements. The work was partly supported by Ministry of Higher Education Malaysia via Fundamental Research Grant Scheme with Grant no: FRGS/1/2020/ICT02/UM/02/4. The work was also partly supported by Technology Innovation Hub, Indian Statistical Institute, Kolkata, India.

References

1. Goodfellow, I., Courville, A., Bengio, Y.: Large-scale feature learning with spike-and-slab sparse coding. arXiv preprint arXiv:1206.6407 (2012)
2. Vignesh, S., Savithadevi, M., Sridevi, M., Sridhar, R.: A novel facial emotion recognition model using segmentation VGG-19 architecture. Int. J. Inf. Technol. **15**(4), 1777–1787 (2023)
3. Fard, A.P., Mahoor, M.H.: Ad-corre: adaptive correlation-based loss for facial expression recognition in the wild. IEEE Access **10**, 26756–26768 (2022)
4. Pecoraro, R., Basile, V., Bono, V.: Local multi-head channel self-attention for facial expression recognition. Information **13**(9), 419 (2022)
5. Khaireddin, Y., Chen, Z.: Facial emotion recognition: state of the art performance on FER2013. arXiv preprint arXiv:2105.03588 (2021)
6. Christopher, P., Martin, K.: Facial expression recognition using convolutional neural networks: state of the art. arXiv preprint arXiv:1612.02903 (2016)
7. Luan, P., The, H.V., Tuan, A.T.: Facial expression recognition using residual masking network. In 2020 25th International Conference on Pattern Recognition (ICPR), pp. 4513–4519. IEEE (2021)
8. Savchenko, A.V., Savchenko, L.V., Makarov, I.: Classifying emotions and engagement in online learning based on a single facial expression recognition neural network. IEEE Trans. Affect. Comput. **13**(4), 2132–2143 (2022)
9. Kollias, D., Zafeiriou, S.: Expression, affect, action unit recognition: Aff-Wild2, multi-task learning and ArcFace. arXiv preprint arXiv:1910.04855 (2019)
10. Wen, Z., Lin, W., Wang, T., Xu, G.: Distract your attention: multi-head cross attention network for facial expression recognition. arXiv preprint arXiv:2109.07270 (2021)
11. Pourmirzaei, M., Montazer, G. A., Esmaili, F.: Using self-supervised auxiliary tasks to improve fine-grained facial representation. arXiv preprint arXiv:2105.06421 (2021)
12. Schoneveld, L., Othmani, A., Abdelkawy, H.: Leveraging recent advances in deep learning for audio-visual emotion recognition. Pattern Recogn. Lett. **146**, 1–7 (2021)
13. Leong, S.C., Tang, Y.M., Lai, C.H., Lee, C.K.M.: Facial expression and body gesture emotions recognition: a systematic review on the use of visual data in affective computing. Comput. Sci. Rev. **48** (2023). https://doi.org/10.1016/j.cosrev.2023.100545
14. Liu, H., Cai, H., Lin, Q., Zhang, X., Li, X., Xiao, H.: FEDA: fine-grained emotion difference analysis for facial expression recognition. Biomed. Sig. Process. Control **79** (2023). https://doi.org/10.1016/j.bspc.2022.104209
15. Verma, M., Mandal, M., Reddy, S.K., Meedimale, Y.R., Vipparthi, S.K.: Efficient neural architecture search for emotions recognition. Exp. Syst. Appl. **224** (2023). https://doi.org/10.1016/j.eswa.2023.119957
16. Daquan, Z., Hou, Q., Chen, Y., Feng, J., Yan, S.: Rethinking bottleneck structure for efficient mobile network design. arXiv arXiv:2007.02269 (2020)

17. He, K., Zhang, X., Ren, S., Sun, J.: Deep residual learning for image recognition. arXiv arXiv: 1512.03385 (2015)
18. Huang, G., Liu, Z., Weinberger, K.Q.: Densely connected convolutional networks. arXiv arXiv:1608.06993 (2016)
19. Woo, S., Park, J., Lee, J., Kweon, I.S.: CBAM: convolutional block attention module. arXiv arXiv:1807.06521 (2018)
20. Chen, T., et al.: ABD-Net: attentive but diverse person re-identification. In Proceedings of the ICCV, pp. 8350–8360 (2019)
21. Vaswani, A., et al.: Attention is all you need. arXiv arXiv:1706.03762 (2017)

Uncertainty-Guided Test-Time Training for Face Forgery Detection

Shenyuan Huang[1,5], Huaibo Huang[5], Zi Wang[1], Nan Xu[5], Aihua Zheng[2,3,4],
and Ran He[5(✉)]

[1] School of Computer Science and Technology, Anhui University, Hefei, China
[2] Information Materials and Intelligent Sensing Laboratory of Anhui Province, Hefei,
China
[3] Anhui Provincial Key Laboratory of Multimodal Cognitive Computation, Hefei,
China
[4] School of Artificial Intelligence, Anhui University, Hefei, China
[5] NLPR, CRIPAC, CASIA, Beijing, China
huaibo.huang@cripac.ia.ac.cn, xunan2015@ia.ac.cn, rhe@nlpr.ia.ac.cn

Abstract. Face forgery detection is becoming increasingly important
in computer vision as facial manipulation technologies cause serious concerns. Recent works have resorted to the frequency domain to develop
face forgery detectors and achieved better generalization achievements.
However, there are still unignorable problems: a) the role of frequency
is not always sufficiently effective and generalized to different forgery
technologies; and b) the network trained on public datasets is unable to
effectively quantify its uncertainty. To address the generalization issue,
we design a Dynamic Dual-spectrum Interaction Network (DDIN) that
allows test-time training with uncertainty guidance. RGB and frequency
features are first interacted in multi-level by using a Frequency-guided
Attention Module (FAM). Then these multi-modal features are merged
with a Dynamic Fusion Module (DFM). Moreover, we further exploit
uncertain perturbations as guidance during the test-time training phase.
The network can dynamically fuse the features with quality discrepancies, thus improving the generalization of forgery detection. Comprehensive evaluations of several benchmark databases corroborate the superior
generalization performance of DDIN.

Keywords: Face Forgery Detection · Frequency Domain · Test-time
training · Generalization

1 Introduction

Recent years have witnessed significant progress in the area of face forgery technology. The quality of fake media has been greatly improved with the development of deep learning technology. At the same time, these forged media may be
abused for malicious purposes, causing severe trust issues and security concerns

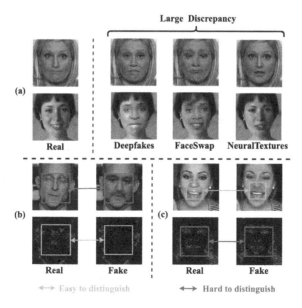

Fig. 1. In the first two rows, the real images are compared to images synthesized by different forgery techniques. In the last two rows, we show the quality difference in RGB and frequency domains. The red box indicates that the forgery traces are hard to recognize, while the green box shows that it is easy to distinguish. (Color figure online)

in our society. Therefore, it is critical to developing effective forgery detection methods.

Most of the existing methods focus on within-database detection [2,20], where forged images in the training set and testing set are manipulated by the same forgery technique. As shown in Fig. 1(a), the styles of the synthesized images from various forgery techniques are quite different. Thus, an ongoing issue of face forgery detection is generalization under out-of-distribution (OOD) data [12]. As shown in Fig. 1(b), the frequency distributions of real and fake images differ significantly in some datasets, but it is difficult to distinguish between the two in the RGB domain. Recent methods [5,17,23,26,29,39] introduced the face forgery frequency network to mine forgery traces in the frequency domain. Chen et al. [5] proposed a similarity model using frequency features to improve the model's performance in unseen domains, and Luo et al. [23] assumed that the high-frequency noise of images can remove colour texture and mine forgery traces and utilize image noises to boost the generalization ability. However, the role of the frequency domain is not always sufficiently effective, and RGB features also contain discriminative forgery information, as shown in Fig. 1(c). The quality discrepancies between frequency and RGB features are less addressed [29].

To alleviate the effects of feature quality discrepancies and model uncertainty, we design a Dynamic Dual-spectrum Interaction Network (DDIN) that allows test-time training with uncertainty guidance. First, in order to explore the forgery region, frequency features are more effective than discriminating only in the RGB domain. We propose a Dynamic Fusion Module (DFM) to use the quality distinction between RGB and frequency domain in an adaptive evaluation. Secondly, to increase model generalization on unseen data, we further fine-tune the trained network by estimating the uncertainty in the test-time training phase.

Spectrum transformation on an RGB image is used to obtain its corresponding frequency image based on *Discrete Cosine Transform* (DCT), and then these RGB and frequency images are input into the transformer-based network. Second, in the multi-level interaction stage, we use a Frequency-guided Attention Module (FAM) to direct the RGB modality from a frequency perspective, allowing us to attach more forgery traces. Thirdly, in the multi-modal fusion stage, we use the Cross-modal Attention Module (CAM) to fuse the features of the dual-stream network's output in order to enrich the information of the forged area. We further propose a Dynamic Fusion Module (DFM) for the dynamic enhancement of this multi-modal information to boost the generalization ability.

Moreover, to learn a more generalizable face forgery detector, we propose Uncertainty-guided Test-time Training (UTT). The key idea is to fine-tune the dynamic fusion module by estimating and exploiting the uncertainty of unseen test data. Specifically, we apply uncertainty-guided perturbations to different branches. The uncertain perturbation causes the network to predict quality weights in a probabilistic manner, and we fine-tune the network based on the distribution bias caused by this uncertainty. The distribution of predictions for forgery features on the training and test sets can be narrowed. Thus, it results in more robust predictions, particularly when the test set contains OOD data.

In brief, the main contributions are as follows:

- We propose a Dynamic Dual-spectrum Interaction Network (DDIN) that allows test-time training with uncertainty guidance to alleviate the effects of feature quality discrepancies and model uncertainty.
- We propose a Frequency-guided Attention Module (FAM) and Dynamic Fusion Module (DFM) in Dynamic Dual-spectrum Interaction Network (DDIN) that can be used to make the model dynamically fuse the features with quality discrepancies.
- We propose an Uncertainty-guided Test-time Training (UTT) by adding uncertain perturbation during the test-time training phase to improve the network generalization of forgery detection.
- Extensive experiments and visualizations demonstrate the effectiveness of our method against state-of-the-art competitors.

2   Related Work

2.1   Face Forgery Detection

In the past few years, face forgery detection has made significant strides, with a number of forgery-spotting models being successively proposed to meet the application's practical requirements. In the earlier stage, methods [1,2,7,13,18,28] are built with a significant emphasis on spotting semantic visual artefacts with sophisticated model designs. Recently, several works have focused on solving the generalizing problem. For instance, methods [5,16] both notice the content-independent low-level features that can uniquely identify their sources and the identity swapping will destroy the origin consistency. Li et al. [16] suggest identifying those subtle features across the facial boundary and Chen et al. [5] turn to discover the spatial-local contradictions. Methods [3,10,25] fuse the low-level frequency pattern learning with CNN to improve the generalizability. Despite the fact that these techniques frequently work, the low-level artefacts they rely on are sensitive to post-processing techniques that differ across datasets, putting their generalizability at risk. Despite the possibility that these features will lead to some advancements, it is very likely that deepfake algorithms will be created in the future in order to create more realistic fakes and pose a bigger threat to social security. Different from existing works, we propose a novel dynamic dual-spectrum interaction network that allows test-time training with uncertainty guidance.

2.2 Test-Time Training Strategy

The concept of test-time training was first presented in [33] for generalization to out-of-distribution test data. In this method, the main classification task is combined with a self-supervised rotation prediction task during training, and only the self-supervised task is used to help improve the visual representation during inference, which indirectly improves semantic classification. Li et al. [19] propose a reconstruction task within the main pose estimation framework, which can be trained by contrasting the reconstructed image with the ground truth gleaned from other frames. Chen et al. [4] proposed one-shot test-time training specially designed for the generalizable deepfake detection task. Nevertheless, despite some positive findings, current TTT methods aim to choose empirical self-supervised tasks, which carry a significant risk of degrading performance when the tasks are not properly chosen [22]. Instead, our UTT method is easy to implement and can avoid the tedious work of selecting an effective self-supervised task, which can significantly boost the deepfake detector's generalization performance and outperform existing solutions in a variety of benchmark datasets.

3 Proposed Method

3.1 Spectrum Transformation

As shown in the left-top in Fig. 2, we apply spectrum transformation that decomposes the input RGB image into frequency components, assisting the network in mining the distinction between real and forged regions.

Without loss of generality, let $X_{rgb} \in \mathbb{R}^{H \times W \times 3}$ denote the RGB input, where H and W are the height and width. First, we apply the Discrete Cosine Transform (DCT) to transform X_{rgb} from RGB into the frequency domain. DCT places

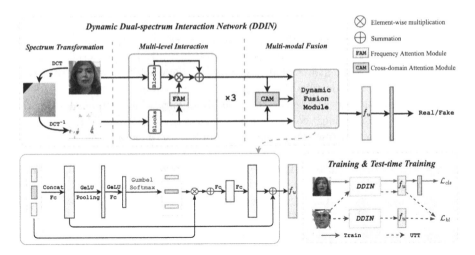

Fig. 2. The framework of our proposed DDIN and the pipeline of UTT.

low-frequency responses in the top-left corner and high-frequency responses in the bottom-right corner. Qian et al. [29] show that the low-frequency band is the first $1/16$ of the spectrum, the middle-frequency band is between $1/16$ and $1/8$ of the spectrum, and the high-frequency band is the last $7/8$ of the spectrum. To amplify subtle artefacts at high frequency, we filter out low and middle-frequency information by setting their frequency band to 0. To preserve shift-invariance and local consistency of natural images, we then invert the high-frequency spectrum back into RGB via IDCT to obtain the desired representation in the frequency domain, which can be formulated as:

$$X_{freq} = \mathcal{D}^{-1}(\mathcal{F}(\mathcal{D}(X_{rgb}))),\tag{1}$$

where $X_{freq} \in \mathbb{R}^{H\times W\times 3}$ denotes the RGB image represented at frequency domain, $\mathcal{D}$ denotes the DCT, $\mathcal{F}$ denotes the filter to obtain high frequency information, and $\mathcal{D}^{-1}$ denotes the IDCT. In this way, the original RGB input is decomposed and recombined frequency-aware data while maintaining the spatial relationship. Finally, we input both RGB and frequency images into the multi-level interaction phase to enhance the forged features.

3.2 Multi-level Interaction

RGB information is useful for locating anomalous textures in forged images, whereas frequency information amplifies subtly manipulated artefacts. To explore more forgery traces, we use a Frequency-guided Attention Module (FAM) based on CBAM [40]. While CBAM gains the attention weights from the RGB images, we exploit the frequency features to obtain the attention maps, to direct the RGB modality from a frequency perspective.

As shown in middle in DDIN at Fig. 2, let $X_{rgb} \in \mathbb{R}^{H\times W\times 3}$ and $x_{freq} \in \mathbb{R}^{H\times W\times 3}$ denotes the RGB input and the frequency input. After feature extraction, we use FAM to derive the frequency attention map. That is:

$$\hat{f} = Conv_{3\times 3}(f_{freq}),\tag{2}$$

$$f_{att} = \sigma(Conv_{7\times7}(CAT(GAP(\hat{f}), GMP(\hat{f})))), \qquad (3)$$

where f_{freq} denotes the frequency feature after feature extraction in Eq. (2), σ denotes the Sigmoid function, GAP and GMP represent global average pooling and global max pooling in Eq. (3), respectively. And CAT concatenates the features along with the depth. We finally choose a 7×7 convolution kernel to extract the forged traces in the frequency domain because it can detect edge information better and cover a larger area than three 3×3 convolution kernels. The attention map f_{att} contains subtle forgery traces in the frequency domain that are difficult to mine in the RGB features. Therefore, we implement f_{att} on the RGB feature f_{rgb}, directing f_{rgb} further mine forgery traces, that is:

$$f_{rgb} = f_{rgb} \oplus (f_{rgb} \otimes f_{att}), \qquad (4)$$

where $\oplus$ represents summation and $\otimes$ represents element-wise multiplication.

In addition, there are three level stages to feature extraction, low-level, mid-level and high-level. The low-level features represent texture forgery information, while the high-level features extract more overall forgery traces. Therefore, we interact with RGB features and frequency features at multi-level obtaining a more comprehensive representation of forged features. Specifically, the frequency domain output f^i_{freq} of the i-th stage is used as the $i+1$-th stage input $\hat{f}^i_{freq}$, and the RGB input $\hat{f}^{i+1}_{rgb}$ is the RGB feature f^i_{rgb} previously guided in the frequency domain, which can be formulated as:

$$\hat{f}^{i+1}_{rgb} = f^i_{rgb} \oplus (\hat{f}^i_{rgb} \otimes f^i_{att}), \quad \hat{f}^{i+1}_{freq} = f^i_{freq}. \qquad (5)$$

Then we input the high-level output features $f_{rgb} \in \mathbb{R}^{h\times w\times c}$ and $f_{freq} \in \mathbb{R}^{h\times w\times c}$ into multi-modal fusion to mine more discriminative information, where h, w and c are the dimensions of these output features.

3.3 Multi-modal Fusion

In recent years the attention mechanism has been broadly applied in natural language processing [37] and computer vision [9]. Inspired by these works, the resulting RGB features are combined with frequency features with a Cross-modal Attention Module (CAM). And considering the role of the frequency domain is not always sufficiently effective, which causes the quality discrepancies between the RGB and frequency feature, we designed a Dynamic Fusion Module (DFM) in the multi-modal fusion stage.

According to Sect. 3.2, the frequency modal should serve as a supporting component. Given RGB features f_{rgb} and frequency features f_{freq}, we implement CAM to perform a preliminary fusion of them into a unified representation by using the query-key-value mechanism. Specifically, we use 1×1 convolutions to embed f_{rgb} into Q and embed f_{freq} into K and V. Then we perform the attention mechanism by flatting them to 2D embeddings $\hat{Q}$, $\hat{K}$ and $\hat{V} \in \mathbb{R}^{\frac{h \times w}{16} \times c}$ along the channel dimension, which can be formulated as:

$$f_{cam} = softmax(\frac{\hat{Q}\hat{K}^T}{\sqrt{h/4 \times w/4 \times c}})\hat{V}, \qquad (6)$$

where f_{cam} denotes the preliminary fusion feature which aggregates the RGB and frequency information. Then, in order to effectively utilize the forged information in f_{rgb}, f_{cam} and f_{freq}, we design a dynamic fusion module in the multi-modal fusion stage. In more details, we input a set $S = \{f_{rgb}, f_{cam}, f_{freq}\}$ into DFM. DFM generates corresponding weights for each branch based on the quality information from all branches, which it then uses to weigh the combined information to combine from various branches.

To obtain the corresponding weights for each branch, we further integrate the three branch features by using two fully connected layers FC_1 and FC_2, global average pooling GAP and active layer GELU function δ, which can be formulated as:

$$f' = FC_1(CAT(f_{rgb}, f_{cam}, f_{freq})), \quad \hat{f} = FC_2(\delta_1(GAP(\delta_2(f')))), \quad (7)$$

where $f' \in \mathbb{R}^{h \times w \times 3c}$ and $\hat{f} \in \mathbb{R}^{1 \times 1 \times c}$. Then we set three fully connected layers F_c^1, F_c^2 and F_c^3 and softmax function to generate quality weights α_i for each branch, which can be formulated as:

$$\alpha_i = \frac{exp(F_c^i(\hat{f}))}{\sum_j^3 expF_c^j(\hat{f})}, i = 1, 2, 3, \quad (8)$$

where $\alpha_i \in \mathbb{R}^{1 \times 1 \times C}$ represents the quality of each branch. Because different branches are contributed differently to mining forged clues, we weigh the fusion features based on the quality and use two linear mapping layers to restore the channel dimension of the dynamic fusion features. The output f_u can be formulated as:

$$f_u = f' + FC_4(FC_3(\sum_i^3 \alpha_i S_i)), i = 1, 2, 3. \quad (9)$$

3.4   Uncertainty-Guided Test-Time Training

The first three sections Sect. 3.1, Sect. 3.2 and Sect. 3.3 describe the DDIN network's mining of forgery traces' quality in the RGB and frequency domains and the dynamic fusion of forgery features to discriminate based on quality differences. However, the trained network's prediction weight is biased towards the quality discrepancies of different modalities of the training set data during dynamic fusion, leading to a bias in the fusion weight of uncertain unseen data, which affects the model's generalization. To improve the network's generalization of forgery detection, we further use uncertain perturbation as guidance during the test-time training phase.

To accomplish this, we introduce a perturbation g drawn from Gumbel(0, 1) in the test-time training phase. The Gumbel(0, 1) distribution can be sampled using inverse transform sampling by drawing $u \sim$ Uniform(0, 1) and computing $g = -\log(-\log(u))$ [11]. We implement g to the DFM to influence the network's perception of intra-modal quality. The uncertain g modifies the quality weight slightly, making it probabilistic rather than deterministic. And the uncertain quality weight β is given by the Gumbel softmax function [14]:

$$\beta_i = \frac{exp((log(F_c^i(\hat{f})) + g_i)/\tau)}{\sum_j^3 exp((log(F_c^j(\hat{f})) + g_j)/\tau)}, i = 1, 2, 3, \qquad (10)$$

where τ is the softmax temperature. The β replaces the α in Eq. (9) and results in an uncertain distribution of the fused feature f_u. In contrast to f_u during training, the distribution of f_u in UTT is uncertain and related to the test set. Based on this uncertainty, we design a self-supervised task in the UTT stage. Specifically, we sample an image x from test-set $\mathbf{D}$ and input it twice to the pre-trained detector $f(\cdot, \theta)$, where the θ is the model parameter. Then we can gain two uncertain fused features f_u^1 and f_u^2. The distributions of these two features match the actual distribution of the model output, but they are influenced by the test set, and the perturbations make them uncertain. The KL loss is used to evaluate the distribution shift caused by uncertainty and to update the model parameters by narrowing the feature distribution gap, which encourages the model to perform well on the test set.

3.5   Loss Function

In the training phase, we flatten the f_u and pass it through the fully connected layer and sigmoid function to obtain the final predicted probability $\hat{y}$. And the classification loss is defined as:

$$\mathcal{L}_{cls} = y \log \hat{y} + (1 - y) \log(1 - \hat{y}), \qquad (11)$$

where y is set to 1 if the image has been manipulated, otherwise it is set to 0.

In the test-time training phase, We add uncertain perturbations to the DFM and obtain two uncertain features denoted as f_u^1 and f_u^2. To narrow the two feature distributions, we use KL divergence loss as follows:

$$\mathcal{L}_{kl} = \mathcal{D}_{kl}(f_u^1 \| f_u^2) = f_u^1 \log(f_u^1) - f_u^1 \log(f_u^2). \qquad (12)$$

4   Experiments

4.1   Experimental Setup

Datasets. We evaluate our proposed method and existing approaches on Face-Forensics++ (FF++) [30], CelebDF [21] and DFDC [8]. FF++ is a face forgery detection dataset consisting of 1000 original videos with real faces, in which 720 videos are used for training, 140 videos are reserved for validation and 140 videos for testing. CelebDF includes 590 real videos and 5,639 high-quality fake videos which are crafted by the improved DeepFake algorithm [36]. DFDC is a largescale dataset which contains 128,154 facial videos of 960 IDs.

Table 1. Quantitative results on Celeb-DF dataset and FaceForensics++ dataset with different quality settings. The best results are shown in **bold**, and the second results are shown in *blue*.

Method	FF++ (C23)		FF++(C40)		Celeb-DF	
	Acc (%)	AUC (%)	Acc (%)	AUC (%)	Acc (%)	AUC (%)
MesoNet [1]	83.10	-	70.47	-	-	-
Multi-task [25]	85.65	85.43	81.30	75.59	-	-
Xception [6]	95.73	96.30	86.86	89.30	97.90	99.73
Face X-ray [17]	-	87.40	-	61.60	-	-
Two-branch [24]	96.43	98.70	86.34	86.59	-	-
RFM [38]	95.69	98.79	87.06	89.83	97.96	**99.94**
F3-Net [29]	97.52	98.10	90.43	93.30	95.95	98.93
Add-Net [42]	96.78	97.74	87.50	91.01	96.93	99.55
FDFL [16]	96.69	99.30	89.00	92.40	-	-
MultiAtt [41]	97.60	99.29	88.69	90.40	97.92	**99.94**
PEL [10]	*97.63*	*99.32*	*90.52*	94.28	-	-
DDIN	97.59	99.31	90.41	*94.47*	*98.02*	99.83
DDIN (+UTT)	**97.69**	**99.39**	**90.84**	**94.80**	**98.20**	*99.93*

Evaluation Metrics. To evaluate our method, we apply the Accuracy score (Acc) and Area Under the Receiver Operating Characteristic Curve (AUC) as our evaluation metrics. To ensure a fair comparison, the results of all comparison methods are taken from their paper.

Implementation Details. We modify MOA-Transformer [27] pre-trained on ImageNet as the backbone network. We use the DLIB [31] for face extraction and alignment. The input shape of images is resized to 224×224 with the data augmentation of randomly erase. The τ in Eq. (10) is set to 1, and the batch size of the training and test-time training phase are all set to 32. We use the Adam optimizer for optimizing the network with $\beta_1 = 0.9$ and $\beta_2 = 0.999$. The learning rates for the training and test-time training phase are set to $1e-5$ and $1e-4$, respectively. We only update the parameters in the DFM and freeze the parameters of other layers during the test-time training phase.

4.2 Experimental Results

Intra-testing. In this section, we first compare our method with state-of-the-art face forgery detection methods on widely used datasets FF++ and Celeb-DF datasets. As shown in Table 1, for the FF++ dataset, our proposed method consistently outperforms all compared opponents by a considerable margin. For example, compared with the state-of-the-art method PEL [10], the AUC of our method exceeds it by 0.10% and 0.52% at all the two quality settings(c23 and

Table 2. Cross-testing in terms of AUC (%) by training on FF++. The best results are shown in **blod**.

Method		Xception [6]	RFM [38]	Add-Net [42]	F3-Net [29]	MultiAtt [41]	PEL [10]	DDIN	DDIN (+UTT)
Test	CelebDF	61.80	65.63	65.29	61.51	67.02	69.18	68.35	**69.32**
	DFDC	63.61	66.01	64.78	64.60	68.01	63.31	68.80	**70.10**

Table 3. Cross-manipulation evaluation on the subsets of FF++(C40) in terms of AUC(%). Grey background indicates intra-dataset results and Cross Avg. means the average of cross-method results. The best results are shown in **blod**.

Method	Train	DF	F2F	FS	NT	Cross Avg.
FDFL[16]		98.91	58.90	66.87	63.61	63.13
MultiAtt[41]		99.51	66.41	67.33	66.01	66.58
DDIN	DF	99.71	61.99	78.08	67.02	69.03
DDIN (+UTT)		**99.78**	66.62	**78.81**	**67.83**	**71.08**
FDFL[16]		67.55	93.06	55.35	66.66	63.19
MultiAtt[41]		73.04	97.96	**65.10**	71.88	70.01
DDIN	F2F	73.85	98.01	64.25	72.49	70.19
DDIN (+UTT)		**77.10**	98.09	64.42	**74.71**	**72.07**
FDFL[16]		75.90	54.64	98.37	49.72	60.09
MultiAtt[41]		82.33	61.65	98.82	54.79	66.26
DDIN	FS	88.20	62.13	98.80	56.63	68.98
DDIN (+UTT)		**89.18**	**62.56**	**98.83**	**58.44**	**70.06**
FDFL[16]		79.09	74.21	53.99	88.54	69.10
MultiAtt[41]		74.56	80.61	60.90	93.34	72.02
DDIN	NT	78.15	81.34	62.67	93.34	74.05
DDIN (+UTT)		**79.57**	**85.73**	**63.22**	**94.17**	**76.04**

c40), and this performance gain is also obtained under Acc. To explain, DDIN considers the quality of the auxiliary discriminant information contained in each branch in the multi-modal fusion stage and improves the network's discriminative ability on the test set in the UTT stage. The above results demonstrate the effectiveness of the proposed DDIN framework and UTT strategy. The above results demonstrate the effectiveness of our proposed method.

Cross-Testing. To evaluate the generalization ability of our method on unknown forgeries, we conduct cross-dataset experiments by training and testing on different datasets. Specifically, we train the models on FF++ and then test them on Celeb-DF and DFDC, respectively. As shown in Table 2, we observe that our method outperforms the other methods well on the unseen dataset. For example, when testing on the DFDC dataset, the AUC score of most previous methods drops to around 70%. The performance mainly benefits from the proposed DDIN framework and UTT fine-turning which focus on quality differences between different modalities, while the uncertainty perturbation guides the model to learn more distribution discrepancies between the train-set and test-set. Instead of overfitting with specific forged patterns as in existing methods, our method fine-tunes the trained model by using the unlabeled test set data to achieve better generalizability.

We further conduct fine-grained cross-testing by training on a specific manipulation technique and testing on the others listed in FF++(C40). As shown in Table 3, we compare our method with approaches that focus on specific forgery patterns like FDFL [16] and MultiAtt [41]. Our method generally outperforms others on unseen forgery types. In comparison, our pre-trained detector can adapt to the test samples via UTT, thus being more effective than the two methods for the generalizable deepfake detection task.

4.3 Ablation Study

Components. As shown in Table 4, we develop several variants and conduct a series of experiments on the FF++(C40) dataset to explore the influence of different components in our proposed method. The frequency-guided attention module used in the multi-level interaction stage can enhance the performance, and it can be improved by adding the proposed frequency-guided attention module or dynamic fusion module, reaching better performance when they are applied to the overall DDIN framework. The results verify that the frequency input is distinct and complementary to the RGB information and the quality discrepancies are negligible.

Table 4. Ablation study of the proposed method on FF++.

Ablation Study	Modules			FF++(C40)	
	FAM	DFM	UTT	AUC (%)	Acc (%)
(a)	-	-	-	92.15	88.51
(b)	✓	-	-	93.43	89.73
(c)	-	✓	-	93.82	90.21
(d)	✓	✓	-	94.47	90.41
(e)	-	✓	✓	94.02	90.23
(f)	✓	✓	✓	**94.80**	**90.84**

Furthermore, uncertainty-guided test-time training is also extremely effective to boost performance. And the best performance is achieved when combining all the proposed components with Acc and AUC of 90.84% and 94.80%, respectively. In addition, before the dynamic fusion module, we investigate the preliminary feature fusion method. Table 5 shows the results of three different scenarios. By comparing a and b, we can observe that the initial feature fusion is required. The result of c shows that the CAM module we use can effectively supplement the RGB and frequency domain feature information.

Table 5. Ablation study of fusion method before dynamic fusion.

Ablation Study	Fusion Method		FF++(C40)	
	Concat	CrossAtt	AUC (%)	Acc (%)
(a)	-	-	93.47	89.79
(b)	✓	-	94.26	90.33
(c)	-	✓	**94.80**	**90.84**

4.4 Visualization

To gain a better understanding of our method's decision-making mechanism, we provide the Grad-CAM [32] visualization on FF++ as shown in Fig. 3. It can be observed that the baseline method MOA-Transformer [27] tends to overlook forged traces in fake faces, particularly those that are concealed within the RGB domain. In contrast, even though it only uses binary labels for training, our method generates distinguishable heatmaps for real and fake faces, with the prominent regions varying in forgery techniques. For example, when detecting images forged with Deepfakes [36] and NeuralTextures [34] technologies, our method focuses on the edge contours of artefacts, which are difficult to detect in the RGB domain. And our method is more sensitive to the abnormal texture information forged by FaceSwap [15] in the eyes region and the inconsistent information forged by Face2Face [35] in the mouth region.

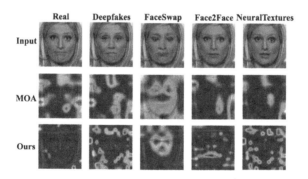

Fig. 3. The Grad-CAM [32] of visualization.

5 Conclusion

In this paper, we have proposed a Dynamic Dual-spectrum Interaction Network (DDIN) that allows test-time training to alleviate the effects of feature quality discrepancies and model uncertainty. The frequency-guided attention module used in multi-level interaction and the dynamic fusion module applied in multi-modal fusion can make the network dynamically fuse the features with quality discrepancies. Meanwhile, the uncertainty-guided test time training is introduced to fine-tune the trained detector by adding uncertain perturbation, which improves the network generalization. Extensive experiments and visualizations demonstrate the effectiveness of our method against its state-of-the-art competitors. In the future, we will explore the use of uncertainty to design self-supervised tasks in other related fields such as forensic attribution.

Acknowledgements. This research is partly supported by National Natural Science Foundation of China (Grant No. 62006228), Youth Innovation Promotion Association CAS (Grant No. 2022132) and the University Synergy Innovation Program of Anhui Province (No. GXXT-2022-036). The authors would like to thank Tong Zheng (AHU) and Jin Liu (ShanghaiTech) for their valuable discussions.

References

1. Afchar, D., Nozick, V., Yamagishi, J., Echizen, I.: MesoNet: a compact facial video forgery detection network. In: WIFS (2018)
2. Amerini, I., Galteri, L., Caldelli, R., Del Bimbo, A.: DeepFake video detection through optical flow based CNN. In: CVPRW (2019)
3. Cao, J., Ma, C., Yao, T., Chen, S., Ding, S., Yang, X.: End-to-end reconstruction-classification learning for face forgery detection. In: CVPR (2022)
4. Chen, L., Zhang, Y., Song, Y., Wang, J., Liu, L.: OST: improving generalization of DeepFake detection via one-shot test-time training. In: NeurIPS (2022)
5. Chen, S., Yao, T., Chen, Y., Ding, S., Li, J., Ji, R.: Local relation learning for face forgery detection. In: AAAI (2021)
6. Chollet, F.: Xception: deep learning with depthwise separable convolutions. In: CVPR (2017)
7. Das, S., Seferbekov, S., Datta, A., Islam, M., Amin, M., et al.: Towards solving the DeepFake problem: an analysis on improving DeepFake detection using dynamic face augmentation. In: ICCV (2021)
8. Dolhansky, B., et al.: The DeepFake detection challenge (DFDC) dataset. arXiv preprint arXiv:2006.07397 (2020)
9. Dosovitskiy, A., et al.: An image is worth 16×16 words: transformers for image recognition at scale. arXiv preprint arXiv:2010.11929 (2020)
10. Gu, Q., Chen, S., Yao, T., Chen, Y., Ding, S., Yi, R.: Exploiting fine-grained face forgery clues via progressive enhancement learning. In: AAAI (2022)
11. Gumbel, E.J.: Statistical theory of extreme values and some practical applications: a series of lectures, vol. 33. US Government Printing Office (1954)
12. Guo, H., Wang, H., Ji, Q.: Uncertainty-guided probabilistic transformer for complex action recognition. In: CVPR (2022)
13. He, R., Zhang, M., Wang, L., Ji, Y., Yin, Q.: Cross-modal subspace learning via pairwise constraints. IEEE TIP **24**(12), 5543–5556 (2015)
14. Jang, E., Gu, S., Poole, B.: Categorical reparameterization with Gumbel-Softmax. arXiv preprint arXiv:1611.01144 (2016)
15. Kowalski, M.: FaceSwap. https://github.com/marekkowalski/faceswap
16. Li, J., Xie, H., Li, J., Wang, Z., Zhang, Y.: Frequency-aware discriminative feature learning supervised by single-center loss for face forgery detection. In: CVPR (2021)

17. Li, L., et al.: Face X-ray for more general face forgery detection. In: CVPR (2020)
18. Li, X., Hou, Y., Wang, P., Gao, Z., Xu, M., Li, W.: Trear: transformer-based RGB-D egocentric action recognition. TCDS **14**(1), 246–252 (2021)
19. Li, Y., Hao, M., Di, Z., Gundavarapu, N.B., Wang, X.: Test-time personalization with a transformer for human pose estimation. In: NeurIPS (2021)
20. Li, Y., Chang, M.C., Lyu, S.: In Ictu Oculi: exposing AI created fake videos by detecting eye blinking. In: WIFS (2018)
21. Li, Y., Yang, X., Sun, P., Qi, H., Lyu, S.: Celeb-DF: a large-scale challenging dataset for DeepFake forensics. In: CVPR (2020)
22. Liu, Y., Kothari, P., van Delft, B., Bellot-Gurlet, B., Mordan, T., Alahi, A.: TTT++: when does self-supervised test-time training fail or thrive? In: NeurIPS (2021)
23. Luo, Y., Zhang, Y., Yan, J., Liu, W.: Generalizing face forgery detection with high-frequency features. In: CVPR (2021)
24. Masi, I., Killekar, A., Mascarenhas, R.M., Gurudatt, S.P., AbdAlmageed, W.: Two-branch recurrent network for isolating Deepfakes in videos. In: Vedaldi, A., Bischof, H., Brox, T., Frahm, J.-M. (eds.) ECCV 2020. LNCS, vol. 12352, pp. 667–684. Springer, Cham (2020). https://doi.org/10.1007/978-3-030-58571-6_39
25. Nguyen, H.H., Fang, F., Yamagishi, J., Echizen, I.: Multi-task learning for detecting and segmenting manipulated facial images and videos. In: BTAS (2019)
26. Nirkin, Y., Wolf, L., Keller, Y., Hassner, T.: DeepFake detection based on discrepancies between faces and their context. IEEE TPAMI **44**, 6111–6121 (2021)
27. Patel, K., Bur, A.M., Li, F., Wang, G.: Aggregating global features into local vision transformer. arXiv preprint arXiv:2201.12903 (2022)
28. Plizzari, C., Cannici, M., Matteucci, M.: Spatial temporal transformer network for skeleton-based action recognition. In: ICPR (2021)
29. Qian, Y., Yin, G., Sheng, L., Chen, Z., Shao, J.: Thinking in frequency: face forgery detection by mining frequency-aware clues. In: Vedaldi, A., Bischof, H., Brox, T., Frahm, J.-M. (eds.) ECCV 2020. LNCS, vol. 12357, pp. 86–103. Springer, Cham (2020). https://doi.org/10.1007/978-3-030-58610-2_6
30. Rossler, A., Cozzolino, D., Verdoliva, L., Riess, C., Thies, J., Nießner, M.: Face-Forensics++: learning to detect manipulated facial images. In: ICCV (2019)
31. Sagonas, C., Antonakos, E., Tzimiropoulos, G., Zafeiriou, S., Pantic, M.: 300 faces in-the-wild challenge: database and results. IVC **47**, 3–18 (2016)
32. Selvaraju, R.R., Cogswell, M., Das, A., Vedantam, R., Parikh, D., Batra, D.: Grad-CAM: visual explanations from deep networks via gradient-based localization. In: ICCV (2017)
33. Sun, Y., Wang, X., Liu, Z., Miller, J., Efros, A., Hardt, M.: Test-time training with self-supervision for generalization under distribution shifts. In: ICML (2020)
34. Thies, J., Zollhöfer, M., Nießner, M.: Deferred neural rendering: image synthesis using neural textures. ACM TOG **38**(4), 1–12 (2019)
35. Thies, J., Zollhofer, M., Stamminger, M., Theobalt, C., Nießner, M.: Face2Face: Real-time face capture and reenactment of RGB videos. In: CVPR (2016)
36. Tora: DeepFakes. https://github.com/deepfakes/faceswap/tree/v2.0.0
37. Vaswani, A., et al.: Attention is all you need. In: NeurIPS (2017)
38. Wang, C., Deng, W.: Representative forgery mining for fake face detection. In: CVPR (2021)
39. Wang, J., et al.: M2TR: multi-modal multi-scale transformers for DeepFake detection. In: ICMR (2022)

40. Woo, S., Park, J., Lee, J.-Y., Kweon, I.S.: CBAM: convolutional block attention module. In: Ferrari, V., Hebert, M., Sminchisescu, C., Weiss, Y. (eds.) ECCV 2018. LNCS, vol. 11211, pp. 3–19. Springer, Cham (2018). https://doi.org/10.1007/978-3-030-01234-2_1
41. Zhao, H., Zhou, W., Chen, D., Wei, T., Zhang, W., Yu, N.: Multi-attentional DeepFake detection. In: CVPR (2021)
42. Zi, B., Chang, M., Chen, J., Ma, X., Jiang, Y.G.: WildDeepfake: a challenging real-world dataset for DeepFake detection. In: ACM MM (2020)

CTC-Net: A Novel Coupled Feature-Enhanced Transformer and Inverted Convolution Network for Medical Image Segmentation

Shixiang Zhang$^{(\boxtimes)}$, Yang Xu, Zebin Wu, and Zhihui Wei

Nanjing University of Science and Technology, 200 Xiaolingwei Street, Nanjing, Jiangsu, China
shixiangzhang@njust.edu.cn

Abstract. In recent years, the Vision Transformer has gradually replaced the CNN as the mainstream method in the field of medical image segmentation due to its powerful long-range dependencies modeling ability. However, the segmentation network leveraging pure transformer performs poor in feature expression because of the lack of convolutional locality. Besides, the channel dimension information are lost in the network. In this paper, we propose a novel segmentation network termed CTC-Net to address these problems. Specifically, we design a feature-enhanced transformer module with spatial-reduction attention to extract the region details in the image patches by the depth-wise convolution. Then, the point-wise convolution is leveraged to capture non-linear relationship in the channel dimension. Furthermore, a parallel convolutional encoder branch and an inverted residual coordinate attention block are designed to mine the clear dependencies of local context, channel dimension features and location information. Extensive experiments on Synapse Multi-organ CT and ACDC (Automatic Cardiac Diagnosis Challenge) datasets show that our method outperforms the methods based on CNN and pure transformers, obtaining up to 1.72% and 0.68% improvement in DSC scores respectively.

Keywords: Medical Image Segmentation · Feature-enhanced Transformer · Dimensional Inverted Convolution · Channel Dimension Feature

1 Introduction

With the increasingly significant role of medical imaging in clinical diagnosis and adjuvant therapy, medical image segmentation undertakes important tasks such as obtaining pathological information and locating required areas [1]. Improving the efficiency of medical image segmentation is conducive to the accuracy of clinical diagnosis results and the advancement of the overall treatment process. For instance, segmenting the heart region in medical images can analyze parameters such as the size and shape of the heart, and accurate segmentation can help

H. Lu et al. (Eds.): ACPR 2023, LNCS 14407, pp. 273–283, 2023.
https://doi.org/10.1007/978-3-031-47637-2_21

doctors diagnose and treat heart diseases. Therefore, there exists much research work in this field to explore more efficient segmentation methods in the past few years. Most of them are based on convolutional networks or pure transformers for research. Our work contributes to more effectively extract different perspectives of features from medical images by combining the advantages of convolutional networks and transformers.

The existing deep learning methods for medical image segmentation are mainly based on fully convolutional networks [2], especially the U-Net [3] model which has far-reaching influence. U-Net [3] consists of a symmetric encoder-decoder with skip connection. The encoder stage extracts the deep features of the image through convolution and max pooling layer-by-layer downsampling. Besides, the decoder stage upsamples the deep features and fuses the feature map fed by skip connection for pixel-level prediction. Some U-Net-based improved variants incorporate new design concepts to achieve better performance in the field of medical image segmentation. U-Net++ [4] redesigns skip connections, adding several convolutional layers and dense connections to reduce the difference in network decoding and encoding feature expression. Res-UNet [5] simplifies the training of deep networks by replacing each convolutional submodule of U-Net [3] with a form with residual connections. Attention-UNet [6] introduces attention mechanism in U-Net [3] to better realize the attention to the salient regions and the suppression of the irrelevant background regions. Due to the local receptive field of convolution and its inherent inductive bias, it is difficult for the segmentation network based on CNN to learn global information and long-range interpixel dependencies.

In order to solve the local limitations of CNNs, ViT (Vision Transformer) [7] has been proposed and applied to image processing tasks. The structure of ViT [7] based on the multi-head self-attention [8] enables it to have a powerful ability to capture long-range relationships. Its performance outperforms CNN when using enough data for self-supervised pre-training. The researchers noticed the potential of ViT [7] and applied it in combination with U-Net [3] to the field of medical image segmentation. TransUNet [9], as a pioneer in this direction, has the advantages of both transformer and U-Net [3]. It serializes the feature map from CNN as input to the transformer layer in the encoder to extract global context information. Then, the encoded deep features are upsampled in the decoder and combined with high-resolution local feature information to improve the segmentation effect of the network. The pure transformer-based U-shaped segmentation network termed Swin-UNet [10] completely abandons CNN and adopts a multi-scale expression form. Actually, it utilizes two consecutive Transformer blocks with shifted windows [11] in each layer to capture contextual information between adjacent windows. Another high-efficiency U-shaped segmentation network based on pure transformer named MISSFormer [12] leverages the ReMix-FFN to improve performance by remixing the local and global information. It also designs a novel transformer context bridge that enhances multi-scale feature context relationships. For the U-shaped segmentation network constructed by pure transformer, the deep features extracted by the encoder are global information. The detailed local information are easily lost in the fixed size of patch after image serialization. Moreover, the methods mentioned above lack consideration of image channel dimension information. The above problems lead to room for improvement in the segmentation efficiency of this type of model.

In this paper, we propose a novel segmentation network termed CTC-Net to integrate the global information and local detail features. Besides, the channel dimension features and location information can be extracted in its encoder to improve the utilization of information contained in feature maps. The works of this paper are summarized as follows:

(1) We design a feature-enhanced transformer module to extract the region details in the image patches by the depth-wise convolution. Besides, we introduce the spatial-reduction attention instead of multi-head attention to reduce the quadratic computational complexity. Finally, the point-wise convolution is leveraged to capture non-linear relationship in the channel dimension instead of linear layer in the MLP module.

(2) We propose a novel convolution parallel encoder branch and introduce an inverted residual coordinate attention (IRCA) block to mine the clear dependencies of channel dimension features and location information. Between inverted dimension transformations by point-wise convolution, we leverage the depth-wise convolution and coordinate attention to extract different types of features in a high-dimensional state.

(3) In order to verify the segmentation efficiency of our proposed model, we conduct experiments on the public medical image segmentation datasets and obtain better performance results.

2   Method

2.1   Overall Architecture

The CTC-Net has a approximately symmetrical structure of four-layers encoder-decoder with bridge of multi-scale features interaction and its overall architecture is presented in Fig. 1. To be concrete, the encoder consisting of convolution branch and transformer branch can capture two types of deep features. Both of two branches utilize overlapping convolution to generate low resolution and high dimensional features, but they have different normalization methods to obtain features from two different directions. Besides, the parallel dual branch of the first encoder layer divides the image into patches of kernel size through overlapping convolution with a stride of 4, while the stride of the rest layers is 2. The last step of each encoder layer is to fuse the features from two branches through concatenating. The whole process can be denoted as:

$$
\begin{aligned}
x_c &= \xi(\delta_{conv}(x)) \\
x_t &= \beta(\delta_{trans}(x)) \\
x_{output} &= Conv_{1\times1}(Concat(x_c, x_t))
\end{aligned}
\tag{1}
$$

where x_c and x_t represent the output features of convolution and transformer branch respectively, δ indicates the downsampling process, ξ and β represent our proposed inverted residual coordinate attention and feature-enhanced transformer respectively.

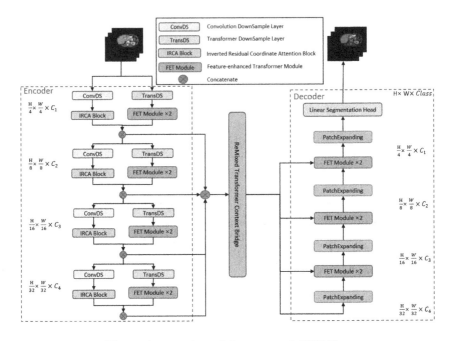

Fig. 1. An overview of the proposed CTC-Net.

There is a skip connection stage between the encoder and decoder. We utilize ReMixed transformer context bridge [12] to capture the local and global dependencies between different scale feature map in the stage. Symmetrical to the encoder, the decoder is realized by four-layer patch expanding [10] and two consecutive feature-enhanced transformer modules in each layer. The patch expanding layer is to reshape the low resolution feature and correspondingly halve the feature channel dimension. Furthermore, the upsampled features are concatenated with the features sent by the transformer context bridge and then enter to the feature-enhanced transformer module. In the final stage of the model, we leverage linear projection to obtain a pixel-wise segmentation prediction.

2.2   Feature-Enhanced Transformer Module

In order to collect the local detailed information in different states and reduce the computational complexity of self-attention, we propose the feature-enhanced transformer module. The structure of original transformer is presented in Fig. 2(a) and the feature-enhanced transformer module is shown in Fig. 2(b).

Firstly, we leverage the local enhancement unit composed of depth-wise convolution to reduce the loss of local detailed information inside the patch. Furthermore, the residual connection [13] is introduced to enhance the generalization of the model. It can be defined as:

$$x_i = \psi(x_i) + x_i \tag{2}$$

where $x_i \in \mathbb{R}^{H_i \times W_i \times C_i}$ represents the shape of the i-th layer feature map, ψ means the depth-wise convolution.

Secondly, after flattening and layer normalizing the feature map, we feed it into the spatial-reduction attention [14] unit. The unit introduces the spatial reduction ratio R to reduce the computational complexity base on the self-attention mechanism. Specifically, the input x_i is generated Q, K, V through three linear layers, and Q, K, V denote respectively the query, key and value. The formula for calculating self-attention is as follows:

$$Attention(Q, K, V) = \sigma(\frac{QK^T}{\sqrt{d_k}})V \tag{3}$$

where $Q, K, V \in \mathbb{R}^{N_i \times C_i}$, d_k is the scale factor and σ represents softmax function.

Then, utilizing the spatial reduction ratio R to makes the K and V of i-th layer reshaped as $\frac{N_i}{R} \times (C_i * R)$. To the end, we set the convolutional layer to bring the channel dimension $(C_i * R)$ back to C_i. In this case, the computational complexity of self-attention is reduced from $O(N^2)$ to $O(\frac{N^2}{R})$, thereby decreasing the overall computational cost of the model.

Finally, for MLP layer of the transformer module, we design a novel inverted residual feed-forward network (IRFFN) unit, which is shown in Fig. 2(c). In detail, we first increase then decrease the channel dimension by point-wise convolution. Between the two steps, we utilize depth-wise convolution to capture the high-dimensional local context information. The implementation process formula is as follows:

$$\begin{aligned} x_i &= \delta(Conv_{1\times1}(x_i)) \\ x_i &= Conv_{1\times1}(\delta(\psi(x_i) + x_i)) \end{aligned} \tag{4}$$

where δ consists of batch normalization and the activation function GELU, ψ is the depth-wise convolution.

2.3 Inverted Residual Coordinate Attention Block

In order to fully extract the channel dimension information and spatial location information of the feature map, we propose inverted residual coordinate attention block working in the convolution branch. It is composed of separable convolution and coordinate attention and represented in Fig. 2(d).

Specifically, we utilize dimension-inverted structure similar to IRFFN. Furthermore, coordinate attention [15] between the depth-wise convolution and the second point-wise convolution captures remote context information interaction

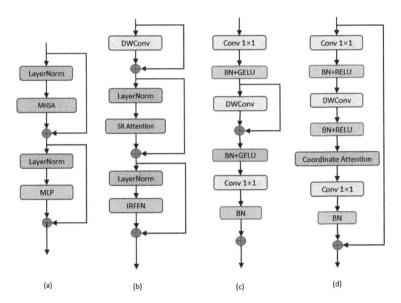

Fig. 2. The structure of modules, from left to right: (a) Original Transformer module, (b) Feature-enhanced Transformer module, (c) Inverted Residual Feed-forward Neural Network unit, (d) Inverted Residual Coordinate Attention block. (The blue plus circle represents the feature addition of residual connection.) (Color figure online)

with precise location by averaging pooling from horizontal and vertical directions, and leverage it to extract the channel dimensional information of feature maps. The coordinate attention can be denoted as follow:

$$
\begin{aligned}
x' &= \mu(Conv(Concatenate[\varphi_h(x_{input}), \varphi_w(x_{input})] \\
x_{output} &= x_{input} \times \theta(Conv(x'_h)) \times \theta(Conv(x'_w))
\end{aligned}
\tag{5}
$$

where φ_h and φ_w respectively represent averaging pooling from horizontal and vertical directions, x'_h and x'_w represent two separate features that split x' along the spatial dimension, μ represents non-linear activation function Swish and θ is the Sigmoid function.

Finally, a residual shortcut is applied in the block to promote the propagation ability of gradient across layers.

3   Experiments and Results

3.1   Datasets

Synapse Multi-organ CT (Synapse). The dataset originates from the MIC-CAI 2015 Multi-Atlas Abdomen Labeling Challenge, including 30 abdominal CT scans, with 3779 axial abdominal clinical CT images. It is divided into 18 training samples and 12 samples for testing, which contains eight abdominal organs (aorta, gallbladder, spleen, left kidney, right kidney, liver, pancreas, spleen, and stomach). In addition, we utilize the average Dice-Similarity Coefficient (DSC) and average 95% Hausdorff Distance (HD95) as evaluation metric.

Automated Cardiac Diagnosis Challenge (ACDC). The ACDC dataset collect 100 MRI scans form different patients by MRI scanner. For MRI image of each patient, label three organs: left ventricle (LV), right ventricle (RV) and myocardium(MYO). The dataset is divided into 70 cases for training, 10 cases for validation and 20 cases for test. Similar to [9], the average Dice-Similarity Coefficient (DSC) is used to evaluate methods.

3.2   Implementation Details

The CTC-Net is implemented based on python 3.7 and Pytorch 1.7.1, and trained on an Nvidia GeForce RTX 3090 GPU with 24 GB of memory. The model is trained on 2D slices from 3D volume data, and the predicted 2D slices are stacked together to reconstruct 3D predictions for evaluation. For all training samples, we use data augmentations such as flips and rotations to increase data diversity. Furthermore, we randomly initialized and train the CTC-Net from scratch, setting the input image size as 224×224. For the Synapse dataset, the initial learning rate is 0.05, the training epoch is 400 and the batch size is 24. For the ACDC dataset, we apply the same setting as [17]. The model utilizes the SGD optimizer with a momentum of 0.9 and weight decay of $1e-4$ for back propagation. We use the combination of weighted cross entropy loss and Dice coefficient loss to supervise the whole training process.

3.3   Comparison with State-of-the-Art Methods

Comparison on the Synapse Dataset. The comparison of the proposed CTC-Net with previous state-of-the-art methods on the Synapse multi-organ CT dataset is shown in Table 1. It should be mentioned that the encoder of TransUnet and Swin-Unet adopt the pre-trained checkpoint on ImageNet [16]. From the table, we can see the results of CNN-based methods: U-Net and Att-Unet are respectively realizing the segmentation accuracy of 74.6% (DSC) and 75.57% (DSC). After transformers are utilized in the segmentation methods, the value of DSC increases and the value of HD95 decreases to prove the ability of transformers. As the latest method, MISSFormer achieves an additional improvement of 5.26% in DSC and 15.96 mm in HD95 compared with Att-Unet. We can also conclude that the CTC-Net realizes accuracy improvement of 1.72% in DSC and 3.31 mm in HD95 compared with MISSFormer, which demonstrates that our method can achieve better segmentation accuracy.

Moreover, we provide the visual results of qualitative comparison with different methods on Synapse dataset, which are presented in Fig. 3. By comparing the results with each other, we can find that our method CTC-Net achieves better regions details prediction due to its enhanced ability of extracting more key information.

Table 1. The Comparison on Synapse multi-organ CT dataset. (dice score % and hausdorff distance mm)

Methods	DSC↑	HD95↓	Aorta	Gallbladder	Kidney (L)	Kidney (R)	Liver	Pancreas	Spleen	Stomach
R50 U-Net [9]	74.68	36.87	84.18	62.84	79.19	71.29	93.35	48.23	84.41	73.92
R50 Att-UNet [9]	75.57	36.97	85.92	63.91	79.20	72.71	93.56	49.37	87.19	74.95
TransUNet [9]	77.16	33.53	**87.62**	61.95	80.04	74.06	94.30	57.16	86.39	75.81
Swin-Unet [10]	77.99	26.98	84.84	64.21	82.30	78.51	93.88	56.50	87.81	75.90
MISSFormer [12]	80.83	21.01	85.94	71.12	83.37	79.20	**94.74**	63.36	90.73	78.17
CTC-Net	**82.55**	**17.70**	87.20	**71.15**	**86.78**	**82.86**	94.56	**64.34**	**92.46**	**81.01**

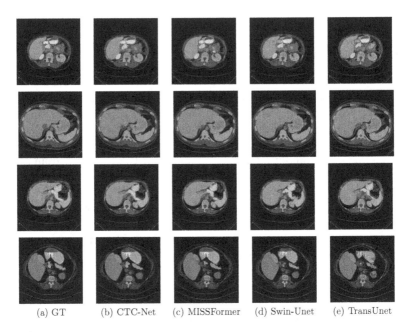

(a) GT   (b) CTC-Net   (c) MISSFormer   (d) Swin-Unet   (e) TransUnet

Fig. 3. The visualization of qualitative comparison results with previous state-of-the-art approaches on Synapse dataset. (GT means ground truth)

Comparison on the ACDC Dataset. The proposed CTC-Net is trained on the ACDC dataset to realize automated cardiac segmentation in the format of MRI. The comparison results are represented in Table 2. In the table, we can draw that our CTC-Net realizes the accuracy improvement of 0.68% in DSC compared with MISSFormer. In addition, the performance of our method exceeds that of the previous classic segmentation network base on CNN and pure transformers.

3.4   Ablation Studies

In order to explore the impact on proposed modules and the rationality of model structure, we conduct ablation studies on the Synapse dataset as follows:

Table 2. The Comparison on ACDC dataset.

Methods	DSC↑	RV	Myo	LV
R50 U-Net [17]	87.60	84.62	84.52	93.68
R50 AttnUNet [17]	86.90	83.27	84.33	93.53
TransUNet [9]	89.71	86.67	87.27	95.18
Swin-Unet [10]	90.00	88.55	85.62	**95.83**
MISSFormer [12]	90.03	87.77	87.32	94.99
CTC-Net	**90.71**	**88.97**	**88.14**	95.03

The Effect of Proposed Modules. To analyse the effect of proposed modules designed for capturing complementary features to promote the segmentation accuracy, we conduct experiments on the Synapse dataset with modules from different designs base on the U-Net architecture. The results of ablation studies is presented in Table 3, which show our CTC-Net architecture with IRCA block can realize better segmentation accuracy.

More specifically, the results in the first three rows of the table demonstrate the effect of using the proposed module individually. The experimental data in the next three rows represents the outcomes of combining them in pairs. It can be observed that effective combinations between modules can enhance segmentation efficiency. For instance, the combination of spatial-reduction attention and IRFFN achieves extra improvements of 3.78% in DSC and reduction of 2.87 mm in HD95 compared to using spatial attenuated attention alone. Similarly, compared to using IRFFN alone, this combination shows 0.39% improvement in DSC and 1.75 mm reduction in HD95. Furthermore, when comparing CTC-Net to the solely utilizing the feature enhanced transformer, the former demonstrates extra improvement of 0.29 % in DSC and reduction of 0.96 mm in HD95.

These above experimental results provide sufficient evidence to support the effectiveness of our proposed module.

Table 3. Ablation study on the effect of proposed modules. (DWConv represents the depth-wise convolution layer, SRAttn and IRFFN mean the spatial-reduction attention unit and inverted residual feed-forward network respectively. IRCA Block is inverted residual coordinate attention block in the parallel branch.)

Architecture	Module	DSC↑	HD95↓	Aorta	Gallbladder	Kidney (L)	Kidney (R)	Liver	Pancreas	Spleen	Stomach
U-Net	DWConv	76.68	26.21	85.14	61.26	80.95	77.11	93.42	52.86	89.30	73.37
U-Net	SRAttn	77.71	20.99	84.82	66.62	83.45	77.21	94.38	51.96	88.78	74.45
U-Net	IRFFN	81.10	19.87	86.78	67.70	84.15	78.07	94.78	62.26	92.32	**82.72**
U-Net	DWConv + SRAttn	78.22	26.61	85.37	69.43	82.41	71.82	94.18	54.41	91.43	76.69
U-Net	SRAttn + IRFFN	81.49	18.12	87.64	68.66	84.73	82.25	94.48	63.65	91.62	78.89
U-Net	DWConv + IRFFN	82.06	19.94	86.40	68.87	84.57	82.08	**95.51**	**67.63**	90.91	80.46
U-Net	Enhanced Transformer [12]	80.83	21.01	85.94	71.12	83.37	79.20	94.74	63.36	90.73	78.17
U-Net	FE Transformer	82.26	18.66	**87.82**	70.07	85.44	**84.17**	94.51	63.67	92.06	80.29
CTC-Net	+IRCA Block	**82.55**	**17.70**	87.20	**71.15**	**86.78**	82.86	94.56	64.34	**92.46**	81.01

The Impact of the Encoder Enhancement Layers. We conduct experiments on the Synapse dataset with different number of encoder layers for finding the more appropriate structure of encoder branch and seek what deep features that transformer need to integrate. The results illustrate that our model CTC-Net with the parallel of four layers has better performance on the score of DSC and correspondingly higher value in HD95, which can be seen from Table 4.

Table 4. Ablation study on the impact of the encoder enhancement layers

Architecture	Enhanced Encoder Layers	DSC↑	HD95↓	Aorta	Gallbladder	Kidney (L)	Kidney (R)	Liver	Pancreas	Spleen	Stomach
CTC-Net	1	82.27	**15.29**	**88.84**	70.43	84.30	79.90	94.31	**66.48**	92.42	**81.51**
CTC-Net	1, 2	82.29	16.20	86.37	70.54	84.99	**84.14**	**94.96**	63.79	92.06	81.46
CTC-Net	1, 2, 3	81.81	17.08	87.22	67.21	**88.17**	81.36	94.90	62.03	92.19	81.39
CTC-Net	1, 2, 3, 4	**82.55**	17.70	87.20	**71.15**	86.78	82.86	94.56	64.34	**92.46**	81.01

4   Conclusion

In this paper, we design a novel network CTC-Net for 2D medical image segmentation. In order to mine the detail features of image and leverage the fusion of local and global information, we propose feature-enhanced transformer as the module for transformer branch. In addition, we design a parallel branch with IRCA block in the encoder to extract the channel dimension features and location information. Experiments on Synapse and ACDC datasets demonstrate that our CTC-Net has better performance than CNN-based methods and pure transformer models.

References

1. Sahiner, B., Pezeshk, A., Hadjiiski, L.M., et al.: Deep learning in medical imaging and radiation therapy. Med. Phys. **46**(1), e1–e36 (2019)
2. Long, J., Shelhamer, E., Darrell, T.: Fully convolutional networks for semantic segmentation. In: Proceedings of the IEEE Conference on Computer Vision and Pattern Recognition, pp. 3431–3440 (2015)
3. Ronneberger, O., Fischer, P., Brox, T.: U-Net: convolutional networks for biomedical image segmentation. In: Navab, N., Hornegger, J., Wells, W.M., Frangi, A.F. (eds.) MICCAI 2015. LNCS, vol. 9351, pp. 234–241. Springer, Cham (2015). https://doi.org/10.1007/978-3-319-24574-4_28
4. Zhou, Z., Siddiquee, M.M.R., Tajbakhsh, N., et al.: UNet++: redesigning skip connections to exploit multiscale features in image segmentation. IEEE Trans. Med. Imaging **39**(6), 1856–1867 (2019)
5. Diakogiannis, F.I., Waldner, F., Caccetta, P., et al.: ResUNet-a: a deep learning framework for semantic segmentation of remotely sensed data. ISPRS J. Photogramm. Remote. Sens. **162**, 94–114 (2020)

6. Oktay, O., Schlemper, J., Folgoc, L.L., et al.: Attention U-Net: learning where to look for the pancreas. arXiv preprint arXiv:1804.03999 (2018)

7. Dosovitskiy, A., Beyer, L., Kolesnikov, A., et al.: An image is worth 16 × 16 words: transformers for image recognition at scale. arXiv preprint arXiv:2010.11929 (2020)

8. Vaswani, A., Shazeer, N., Parmar, N., et al. : Attention is all you need. In: Advances in Neural Information Processing Systems, vol. 30 (2017)

9. Chen, J., Lu, Y., Yu, Q., et al.: TransUNet: transformers make strong encoders for medical image segmentation. arXiv preprint arXiv:2102.04306 (2021)

10. Cao, H., et al.: Swin-Unet: Unet-like pure transformer for medical image segmentation. In: Karlinsky, L., Michaeli, T., Nishino, K. (eds.) Proceedings of the Computer Vision, ECCV 2022 Workshops, Part III, Tel Aviv, Israel, 23–27 October 2022, pp. 205–218. Springer, Cham (2023). https://doi.org/10.1007/978-3-031-25066-8_9

11. Liu, Z., Lin, Y., Cao, Y., et al.: Swin transformer: hierarchical vision transformer using shifted windows. In: Proceedings of the IEEE/CVF International Conference on Computer Vision, pp. 10012–10022 (2021)

12. Huang, X., Deng, Z., Li, D., et al.: MISSFormer: an effective transformer for 2D medical image segmentation. IEEE Trans. Med. Imaging **42**, 1484–1494 (2022)

13. He, K., Zhang, X., Ren, S., et al.: Deep residual learning for image recognition. In: Proceedings of the IEEE Conference on Computer Vision and Pattern Recognition, pp. 770–778 (2016)

14. Wang, W., Xie, E., Li, X., et al.: Pyramid vision transformer: a versatile backbone for dense prediction without convolutions. In: Proceedings of the IEEE/CVF International Conference on Computer Vision, pp. 568–578 (2021)

15. Hou, Q., Zhou, D., Feng, J.: Coordinate attention for efficient mobile network design. In: Proceedings of the IEEE/CVF Conference on Computer Vision and Pattern Recognition, pp. 13713–13722 (2021)

16. Deng, J., Dong, W., Socher, R., et al. : ImageNet: a large-scale hierarchical image database. In: 2009 IEEE Conference on Computer Vision and Pattern Recognition, pp. 248–255. IEEE (2019)

17. Wang, H., Xie, S., Lin, L., et al.: Mixed transformer U-Net for medical image segmentation. In: 2022 IEEE International Conference on Acoustics, Speech and Signal Processing (ICASSP). ICASSP 2022, pp. 2390–2394. IEEE (2022)

EEG Emotion Recognition Based on Temporal-Spatial Features and Adaptive Attention of EEG Electrodes

Wenxia Qi[1,2], Xingfu Wang[1,2], and Wei Wang[1,2(✉)]

[1] Technology and Engineering Center for Space Utilization, Chinese Academy of Sciences, Beijing, China
{qiwenxia20,wangxingfu21}@mails.ucas.ac.cn
[2] University of Chinese Academy of Sciences, Beijing, China
wangwei@csu.ac.cn

Abstract. EEG signals are more objective in reflecting human emotions, compared to facial expression and speech which can be disguised. Therefore, EEG emotion recognition is a well-worthy research area. The previous recognition methods fail to fully extract the temporal and spatial information in EEG signals, while ignoring the differences of different EEG channels contributing to emotion recognition. Based on this, a new EEG emotion recognition method is proposed in this paper. The method achieves auto-assignment of EEG channel weights by spatial attention mechanism, extracts spatial and temporal features by continuous convolutional block and LSTM, and achieves feature classification by introducing L2-SVM in the last layer of the model. Finally, we have experimented extensively on the DEAP public dataset, and the experimental results show that our method has an average accuracy of 98.93% and 98.95% in valence and arousal, with a minimum accuracy of 93.37% and a maximum accuracy of 99.88%. Its performance is better than the previous methods under subject-dependent condition, which indicates that the method proposed in this paper provides a feasible solution for the emotion recognition task based on physiological signals.

Keywords: Emotion Recognition · Deep learning · Electroencephalography (EEG) · Differential Entropy (DE)

1 Introduction

Emotions play a very important role in our daily life. In addition to reflecting people's current physiological and psychological states, emotion is also a critical factor in determining people's cognitive ability, communication ability and decision-making ability. Emotion recognition technology can automatically recognize human emotions through certain algorithms, which will contribute to solving numerous challenges in the fields of education, transportation, medical care, sales, etc. Compared with signals that can be easily artifacted, such as facial expressions, speech, and body postures, EEG signals are generated spontaneously by the human body, and their identification results are more objective and reliable. As a result, many researchers have conducted studies on EEG emotion recognition.

Emotion recognition is essentially a pattern recognition problem, and its accuracy is closely related to the extracted features. Thus feature engineering has been a critical process in emotion recognition. Traditionally, the characterization of EEG has been studied from a linear perspective, and many metrics have been proposed to characterize it. In this respect, frequency features such as power spectral density and asymmetry of the cerebral hemispheres in different frequency bands have been widely used [8]. However, linear metrics can only provide limited information from the EEG signal and cannot represent the nonlinear dynamical system features it has, so in recent years some features describing nonlinear dynamical systems such as correlation dimension, approximate entropy, and K-C complexity have appeared in research on emotion recognition [7,13]. In addition, Sharma et al. [17] used third-order cumulants (ToC) to explore the nonlinear dynamical properties of each sub-band signal and then used BiLSTM to classify emotions.

With the wide application of deep learning techniques in areas such as image and text, many researchers began to use end-to-end approaches to learn emotional EEG features for emotion recognition. Tripathi et al [22] firstly used DNN and CNN to classify EEG emotions and demonstrated that the neural network can also be a robust classifier of temporal EEG signals. Yang et al. [25] recombined DE features from multiple bands in EEG signals and used continuous convolutional neural networks as classifiers. Li et al. [12] proposed a Bi-hemisphere Domain Adversarial Neural Network (BiDANN) model, which learns remarkable information related to emotions from both brain hemispheres. Song et al. [20] proposed a Dynamical Graph Convolutional Neural Networks (DGCNN) model, which uses a graph to model a multichannel EEG and dynamically learn the intrinsic relationships between different channels. To obtain more effective EEG features, several researchers have introduced attentional mechanisms into the model. For example, Zhang et al. [26] proposed a convolutional recurrent attention model, for learning the high-level EEG feature representation and exploring the temporal dynamics.

However, the above methods have not fully utilized the emotion information in EEG signals. On the one hand, the EEG, as a temporal signal, has emotion-related temporal information within it. On the other hand, different EEG channels contribute differently to emotion recognition. Most studies have not fully considered these two points. In addition, some of the large networks such as Graph Convolutional Networks and Capsule Networks greatly increase the complexity and computation of the model while improving the recognition accuracy. Based on this, this paper proposes a new method for EEG emotion recognition, and the main contributions are summarized as follows:

1. We propose a model for EEG feature extraction and classification, named CALS, to extract both spatial and temporal emotional features from EEG signals.

2. We propose an EEG channel attention method, which first maps EEG channels to the 2D plane, and then realizes automatic weight assignment of EEG channels through adaptive spatial attention block.
3. We perform experiments on the publicly dataset DEAP. The results show that the proposed method in this paper achieves 98.93% and 98.95% recognition accuracy in valence and arousal, respectively.

2   Proposed Methods

The overall framework of emotion recognition proposed in this paper is shown in Fig. 1, which is roughly divided into two processes: one is feature construction, and the other is to perform the feature extraction and classification by the model CALS proposed in this paper. The detailed processing steps are described in 2.1 and 2.2, respectively.

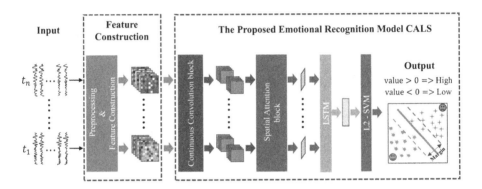

Fig. 1. The overall framework of the proposed emotion recognition method.

2.1   Feature Construction

Since the 1D EEG signal loses certain information, such as spatial information, we enhance the useful information by feature construction to improve the recognition accuracy. Through the feature construction, we transform the 1-D time-series signal into a 3-D input with time-space-frequency-nonlinear dynamical system features. The overall process is shown in Fig. 2.

Frequency Band Decomposition . The correlation between different frequency components of the EEG and different emotion types is one of the key scientific questions in cognitive neuroscience, which is also crucial for building effective recognition models. In particular, Theta (4–8 Hz), Alpha (8–13 Hz), Beta (13–30 Hz) and Gamma (30–45 Hz) frequency bands are closely correlated with emotions.

Moreover, it has been confirmed [1,3] that Beta-2 band(18–22 Hz), Beta-3 band (22–30 Hz), and Gamma band (30–45 Hz) have significant correlation with emotion. Based on this, instead of extracting only the 4 bands of Theta, Alpha, Beta and Gamma as in the previous work, we decomposed the Beta band into 3 bands of Beta-1, Beta-2, and Beta-3. Finally, we extracted six frequency bands from each channel of the original signal by a third-order Butterworth bandpass filter.

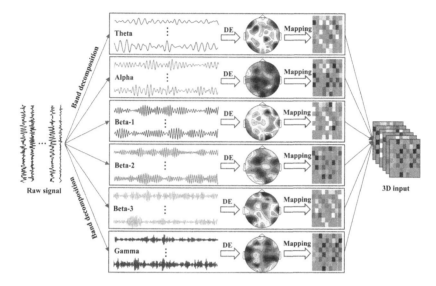

Fig. 2. Feature construction process of 1D time-series data into 3D input.

Calculation of Nonlinear Dynamics Features - Differential Entropy.
Duan et al. [4] first introduced Differential entropy (DE) to EEG-based emotion recognition, and its validity and robustness have been extensively validated in many studies and has been shown to have advantages over PSD [27]. This is because the low-frequency energy of EEG data is higher than the high-frequency energy, and DE has a balanced ability to distinguish the low-frequency and high-frequency energy of EEG patterns [11].

For an EEG signal x of a specific length which approximately obeys a Gaussian distribution $N(u, \sigma^2)$, a fixed-length signal x, the differential entropy DE_{band_i} of the signal in the frequency band $band_i$ [19] can be calculated as (1),

$$DE_{band_i} = \frac{1}{2} log(2\pi e \sigma^2_{band_i})$$
(1)

where $\sigma^2_{band_i}$ represents the signal variance of a fixed length EEG signal x in the frequency band $band_i$ range, and e denotes the Euler constant.

The differential entropy in the six frequency bands and their corresponding EEG topographies are shown in Fig. 2. In addition, The EEG signal is susceptible to the external environment, so we calibrated the experimental signal using the baseline signal (the resting signal obtained before the start of each experiment) [25], taking the difference between the DE value of the experimental signal and the baseline signal as the final DE feature.

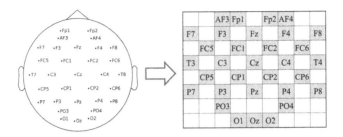

Fig. 3. 2D mapping of 32 EEG channels.

2D Mapping. The 32 electrodes of EEG channels have the relatively fixed position in 3D space, but the electrodes are arranged sequentially in the original sample data, which loses the spatial information in the EEG signal. For this reason, we increase the spatial resolution of the EEG signal by mapping the 32 EEG signals into a 2D plane according to the relative positions in 3-dimensional space. The mapping process is shown in Fig. 3.

2.2 The Construction of Proposed Model CALS

In this section, the four parts of the deep learning model CALS proposed in this paper are described in detail: the continuous convolution block, the adaptive spatial attention block, the two-layer LSTM block, and the L2-SVM layer.

Continuous Convolution Block. Inspired by yang et al. [25] we discarded the pooling layer that follows the convolutional layer in traditional CNNs to better preserve the effective information. We designed a continuous convolutional block for the extraction of high-level features, which consists of four convolutional layers with different receptive fields, as shown in Fig. 4.

Adaptive Spatial Attention Block. Each brain region (electrode channel) has certain differences in the reflection of emotions. Inspired by CBAM [23], in order to obtain a more precise feature representation, we introduced an adaptive spatial attention module, which automatically assigns weights to the 32 EEG channels based on importance. Therefore, the model can focus on those EEG channels which contribute more to emotion recognition, while suppressing those which contribute less. The processing flow is shown in Fig. 4.

First, as shown in (2) and (3), feature maps F_{GMP}, $F_{GAP} \in \mathbb{R}^{H \times W \times 1}$ are obtained by global max pooling and global average pooling along the channel dimension of the feature map $F \in \mathbb{R}^{H \times W \times C}$, respectively. Max pooling can capture the difference features, while average pooling can capture the universal features. Then, as shown in (4) and (5), the spatial weight matrix $M_s(F) \in \mathbb{R}^{H \times W \times 1}$ can be obtained by a 9×9 convolution layer and Sigmoid function, and the weighted new feature $F' \in \mathbb{R}^{H \times W \times C}$ can be obtained by multiplying M_s with the original feature F. Finally, the 2×2 maximum pooling layer and the fully connected layer are used to obtain the 1D vector, which will be used as one of the n time steps of the LSTM later.

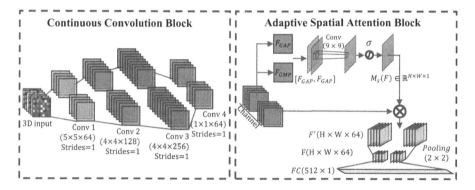

Fig. 4. The structure of the continuous convolution block and the adaptive spatial attention block.

$$F_{GMP} = MaxPooling_{1 \times C}(F) \tag{2}$$

$$F_{GAP} = AvgPooling_{1 \times C}(F) \tag{3}$$

$$M_s(F) = \sigma(f^{9 \times 9}([F_{GMP}, F_{GAP}])) \tag{4}$$

$$F' = F \cdot M_s(F) \tag{5}$$

LSTM Block. Neurons in Long short-term memory network (LSTM) [6] have the advantage of retaining long-time memory, which means that, for EEG signals, LSTM networks can retain both long-time and short-time emotional features. Based on this, we cascade a two-layer LSTM behind the adaptive attention module with 128 cells in the first layer, 64 cells in the second layer and 6 time-steps. Finally, the output of the last hidden state (64 × 1 vector) is used as the final output feature.

L2-SVM Layer. The top layer of traditional deep learning models mostly uses the softmax function for prediction, while minimizing the cross-entropy loss function to make its output values fit the true probability distribution as much as possible. For the binary classification problem, given a set of training samples $(x_i, y_i), i \in 1, \ldots, N, x_i \in \mathbb{R}^D, y_i \in \{0, 1\}$, assume that p_i denotes the probability that sample x_i is correctly predicted, then the probability of incorrect prediction is $1 - p_i$, at this time, the cross-entropy loss function of each class is shown in the following (6).

$$Loss = \frac{1}{N} \sum_i -[y_i log(p_i) + (1 - y_i) log(1 - p_i)] \tag{6}$$

It can be seen that the cross-entropy loss function is a self-probability model that considers the global data, which means that the final classification hyperplane obtained will be disturbed by each sample. This is very disadvantageous for the EEG signal which is inherently non-smooth and multi-noise in nature. For this reason, we use a linear support vector machine to replace the softmax layer commonly used in deep learning model, and tang et al. [21] used this approach to obtain better performance than softmax on image datasets.

Unlike the softmax classifier, the classification performance of L2-SVM is mainly influenced by the support vectors, and the non-support vectors do not cause changes in the decision plane. Accordingly, we need to minimize a marginal-based loss instead of a cross-entropy loss. For a given set of training samples $(x_i, y_i), i \in 1, \ldots, N, x_i \in \mathbb{R}^D, y_i \in \{-1, 1\}$, the support vector machine can be represented as solving the constrained optimization problem represented by the following (7), where ξ_i is the slack variable which penalizes data points and C is the penalty factor. For linear L1-SVM, L2-SVM, it can be expressed as solving the unconstrained optimization problem represented by the following (8).

$$\min_{w, \xi_i} \frac{1}{2} w^T w + C \sum_{i=1}^{N} \xi_i , \quad s.t. \begin{cases} y_i w^T x_i \geqslant 1 - \xi_i, \forall i \in 1, \ldots, N \\ \xi_i \geqslant 0, \forall i \in 1, \ldots, N \end{cases} \tag{7}$$

$$\min_{w} f(w) = \frac{1}{2} w^T w + C \sum_{i=1}^{N} \xi(w, x_i, y_i) ,$$

$$\xi(w, x_i, y_i) = \begin{cases} \max(0, 1 - y_i w^T x_i), & L1 - SVM \\ \max(0, 1 - y_i w^T x_i)^2, & L2 - SVM \end{cases} \tag{8}$$

Since L1-SVM is not differentiable which cannot be trained by back-propagation, we finally use L2-SVM and the optimization objective is represented by the following (9):

$$\min_{w} f(w) = \frac{1}{2} w^T w + C \sum_{i=1}^{N} \max(0, 1 - y_i w^T x_i)^2 \tag{9}$$

3   Experiments and Results

This section presents the experiments and classification results based on the DEAP dataset. First, the dataset we used, DEAP, is introduced in Sect. 3.1.

Then the experimental settings are described in Sect. 3.2. Finally, the results of our experiments are shown in Sect. 3.3.

3.1 Data Materials

The DEAP emotion database is authoritative and rich in data, which is highly favored by experts and scholars in this research area, and some signal processing methods as well as machine learning algorithms have been applied in many studies. Therefore, all studies and experiments in this paper are based on the DEAP emotion database.

The DEAP [9] database was proposed by Koelstra et al. in 2012, which contains 32 channels of EEG signals and 8 channels of peripheral physiological signals from 32 subjects. To ensure the authority and richness of the data, the team carefully selected 40 different types of music videos, and only extracted the most emotionally stimulating 1-minute clips. Therefore, each subject will be asked to perform 40 experiments of 1 min long. After each experiment, subjects were required to give a score (rating 1-9) on each of the four dimensions: value, arousal, dominance, and liking.

3.2 Experimental Settings

In this paper, the EEG signals of 32 channels in the DEAP dataset were used as experimental data. For the dimensional representation model of emotion, the most widely recognized one is the Valence-Arousal (VA) emotion representation proposed by Russell [16], so we adopt validity and arousal as evaluation indexes in this paper. In each dimension, labels were classified into two categories with a threshold of 5: signal with $rating > 5$ is labeled as "high" and $rating \leq 5$ is labeled as "low". In addition, EEG emotion recognition can be either subject-independent or subject-dependent [15]. In this paper, we focus on subject- dependent EEG emotion recognition.

All experiments were done based on Python, and the network structure was built using the deep learning framework Tensorflow 2.5. In order to verify the effectiveness of the method in this paper, a large number of experiments are conducted on the DEAP dataset, and the accuracy and loss values of the model are obtained by a 10-fold cross-validation strategy to evaluate the performance of the model.

3.3 Results and Analysis

Overall Performance. For each of the 32 subjects in the DEAP dataset, we constructed two classification tasks, Low/High Valence and Low/High Arousal (LA/HA), which means there were 64 classification tasks performed in total. For each classification task, we used a 10-fold cross-validation strategy to obtain loss and accuracy values, and the average of the 10 results was used as the final result of the current experiment. The accuracy and loss results for the 64 experiments with 32 subjects are shown in Fig. 5 and Fig. 6.

The experimental results show that our method has an average accuracy of 98.93% and 98.95% in valence and arousal, with a minimum accuracy of 93.37% and a maximum accuracy of 99.88%. In addition, we visualized data separability at different phases in 2D and 3D using t-distributed stochastic neighbor embedding (t-SNE). As shown in Fig. 7, the output features of the last layer of the CALS model show a clear separability compared to the original data and the 3D data after feature construction. All the above results show that the emotion recognition method proposed in this paper can effectively extract emotion-related features.

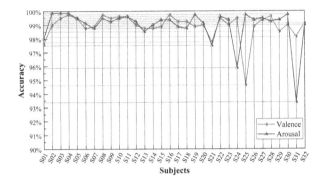

Fig. 5. The average accuracy of the 10-fold cross-validation for each subject.

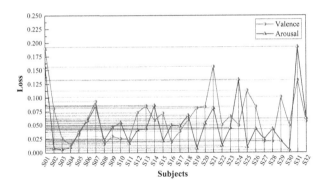

Fig. 6. The average loss of the 10-fold cross-validation for each subject.

Comparison with Previous Studies. In order to illustrate the effectiveness of our proposed method, we compared it with various state of arts of related

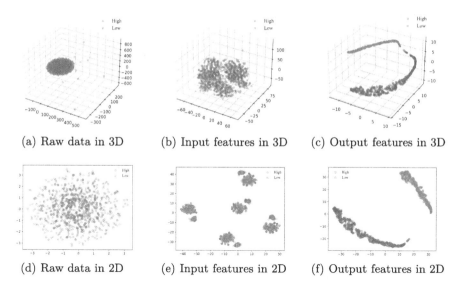

(a) Raw data in 3D   (b) Input features in 3D   (c) Output features in 3D

(d) Raw data in 2D   (e) Input features in 2D   (f) Output features in 2D

Fig. 7. 3D and 2D visualization of data separability in 3 stages: raw time-series data, Input features after feature construction, and the output features of CALS.

works based on DEAP dataset. As shown in Table 1, our method shows obvious strengths in the recognition accuracy of both the valence and the arousal dimension.

Compared to models based only on cnn or lstm, the recognition accuracy of our method has a significant advantage. This is mainly attributed to the CALS extracting both spatial and temporal features from EEG, which fully utilizes the emotional information in the EEG signals. Notably, compared to the hybrid models CNN-RNN and 4D-CRNN, which are also based on CNN and RNN, the recognition accuracy of our method is 9% higher than that of CNN-RNN and 3% higher than that of 4D-CRNN. This mainly contributes to 2 factors: first, the EEG channel attention mechanism enhances the extraction of useful features, second, the introduction of L2-SVM in the last layer of the model improves the generalization ability.

In addition, we further calculate the FLOPs and Params of the top-performing MTCA-CapsNet model and our proposed model, and the results are shown in Table 2. It can be seen that the accuracy of our method is 1.61% higher than MTCA-CapsNet, while at the same time, the number of parameters and the model size of our method are only about 1/4 of those of the MTCA-CapsNet.

Exploration of Generalization Ability. To test the generalization performance of our proposed method, we tested it on a dataset containing different numbers of individual subjects. A total of seven datasets were obtained by performing two dichotomies on 32 subjects. Among them, four datasets merged the data of 8 subjects named s01-s08, s09-s16, s17-s24, s25-s32, two datasets merged

Table 1. Comparison of the proposed method with various state of arts of related works in valence and arousal.

Studies	Model	Valence	Arousal
Xing et al. [24]	SAE+LSTM	81.10%	74.38%
Chen et al. [2]	CNN-RNN	93.64%	93.26%
Yang et al. [25]	Continuous CNN	89.45%	90.24%
Sharma et al. [17]	Bi-LSTM	84.16%	85.21%
Shen et al. [18]	4D-CRNN	94.22%	94.58%
Gao et al. [5]	Dense CNN	92.24%	92.92%
Pan et al. [14]	FBCCNN	90.26%	88.90%
Li et al. [10]	MTCA-CapsNet	97.41%	97.25%
Ours	**CALS**	**98.93%**	**98.95%**

Table 2. Comparison of the MTCA-CapsNet and our model on FLOPs and params.

Studies	Model	FLOPs	params
Li et al. [10]	MTCA-CapsNet	2.438 G	5.330 M
Ours	**CALS**	**0.592 G**	**1.581 M**

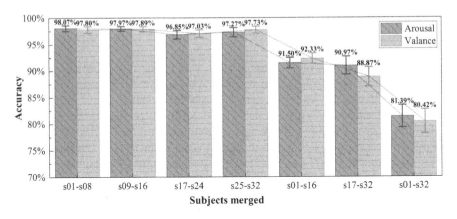

Fig. 8. The performance of the proposed method on datasets merging different numbers of subjects.

the data of 16 subjects named s01-s16, s16-s32, and one dataset merged the data of all 32 subjects named s01-s32. We performed 10 cross-validations on each of these 8 datasets, and the results are shown in Fig. 8. As the number of combined subjects increased, the average recognition accuracy of valence and arousal gradually decreased, while the experimental error gradually increased. Nevertheless, our method achieved a relatively positive result with a recognition accuracy of 80.42% in valence and 81.38% in arousal on the dataset merging all 32 subjects.

4   Conclusion

In this paper, we propose an emotion recognition method based on EEG signals. We validate the effectiveness of the method on the DEAP public dataset, and its recognition accuracies in valence and arousal are respectively 98.93% and 98.95%, which are both better than other methods. Although this study achieved high classification performance in EEG-based emotion recognition, its feature construction process is complicated and not suitable for the real-time emotion recognition task. Therefore, the next study of our research will further simplify the model to improve the performance of real-time emotion recognition.

References

1. Aftanas, L., Reva, N., Savotina, L., Makhnev, V.: Neurophysiological correlates of induced discrete emotions in humans: an individually oriented analysis. Neurosci. Behav. Physiol. **36**, 119–130 (2006)
2. Chen, J., Jiang, D., Zhang, Y., Zhang, P.: Emotion recognition from spatiotemporal EEG representations with hybrid convolutional recurrent neural networks via wearable multi-channel headset. Comput. Commun. **154**, 58–65 (2020)
3. Daly, I., et al.: Neural correlates of emotional responses to music: an EEG study. Neurosci. Lett. **573**, 52–57 (2014)
4. Duan, R.N., Zhu, J.Y., Lu, B.L.: Differential entropy feature for eeg-based emotion classification. In: 2013 6th International IEEE/EMBS Conference on Neural Engineering (NER), pp. 81–84. IEEE (2013)
5. Gao, Z., Wang, X., Yang, Y., Li, Y., Ma, K., Chen, G.: A channel-fused dense convolutional network for eeg-based emotion recognition. IEEE Trans. Cognit. Developm. Syst. **13**(4), 945–954 (2020)
6. Hochreiter, S., Schmidhuber, J.: Long short-term memory. Neural Comput. **9**(8), 1735–1780 (1997)
7. Hosseinifard, B., Moradi, M.H., Rostami, R.: Classifying depression patients and normal subjects using machine learning techniques and nonlinear features from eeg signal. Comput. Methods Programs Biomed. **109**(3), 339–345 (2013)
8. Kim, M.K., Kim, M., Oh, E., Kim, S.P.: A review on the computational methods for emotional state estimation from the human eeg. In: Computational and Mathematical Methods in Medicine (2013) (2013)
9. Koelstra, S., et al.: Deap: a database for emotion analysis; using physiological signals. IEEE Trans. Affect. Comput. **3**(1), 18–31 (2011)
10. Li, C., et al.: Emotion recognition from eeg based on multi-task learning with capsule network and attention mechanism. Comput. Biol. Med. **143**, 105303 (2022)
11. Li, X., et al.: Eeg based emotion recognition: a tutorial and review. ACM Comput. Surv. **55**(4), 1–57 (2022)
12. Li, Y., Zheng, W., Zong, Y., Cui, Z., Zhang, T., Zhou, X.: A bi-hemisphere domain adversarial neural network model for eeg emotion recognition. IEEE Trans. Affect. Comput. **12**(2), 494–504 (2018)
13. Liu, Y., Sourina, O.: Eeg-based subject-dependent emotion recognition algorithm using fractal dimension. In: 2014 IEEE International Conference on Systems, Man, and Cybernetics (SMC), pp. 3166–3171. IEEE (2014)

14. Pan, B., Zheng, W., et al.: Emotion recognition based on eeg using generative adversarial nets and convolutional neural network. In: Computational and Mathematical Methods in Medicine (2021) (2021)

15. Piho, L., Tjahjadi, T.: A mutual information based adaptive windowing of informative eeg for emotion recognition. IEEE Trans. Affect. Comput. **11**(4), 722–735 (2018)

16. Russell, J.A.: A circumplex model of affect. J. Pers. Soc. Psychol. **39**(6), 1161 (1980)

17. Sharma, R., Pachori, R.B., Sircar, P.: Automated emotion recognition based on higher order statistics and deep learning algorithm. Biomed. Signal Process. Control **58**, 101867 (2020)

18. Shen, F., Dai, G., Lin, G., Zhang, J., Kong, W., Zeng, H.: Eeg-based emotion recognition using 4d convolutional recurrent neural network. Cogn. Neurodyn. **14**, 815–828 (2020)

19. Shi, L.C., Jiao, Y.Y., Lu, B.L.: Differential entropy feature for eeg-based vigilance estimation. In: 2013 35th Annual International Conference of the IEEE Engineering in Medicine and Biology Society (EMBC), pp. 6627–6630. IEEE (2013)

20. Song, T., Zheng, W., Song, P., Cui, Z.: Eeg emotion recognition using dynamical graph convolutional neural networks. IEEE Trans. Affect. Comput. **11**(3), 532–541 (2018)

21. Tang, Y.: Deep learning using linear support vector machines. arXiv preprint arXiv:1306.0239 (2013)

22. Tripathi, S., Acharya, S., Sharma, R., Mittal, S., Bhattacharya, S.: Using deep and convolutional neural networks for accurate emotion classification on deap data. In: Proceedings of the AAAI Conference on Artificial Intelligence, vol. 31, pp. 4746–4752 (2017)

23. Woo, S., Park, J., Lee, J.-Y., Kweon, I.S.: CBAM: convolutional block attention module. In: Ferrari, V., Hebert, M., Sminchisescu, C., Weiss, Y. (eds.) ECCV 2018. LNCS, vol. 11211, pp. 3–19. Springer, Cham (2018). https://doi.org/10.1007/978-3-030-01234-2_1

24. Xing, X., Li, Z., Xu, T., Shu, L., Hu, B., Xu, X.: Sae+ lstm: a new framework for emotion recognition from multi-channel eeg. Front. Neurorobot. **13**, 37 (2019)

25. Yang, Y., Wu, Q., Fu, Y., Chen, X.: Continuous convolutional neural network with 3D input for EEG-based emotion recognition. In: Cheng, L., Leung, A.C.S., Ozawa, S. (eds.) ICONIP 2018. LNCS, vol. 11307, pp. 433–443. Springer, Cham (2018). https://doi.org/10.1007/978-3-030-04239-4_39

26. Zhang, D., Yao, L., Chen, K., Monaghan, J.: A convolutional recurrent attention model for subject-independent eeg signal analysis. IEEE Signal Process. Lett. **26**(5), 715–719 (2019)

27. Zheng, W.L., Lu, B.L.: Investigating critical frequency bands and channels for eeg-based emotion recognition with deep neural networks. IEEE Trans. Auton. Ment. Dev. **7**(3), 162–175 (2015)

Replaying Styles for Continual Semantic Segmentation Across Domains

Yao Deng and Xiang Xiang[✉]

Key Lab of Image Processing and Intelligent Control, Ministry of Education,
School of Artificial Intelligence and Automation,
Huazhong University of Science and Technology, Wuhan 430074, China
xex@hust.edu.cn

Abstract. In the context of Domain Incremental Learning for Semantic Segmentation, catastrophic forgetting is a significant issue when a model learns new geographical domains. While replay-based approaches have been commonly used to mitigate this problem by allowing the model to review past knowledge, they require additional storage space for old data, which may not be feasible in real-world applications. To address this limitation, we propose a style replay method that leverages the characteristics of low-level representations in CNN to require only one style feature for each domain, leading to a significant reduction in storage overhead. By fusing the style features of past domains with the semantic features of current data, our method enables style transfer for new domain data, thereby improving the model's generalization ability to the domain. Through extensive experimental evaluations on various autonomous driving datasets, we demonstrate the efficacy of our proposed method in addressing the challenges of continual semantic segmentation under both label and domain shift, outperforming the previous state-of-the-art methods.

Keywords: Incremental Learning · Semantic Segmentation · Domain Adaptation

1 Introduction

In recent years, deep neural networks have exhibited remarkable potential across diverse industries and academic domains, particularly in the realm of computer vision tasks. Among the various tasks in computer vision, semantic segmentation has emerged as a prominent research direction, having achieved significant progress with applications in fields such as autonomous driving. However, while deep models may demonstrate high performance within a specific task, they often struggle when adapting to changing environments and confronted with an increasing number of tasks. The primary challenge arises from models' tendency to experience catastrophic forgetting of previously acquired knowledge (Fig. 1).

H. Lu et al. (Eds.): ACPR 2023, LNCS 14407, pp. 297–311, 2023.
https://doi.org/10.1007/978-3-031-47637-2_23

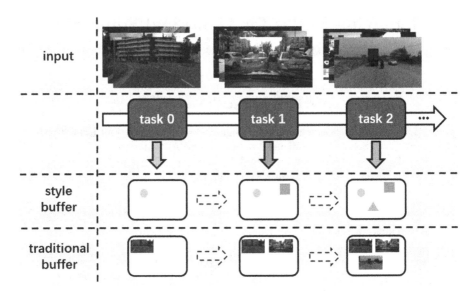

Fig. 1. The setting of domain incremental semantic segmentation and a comparison between traditional replay and our method.

For instance, in an autonomous driving system, when encountering an unfamiliar geographic environment, *i.e.*, data from a previously unobserved domain, the system must adjust to the new environment while retaining its knowledge of the geographic environments it has encountered previously. This necessitates the ability of the system to perform domain incremental learning. In contrast to domain adaptation, which aims to achieve high performance on both the source and target domain, domain incremental learning necessitates the model to achieve satisfactory outcomes in a sequence of gradually arriving domains.

Many methods have been proposed in the realm of incremental learning to address catastrophic forgetting, with replay-based approaches yielding superior results. The fundamental concept underlying such methods is that, when training a new task, a representative subset of the previous data is preserved and leveraged by the model to revisit previously learned knowledge. However, this technique suffers from certain limitations in practical scenarios: (1) replay samples entail additional storage requirements, and the number of samples to be retained increases incrementally as new tasks are introduced, thereby exacerbating the storage burden of old task samples; (2) if the total number of replay samples is fixed, the number of tasks storing samples in memory increases gradually with the appearance of new tasks. To maintain the total number of samples, samples from each task must be selectively removed, resulting in an imbalance between the number of samples from the current and old tasks. Consequently, the model is more inclined to learn the knowledge of the current domain during the training process. While generative replay can alleviate the storage space constraint by producing synthetic samples of old tasks to be employed in training, it still necessitates the training of a separate generative model to support the incremental model.

In order to address the need for realistic scenarios, we propose a domain incremental semantic segmentation method that adds little additional storage overhead. Our approach leverages the characteristics of low-level features in CNN to extract a style feature for each domain, which is then saved. To train a new task, the fused features with current data semantics under the old domain style are added to the training set via feature fusion. By storing only one feature map containing style information for each domain, our method significantly reduces storage space. The benefits of domain styling are multifaceted. Firstly, our approach enables predictive models to experience past input distributions under supervision or pseudo-supervision, thereby mitigating the problem of catastrophic forgetting at the domain level. Secondly, our approach aims to learn new classes in old domains without direct supervision in those domains, while retaining knowledge of old classes to alleviate semantic-level catastrophic forgetting. Additionally, by obtaining variable input distributions, our approach encourages the predictive model to extend its ability to adapt to unseen domains, which is crucial in continual learning models involving domain shift.

In summary, our key contributions can be outlined as follows:

(1) Our proposed method involves extracting domain-specific styles from the shallow features of a network. This allows us to obtain style feature maps for different domains, which can then be fused with semantic features to enable style transfer.

(2) We utilize fused features that incorporate different domain styles to augment the training process. This effectively mitigates the problem of catastrophic forgetting of previous domain knowledge by the model, thereby enhancing its robustness.

(3) Experiments on various autonomous driving datasets demonstrate the efficacy of our proposed method in addressing the challenges of continual semantic segmentation under both lable and domain shift, outperforming previous State-of-the-Art (SOTA) methods.

2   Related Works

2.1   Semantic Segmentation

In the field of computer vision, semantic segmentation is a fundamental task that has made significant strides in recent years. This progress can be attributed to the rapid advancement of deep learning algorithms, which have led to the development of various techniques aimed at enhancing the performance of semantic segmentation. These techniques include the encoder-decoder [3,8,14,24] structure, dilated convolution [4,5], pyramid structure [32,35], attention mechanism [9,31,36], and transformers [6,25,28,34]. Besides, some recent studies have emphasized the importance of computational resources, in addition to accuracy. To fulfill this need, our study employs a lightweight network as the backbone for our semantic segmentation model.

2.2   Incremental Learning

Incremental Learning (IL) in computer vision involves continuously processing real-world information while retaining previously learned knowledge. For image classification tasks, existing IL methods can be broadly categorized into three categories [7]: replay-based [2,19,20,22], regularization-based [1,13,30], and parameter-isolation-based [16,17,21] methods. Replay-based approaches retain some old data to enable the model to review previously learned knowledge when training a new task. Regularization-based approaches protect old knowledge from being overwritten by new knowledge by imposing constraints on the loss function of the new task. Parameter-isolation-based approaches are used for task-specific learning by introducing a larger number of parameters and computational volumes with different parameters. These methods have been extensively studied and have shown promising results.

2.3   Domain Adaptation

Our work is primarily concerned with addressing domain shift between tasks, and as such, it is related to the field of domain adaptation for semantic segmentation [18,26,27,29,33]. Specifically, we note that prior research in this area includes the proposal by [33] of a multi-source adaptation framework that generates adapted domains with semantic consistency, aligning them towards the target, and performing feature-level alignment between the aggregated domain and target domain. Similarly, [29] presented an unsupervised domain adaptation method that reduces the distribution discrepancy between the source and target by swapping their low-frequency spectra, demonstrating its effectiveness in tasks where densely annotated images are difficult to obtain in real domains. However, it is important to highlight that our work differs from traditional domain adaptation approaches, as we aim to retain source domain performance while simultaneously learning from the target domain.

3   Method

3.1   Problem Formulation

In incremental learning, T tasks are presented sequentially, each corresponding to a different dataset of domains $\mathcal{D}_1, \mathcal{D}_2, ..., \mathcal{D}_t, ..., \mathcal{D}_T$ with label spaces $\mathcal{Y}_1, \mathcal{Y}_2, ..., \mathcal{Y}_t, ..., \mathcal{Y}_T$, respectively. A domain $\mathcal{D}_t$ represents image data collected from a particular geographic road environment, and $\mathcal{Y}_t$ represents the semantic label space of the classes present in that domain. Considering the general case of non-overlapping label spaces, $\mathcal{Y}_t$ will either have a full overlap or a partial overlap w.r.t. $\mathcal{Y}_{t-1}$. $\mathcal{Y}_t$ may contain novel classes that were not present in $\mathcal{Y}_{t-1}$ and $\mathcal{Y}_{t-1}$ may also have novel classes absent in $\mathcal{Y}_t$. $\mathcal{D}_t$ has a domain shift with respect to $\mathcal{D}_{t-1}$, as expected.

   Our objective is to train a segmentation network $\mathcal{S}$ that learns to classify data on each domain $\mathcal{D}_t$, sequentially. More formally, we aim to learn $\mathcal{S} : \mathcal{X}_{0:t} \rightarrow \mathcal{Y}_{0:t}$

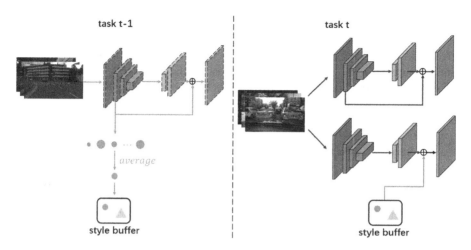

Fig. 2. Overall framework of our domain incremental semantic segmentation method.

to recognize all the semantic classes $\mathcal{Y}_{0:t} = \bigcup_{k=0}^{t} \mathcal{Y}_k$ observed up to the current step t on all the image domains $\mathcal{D}_{0:t} = \bigcup_{k=0}^{t} \mathcal{D}_k$ experienced so far.

3.2   Style Extraction from Low-Level Representations

The appearance of an image can be influenced by various low-level factors such as the equipment used to capture it and the lighting conditions present in the environment. These factors can affect the image's style, but not necessarily its semantic content. Deep learning models are primarily designed to learn semantic features for understanding the content of an image, rather than low-level stylistic elements.

However, if a model is only trained on a specific domain that lacks variation in these low-level factors, it may not be able to generalize well to new data with different stylistic characteristics. This is because the model has not been exposed to a sufficiently diverse range of image styles during training. As a consequence, introducing greater diversity in the input data domain during the training process can enhance a model's ability to achieve improved generalization across diverse domains. FDA [29] builds upon this concept by leveraging the low-frequency component of the image frequency domain, which is considered as a distinctive feature of the domain, to facilitate style transfer. Specifically, FDA replaces the corresponding low-frequency component of the current domain image with that of the target domain, thereby achieving style transfer and generating an image with diverse domain.

Despite its efficacy in image style transfer, the FDA has certain limitations that are particularly relevant in the context of domain incremental settings. Firstly, the size of the frequency domain region that is utilized for style replacement varies across different datasets, and this hyperparameter must be continually adjusted as new datasets are added during the incremental process. This necessitates a significant amount of manual intervention and makes the incremental process more challenging to manage effectively. Secondly, style information extracted through FDA is incomplete. As the method operates solely on frequency domain of images, it can only extract stylistic features that are present in this domain. Such limitation restricts the ability of the model to capture more complex and nuanced stylistic characteristics that may be present in the images across different domains.

Building upon recent work on the principles of forgetting in domain incremental semantic segmentation [11], we propose a novel approach for extracting domain-specific style information that leverages the low-level representations of the network. We exploit the fact that shallow networks are closer to the input, have a smaller perceptual field, and are more attuned to image details, thereby containing rich style information. Conversely, deep network features contain more semantic information. However, given that shallow and deep features are located at different levels in the network, a structural modification of the network is required to enable the fusion of domain-specific style features with the semantic features of the input image. Our approach aims to address this challenge by proposing a novel network architecture that facilitates the extraction and integration of style information from different domains, while also preserving the semantic content of the input image.

Specifically, the original model is divided into three parts: $\mathcal{S}(\mathbf{x}) = f \circ g \circ h(\mathbf{x})$, where h is the shallow module of the network for extracting style features, g is the intermediate layer of the model for extracting features that contain more semantic information, and f is the deep module of the network for fusing semantic and style features, then the output of the current network is:

$$\mathcal{S}(\mathbf{x}) = f[h(\mathbf{x}) + g(h(\mathbf{x}))]. \tag{1}$$

In contrast to the style migration method employed by FDA, our proposed approach utilizes network-extracted features as style features, instead of solely relying on the frequency domain component. This approach offers a more comprehensive representation of domain information, enabling the extraction of features that describe domain style characteristics beyond those captured in the frequency domain. Furthermore, the hyperparameters in the FDA method require readjustment for different datasets, whereas the features learned by the network in our approach can reduce the need for such adjustments. This is because the network-learned features are capable of capturing the complex and dynamic relationships between the input images and their corresponding stylistic characteristics, thereby reducing the dependence on manually tuned hyperparameters.

3.3   Replaying Styles for Knowledge Preservation

Our approach involves regarding the shallow features of the network as domain-specific style features, which can be extracted and stored as feature maps representing the style of each domain. Specifically, during task t, the average style features of all input data for the current task are extracted by the trained model and saved as the style features of the k-th domain:

$$H_k = \frac{1}{N} \sum_{\mathbf{x_k} \in \mathcal{D}_k} h(\mathbf{x_k}). \tag{2}$$

We preserve the style features of each task, which are stored as a style memory $\mathcal{M}_{0:t-1} = \{H_k | k < t\}$. During each incremental step, this style memory can be accessed to retrieve key information characterizing the style of the past domain, without the need to directly access the original data.

Upon the arrival of the new task t, we are able to obtain the features of the current input in the past style by feature fusion. Specifically, the output of fused feature with the k-th$(k < t)$ style is denoted as:

$$\mathcal{S}^k(\mathbf{x_t}) = f[H_k + g(h(\mathbf{x_t}))]. \tag{3}$$

At this stage, we have access to the fused feature corresponding to the past domains, which can be used to supervise the model and thereby retain the knowledge of the old domains. To acquire knowledge in current domain, we train the model on the loss given as:

$$\mathcal{L}_{ce} = \frac{1}{N} \sum_{\mathbf{x_t} \in \mathcal{D_t}} \phi(y_t, \mathcal{S}(\mathbf{x_t})), \tag{4}$$

where ϕ is the softmax cross-entropy loss.

To address the challenge of limited input data from past domains, our approach involves generating features of the current task in the style of the past domains. This process enables the retention of low-level style statistics similar to those of the past domains, compensating for the lack of available input data. We preserve previous domain knowledge by optimize:

$$\mathcal{L}_1 = \frac{1}{t} \sum_{k<t} \frac{1}{N} \sum_{\mathbf{x_t} \in \mathcal{D_t}} \phi(y_t, \mathcal{S}^k(\mathbf{x_t})). \tag{5}$$

Furthermore, it is possible that certain classes of past tasks may be underrepresented or even completely absent in the new task. To address this challenge and retain the knowledge gained from the previous classes, our approach involves retaining the model of the previous task as the teacher model $\mathcal{T}$ and acquiring such knowledge through the use of the distillation loss ψ:

$$\mathcal{L}_2 = \frac{1}{N} \sum_{\mathbf{x_t} \in \mathcal{D_t}} \psi(\mathcal{T}(\mathbf{x}_t), \mathcal{S}(\mathbf{x_t})). \tag{6}$$

In a similar manner, our approach also employs knowledge distillation to retain the knowledge of old classes under past domains:

$$\mathcal{L}_3 = \frac{1}{t} \sum_{k<t} \frac{1}{N} \sum_{\mathbf{x_t} \in \mathcal{D_t}} \psi(\mathcal{T}(\mathbf{x}_t), \mathcal{S}^k(\mathbf{x_t})). \tag{7}$$

Therefore, the total loss of our work is denoted as:

$$\mathcal{L}_{all} = \mathcal{L}_{ce} + \lambda_1 \mathcal{L}_1 + \lambda_2 \mathcal{L}_2 + \lambda_3 \mathcal{L}_3, \tag{8}$$

304 Y. Deng and X. Xiang

where λ_1, λ_2 and λ_3 are balanced weights. The overall framework of our method is illustrated in Fig. 2.

In comparison to traditional replay-based methods, our proposed approach requires significantly less storage space, as it only saves the stylistic features of each domain instead of multiple images under each task. This reduction in storage requirements is made possible by the ability of our approach to generate data of past styles by combining the saved style features with the semantic features of the current task. Traditional replay-based methods suffer from a decrease in the number of samples per task as the number of tasks increases, if the size of the memory is fixed. Alternatively, if the number of samples per task is fixed, the size of the memory increases rapidly. Our approach, however, enables efficient recall of domain-specific information without requiring additional storage space or memory resources. This not only reduces storage space occupation but also enhances the storage efficiency and generalization performance of the model.

4 Experiments

4.1 Datasets

Following [10], we conduct our experiments on three datasets, with domain shift and possibly label shift between them. The datasets were collected from diverse geographic locations, capturing various urban driving scenarios. The Cityscapes dataset (CS) is a prominent autonomous driving dataset consisting of daytime images with 19 labels, obtained from 50 different cities situated in Central Europe. The Berkeley Deep Drive dataset (BDD) encompasses a wider range of road scenes, including residential areas, highways, and urban streets, and was captured under varying weather conditions at different times of the day. The BDD provides 7000 training and 1000 validation images. The Indian Driving Dataset (IDD) comprises driving scenes from Indian cities and their outskirts, covering highly unstructured road environments and featuring unique labels such as billboard, auto-rickshaw, and animal, among others. The IDD contains 6993 training and 781 validation images and is classified into 26 labels under IDD level 3. For our experiment, we utilize 19 labels from Cityscapes and BDD100k and 26 labels from IDD level 3. We frame the process of incrementally performing the task on three distinct datasets as an approach that addresses multiple domains.

4.2 Evaluation Metrics

Mean Intersection-over-Union (mIoU) metric is widely used to evaluate the semantic segmentation performance of a model on each dataset. Besides, inspired by [10,12], we resort to the average per-task drop with respect to the corresponding single-task baseline to quantify the overall IL performance of a model:

$$\Delta_d\% = \frac{1}{T} \sum_{t=1}^{T} \frac{\mathcal{A}_s - \mathcal{A}_m}{\mathcal{A}_s}, \tag{9}$$

where $\mathcal{A}_s$ and $\mathcal{A}_m$ stand for the mIoU of model individual trained on each task and current model respectively.

4.3   Implementation Details

We use ERFNet [23], a lightweight network for real-time semantic segmentation, as the backbone of our experiment, which is more relevant to realistic scenarios. In all experiments, the segmentation model is pre-trained on ImageNet. We use the Adam optimizer and learning rate set to 5e−4. Weight decay is fixed to 1e−4, and we employ a polynomial decay of power 0.9 for learning rate scheduling. We train for 150 epochs at each learning step with a batch size of 6.

Table 1. Comparison experiments on CS → BDD → IDD.

IL Step	Step 1	Step 2			Step 3			
	CS	CS → BDD			CS → BDD → IDD			
Method	CS	CS	BDD	$\Delta_d\%(\downarrow)$	CS	BDD	IDD	$\Delta_d\%(\downarrow)$
Single-task	67.51	67.51	49.54	–	67.51	49.54	62.24	–
FT	67.51	55.75	55.42	2.78	41.16	35.80	55.95	25.63
LwF [15]	67.51	55.82	50.50	7.69	46.70	42.62	55.02	18.80
MDIL [10]	67.31	58.03	54.26	2.26	47.89	42.96	54.93	18.03
Ours	68.46	59.05	55.22	0.53	50.24	44.15	54.94	16.06

Table 2. Comparison experiments on domain adaptation with MDIL.

IL Step	Step 1	Step 2		
	CS	CS → BDD		
Method	CS	CS	BDD	$\Delta_d\%(\downarrow)$
Single-task	67.51	67.51	49.54	–
MDIL (w-prior)	67.31	58.03	54.26	2.26
MDIL (wo-prior)	68.31	58.18	54.28	2.13
Ours	68.46	59.05	55.22	0.53

4.4   Comparison with State-of-the-Art

In our study, we evaluate the effectiveness of our proposed method by comparing it with several baselines. The single-task baseline, which involves training datasets independently on separate models, serves as a benchmark for incremental learning (IL) performance. We employ this baseline to calculate the average per-task drop $\Delta_d\%$, which quantifies the overall performance of IL. Another standard baseline in IL is fine-tuning (FT), whereby a model is fine-tuned on the newer task without any explicit effort to mitigate catastrophic forgetting. Additionally, we compare our method with other existing IL techniques, including Learning without Forgetting (LwF) [15], which uses a regularization term in the loss function to retain past task knowledge, and Multi-Domain Incremental

Learning (MDIL) [10], which assigns different parameters for inference to data from different domains. To ensure fairness, we modify the MDIL setting by not providing explicit information about the domain of the input data during the inference phase, as the prior knowledge of data source can significantly enhance the performance of IL. Furthermore, we compare the domain adaptation performance of MDIL with our proposed method and find that our method outperforms MDIL, even when prior knowledge is added to the latter (see Table 2).

Table 3. Comparison experiments on BDD → IDD → CS.

IL Step	Step 1	Step 2			Step 3			
	BDD	BDD → IDD			BDD → IDD → CS			
Method	BDD	BDD	IDD	$\Delta_d\%(\downarrow)$	BDD	IDD	CS	$\Delta_d\%(\downarrow)$
Single-task	49.54	49.54	62.24	–	49.54	62.24	67.51	–
FT	49.54	41.36	55.39	13.76	33.48	48.22	54.01	24.98
LwF [15]	49.54	42.98	53.56	13.59	34.96	49.13	53.87	23.57
MDIL [10]	49.54	43.55	54.73	12.08	35.12	49.59	54.13	23.08
Ours	51.02	44.11	55.26	11.09	36.08	50.33	55.34	21.44

Table 4. Comparison experiments on IDD → CS → BDD.

IL Step	Step 1	Step 2			Step 3			
	IDD	IDD → CS			IDD → CS → BDD			
Method	IDD	IDD	CS	$\Delta_d\%(\downarrow)$	IDD	CS	BDD	$\Delta_d\%(\downarrow)$
Single-task	62.24	62.24	67.51	–	62.24	67.51	49.54	–
FT	62.24	53.04	55.13	16.56	47.87	48.04	43.83	21.15
LwF [15]	62.24	53.98	54.69	16.13	48.44	48.96	43.54	20.76
MDIL [10]	62.24	54.12	55.21	15.64	49.66	49.37	44.12	19.34
Ours	63.15	55.73	56.24	13.58	50.13	50.42	45.33	17.57

Experiments on settings CS → BDD → IDD are shown in Table 1. During fine-tuning, it has been observed that the model's performance on subsequent incremental datasets decreases due to the absence of training data that has already been exposed to the task. This phenomenon, known as catastrophic forgetting, persists even when the learning rate is set to a low value. However, during stage 2 of our approach, we observed an improvement in the fine-tuning performance on the BDD dataset by 5.88% compared to the model trained solely on the BDD dataset. This can be attributed to the pre-training stage of the CS dataset in stage 1, which can be considered as a form of pre-training that allows the model to converge to the optimal point more efficiently during fine-tuning on the BDD dataset.

In our comparative analysis of various methods, LwF was found to be effective in mitigating catastrophic forgetting, with a lower level of forgetting in stage

3 compared to fine-tuning. However, LwF exhibited a higher level of forgetting in stage 2 (7.69%) than the fine-tuning method. This suggests that the simple regularization approach used in LwF, which constrains the loss function of the new task to protect old knowledge from being overwritten by new knowledge, does not effectively address domain bias present in domain adaptation. On the other hand, the MDIL method showed improvement in its ability to handle catastrophic forgetting, with lower levels of forgetting observed in both stages 2 and 3 (2.26% and 18.03%, respectively). This method employs parametric isolation to retain more knowledge of the seen dataset and demonstrates better results in dealing with both domain offset and label offset problems. The impact of our proposed method on alleviating forgetting in both incremental stages was superior to that of other methods (0.53% and 16.06%). Additionally, we conducted experiments by altering the order in which the datasets were experienced to demonstrate the generality of our proposed method. Experiments on BDD → IDD → CS and IDD → CS → BDD are illustrated in Tables 3 and Table 4.

Table 5. Ablation study of feature fusion.

IL Step	Step 1	Step 2		Step 3		
	CS	CS → BDD		CS → BDD → IDD		
	CS	CS	BDD	CS	BDD	IDD
Single-task	67.51	67.51	49.54	67.51	49.54	62.24
$\mathcal{L}_{ce}$ (wo-fusion)	67.51	55.75	55.42	41.16	35.80	55.95
$\mathcal{L}_{ce}$ (w-fusion)	68.46	56.88	55.88	41.94	36.74	56.03

Table 6. Ablation study of loss.

IL Step	Step 1	Step 2		Step 3		
	CS	CS → BDD		CS → BDD → IDD		
	CS	CS	BDD	CS	BDD	IDD
Single-task	67.51	67.51	49.54	67.51	49.54	62.24
$\mathcal{L}_{ce}$	68.46	56.88	55.88	41.94	36.74	56.03
$\mathcal{L}_{ce} + \mathcal{L}_1$	68.46	57.08	57.22	41.10	34.42	56.90
$\mathcal{L}_{ce} + \mathcal{L}_2$	68.46	57.64	56.88	45.94	41.78	54.06
$\mathcal{L}_{ce} + \mathcal{L}_3$	68.46	57.29	56.73	45.86	42.46	54.12
$\mathcal{L}_{ce} + \mathcal{L}_1 + \mathcal{L}_2$	68.46	58.46	56.19	49.88	43.54	53.35
$\mathcal{L}_{ce} + \mathcal{L}_1 + \mathcal{L}_3$	68.46	58.14	56.41	50.17	43.96	53.49
$\mathcal{L}_{ce} + \mathcal{L}_2 + \mathcal{L}_3$	68.46	58.64	55.87	50.29	43.88	53.04
$\mathcal{L}_{ce} + \mathcal{L}_1 + \mathcal{L}_2 + \mathcal{L}_3$	68.46	59.05	55.22	50.24	44.15	54.94

4.5 Ablation Study

In this section, we perform an ablation study on feature fusion (Table 5) and training loss (Table 6). Our results indicate that incorporating feature fusion can effectively enhance the segmentation performance, as low-level, image-detail-related features play a crucial role in achieving fine-grained image segmentation. Moreover, the segmentation performance of the model tends to improve as each loss is gradually added to the overall loss function. In particular, the addition of distillation losses $\mathcal{L}_2$ and $\mathcal{L}_3$, which are designed to assist the model in retaining old knowledge, as well as loss $\mathcal{L}_1$, which aims to alleviate the model's forgetfulness of information in the old domain, led to improved performance of the model during incremental learning. These experiments demonstrate the effectiveness of each partial loss in mitigating catastrophic forgetting and enhancing the segmentation performance of the model.

5 Conclusion

We propose a method to address the problem of catastrophic forgetting in domain incremental semantic segmentation. Our approach leverages the low-level features of CNN to retain domain-specific features that contain rich image details as stylized features of the domain. This allows us to fuse the deep features that contain more semantic information, thereby altering the data distribution and enhancing the model's robustness when new domain data is encountered. Compared with general replay-based methods, our approach does not require the retention of samples from previous stages, resulting in significant storage space savings. Furthermore, our approach does not rely on generative models to obtain pseudo-samples of past tasks, thereby eliminating the need for additional auxiliary generative models and associated storage space. We verify the effectiveness of our method for domain incremental semantic segmentation and our method outperforms SOTA.

Acknowledgements. This research was supported by the Natural Science Fund of Hubei Province under Grant 2022CFB823, the HUST Independent Innovation Research Fund under Grant 2021XXJS096, the Alibaba Innovation Research program under Grant CRAQ7WHZ11220001-20978282, and grants from the Key Lab of Image Processing and Intelligent Control, Ministry of Education, China.

References

1. Aljundi, R., Babiloni, F., Elhoseiny, M., Rohrbach, M., Tuytelaars, T.: Memory aware synapses: learning what (not) to forget. In: Ferrari, V., Hebert, M., Sminchisescu, C., Weiss, Y. (eds.) ECCV 2018. LNCS, vol. 11207, pp. 144–161. Springer, Cham (2018). https://doi.org/10.1007/978-3-030-01219-9_9
2. Aljundi, R., Lin, M., Goujaud, B., Bengio, Y.: Gradient based sample selection for online continual learning. In: Advances in Neural Information Processing Systems, vol. 32 (2019)

3. Badrinarayanan, V., Kendall, A., Cipolla, R.: SegNet: a deep convolutional encoder-decoder architecture for image segmentation. IEEE Trans. Pattern Anal. Mach. Intell. **39**(12), 2481–2495 (2017)
4. Chen, L.C., Papandreou, G., Kokkinos, I., Murphy, K., Yuille, A.L.: Semantic image segmentation with deep convolutional nets and fully connected CRFs. arXiv preprint arXiv:1412.7062 (2014)
5. Chen, L.C., Papandreou, G., Schroff, F., Adam, H.: Rethinking atrous convolution for semantic image segmentation. arXiv preprint arXiv:1706.05587 (2017)
6. Cheng, B., Misra, I., Schwing, A.G., Kirillov, A., Girdhar, R.: Masked-attention mask transformer for universal image segmentation. In: Proceedings of the IEEE/CVF Conference on Computer Vision and Pattern Recognition, pp. 1290–1299 (2022)
7. De Lange, M., et al.: Continual learning: a comparative study on how to defy forgetting in classification tasks. arXiv preprint arXiv:1909.08383, vol. 2(6), p. 2 (2019)
8. Fan, M., et al.: Rethinking BiSeNet for real-time semantic segmentation. In: Proceedings of the IEEE/CVF Conference on Computer Vision and Pattern Recognition, pp. 9716–9725 (2021)
9. Fu, J., et al.: Dual attention network for scene segmentation. In: Proceedings of the IEEE/CVF Conference on Computer Vision and Pattern Recognition, pp. 3146–3154 (2019)
10. Garg, P., Saluja, R., Balasubramanian, V.N., Arora, C., Subramanian, A., Jawahar, C.: Multi-domain incremental learning for semantic segmentation. In: Proceedings of the IEEE/CVF Winter Conference on Applications of Computer Vision, pp. 761–771 (2022)
11. Kalb, T., Beyerer, J.: Principles of forgetting in domain-incremental semantic segmentation in adverse weather conditions. In: Proceedings of the IEEE/CVF Conference on Computer Vision and Pattern Recognition, pp. 19508–19518 (2023)
12. Kanakis, M., Bruggemann, D., Saha, S., Georgoulis, S., Obukhov, A., Van Gool, L.: Reparameterizing convolutions for incremental multi-task learning without task interference. In: Vedaldi, A., Bischof, H., Brox, T., Frahm, J.M. (eds.) Computer Vision-ECCV 2020: 16th European Conference, Glasgow, UK, 23–28 August 2020, Proceedings, Part XX 16, pp. 689–707. Springer, Cham (2020). https://doi.org/10.1007/978-3-030-58565-5_41
13. Kirkpatrick, J., et al.: Overcoming catastrophic forgetting in neural networks. Proc. Natl. Acad. Sci. **114**(13), 3521–3526 (2017)
14. Li, X., et al.: Semantic flow for fast and accurate scene parsing. In: Vedaldi, A., Bischof, H., Brox, T., Frahm, J.M. (eds.) Computer Vision-ECCV 2020: 16th European Conference, Glasgow, UK, 23–28 August 2020, Proceedings, Part I 16, pp. 775–793. Springer, Cham (2020). https://doi.org/10.1007/978-3-030-58452-8_45
15. Li, Z., Hoiem, D.: Learning without forgetting. IEEE Trans. Pattern Anal. Mach. Intell. **40**(12), 2935–2947 (2017)
16. Mallya, A., Davis, D., Lazebnik, S.: Piggyback: adapting a single network to multiple tasks by learning to mask weights. In: Ferrari, V., Hebert, M., Sminchisescu, C., Weiss, Y. (eds.) ECCV 2018. LNCS, vol. 11208, pp. 72–88. Springer, Cham (2018). https://doi.org/10.1007/978-3-030-01225-0_5
17. Mallya, A., Lazebnik, S.: PackNet: adding multiple tasks to a single network by iterative pruning. In: Proceedings of the IEEE Conference on Computer Vision and Pattern Recognition, pp. 7765–7773 (2018)

18. Mei, K., Zhu, C., Zou, J., Zhang, S.: Instance adaptive self-training for unsupervised domain adaptation. In: Vedaldi, A., Bischof, H., Brox, T., Frahm, J.M. (eds.) Computer Vision-ECCV 2020: 16th European Conference, Glasgow, UK, 23–28 August 2020, Proceedings, Part XXVI 16, pp. 415–430. Springer, Cham (2020). https://doi.org/10.1007/978-3-030-58574-7_25
19. Odena, A., Olah, C., Shlens, J.: Conditional image synthesis with auxiliary classifier GANs. In: International Conference on Machine Learning, pp. 2642–2651. PMLR (2017)
20. Ostapenko, O., Puscas, M., Klein, T., Jahnichen, P., Nabi, M.: Learning to remember: a synaptic plasticity driven framework for continual learning. In: Proceedings of the IEEE/CVF Conference on Computer Vision and Pattern Recognition, pp. 11321–11329 (2019)
21. Rebuffi, S.A., Bilen, H., Vedaldi, A.: Efficient parametrization of multi-domain deep neural networks. In: Proceedings of the IEEE Conference on Computer Vision and Pattern Recognition, pp. 8119–8127 (2018)
22. Rebuffi, S.A., Kolesnikov, A., Sperl, G., Lampert, C.H.: iCaRL: incremental classifier and representation learning. In: Proceedings of the IEEE Conference on Computer Vision and Pattern Recognition, pp. 2001–2010 (2017)
23. Romera, E., Alvarez, J.M., Bergasa, L.M., Arroyo, R.: ERFNet: efficient residual factorized convnet for real-time semantic segmentation. IEEE Trans. Intell. Transp. Syst. 19(1), 263–272 (2017)
24. Ronneberger, O., Fischer, P., Brox, T.: U-Net: convolutional networks for biomedical image segmentation. In: Navab, N., Hornegger, J., Wells, W., Frangi, A. (eds.) Medical Image Computing and Computer-Assisted Intervention-MICCAI 2015: 18th International Conference, Munich, Germany, 5–9 October 2015, Proceedings, Part III 18, pp. 234–241. Springer, Cham (2015). https://doi.org/10.1007/978-3-319-24574-4_28
25. Strudel, R., Garcia, R., Laptev, I., Schmid, C.: Segmenter: transformer for semantic segmentation. In: Proceedings of the IEEE/CVF International Conference on Computer Vision, pp. 7262–7272 (2021)
26. Vu, T.H., Jain, H., Bucher, M., Cord, M., Pérez, P.: ADVENT: adversarial entropy minimization for domain adaptation in semantic segmentation. In: Proceedings of the IEEE/CVF Conference on Computer Vision and Pattern Recognition, pp. 2517–2526 (2019)
27. Wu, Z., Wang, X., Gonzalez, J.E., Goldstein, T., Davis, L.S.: ACE: adapting to changing environments for semantic segmentation. In: Proceedings of the IEEE/CVF International Conference on Computer Vision, pp. 2121–2130 (2019)
28. Xie, E., Wang, W., Yu, Z., Anandkumar, A., Alvarez, J.M., Luo, P.: SegFormer: simple and efficient design for semantic segmentation with transformers. Adv. Neural. Inf. Process. Syst. 34, 12077–12090 (2021)
29. Yang, Y., Soatto, S.: FDA: Fourier domain adaptation for semantic segmentation. In: Proceedings of the IEEE/CVF Conference on Computer Vision and Pattern Recognition, pp. 4085–4095 (2020)
30. Zenke, F., Poole, B., Ganguli, S.: Continual learning through synaptic intelligence. In: International Conference on Machine Learning, pp. 3987–3995. PMLR (2017)
31. Zhang, F., et al.: ACFNet: attentional class feature network for semantic segmentation. In: Proceedings of the IEEE/CVF International Conference on Computer Vision, pp. 6798–6807 (2019)
32. Zhao, H., Shi, J., Qi, X., Wang, X., Jia, J.: Pyramid scene parsing network. In: Proceedings of the IEEE Conference on Computer Vision and Pattern Recognition, pp. 2881–2890 (2017)

33. Zhao, S., et al.: Multi-source domain adaptation for semantic segmentation. In: Advances in Neural Information Processing Systems, vol. 32 (2019)
34. Zheng, S., et al.: Rethinking semantic segmentation from a sequence-to-sequence perspective with transformers. In: Proceedings of the IEEE/CVF Conference on Computer Vision and Pattern Recognition, pp. 6881–6890 (2021)
35. Zhou, B., Zhao, H., Puig, X., Fidler, S., Barriuso, A., Torralba, A.: Scene parsing through ADE20K dataset. In: Proceedings of the IEEE Conference on Computer Vision and Pattern Recognition, pp. 633–641 (2017)
36. Zhu, Z., Xu, M., Bai, S., Huang, T., Bai, X.: Asymmetric non-local neural networks for semantic segmentation. In: Proceedings of the IEEE/CVF International Conference on Computer Vision, pp. 593–602 (2019)

ABFNet: Attention Bottlenecks Fusion Network for Multimodal Brain Tumor Segmentation

Ning Li[1], Minghui Chen[1], Guohua Zhao[2,3], Lei Yang[1], Ling Ma[1],
Jingliang Cheng[2,3(✉)], and Huiqin Jiang[1]

[1] Zhengzhou University, Zhengzhou, China
Ln_student@gs.zzu.edu.cn, cmhemail2000@163.com,
{nscczzyanglei,ielma,iehqjiang}@zzu.edu.cn
[2] Department of Magnetic Resonance Imaging, The First Affiliated Hospital of
Zhengzhou University, Zhengzhou 450052, China
ghzhao@ha.edu.cn
[3] Henan Engineering Research Center of Medical Imaging Intelligent Diagnosis and
Treatment, Zhengzhou 450052, China
fccchengjl@zzu.edu.cn

Abstract. Brain tumor segmentation based on multimodal magnetic resonance imaging (MRI) is a crucial step in the early diagnosis and prognosis evaluation of glioma. Current multimodal brain tumor segmentation algorithms only perform simple concatenation of multimodal information and fail to utilize their complementary information, resulting in limited segmentation accuracy. To address this problem, we design an Attention Bottlenecks Fusion Network (ABFNet) to segment brain tumor based on MRI by fusing multimodal complementary information. Firstly, based on the encoder-decoder architecture, we utilize multiple CNN encoders to extract modality-specific features. Then, a Bottleneck Fusion Transformer (BFT) module is introduced, which uses Transformer-style to fuse information from different modalities through a small number of potential bottleneck tokens, forcing each modality to condense the most necessary information and share it. Lastly, Fusion Connection Gating (FCG) is proposed to fuse modality-specific features from different levels through concatenation and convolutional operations. Multi-scale features utilized in FCG can enrich features and enhance the discriminability of every modality. Experiments are conducted on datasets BraTS2020 and BraTS2018. On BraTS2020, the DSC of our method on complete tumor, core tumor and enhancing tumor are 92.95%, 91.64% and 79.62%. On BraTS2018, the corresponding results are 90.12%, 83.40% and 70.56%. And experiments of modalities missing situations are conducted, showing the robustness and effectiveness of our method.

Keywords: Multimodal Brain Tumor Segmentation · Bottleneck Fusion Transformer · Fusion Connection Gating

H. Lu et al. (Eds.): ACPR 2023, LNCS 14407, pp. 312–325, 2023.
https://doi.org/10.1007/978-3-031-47637-2_24

1   Introduction

Glioma is the most common malignant brain tumor with a high incidence and low survival rate [1,2]. Accurate segmentation of brain tumor is crucial for the diagnosis, treatment and prognosis evaluation of glioma. MRI is the most commonly used technique in brain tumor diagnostics, offering abundant multimodal imaging information. Fluid Attenuated Inversion Recovery (Flair), Contrast-enhanced T1-Weighted (T1c), T1-Weighted (T1) and T2-Weighted (T2) are the most commonly used MRI sequences [3], as shown in Fig. 1. Each modality contributes differently to brain tumor segmentation. For example, the Flair images show the surrounding tumor well and show the edema area clearly. The T1 images focus on details within soft tissues, while the T2 images can highlight lesion areas [4–6]. Therefore, designing an effective feature fusion module that fully utilizes multimodal MRI images information for accurate brain tumor segmentation is of great significance.

Convolution neural networks (CNNs) have been widely used in multimodal brain tumor segmentation due to their powerful representation ability and parameter sharing characteristics [7,8]. Among them, U-Net [9] is the most commonly used network. U-Net utilizes an encoder-decoder architecture and skip connections to effectively extract and reuse multi-scale image features, which has achieved outstanding performance in brain tumor segmentation [10]. Based on the U-Net, several networks are proposed to further improve brain tumor segmentation performance. For instance, Isensee et al. [11] design a cascaded U-Net framework that adaptively adjusts the size and depth of the network according to the dataset, and improves the universality of U-Net. Çiçek et al. [12] extend 2D convolutions in U-Net to 3D convolutions, and achieve better performance by fully utilizing 3D information of multimodal MRI images compared to 2D networks. However, CNNs are limited in their ability to model global information due to their restricted receptive fields, which only allow them to focus on local features of images and cannot model long sequences. In contrast, Transformer-based [23] networks overcome the shortcomings of CNNs. They model long-range dependencies through the attention mechanism, which can effectively capture global features [13,14]. For example, Hatamizadeh et al. propose UNETR [15], which uses Transformer as encoder to effectively capture global contextual features at multiple scales. However, Transformer performs worse than CNN on small-scale datasets due to the lack of inductive bias. To solve this problem, Wang et al. [16] introduce a network called TransBTS that jointly uses 3D CNN and Transformer. It utilizes the inductive bias of CNN, enabling the model to perform well even on small-scale datasets. The network also leverages both local and global features from multimodal MRI images for brain tumor segmentation.

Previous methods have achieved some success in multimodal brain tumor segmentation. However, when fusing multimodal information, they simply concatenate the modalities without considering redundancy and complementarity among them. This results in the ineffective use of complementary information. To address this issue, recent works [17–20] have been conducted on multimodal feature fusion, and have improve brain tumor segmentation accuracy indeed.

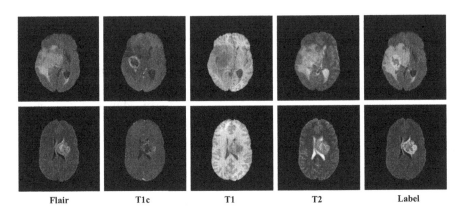

Flair   T1c   T1   T2   Label

Fig. 1. From left to right: Flair, T1c, T1, T2 and ground truth segmentation of brain tumors. Red color in labels corresponds to enhancing tumor, yellow corresponds to necrosis, and green corresponds to edema. (Color figure online)

Zhang et al. [17] propose an architecture for incomplete multimodal learning. It utilizes 3D CNN and Transformer as encoders to extract both local and global features from different modalities, and Transformer is used to model the relationships among different modality features to obtain fused modality features with global semantics. But it still fails to address the issue of information redundancy. Ding et al. [18] design a region-aware fusion module, using the attention mechanism to give different attention to different modalities of each tumor subregion. It can obtain heterogeneity characteristics of the tumor region, reducing the redundancy of information in fusion process. However, this fusion method only explores the relationships between different modalities and tumor subregions, without considering the long-range dependencies among different modalities.

In this paper, we propose ABFNet, which considers the long-range dependencies among modalities and utilizes complementary information from multimodal MRI for brain tumor segmentation. Firstly, an encoder-decoder architecture with multiple 3D CNN encoders is adopted to capture modality-specific multi-scale spatial features. Secondly, a BFT is designed to explore long-distance dependencies between high-level features from different modalities. In BFT, high-level feature information from different modalities is exchanged through introduced bottleneck fusion tokens, which enables the model to integrate and compress information from each modality and share necessary information. Then, we design FCG to concatenate different modal features at various stages of encoders, and perform convolution to obtain multi-scale features containing multimodal information. Finally, we concatenate features from FCG with the upsampling features from 3D CNN decoder, and use 3D CNN decoder to gradually restore the feature maps to the original image resolution size.

Overall, our contributions are fourfold:

– An Attention Bottlenecks Fusion Network (ABFNet) is designed for brain tumor segmentation. Specifically, a Bottleneck Fusion Transformer (BFT) module is proposed to explore long-distance dependency relationships between different modalities.

- A Fusion Connection Gating (FCG) is designed to obtain multi-scale features containing multimodal information for decoder to produce the final segmentation results.
- Compared with state-of-the-art extensively using the BraTS2020 and BraTS2018 datasets, ABFNet achieves superior segmentation accuracy.
- Experiments on scenarios of modalities missing are conducted, and the results show that our network has certain effectiveness.

2   Method

In this paper, we propose an ABFNet architecture to improve accuracy of brain tumor segmentation. Similar to the encoder-decoder structure of 3D U-Net [12], multiple 3D CNN encoders of ABFNet are used to extract local feature maps of different modal images, and a 3D CNN decoder is used to extract the upsampling feature maps after multimodal feature fusion and produce the final segmentation result. Feature fusion is primarily accomplished within the BFT module. Additionally, multi-scale features of different modalities from multiple encoders are fused with upsampling features from 3D CNN decoder through the proposed FCG, progressively refining the final segmentation result. The overview of ABFNet is illustrated in Fig. 2, and we will introduce each component in detail.

2.1   CNN Encoder

Similar to the encoder path of 3D U-Net [12], we use multiple convolution encoders to extract local contextual features of each modality. The convolution encoder consists of five stages, and each stage includes three convolutional blocks. The first convolution block of the first stage consists of one convolution with kernel size of 3, padding of 1 and stride of 1, and the first convolution block in other stages consists of one convolution with kernel size of 3 and stride of 2 to downsample the feature maps. The other two convolution blocks contain batch normalization, ReLU and a convolution with kernel size of 3 and stride of 1. Given an input of MRI scan $X_m \in \mathbb{R}^{C \times H \times W \times D}$ with a spatial resolution of $H \times W$, depth dimension D and C channels, we employ encoder E_m to generate local context feature map F_m^i capturing spatial and depth information of different modalities and different scales. It can be expressed as follows.

$$F_m^i = E_m(X_m; \theta_m^E) \tag{1}$$

Here, $F_m^i \in \mathbb{R}^{Ci \times \frac{H}{2^{i-1}} \times \frac{W}{2^{i-1}} \times \frac{D}{2^{i-1}}}$ represents high-level features of different modalities and Ci is the channel dimension of each stage in each encoder. $m \in M = \{Flair, T1c, T1, T2\}$ denotes different modality. θ_m^E indicates corresponding parameters of each convolution encoder, and $i \in [1, 5]$ means that each convolution encoder is composed of 5 stages. The number of filters at each stage in each encoder is 8, 16, 32, 64, and 128, respectively.

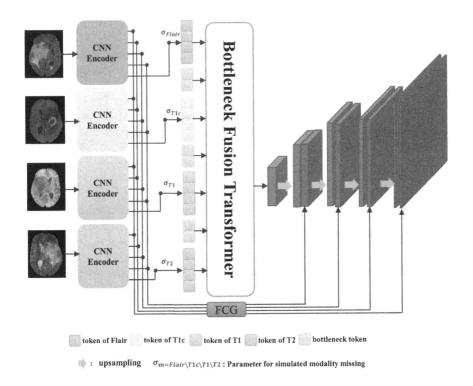

Fig. 2. Overview of the proposed ABFNet. We design a BFT module that forces the fusion of features from different modalities through a small number of potential bottlenecks. And, we propose a FCG module to obtain multi-scale features containing multimodal information for decoder to produce the final segmentation results.

2.2   Bottleneck Fusion Transformer

Most existing methods adopt concatenation to fuse multimodal features, which cannot effectively explore the correlation and complementary information between modalities. To this end, we propose a BFT module that fuses high-level features of different modalities from encoders, inspired by [21,22]. As illustrated in Fig. 3, we utilize a reduced number of latent bottleneck tokens to encode information of input sequence, where the length of tokens is typically much smaller than input and output. And, Transformer blocks are used to encode features of each modality, mapping them to latent bottleneck tokens. The output of the previous Transformer block serves as the initial latent bottleneck tokens for the next Transformer block, until information of all modalities is fused. In general, features of different modalities are fused through tight bottleneck fusion tokens. It forces the model to collect and compress information from each modality, effectively reducing information redundancy and share necessary complementary information with other modalities.

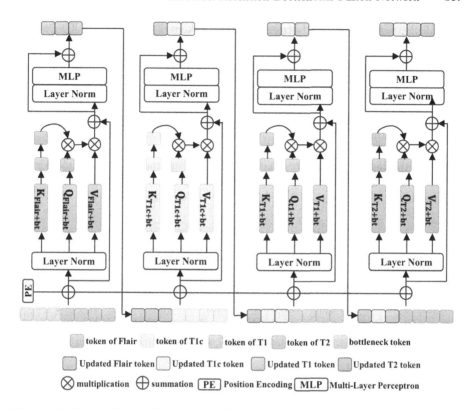

Fig. 3. Bottleneck Fusion Transformer. The introduced fusion bottleneck tokens are used as input to the BFT module along with the high-level feature sequences of MRI images. The output of each modality is used as the input of another modality.

Input images of each modality gradually encoded by multiple encoders into high-level features $F_m^5 \in \mathbb{R}^{C5 \times \frac{H}{16} \times \frac{W}{16} \times \frac{D}{16}}$ ($C5 = 128$), $m \in M$, and then BFT is used to model the long-range correlation between them. The specific implementation process of BFT module is as follows. Firstly, a $3 \times 3 \times 3$ convolutional layer is used to increase the channel dimension of F_m^5 from 128 to K = 512, and reshape the F_m^5 into one-dimensional tokens $F_m^{5'} \in \mathbb{R}^{C5 \times \frac{HWD}{16}}$, because the input of a standard Transformer layer must be a one-dimensional token sequence [23]. Secondly, to preserve spatial positional information of the high-level feature tokens, a one-dimensional learnable positional encoding variable [24] and the high-level feature tokens are both used as inputs to the BFT module. We express a Transformer layer, including Multi-Head Attention(MSA), Multilayer Perceptron(MLP) and Layer Normalization(LN), $Z_{out} = Transformer(Z)$ as follows.

$$y = MSA(LN(Z)) + Z \tag{2}$$

$$Z_{out} = MLP(LN(y)) + y \tag{3}$$

Thirdly, a small set of S bottleneck fusion tokens $Z_{bt} = [Z_{bt}^1, Z_{bt}^2, Z_{bt}^3, ..., Z_{bt}^S]$ are introduced to the high-level feature tokens $F_m^{5'}$. The input to the BFT module is as follows.

$$Z = [\sigma_m F_m^{5'} \parallel Z_{bt}] \tag{4}$$

Here, $\sigma_m \in \{0, 1\}, m \in M$ is a parameter that simulates the absence of different modalities. In reallife scenarios, it is common to encounter missing modalities. Therefore, when modalities are missing, the corresponding σ_m is set to 0, and the high-level feature tokens of the missing modalities are set to zero vectors. $\parallel$ represents concatenation of different modalities tokens. Finally, after feeding the input Z into the BFT module, the output is calculated as follows.

$$\left[\widehat{Z}_m \parallel \widehat{Z}_{btm}\right] = Tranformer\left([Z_m \parallel Z_{bt}]; \theta_m\right) \tag{5}$$

$$Z_{bt}^{next} = avg\left(\widehat{Z}_{btm}\right) \tag{6}$$

Here, θ_m is the corresponding parameter of BFT module. The high-level feature tokens of each modality can only exchange information through bottleneck fusion tokens. $\widehat{Z}_m$ means $\sigma_m F_m^{5'}$ after being updated by the BFT. The temporary bottleneck fusion tokens $\widehat{Z}_{btm}$ are updated simultaneously with the high-level feature tokens $\sigma_m F_m^{5'}$. Z_{bt}^{next} denote the initial bottleneck fusion tokens of the next layer of the BFT. The more detailed calculation process of (5) is as follows.

$$\left[\widehat{Z}_{Flair} \parallel \widehat{Z}_{btFlair}\right] = Transformer\left(\left[\sigma_{Flair} F_{Flair}^{5'} \parallel Z_{bt}\right]; \theta_{Flair}\right) \tag{7}$$

$$\left[\widehat{Z}_{T1c} \parallel \widehat{Z}_{btT1c}\right] = Transformer\left(\left[\sigma_{T1c} F_{T1c}^{5'} \parallel \widehat{Z}_{btFlair}\right]; \theta_{T1c}\right) \tag{8}$$

$$\left[\widehat{Z}_{T1} \parallel \widehat{Z}_{btT1}\right] = Transformer\left(\left[\sigma_{T1} F_{T1}^{5'} \parallel \widehat{Z}_{btT1c}\right]; \theta_{T1}\right) \tag{9}$$

$$\left[\widehat{Z}_{T2} \parallel \widehat{Z}_{btT2}\right] = Transformer\left(\left[\sigma_{T2} F_{T2}^{5'} \parallel \widehat{Z}_{btT1}\right]; \theta_{T2}\right) \tag{10}$$

The output of the BFT module is $F_{last} = \widehat{Z}_{T2} \in \mathbb{R}^{K \times \frac{HWD}{16}}$, which is the result of fusing features of all modalities together.

2.3   Fusion Connection Gating

Modality-specific shallow local discriminative features and deep global high-level semantic features are obtained by multiple 3D CNN encoders through multiple convolutions and downsampling [25]. However, most methods only directly concatenate multi-scale features and decoder features, resulting in semantic feature gaps. To address this problem, FCG is proposed to concatenate different modality features at different levels, and fuse multi-scale features of different modalities through convolutions. The fused multi-scale features are concatenated with the upsampling features of the decoder to gradually obtain the final segmentation results.

Different modality and scale feature maps F_m^i are obtained from encoders. We concatenate the features of different modalities at different stages, as shown in (11).

$$F^i = \left[F_{Flair}^i \parallel F_{T1c}^i \parallel F_{T1}^i \parallel F_{T2}^i \right] \tag{11}$$

We apply three convolutional layers to the concatenated features F^i to obtain the fused features of different modalities at different stages, as shown in (12).

$$F_{FCG}^i = FCG\left(F^i\right) = conv_{k1}^1 \left(conv_{k3}^1 \left(conv_{k1}^1 \left(F^i\right)\right)\right) \tag{12}$$

Here, $conv_{k1}^1$ indicates a convolution with kernel size of 1, and $conv_{k3}^1$ shows a convolution with kernel size of 3. Finally, F_{FCG}^i is used for the segmentation of the decoder. We concatenate the fused features F_{FCG}^i with the upsampling features of the decoder, gradually restoring the feature maps to original image resolution.

2.4 CNN Decoder

Based on the encoder-decoder architecture, we utlize multiple encoders to extract local feature maps of different modalities, and use a decoder to decode the fused feature map of modalities to obtain the final segmentation result. Symmetric to the encoder, the decoder also consists of five stages. The high-level feature tokens F_{last} from the BFT are unfolded into a high-level 4D feature map $F_{4D} \in \mathbb{R}^{K \times \frac{H}{16} \times \frac{W}{16} \times \frac{D}{16}}$. Then, convolutions and upsampling are used to gradually restore the high-level 4D feature map F_{4D} to the resolution of the network input image. At each upsampling layer, the size of the feature map is doubled while the number of channels is reduced by half of input. At each stage of the decoder, the input is a concatenation of the output features from the FCG and the upsampling features from the previous decoder stage.

3 Experiments

3.1 Dataset and Evaluation Metrics

To validate the effectiveness of the proposed ABFNet, experiments are conducted on two datasets from Multimodal Brain Tumor Segmentation Challenge (BraTS), i.e., BraTS2020 and BraTS2018 [27,28]. BraTS2020 training dataset contains 369 subjects and each subject contains four modalities: Flair, T1c, T1, T2 and expert segmentation images. The ground truth segmentation images are divided into 4 classes with labels - 0: background and non-tumor region, 1: Necrosis, 2: Edema, and 4: enhancing tumor (ET) [1]. According to the practical clinical application, for the multi-class brain tumor segmentation task, automatic image segmentation is performed by labeling complete tumor (containing all labels except background and non-tumor region), core tumor (consisting of Necrosis and ET), and enhancing tumor (containing only ET) [29]. BraTS2018 training dataset contains 285 subjects and other information are the same as BraTS2020.

Dice Similarity Coefficient (DSC) [30] effectively measures the coincidence degree between the segmentation results and the ground truth labels, reflects the similarity between the experimental segmentation results and the expert manual segmentation results, and can more effectively reflect the accuracy of segmentation methods. The specific calculation is as follows.

$$DSC = \frac{Y \cap \widehat{Y}}{\left(Y + \widehat{Y}\right)/2} \qquad (13)$$

Here, Y is he ground truth labels, $\widehat{Y}$ is the segmentation result of segmentation methods. The range of DSC is [0,1]. 0 means that the segmentation result area of the method completely deviates from the actual doctor's marker area, and 1 indicates that the segmentation result area of the method completely coincides with the actual doctor's marker area.

3.2   Baseline Methods and Settings

We compare the proposed ABFNet with baseline methods, the following is an overview of the methods. And the hyperparameters and details of experiments are shown in Table 1.

- 3D U-Net [12]: A CNN-based model which fusion multimodal information by concatenation.
- nnUNet [11]: A model that fuses multimodal images in the early stage of the network.
- TransBTS [16]: An early fusion model which combines CNN-Transformer.
- mmFormer [17]: A hybrid CNN-Transformer network that sends concatenated features to Transformer to model the relationship among modalities.
- RFNet [18]: A network exploring relationships between modalities and tumor subregions using region-aware fusion module.

3.3   Experiment Results

To validate the effectiveness and robustness of the proposed method, experiments are conducted from four perspectives.

The ABFNet Is Compared with the Following Baselines. We compare the proposed model with five baseline models on BraTS2020 and BraTS2018, results as presented in Table 2. And the visualizations of segmentation results on BraTS2020 are shown in Fig. 4.

Table 1. Experiment hyperparameters and details setting.

Description	Value
Input images size	$128 \times 128 \times 128$
Number of training epoch	1000
Optimizer	Adam, $\beta_1 = 0.9, \beta_2 = 0.99, weightdecay = 1e^{-5}$
Bottleneck tokens	$S = 16$
Initializing bottleneck tokens	Gaussian distribution [21, 24]
Learning rate	$2e^{-4} \times 1 - \frac{epoch}{max\_epoch}^p, p = 0.9$
Loss function	dice loss and weighted cross-entropy loss [26]
Data augmentation	random rotations, intensity shift, mirror flipping

Table 2. The proposed method ABFNet is compared with the state-of-art models on BraTS2020 and BraTS2018.

Method	BraTS2020			BraTS2018		
	DSC (%)			DSC (%)		
	Complete	Core	enhancing	Complete	Core	Enhancing
3D U-Net [12]	88.76	82.67	80.65	86.69	80.67	69.73
nnUNet [11]	90.33	84.93	**82.02**	90.08	80.21	**71.39**
TransBTS [16]	89.02	84.75	73.84	87.86	82.45	69.29
mmFormer [17]	91.12	87.90	74.22	89.95	82.74	67.98
RFNet [18]	90.90	85.01	74.90	89.84	81.02	69.15
ABFNet	**92.95**	**91.64**	79.62	**90.12**	**83.40**	70.56

Ablation Study. In Table 3, we conduct ablation experiments on BraTS2020 to study how FCG and BFT improve the performance of the proposed model. And to explore the impact of the bottleneck fusion tokens introduced in BFT, experiments with S=4,16,32,256,512 are conducted on BraTS2020.

Experiment with Different Activation Functions. ReLU, LeakyReLU and ELU are three commonly used activation functions in CNN. In Table 4, they are respectively used as the activation function of ABFNet for experiments to explore influence of them on the segmentation accuracy.

Modality Missing Simulation Experiment. In clinical practice, the problem of missing modes often occurs due to different scanning schemes and actual conditions of patients, which will affect the performance of models. Therefore, we simulate different modality missing scenarios and compare with state-of-the-art methods to demonstrate the robustness of ABFNet, as shown in Table 5.

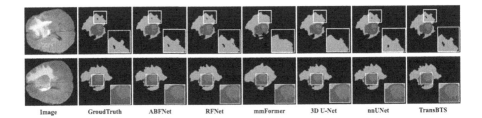

| Image | GroudTruth | ABFNet | RFNet | mmFormer | 3D U-Net | nnUNet | TransBTS |

Fig. 4. The visual comparison results on BraTS2020.

Table 3. Validate the influence of FCG, BFT and the number of S on the proposed model on the dataset BraTS2020.

FCG	BFT	Number of S	DSC(%)		
			Com-plete	Core	Enhan-cing
			89.73	85.25	71.80
✓			92.11	90.36	76.05
	✓	16	92.17	90.72	78.89
✓	✓	4	92.90	91.01	76.01
✓	✓	16	**92.95**	**91.64**	**79.62**
✓	✓	32	92.53	91.18	76.17
✓	✓	256	92.84	91.23	77.03
✓	✓	512	92.74	91.38	77.09

Table 4. Validate the influence of different Activation Functions (AF) the dataset BraTS2020.

AF	DSC(%)		
	Complete	Core	Enhan-cing
ReLU	92.95	91.62	78.52
LReLU	**92.95**	**91.64**	**79.62**
ELU	92.43	91.05	77.48

3.4 Result Analysis

Analysis of Comparison Results. We compare the proposed model with five baseline models on BraTS2020 and BraTS2018, results as presented in Table 2. The proposed method ABFNet demonstrates significant performance enhancement on BraTS2020 dataset, with DSC of 92.95% and 91.64% for complete tumor and core tumor, respectively, outperforming the five baseline models. The enhancing tumor segmentation achieves 79.62%, surpassing TransBTS, mmFormer, and RFNet. We also visualize the segmentation results on the BraTS2020 dataset, as shown in Fig. 4. It can be observed that the proposed model outperforms the baseline models in segmenting challenging regions. In addition, as can be seen from Table 5, our method outperforms RFNet and mmFormer in segmenting complete, core and enhancing tumors on all 15 possible modalities combinations.

Analysis of Ablation Study. As we can see from Table 3, the BFT module increases the DSC of the three tumor regions by 2.44%, 5.47%, and 7.09%, respectively. This indicates that BFT effectively utilizes the complementary information between different modalities and reduces information redundancy. The FCG module has increased the DSC of the three tumor regions by 2.38%, 5.11%, and 4.25% respectively. This highlights the importance of utilizing multi-scale features for segmentation. Moreover, we investigate the impact of the number of fusion bottleneck tokens in BFT. We experiment with S = 4, 16, 32, 256 and 512,

Table 5. On BraTS2020, the proposed method is compared with state-of-art models RFNet and mmFormer. ✓ and ✗ denote available and missing modalities, respectively.

Modalities	DSC(%)								
	Complete			Core			Enhancing		
F T1c T1 T2	[18]	[17]	ours	[18]	[17]	ours	[18]	[17]	ours
✓ ✓ ✓ ✓	90.90	91.12	**92.95**	85.01	87.90	**91.64**	74.90	74.22	**79.62**
✗ ✓ ✓ ✓	88.21	88.60	**90.28**	83.31	87.30	**91.52**	75.00	74.18	**76.71**
✓ ✓ ✗ ✓	90.41	90.99	**92.86**	72.83	87.98	**90.69**	77.15	74.15	**78.43**
✓ ✗ ✓ ✓	90.39	90.93	**92.58**	74.12	77.99	**85.29**	48.51	57.96	**70.95**
✓ ✓ ✓ ✗	90.47	90.46	**92.87**	84.08	88.12	**91.64**	74.42	74.06	**76.77**
✓ ✓ ✗ ✗	89.58	89.86	**92.80**	72.38	88.07	**91.56**	75.72	73.82	**77.58**
✓ ✗ ✗ ✓	89.57	90.56	**92.41**	73.21	76.61	**85.03**	47.85	55.76	**69.89**
✗ ✗ ✓ ✓	87.86	88.12	**89.69**	72.55	75.82	**84.03**	45.68	56.22	**68.49**
✓ ✗ ✓ ✗	89.76	90.11	**92.46**	71.74	76.29	**85.03**	40.37	52.35	**69.71**
✗ ✓ ✓ ✗	80.40	82.17	**87.18**	82.88	85.90	**91.08**	74.18	72.64	**77.53**
✗ ✓ ✗ ✓	87.49	88.10	**89.93**	83.08	87.39	**91.44**	74.02	73.91	**77.35**
✓ ✗ ✗ ✗	87.33	88.45	**92.14**	68.85	73.17	**84.21**	38.92	45.19	**65.84**
✗ ✗ ✓ ✗	76.03	79.44	**85.76**	63.56	69.53	**82.58**	35.25	44.83	**64.87**
✗ ✓ ✗ ✗	76.21	79.38	**86.23**	82.44	86.32	**90.61**	71.22	74.17	**76.96**
✗ ✗ ✗ ✓	86.00	86.52	**88.57**	70.62	73.58	**82.46**	46.36	49.95	**61.35**
Average	86.70	87.65	**90.58**	76.04	81.46	**87.92**	59.97	63.56	**72.80**

and find that the best performance is achieved with S=16. Hence, the number of tokens to S=16 is choosed for all experiments with BFT.

Analysis of Activation Function. In Table 4, when LeakyReLU is used, the segmentation accuracy of the model is the highest, followed by ReLU, and ELU is the worst. Therefore, the CNN part of ABFNet uses LeakyReLU.

4 Conclusion

In this work, we propose a multimodal feature fusion network ABFNet to segment brain tumor. A BFT module is introduced to fuse information from different modalities, leading to excellent performance. Besides, a FCG module is designed to obtain multi-scale features for high-precision segmentation. Our framework is modality-independent and can be extended to other disease classes with multimodal data. Although our work has made progress, it only considers the correlation between modalities and does not consider the relationship between modalities and tumor subregions. In the future, the influence of two pairs of factors on brain tumor segmentation will be considered simultaneously in order to obtain more accurate results.

References

1. Maji, D., Sigedar, P., Singh, M.: Attention Res-UNet with Guided Decoder for semantic segmentation of brain tumors. Biomed. Signal Process. Control **71**, 103077 (2022)

2. Tandel, G.S., Biswas, M., Kakde, O.G., Tiwari, A., Suri, H.S., Turk, M., Laird, J.R., Asare, C.K., Ankrah, A.A., Khanna, N., et al.: A review on a deep learning perspective in brain cancer classification. Cancers **11**(1), 111 (2019)

3. Bakas, S., et al.: Identifying the best machine learning algorithms for brain tumor segmentation, progression assessment, and overall survival prediction in the brats challenge. arXiv preprint (2018)

4. Zhang, D., Huang, G., Zhang, Q., Han, J., Han, J., Wang, Y., Yu, Y.: Exploring task structure for brain tumor segmentation from multi-modality mr images. IEEE Trans. Image Process. **29**, 9032–9043 (2020)

5. Menze, B.H., Jakab, A., Bauer, S., et al.: The multimodal brain tumor image segmentation benchmark (BRATS). IEEE Trans. Med. Imaging **34**(10), 1993–2024 (2014)

6. Pereira, S., Pinto, A., Alves, V., Silva, C.A.: Brain tumor segmentation using convolutional neural networks in MRI images. IEEE Trans. Med. Imaging **35**(5), 1240–1251 (2016)

7. Isensee, F., Jaeger, P.F., Kohl, S.A., Petersen, J., Maier-Hein, K.H.: nnU-Net: a self-configuring method for deep learning-based biomedical image segmentation. Nat. Methods **18**(2), 203–211 (2021)

8. Zhou, T., Fu, H., Chen, G., Shen, J., Shao, L.: Hi-net: hybrid-fusion network for multi-modal mr image synthesis. IEEE Trans. Med. Imaging **39**(9), 2772–2781 (2020)

9. Ronneberger, O., Fischer, P., Brox, T.: U-Net: convolutional networks for biomedical image segmentation. In: Navab, N., Hornegger, J., Wells, W.M., Frangi, A.F. (eds.) MICCAI 2015. LNCS, vol. 9351, pp. 234–241. Springer, Cham (2015). https://doi.org/10.1007/978-3-319-24574-4_28

10. Zhang, J., Lv, X., Zhang, H., Liu, B.: AResU-Net: Attention residual U-Net for brain tumor segmentation. Symmetry **12**(5), 721 (2020)

11. Luu, H.M., Park, S.H.: Extending nn-UNet for brain tumor segmentation. In: Crimi, A., Bakas, S. (eds.) BrainLes 2021. LNCS, vol. 12963, pp. 173–186. Springer, Cham (2022). https://doi.org/10.1007/978-3-031-09002-8_16

12. Çiçek, Ö., Abdulkadir, A., Lienkamp, S.S., Brox, T., Ronneberger, O.: 3D U-Net: learning dense volumetric segmentation from sparse annotation. In: Ourselin, S., Joskowicz, L., Sabuncu, M.R., Unal, G., Wells, W. (eds.) MICCAI 2016. LNCS, vol. 9901, pp. 424–432. Springer, Cham (2016). https://doi.org/10.1007/978-3-319-46723-8_49

13. Schlemper, J., et al.: Attention gated networks: learning to leverage salient regions in medical images. Med. Image Anal. **53**, 197–207 (2019)

14. Jia, Q., Shu, H.: BiTr-Unet: a CNN-transformer combined network for MRI brain tumor segmentation. In: Crimi, A., Bakas, S. (eds.) BrainLes 2021. LNCS, vol. 12963, pp. 3–14. Springer, Cham (2022). https://doi.org/10.1007/978-3-031-09002-8_1

15. Hatamizadeh, A., et al.: Unetr: transformers for 3d medical image segmentation. In: Proceedings of the IEEE/CVF Winter Conference on Applications of Computer Vision, pp. 574–584 (2022)

16. Wang, W., Chen, C., Ding, M., Yu, H., Zha, S., Li, J.: TransBTS: multimodal brain tumor segmentation using transformer. In: de Bruijne, M., et al. (eds.) MICCAI 2021. LNCS, vol. 12901, pp. 109–119. Springer, Cham (2021). https://doi.org/10.1007/978-3-030-87193-2_11

17. Zhang, Y., He, N., Yang, J., Li, Y., Wei, D., et al.: mmFormer: multimodal medical transformer for incomplete multimodal learning of brain tumor segmentation. In: Wang, L., Dou, Q., Fletcher, P.T., Speidel, S., Li, S. (eds.) MICCAI 2022. LNCS, vol. 13435, pp. 107–117. Springer, Cham (2022)

18. Ding, Y., Yu, X., Yang, Y.: RFNet: Region-aware fusion network for incomplete multi-modal brain tumor segmentation. In: Proceedings of the IEEE/CVF International Conference on Computer Vision, pp. 3975–3984 (2021)

19. Dolz, J., Gopinath, K., Yuan, J., Lombaert, H., Desrosiers, C., Ayed, I.B.: HyperDense-Net: a hyper-densely connected CNN for multi-modal image segmentation. IEEE Trans. Med. Imaging **38**(5), 1116–1126 (2018)

20. Xing, Z., Yu, L., Wan, L., Han, T., Zhu, L.: NestedFormer: nested modality-aware transformer for brain tumor segmentation. In: Wang, L., Dou, Q., Fletcher, P.T., Speidel, S., Li, S. (eds.) MICCAI 2022. LNCS, vol. 13435, pp. 140–150. Springer, Cham (2022)

21. Nagrani, A., Yang, S., Arnab, A., Jansen, A., Schmid, C., Sun, C.: Attention bottlenecks for multimodal fusion. Adv. Neural. Inf. Process. Syst. **34**, 14200–14213 (2021)

22. Jaegle, A., et al.: Perceiver io: a general architecture for structured inputs & outputs (2021)

23. Vaswani, A., et al.: Attention is all you need. In: Advances in Neural Information Processing Systems 30 (2017)

24. Dosovitskiy, A., et al.: An image is worth 16x16 words: Transformers for image recognition at scale (2020)

25. Tang, W., He, F., Liu, Y., Duan, Y.: Matr: multimodal medical image fusion via multiscale adaptive transformer. IEEE Trans. Image Process. **31**, 5134–5149 (2022)

26. Chen, C., Dou, Q., Jin, Y., Chen, H., Qin, J., Heng, P.-A.: Robust multimodal brain tumor segmentation via feature disentanglement and gated fusion. In: Shen, D., et al. (eds.) MICCAI 2019. LNCS, vol. 11766, pp. 447–456. Springer, Cham (2019). https://doi.org/10.1007/978-3-030-32248-9_50

27. Bakas, S., et al.: Advancing the cancer genome atlas glioma MRI collections with expert segmentation labels and radiomic features. Sci. Data **4**(1), 1–13 (2017)

28. Xie, Y., Zhang, J., Shen, C., Xia, Y.: CoTr: efficiently bridging CNN and transformer for 3D medical image segmentation. In: de Bruijne, M., et al. (eds.) MICCAI 2021. LNCS, vol. 12903, pp. 171–180. Springer, Cham (2021). https://doi.org/10.1007/978-3-030-87199-4_16

29. Zhang, Y., et al.: Modality-aware mutual learning for multi-modal medical image segmentation. In: de Bruijne, M., et al. (eds.) MICCAI 2021. LNCS, vol. 12901, pp. 589–599. Springer, Cham (2021). https://doi.org/10.1007/978-3-030-87193-2_56

30. Dice, L.R.: Measures of the amount of ecologic association between species. Ecology **26**(3), 297–302 (1945)

Efficient Tensor Low-Rank Representation with a Closed Form Solution

Yaozu Kan, Gui-Fu Lu[(✉)], Yangfan Du, and Guangyan Ji

School of Computer Science and Information, AnHui Polytechnic University,
WuHu 241000, AnHui, China
lu-guifu@ahpu.edu.cn

Abstract. In recent years, many tensor data processing methods have emerged. Tensor low-rank representation (TLRR) is a recently proposed tensor-based clustering method, and its clustering performance is promising. However, its calculation efficiency is low because its optimization procedure is iterative and needs to calculate tensor product, tensor singular value decomposition (t-SVD) and tensor product (t-product) in each iteration. To address the problem, we propose an efficient TLRR with a closed form solution (ETLRR/CFS). That is, we do not need an iterative procedure for finding the solution to ETLRR/CFS and only need one step to obtain the solution to ETLRR/CFS. Then, the computation efficiency is greatly improved. Specifically, we propose a novel objective function, which integrates tensor nuclear norm (TNN) and Frobenius norm into a unified framework, and give its closed form solution. Experiment results on several datasets shows that ETLRR/CFS not only is much faster than TLRR and its improved methods but can obtain similar clustering performance.

Keywords: Low-rank Representation · Tensor Data Clustering · Closed Form Solution · Tensor Nuclear Norm

1 Introduction

Nowadays, with the continuous development of various electronic products and the Internet, various types of high-dimensional data, e.g., images, network text, video, etc., continue to emerge. For machine learning and image processing algorithms, high-dimensional data will increase computational complexity and affect algorithm performance due to noise effects and redundant features, which is often called the curse of dimensionality [1]. In fact, these high-dimensional data are usually located in the low-dimensional structure. For example, face images are affected by different illumination and occlusion, but face images of a person are essentially located in the same subspace [2]. Therefore, how to find the low-dimensional subspace of data becomes the key to solving the problem.

To solve the above problem, in general, it is necessary to find the low-dimensional subspace of data, and then divide the data into their respective subspace, usually called subspace clustering (SC). SC can not only remove noise from raw data, but also process low-dimensional data more effectively. SC has been used in motion segmentation [3, 4] and scene clustering [5], etc. [6, 7]. Among all the SC methods, there are two representative methods, i.e., sparse SC (SSC) [8]and low-rank representation (LRR) [9]. SSC is triggered by sparse representation [10], and LRR is transformed from robust principal component analysis (RPCA) [11]. SSC and LRR are both very important and representative methods in SC. Their main difference is that SSC imposes L1-norm constraint on coefficient representations, while LRR imposes low-rank constraint on coefficient representations. SSC and LRR can effectively recover multiple subspace structures of data. In addition, LRR has developed several variants, using additional regularization terms to find low-rank structures [12–18]. Clustering tools such as normalized cut (Ncut) [19] are implemented on the low-rank representation coefficient matrix to complete the final clustering. Even if the data is polluted by various kinds of noise, these methods can still achieve good results. Generally, LRR uses the Augmented Lagrange Multiplier (ALM) [20] method to obtain its solution. Later P. Favarob et al. proposed an improved method of LRR [21], which greatly improved the efficiency of LRR algorithm and obtained better clustering results.

However, these methods are matrix-based ones. With the continuous increase of data dimensions and the increasing scale, these methods need to compress the data into a matrix. This operation destroys the intrinsic structure of the data [20, 22], and then some information will be lost in the compression process [23, 24]. Besides, their computational complexities are also high, and the computational efficiencies are not satisfactory. In order to solve these problems, people began to study the SC algorithm based on tensor. Kilmer et al. proposed some tensor operation related definitions such as t-product, t-SVD and tensor nuclear norm (TNN) [25–27], on which Lu et al. extended RPCA to tensor RPCA (TRPCA) [22]. Experimental results show that TRPCA has good performance. Recently, tensor LRR (TLRR) [28] is proposed, which is a generalization of LRR. TLRR can effectively restore the low rank structure of a tensor data and deduce the sample clustering. Similarly, TLRR also used the ALM [20] to optimize its algorithm. However, it needs many iterations to obtain its solution and needs to compute t-product and t-SVD in each iteration. It is not difficult to see that the computational complexity of TLRR is high and the computational speed is low. In addition, there are some improved algorithms of TLRR, such as enhanced TLRR (ETLRR) [29] and tensor low-rank sparse representation (TLRSR) [7], etc. Considering that TLRR only considers Laplace noise hidden in data, ETLRR can both consider Laplacian noise and Gaussian noise among data and can better recover the low-rank structure of the data. TLRSR argues that TLRR only considers the global structure of data. To capture the local structure of the data, TLRSR applies sparse constraints to the coefficient tensor based on TLRR. Although these algorithms can get better results than TLRR, their computational complexity is still very high.

To address the problem of TLRR and its improved algorithm, we propose an efficient tensor low-rank representation with a closed form solution (ETLRR/CFS) to improve the computational efficiency of TLRR. Totally different from TLRR and its some improved methods, the solution to ETLRR/CFS is a closed form solution. That is, it does not need an iterative procedure for finding the solution to ETLRR/CFS and only need one step to obtain the solution to ETLRR/CFS. Then, its calculation speed is very fast and computational complexity is very low. Specifically, we propose a novel objective function, which integrates TNN and Frobenius norm into a unified framework. We also give its closed solution. According to the experimental results, ETLRR/CFS not only is much faster than TLRR and its improved methods but can obtain similar clustering performance. The main contributions of this paper are as follows:

1. We propose a novel tensor-based SC method, i.e., ETLRR/CFS.
2. The theoretical derivation of ETLRR/CFS demonstrates that it has a closed form solution. That is, it only needs one step to obtain its final solution, which greatly improves its computational efficiency.
3. The experiment results on six datasets verify that our algorithm has high efficiency and good performance.

2 Notations and Preliminaries

In this section, we first summarize all the symbols in Table 1 and introduce some definitions used in this paper.

Table 1. Summary of notation.

Notation	Description	Notation	Description
a	A scalar	A	A matrix
a	A vector	$\mathcal{A}$	A tensor
rank(A)	Rank of matrix A	$\mathcal{A}(:,:,k)$	kth frontal slice
$\|A\|_*$	Matrix nuclear norm	$\|A\|_F$	$\|A\|_F = \sqrt{\sum_{i=1}^{m}\sum_{j=1}^{n} A_{i,j}^2}$
I	Identity matrix	$\|A\|_{2,1}$	$\|A\|_{2,1} = \sum_{j=1}^{N}\sqrt{\sum_{i=1}^{N} A_{i,j}^2}$
$\|A\|_1$	$\|A\|_1 = \sum_{i,j}|a_{i,j}|$	$\|A\|_2$	$\|A\|_2 = (\sum_i |a_i|^2)^{1/2}$
0	Matrix with entry value 0	$\|\mathcal{A}\|_F$	$\|\mathcal{A}\|_F = \sqrt{\sum_{k=1}^{n_3}\sum_{j=1}^{n_2}\sum_{i=1}^{n_1} \mathcal{A}_{i,j,k}^2}$
$\overline{\mathcal{A}} = fft(\mathcal{A},[\ ],3)$	Fourier transform	$\mathcal{A} = ifft(\overline{\mathcal{A}},[\ ],3)$	Inverse Fourier transform

Definition 1 (T-product)

Let $\mathcal{X} \in R^{n_1 \times l \times n_3}$, $\mathcal{Y} \in R^{l \times n_2 \times n_3}$. Then the t-product $\mathcal{X} * \mathcal{Y}$ is defined to be a tensor of size $n_1 \times n_2 \times n_3$,

$$\mathcal{X} * \mathcal{Y} = fold(bcirc(\mathcal{X}) \cdot unfold(\mathcal{Y})) \tag{1}$$

Theorem 1 (t-SVD)
Assume that $\mathcal{X} \in R^{n_1 \times n_2 \times n_3}$. Then it can be factored as

$$\mathcal{X} = \mathcal{U} * \mathcal{S} * \mathcal{V}^* \tag{2}$$

where $\mathcal{U} \in R^{n_1 \times n_1 \times n_3}$ and $\mathcal{V} \in R^{n_2 \times n_2 \times n_3}$ are orthogonal tensor, $\mathcal{S} \in R^{n_1 \times n_2 \times n_3}$ is a f-diagonal tensor.

Definition 2 (Tensor nuclear norm)
The tensor nuclear norm $\|\mathcal{X}\|_*$ of a tensor $\mathcal{X} \in R^{n_1 \times n_2 \times n_3}$ is defined as

$$\|\mathcal{X}\|_* = \frac{1}{n_3} \sum_{i=1}^{n_3} \|\overline{X}^{(i)}\|_* = \frac{1}{n_3} \|\overline{X}\|_* \tag{3}$$

Lemma 1 Suppose $\mathcal{Y} \in R^{n_1 \times n_2 \times n_3}$, $\mathcal{X} \in R^{n_1 \times n_2 \times n_3}$ are two arbitrary tensors. Let $\mathcal{F} = \mathcal{X} * \mathcal{Y}$ then we have:

1. $\|\mathcal{X}\|_{\mathcal{F}}^2 = \frac{1}{n_3}\|\overline{X}\|_F^2$
2. $\mathcal{F} = \mathcal{X} * \mathcal{Y}$ and $\overline{F} = \overline{X}\overline{Y}$ are equivalent to each other.

3   Related Work

In this section, we will introduce LRR, TLRR, ETLRR and TLRSR which are very relevant to our proposed.

3.1   Low-Rank Representation (LRR)

LRR and RPCA assume data consists of clean data and noise data. To be able to get a clean low-rank data from the raw data, the rank minimization problem is proposed:

$$\min_{D,E} rank(D) + \lambda\|E\|_\ell \quad s.t. \quad X = D + E \tag{4}$$

where $\lambda > 0$ is a parameter and $\|\cdot\|_\ell$ is a regularization strategy. In fact, (4) is the objective of RPCA [5]. Further, LRR argues that clean data is obtained by multiplying the dictionary with the coefficient representation matrix as follows:

$$\min_{Z,E} rank(Z) + \lambda\|E\|_\ell \quad s.t. \quad X = XZ + E \tag{5}$$

where Z represents low-rank structure. Since solving Eq. (5) is a NP problem, the nuclear norm is used to replace the rank function in LRR, and the L$_{21}$-norm is used for noise E. Finally, we get the LRR convex optimization problem:

$$\min_{Z,E} \|Z\|_* + \lambda\|E\|_{2,1} \quad s.t. \quad X = XZ + E \tag{6}$$

ALM is used for solving LRR.

3.2 Tensor Low-Rank Representation (TLRR)

Based on the TNN proposed by [22], LRR is extended to the TLRR. Zhou et al. proposed TLRR, which is similar to LRR:

$$\min_{\mathcal{L},\mathcal{E}} \|\mathcal{L}\|_* + \lambda\|\mathcal{E}\|_1 \quad s.t. \quad \mathcal{X} = \mathcal{D} * \mathcal{L} + \mathcal{E} \tag{7}$$

where $\mathcal{X}$ is the raw data, $\mathcal{L}$ is a low-rank tensor structure, $\mathcal{E}$ is a sparse noise tensor, and $\mathcal{D}$ represents the dictionary. When raw data is used as a dictionary, TLRR is called simple TLRR (STLRR). When the clean data estimated by TRPCA is used as a dictionary, TLRR is called robust TLRR(RTLRR). ADMM is also used for solving TLRR.

3.3 Enhanced Tensor Low-Rank Representation (ETLRR)

ETLRR [29] is an improved method of TLRR. Unlike the original TLRR algorithm which only considers one type of Laplacian noise, ETLRR considers both Laplacian and Gaussian noise. The objective function of ETLRR is

$$\min_{\mathcal{L},\mathcal{E},\mathcal{N}} \|\mathcal{L}\|_* + \alpha\|\mathcal{E}\|_1 + \beta\|\mathcal{N}\|_1 \quad s.t. \quad \mathcal{X} = \mathcal{D} * \mathcal{L} + \mathcal{E} + \mathcal{N} \tag{8}$$

where $\mathcal{N}$ is a Gaussian noise tensor. Similarly, the ADMM method is also used to optimize ETLRR.

3.4 Tensor Low-Rank Sparse Representation (TLRSR)

TLRSR [7] is also an improved method of TLRR. They argue that TLRR only takes into account the global structure of samples and ignores the local structure of sample. TLRSR captures the global structure by applying TNN constraints to the coefficient representation and the local structure by using sparse constraints. The objective function of TLRSR is as follows:

$$\min_{\mathcal{L},\mathcal{E}} \|\mathcal{L}\|_* + \alpha\|\mathcal{L}\|_1 + \beta\|\mathcal{E}\|_l \quad s.t. \quad \mathcal{X} = \mathcal{D} * \mathcal{L} + \mathcal{E} \tag{9}$$

where l represents the tensor norm, e.g., tensor L_1-norm and L_{21}-norm. Similarly, the ADMM method is also used to optimize TLRSR.

4 Efficient Tensor Low-Rank Representation with a Closed Form Solution (ETLRR/CFS)

TLRR can achieve good clustering performance, but it requires several iterations. Moreover, a lot of t-product and t-SVD need to be calculated in the iterative process, so the computational complexity of TLRR is high and the computational speed is slow. Therefore, we propose the ETLRR/CFS method, which can greatly improve the calculation efficiency. It only takes one step to obtain its solution, and then the computational efficiency is greatly improved. Besides, the clustering performance of ETLRR/CFS is comparable to the state-of-the-art methods.

Suppose $\mathcal{X} \in R^{n_1 \times n_2 \times n_3}$ is the raw data set, the usual formula for finding the low-rank structure of $\mathcal{X}$ is as follows:

$$\min_{\mathcal{A},\mathcal{C}} \|\mathcal{C}\|_{TNN} + \frac{\lambda}{2}\|\mathcal{E}\|_l \quad s.t. \quad \mathcal{X} = \mathcal{X} * \mathcal{C} + \mathcal{E} \tag{10}$$

where $\mathcal{C}$ represents the low-rank structure of $\mathcal{X}$, and $\|\cdot\|_l$ represents the regularization strategy representing various noises. For example, in TLRR, the L_1-norm is used to measure Laplacian noise, while in ETLRR, the L_1-norm and L_2-norm are both used to measure Laplacian noise and Gaussian noise. However, although good experimental results can be obtained by both methods, the computational speed is relatively low. Therefore, in order to be able to get a closed form solution, we use the Frobenius norm instead of the L1-norm in TLRR. Then (12) can be rewritten as:

$$\min_{\mathcal{A},\mathcal{C}} \|\mathcal{C}\|_{TNN} + \frac{\lambda}{2}\|\mathcal{E}\|_F^2 \quad s.t. \quad \mathcal{X} = \mathcal{X} * \mathcal{C} + \mathcal{E} \tag{11}$$

In general, many algorithms use raw data as dictionaries. In fact, there generally are some noises in raw data. Therefore, we divide the raw data into clean data and noise, i.e., $\mathcal{X} = \mathcal{A} + \mathcal{E}$, where $\mathcal{A}$ is the clean data tensor and $\mathcal{E}$ is the noise tensor. Then, we reformulate (13) as follows.:

$$\min_{\mathcal{A},\mathcal{C}} \|\mathcal{C}\|_{TNN} + \frac{\tau}{2}\|\mathcal{E}\|_F^2 \quad s.t. \quad \mathcal{A} = \mathcal{A} * \mathcal{C}, \mathcal{X} = \mathcal{A} + \mathcal{E} \tag{12}$$

where $\mathcal{E}$ represents noise. Finally, we can relax the equality constraint in Eq. (12) And convert Eq. 12 Into the following equation:

$$\min_{\mathcal{A},\mathcal{C}} \|\mathcal{C}\|_{TNN} + \frac{\tau}{2}\|\mathcal{A} - \mathcal{A} * \mathcal{C}\|_F^2 + \frac{\alpha}{2}\|\mathcal{X} - \mathcal{A}\|_F^2 \tag{13}$$

(13) is the finally objection function of ETLRR/CFS, which can be solved by Theorem 1.

Theorem 1. Let $\mathcal{X} = \mathcal{U} * \mathcal{S} * \mathcal{V}^T$ be the t-SVD of a given tensor $\mathcal{A}$. The optimal solution to (13) is

$$\mathcal{A} = \mathcal{U} * \mathcal{D} * \mathcal{V}^T \tag{14}$$

and

$$\mathcal{C} = \mathcal{V} * \mathcal{T} * \mathcal{V}^T \tag{15}$$

where $\mathcal{D}$ is an $n_1 \times n_2 \times n_3$ f-diagonal tensor and its diagonal entry, i.e., $\mathcal{D}(i,i,j)$ is computed as

$$S(i,i,j) = \varphi(\mathcal{D}(i,i,j)) = \begin{cases} \mathcal{D}(i,i,j) + \frac{1}{\alpha\tau\mathcal{D}^3(i,i,j)}, \mathcal{D}(i,i,j) > \frac{1}{\sqrt{\tau}} \\ \mathcal{D}(i,i,j) + \frac{\tau}{\alpha\mathcal{D}(i,i,j)}S(i,i,j), \mathcal{D}(i,i,j) \leq \frac{1}{\sqrt{\tau}} \end{cases} \tag{16}$$

$\mathcal{T}$ is also an $n_1 \times n_2 \times n_3$ f-diagonal tensor and its diagonal entry, i.e., $\mathcal{T}(i,i,j)$, in Fourier domain, is computed as

$$\mathcal{T}(i,i,j) = \begin{cases} 1 - \frac{1}{\tau\mathcal{D}^2(i,i,j)}, \mathcal{D}(i,i,j) > \frac{1}{\sqrt{\tau}} \\ 0, (i,i,j) \leq \frac{1}{\sqrt{\tau}} \end{cases} \tag{17}$$

Before proving Theorem 1, we first give Lemma 2.

Lemma 2. [21] Let $D = U\Sigma V^T$ be the SVD of the data matrix D. The optimal solution to

$$\min_{A,C}\|C\|_* + \frac{\tau}{2}\|A - AC\|_F^2 + \frac{\alpha}{2}\|D - A\|_F^2 \tag{18}$$

is given by $\hat{A} = U\Lambda V^T$ and $\hat{C} = V_1(I - \frac{1}{\tau}\Lambda_1^{-2})V_1^T$, where each entry of $\Lambda = diag(\lambda_1, ..., \lambda_n)$ is obtained from on entry of $\Sigma = diag(\sigma_1, ..., \sigma_n)$ as the solution to

$$\sigma = \psi(\lambda) = \begin{cases} \lambda + \frac{1}{\alpha\tau}\lambda^{-3} if \lambda > 1/\sqrt{\tau} \\ \lambda + \frac{1}{\alpha}\lambda if \lambda \le 1/\sqrt{\tau} \end{cases} \tag{19}$$

that minimizes the cost, and the matrices $U = [U_1 U_2]$, $\Lambda = diag(\Lambda_1, \Lambda_2)$ and $V = [V_1 V_2]$ are partitioned according to the sets $I_1 = \{i : \lambda_i > 1/\sqrt{\tau}\}$ and $I_2 = \{i : \lambda_i \le 1/\sqrt{\tau}\}$.

Now we give the detail proof of Theorem 1.

Proof: In Fourier domain, (13) can be reformulated as:

$$arg \min_{A,C}\|C\|_{TNN} + \frac{\tau}{2}\|A - A * C\|_F^2 + \frac{\alpha}{2}\|X - A\|_F^2$$

$$= arg \min_{A,C} \frac{1}{n_3}\left(\|\overline{C}\|_* + \frac{\tau}{2}\|\overline{A} - \overline{A} * \overline{C}\|_F^2 + \frac{\alpha}{2}\|\overline{X} - \overline{A}\|_F^2\right)$$

$$= arg \min_{\overline{A}^{(i)},\overline{C}^{(i)}} \frac{1}{n_3}\sum_{j=1}^{n_3}\left(\|\overline{C}^{(j)}\|_* + \frac{\tau}{2}\|\overline{A}^{(j)} - \overline{A}^{(j)} * \overline{C}^{(j)}\|_F^2 + \frac{\alpha}{2}\|\overline{X}^{(j)} - \overline{A}^{(j)}\|_F^2\right) \tag{20}$$

Let $\overline{X}^{(j)} = \overline{U}^{(j)}\overline{S}^{(j)}\overline{V}^{(j)T}$ be the SVD of $\overline{X}^{(i)}$, then we can solve this problem by Lemma 2:

$$\overline{A}^{(j)} = \overline{U}^{(j)}\overline{D}^{(j)}\overline{V}^{(j)T} \tag{21}$$

and

$$\overline{C}^{(j)} = \overline{V}_1^{(j)}\overline{T}^{(j)}\left(\overline{V}_1^{(j)}\right)^T \tag{22}$$

where each entry of $\overline{D}^{(j)} = diag\left(\overline{\lambda}_1^{(j)}...,\overline{\lambda}_n^{(j)}\right)$ is obtained from one entry of $\overline{S}^{(j)} = diag\left(\overline{\sigma}_1^{(j)}...,\overline{\sigma}_n^{(j)}\right)$ as the solution to

$$\overline{\sigma}^{(j)} = \varphi\left(\overline{\lambda}^{(j)}\right) = \begin{cases} \overline{\lambda}^{(j)} + \frac{1}{\alpha\tau}(\overline{\lambda}^{(j)})^{-3}, \overline{\lambda}^{(j)} > \frac{1}{\sqrt{\tau}} \\ \overline{\lambda}^{(j)} + \frac{\tau}{\alpha}\overline{\lambda}^{(j)}, \overline{\lambda}^{(j)} \le \frac{1}{\sqrt{\tau}} \end{cases} \tag{23}$$

that minimizes the cost, and the where $\overline{U}^{(j)} = \left[\overline{U}_1^{(j)} \overline{U}_2^{(j)}\right]$, $\overline{\Sigma}^{(j)} = diag\left(\overline{D}_1^{(j)} \overline{D}_2^{(j)}\right)$, and $\overline{V}^{(j)} = \left[\overline{V}_1^{(j)} \overline{V}_2^{(j)}\right]$ are partitioned according to the sets $I_1 = \{i : \overline{\lambda}_i > \sqrt{\tau}\}$ and $I_2 = \{i : \overline{\lambda}_i \le \sqrt{\tau}\}$. Let

$$\overline{D}(i, i, j) = \overline{\lambda}_i^{(j)} \tag{24}$$

and

$$\bar{T}^{(j)} = diag\left(I - \frac{1}{\tau}\left(\bar{D}_1^{(j)}\right)^{-2} \quad \mathbf{0}\right) \tag{25}$$

Where $\mathbf{0}$ is a zero matrix with the same size as $\overline{\Lambda}_2^{(i)}$. Let $\mathcal{T} = ifft\left(\overline{\mathcal{T}}, [], 3\right)$, where $\overline{\mathcal{T}}$ is a tensor, whose frontal slice is $T^{(i)}$. Then we can obtain $\mathcal{C} = \mathcal{V} * \mathcal{T} * \mathcal{V}^T$ and $\mathcal{A} = \mathcal{U} * \mathcal{D} * \mathcal{V}^T$ are solution to (13).

According to Theorem 1, we give the following algorithm 1 to solve ETLRR/CFS.

Algorithm 1: ETLRR/CFS

Input: The original data$\mathcal{X} \in R^{n_1 \times n_2 \times n_3}$, α, τ

Initialize:$\mathcal{A} = \mathcal{C} = 0$

1.Computer $\overline{\mathcal{X}} = fft(\mathcal{X}, [], 3)$

2.Perform t-SVD of $\overline{\mathcal{X}}$, i.e., $\overline{\mathcal{X}} = \overline{\mathcal{U}} * \overline{\mathcal{S}} * \overline{\mathcal{V}}^T$

3.Computer $\overline{\mathcal{D}}$ by using (20);

4.Computer $\overline{\mathcal{T}}$ by using (22);

5.Computer:$\overline{\mathcal{A}} = \overline{\mathcal{U}} * \overline{\mathcal{D}} * \overline{\mathcal{V}}^T$;

6.Computer:$\overline{\mathcal{C}} = \overline{\mathcal{V}} * \overline{\mathcal{T}} * \overline{\mathcal{V}}^T$;

7.Computer: $\mathcal{A} = ifft(\overline{\mathcal{A}}, [], 3)$

8.Computer: $\mathcal{C} = ifft(\overline{\mathcal{C}}, [], 3)$

Output: $\mathcal{A}, \mathcal{C}$

By using Algorithm 1, we can get the low-rank structure $\mathcal{C}$. Note that the representation coefficient of $\mathcal{X}^{(j)}$ for the front slice of each $\mathcal{X}$ is $\mathcal{C}^{(j)}$. So, we can use these front slices to construct the similarity matrix S, which is constructed as follows:

$$S = \frac{1}{2n_3}\sum_{j=1}^{n_3} \left(\left|\mathcal{C}^{(j)*}\right| + \left|\mathcal{C}^{(j)}\right|\right) \tag{26}$$

We can use Algorithm 2 to obtain the final clustering results.

Algorithm 2: ETLRR/CFS for clustering

Input: The original data $\mathcal{X} \in R^{n_1 \times n_2 \times n_3}$, number c of clusters

Output: cluster results

1.obtain the optimal solution $\mathcal{A}, \mathcal{C}$ of (11) by Algorithm 1.

2.Construct a similarity matrix $S$by (23).

3. Cluster the samples into c clusters by performing Ncut.

4.1 Computational Complexity Analysis and Comparison

According to the description of algorithm 1, the complexity of our algorithm mainly focuses on Fourier transformation and t-SVD. So, we mainly consider these two parts when discussing the complexity. Specifically, assuming the original data $\mathcal{X} \in R^{n_1 \times n_2 \times n_3}$, the complexity of its Fourier transform is $O(n_1 n_2 n_3 log(n_1 n_2 n_3))$, the complexity of t-SVD is $O(n_3 n_1^2 n_2)$, so the complexity of ETLRR/CFS is $O(n_1 n_2 n_3 log(n_1 n_2 n_3) + n_3 n_1^2 n_2)$. Then, we give the computational complexity of partially tensor-based algorithms. The computational complexity of ETLRR and TLRSR is $O(t(r(n_1 + n_2)n_3 log(n_3) + rn_3 n_1 n_2))$, where t is the number of iterations and r is the tubal rank of dictionary. The computational complexity of TLRR is $O(r(n_1 + n_2)n_3 log(n_3) + rn_3 n_1 n_2)$.

5 Experiments

In this section, we compare ETLRR/CFS with several different methods on different datasets to demonstrate the superior performance of ETLRR/CFS. All experiments are implemented in Matlab 2019b on the computer with i7-8750 H, 2.20 GHz CPU and 16 GB of memory.

5.1 Data Sets Description

In our experiment, we used several data sets, i.e., ORL, YaleB, ExtendYaleB, FRDUE, Yale to test the performance of ETLRR/CFS. Details of the data set are shown in Table 2.

Table 2. Statistics of datasets.

Dataset	#Images	#Clusters	#Per cluster	Size
ExtendYaleB	840	28	30	80×60
ORl	400	40	10	32×32
Yale	165	15	11	32×32
YaleB	650	10	65	50×50
FRDUE (100)	1980	99	20	25×22
FRDUE (all)	3040	152	20	25×22

5.2 Compared Methods

The ETLRR/CFS is compared with several methods, i.e., SSC, LRR, S-TLRR, R-TLRR, ETLRR and TLRSR. For the comparison method, we use the parameters recommended in their papers.

SSC [8]: SSC algorithm assumes that every point can be represented using a linear combination of other points.

LRR [9]: LRR obtains the low-rank structure of the original data by applying low-rank constraints to the coefficient matrix.

S-TLRR and R-TLRR [28]: Zhou et al. extends LRR to the tensor LRR based on some tensor operations. When using raw data as a dictionary, TLRR is called STLRR and when data preprocessed by TRPCA is used as a dictionary, TLRR is called RTLRR.

ETLRR [29]: ETLRR takes into account the influence of Gaussian noise on data more than TLRR. By processing more noise, more accurate results can be obtained.

TLRSR [7]: On the basis of TLRR, TLRSR adds sparse representation constraint to the coefficient representation tensor. This ensures that the coefficient representation tensor captures the global and local structure. Therefore, TLRSR can better recover the low-rank structure of data and achieve better clustering performance.

5.3 Evaluation Method

In this paper, we used three clustering metrics i.e., the accuracy (ACC), the normalized mutual information (NMI), the purity (PUR) to measure the clustering performance of the algorithm. We will repeat each experiment 10 times and show the average performance. For all of the above measures, their values range in [0–1], and if the value is bigger, the clustering effect is better. In addition, to compare the algorithm's computational complexity, we use time (seconds) to compare algorithm speed, and if the value is shorter, the speed is faster.

5.4 Parameter Analysis

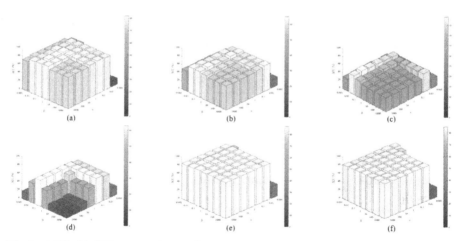

Fig. 1. ACC with different α and τ on all data sets. (a) ACC on ExtendYaleB; (b) ACC on ORL; (c) ACC on Yale; (d) ACC on YaleB; (e) ACC on FRDUE (100); (f) ACC on FRDUE (all).

For α and τ in the ETLRR/CFS method, we first search on [0.001, 0.01, 0.1, 1, 10, 100, 1000] and then fine-tune the parameters. In ExtendYaleB $\alpha = 1, \tau = 0.3$;

$\alpha = 0.1, \tau = 0.06$ in ORL; $\alpha = 1, \tau = 0.02$ in Yale; $\alpha = 0.05, \tau = 0.13$ in YaleB; $\alpha = 1, \tau = 0.1$ in FRDUE(100); $\alpha = 1, \tau = 1$ in FRDUE(all). In Fig. 1, we show the ACC with different α and τ on all data sets. From Fig. 1, it is not difficult to see that ETLRR/CFS are not sensitive to parameters, and with the change of α and τ, ETLRR/CFS have better clustering performance.

5.5   Experimental Analysis

Table 3 shows the performances of all the compared algorithm on different data sets with the best performance highlighted in bold. It can be seen that: (1) the clustering performances of matrix-based low-rank representation methods, i.e., SSC, LRR, are generally not as good as those of tensor-based low-rank representation methods, i.e., TLRR, ETLRR, TLRSR. This indicates that if the tensor data is compressed into a matrix, the tensor structure of the tensor data will be destroyed, and some information will be lost in the compression process; (2) In general, our algorithm has achieved good clustering performance on all data sets. For example, on FRDUE and FRDUE100, our algorithm works best. On the other data sets, such as ExtendYaleB, ORL, etc. our algorithm is not the best, but it is close to the best.

Table 3. Experimental results of clustering performance

Dataset	Metric	SSC	LRR	S-TLRR	R-TLRR	ETLRR	TLRSR	ETLRR/CFS
ExtendYaleB	ACC	0.680	0.707	0.829	0.839	0.841	0.832	0.817
	NMI	0.837	0.787	0.889	0.908	0.904	0.900	0.879
	PUR	0.737	0.731	0.843	0.860	0.861	0.853	0.831
ORL	ACC	0.684	0.659	0.603	0.558	0.619	0.620	0.655
	NMI	0.836	0.805	0.748	0.719	0.777	0.775	0.791
	PUR	0.837	0.693	0.632	0.591	0.649	0.651	0.684
Yale	ACC	0.631	0.523	0.377	0.369	0.484	0.524	0.520
	NMI	0.559	0.572	0.436	0.435	0.537	0.559	0.564
	PUR	0.632	0.546	0.409	0.394	0.514	0.549	0.545
YaleB	ACC	0.761	0.443	0.478	0.613	0.725	0.740	0.719
	NMI	0.683	0.380	0.452	0.599	0.673	0.684	0.669
	PUR	0.761	0.470	0.485	0.613	0.729	0.741	0.720
FRDUE (100)	ACC	0.776	0.779	0.867	0.849	0.866	0.870	0.870
	NMI	0.902	0.915	0.956	0.949	0.957	0.961	0.958
	PUR	0.838	0.829	0.894	0.879	0.893	0.899	0.897
FRDUE (all)	ACC	0.741	0.701	0.843	0.830	0.839	0.845	0.847
	NMI	0.879	0.905	0.950	0.944	0.951	0.955	0.952
	PUR	0.813	0.723	0.875	0.862	0.870	0.876	0.877

Table 4. Algorithm time experiment results.

Dataset	SSC	LRR	S-TLRR	R-TLRR	ETLRR	TLRSR	ETLRR/CFS
ExtendYaleB	205.361	75.947	272.847	311.053	189.495	966.737	4.671
ORL	88.569	21.490	25.967	30.754	19.026	92.454	0.343
Yale	61.681	6.240	13.716	16.264	35.281	47.869	0.069
YaleB	61.747	41.943	35.338	37.107	30.750	109.934	0.222
FRDUE (100)	63.702	433.336	49.397	60.106	41.042	371.229	5.908
FRDUE (all)	145.037	421.191	84.706	106.693	73.843	383.626	14.807

Table 4 shows the operation times of each algorithm on different data sets. Comparing ETLRR/CFS with TLRR, ETLRR and TLRSR on all data sets, we can see that ETLRR/CFS is the fastest, several or even tens of times faster than the other methods. From Table 3 and 4, we can obtain that ETLRR/CFS not only is much faster than TLRR and its improved methods but can obtain similar clustering performance.

6 Conclusion

In this paper, we propose an ETLRR/CFS method. Most of the low-rank tensor representation methods proposed in the past need a lot of time for calculation. Although good results can be achieved, the calculation speed is slow because they need many iterations to obtain its solution and needs to compute t-product and t-SVD in each iteration. Therefore, we propose a low-rank tensor representation algorithm with closed-form solutions. ETLRR/CFS can not only achieve clustering performance as the previous algorithms, but also calculate the results in one step, which means that its calculation speed is very fast. We compared the ETLRR/CFS method with several other methods on six data sets. Experimental results demonstrate the efficiency and effectiveness of ETLRR/CFS.

Acknowledgments. This research was supported by NSFC (No. 61976005) and the Natural Science Research Project of Anhui Province University (No. 2022AH050970).

References

1. Elhamifar, E., Vidal, R.: Sparse subspace clustering: algorithm, theory, and applications. IEEE Trans. Pattern Anal. Mach. Intell. **35**, 2765–2781 (2013)
2. Basri, R., Jacobs, D.W.: Lambertian reflectance and linear subspaces. IEEE Trans. Pattern Anal. Mach. Intell. **25**, 218–233 (2003)
3. Lu, C.Y., Min, H., Zhao, Z.Q., Zhu, L., Huang, D.S., Yan, S.: Robust and efficient subspace segmentation via least squares regression. In: Fitzgibbon, A., Lazebnik, S., Perona, P., Sato, Y., Schmid, C. (eds.) Computer Vision – ECCV 2012. ECCV 2012. LNCS, vol. 7578, pp. 347–360. Springer, Berlin (2012). https://doi.org/10.1007/978-3-642-33786-4_26
4. Hu, H., Lin, Z., Feng, J., Zhou, J.: Smooth representation clustering. In: Proceedings of the IEEE Conference on Computer Vision and Pattern Recognition, pp. 3834–3841 (2014)

5. Greene, D., Cunningham, P.: Practical solutions to the problem of diagonal dominance in kernel document clustering. In: Proceedings of the 23rd International Conference on Machine Learning, pp. 377–384 (2006)

6. Ma, Y., Derksen, H., Hong, W., Wright, J.: Segmentation of multivariate mixed data via lossy data coding and compression. IEEE Trans. Pattern Anal. Mach. Intell. **29**, 1546–1562 (2007)

7. Du, S., Shi, Y., Shan, G., Wang, W., Ma, Y.: Tensor low-rank sparse representation for tensor subspace learning. Knowl.-Based Syst. **440**, 351–364 (2021)

8. Vidal, E.E.R.: Sparse subspace clustering. In: IEEE Conference on Computer Vision and Pattern Recognition (CVPR), pp. 2790–2797 (2009)

9. Liu, G., Lin, Z., Yu, Y.: Robust subspace segmentation by low-rank representation. In: Proceedings of the 27th International Conference on Machine Learning (ICML-10), pp. 663–670 (2010)

10. Wright, J., Yang, A.Y., Ganesh, A., Sastry, S.S., Ma, Y.: Robust face recognition via sparse representation. IEEE Trans. Pattern Anal. Mach. Intell. **31**, 210–227 (2018)

11. Candès, E.J., Li, X., Ma, Y., Wright, J.: Robust principal component analysis?. J. ACM **58**, 1–37 (2011)

12. Du, S., Ma, Y., Ma, Y.: Graph regularized compact low rank representation for subspace clustering. Knowl.-Based Syst. **118**, 56–69 (2017)

13. He, W., Chen, J.X., Zhang, W.: Low-rank representation with graph regularization for subspace clustering. Soft Comput. **21**, 1569–1581 (2017). https://doi.org/10.1007/s00500-015-1869-0

14. Wang, Q., He, X. and Li, X.: Locality and structure regularized low rank representation for hyperspectral image classification. IEEE Trans. Geosci. Remote Sens. **57**, 911–923 (2018)

15. Wen, J., Fang, X., Xu, Y., Tian, C., Fei, L.: Low-rank representation with adaptive graph regularization. Neural Netw. **108**, 83–96 (2018)

16. Ding, Y., Chong, Y. and Pan, S.: Sparse and low-rank representation with key connectivity for hyperspectral image classification. IEEE J. Sel. Top. Appl. Earth Obser. Remote Sens. **13**, 5609–5622 (2020)

17. Chen, J., Mao, H., Wang, Z., Zhang, X.: Low-rank representation with adaptive dictionary learning for subspace clustering. Knowl.-Based Syst. **223**, 107053 (2021)

18. Cai, B., Lu, G.-F.: Tensor subspace clustering using consensus tensor low-rank representation. Inf. Sci. **609**, 46–59 (2022)

19. Shi, J., Malik, J.: Normalized cuts and image segmentation. IEEE Trans. Pattern Anal. Mach. Intell. **22**(8), 888–905 (2000)

20. Bertsekas, D.P.: Constrained Optimization and Lagrange Multiplier Methods. Academic Press, Cambridge (2014)

21. Favaro, P., Vidal, R., Ravichandran, A.: A closed form solution to robust subspace estimation and clustering. In: CVPR 2011, pp. 1801–1807. IEEE (2011)

22. Lu, C., Feng, J., Chen, Y., Liu, W., Lin, Z., Yan, S.: Tensor robust principal component analysis: exact recovery of corrupted low-rank tensors via convex optimization. In: Proceedings of the IEEE Conference on Computer Vision and Pattern Recognition, pp. 5249–5257 (2016)

23. Yang, J., Luo, L., Qian, J., Tai, Y., Zhang, F., Xu, Y.: Nuclear norm based matrix regression with applications to face recognition with occlusion and illumination changes. IEEE Trans. Pattern Anal. Mach. Intell. **39**, 56–171 (2016)

24. Lu, Y., Lai, Z., Li, X., Wong, W.K., Yuan, C., Zhang, D.: Low-rank 2-D neighborhood preserving projection for enhanced robust image representation. IEEE Trans. Cybern. **49**, 1859–1872 (2018)

25. Kilmer, M.E., Martin, C.D.: Factorization strategies for third-order tensors. Linear Algebra Appl. **435**, 641–658 (2011)

26. Kilmer, M.E., Braman, K., Hao, N., Hoover, R.C.: Third-order tensors as operators on matrices: A theoretical and computational framework with applications in imaging. SIAM J. Matrix Anal. Appl. **34**, 148–172 (2013)
27. Kernfeld, E., Kilmer, M., Aeron, S.: Tensor–tensor products with invertible linear transforms. Linear Algebra Appl. **485**, 545–570 (2015)
28. Zhou, P., Lu, C., Feng, J., Lin, Z., Yan, S.: Tensor low-rank representation for data recovery and clustering. IEEE Trans. Pattern Anal. Mach. Intell. **43**(5) 1718–1732 (2019)
29. Du, S., Liu, B., Shan, G., Shi, Y., Wang, W.: Enhanced tensor low-rank representation for clustering and denoising. Knowl.-Based Syst. **243**, 108468 (2022)

Fine-Grained Face Sketch-Photo Synthesis with Text-Guided Diffusion Models

Jin Liu[1,2], Huaibo Huang[2], Jie Cao[2], Junxian Duan[2], and Ran He[1,2(✉)]

[1] School of Information Science and Technology, ShanghaiTech University, Shanghai, China
liujin2@shanghaitech.edu.cn
[2] CRIPAC & MAIS, Institute of Automation, Chinese Academy of Sciences, Beijing, China
{huaibo.huang,jie.cao,junxian.duan}@cripac.ia.ac.cn, rhe@nlpr.ia.ac.cn

Abstract. Face sketch-photo synthesis involves generating face photos from input face sketches. However, existing Generative Adversarial Networks (GANs)-based methods struggle to produce high-quality images due to artifacts and lack of detail caused by training difficulties. Additionally, prior approaches exhibit fixed and monotonous image styles, limiting practical usability. Drawing inspiration from recent successes in Diffusion Probability Models (DPMs) for image generation, we present a novel DPMs-based framework. This framework produces detailed face photos from input sketches while allowing control over facial attributes using textual descriptions. Our framework employs a U-Net, a semantic sketch encoder for extracting information from input sketches, and a text encoder to convert textual descriptions into text features. Furthermore, we incorporate a cross-attention mechanism within the U-Net to integrate text features. Experimental results demonstrate the effectiveness of our model, showcasing its ability to generate high-fidelity face photos while surpassing alternative methods in qualitative and quantitative evaluations.

Keywords: Diffusion Models · Face Sketch-Photo Synthesis · Text-to-Image Synthesis

1 Introduction

Face sketch-photo synthesis involves the conversion of face images from the sketch domain to the photo domain and vice versa. This task holds significant practical implications [17,43]. One notable application lies in law enforcement [29], where artists generate sketches of suspects based on verbal descriptions provided by witnesses, aiding in suspect identification. However, the inherent disparity between face photos and face sketches often results in inaccuracies when utilizing photo-based face recognition methods [8,9]. Consequently, the concept of face sketch-photo synthesis emerged to bridge this domain gap and enhance the precision of comparing similarities between face sketches and photos.

Recent research has focused on the development of methods utilizing Generative Adversarial Networks (GANs) [6]. These methods train the generator through a combination of adversarial loss and reconstruction loss. Through experimentation with various model architectures, these techniques have demonstrated enhanced performance levels on benchmark datasets. For example, Wang et al. [31] introduced a multi-adversarial network designed for synthesizing images across different scales. Zhang et al. [38] proposed a multi-domain adversarial learning approach to facilitate cross-domain mapping. In addition, Yu et al. [34] presented a composition-aided generative adversarial network to leverage facial composition information. Nonetheless, the effectiveness of these GAN-based methodologies is hindered by challenges in training, often leading to the generation of subpar quality images. Furthermore, sketches are inherently limited in conveying color information such as skin tone and hair color. Consequently, this deficiency may contribute to the production of synthesized images with erroneous color information, thereby negatively impacting the accuracy of face recognition.

To address the limitations inherent in the aforementioned methodologies, we introduce an innovative framework based on Diffusion Probability Models (DPMs) for synthesizing fine-grained face photos from input sketches and textual descriptions. Our framework adopts the standard diffusion denoising approach and integrates a Sketch Semantic Encoder alongside a cross-attention mechanism. These components facilitate the extraction of sketch features and the integration of comprehensive textual information, respectively. The Sketch Semantic Encoder employs the structural architecture of the down-sampling section within a U-Net model. This structure is enhanced through the incorporation of an additional down-sampling block, which compresses the 3-dimensional feature map into a singular 1-dimensional vector. To maximize the utility of the features extracted by the Sketch Semantic Encoder, we have introduced a straightforward technique named **Semantic Control**. This technique effectively integrates these features into the U-Net architecture. During the training process, a batch of noisy face photos, accompanied by corresponding sketch images and textual descriptions, are input into the denoising network. This network is subsequently trained to accurately predict the noise terms that were initially introduced to the face photos. In the generation phase, the framework initiates with pure Gaussian noise and progressively eliminates the noise components estimated by the conditioned denoising network. The final outcome is a noise-free facial photograph that aligns seamlessly with the provided sketch and text conditions.

Furthermore, the stochastic nature of DPMs makes it inherently capable of generating diverse results. Even conditioned on the same pair of face sketch and text, the output face photos will differ with different initial Gaussian noises or different sample strategies. In addition, the sample strategy is also highly related to the convergence of the sample results, where small sampling steps will produce higher image quality generally. During the training stage, we adopt the strategy from [12] that random drops text condition with probability p. This strategy allows more free text control, i.e., the proposed model is capable of synthesizing high-quality face photo images with or without text condition, as shown in Fig. 4. Besides, we also adopt the Diffusion Denoising Implicit Model (DDIM) [27] sample strategy, which achieves better balance between sample speed and sample quality.

We conduct experiments on the CUFS [32] dataset. Both quantitative and qualitative results demonstrates our framework can generate high-fidelity and fine-grained face photos conditioned on face sketches and text descriptions, achieving superior performance compared with previous methods.

Furthermore, the intrinsic stochastic nature of DPMs inherently empowers it to yield diverse outcomes. Even when conditioned on identical face sketch and text pairs, the resultant face photos will exhibit variations due to disparities in initial Gaussian noises or distinct sampling strategies. Moreover, the chosen sampling strategy significantly impacts the convergence of sample outcomes, wherein longer sampling steps tend to yield higher image quality. In the training phase, we implement a strategy derived from [12], which introduces a probability p of randomly omitting the text condition. This technique affords greater flexibility in textual control, enabling our proposed model to generate high-quality face photos with or without the presence of textual conditions, as exemplified in Fig. 4. Additionally, we incorporate the sampling strategy from the Diffusion Denoising Implicit Model (DDIM) [27], which strikes a harmonious balance between sample speed and quality.

Our experimental evaluation is conducted using the CUFS [32] dataset. Both quantitative and qualitative assessments unequivocally demonstrate the prowess of our framework in producing high-fidelity and fine-grained face photos, guided by face sketches and textual descriptions. Our method achieving superior performance compared with previous methods.

The main contributions of our work are summarized as follows:

- We introduce a novel face sketch-text conditioned diffusion probabilistic model. This innovative model possesses the capability to generate high-fidelity face photos guided by provided face sketches and text descriptions.
- In pursuit of improved identity preservation, we present Semantic Control—an uncomplicated yet highly effective approach to seamlessly incorporate sketch semantic features into the framework of DPMs.
- Extensive experiments on the benchmark datasets demonstrate the effectiveness of the proposed framework, achieving new state-of-the-art performance on the quantitative evaluations.

2 Related Work

Face Sketch-Photo Synthesis. The initial explorations within this field predominantly centered on sampler-based methodologies [32,33,40]. These methods operate by assembling images through the combination of patches extracted from a training dataset. This approach often involves the application of Markov random field (MRF) or Markov weight field (MWF) models. For instance, Wang et al. [32] employed an MRF approach to select potential image patch candidates. Meanwhile, Xiao et al. [33] focused on the selection of patches within the subspace of either sketches or photographs. Building upon this foundation, Zhou et al. [40] advanced the field by introducing an MWF model. An alternative direction was pursued by Peng et al. [20], who proposed a super-pixel-based method for segmenting images into patches. However, these methodologies are burdened with several limitations. Particularly, they struggle to identify an optimal composition of patches for the synthesis of high-quality images, frequently giving rise to evident seams or other undesirable artifacts. More recently, the landscape has witnessed the emergence of numerous deep learning-based approaches [31,34,35,42,43]. For instance, Wang et al. [31] introduced a multiple-discriminator network that leverages adversarial supervision within hidden states. Similarly, Zhu et al. [43] proposed a knowledge transfer framework aimed at training task-specific student networks via pre-trained teacher networks. Addressing the domain of style transfer, Peng et al. [21] devised a universal face photo-sketch style transfer framework devoid of source domain training requirements. Concurrently, researchers have concentrated on the preservation of intricate facial features and identity information. Lin et al. [15], [?] introduced identity-aware models and feature injection techniques. In a parallel pursuit, Duan et al. [5] advanced a multi-scale self-attention residual learning framework that harnesses features at various scales. A recent addition by Yu et al. [35] encompasses the development of an efficient transformer-based network tailored to face sketch-photo synthesis. Despite these advancements, the recurrent utilization of adversarial training techniques within these approaches often engenders training instability, thereby yielding suboptimal outcomes of reduced quality.

Diffusion Probability Models. Diffusion Probability Models (DPMs) [11,26] learn a parameterized Markov chain to map a Gaussian distribution to a target data distribution, and generates high-quality samples through sequential stochastic transitions. By using maximum likelihood training instead of the adversarial training, DPMs produce high-quality and diverse images. These methods have been shown to outperform GANs on many image generative benchmarks [4,27,28]. While many text-conditional DPMs [7,19,24] have been proposed for text-to-image synthesis. And several works [1,30] have explored the application of DPMs in synthesizing objectives of nature scenario images conditioned on sketch images. However, there are few discussion regarding text-conditioned face sketch-photo synthesis.

Image to Image Translation. In the field of image-to-image translation, a series of recent studies have effectively showcased the efficacy of Diffusion Probability Models (DPMs) [2,3,14,18,25,39]. methods. For instance, Choi et al. [2] introduced a pioneering training-free approach for image-to-image translation. Their methodology harnesses a pre-trained DPMs, wherein the noise terms estimated at each step of the sample process are substituted with corresponding information extracted from the noised input images. This strategy effectively steers the DPMs towards generating high-quality images, obviating the necessity for additional training efforts. Similarly, Meng et al. [18] devised a training-free technique that samples an image from a noised input image, resulting in output images harmonizing with the semantic attributes of the input images. In the pursuit of meaningful latent representations, Preechakul et al. [22] proposed Diffusion Autoencoder. This innovation employs a DPMs-based methodology to encode images into two-part latent codes and subsequently reconstructs images from these latent codes. This not only facilitates image manipulation but also extends readily to various image-to-image translation tasks. Collectively, these studies underscore the versatility and potential of DPM-based techniques in delivering results that stand on par with prevailing image-to-image translation approaches. Moreover, supplementary contributions by Saharia et al. [25], Li et al. [14], Chung et al. [3], and Zhao et al. [39] reinforce the efficacy of DPM-based methods across diverse image-to-image translation tasks, thereby accentuating their value within the domain.

3   Methods

In this paper, we introduce the **F**ace **S**ketch-**T**ext Guided **D**iffusion (**FSTD**) framework, a pioneering approach for generating face images conditioned on both face sketches and text descriptions using diffusion probabilistic models. Our framework excels in producing high-fidelity face images by leveraging the provided face sketch and corresponding text description. The subsequent sections of this paper are structured as follows: Firstly, we provide a concise overview of conditional denoising diffusion probabilistic models. Subsequently, we elucidate the architecture and design specifics underpinning the proposed framework.

3.1   Preliminaries

We first briefly review the theory of conditional diffusion probabilistic models. Consider x_0 as a data point drawn from the conditional distribution $p(x_0|y)$. The forward diffusion process mirrors the unconditional diffusion model, resembling a Markov chain that gradually introduces noise to x_0 during successive time steps, denoted as t:

$$q\left(x_T \mid x_0\right) := \prod_{t=1}^{T} q\left(x_t \mid x_{t-1}\right), \tag{1}$$

$$q\left(x_t \mid x_{t-1}\right) := \mathcal{N}\left(x_t; \sqrt{1-\beta_t}x_{t-1}, \beta_t \mathbf{I}\right), \tag{2}$$

where β is a set of pre-defined sample schedule constants and $\beta_t \in (0,1)$. With the notation $\alpha_t := 1 - \beta_t$ and $\overline{\alpha_t} := \prod_{s=1}^{t} \alpha_s$, the multi-step forward processes can be defined in one step:

$$q\left(x_T \mid x_0\right) := \mathcal{N}\left(x_t; \sqrt{\bar{\alpha}_t}x_0, \sqrt{1-\bar{\alpha}_t}\mathbf{I}\right) \tag{3}$$

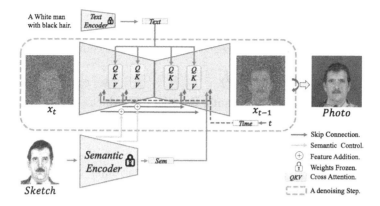

Fig. 1. Architecture of proposed framework, When provided with a face sketch and a corresponding text description, our proposed model can produce a fine-grained face photo that aligns with both the contour of the sketch and the given text description, after undergoing sufficient denoising steps.

Accordingly, the reverse process of conditional diffusion model is a approximated Markov chain with learned Gaussian transition, by starting from $p\left(\mathbf{x}_T\right) = \mathcal{N}(x_T; 0, \boldsymbol{I})$:

$$p_\theta\left(\mathbf{x}_{0:T} \mid \mathbf{y}\right) = p\left(\mathbf{x}_T\right) \prod_{t=1}^{T} p_\theta\left(\mathbf{x}_{t-1} \mid \mathbf{x}_t, \mathbf{y}\right), \tag{4}$$

$$p_\theta\left(\mathbf{x}_{t-1} \mid \mathbf{x}_t, \mathbf{y}\right) = \mathcal{N}\left(\mathbf{x}_{t-1}; \boldsymbol{\mu}_\theta\left(\mathbf{x}_t, \mathbf{y}, t\right), \sigma_t^2 \boldsymbol{I}\right), \tag{5}$$

where

$$\boldsymbol{\mu}_\theta\left(\mathbf{x}_t, \mathbf{y}, t\right) := \frac{1}{\sqrt{\alpha_t}}\left(\boldsymbol{x}_t - \frac{1-\alpha_t}{\sqrt{1-\bar{\alpha}_t}}\epsilon_\theta\left(\boldsymbol{x}_t, \mathbf{y}, t\right)\right). \tag{6}$$

Here, $\epsilon_\theta\left(\boldsymbol{x}_t, \mathbf{y}, t\right)$ is the conditional diffusion model trained to optimize the following objective:

$$L(\theta) = \mathbb{E}_{t,y,x_0,\epsilon}\left[\|\epsilon - \epsilon_\theta\left(\boldsymbol{x}_t, \mathbf{y}, t\right)\|^2\right], \tag{7}$$

where $\epsilon \sim \mathcal{N}(\mathbf{0}, \boldsymbol{I})$, and it is the noise term used in (3) for sampling x_t.

3.2   Face Sketch-Text Guided Diffusion

Figure 1 illustrates the sampling procedure of proposed FSTD framework. The framework combines a U-Net for noise estimation, a text encoder, and a semantic encoder for face sketch-text conditioning. In addition, a straightforward operation called Semantic Control was proposed for integrating sketch semantic information. It is worth noting that our U-Net design follows the architecture of the DPMs standard framework, and the detailed structure can be referenced in [11, 22].

Semantic Encoder. Given a paired data $(x, y, text)$, where $x \in \mathbb{R}^{C \times H \times W}$ is the face photo, $y \in \mathbb{R}^{C \times H \times W}$ is the face sketch and $text$ is the text prompt of the face, the face sketch y will be encoded into a latent code:

$$f_y = Enc(y), \tag{8}$$

where Enc is an off-the-shelf Semantic Encoder [22], which can extract semantic information from the input sketch images, and $f_y \in \mathbb{R}^D$ is the semantic feature of the face sketch.

Semantic Control. We introduce a Semantic Controlling into the U-Net. This is able to replace the time consuming DDIM encoding operation, while the semantic details are maintained. In Fig. 2, we demonstrates how the Semantic Controlling is performed. The skip connection in the U-Net not only using the information from the down sample block but the features of the Semantic Encoder at same scale. This requires that the **Semantic Encoder** not only output the semantic feature vector f_y but the intermediate feature maps:

$$f_y, m_y = Enc(y), \tag{9}$$

where m_y is a set of the intermediate feature maps of the Semantic Encoder in different scale.

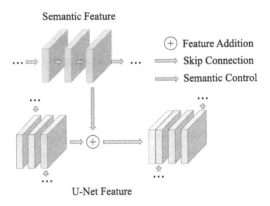

Fig. 2. Illustration of Semantic Control.

Text Control. For text controlling, we first use a CLIP text encoder [23] for encoding a text description into a text feature:

$$f_{text} = CLIP(text). \tag{10}$$

For integrating text feature, we deploy cross attention mechanism in the U-Net. Notably, our cross attention operations are only used in specific intermediate feature maps, in our case, we only use it when spacial resolution of the feature maps is 16×16, for balancing computational consumption and performance.

$$h = CrossAttn(h, f_{text})$$
$$= Softmax(Q(h), K(f_{text})^T) \cdot V(f_{text}), \tag{11}$$

where h are the specific intermediate feature maps in the U-Net.

Loss Functions. The training of our **FSTD** only need a Mean-Squared Error (MSE) loss. While the paired data $(x, y, text)$ is given, the face photo will be noised with a standard Gaussian noise:

$$x_t = \sqrt{\bar{\alpha}_t} x_0 + \sqrt{1 - \bar{\alpha}_t} \epsilon, \tag{12}$$

where $\epsilon \sim \mathcal{N}(\mathbf{0}, \mathbf{I})$, α_t is the same schedule constants defined in (3), and t is the time step random sampled from $\{0, 1, ..., T\}$.

An one-step noise estimating of our conditional diffusion model is formulated as:

$$\hat{\epsilon} = \epsilon_\theta(x_t, f_y, m_y, f_{text}, t), \tag{13}$$

where f_y, m_y and f_{text} are the features extracted from (9) and (10) separately. And the MSE loss computed via:

$$\mathcal{L}_{MSE} = \mathbb{E}_\epsilon \left[\|\hat{\epsilon} - \epsilon\|^2 \right]. \tag{14}$$

Flexible Guidance. Previous work [12] trained a weights-shared diffusion model for classifier-free guidance, using both conditional and unconditional models to generate a sample. We adopt this strategy for flexibly controlling of text prompts. In the training procedure, we randomly replaced text conditions with an empty string with a probability of p, where we set to 0.1 in our experiments, and during sampling. This allows our FSTD to produce face photos with only the face sketch guidance while the text descriptions are not provided. Our training procedure is detailed in Algorithm 1.

Algorithm 1. Training Procedure.

1: **while** not converged **do**
2:      $(\mathbf{x}, \mathbf{y}, \mathbf{text}) \sim \mathbf{Data}(\mathcal{D})$;
3:      $\epsilon \sim \mathcal{N}(0, \mathbf{I}), t \sim$ uniform$\{1, 2, ..., T\}$;
4:      $\mathbf{text} = (\mathbf{text})$ if rand() > 0.1, else $(\emptyset)$;
5:      $\mathbf{x_t} = \sqrt{\alpha_t} \mathbf{x} + \sqrt{1 - \alpha_t} \epsilon$;
6:      $\mathcal{L}_{\mathrm{MSE}} = \mathbb{E}_\epsilon \left[\|\epsilon_\theta(x_t, \mathbf{y}, \mathbf{text}, t) - \epsilon\|^2 \right]$;
7:      Take a gradient descent step on $\nabla_\theta \mathcal{L}_{\mathrm{MSE}}$
8: **end while**

Algorithm 2. DDIM Sample with CFG.

Input: $y, text,$ and CFG weight: w

1: $x_T \sim \mathcal{N}(0, \mathbf{I})$;
2: **for** $t = T, \ldots, 1$ **do**
3:    $\hat{\epsilon}_c = \epsilon_\theta(x_t, y, text, t)$;   ▷ Text conditional
4:    $\hat{\epsilon}_u = \epsilon_\theta(x_t, y, t)$;   ▷ Text unconditional
5:    $\hat{\epsilon} = (1 + w)\hat{\epsilon}_c - w\hat{\epsilon}_u$;
6:    $\hat{x}_0 = \frac{1}{\bar{\alpha}_t}(x_t - \sqrt{1 - \bar{\alpha}_t}\hat{\epsilon})$;   ▷ Predict x_0
7:    $x_{t-1} = \sqrt{\bar{\alpha}_{t-1}}\hat{x}_0 + \sqrt{1 - \bar{\alpha}_{t-1}}\hat{\epsilon}$;
8: **end for**

---
return x_0

DDIM Sample. DDIM [27] introduced a new sample strategy with faster convergence speed. This strategy only requires modifications to some terms in the original DDPM sample strategy. The sample processes for both DDPM and DDIM are presented in (15) and (16), respectively. The DDIM sample process involves using the estimated noise $\hat{\epsilon}$ from (13) and predicting the clean image x_0 by one-step denoising, i.e., $\frac{1}{\bar{\alpha}_t}(x_t - \sqrt{1 - \bar{\alpha}_t}\hat{\epsilon})$, which is the reverse version of (12).

$$x_{t-1} = \frac{1}{\sqrt{\alpha_t}}\left(x_t - \frac{1 - \alpha_t}{\sqrt{1 - \bar{\alpha}_t}}\hat{\epsilon}\right) + \sigma_t^2\epsilon, \tag{15}$$

$$x_{t-1} = \sqrt{\frac{\bar{\alpha}_{t-1}}{\bar{\alpha}_t}}\left(x_t - \sqrt{1 - \bar{\alpha}_t}\hat{\epsilon}\right) + \sqrt{1 - \bar{\alpha}_{t-1}}\hat{\epsilon}, \tag{16}$$

where $\hat{\epsilon}$ is the estimated noise obtained in (13). The detailed DDIM sample procedure with Classifier-free guidance is presented in Algorithm 2.

4   Experiments

4.1   Experimental Settings

Datasets. We mainly conducting our experiments on the Chinese University of Hong Kong Face Sketch (CUFS) dataset [32]. This dataset encompasses 606 well-aligned face photo-sketch pairs derived from three distinct subsets: 188 pairs from the CUHK student dataset, 123 pairs from the AR dataset, and 295 pairs from the XM2VTS dataset. Each face photo-sketch pair consists of a face sketch, meticulously hand-drawn by an artist to match the corresponding frontal face photo, taken under normal lighting conditions. We follow the setting in previous work [34], using 268 face photo-sketch pairs for training and the rest 338 pairs for testing. However the original version of the CUFS dataset has no text descriptions for face photos, thus we label the captions by the attributes predicted from a multiple face attributes classification model.

Implementation Details. Our model was implemented using the PyTorch framework and the experiments were conducted on an NVIDIA TITAN RTX GPU. Given the challenge of training diffusion models with limited data, we leveraged pre-trained weights from the FFHQ dataset [22] to enhance training stability. Throughout the experiments, we fine-tuned the model utilizing an AdamW optimizer [16] with betas set to (0.9, 0.999). The learning rate was configured at 0.0001, the batch size was established as 16, and a total of 100,000 iterative steps were executed for training. During the training process, we integrated an exponential moving average (EMA) mechanism with a decay factor of 0.9999 to facilitate updates to the denoising network weights.

Criteria. This study employs three performance metrics to comprehensively assess the effectiveness of our proposed method. These metrics encompass the Fréchet Inception distance (FID) [10] for gauging visual quality, the Feature Similarity Index Metric (FSIM) [36] for quantifying the similarity between generated face photos and authentic face photos, and the Learned Perceptual Image Patch Similarity (LPIPS) [37] for evaluating image diversity. To ensure a thorough evaluation, we compute the LPIPS value using three distinct classification networks: AlexNet, SqueezeNet, and VGGNet.

Table 1. Quantitative comparison of face photos synthesized on the CUFS Dataset. The best and second best of each metrics will be highlighted in **boldface** and underline format, respectively. ↓ indicates the lower is better, and ↑ higher is better.

Methods	FID ↓	FSIM ↑	LPIPS(squeeze) ↓	LPIPS(vgg) ↓	LPIPS(alex) ↓
Pix2Pix [13]	125.00	0.7670	0.1837	0.3537	0.2005
CycleGAN [41]	104.59	0.7385	0.2100	0.3891	0.2104
PS2MAN [31]	87.68	0.7768	0.2164	0.3281	0.2471
SCA-GAN [34]	103.66	**0.7984**	<u>0.1384</u>	0.2781	0.1521
KD [42]	55.60	0.7844	0.1583	0.2862	0.1847
KDGAN [42]	<u>44.47</u>	0.7761	0.1483	<u>0.2832</u>	<u>0.1729</u>
Our	**29.47**	<u>0.7959</u>	**0.1173**	**0.2417**	**0.1331**

4.2 Comparison with Previous Methods

We compare our method with several state-of-the-art methods on face photo synthesis, and we use the results or codes of these methods released by their corresponding authors.

Comparison on CUFS Dataset. We selected six state-of-the-art methods to conduct comparisons on the CUFS dataset. These methods include CycleGAN [41], Pix2Pix [13], PS2MAN [31], SCA-GAN [34], KD [42], and KDGAN [42]. The qualitative results of the synthesized face photo images are visually presented in

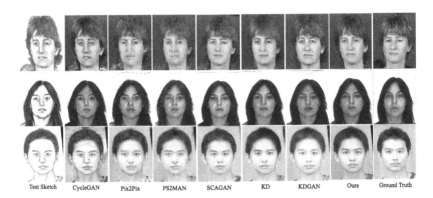

| Test Sketch | CycleGAN | Pix2Pix | PS2MAN | SCAGAN | KD | KDGAN | Ours | Ground Truth |

Fig. 3. Comparison results of synthesized face photos on the CUFS dataset. From top to bottom, the examples are selected from the XM2VTS dataset, the AR dataset, and the CUHK student dataset, separately.

Fig. 3. The synthesized results produced by CycleGAN, Pix2Pix, and PS2MAN exhibit unclear facial details, distorted colors, and messy textures. While SCA-GAN's generated photos demonstrate improved structural integrity owing to the incorporation of pixel-wise face labels during both training and inference, certain regions such as hair still suffer from suboptimal texture quality. KD yields images with fewer deformations and artifacts due to its utilization of two pretrained teacher networks to provide semantic guidance to a CNN-based student network. However, undesired artifacts on facial regions remain present. Leveraging adversarial loss during training, KDGAN enhances the perceptual quality of synthesized photos. Nevertheless, inaccuracies in color reproduction continue to impact image quality. In contrast to the aforementioned CNN-based approaches, our FSTD model excels in synthesizing more realistic face photos endowed with natural textures and well-defined details.

The quantitative assessment on the CUFS dataset is shown in Table 1. As compared to other methods, our FSTD has demonstrated a substantial decrease in the FID score to 29.47. Additionally, FSTD achieves superior scores in all three variants of LPIPS score, which is highly consistent with human perception, the lower indicating better perceptual quality of the synthesized face photos. Furthermore, the FSTD model achieved the second-best performance in the FSIM metric, just behind the result of SCA-GAN. The primary reason for this is that SCA-GAN generates a face photo not only from the input sketch but also from the facial composition of the corresponding face photo, making the synthesized results more aligned with the face photo, which can be observed in the results generated by SCA-GAN in Fig. 3. The comparison results provide compelling evidence of the superior performance of FSTD in generating high-quality face photos.

Ablation Studies. To verify the effectiveness of the incorporated components within our framework, we performed ablative experiments and conducted a comparative analysis of the outcomes. The comparison results of our ablation study

Table 2. Ablation studies on the CUFS dataset. Where SC indicates training with The Semantic Control, CA indicates training with Cross Attention, and CFG indicates training and sampling with Classifier-Free Guidance.

Settings			Metrics				
SC	CA	CFG	FID ↓	FSIM ↑	LIPIS(squeeze) ↓	LIPIS(vgg) ↓	LIPIS(alex) ↓
			<u>36.31</u>	0.7748	0.1622	0.2741	0.1407
✓			36.49	0.7933	0.1329	0.2584	0.1475
✓	✓		36.84	**0.7979**	<u>0.1251</u>	<u>0.2465</u>	<u>0.1394</u>
✓	✓	✓	**29.47**	<u>0.7959</u>	**0.1173**	**0.2417**	**0.1331**

are presented in Table 2. Our investigation underscores that the inclusion of both the Semantic Control and Cross Attention mechanisms leads to a notable improvement, with the FSIM score experiencing a substantial 2.39% increase. Furthermore, the integration of the classifier-free guidance strategy [12] yields significant improvements. Specifically, the FID score demonstrates a significant reduction from 36.84 to 29.47. Similarly, the LIPIS scores register reductions of approximately 4.49%, 3.24%, and 0.76% across different metrics. These comparative outcomes firmly establish the effectiveness of the Semantic Control, Cross Attention mechanisms, and Classifier-free guidance strategy. These components, pivotal to our proposed approach, collectively contribute to the enhanced performance observed.

Fig. 4. Illustration of diversity fine-grained face photo synthesis. (a)The comparison results of without or with text guidance. (b)The synthesized photos with different textual descriptions.

4.3   Text Control

Our FSTD framework excels in producing intricate, finely detailed face photos while being guided by diverse text prompts. Figure 4 showcases the outcomes of our synthesized face images, each corresponding to different text prompts. In

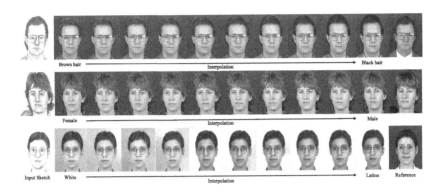

Fig. 5. Illustration of the text feature interpolation. The first column is the input face sketch, The second to eleventh columns are the images generated using different text features. And the last column is the reference images.

Fig. 4(a), the absence of a text prompt results in a neutral output due to the lack of text-derived guidance. Conversely, when specific text prompts are provided, our model adeptly generates images in line with the intended attributes. Figure 4(b) underscores our model's prowess in fine-grained face photo synthesis, enabling the creation of distinct appearances aligned with distinct text cues while retaining the core features of the original image.

To further demonstrate the text controlling ability of our model, we present interpolation results of text features in Fig. 5. These visualizations illuminate the evolution of generated images in response to varying text features. These results emphasize our model's ability to seamlessly produce realistic images based on interpolated text features.

5   Conclusions

In this paper, we propose a novel framework named Face Sketch-Text Guided Diffusion (FSTD) for face sketch-photo synthesis. Specifically, the use of Semantic Control and Cross Attention mechanisms in the proposed network makes our FSTD is able to fully take advantage of the semantic information extracted from the input face sketch and the global style information of the input text prompts while generating a fine-grained face photo. Furthermore, we introduce classifier-free guidance into our training and sampling procedure, which improves the flexibility of text control and significantly decreases the FID score and LIPIS metrics. Extensive experiments on the benchmark datasets demonstrate the effectiveness of our method. Our method achieves state-of-the-art performance in terms of FID and LPIPS metrics and shows better visual quality of synthetic images compared with previous methods.

Acknowledgment. This research is supported in part by the National Natural Science Foundation of China under grants No. 62206277 and No. 62006228, and in part by the Youth Innovation Promotion Association CAS (Grant No. 2022132).

References

1. Cheng, S.I., Chen, Y.J., Chiu, W.C., Tseng, H.Y., Lee, H.Y.: Adaptively-realistic image generation from stroke and sketch with diffusion model. In: WACV (2023)
2. Choi, J., Kim, S., Jeong, Y., Gwon, Y., Yoon, S.: Ilvr: conditioning method for denoising diffusion probabilistic models. In: ICCV (2021)
3. Chung, H., Sim, B., Ryu, D., Ye, J.C.: Improving diffusion models for inverse problems using manifold constraints. In: NeurIPS (2022)
4. Dhariwal, P., Nichol, A.: Diffusion models beat GANs on image synthesis. In: NeurIPS, vol. 34 (2021)
5. Duan, S., Chen, Z., Wu, Q.M.J., Cai, L., Lu, D.: Multi-scale gradients self-attention residual learning for face photo-sketch transformation. In: IEEE TIFS (2021)
6. Goodfellow, I.J., et al.: Generative adversarial networks. arXiv preprint arXiv:1406.2661 (2014)
7. Gu, S., et al.: Vector quantized diffusion model for text-to-image synthesis. In: CVPR (2022)
8. He, R., Hu, B.-G., Yuan, X.-T.: Robust discriminant analysis based on nonparametric maximum entropy. In: Zhou, Z.-H., Washio, T. (eds.) ACML 2009. LNCS (LNAI), vol. 5828, pp. 120–134. Springer, Heidelberg (2009). https://doi.org/10.1007/978-3-642-05224-8_11
9. He, R., Zhang, M., Wang, L., Ji, Y., Yin, Q.: Cross-modal subspace learning via pairwise constraints. IEEE Trans. Image Process. **24**(12), 5543–5556 (2015)
10. Heusel, M., Ramsauer, H., Unterthiner, T., Nessler, B., Hochreiter, S.: GANs trained by a two time-scale update rule converge to a local NASH equilibrium. In: NeurIPS (2017)
11. Ho, J., Jain, A., Abbeel, P.: Denoising diffusion probabilistic models. In: NeurIPS (2020)
12. Ho, J., Salimans, T.: Classifier-free diffusion guidance. In: NeurIPSW (2021)
13. Isola, P., Zhu, J.Y., Zhou, T., Efros, A.A.: Image-to-image translation with conditional adversarial networks. In: CVPR (2017)
14. Li, H., Yang, Y., Chang, M., Chen, S., Feng, H., Xu, Z., Li, Q., Chen, Y.: SRDiff: single image super-resolution with diffusion probabilistic models. In: Neurocomputing (2022)
15. Lin, Y., Ling, S., Fu, K., Cheng, P.: An identity-preserved model for face sketch-photo synthesis. In: IEEE LSP (2020)
16. Loshchilov, I., Hutter, F.: Decoupled weight decay regularization. In: ICLR (2019)
17. Luo, M., Wu, H., Huang, H., He, W., He, R.: Memory-modulated transformer network for heterogeneous face recognition. In: IEEE TIFS (2022)
18. Meng, C., et al.: SDEdit: guided image synthesis and editing with stochastic differential equations. In: ICLR (2021)
19. Nichol, A., et al.: Glide: towards photorealistic image generation and editing with text-guided diffusion models. In: ICML (2022)
20. Peng, C., Gao, X., Wang, N., Li, J.: Superpixel-based face sketch–photo synthesis. In: IEEE TCSVT (2017)
21. Peng, C., Wang, N., Li, J., Gao, X.: Universal face photo-sketch style transfer via multiview domain translation. In: IEEE TIP (2020)

22. Preechakul, K., Chatthee, N., Wizadwongsa, S., Suwajanakorn, S.: Diffusion autoencoders: toward a meaningful and decodable representation. In: CVPR (2022)
23. Radford, A., et al.: Learning transferable visual models from natural language supervision. In: ICML (2021)
24. Rombach, R., Blattmann, A., Lorenz, D., Esser, P., Ommer, B.: High-resolution image synthesis with latent diffusion models. In: CVPR (2022)
25. Saharia, C., Ho, J., Chan, W., Salimans, T., Fleet, D.J., Norouzi, M.: Image super-resolution via iterative refinement. In: IEEE TPAMI (2022)
26. Sohl-Dickstein, J., Weiss, E., Maheswaranathan, N., Ganguli, S.: Deep unsupervised learning using nonequilibrium thermodynamics. In: ICML (2015)
27. Song, J., Meng, C., Ermon, S.: Denoising diffusion implicit models. In: ICLR (2021)
28. Song, Y., Sohl-Dickstein, J., Kingma, D.P., Kumar, A., Ermon, S., Poole, B.: Score-based generative modeling through stochastic differential equations. In: ICLR (2021)
29. Tang, X., Wang, X.: Face sketch recognition. In: IEEE TCSVT (2004)
30. Voynov, A., Aberman, K., Cohen-Or, D.: Sketch-guided text-to-image diffusion models. arXiv preprint arXiv:2211.13752 (2022)
31. Wang, L., Sindagi, V., Patel, V.: High-quality facial photo-sketch synthesis using multi-adversarial networks. In: FG (2018)
32. Wang, X., Tang, X.: Face photo-sketch synthesis and recognition. In: IEEE TPAMI (2008)
33. Xiao, B., Gao, X., Tao, D., Yuan, Y., Li, J.: Photo-sketch synthesis and recognition based on subspace learning. In: Neurocomputing (2010)
34. Yu, J., et al.: Toward realistic face photo–sketch synthesis via composition-aided GANs. In: IEEE TCYB (2021)
35. Yu, W., Zhu, M., Wang, N., Wang, X., Gao, X.: An efficient transformer based on global and local self-attention for face photo-sketch synthesis. In: IEEE TIP (2023)
36. Zhang, L., Zhang, L., Mou, X., Zhang, D.: FSIM: a feature similarity index for image quality assessment. In: IEEE TIP (2011)
37. Zhang, R., Isola, P., Efros, A.A., Shechtman, E., Wang, O.: The unreasonable effectiveness of deep features as a perceptual metric. In: CVPR (2018)
38. Zhang, S., Ji, R., Hu, J., Lu, X., Li, X.: Face sketch synthesis by multidomain adversarial learning. In: IEEE TNNLS (2018)
39. Zhao, M., Bao, F., Li, C., Zhu, J.: EGSDE: unpaired image-to-image translation via energy-guided stochastic differential equations. In: NeurIPS (2022)
40. Zhou, H., Kuang, Z., Wong, K.Y.K.: Markov weight fields for face sketch synthesis. In: CVPR (2012)
41. Zhu, J.Y., Park, T., Isola, P., Efros, A.A.: Unpaired image-to-image translation using cycle-consistent adversarial networks. In: ICCV (2017)
42. Zhu, M., Li, J., Wang, N., Gao, X.: Knowledge distillation for face photo–sketch synthesis. In: IEEE TNNLS (2022)
43. Zhu, M., Wang, N., Gao, X., Li, J., Li, Z.: Face photo-sketch synthesis via knowledge transfer. In: IJCAI (2019)

MMFA-Net: A New Brain Tumor Segmentation Method Based on Multi-modal Multi-scale Feature Aggregation

Yulin Dong[1], Zhizhuo Jiang[1], and Yu Liu[2(✉)]

[1] Tsinghua Shenzhen International Graduate School, Shenzhen, China
dongyl21@mails.tsinghua.edu.cn, jiangzhizhuo@sz.tsinghua.edu.cn
[2] Department of Electronic Engineering, Tsinghua University, Beijing, China
liuyu77360132@126.com

Abstract. Precise brain tumor segmentation is crucial for brain cancer diagnosis. Magnetic resonance imaging (MRI) plays an essential role in tumor segmentation due to the abundant information in multi-model data. However, current deep learning-based image segmentation methods expose their limitations in fully extracting and utilizing the comprehensive information from multi-modal MRI. To tackle this issue, we propose a multi-modal multi-scale feature aggregation network (MMFA-Net) for brain tumor segmentation in MRI images. A well-designed dual-branch framework employing spatial location activation (SPA) module is proposed in MMFA-Net to share the location information of the lesion area extracted by each branch. Moreover, the multi-scale feature aggregation (MFA) module is developed to fuse the global and local information to improve the performance of brain tumor segmentation. Extensive experimental results based on the public BraTS2020, BraTS2021, and ISBI datasets indicate that the proposed MMFA-Net exhibits superior performance compared to several state-of-the-art methods in the domain of multi-modal brain tumor segmentation. This superiority is most evident in the Dice Score and 95%-Hausdorff Distance (HD95) metrics, where MMFA-Net demonstrates an average improvement of 2.5% in the Dice score on tumor segmentation.

Keywords: Brain tumor segmentation · Multi-model MRI fusion · Multi-scale feature aggregation

1 Introduction

Since the beginning of the 20th century, malignant tumors have become the "number one killer" that threatens human health, with the highest mortality

---

Y. Dong and Z. Jiang—Contributed equally.

© The Author(s), under exclusive license to Springer Nature Switzerland AG 2023
H. Lu et al. (Eds.): ACPR 2023, LNCS 14407, pp. 355–366, 2023.
https://doi.org/10.1007/978-3-031-47637-2_27

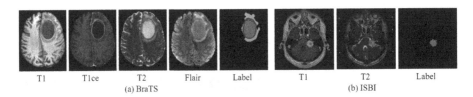

T1   T1ce   T2   Flair   Label   T1   T2   Label

(a) BraTS   (b) ISBI

Fig. 1. Multi-modal MRIs for (a) BraTS; and (b) ISBI.

rate among all causes of death [13,16]. Brain tumors, one of the most common types of cancer in the world, seriously endanger people's lives [8]. In today's clinical diagnosis of brain tumors, multi-modal MRI has been widely used by doctors due to its high resolution and clear soft tissue structure, allowing them to obtain important information about tumors, including size and shape. Meanwhile, MRI is safe because of its protection from ionizing radiation [2]. Therefore, MRI has been widely adopted in brain tumor imaging. When using MRI for brain tumors, four different modalities of images can be obtained by changing the imaging parameters, including T1 image, T2 image, T1c image, and FLAIR image (MRI images of different modalities and their segmentation pictures are showed in Fig. 1). Multiple modalities of images show different properties in different lesion areas. Brain tumor images based on multi-modal MRI allow doctors to obtain more information and make adequate judgments according to the boundary and morphology of the tumor lesion areas. Therefore, automatic brain tumor segmentation will greatly help doctors improve the speed, difficulty, and accuracy of diagnosis, and it has strong practical significance.

In recent years, with the development of deep learning, convolutional neural networks have achieved outstanding results in image segmentation. Among them, U-Net [11] has shown powerful ability in the field of medical image segmentation. And its encoder-decoder with skip-connection architecture has become the mainstream framework for brain tumor segmentation. Many subsequent network models use it as the backbone network and achieve satisfactory performance, such as 3D UNet [4], SegResNet [9] and nnUNet [6]. Recently, with the rise of Transformer [14], Transformer-based models have achieved state-of-the-art performance in many fields. Recent studies have applied transformers to their own networks in tumor segmentation tasks [14], such as SwinUNet [3], UNETR [5] and SegTransVAE [10]. In the realm of image segmentation, SwinUNet [3] constructs a symmetric encoder-decoder framework with skip connections, which is centered around the Swin Transformer block. This architecture incorporates a local-to-global self-attention scheme within the encoder. In the decoding phase, global characteristics are up-scaled to match the input resolution, thereby facilitating precise pixel-level segmentation predictions. Alternatively, UNETR [5] employs a standalone transformer in its encoder structure to extract contextual information from embedded input patches. The learned representations, sourced from the transformer encoder, are then integrated with the decoder through multi-resolution skip connections, consequently enabling the generation of segmentation outcomes. A different approach is taken by SegTransVAE [10] which bases its architecture on the encoder-decoder model. This method effectively utilizes a transformer coupled with a variational autoencoder (VAE) branch. The addition of the VAE branch to the network permits the concurrent reconstruction of input images and the execution of segmentation. This composition results in a unique method of segmenting and reconstructing input data. However, the above-mentioned methods only enhance the effect of the feature extraction, and ignore the fusion of the complementary characteristics of multi-modal MRI data.

To effectively integrate the semantic information from multiple modalities of MRI data, recent methods have applied fusion processing at different stages in the network. Some methods join different modality data at the input stage, known as early fusion, but neglect potential connections between the modalities. To leverage the entirety of available information, certain methodologies adopt a mid-fusion approach. This approach fuses modality-specific features extracted by disparate encoders at an intermediate stage within the network. As an exemplar, NestedFormer [17] employs nested multi-modal fusion on high-level features derived from various modalities, based on a multi-encoder and single-decoder architecture. Furthermore, it utilizes modality-sensitive gating at lower scales to enhance the efficiency of skip connections. Nevertheless, existing methods ignore the relationship between features with various scales.

In this paper, we propose MMFA-Net, a new multi-modal multi-scale medical image segmentation network for brain tumor segmentation. Firstly, a dual-branch network structure is designed to independently extract features from MRI images in different modalities. Secondly, we design the Spatial Position Activation (SPA) module between two encoder branches to improve the feature extraction. This module enables that the information extracted from one branch guides the feature extraction of another branch by fusing the knowledge of approximate tumor position. SPA allows MMFA-Net focus on the salient features at the same time in corresponding regions of different modalities. Furthermore, multi-scale feature aggregation (MFA) module is designed to fuse multi-scale features of multi-modal data. The channel and spatial attention is used as a parallel structure to better utilize the different dimensional information of data in different modalities for downstream tasks. Extensive experiments on three brain tumor segmentation datasets: BraTS2020 [7], BraTS20211 [1], and ISBI [12] demonstrate that MMFA-Net exhibits outstanding performance across various training data volumes, outperforming the state-of-the-art methods in the Dice metric and HD95 metric.

2 Method

In this section, the proposed multi-modal medical image segmentation network, i.e., MMFA-Net is elaborated. The architecture of MMFA-Net is shown in Fig. 2. The main contributions of this work can be summarized in the following three aspects 1) the dual-branch network (DBN) is well-designed to extract the specific features corresponding to different modality, which promotes MMFA-Net to capture information from multi-modal MRI data. 2) the spatial position activation

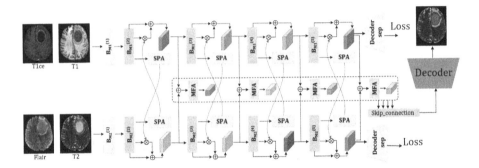

Fig. 2. An overview of the proposed MMFA-Net. $B_{M1}^{(i)}$ and $B_{M2}^{(i)} (i \in \{1, 2, 3, 4, 5\})$ are independent convolution blocks, SPA is Spatial Position Activation module, and MFA is Multi-scale Feature Aggregation module. $\oplus$ is broadcast element-wise addition, and $\otimes$ is matrix multiplication.

(SPA) module is developed to fuse the position information of different modalities, thereby improving the accuracy. and 3) the multi-scale feature aggregation (MFA) module is proposed to capture global and local information by concatenating the features of different scales. We will elaborate them in the following.

2.1 Dual-Branch Network

This work focuses on multi-modal medical image segmentation using MRI data, which typically includes four modalities: T1, T2, T1c, and Flair. T1 and T2 modalities are often used in daily clinical diagnosis because more information can be obtained by comparing the two modalities. Therefore, we merge T1 and T1c modalities into one branch, T2 and Flair modalities are combined as the input of another branch, as shown in Fig. 2. Inspired by the Nestedformer [17], we employ a dual-branch network that can independently extract modality-specific features from data in different modalities. In medical images, the detailed information such as contour position play a crucial role in accurate segmentation. To extract these details, convolution is used in the encoding stage. The local receptive field of convolution effectively captures such detailed information. Moreover, sharing parameters among convolutional layers can significantly reduce the network's parameters. In the proposed MMFA-Net, 3D U-Net [4] is employed as the backbone network in the encoder part. The two branches of the new MMFA-Net are indicated as M1 and M2, in which the independent convolution blocks are denoted by $B_{M1}^{(i)} (i \in \{1, 2, 3, 4, 5\})$ and $B_{M2}^{(i)} (i \in \{1, 2, 3, 4, 5\})$ respectively.

The features extracted from each branch in our dual-branch network are directly transferred into the decoder without any fusion. Thus, the original characteristics of multi-modal data are preserved. The architecture of the decoding module closely resembles that of the 3D U-Net [4], which upsamples the feature map to match the size of the input image. The loss of the two branches is calculated and compose the overall loss to enhance the accuracy of the predictions.

2.2 Spatial Position Activation (SPA) Module

In the feature extraction stage, the extracted features, such as the contour position information of the brain tumor, of the two branches are shared through the SPA module. Since data in different modalities focus on different lesion areas, SPA module enables that the current branch shares the position information of the lesion area to another branch to focus on the spatially salient features of the current modality. Specifically, the output features F_{M1}^i and F_{M2}^i of Block i ($i \in \{1, 2, 3, 4, 5\}$) of the encoder are input into SPA module to obtain shared information $S_{M1}^i \in \mathbb{R}^{1 \times H' \times W' \times D'}$ and $S_{M2}^i \in \mathbb{R}^{1 \times H' \times W' \times D'}$ respectively. Then the feature calculation method of the final output of each scale i ($i \in \{1, 2, 3, 4, 5\}$) is respectively:

$$F'_{M1} = F_{M1}^i \oplus S_{M2}^i \otimes F_{M1}^i \tag{1}$$

$$F'_{M2} = F_{M2}^i \oplus S_{M1}^i \otimes F_{M2}^i \tag{2}$$

where $\oplus$ and $\otimes$ denote the operation of element-wise addition and element-wise multiplication, respectively.

In a word, the dual-branch network achieves comprehensive information fusion from each branch by employing the SPA module while eliminating the information loss caused by single modal data.

2.3 Multi-scale Feature Aggregation (MFA) Module

In this subsection, the MFA module is well designed to ensure the effective fusion of multi-scale features. Figure 3 shows the whole structure of the proposed MFA module. The input of MFA is the aggregated feature F_i of two different network branches, $F_i = F_{M1}^i + F_{M2}^i (i \in \{1, 2, 3, 4, 5\}) \in \mathbb{R}^{C \times H \times W \times D}$. Then, the local and global information are complementary fused through MFA module from the input fusion feature F_i. More precisely, the MFA module builds a pyramid structure based on convolution layers. Firstly, a global average pooling layer and a $7 \times 7 \times 7$ 3D convolutional layer is used to extract a global representation. Then, a $3 \times 3 \times 3$ 3D convolutional layer and a $5 \times 5 \times 5$ 3D convolutional layer is used to capture the local detail information of the feature. Finally, the output of these multi-scale convolutional layers is concatenated after being up-sampled to $H \times W \times D$, and the concatenated features are passed through a $1 \times 1 \times 1$ convolutional layer to obtain the feature $F_{fuse} \in \mathbb{R}^{C \times H \times W \times D}$. Then, the feature $F_{fuse} \in \mathbb{R}^{C \times H \times W \times D}$ undergoes an attention layer for feature reconstruction. Specifically, given the feature map $F_{fuse} \in \mathbb{R}^{C \times H \times W \times D}$, the attention module uses the input features to infer the 1D attention map $A_c \in \mathbb{R}^{C \times 1 \times 1 \times 1}$ on the channel and the attention map $A_s \in \mathbb{R}^{1 \times H \times W \times D}$ on the 2D space. The general calculation method is as follows:

$$F_{Attn} = [A_c(F_{fuse}) \otimes F_{fuse}, A_s(F_{fuse}) \otimes F_{fuse}] \tag{3}$$

where $[\cdot, \cdot]$ denotes concatenation operation, $\otimes$ denotes element-wise multiplication.

The final output features are:

$$F_{out} = F_{Attn} \oplus F_i \tag{4}$$

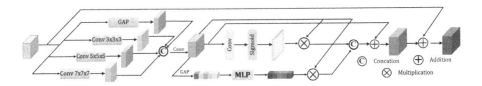

Fig. 3. Multi-scale Feature Aggregation module (MFA)

3 Experiment

In this section, we first introduce the overall settings including implementation details, datasets and evaluation metrics. Then, extensive experiments are conducted to compare the segmentation accuracy with several state-of-the-art methods. Finally, we conduct the ablation study to investigate the effectiveness of components in our method.

3.1 Implementation Details

The new MMFA-Net was implemented in PyTorch 1.12.1 on eight NVIDIA GeForce RTX-3090-24 GB GPUs and eight Tesla V100-SXM3-32GB GPUs. We use the adam algorithm as our optimizer, batchsize is set to 8, learning rate is set to 2e−4 and all experiments run for 300 epochs. The input size of all experiments is $128 \times 128 \times 128$. RandCrop3D, RandomRotion, RandomIntensityChange, RandomFlip are employed for data augmentation.

3.2 Datasets

To evaluate the performance of each of the aforementioned methods, three public brain tumor segmentation datasets, namely, BraTS2020 [7], BraTS2021 [1], and the International Symposium on Biomedical Imaging (ISBI) challenge dataset [12], are utilized.

BraTS2020 Dataset. The BraTS2020 dataset provides a training dataset of 369 aligned, multi-modal MRI data including T1, T1ce, T2, and FLAIR modalities, each accompanied by expert segmentation masks encapsulating whole tumor (WT), enhancing tumor (ET), and tumor core (TC). Each modality contains a volumetric configuration of $155 \times 240 \times 240$ and is preprocessed through resampling and co-registration. The objective of the segmentation task is to isolate the WT, ET, and TC regions. For this evaluation, the dataset is bifurcated into 300 cases for training/validation and the remaining 69 cases for testing.

BraTS2021 Dataset. The BraTS2021 dataset maintains the same format as its predecessor, but differs in terms of the number of training cases, containing 1251 cases for training and 219 for validation. Notably, the validation data of BraTS2021 is withheld, with the ground truth not provided. In the context of this study, the 1251 cases are divided into 1000 cases for training/validation and 251 cases for testing.

ISBI Dataset. The ISBI dataset, sourced from The Cancer Imaging Archive Public Access, comprises a labeled collection of MRI images, collected from 242 consecutive patients. The structural images include contrast-enhanced T1-weighted (ceT1) and high-resolution T2-weighted (hrT2) images. Manual segmentation of all structures was performed in consensus by the attending neurosurgeon and physicist, using both ceT1 and hrT2 images as references. We manually convert the original DICOM images and JSON contour lines into NIFTI format and register the real labels of the hrT2 modality to the ceT1 modality. In this study, the 242 cases were split into 200 cases for training/validation and 42 cases for testing.

3.3 Evaluation Metrics

The evaluation of the aforementioned methods employs two quantitative metrics: the Dice score and the 95%-Hausdorff distance (HD95). The Dice score, ranging from 0 to 1, quantifies the overlap rate between the predicted outcomes and ground truth, with higher values signifying greater accuracy. The HD95, meanwhile, measures the distance disparity the predicted outcomes and ground truth, offering a higher sensitivity than the Dice score [15]. Lower HD95 values indicate better performance.

3.4 Comparison

The proposed MMFA-Net is compared against several SOTA segmentation methods, including 3D-UNet [4], nnUNet [6], SwinUNet [3], UNETR [5], SegTransVAE [10] and NestedFormer [17]. To ensure the fairness of the results, all methods are trained for a maximum of 300 epochs on each dataset.

Performance Comparison on BraTS2020 Dataset. Table 1 presents the Dice and HD95 scores on three target regions (WT, TC, and ET), as well as the average scores across all methods applied to the BraTS2020 dataset. Apparently, our MMFA-Net achieves the higher Dice score on each region, the lower HD95 scores on each region. Therefore, MMFA-Net achieves better averaging Dice and HD95 scores compared with the SOTA methods such as Nestedformer [17].

Table 1. Performance Comparison on BraTS2020 Dataset.

Methods	Dice Score ↑				HD95 Score ↓			
	WT	TC	ET	Avg	WT	TC	ET	Avg
3D UNet [4]	0.882	0.830	0.782	0.831	5.113	6.604	6.715	6.144
nnUNet [6]	0.907	0.848	0.814	0.856	6.94	5.069	5.851	5.953
SwinUNet [3]	0.872	0.809	0.744	0.808	6.752	8.071	10.64	8.488
UNETR [5]	0.899	0.842	0.788	0.843	4.314	5.843	5.598	5.251
SegTransVAE [10]	0.841	0.777	0.713	0.777	10.05	7.74	6.17	7.987
NestedFormer [17]	0.920	0.864	0.800	0.861	4.567	5.316	5.269	5.051
Ours	**0.921**	**0.884**	**0.852**	**0.886**	**2.23**	**2.33**	**2.29**	**2.283**

Table 2. Performance Comparison on BraTS2021 Dataset.

Methods	Dice Score ↑				HD95 Score ↓			
	WT	TC	ET	Avg	WT	TC	ET	Avg
3D UNet [4]	0.911	0.850	0.807	0.856	6.20	8.99	4.83	6.67
UNETR [5]	0.895	0.851	0.822	0.856	7.62	13.18	5.63	8.81
SegTransVAE [10]	0.926	0.905	0.854	0.895	3.57	5.84	2.89	4.10
NestedFormer [17]	0.934	0.908	0.877	0.906	5.98	4.54	3.53	4.68
Ours	**0.943**	**0.930**	**0.892**	**0.922**	**1.445**	**1.220**	**1.709**	**1.46**

Performance Comparison on BraTS2021 Dataset. In Table 2, the Dice and HD95 scores for the same regions, as well as the average scores across all methods on the BraTS2021 dataset, are reported. Notably, our proposed MMFA-Net achieves better Dice score and HD95 scores across all regions. Further, it exhibits superior quantitative performance, with average Dice and HD95 scores amounting to 0.922 and 1.46, respectively.

Table 3. Performance Comparison on IBSI Dataset.

Methods	Dice Score ↑	HD95 Score ↓
3D UNet [4]	0.8112	8.2932
UNETR [5]	0.8581	1.9824
SegTransVAE [10]	0.6889	8.0875
NestedFormer [17]	0.8949	3.6215
Ours	**0.9169**	**1.4866**

Performance Comparison on ISBI Dataset. Table 3 lists the Dice and HD95 scores for MMFA-Net and comparative methods applied to tumor regions on the ISBI dataset, in addition to the average metrics. Of all methods evaluated, ours delivers a higher average Dice score of 0.9169 for tumor segmentation and a lower HD95 score of 1.4866.

Visual Comparisons on BraTS2020, BraTS2020 and ISBI. Figure 4 provides a visual comparison of the segmentation results predicted by MMFA-Net and state-of-the-art methods on BraTS2020, BraTS2021, and ISBI datasets. These visualization results suggest that MMFA-Net outperforms the other compared methods in terms of the precision of brain tumor segmentation. The reason behind is that our DBN and SPA module can better extract the features of different scales and different modalities, and MFA module can better fuse the global and local information from these features.

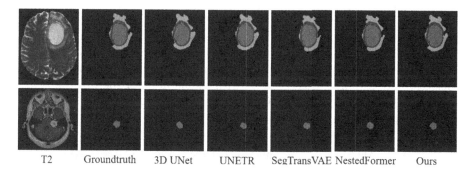

| T2 | Groundtruth | 3D UNet | UNETR | SegTransVAE | NestedFormer | Ours |

Fig. 4. The visual comparison results on BraTS and ISBI dataset.

3.5 Ablation Study

Ablation studies were conducted on the BraTS2020 dataset to assess the effect of different input combinations for multimodal data in our approach. As shown in Table 4, T1+T1ce and T2+Flair achieved the highest Dice score of 0.921 based on the inputs received from doctors.

Furthermore, we carried out ablation studies on the BraTS2021 dataset to evaluate the contribution of the well-designed modules in our approach. Table 5 provides a comparison of the single-branch and dual-branch encoder backbones and the effect of the proposed SPA and MFA modules.

A single-branch network (SBN) is used in SBN-1 to extract features and DBN-1 use a DBN instead. By comparing the results of this group, it can be clearly seen that DBN has better multi-modal feature extraction ability than SBN.

Table 4. Effect of different input combinations for multimodal data.

input combinations		Dice Score ↑			
Input 1	Input 2	WT	TC	ET	Avg
T1+T2	T1ce+Flair	0.921	0.870	0.823	0.871
T1+Flair	T1ce+T2	0.906	0.851	0.808	0.855
T1+T1ce	T2+Flair	**0.921**	**0.884**	**0.852**	**0.886**

DBN-1 and DBN-2 use a DBN to extract features of different modal images and compare the effects of the SPA modules. DBN-3 and MMFA-Net use a DBN and FMA modules and compare the effects of the SPA modules. By comparing the results of the above two groups, we can see that the addition of the SPA modules boosts the feature extraction ability of the network for different modal images and increases the accuracy of model predictions.

SBN-1 and SBN-2 utilize a SBN to extract features of different modal images and compare the effect of the MFA module. DBN-1 and DBN-3 use a DBN to extract features of different modal images and compare the effects of the FMA modules. DBN-2 and MMFA-Net use a DBN and SPA modules and compare the effects of the FMA modules. By comparing the results of the above three groups, it can be seen that the models with the addition of the MFA modules have shown better performance, and can more comprehensively fuse global and local information.

Table 5. Ablation study for different modules on BraTS 2021 Dataset.

Network	DBN	SPA	MFA	Dice Score ↑			
				WT	TC	ET	Avg
SBN-1				0.924	0.918	0.850	0.987
SBN-2			✔	0.934	0.923	0.886	0.914
DBN-1	✔			0.928	0.922	0.853	0.901
DBN-2	✔	✔		0.939	0.923	0.889	0.917
DBN-3	✔		✔	0.934	0.926	0.886	0.915
MMFA-Net	✔	✔	✔	**0.943**	**0.929**	**0.892**	**0.921**

4   Conclusion

In this paper, we propose an new multi-scale feature aggregation network based on multi-modal MRI data for medical image segmentation, named by MMFA-Net. Specifically, a dual-branch network structure is designed to independently extract semantic features from MRI images in different modalities. Meanwhile,

SPA module is developed to fuse the position information of different modalities between two branches. Finally, the features of different scales extracted by the network are concatenated through the MFA module to obtain rich global and local information. And the abundant information is combined to further increase the segmentation accuracy. Generally, the multi-scale features of brain tumors based on the multi-modal MRI data are extracted and fused in the proposed MMFA-Net to improve the segmentation performance of lesion area. Experimental results on three datasets demonstrate the superiority of the proposed MMFA-Net when compared to state-of-the-art methods including 3D UNet [11], UNETR [5], SegresnetVAE [10] and NestedFormer [17]. The average Dice score has an increase of about three percent.

Nevertheless, our study is subject to several limitations. On one hand, in routine clinical diagnostics, it is challenging to obtain a substantial amount of expert-annotated MRI data for training. Insufficient data or significant label errors can adversely affect the precision of the model. On the other hand, while our model demonstrates exemplary performance in brain tumor segmentation, it remains uncertain whether this efficacy can be replicated in tumor segmentation tasks for other anatomical regions. Consequently, our subsequent research will prioritize investigations into small-sample training and enhancing the model's generalizability.

References

1. Baid, U., et al.: The RSNA-ASNR-MICCAI BraTS 2021 benchmark on brain tumor segmentation and radiogenomic classification. arXiv preprint arXiv:2107.02314 (2021)
2. Bakas, S., et al.: Advancing the cancer genome atlas glioma MRI collections with expert segmentation labels and radiomic features. Sci. Data **4**(1), 1–13 (2017)
3. Cao, H., et al.: Swin-Unet: Unet-like pure transformer for medical image segmentation. arXiv preprint arXiv:2105.05537 (2021)
4. Çiçek, Ö., Abdulkadir, A., Lienkamp, S.S., Brox, T., Ronneberger, O.: 3D U-Net: learning dense volumetric segmentation from sparse annotation. In: Ourselin, S., Joskowicz, L., Sabuncu, M.R., Unal, G., Wells, W. (eds.) MICCAI 2016. LNCS, vol. 9901, pp. 424–432. Springer, Cham (2016). https://doi.org/10.1007/978-3-319-46723-8_49
5. Hatamizadeh, A., et al.: UNETR: transformers for 3D medical image segmentation. In: Proceedings of the IEEE/CVF Winter Conference on Applications of Computer Vision, pp. 574–584 (2022)
6. Isensee, F., Jaeger, P.F., Kohl, S.A., Petersen, J., Maier-Hein, K.H.: nnU-Net: a self-configuring method for deep learning-based biomedical image segmentation. Nat. Methods **18**(2), 203–211 (2021)
7. Menze, B.H., et al.: The multimodal brain tumor image segmentation benchmark (BRATS). IEEE Trans. Med. Imaging **34**(10), 1993–2024 (2014)
8. Miller, K.D., et al.: Brain and other central nervous system tumor statistics, 2021. CA Cancer J. Clin. **71**(5), 381–406 (2021)
9. Myronenko, A.: 3D MRI brain tumor segmentation using autoencoder regularization. In: Crimi, A., Bakas, S., Kuijf, H., Keyvan, F., Reyes, M., van Walsum,

T. (eds.) BrainLes 2018. LNCS, vol. 11384, pp. 311–320. Springer, Cham (2019). https://doi.org/10.1007/978-3-030-11726-9_28

10. Pham, Q.D., et al.: SegTransVAE: hybrid CNN-transformer with regularization for medical image segmentation. In: 2022 IEEE 19th International Symposium on Biomedical Imaging (ISBI), pp. 1–5. IEEE (2022)

11. Ronneberger, O., Fischer, P., Brox, T.: U-Net: convolutional networks for biomedical image segmentation. In: Navab, N., Hornegger, J., Wells, W.M., Frangi, A.F. (eds.) MICCAI 2015. LNCS, vol. 9351, pp. 234–241. Springer, Cham (2015). https://doi.org/10.1007/978-3-319-24574-4_28

12. Shapey, J., et al.: Segmentation of vestibular schwannoma from magnetic resonance imaging: an open annotated dataset and baseline algorithm. The Cancer Imaging Archive (2021)

13. Siegel, R.L., Miller, K.D., Wagle, N.S., Jemal, A.: Cancer statistics, 2023. CA Cancer J. Clin. **73**(1), 17–48 (2023)

14. Vaswani, A., et al.: Attention is all you need. In: Advances in Neural Information Processing Systems, vol. 30 (2017)

15. Wang, W., Chen, C., Ding, M., Yu, H., Zha, S., Li, J.: TransBTS: multimodal brain tumor segmentation using transformer. In: de Bruijne, M., et al. (eds.) MICCAI 2021. LNCS, vol. 12901, pp. 109–119. Springer, Cham (2021). https://doi.org/10.1007/978-3-030-87193-2_11

16. Xia, C., et al.: Cancer statistics in China and United States, 2022: profiles, trends, and determinants. Chin. Med. J. **135**(05), 584–590 (2022)

17. Xing, Z., Yu, L., Wan, L., Han, T., Zhu, L.: NestedFormer: nested modality-aware transformer for brain tumor segmentation. In: Wang, L., Dou, Q., Fletcher, P.T., Speidel, S., Li, S. (eds.) International Conference on Medical Image Computing and Computer-Assisted Intervention, pp. 140–150. Springer, Cham (2022). https://doi.org/10.1007/978-3-031-16443-9_14

Diffusion Init: Stronger Initialisation of Decision-Based Black-Box Attacks for Visual Object Tracking

Renjie Wang[1], Tianyang Xu[1]($\boxtimes$), Shaochuan Zhao[1], Xiao-Jun Wu[1], and Josef Kittler[2]

[1] School of Artificial Intelligence and Computer Science, Jiangnan University, Wuxi, Jiangsu, China
tianyang_xu@163.com
[2] Centre for Vision, Speech and Signal Processing, University of Surrey, Guildford GU2 7XH, UK

Abstract. Adversarial attacks have emerged in the field of visual object tracking to mislead the tracker and result in its failure. Black-box attacks in particular have attracted increasing attention for their affinity with real-world applications. In the paradigm of decision-based black-box attacks, the magnitude of perturbation is gradually amplified, while the optimisation direction is predefined by an initial adversarial sample. Considering the pivotal role played by the initial adversarial sample in determining the success of an attack, we utilise the noise generated from the reverse process of a diffusion model as a better attacking direction. On the one hand, the diffusion model generates Gaussian noise, which formulate global information interaction, with a comprehensive impact on Transformer-based trackers. On the other hand, the diffusion model pays more attention to the target region during the inverse process, resulting in a more powerful perturbation of the target object. Our method, which is widely applicable, has been validated on a range of trackers using several benchmarking datasets. It is shown to deliver more extensive tracking performance degradation, compared to other state-of-the-art methods. We also investigate different approaches to the problem of generating the initial adversarial sample, confirming the effectiveness and rationality of our proposed diffusion initialisation method.

Keywords: Adversarial Attack · Diffusion Model · Visual Object Tracking

1 Introduction

Visual object tracking is a crucial branch of computer vision, with broad applications, including but not limited to video surveillance, virtual reality, human-computer interaction, image comprehension, and autonomous driving. With

This work is supported in part by the National Natural Science Foundation of China (Grant No. 62106089, 62020106012).

the rapid development and widespread adoption of deep learning, deep models [3,16,19,29–31] have recently been demonstrated to offer significantly advanced visual tracking performance. However, these models lack interpretability as their internal mechanisms are difficult to rationalise. Consequently, ensuring the security and reliability of these models is challenging.

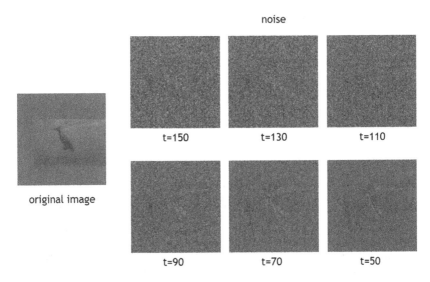

Fig. 1. Showcasing the visualisation of the effect of noise, during the reverse process of the diffusion model. The noise is obtained by subtracting the original image from the current image, with colour normalisation for enhanced clarity, where t denotes the time step.

The goal of adversarial attacks on visual object tracking is to shift the predicted bounding box from the target by adding imperceptible perturbations to the clean image. In general, adversarial attacks can be categorised into white-box attacks and black-box attacks. White-box attacks [6,10,14,17,32] can use the full knowledge of the model architecture, parameters, and gradient. In contrast, black-box attacks, cannot access the internal information of the model assaulted, which fits the real-world application more realistically. Specifically, black-box attacks can be divided into two categories: transfer-based black-box attacks [2,22] and decision-based black-box attacks [4,5,9,18]. A transfer-based black-box attack method attacks a substituted (surrogate) model to learn appropriate perturbations and then applies them to the target model to mislead its decisions. However, finding surrogate models in the real world is not easy. In contrast, a decision-based black-box attack interferes with the optimisation process of the adversarial perturbations by directly changing the output decisions. Therefore, decision-based black-box attacks are more in line with real-world settings than transfer-based black-box attacks. Our study in this paper focuses on decision-based black-box attacks.

Among decision-based black-box attack methods, IoU Attack [15] was the first proposed for attacking a visual tracking algorithm. To be specific, an adversarial example, corrupted by Heavy noise (similar to pulse noise) is selected as initialisation. Then, random perturbations with a Gaussian distribution are added to the sample. The attacker aims to find the most adversarial perturbations with a magnitude constraint on the noise level. After that, the noise level is amplified and the optimal perturbations at the new level are computed. Ideally, the Intersection over Union (IoU) score between the bounding boxes generated by the clean image and the adversarial image progressively decreases with the number of iterations. Considering the high-speed requirement of visual object tracking in video, once the IoU score is sufficiently small or the iteration number reaches its upper limit, the perturbation update is terminated.

Note that the effectiveness of decision-based black-box attacks largely depends on the initial adversarial sample, as it actually plays the role of 'exemplar' that determines the direction of optimisation. In this context, selecting a high-quality initial adversarial sample is crucial to a successful attack.

As an increasing number of advanced trackers adopt the Transformer as a backbone component, attacks become more difficult, as the extreme noise distributions, such as Heavy noise, do not work when well with Transformer-based trackers. To overcome this limitation, we propose substituting Heavy noise with a noise generated by a diffusion model to enhance the attack effectiveness. Firstly, the diffusion model generates Gaussian noise, which impacts more severely on the global interactions between the patches of Transformer-based trackers, especially compared to the Heavy noise characterised by extreme distributions. Secondly, the diffusion model introduces more variations in the target location during the reversed image reconstruction process, leading to a higher level of noise at the target location. By leveraging these effects, generating the initial adversarial sample by the diffusion model leads to a greater performance degradation. We verify the merits of our method on various benchmarks and trackers, and compare the impact of Gaussian noise, Poisson noise, and Pulse noise initialisation, on the effectiveness of our approach.

2 Related Work

2.1 Transformer-Based Visual Object Tracker

Thanks to the recent significant advances made in Transformer architectures, modern visual object trackers have shifted their attention from convolutional neural networks (CNNs) [3,16,27] to Transformers [19,28,31]. The robust performance of transformer-based trackers, demonstrated on various benchmarking datasets, owes to the unique transformer capacity to model global interactions among local patches. A noteworthy and representative tracker adopting the transformer architecture is STARK [31]. To be specific, the encoder of STARK aggregates the global feature dependencies between the target object and the search region, while the decoder learns a query embedding to predict the spatial location of the target object. By updating the template image across the video sequence, the encoder is able to capture an improved discriminative feature representation for the scenario. Using the transformer encoding, a tracking head is designed to obtain the final bounding box by predicting the upper-left and lower-right corner point heat maps, thus avoiding any complex and hyper-parameter-sensitive post-processing.

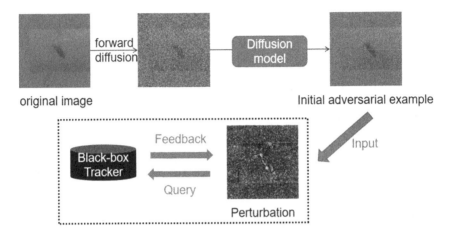

Fig. 2. Illustration of the methodology employed in Diffusion Init.

ToMP [19] is another typical tracker utilising the Transformer architecture. It stands out from the rest by incorporating Discriminative Correlation Filters (DCFs) approach to dynamically update the target model, improving the spatio-temporal model capacity. It bridges the gap between Transformer and DCF tracking, providing a more powerful representation for online trackers. Furthermore, a parallel two-stage tracking process is proposed to decouple the target localisation and target box regression, resulting in more robust and accurate tracking results.

2.2   Decision-Based Attack

The algorithms of decision-based black-box attacks [4,5,9,18] essentially take an initial adversarial sample to confuse the model and iteratively reduce the magnitude of the perturbations. However, this approach is not suitable for tracking, as the volume of queries conflicts with the real-time requirement. Instead, it is more convenient to add noise continuously to the original images to achieve the desired perturbations, or just stop searching when the time is up.

IoU Attack [15] proposes an effective way to use decision-based black-box attacks in tracking tasks, which is essentially a variant of the Boundary Attack [4]. The process of learning perturbations changes from compressing perturbations to progressively increasing the noise level. The classification prediction is then transformed into a bounding box estimation, and the inspection category is replaced with the IoU value between bounding boxes. Thanks to the adaption from the image classification task to the object tracking task, the quality of the initial adversarial sample plays a more crucial role in terms of the attack effectiveness.

2.3   Diffusion Model

Diffusion models [8,11,23] take inspiration from the physical phenomenon of diffusion. The idea behind diffusion models is to continuously add noise to an image until it becomes pure noise, and then the model tries to learn the denoising process to restore the image. Visual Counterfactual Explanations [1,13] and Face Morphing Attack [7] have taken advantage of the realism of the images generated by diffusion models to achieve better results. In spite of sharing the goal of adversarial attacks, they essentially use diffusion models to accomplish a generative task. However, the process of denoising can lead to semantic changes. In contrast, adversarial purification [21,24,25] aims to eliminate perturbations in adversarial samples by adding sufficient noise to overwhelm the perturbations and then denoising to restore the image. Many efforts in adversarial purification have overlooked the attack capabilities of the diffusion model. We have observed that not completely removing the noise during the reverse process results in more aggressive noise compared to the noise added during the forward process. Additionally, the magnitude of the noise obtained during the reverse process is much smaller than the noise added during the forward process.

3   Diffusion Init

3.1   Motivation

Unlike classification tasks, where the goal is to simply make the model misclassify the target class, attacks in the tracking domain aim to result in as many bounding box shifts from the real target as possible. However, the effect of the decision-based black box attacks depends heavily on the initial adversarial example, so it is particularly important to find the most aggressive example. Due to their exceptional performance, Transformer trackers are now the method of choice in visual object tracking. However, Transformer trackers are more resilient to Heavy noise, such as impulse noise, and an alternative form of perturbation is required. Considering the global interaction among patches in the Transformer structure, Gaussian noise appears to be more suitable than Heavy noise as an initial adversarial sample for decision-based black-box attacks.

Moreover, the diffusion model can reveal more semantic information than just simple Gaussian noise. It induces a significant variation in the target location during the reverse process, as depicted in Fig. 1. It is worth noting that the proportion of noise at the target location amplifies throughout the reverse process. The resulting noise is not only globally dispersed but also heavier at the target location, both of which can contribute to a heightened performance degradation in decision-based black-box attacks when used as the initial adversarial sample.

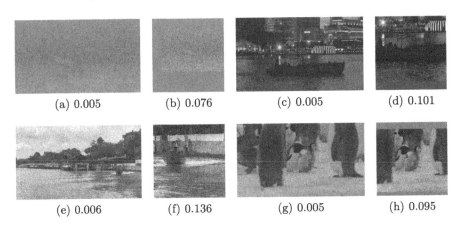

(a) 0.005   (b) 0.076   (c) 0.005   (d) 0.101

(e) 0.006   (f) 0.136   (g) 0.005   (h) 0.095

Fig. 3. Examples of an attack that targeted the original image, resulting in a highly noisy search region. The image on the left depicts the original image, while the image on the right represents the search region. The numerical value displayed beneath each image represents the ratio of l_2-norm magnitude of the adversarial sample measured with reference to the clean original image or a clean search region.

3.2   Diffusion Init

The image generation process of the diffusion model comprises two fundamental stages: the forward diffusion process, where noise is injected into the image, and the reverse diffusion process, which aims to denoise and restore the image.

Given an original image, denoted as x_0, which follows the distribution $q(x)$, a Gaussian noise is progressively added to the image along the time step t. The standard deviation of the noise is determined by β_t, while the mean is determined by a fixed value of β_t and the data x_t at the current time step. The magnitude of each step is regulated by a variance schedule $\{\beta_t \in (0,1)\}_{t=1}^{T}$. This update operates as a Markov chain process and does not involve any learnable parameters. As the time step t increases, the final data distribution x_T converges to an independent Gaussian distribution. This entire process, spanning from x_0 to x_T, can be defined as:

$$q(x_t|x_{t-1}) = \mathcal{N}(x_t; \sqrt{1-\beta_t}x_{t-1}, \beta_t I) \tag{1}$$

$$q(x_{1:T}|x_0) = \prod_{t=1}^{T} q(x_t|x_{t-1}) \tag{2}$$

By the technique of reparameterisation, denoted as $\alpha_t = 1-\beta_t$, $\bar{\alpha}_t = \prod_{s=1}^{t} \alpha_s$, we can derive

$$x_t = \sqrt{\bar{\alpha}_t}x_0 + \sqrt{1-\bar{\alpha}_t}\epsilon \tag{3}$$

Algorithm 1. Diffusion Init

Input: Diffusion model ϵ_θ; Variance β_t; Number of the forward process steps n;
    Reverse termination step s; Input video V with M frames; Maximum perturba-
    tion L_2 norm $L_2 MAX$;
Output: Adversarial sample of M frames;
 1: **for** $f = 2$ **to** M **do**
 2:    Get current frame x_0
 3:    Obtain x_n by (3)
 4:    **for** t $=$ n **to** s **do**
 5:       Obtain x_{t-1} by (7)
 6:    **end for**
 7:    Calculate IoU_s
 8:    $x_a dv = x_s$
 9:    Calculate $\text{IoU}_a dv$
10:    **while** $\|x_{adv} - x_0\|_2 < L_2 MAX$ **and** $\text{IoU}_{x_s} < \text{IoU}_{adv}$ **do**
11:       Learning perturbations along the tangential direction
12:       Learning perturbations along the normal direction
13:       Get adversarial example x_{adv}
14:       Calculate $\text{IoU}_a dv$
15:    **end while**
16:    **return** x_{adv}
17: **end for**

---

where ϵ represents the standard Gaussian noise. By utilising this equation, we can efficiently obtain x_t in a single step.

The reverse process aims to restore the original data from the Gaussian distribution. When β_t is sufficiently small, each small step of the reverse process $p_\theta(x_{t-1}|x_t)$ can also be derived as a Gaussian distribution. The learnt model p_θ approximates these conditional probabilities, as

$$p_\theta(x_{t-1}|x_t) = \mathcal{N}(x_{t-1}; \mu_\theta(x_t, t), \Sigma_\theta(x_t, t)) \tag{4}$$

The reverse diffusion process can be summarised as follows:

$$p_\theta(x_{0:T}) = p(x_T) \prod_{t=1}^{T} p_\theta(x_{t-1}|x_t) \tag{5}$$

It is realised by a network which estimates the parameter θ. For $p_\theta(x_{t-1}|x_t)$, the variance (given as β_t initially) is known. The requirement is to obtain the mean $\mu_\theta(x_t, t)$ to define the posterior probability of the reverse process. The term $\mu_\theta(x_t, t)$ can be characterised as follows:

$$\mu_\theta(x_t, t) = \frac{1}{\sqrt{\alpha_t}}(x_t - \frac{\beta_t}{\sqrt{1 - \bar{\alpha}_t}}\epsilon_\theta(x_t, t)), \tag{6}$$

where ϵ_θ is a learned gradient of the data density. At this juncture, we can determine the posterior probability, $p_\theta(x_{t-1}|x_t)$, while the computation of the samples x_{t-1} can be expressed as follows:

$$x_{t-1} = \mu_\theta(x_t, t) + \sigma_t z,   \text{(7)}$$

where $\sigma_t = \sqrt{\beta_t}$ and $z \sim \mathcal{N}(0, I)$.

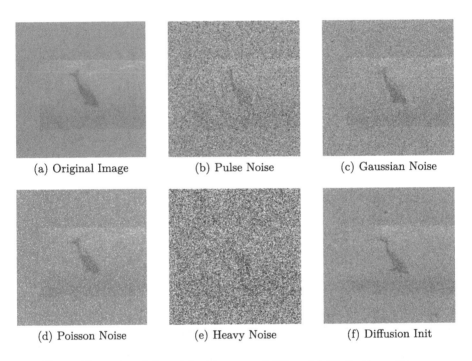

(a) Original Image   (b) Pulse Noise   (c) Gaussian Noise

(d) Poisson Noise   (e) Heavy Noise   (f) Diffusion Init

Fig. 4. Examples of the original image and different initialisation settings.

Figure 2 provides a visual representation of the methodology employed in Diffusion Init. Algorithm 1 presents the pseudocode implementation of the Diffusion Init. Initially, a clean search region is utilised to derive x_n through (3). Subsequently, (7) is employed to iteratively execute the reverse diffusion process for the optimisation of the initial adversarial example x_s. The learning of perturbations forwards along the tangential and normal directions [15] proceeds in an iterative manner until the L_2 norm of the perturbation exceeds the set maximum limit, or the IoU score between bounding boxes generated from benign and adversarial examples is lower than a threshold.

4   Experiments

4.1   Experimental Settings

Datasets. We evaluated the performance of our Diffusion Init method on three datasets, each representing sequences of different lengths: GOT-10K [12], OTB100 [26], and UAV123 [20].

Deployment of Trackers. To validate the efficacy of our methodology, we employ two Transformer-based trackers, *i.e.*, STARK [31] and ToMP [19]. STARK has two versions: STARK-S fixes the template from the first frame, while STARK-ST dynamically updates the templates. On the other hand, ToMP is used as a representative of a DCF-based tracker. Therefore, we validate the effectiveness of our method on STARK-S, STARK-ST, and ToMP from the generalisation point of view.

Deployment of the Diffusion Model. For its powerful image generation ability in realistic scenarios, a pre-trained diffusion model [8] is employed as the main component of Diffusion Init. Notice that, the timestep t is a key hyperparameter in the diffusion model. As illustrated in Fig. 1, after 100 timesteps of the reverse process, the noise level on the target area is obviously higher than that on the background. However, as the number of reverse steps increases, not only the noise level of the target area becomes consistent with the background, the time costs are unaffordable for tracking task. Additionally, selecting a larger timestep leads to excessive modifications of the image content, while a small timestep results in an insufficient noise level in the initial adversarial example. Therefore, we select $s = 50, n = 150$ to obtain the initial adversarial example.

Implementation Details. Previous black-box attacks in the realm of visual object tracking act on the full-size image. However, it is important to note that the actual input to the network is the search region which is cropped from the full-size image and then resized according to the predicted bounding box of the previous frame. Through our investigations, the resize operation basically leads to amplifying the perturbation in the search region, resulting in a significant increase in the noise level, as shown in Fig. 3. For a fair comparison, we focus our attacks on the search region and set similar L_2MAX with the perturbations on the resized image of [15].

4.2 Overall Attack Results

GOT-10k. GOT-10k [12] is a comprehensive tracking dataset that offers an extensive collection of common moving objects. It leverages the WordNet structure as its foundation, encompassing over 560 classes of moving objects and 87 distinct motion patterns. This broad range of categories surpasses other datasets of comparable size. Eeach object's bounding box is meticulously labelled through manual annotation. With over 1.5 million bounding boxes available, this dataset ensures consistent training and a reliable evaluation of deep trackers. Two main metrics, i.e., AO and SR, are used for evaluation. AO represents the average overlap between all ground truth and estimated bounding boxes, while SR measures the percentage of successfully tracked frames with overlaps exceeding a certain threshold (e.g., 0.5).

Table 1 shows the results of measuring the performance degradation before and after black-box attacks. We conducted tests using different initialisation

Table 1. A comparison of the tracking results using Heavy noise, and Diffusion Init of STARK [31], ToMP [19] respectively on the GOT-10K [12] dataset.

Trackers	AO			$SR_{0.50}$			$SR_{0.75}$		
	Orig.	Heavy.	Diff.	Orig.	Heavy.	Diff.	Orig.	Heavy.	Diff.
STARK-S	0.671	0.655	**0.649**	0.761	0.740	**0.734**	0.609	0.598	**0.594**
STARK-ST	0.680	0.664	**0.659**	0.776	0.754	**0.748**	0.620	0.609	**0.604**
ToMP	0.724	0.703	**0.682**	0.841	0.817	**0.792**	0.655	0.643	**0.615**

methods, such as random Heavy noise, which is adopted by [15] and our proposed diffusion init, to generate adversarial samples. Our method achieves a greater performance degradation, compared to the use of Heavy noise on various compromised trackers. For the original performance of the trackers, the AO score decreases by 2.2% on STARK-S and 2.1% on STARK-ST. In particular, compared to Heavy noise, the AO score is reduced by 1.1% on ToMP.

Table 2. A comparison of the tracking results achieved by STARK [31] and ToMP [19], respectively, on the original sequences from the OTB100 [26] dataset, on the same sequences attacked using Heavy noise initialisation, and with Diffusion Init

Trackers	Success			Precision		
	Orig.	Heavy.	Diff.	Orig.	Heavy.	Diff.
STARK-S	0.663	0.657	**0.653**	0.860	0.857	**0.853**
STARK-ST	0.673	0.668	**0.659**	0.879	0.878	**0.862**
ToMP	0.700	0.692	**0.683**	0.907	0.897	**0.885**

OTB100. OTB100 [26] is one of the most widely used benchmarks for visual object tracking, consisting of 100 well-annotated video sequences. Two main metrics, *i.e.*, success and precision, are used for evaluation. The success rate calculation involves computing the intersection over union (IoU) of pixels within the predicted bounding box and the ground truth bounding box. Precision is defined as the Euclidean distance between the predicted bounding box centre and the ground truth bounding box centre. As shown in Table 2, our method results in performance degeneration that surpasses that of the Heavy noise method in all cases. In terms of the Success rate metric, our method shows a decrease of 1.0% on STARK-S, 1.4% on STARK-ST, and compared to Heavy noise, a decrease by 0.9% on ToMP. In terms of the Precision metric, our method achieves a decrease of 0.7% on STARK-S, and compared to Heavy noise, reduces the performance by 1.6% on STARK-ST, and 1.2% on ToMP.

Table 3. A comparison of the tracking results obtained by STARK [31], and ToMP [19] respectively, on the original sequences from the UAV123 [20] dataset, and on the same sequences attacked with the Heavy noise, and Diffusion Init initialisation.

Trackers	Success			Precision		
	Orig.	Heavy.	Diff.	Orig.	Heavy.	Diff.
STARK-S	0.690	0.677	**0.676**	0.896	0.889	**0.886**
STARK-ST	0.688	0.679	**0.670**	0.903	0.893	**0.883**
ToMP	0.680	0.672	**0.644**	0.877	0.870	**0.833**

UAV123. The UAV123 [20] dataset consists of 91 drone videos, some of which are long sequences split into three or four shorter segments for repeated use, resulting in a total of 123 sequences. The evaluation has two main metrics, success rate and precision. As shown in Table 3, our method results in performance degradation that surpasses that of the Heavy noise method in all cases. Our solution achieves a decrease of the Success rate by 2.4% on STARK-S, and compared to Heavy noise, a reduction of 0.9% on STARK-ST, and 2.8% on ToMP. In terms of the Precision metric, our method is 1.0% better on STARK-S, and compared to Heavy noise, it achieves a decrease of 1.0% on STARK-ST, and 3.7% on ToMP.

Table 4. A comparison of the tracking results obtained by ToMP [19] on the original sequences in the GOT-10K [12] dataset, and on those attacked with different initialisation methods.

	AO	$SR_{0.50}$	$SR_{0.75}$
ToMP	0.724	0.841	0.655
Pulse Noise	0.701	0.815	0.638
Gaussian Noise	0.691	0.805	0.624
Poisson Noise	0.731	0.849	0.667
Heavy Noise	0.703	0.817	0.643
Ours	**0.682**	**0.792**	**0.615**

4.3 Ablation Studies

To explore the characteristics of the different kinds of initialisation, we compared the impact of Pulse noise, Gaussian noise, Poisson noise, Heavy noise [15], and Diffusion Init at the same L_2 norm constraint level, as illustrated in Fig. 4. According to Table 4, our method exhibits the most significant performance degradation among all the initialisation methods. Furthermore, due to the similar characteristics of Heavy noise and Pulse noise, they deliver similar performance.

The reason behind the Poisson noise producing an enhanced tracker accuracy is that the black box attack is based on the raw tracker performance, rather than on the groundtruth, so the attack direction does not necessarily align with the accuracy degradation. The performance degradation caused by Gaussian noise is also substantial. Considering that the forward diffusion process also introduces Gaussian noise, the fact that our method leads to even greater performance degradation than Gaussian noise proves that the noise is more aggressive after the reverse diffusion process.

5 Conclusion

This paper delves into the efficacy of the proposed method advocating a careful selection of the initial adversarial sample in decision-based black-box attacks. We show that the use of a diffusion process to generate the initialisation of the data perturbation amplifies its aggressiveness, leading to a performance degradation. We substantiate the effectiveness of our approach through the evaluation of different trackers on benchmarking datasets, and compare their performance on the original sequences, and those attacked with the commonly used Heavy noise initialisation, and the proposed Diffusion Init. In a future study, more refined approaches will be developed to harness the potential of the diffusion model for adversarial attacks.

References

1. Augustin, M., Boreiko, V., Croce, F., Hein, M.: Diffusion visual counterfactual explanations. In: Oh, A.H., Agarwal, A., Belgrave, D., Cho, K. (eds.) Advances in Neural Information Processing Systems (NeurIPS) (2022)
2. Bai, S., Li, Y., Zhou, Y., Li, Q., Torr, P.S.: Adversarial metric attack and defense for person re-identification. IEEE Trans. Pattern Anal. Mach. Intell. (TPAMI) **43**(06), 2119–2126 (2021)
3. Bhat, G., Danelljan, M., Gool, L.V., Timofte, R.: Learning discriminative model prediction for tracking. In: International Conference on Computer Vision (ICCV), pp. 6182–6191 (2019)
4. Brendel, W., Rauber, J., Bethge, M.: Decision-based adversarial attacks: reliable attacks against black-box machine learning models. In: International Conference on Learning Representations (ICLR) (2018)
5. Chen, J., Jordan, M.I., Wainwright, M.J.: HopSkipJumpAttack: a query-efficient decision-based attack. In: IEEE Symposium on Security and Privacy (SP), pp. 1277–1294. IEEE (2020)
6. Chen, X., Yan, X., Zheng, F., Jiang, Y., Ji, R.: One-shot adversarial attacks on visual tracking with dual attention. In: Conference on Computer Vision and Pattern Recognition (CVPR) (2020)
7. Damer, N., Fang, M., Siebke, P., Kolf, J.N., Huber, M., Boutros, F.: MorDIFF: recognition vulnerability and attack detectability of face morphing attacks created by diffusion autoencoders (2023)

8. Dhariwal, P., Nichol, A.: Diffusion models beat GANs on image synthesis. In: Advances in Neural Information Processing Systems (NIPS), vol. 34, pp. 8780–8794 (2021)
9. Dong, Y., et al.: Efficient decision-based black-box adversarial attacks on face recognition. In: Conference on Computer Vision and Pattern Recognition (CVPR), pp. 7714–7722 (2019)
10. Guo, Q., et al.: SPARK: spatial-aware online incremental attack against visual tracking. In: Vedaldi, A., Bischof, H., Brox, T., Frahm, J.-M. (eds.) ECCV 2020. LNCS, vol. 12370, pp. 202–219. Springer, Cham (2020). https://doi.org/10.1007/978-3-030-58595-2_13
11. Ho, J., Jain, A., Abbeel, P.: Denoising diffusion probabilistic models. In: Advances in Neural Information Processing Systems (NeurIPS), vol. 33, pp. 6840–6851 (2020)
12. Huang, L., Zhao, X., Huang, K.: GOT-10k: a large high-diversity benchmark for generic object tracking in the wild. IEEE Trans. Pattern Anal. Mach. Intell. **43**(5), 1562–1577 (2021)
13. Jeanneret, G., Simon, L., Jurie, F.: Adversarial counterfactual visual explanations. In: Conference on Computer Vision and Pattern Recognition (CVPR), pp. 16425–16435 (2023)
14. Jia, S., Ma, C., Song, Y., Yang, X.: Robust tracking against adversarial attacks. In: Vedaldi, A., Bischof, H., Brox, T., Frahm, J.-M. (eds.) ECCV 2020. LNCS, vol. 12364, pp. 69–84. Springer, Cham (2020). https://doi.org/10.1007/978-3-030-58529-7_5
15. Jia, S., Song, Y., Ma, C., Yang, X.: IoU attack: towards temporally coherent black-box adversarial attack for visual object tracking. In: Conference on Computer Vision and Pattern Recognition (CVPR) (2021)
16. Li, B., Wu, W., Wang, Q., Zhang, F., Xing, J., Yan, J.: SiamRPN++: evolution of Siamese visual tracking with very deep networks. In: Conference on Computer Vision and Pattern Recognition (CVPR), pp. 4277–4286 (2019)
17. Liang, S., Wei, X., Yao, S., Cao, X.: Efficient adversarial attacks for visual object tracking. In: Vedaldi, A., Bischof, H., Brox, T., Frahm, J.-M. (eds.) ECCV 2020. LNCS, vol. 12371, pp. 34–50. Springer, Cham (2020). https://doi.org/10.1007/978-3-030-58574-7_3
18. Maho, T., Furon, T., Merrer, E.L.: SurFree: a fast surrogate-free black-box attack. Conference on Computer Vision and Pattern Recognition (CVPR), pp. 10425–10434 (2020)
19. Mayer, C., et al.: Transforming model prediction for tracking. In: Conference on Computer Vision and Pattern Recognition (CVPR), pp. 8731–8740, June 2022
20. Mueller, M., Smith, N., Ghanem, B.: A benchmark and simulator for UAV tracking. In: Leibe, B., Matas, J., Sebe, N., Welling, M. (eds.) ECCV 2016. LNCS, vol. 9905, pp. 445–461. Springer, Cham (2016). https://doi.org/10.1007/978-3-319-46448-0_27
21. Nie, W., Guo, B., Huang, Y., Xiao, C., Vahdat, A., Anandkumar, A.: Diffusion models for adversarial purification. In: International Conference on Machine Learning (ICML) (2022)
22. Papernot, N., McDaniel, P., Goodfellow, I., Jha, S., Celik, Z.B., Swami, A.: Practical black-box attacks against machine learning. In: Proceedings of the 2017 ACM on Asia Conference on Computer and Communications Security, pp. 506–519 (2017)
23. Song, J., Meng, C., Ermon, S.: Denoising diffusion implicit models. In: International Conference on Learning Representations (ICLR) (2021)
24. Wang, J., Lyu, Z., Lin, D., Dai, B., Fu, H.: Guided diffusion model for adversarial purification (2022)

25. Wu, Q., Ye, H., Gu, Y.: Guided diffusion model for adversarial purification from random noise (2022)
26. Wu, Y., Lim, J., Yang, M.H.: Object tracking benchmark. IEEE Trans. Pattern Anal. Mach. Intell. (TPAMI) **37**(9), 1834–1848 (2015)
27. Xu, T., Feng, Z., Wu, X.J., Kittler, J.: Adaptive channel selection for robust visual object tracking with discriminative correlation filters. Int. J. Comput. Vision **129**, 1359–1375 (2021)
28. Xu, T., Feng, Z., Wu, X.J., Kittler, J.: Toward robust visual object tracking with independent target-agnostic detection and effective Siamese cross-task interaction. IEEE Trans. Image Process. **32**, 1541–1554 (2023)
29. Xu, T., Wu, X.J., Kittler, J.: Non-negative subspace representation learning scheme for correlation filter based tracking. In: 2018 24th International Conference on Pattern Recognition (ICPR), pp. 1888–1893. IEEE (2018)
30. Xu, T., Zhu, X.F., Wu, X.J.: Learning spatio-temporal discriminative model for affine subspace based visual object tracking. Vis. Intell. **1**(1), 4 (2023)
31. Yan, B., Peng, H., Fu, J., Wang, D., Lu, H.: Learning spatio-temporal transformer for visual tracking. In: International Conference on Computer Vision (ICCV), pp. 10448–10457 (2021)
32. Yan, B., Wang, D., Lu, H., Yang, X.: Cooling-shrinking attack: blinding the tracker with imperceptible noises. In: Conference on Computer Vision and Pattern Recognition (CVPR), pp. 987–996 (2020)

MMID: Combining Maximized the Mutual Information and Diffusion Model for Image Super-Resolution

Yu Shi[1], Hu Tan[1], Song Gao[2], Yunyun Dong[2], Wei Zhou[2],
and Ruxin Wang[3(✉)]

[1] Engineering Research Center of Cyberspace, Yunnan University, Kunming, China
{shiyu,tanhu}@mail.ynu.edu.cn
[2] National Pilot School of Software, Engineering Research Center of Cyberspace,
Yunnan University, Kunming, China
{gaos,dongyy929,zwei}@ynu.edu.cn
[3] Alibaba Group, Beijing, China
rosinwang@gmail.com

Abstract. The Denoising Diffusion Probabilistic Models (DDPM) [11] have shown promise in recovering realistic details for single image super-resolution (SISR). However, the diffusion model's recovery results often suffer from unpleasant artifacts due to the optimization objective of DDPM, which relies on the L_p norm distance and is sensitive to data uncertainty. To address this issue, we propose a novel method named MMID (Maximize the Mutual Information for Diffusion model). MMID enhances the relationship between the input and output by maximizing their mutual information. This helps to alleviate the problem of instability arising from the L_p norm optimization, where the same input may yield multiple output possibilities. Moreover, this paper incorporates the Convolutional visual Transformer (CvT) network structure into the conventional U-Net to form the CTU-Net model, which improves the quality of image restoration. The proposed MMID approach offers a novel and powerful solution, enabling the diffusion model to achieve significantly better performance in super-resolution tasks.

Keywords: Super-resolution · Diffusion model · Mutual information

1 Introduction

Single image super-resolution reconstruction aims to generate a high-resolution (HR) image with clear detailed features from a given low-resolution (LR) image. High resolution means a high density of pixels in an image, which provides more detail that is essential for practical applications. However, single image super-resolution reconstruction is challenging because it is an ill-posed problem that has usually no stable and unique solution, with multiple outputs corresponding

H. Lu et al. (Eds.): ACPR 2023, LNCS 14407, pp. 381–395, 2023.
https://doi.org/10.1007/978-3-031-47637-2_29

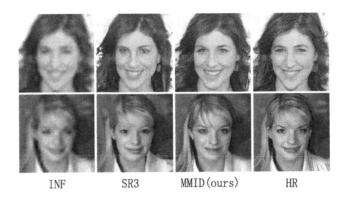

INF   SR3   MMID(ours)   HR

Fig. 1. The results of the MMID (64–512) trained on FFHQ and applied to images outside the training set.

to one input in many cases. This is due to the uncertainty of the L_p norm as an objective function during training. The output of the L_2 norm is interpreted as the possible average to account for the uncertainty in the prediction, while the L_1 norm is used to predict the median of all such results. The uncertainty of the L_p norm in the regression-based SISR methods hinders them from producing rich high-frequency information. Therefore, it is essential to find out how these real detailed textures can be generated.

Deep generative models have achieved excellent performance in learning the complex empirical distribution of images. They can sample high-quality images with complex textures and are often combined with super-resolution tasks to generate high-resolution images with abundant details. Since the proposal of Generative Adversarial Networks (GANs), generative-model-based SISR methods [14,18,23,24] have been dominated by GANs. However, GANs require well-designed regularization and optimization techniques to address the instability and mode collapse during training. Therefore, a superior generative model is required for the SISR task. Diffusion probability models (DPMs) have shown impressive capabilities in image synthesis and image restoration, especially denoising diffusion probabilistic models (DDPMs). They have also shown promise in SISR tasks, such as SR3 (Super-Resolution via Repeated Refinement) [22]. However, the diffusion model introduces unpleasant artifacts when generating image details, which are undesirable for the user. We discovered through experiments that using the L_p norm as the optimization objective caused this problem, as it was affected by the uncertainty of one-to-many mapping between inputs and outputs. To address this problem, we propose to increase the correlation between model inputs and outputs, so that the model can learn more valid information from the input image.

Inspired by the above, we propose MMID to maximize the mutual information between the inputs and outputs of the deep neural network. We modified the training objective function by adding a regularization term that maximizes the JS (Jensen-Shannon) distance between the joint and marginal probability distributions of the inputs and outputs to achieve this goal. That is, we add a regularization term to the L_p norm at training time to restrict the diffusion model from generating artifacts that do not match the input information.

MMID has achieved good results in super-resolution tasks and also effectively mitigated the problem of artifact generation. However, when we recover images with larger resolution, the reconstruction results are accompanied by more noise. To further improve the reconstruction effect of the model, we propose to improve the traditional U-Net [21]. We found that the limitation of U-Net is due to the inability of Convolutional Neural Networks (CNNs) to capture long-range features and to obtain more contextual information. Therefore, we introduced the structure of the vision transformer (ViT) [8] to U-Net while maintaining the inductive bias of CNNs to improve performance and robustness. We propose a new structure CTU-Net that incorporates the convolution structure with the transformer feature into U-Net.

In summary, this paper makes three contributions. (1) We propose a novel diffusion probability model MMID for SISR tasks, which reduces artifact generation by maximizing mutual information while generating rich high-frequency information. (2) We improve the traditional U-Net and propose the CTU-Net with the advantage of Transformer. (3) We show that the proposed MMID framework is highly flexible and can be applied to different diffusion models to improve the results.

2   Related Work

2.1   Super-Resolution

Since SRCNN [7], the first deep convolutional neural network for SISR, achieved excellent performance, many neural networks have been proposed for single image super-resolution. These networks generally fall into two categories: regression-based [5,7,15,28] and generative model-based [9,14,17,22].

2.2   Regression-Based SISR Method

Regression-based SISR method. In the present study, the regression-based SISR method is applied to optimize the output of the model to the original high-resolution image HR through various pixel-level distance measures, such as L_p norm loss and structural similarity (SSIM). Following SRCNN [7], researchers have developed deeper and more complex artificial neural network models to enhance the output performance. For instance, RCAN [28] and HAT [5] improve network performance by designing complex channel attention, global attention, and deeper convolutional layer structures.

2.3   Generative-Based SISR Methods

These SISR methods produce high-quality images by regulating the generator's generation ability.

GAN-SR Method. Researchers have recently made significant progress in the adversarial training of SRGAN [14] with SRResNet [14] as the generator. Moreover, many methods have been developed to control the generator's output details, and these GAN-SR methods improve the output quality. For instance, ESRGAN [24] refines the deep residual network to enhance the image generation effect in SISR. SPSR [18] introduces a gradient restoration branch to control the generator's image structure for a better output.

Flow-Based. Models map a simple prior distribution to a complex data distribution through a series of invertible transformations (bijective functions). SRFlow [17] uses this model to sample a realistic high-resolution image by learning a conditional distribution given a low-resolution image. However, this model is computationally expensive for high-resolution image generation, and flow-based methods often produce sub-optimal sample quality.

VAE-SR. Applying the hidden space of VAE to super-resolution tasks. For example, SrVae [9] extends VAE by adding a random variable that represents a downsampled version of the original image and uses a log-likelihood function as the learning objective. VAE is a network of encoders that maps a real sample to a desired data distribution, and a network of decoders that reconstructs a generated sample from this distribution. However, this process requires sufficient real samples and large network parameters to fit the ideal data distribution, which is challenging. Therefore, it often needs a more complex network structure and produces unsatisfactory results in super-resolution tasks.

DDPM (Denoising Diffusion Probabilistic Model) consists of a forward diffusion process and a backward generation process. The forward diffusion process gradually adds Gaussian noise to an image until it becomes random noise, while the backward generation process is a denoising process. It starts from random noise and gradually denoises it until an image is generated, which is the part to be trained. This generative model avoids the problem of mode collapse that GAN faces when the number of parameters increases. SR3 is the first method to apply this diffusion model to SISR tasks. It produces a high-fidelity image with texture details by upsampling the low-resolution image LR to the pixel space of the high-resolution image HR by bicubic interpolation and then continuously adding noise to remove the blur. With the success of SR3, more DDPM-SR methods have been proposed.

Each generative model has its own strengths and weaknesses. They are often used in SISR tasks to generate rich details that improve the output image quality. Therefore, finding a suitable generative model for super-resolution is essential. Diffusion probabilistic model (DPM) has demonstrated impressive performance in image synthesis and restoration, especially DDPM. However, when applying DDPM to super-resolution tasks, artifacts appear. We suspect that the uncertainty of the L_p norm causes these artifacts. To address this issue, we start from maximizing the correlation between input and output, that is, maximizing the mutual information between model input and output.

3   Methodology

This section starts with a review of the fundamentals of diffusion models, including the forward process and training objectives. After a study on the basics of mutual information, the design of maximizing mutual information will be explained in detail. Finally, the proposed CTU-Net structure will be demonstrated.

3.1   Preliminaries

We first describe the basic setup of super-resolution. As shown in Fig. 2, a high-resolution image (HR) and a low-resolution image (LR) are prepared. LR is obtained by downsampling the image HR through bicubic interpolation, whereas the conditional input image (INF) is upsampled by LR to the HR pixel level through bicubic interpolation. The super resolution (SR) image is obtained after the reconstruction of LR by the model.

Conditional Denoising Diffusion Model. Diffusion Model belongs to the probabilistic model category. It aims to corrupt the data distribution by iteratively adding Gaussian noise, and then learn to reconstruct the data distribution at each corruption step.

The forward process follows a fixed-length Markov chain of T states, where t represents a state in the chain. It starts from image $x := x_0$ and generates a series of noise images $\{x_t | t \in [1, T]\}$, where $x_t = \alpha_t x_0 + (1 - \alpha_t)\epsilon$, ϵ follows Gaussian distribution, and α_t decreases gradually with t.

The denoising operation reverses the forward process. It starts from the noise $z := x_T \sim N(0, I)$ and gradually denoises the input x_t at time t. The denoising model is a sequence of equally weighted denoising autoencoders $\epsilon_\theta(x_t, t)$, which are trained to predict a denoised version of their input x_t. The objective function for the generative process can be simplified as:

$$L_{DM} = \mathbb{E}_{x,\epsilon \sim \mathcal{N}(0,1),t} \left[\| \epsilon - \epsilon_\theta\left(x_t, t\right) \|_2^2 \right] \tag{1}$$

We apply the conditional diffusion model to perform image super-resolution. In this process, we obtain the super-resolved images SR by minimizing the following loss function and using the final noise image x_{inf} as the input for the denoising steps.

$$L_{DM} = \mathbb{E}_{x,\epsilon \sim \mathcal{N}(0,1),t} \left[\| \epsilon - \epsilon_\theta\left(x_t, x_{inf}, t\right) \|_2^2 \right] \tag{2}$$

To improve the quality of restored images, we use diffusion models to progressively sharpen the noisy conditional image x_{inf}. These models are effective and flexible for image restoration and reconstruction.

Mutual Information. As a measure of the interdependence between two random variables, mutual information is denoted as $\mathcal{I}(X, Y)$. It is used to measure the information shared by two random variables: the degree to which the uncertainty of the random variable Y is reduced when the random variable X is known, and the degree to which the uncertainty of the random variable X is reduced when the degree to which the random variable Y is known.

Entropy: It is a measurement of uncertainty, which can be expressed as:

$$H(X) = -\sum_{x \in X} P(x) log P(x) \tag{3}$$

Conditional Entropy: It measures the uncertainty of X when Y is given, indicating uncertainty of random variable X under the condition that the random variable Y is known. It can be expressed as:

$$H(X \mid Y) = -\sum_{x \in X} \sum_{y \in Y} P(x, y) \log P(x \mid y) \tag{4}$$

Mutual Information: When the entropy H(X) and the conditional entropy H(X—Y) are known, mutual information can be defined as the reduction in the uncertainty of X by given Y:

$$I(X, Y) = H(X) - H(X \mid Y) = \sum_{x \in X} \sum_{y \in Y} P(x, y) \left(\log \frac{P(x, y)}{P(x)P(y)} \right) \tag{5}$$

To summarize, we use mutual information maximization as a regularization term to optimize the output uncertainty reduction given the input during training.

3.2   Maximizing Mutual Information for Diffusion Model

We first describe the general setup for training ϵ_θ: $x_t \to y_t$, where x_t and y_t is the input and output of network ϵ with parameters θ. According to Eq (2), the diffusion model ϵ_θ takes x_t, x_{inf} and t as inputs. Because of the x_{inf} and the t have not effect to the mutual information, so the input of ϵ_θ can be seen as x_t simply, and the output is y_t. Let x_t and y_t be the domain and range of continuous and (almost everywhere) differentiable parametric functions. We assume that $\mathbf{X_t} := \left\{ x_t^{(i)} \right\}_{i=1}^{N}$ is a set of training examples in the input space with empirical distribution $\mathbb{P}_{X_t}$. Then, $\mathbb{P}_{Y_t}$ and $\mathbb{P}_{X_t \otimes Y_t}$ denote the marginal and joint distributions of $\mathbf{Y_t} := \left\{ y_t^{(i)} \right\}_{i=1}^{N}$, respectively.

We propose adding a regularization term to the original optimization objective L_p norm of the diffusion model to obtain high-quality reconstruction results with rich texture details. This term aims to reduce the output uncertainty given the known inputs. The optimization objectives are as follows:

$$loss = \alpha L_{DM} - \beta I_{\theta,\psi}^{(JSD)} \tag{6}$$

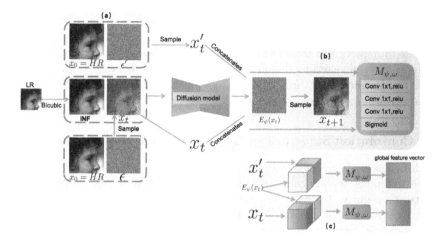

Fig. 2. The overall structure of MMID.

We minimize this function to optimize our network ϵ_θ.

This method is based on MINE [3], which estimates the mutual information through a neural network and computes its lower bound using the DV [2] representation of the KL (Kullback-Leibler) divergence. It can be expressed as:

$$\mathcal{I}(X_t; Y_t) \geq \mathcal{I}_\psi^{(DV)}(X_t; Y_t) := \mathbb{E}_{\mathbb{P}_{X_t Y_t}} \left[M_\psi(x_t, y_t) \right] - \log \mathbb{E}_{\mathbb{P}_{X_t \otimes Y_t}} \left[e^{M_\psi(x_t, y_t)} \right] \quad (7)$$

where, M represents a neural network represented by ψ, which is used to estimate the mutual information. However, our experiments showed that the function was hard to control during optimization and sometimes produced infinite results that terminated the experiment prematurely. Moreover, estimating the mutual information was unnecessary because our goal was to maximize the effective information between the input and output at time t in the Markov chain, which was equivalent to maximizing the mutual information. Therefore, the formula of Shannon mutual information [10] was used:

$$\mathcal{I}_{\omega,\psi}^{(JSD)}(X_t; Y_t) := \mathbb{E}_{\mathbb{P}_{X_t Y_t}} \left[-\mathrm{sp}\left(-M_{\omega,\psi}(x_t, y_t) \right) \right] - \mathbb{E}_{\mathbb{P}_{X_t} \otimes \mathbb{P}_{Y_t}} \left[\mathrm{sp}\left(M_{\omega,\psi}(x_t', y_t) \right) \right] \quad (8)$$

Let x_t' denote another sample from the distribution $\mathbb{P}_{X_t}$ at time t, different from x_t, as shown in Fig. 2(a). $sp(z) = log(1 + e^z)$ represents the softplus function. M is a neural network with parameters ψ for estimating the mutual information.

Compared with KL divergence, maximizing JS divergence is more stable and effective because it has a log2 upper bound. To further illustrate our process, an additional description of Fig. 2:

– Fig. 2(a) depicts the sampling process of x_t'. Firstly, another result ϵ' different from the noise ϵ is sampled from the normal distribution. Then, re-sampling is performed in $\mathbb{P}_{X_t}$ according to the sampling result to obtain x_t'.

– Fig. 2(b) depicts the basic structure of M_ψ, which consists of three 1×1 convolution kernels.
– Fig. 2(c) depicts the transformation process of the global feature vector. x'_t and x_t are connected to the output y_t from the channel dimension, and they are transformed into the global feature vectors whose channel dimension is one feature pixel invariant through M_ψ respectively.

3.3   Convolution Structure with the Transform Feature into U-Net

The diffusion model generates an image through T steps of reconstruction, which aim to minimize the information loss at each step. However, a deeper network structure is required to enable the neural network to simulate complex functions, which reduces the dimensions of the intermediate features to a much lower level than the input and output. This leads to information loss, which is one of the reasons for the image blur generated by the VAE model. Therefore, we use U-Net with skip connections as the basic model of our network structure in the diffusion model.

Figure 3 shows its main structure. It includes the basic Block module, the upsampling and downsampling modules, and the Convolutional Transformer Block (CvT) module. The basic Block module comprises two residual blocks, each of which contains two 3×3 convolutional layers and one batch normalization layer. The main part of U-Net consists of multiple Block modules that extract and learn features from input images. The downsampling module, implemented by a 3×3 convolutional layer with a stride of 2, halves the resolution of the feature map. The upsampling module, conversely, restores the resolution of the feature map to its original size using nearest-neighbor interpolation.

The CvT module is a novel module that combines convolution and self-attention mechanisms. It enhances the performance and robustness of the network while preserving the translational invariance of convolutional neural networks. We apply the CvT module to the lower-dimensional part of the feature map in the U-Net network, which is obtained after three downsampling operations. The CvT module consists of multiple Convolutional Transformer Blocks (CvT Blocks), each of which contains a depth-wise separable convolutional layer and a multi-head self-attention layer. The depth-wise separable convolutional layer performs linear projection of queries, keys, and values, while the multi-head self-attention layer facilitates global information interaction on the feature map.

CTU-Net has higher computational cost than U-Net, but it produces better output results in the DDPM-SR task due to its advantages of long-distance dependency and input adaptation. This property introduces an inductive bias for the CNN to adapt to different input image sizes while preserving the translation invariance of the CNN network.

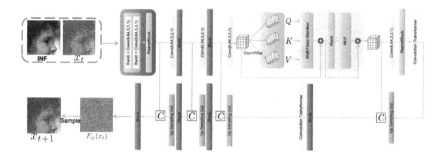

Fig. 3. The overall structure of CTU-Net.

4   Experiments

To evaluate the effectiveness of MMID in image super-resolution, we conducted super-resolution experiments on low-resolution faces and natural images. For faces, we performed 8x upsampling experiments to illustrate the effectiveness of MMID. For natural images, we performed 4x upsampling experiments.

- Face 8x super-resolution at 16–128 and 64–512 trained on FFHQ [13] and evaluated on CelebA-HQ [16]. Also, a comparison was drawn against the regression baseline model that shared the same architecture as SR3 but was trained with a L_2 loss.
- Natural image 4x super-resolution at 32–128 trained on either DIV2K(800 images) [1] dataset, and the resolution of HR patches was 128×128. Three benchmarks were applied for evaluation, including Set5 [4], Set14 [26] and Urban100 [12].

Backbones and Compared Methods. To demonstrate the effectiveness of MMID reasonably, we used the conventional U-Net for comparison experiments. We obtained MMID 16–128 and MMID 64–512 on the face dataset. We compared MMID 16–128 with PULSE [19], FSRNET [6] and SR3 16–128, which could super-resolve face images by a factor of 8 satisfactorily. The diffusion model performs well in large scale super-resolution tasks, but it produces noisier images for larger image sizes. By observing the MMID 64–512 results, we find that the mutual information helps to mitigate, but the noise is still present. Therefore, the network structure CTU-Net is proposed in this study to deal with the 4x SISR task and compare it with SRGAN [14], SFTGAN [23], ESRGAN [24], SPSR [18] and SwinIR [15]+$\mathcal{L}_{GAN}$, which are also generative models. We also showed that the generative output results for the SISR task were more satisfactory than the simple regression-based outputs of RCAN [28] and HAT [5]. We conducted a comparative experiment on them.

Training Details. The experiments were carried out on NVIDIA GTX 3090Ti GPU with PyTorch and the batch size was 4. As described in the previous

Fig. 4. The results of the CTU-Net model trained on DIV2K and applied to images outside the training set.

study, all images were preprocessed for downsampling and upsampling through the MATLAB bicubic kernel. The checkpoints were selected for the regression, MMID according to the peak-PSNR on the held out set. In the training process, the and in the loss were set to 1.0 and 5e−3, respectively. For the N-layer CvT structure in the CTU-Net model, it was set to 6. The Adam optimizer with a linear warmup schedule over 10k training steps was used, which is followed by a fixed learning rate of 1e−4 for 8x MMID, 1e−5 for regression models.

Evaluation Metrics. The GAN-SR results were compared in terms of both perceptual quality and reconstruction accuracy. As for the former, LPIPS [27] was used as a measure. LPIPS was validated as effective in evaluating GAN-SR results. For a comparison between the output of the generative model and that of the traditional simple regression, NIQE [20] was used to evaluate image quality in vision tasks. As for the latter, the PSNR and SSIM [25] indices in the Y channel in the YCbCr space were computed.

4.1 Qualitative Results

Face Images. Figure 1 and Fig. 5 shows the output results of test images of the face super-resolution model SR3 (16–128 and 64–512) and MMID (16–128 and 64–512). The detailed structure inferred can be seen clearly from the 8x magnification factor. Since one output corresponds to multiple inputs due to the large magnification, it is not expected to be exactly the same as the original image.

Natural Images. Figure 4 presents the 4x test results of the super-resolution model CTU-Net at DIV2K 100. Although the image based on simple regression is

Fig. 5. The results of the MMID (64–512) trained on FFHQ and applied to images outside the training set.

Table 1. PSNR & SSIM on 16–128 face super-resolution. Consistency measures MSE (x10⁻5) between the low-resolution inputs and the down-sampled super-resolution outputs.

CelebaHQ [16] 16–128	PSNR	SSIM	Consistency
PULSE [19]	16.88	0.44	161.1
FSRNET [6]	23.01	0.62	33.8
Regression [22]	23.96	**0.69**	2.71
SR3 [22]	23.04	0.65	2.68
MMID (ours)	**24.00**	0.65	**2.63**
CelebaHQ [16] **64–512**	**PSNR**	**SSIM**	**LPIPS**
SR3 [22]	19.87	0.44	0.3455
MMID (ours)	**24.36**	**0.58**	**0.2702**

found more consistent with the original image, it is lacking in texture details and blurred. The output of CTU-Net model has more details and a clearer texture.

4.2 Quantitative Comparison

Table 1 shows a quantitative comparison between the state-of-the-art 8x face super-resolution methods and our MMID (16–128 and 64–512). It can be seen from the table that our proposed maximize mutual information combined with diffusion model improves the accuracy of reconstruction to some extent (PSNR, SSIM, Consistency) on the basis of Conventional U-Net backbone network. The improvement is reflected in the 64–512 tasks, and in the comparison of perceptual quality (LPIPS) with SR3. For the task of 16–128, the amount of image information is less due to the smaller input image, making it more difficult to perform the task. The higher values of psnr and ssim for regression-based Regression result from the fact that its U-Net network maximizes the preservation of the basic structure of the original image. However, the output results obtained are affected by the L_p norm loss problem, which lacks detailed texture and is blurred. Although the relative generative-based PULSE, FSRNET, SR3, and MMID are inferior to the simple regression-based values in terms of reconstruction accuracy, their output is clearer and contains more texture details. Among

Table 2. Comparison of LPIPS between GAN-SR method and the proposed CTU-Net on natural image dataset.

Dataset	bicubic	SRGAN [14]	SFTGAN [23]	ESRGAN [24]	SPSR [18]	SwinIR [15] + LGAN	CTU-Net
Set5 [4]	0.2969	0.0753	0.08	0.0758	0.0647	0.0656	0.0648
Set14 [26]	0.385	0.1327	0.1313	0.1241	0.1207	0.116	0.1141
Urban100 [12]	0.4201	0.1439	0.1343	0.1229	0.1184	0.1077	0.1073

Table 3. Comparison of NIQE between regression-based methods and the proposed CTU-Net on natural image dataset.

Dataset	HR	bicubic	RCAN [28]	HAT [5]	CTU-Net
Set5 [4]	8.7552	12.4632	11.9708	11.5083	**9.7496**
Set14 [26]	7.3229	13.9131	11.5424	11.1034	**9.7164**
Urban100 [12]	6.1754	13.2011	9.5878	8.8818	**7.7199**

these methods, our proposed MMID produces better numerical performance and experimental output free of unpleasant artifacts. To further illustrate the effectiveness of our MMID in dealing with the problem caused by L_p norm loss, we reduced the difficulty of the task and changed the input image to 64×64. It contains more valid information and shows a more significant improvement in both reconstruction accuracy and perceptual quality (LPIPS) on experimental values.

In Table 2, the state-of-the-art GAN-SR methods are quantitatively compared with our CTU-Net. It can be seen from the table that our proposed CTU-Net performs well in perceptual quality (LPIPS) on several test datasets (Set5, Set14, Urban100) in the 4x task. Specifically, SPSR performs the best LPIPS values on the Set5 dataset due to its additional network branches that recover the gradient map of the images. SRGAN introduces GAN into the super-resolution task to solve the blurring of output texture caused by L_p norm loss in simple regression. Then, SFTGAN, ESRGAN, etc. were used to control GAN for the generation of clearer and more reasonable image textures through different ways. Given the effectiveness of transformer in vision tasks, SwinIR has achieved satisfactory results in performing super-resolution tasks through the long-range dependence of transformer. Also, with the generative power of GAN on top of it (SwinIR+L_{GAN}), it demonstrates an equally strong generative power and achieves better numerical performance in LPIPS. Meanwhile, our proposed CTU-Net performs fairly well in terms of LPIPS values on other test datasets. It was further illustrated that the simple regression-based super-resolution method has a poorer quality of output image than the generative-based one due to the limitation of the L_p norm loss, despite a better numerical tableau in terms of reconstruction accuracy. In Table 3, the image quality criterion NIQE is applied to demonstrate that the generative-based super-resolution method is superior to the regression method (RCAN, HAT), and the value of NIQE is more comparable to the original image.

5   Conclusion

This paper investigates the causes of artifacts in the super-resolution results generated by the DDPM-based SISR method. We attribute them to the uncertainty problem of multiple outputs corresponding to one input due to the L_p norm loss, and propose a maximizing mutual information strategy to solve this problem. We design a framework to maximize the mutual information between model inputs and outputs during the training of the DDPM-SR model. Moreover, we enhance the U-Net network structure of the diffusion model by incorporating the advantages of transform's input adaptation and long-distance dependency. The proposed MMID approach can be easily integrated into different DDPM models for generation and SISR tasks. Extensive experiments on widely used datasets demonstrate that MMID outperforms existing GAN-SR methods in terms of training stability and quality.

References

1. Agustsson, E., Timofte, R.: NTIRE 2017 challenge on single image super-resolution: dataset and study. In: 2017 IEEE Conference on Computer Vision and Pattern Recognition Workshops, CVPR Workshops 2017, Honolulu, HI, USA, 21–26 July 2017 (2017)
2. Ahuja, K.: Estimating Kullback-Leibler divergence using kernel machines. In: 53rd Asilomar Conference on Signals, Systems, and Computers, ACSCC 2019, Pacific Grove, CA, USA, 3–6 November 2019 (2019)
3. Belghazi, M.I., et al.: Mutual information neural estimation. In: Proceedings of the 35th International Conference on Machine Learning, ICML 2018, Stockholmsmässan, Stockholm, Sweden, 10–15 July 2018 (2018)
4. Bevilacqua, M., Roumy, A., Guillemot, C., Alberi-Morel, M.: Low-complexity single-image super-resolution based on nonnegative neighbor embedding. In: British Machine Vision Conference, BMVC 2012, Surrey, UK, 3–7 September 2012 (2012)
5. Chen, X., Wang, X., Zhou, J., Dong, C.: Activating more pixels in image super-resolution transformer. CoRR (2022)
6. Chen, Y., Tai, Y., Liu, X., Shen, C., Yang, J.: FSRNet: end-to-end learning face super-resolution with facial priors. In: 2018 IEEE Conference on Computer Vision and Pattern Recognition, CVPR 2018, Salt Lake City, UT, USA, 18–22 June 2018 (2018)
7. Dong, C., Loy, C.C., He, K., Tang, X.: Learning a deep convolutional network for image super-resolution. In: Fleet, D., Pajdla, T., Schiele, B., Tuytelaars, T. (eds.) ECCV 2014. LNCS, vol. 8692, pp. 184–199. Springer, Cham (2014). https://doi.org/10.1007/978-3-319-10593-2_13
8. Dosovitskiy, A., et al.: An image is worth 16x16 words: transformers for image recognition at scale. In: 9th International Conference on Learning Representations, ICLR 2021, Virtual Event, Austria, 3–7 May 2021 (2021)

9. Gatopoulos, I., Stol, M., Tomczak, J.M.: Super-resolution variational auto-encoders. CoRR (2020)
10. Hjelm, R.D., et al.: Learning deep representations by mutual information estimation and maximization. In: 7th International Conference on Learning Representations, ICLR 2019, New Orleans, LA, USA, 6–9 May 2019 (2019)
11. Ho, J., Jain, A., Abbeel, P.: Denoising diffusion probabilistic models. In: Advances in Neural Information Processing Systems 33: Annual Conference on Neural Information Processing Systems 2020, NeurIPS 2020, 6–12 December 2020, virtual (2020)
12. Huang, J., Singh, A., Ahuja, N.: Single image super-resolution from transformed self-exemplars. In: IEEE Conference on Computer Vision and Pattern Recognition, CVPR 2015, Boston, MA, USA, 7–12 June 2015 (2015)
13. Karras, T., Laine, S., Aila, T.: A style-based generator architecture for generative adversarial networks. In: IEEE Conference on Computer Vision and Pattern Recognition, CVPR 2019, Long Beach, CA, USA, 16–20 June 2019 (2019)
14. Ledig, C., et al.: Photo-realistic single image super-resolution using a generative adversarial network. In: 2017 IEEE Conference on Computer Vision and Pattern Recognition, CVPR 2017, Honolulu, HI, USA, 21–26 July 2017 (2017)
15. Liang, J., Cao, J., Sun, G., Zhang, K., Gool, L.V., Timofte, R.: SwinIR: image restoration using Swin transformer. In: IEEE/CVF International Conference on Computer Vision Workshops, ICCVW 2021, Montreal, BC, Canada, 11–17 October 2021 (2021)
16. Liu, Z., Luo, P., Wang, X., Tang, X.: Deep learning face attributes in the wild. In: 2015 IEEE International Conference on Computer Vision, ICCV 2015, Santiago, Chile, 7–13 December 2015 (2015)
17. Lugmayr, A., Danelljan, M., Van Gool, L., Timofte, R.: SRFlow: learning the super-resolution space with normalizing flow. In: Vedaldi, A., Bischof, H., Brox, T., Frahm, J.-M. (eds.) ECCV 2020. LNCS, vol. 12350, pp. 715–732. Springer, Cham (2020). https://doi.org/10.1007/978-3-030-58558-7_42
18. Ma, C., Rao, Y., Cheng, Y., Chen, C., Lu, J., Zhou, J.: Structure-preserving super resolution with gradient guidance. In: 2020 IEEE/CVF Conference on Computer Vision and Pattern Recognition, CVPR 2020, Seattle, WA, USA, 13–19 June 2020 (2020)
19. Menon, S., Damian, A., Hu, S., Ravi, N., Rudin, C.: PULSE: self-supervised photo upsampling via latent space exploration of generative models. In: 2020 IEEE/CVF Conference on Computer Vision and Pattern Recognition, CVPR 2020, Seattle, WA, USA, 13–19 June 2020 (2020)
20. Mittal, A., Soundararajan, R., Bovik, A.C.: Making a "completely blind" image quality analyzer. IEEE Signal Process. Lett. (2013)
21. Ronneberger, O., Fischer, P., Brox, T.: U-Net: convolutional networks for biomedical image segmentation. In: Navab, N., Hornegger, J., Wells, W.M., Frangi, A.F. (eds.) MICCAI 2015. LNCS, vol. 9351, pp. 234–241. Springer, Cham (2015). https://doi.org/10.1007/978-3-319-24574-4_28
22. Saharia, C., Ho, J., Chan, W., Salimans, T., Fleet, D.J., Norouzi, M.: Image super-resolution via iterative refinement. IEEE Trans. Pattern Anal. Mach. Intell. (2023)
23. Wang, X., Yu, K., Dong, C., Loy, C.C.: Recovering realistic texture in image super-resolution by deep spatial feature transform. In: 2018 IEEE Conference on Computer Vision and Pattern Recognition, CVPR 2018, Salt Lake City, UT, USA, 18–22 June 2018 (2018)

24. Wang, X., et al.: ESRGAN: enhanced super-resolution generative adversarial networks. In: Leal-Taixé, L., Roth, S. (eds.) ECCV 2018. LNCS, vol. 11133, pp. 63–79. Springer, Cham (2019). https://doi.org/10.1007/978-3-030-11021-5_5
25. Wang, Z., Bovik, A.C., Sheikh, H.R., Simoncelli, E.P.: Image quality assessment: from error visibility to structural similarity. IEEE Trans. Image Process. (2004)
26. Zeyde, R., Elad, M., Protter, M.: On single image scale-up using sparse-representations. In: Boissonnat, J.-D., et al. (eds.) Curves and Surfaces 2010. LNCS, vol. 6920, pp. 711–730. Springer, Heidelberg (2012). https://doi.org/10.1007/978-3-642-27413-8_47
27. Zhang, R., Isola, P., Efros, A.A., Shechtman, E., Wang, O.: The unreasonable effectiveness of deep features as a perceptual metric. In: 2018 IEEE Conference on Computer Vision and Pattern Recognition, CVPR 2018, Salt Lake City, UT, USA, 18–22 June 2018 (2018)
28. Zhang, Y., Li, K., Li, K., Wang, L., Zhong, B., Fu, Y.: Image Super-resolution using very deep residual channel attention networks. In: Ferrari, V., Hebert, M., Sminchisescu, C., Weiss, Y. (eds.) ECCV 2018. LNCS, vol. 11211, pp. 294–310. Springer, Cham (2018). https://doi.org/10.1007/978-3-030-01234-2_18

Fibrosis Grading Methods for Renal Whole Slide Images Based on Uncertainty Estimation

Ke Tang[1], Xiuxiu Hu[2], Pingsheng Chen[2], and Siyu Xia[1(✉)]

[1] School of Automation, Southeast University, Nanjing 210096, China
xsy@seu.edu.cn

[2] Department of Pathology, School of Medicine, Southeast University, Nanjing 210096, China

Abstract. Fibrosis gradings are a valuable indicator to provide diagnostic information for chronic kidney disease. The assessment of the percentage of renal fibrosis by physicians is based mainly on visual estimation, which is highly subjective and varies widely between physicians, hence the need for objective and reliable morphological assessment algorithms. For ultra-high resolution images, acquiring patch-level labels imposes a heavy annotation burden; conversely, indiscriminately assigning WSI-level labels to each patch poses a significant label noise problem. In this paper, we propose a weakly supervised two-stage framework. In the first stage (Patches Selection Stage), patches with low uncertainty, i.e., strongly correlated with WSI labels, are screened using approximate Bayesian inference. In the subsequent second stage (Decision Aggregation Stage), low uncertainty patches are merged into a large map and fed into a classification network to obtain WSI-level diagnostic results. The uncertainty estimation efficiently targets local regions of interest in high-resolution pathology slice images and excludes noise unrelated to WSI labels. We compared this method with previous methods for grading renal fibrosis in a self-constructed dataset of renal pathology provided by the Institute of Nephrology, Southeast University. We used the quadratic weighted kappa coefficient as a grading consistency evaluation index. The results show that this method is superior in accuracy and kappa consistency.

Keywords: Uncertainty Estimation · Weakly Supervised · WSI Classification · Renal Fibrosis

1 Introduction

Renal puncture biopsy is an essential part of the clinical work-up of kidney disease, where the interstitial fibrosis rating of a kidney biopsy is a powerful indicator to provide diagnostic information for chronic kidney disease. Pathologists estimate the degree of kidney disease by visually measuring the percentage of fibrosis in the entire large picture. The degree of renal cortical lesions is graded according to the Banff classification definition according to the percentage of fibrosis as follows: $0\% - 5\%$ (none or mild), $6\% - 25\%$ (mild), $26\% - 50\%$

H. Lu et al. (Eds.): ACPR 2023, LNCS 14407, pp. 396–408, 2023.
https://doi.org/10.1007/978-3-031-47637-2_30

(moderate), and $> 50\%$ (severe). The percentage of fibrosis is based on the pathologist's visual estimate of the cortical area of the kidney and is, therefore, highly subjective. The variability in assessment by different pathologists can be significant. Therefore, it is necessary to improve the objective reliability of the fibrosis ratings by using appropriate morphological assessment algorithms.

Deep learning-based methods have demonstrated greater accuracy and stability than traditional image processing algorithms based on feature extraction. However, the following difficulties are encountered when performing WSI lesion grading assessments:

Firstly, ultra-high resolution WSIs (hundreds of thousands of pixels in size) cannot be directly invested in neural networks. In addition, unlike surgically excised sections, the tissue obtained from kidney puncture biopsies are usually long strips. The entire WSI is empty and less dense regarding information. Therefore, suitable solutions are needed to efficiently target localized areas of interest.

A second difficulty is that the grading task differs from the usual task of lesion classification. Renal fibrosis lesions are a continuous process. Although the Banff classification artificially divides it into four lesion stages, in practice, there will be cases that are at the junction of the grades and difficult to identify. The consequences of incorrect grading can be severe. Over-grading can cause unnecessary anxiety and over-treatment, while under-grading can cause patients to become complacent and delay optimal treatment.

For the above reasons, we propose a weakly supervised two-stage framework, as shown in Fig. 1. In the first stage (Patches Selection Stage), the patches strongly correlated with WSI labels are selected using approximate Bayesian inference to exclude the effect of patch-level label noise from weak labels in multi-instance learning. In the subsequent second stage (Decision Aggregation Stage), the strongly correlated patches are stitched into one big picture by appropriate data pre-processing techniques and then fed into the classification network for the final WSI-level evaluation results. The main contributions of this work are summarized as follows:

(I) We propose a weakly supervised two-stage framework for the ultra-high resolution WSI grading task. Experimental results show that our method can retain more high-resolution texture information with higher accuracy than the method of directly encoding the global map.

(II) We use the Monte Carlo dropout method to approximate Bayesian inference for uncertainty estimation to filter out patches with low uncertainty, i.e., high correlation with WSI-level labels. The results show that the strategy effectively excludes the influence of label noise from weak labels.

(III) We introduce ordinal regression loss functions and squared weighted κ evaluation metrics. With such a loss function and evaluation system, larger grading errors result in heavier penalties, thus better fitting the needs of the grading task.

2 Related Works

2.1 Algorithms Applied to Renal Whole Slide Images

In recent years, several teams have reported their work on ultra-high resolution renal biopsy images, including tasks such as automatic quantification of renal fibrosis, glomerular detection, and segmentation of important kidney tissue structures. In general, these algorithms can be divided into two main categories: traditional image processing algorithms based on feature extraction and deep learning-based approaches. Farris et al. developed a Positive Pixel Count algorithm (PPC) within the self-built HistomicksTK framework [5]. They used the Pearson correlation coefficient to assess the correlation between algorithmic and physician grading results. Unfortunately, the resulting correlation was low, with a correlation coefficient of $\kappa = 0.46$. Traditional image processing algorithms are susceptible to extraneous factors, such as the concentration of staining reagents and the scanning light, making them less robust [7]. Furthermore, due to lesions, the algorithm has difficulty distinguishing between typical fibrous structures, such as glomeruli or tubular basement membranes, and interstitial fibrosis, which can lead to an erroneous overestimation of the extent of fibrosis.

Deep learning-based methods have shown greater accuracy and stability. Ginley et al. used a U-net segmentation network with DeepLab v2 as the baseline to segment renal fibrosis and tubular atrophy areas (IFTA) under a pixel-level mask. They divided the enclosed IFTA area by the total cortical area as the renal percentage of fibrosis [9]. However, renal fibrotic lesions cannot be considered a strictly contiguous domain. Furthermore, pixel-level mask annotation, a heavy burden for physicians, is not readily available in large quantities. In contrast, weakly supervised WSI classification based on Slide-level labeling is a better approach. Inspired by the work in [2], Zheng et al. developed global and local collaborative networks for weakly supervised multi-instance learning [16]. However, indiscriminately treating all patch labels as identical is bound to introduce a large amount of label noise. Therefore, suitable schemes are needed to efficiently target local regions of interest and exclude noise that is not related to WSI labels.

2.2 Weakly Supervised Learning-Based Approaches to WSIs Classification

Histopathological image classification usually follows the Multiple Instance Learning (MIL) frameworks, also called the bag-of-words model. The whole WSI is considered a bag; the hundreds of cut patches are called words or instances. Hou et al. train each patch, construct the predictions as a grey-scale histogram, and train a classification model using the histogram [10]. Courtiol et al. use RNNs to aggregate patch-level features to synthesize WSI-level decisions [4]. Lu et al. merged domain knowledge into instance-level K-means clustering to add further supervision to improve data utilization efficiency [12]. However, this clustering is based on the assumption that different cancer subtypes are mutually exclusive in the classification process. Unsupervised clustering does not work well for this task, as renal fibrosis lesions are continuous variations, and the lesion patterns of each grade cannot meet the mutually exclusive requirement.

In addition to multi-instance learning, another option is to borrow ideas from Vision Transformer and use self-attention to allow the network to learn the structure of pathological image features spontaneously. Inspired by multi-scale feature pyramids, Chen et al. used a hierarchical pre-training strategy to encode the relationship between words and bags hierarchically, using 10,678 WSIs to pre-train the massive scale ViT architecture to obtain feature encoders and then fine-tune the model in a downstream weakly supervised classification task [1]. To reduce data requirements and computational overhead, Mehta et al. first pre-encoded the full WSI map with a pre-trained CNN to reduce the sequence length to be input, thereby reducing the model size [13]. However, the whole slide obtained from the puncture biopsy is empty with low information density, and more details will be inevitably lost by direct precoding the whole image with CNN.

3   Methods

This paper proposes an automatic framework for grading fibrosis in ultra-high resolution renal biopsy sections based on approximate Bayesian inference. Figure 1 shows that the framework is divided into two phases. In the first stage (Patches Selection Stage), the Monte Carlo dropout method is used to approximate Bayesian inference, perform uncertainty estimation, and screen out patches with low uncertainty, i.e., high correlation with WSI labels; in the second stage (decision aggregation stage), the top N^2 patches most relevant to WSI labels are extracted, stitched into an $N \times N$ large graph, and then put into the classification network for decision aggregation to obtain the fibrosis grading assessment results of WSI.

3.1   Patches Selection Stage

In the first patches selection stage, the WSI is cut into hundreds of patches that do not overlap under a 10x tiled field of view. Invalid background patches are filtered out using positive pixel counting, leaving patches that contain tissue. a WSI-level label is assigned to each patch individually, which is a weakly supervised label for the classification network. The lightweight model EifficientNet [14] proposed by M. Tan et al. was chosen here to save the time required for subsequent variational inference. Subsequently, to achieve uncertainty estimation, we followed the last pooling layer of EifficientNet with two other fully connected layers, each followed by a ReLu nonlinear activation layer and a Dropout layer, and the dropout rate was set to 0.5.

Monte Carlo Dropout and Variational Inference. For the same model, we can let it make T predictions for the same sample and capture the perceptual

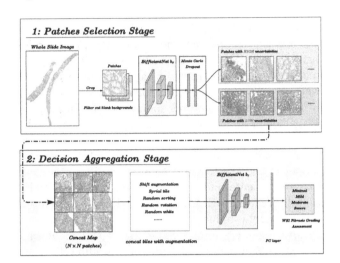

Fig. 1. The proposed weakly supervised two-stage framework. In the first stage (Patches Selection Stage), patches strongly correlated with WSI-level labels are screened out using approximate Bayesian inference to exclude the effect of patch-level label noise from weak labels in multi-instance learning. In the subsequent second stage (Decision Aggregation Stage), the strongly correlated patches are stitched together into one big picture by appropriate data pre-processing techniques and then fed into the classification network for decision aggregation to obtain WSI-level diagnostic assessment results.

uncertainty of the model if these T predictions are different [11]. We can make the model parameter values obey some distribution, and by sampling T times in this distribution, we can obtain T sets of different model parameters.

The Dropout layer of a neural network was initially used as a regularization technique that could effectively prevent model overfitting. Gal Y et al. were surprised that the Dropout strategy could also be used as an approximate Bayesian inference for deep Gaussian Processes (GP) [8]. The dropout rate is set to 0.5 in this paper. The neurons in this network layer have a half probability of deactivating; therefore, the layer's parameters conform to the Bernoulli distribution. So, approximate Variational Inference (VI) for large and complex models can be accomplished by sampling T times from the approximate posterior sample as long as the dropout is still turned on at prediction time. For T predictions, the probabilities can be approximated using Monte Carlo integration as follows:

$$p\left(y = c\right) \approx \frac{1}{T} \sum_{t=1}^{T} Softmax \left(f^{\widehat{W_t}}\left(x\right)\right) \tag{1}$$

where $\widehat{W_t}$ is the Dropout distribution [8].

We use predictive entropy [15] to measure the uncertainty of each patch.

$$p_c = \frac{1}{T} \sum_{t=1}^{T} p_c^t H(p) = -\sum_{c=1}^{C} p_c \log p_c \tag{2}$$

where p_c^t represents the *softmax* probability of the c th class at the t th prediction. The sample is divided into C classes in total. The prediction entropy then takes a value between 0 and 1; the closer to 1, the greater the uncertainty and the lower the confidence in the sample prediction. From this, the top N^2 patches that are most relevant to the WSI labels can be selected based on the uncertainty estimate and remitted to the second stage.

3.2   Decision Aggregation Stage

In the first stage, MC dropout and variational inference obtained N^2 patches with low uncertainty. These patches were stitched together to obtain a $N \times N$ concatenate map. We used some tricks to further data augmentation before feeding the concatenate map into the classification network.

Concat Tile with Augmentation

Shift Augmentation. When cutting WSIs as $w_p \times w_p$ patches, some cut-edge information is inevitably lost. To compensate for this loss, we set up two cut modes, as shown in Fig. 2a , where the starting point of the cut differs by $\frac{w_p}{2}$ in the horizontal and vertical directions, respectively. For the actual training, with probability $p = 0.5$, the patches of mode1 or mode2 are allowed to participate in the whole process, thus compensating for the loss of cut-edge information.

Sprial Tile. With low to high uncertainty, the N^2 patches obtained in the first stage are arranged spirally from the center towards the outer perimeter, as shown in Fig. 2b. The patches with higher prediction confidence are placed in the middle of the image so that important information will be noticed.

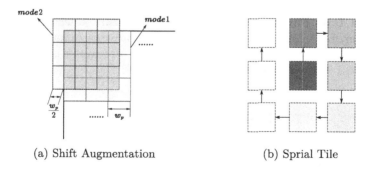

(a) Shift Augmentation   (b) Sprial Tile

Fig. 2. Data pre-processing. We used some tricks to further data augmentation before feeding the concatenate map into the classification network.

Random Sorting, Random Rotation and Random White. Random sorting with $p = 0.5$ probability for patches, random rotation by 90 degrees operation, respectively. Random whitening with probability $p = 0.2$. Further augmentation of the concatenate map.

In addition, we try more data augmentation strategies for the whole concatenate map, including transpose, horizontal flip, vertical flip, random rotation, random translation, non-rigid transformation, and other operations.

After data augmentation, the concatenate map is fed into $EifficientNet\ b_1$, which eventually passes through the fully connected layers and $softmax$ layers to obtain the WSI fibrosis grading assessment results.

3.3   Loss Function

Loss Functions for Grading Tasks. The categories were mutually exclusive in previous pathological classification tasks, and there was no concept of order. Therefore cross-entropy loss L_{CE} was commonly used.

However, renal fibrosis lesions are a continuous process. Assuming a sample with a ground truth of minimal (Grade $= 0$), if the neural network predicts it as severe (Grade $= 3$), it deserves to be penalized more than if it is predicted as mild (Grade $= 1$), which cannot be satisfied by L_{CE}.

One option is to treat the grading task as a regression task, using a mean squared loss function L_{MSE}.

Another option is to use an ordinal regression loss function L_{OR} [3]. It considers the properties of both the classification task and the regression task. For a standard classification neural network that does not consider category order, if the input x belongs to category k, then x can be encoded as a one-hot form $t = (0, ..., 0, 1, 0, ..., 0)$, i.e., only the t_kth element is 1, and all other elements are 0. Then for a classification network considering the order of categories, x can be encoded as $t = (1, ..., 1, 1, 0, ..., 1, 1, 0, ..., 0)$, setting the first k elements to 1 and the rest to 0. It transforms the ordinal regression task into a multi-label classification task, computed using a cross-entropy loss function. In the experimental section of Sect. 5, we will show the impact of each loss function on the model performance.

Weighted Loss Function. Pathology images usually suffer from an uneven distribution of categories, where the number of negative cases (or mild cases) will be much higher than the number of positive cases (or severe cases). Therefore a weighted loss function can be applied as follows:

$$L_w = \sum_{c=1}^{C} \left(\frac{N}{N_c} \right)^k L_c \tag{3}$$

where the weight term $n_c = \left(\frac{N}{N_c} \right)^k$ balances the loss L_c for each category c. N is the total number of data sets, N_c is the amount of data belonging to category c, and k is a factor controlling the importance of category balance. In this paper, $k = 2$.

4   Experiments and Results

4.1   Datasets

Our experiment used a self-constructed data set of renal pathology provided by the Institute of Nephrology, Southeast University. Sections were stained with Sirius Red for the 465 cases diagnosed as renal fibrosis. Each WSI was assigned a grade label according to the Banff classification [6]. The grade assessment was performed by specialist renal pathologists, with three pathologists evaluating each WSI using the Back-to-Back method, i.e., two experts reviewed each WSI first, reserving cases for concordance. If there is disagreement, it is referred to a third expert for review, following the majority voting principle. If the three pathologists could not agree at all, the case was discarded. The internal consistency of pathologists was 0.906.

Among the 465 WSIs, 98 cases were selected as the test set, and the remaining 367 cases were the training and validation sets, using five-fold cross-validation. The specific division details are shown in Table 1.

Table 1. Datasets division.

Grade	minimal	mild	moderate	severe	All
Training & Validation	120	136	80	31	367
Testing	25	25	25	23	98

Data Pre-processing

Segmentation. For each WSI, convert it from RGB space to HSV space. Use the Saturation channel to generate a binary mask for the foreground of the tissue area based on a certain threshold. The mask edges are smoothed by median filtering and morphological closure operations.

Cropping. Downsample the original image (40x resolution) to 10x resolution (commonly used for physicians) and crop patches from within the split contour at 224 × 224. As mentioned in Sect. 3, the original image is cropped in two modes to achieve shift augmentation.

Implementation Details. We experimented with the NVIDIA GeForce RTX 3090, used EfficientNet-B0 as the baseline for patch classification in stage one, and trained 100 epochs per round. We will discuss the impact of the variational inference parameter T on the model's performance later in Sect. 5. The concatenate map was resized to 240 × 240 in the subsequent decision aggregation phase and fed into the EfficientNet-B1 classification network, with 50 epochs per round. The training was performed with a warm-up strategy (first 10 steps of epoch 0) and an early stop strategy (early stop if the validation set loss did not improve within 10 epochs).

4.2   Results

Evaluation Indicators. We use balanced accuracy (BACC) with squared weighted kappa index (QWK) as an evaluation metric. BACC is typically used to deal with unbalanced data sets by taking the average of the results after each category's accuracy has been calculated and balancing the sample size for each category to eliminate potential bias from unbalanced sample sizes.

The QWK fits the hierarchical task better than BACC, as the orderliness of the different classifications should be considered. Linearly weighted (linear) considers the difference between every two levels to be equal, whereas square-weighted QWK squares the weights of the linear weights, amplifying the degree of inconsistency determination, with weights calculated as follows:

$$w_{i,j} = \frac{(i-j)^2}{(N-1)^2} \tag{4}$$

The κ consistency factor is calculated as follows:

$$\kappa = 1 - \frac{\sum_{i,j} w_{i,j} O_{i,j}}{\sum_{i,j} w_{i,j} E_{i,j}} \tag{5}$$

where O_{ij} represents the overall consistency of classification results, and E_{ij} represents the consistency of expected results under the random classification assumption.

Table 2. Effect of Hyperparameters. We explored the effect of two hyperparameters on the model's performance in a five-fold cross-validation.

Parameter T

	T=4	T=5	T=6	T=7	T=8	T=9	**T=10**	T=11	T=12
BACC	0.6974	0.7031	0.7201	0.7315	0.7312	0.7478	**0.7603**	0.7482	0.7468
QWK	0.766	0.7912	0.8309	0.8422	0.8498	0.8564	**0.8699**	0.8604	0.8599

Parameter N

	N=5	N=6	N=7	**N=8**	N=9	N=10	N=11
BACC	0.5645	0.6774	0.7312	**0.7603**	0.7478	0.722	0.6533
QWK	0.7738	0.8171	0.8472	**0.8699**	0.8573	0.8446	0.8041

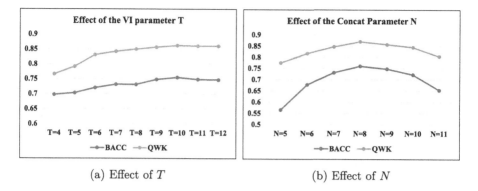

(a) Effect of T (b) Effect of N

Fig. 3. Effect of Hyperparameters. (a) Effect of T: an increasing value of T results in more accurate uncertainty estimates and increases validation time overhead. (b) Effect of N: when the hyperparameter N is too tiny, the concatenate map is not informative enough; relatively, the information density of the concatenate map will need to be higher when.

Effect of Hyperparameters. We explored the effect of two hyperparameters on the model's performance in a five-fold cross-validation. Table 2 shows quantitatively the effect of the parameters on model performance. Figure 3 shows qualitatively. An increasing value of T results in more accurate uncertainty estimates and increases validation time overhead. Considering the model performance and time overhead, the final value of $T = 10$ is taken. With $N \times N$ patches stitched into concatenate map, when the hyperparameter N is too tiny, the concatenate map is not informative enough; relatively, when N is too large, the concatenate map is too empty and too much information is lost after downsampling. In the end, $N = 8$, i.e., 64 patches, are stitched together as a concatenate map.

Ablation Study

Selection Principles Based on Uncertainty Estimates. We validated the effect of the uncertainty estimation-based(UE) patches selection principle in the testing set by comparing it with the positive pixel count-based(PPC) rule. Compared to the PPC, the UE method excluded the interference of normal fibrotic tissues such as blood vessels, glomeruli, and renal peritoneum, as shown in Fig. 4. The BACC and QWK of UE were 0.7548 and 0.8619, respectively, while those of PPC were 0.6903 and 0.8069, with the former showing a significant improvement over the latter.

Data Enhancement Strategies. Table 3 shows the impact of the data preprocessing techniques mentioned in Sect. 3. Shift augmentation, random sorting, and whole concatenate map augmentation are the most noticeable improvements. Spiral tile and Random rotation are also worthwhile strategies. Random white introduces a degradation, which we speculate is because it randomly discards

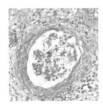   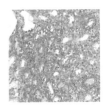

(a) Glomeruli.	(b) Renal medulla.	(c) Blood Vessels.	(d) Severe Fibrosis.
$p = 0.53$	$p = 0.70$	$p = 0.58$	$p = 0.11$

Fig. 4. Effect of the Uncertainty Estimation. The UE method excluded the interference of normal fibrotic tissues with high uncertainty, such as (a) glomeruli ($p = 0.53$), (b) renal peritoneum ($p = 0.70$), and (c) blood vessels ($p = 0.58$), saving low-uncertainty patches ((d) severe fibrosis ($p = 0.11$)).

critical information patches, leading to an increase in overall decision-making errors. Therefore this strategy was eventually discarded in favor of other strategies.

Loss Functions. In Sect. 3, we introduce three loss functions, namely the cross-entropy loss function L_{CE}, the mean squared error loss function L_{MSE}, and the ordinal regression loss function L_{OR}. Table 4 shows the effect of the loss functions on the model performance. The comparison shows that the best strategy is first to use L_{CE} as the optimization target in the Patches Selection Stage, which can reduce the learning difficulty of the network, and then use L_{OR} in the Decision Aggregation Stage, which can learn the monotonicity of the ordinal regression task from the less noisy patches.

Table 3. Data Pre-processing

	BACC	QWK
No Augmentation	0.629	0.7073
Whole Concat Map	0.6714	0.7663
Shift	0.7049	0.8384
Shift+Sprial Tile	0.7162	0.8401
Shift+Random Sort.	0.7446	0.8535
Shift+Random Rota.	0.7081	0.8344
Shift+Random Whit.	0.6837	0.822

Table 4. Loss Function

	BACC	QWK
CE	0.6407	0.6925
MSE	0.6389	0.7314
OR	0.6354	0.7441
CE+OR	**0.7548**	**0.8619**
CE+MSE	0.6822	0.8065

Comparison with Other Methods. We compare our approach with several recent works mentioned in Sect. 2: AJPA, a global-local collaboration framework [16]; CLAM, a multi-instance framework based on clustering and attention pooling [12]; and HATNet, a lightweight Transformer architecture pre-coded by pre-trained CNNs [13]. The results are shown in Table 5. The model in this paper achieves state-of-art performance.

Table 5. Comparison with Other Weakly Supervised Classification Methods

	BACC	QWK
AJPA [16]	0.5161	0.7073
CLAM [12]	0.6059	0.7506
HATNet [13]	0.5873	0.7617
AJPA + L_{OR}	0.6515	0.7443
CLAM + L_{OR}	0.7101	0.8267
HATNet + L_{OR}	0.7159	0.8145
Ours	**0.7548**	**0.8619**

5 Conclusion

In this paper, we develop a weakly supervised two-stage framework for classifying ultra-high resolution kidney pathology images. We used uncertainty estimation to exclude noisy patches and generated uncertainty visualization maps to increase the interpretability of the neural network classification results and to help physicians qualitatively target regions of interest. Although this study achieved high performance in grading renal fibrosis, it did not validate the robustness of the model in an external dataset from other laboratories. In addition, further extension of the present framework to other pathological grading tasks, not limited to chronic kidney disease, could be attempted.

References

1. Chen, R.J., et al.: Scaling vision transformers to gigapixel images via hierarchical self-supervised learning. In: Proceedings of the IEEE/CVF Conference on Computer Vision and Pattern Recognition, pp. 16144–16155 (2022)
2. Chen, W., Jiang, Z., Wang, Z., Cui, K., Qian, X.: Collaborative global-local networks for memory-efficient segmentation of ultra-high resolution images. In: Proceedings of the IEEE/CVF conference on computer vision and pattern recognition, pp. 8924–8933 (2019)
3. Cheng, J., Wang, Z., Pollastri, G.: A neural network approach to ordinal regression. In: 2008 IEEE International Joint Conference on Neural Networks (IEEE world congress on computational intelligence), pp. 1279–1284. IEEE (2008)
4. Courtiol, P., et al.: Deep learning-based classification of mesothelioma improves prediction of patient outcome. Nat. Med. **25**(10), 1519–1525 (2019)
5. Farris, A.B., et al.: Morphometric and visual evaluation of fibrosis in renal biopsies. J. Am. Soc. Nephrol. **22**(1), 176–186 (2011)
6. Farris, A.B., et al.: Banff digital pathology working group: going digital in transplant pathology. Am. J. Transplant. **20**(9), 2392–2399 (2020)
7. Farris, A.B., Vizcarra, J., Amgad, M., Cooper, L.A.D., Gutman, D., Hogan, J.: Image analysis pipeline for renal allograft evaluation and fibrosis quantification. Kidney Int. Reports **6**(7), 1878–1887 (2021)

8. Gal, Y., Ghahramani, Z.: Dropout as a Bayesian approximation: representing model uncertainty in deep learning. In: International Conference on Machine Learning, pp. 1050–1059. PMLR (2016)

9. Ginley, B., et al.: Automated computational detection of interstitial fibrosis, tubular atrophy, and glomerulosclerosis. J. Am. Soc. Nephrol. **32**(4), 837–850 (2021)

10. Hou, L., Samaras, D., Kurc, T.M., Gao, Y., Davis, J.E., Saltz, J.H.: Patch-based convolutional neural network for whole slide tissue image classification. In: Proceedings of the IEEE Conference on Computer Vision and Pattern Recognition, pp. 2424–2433 (2016)

11. Kendall, A., Gal, Y.: What uncertainties do we need in Bayesian deep learning for computer vision? In: Advances in Neural Information Processing Systems 30 (2017)

12. Lu, M.Y., Williamson, D.F., Chen, T.Y., Chen, R.J., Barbieri, M., Mahmood, F.: Data-efficient and weakly supervised computational pathology on whole-slide images. Nature Biomed. Eng. **5**(6), 555–570 (2021)

13. Mehta, S., et al.: End-to-end diagnosis of breast biopsy images with transformers. Med. Image Anal. **79**, 102466 (2022)

14. Tan, M., Le, Q.: Efficientnet: rethinking model scaling for convolutional neural networks. In: International Conference on Machine Learning, pp. 6105–6114. PMLR (2019)

15. Yu, L., Wang, S., Li, X., Fu, C.-W., Heng, P.-A.: Uncertainty-aware self-ensembling model for semi-supervised 3D left atrium segmentation. In: Shen, D., et al. (eds.) MICCAI 2019. LNCS, vol. 11765, pp. 605–613. Springer, Cham (2019). https://doi.org/10.1007/978-3-030-32245-8_67

16. Zheng, Y., et al.: Deep-learning-driven quantification of interstitial fibrosis in digitized kidney biopsies. Am. J. Pathol. **191**(8), 1442–1453 (2021)

Zooplankton Classification Using Hierarchical Attention Branch Network

Koichi Ito[1]($\boxtimes$), Kanta Miura[1], Takafumi Aoki[1], Yurie Otake[2],
Wataru Makino[2], and Jotaro Urabe[2]

[1] Graduate School of Information Sciences, Tohoku University, 6-6-05,
Aramaki Aza Aoba, Sendai 9808579, Japan
`ito@aoki.ecei.tohoku.ac.jp`
[2] Graduate School of Life Sciences, Tohoku University, 6-3, Aramaki Aza Aoba,
Sendai 9808578, Japan

Abstract. Plankton is recognized as one of the most important indicators of the health of aquatic ecosystems and water quality. Surveys of plankton populations in oceans and lakes have been conducted manually. Plankton classification methods using deep learning have been developed to automatically classify plankton images. These methods do not sufficiently take into account the bias in the species included in the dataset or the similarity of their shapes. In this paper, we propose a hierarchical attention branch network (H-ABN) to utilize that plankton are hierarchically named according to their taxonomic ranks. We demonstrate the effectiveness of the proposed method through experiments using a zooplankton dataset collected from lakes and ponds in Japan.

Keywords: image classification · plankton · taxonomy · attention branch network · convolutional neural network

1 Introduction

Zooplankton play a fundamental role in aquatic ecosystem services, for example, regulating water quality by eating algae and linking lower and higher trophic levels [18]. In recent years, aquatic ecosystems have become a serious environmental problem due to the decrease in biodiversity caused by the increase in alien species and the occurrence of nuisance algae. Therefore, plankton, including zooplankton, have been monitored periodically in economically important oceans, lakes, and reservoirs. On the other hand, it is difficult to conduct periodic and accurate plankton monitoring due to the limited number of experts who have the skills to identify the large amount of plankton contained in the collected samples. In addition, plankton communities need to be monitored frequently since they vary within a few days, however, accurate identification and enumeration at high frequencies is difficult even for experts.

To address the above problems, automated plankton monitoring systems using machine learning techniques have been investigated. The methods using

© The Author(s), under exclusive license to Springer Nature Switzerland AG 2023
H. Lu et al. (Eds.): ACPR 2023, LNCS 14407, pp. 409–419, 2023.
https://doi.org/10.1007/978-3-031-47637-2_31

hand-crafted features have been proposed as typical plankton image classification methods using machine learning [9,16,20]. Examples of typical hand-crafted features include Scale-Invariant Feature Transform (SIFT) and Histogram of Oriented Gradients (HOG). Plankton images are classified from extracted features using discriminators such as Support Vector Machine (SVM) and Random Forest. Due to the generality of hand-crafted features, they are not necessarily suitable for plankton image classification, and the classification accuracy is low. With the rapid development of deep learning [8], Convolutional Neural Network (CNN)-based methods have recently been proposed for automated plankton image classification [3,5,7,12–14]. Plankton images can be classified more accurately than methods using hand-crafted features since features are extracted from plankton images based on training using a large amount of data. These methods only utilize CNNs for image recognition to classify plankton images, and do not fully consider label bias or similarity of plankton shapes in the dataset. Although plankton are classified hierarchically based on taxonomic ranks, only one label is given to each plankton image in the available datasets.

In this paper, we consider the plankton image classification by taking into account the taxonomic ranks of the plankton. The taxonomic ranks of plankton are often determined based on their shapes. We expect that it is effective to classify images hierarchically according to the taxonomic ranks. Therefore, we propose a plankton image classification method using Attention Branch Network (ABN) [6], which can apply attention to regions of interests, in a hierarchical form to classify plankton images with high accuracy. We also construct a plankton image dataset by annotating labels based on the taxonomic ranks to samples collected in Japanese lakes and marshes to classify plankton images according to the taxonomic ranks. We demonstrate the effectiveness of the proposed method in plankton image classification through performance evaluation experiments using the constructed plankton image dataset.

2   Related Work

This section gives an overview of plankton image datasets and plankton image classification using CNNs.

2.1   Plankton Image Datasets

Table 1 summarizes the plankton image dataset. WHOI-Plankton [2] is a dataset of 3,272,578 images consisting of 103 classes of zooplankton and phytoplankton collected at Martha's Vineyard. WHOI [17] is a dataset of 6,600 images consisting of 22 classes of zooplankton and phytoplankton collected at Woods Hole Harbor. The images in both datasets were taken with an underwater microscope (In Situ Ichthyoplankton Imaging System: ISIIS), and are therefore blurred. ZooScan [9] is a dataset of 3,771 images consisting of 20 classes of zooplankton collected at Villefranche-sur-Mer Bay. The images in this dataset were scanned using a

Table 1. Summary of plankton image datasets for plankton image classification, where "P" and "Z" indicate phytoplankton and zooplankton, respectively.

Dataset	# of images	# of classes	Image size [px.]	Location	Type
WHOI-Plankton [2]	3,272,578	103	54×139	Sea	P, Z
WHOI [17]	6,600	22	156×367	Sea	P, Z
ZooScan [9]	3,771	20	143×154	Sea	Z
Kaggle [1]	30,336	121	67×73	Sea	P, Z
BearingSea [3]	17,920	7	425×411	Sea	Z
ZooLake [11]	17,943	35	123×121	Lake	Z
Ours	35,820	76	191×190	Lake	Z

consumer product, ZooScan[1]. The background is clear due to the free of dust and other impurities, however, the resolution of the images is low. Kaggle [1] is a dataset of 30,336 images consisting of 121 classes of zooplankton and phytoplankton collected at Florida Strait. The images are blurred since they were taken by ISIIS as well as WHOI-Plankton and WHOI. BearingSea [3] is a dataset of 17,920 images consisting of 7 classes of zooplankton collected at Southeastern Bering Sea. The images in this dataset were taken using the zooplankton visualization and imaging system (ZOOVIS), which is a high-resolution digital imaging system that can acquire images of plankton underwater. ZooLake [11] is a dataset of 17,943 images consisting of 35 classes of zooplankton collected at Lake Greifensee. The images were taken using an underwater microscope (Dual-magnification Scripps Plankton Camera: DSPC), and the image quality is higher than that of other datasets. Although the plankton nomenclature is based on taxonomic ranks, only one label, such as species, is assigned to any of the datasets. Hierarchical labels are important for plankton image classification, since plankton taxonomic ranks are associated with their shapes. Therefore, we construct a new plankton image dataset with high resolution images using optical microscopy and hierarchical labels assigned according to the plankton taxonomic ranks. The details of our dataset are described in Sect. 4.

2.2 Plankton Image Classification Using CNNs

We provide an overview of plankton image classification methods using CNNs. Luo et al. classified plankton images extracted by k-means into 108 types of plankton using SparseConvNet [14]. Ellen et al. improved the classification accuracy by adding metadata obtained during data acquisition to the fully-connected layer for VGG16 [5]. Cheng et al. detected plankton using MSER and classified them with SVM using features extracted by CNN [3]. Lumini et al. propose a method to ensemble features extracted by multiple pre-trained CNNs [12,13]. González et al. propose a method using ResNet [10] and analyze the counting

---
[1] http://www.zooscan.com.

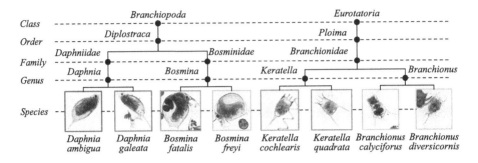

Fig. 1. Example of taxonomic ranks of plankton.

plankton for time-series data. All of the methods only utilize CNNs used in image classification, and none of them have considered the characteristics of plankton. In addition, these methods use plankton data collected at the same location for training and test, and therefore, the generalizability of the classification methods has not been correctly evaluated.

3   Hierarchical Plankton Image Classification

We present the proposed method for classifying plankton images with labels based on the taxonomic ranks. The following describes the plankton taxonomic ranks, ABN, which is the fundamental of the proposed method, and the hierarchical ABN.

3.1   Taxonomic Ranks of Plankton

A hierarchical nomenclature based on taxonomy such as *class*, *order*, *family*, *genus*, and *species* is used for plankton. An example of the hierarchical structure of plankton taxonomic ranks is shown in Fig. 1. Plankton of the same *genus* have very similar shapes, even though they belong to different *species*. Thus, the taxonomic rank of plankton is based on its shape, which may be useful for plankton image classification. In this paper, we use five taxonomic ranks of plankton: *class*, *order*, *family*, *genus*, and *species* .

3.2   Attention Branch Network

The proposed method utilizes Attention Branck Network (ABN) [6], which provides feedback on the attention map generated from the feature map, to classify plankton images considering the shape of the plankton. ABN is an attention mechanism based on a heat map of the region of interest in CNN, consisting of the attention branch and perception branch. The attention branch performs class classification based on the input feature map and generates an attention map that represents the region of interest in CNN. The perception branch performs

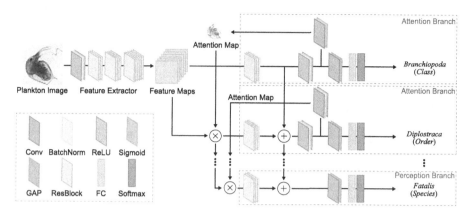

Fig. 2. Overview of the proposed method consisting of ResNet and H-ABN, which is the case of using 5 ranks from *class* to *species*.

class classification based on the features that emphasize the region of interest by multiplying the feature map and the attention map. ABN not only improves the accuracy of general image classification, but has also been demonstrated to be effective in Fine-Grained Recognition for CompCars [19]. Since plankton images often have a uniform background, the attention map indicates the shape of the plankton (or a local region that is useful for classification). By applying ABN from the top to the bottom according to the hierarchical labels of plankton, we expect that plankton images can be classified in consideration of the taxonomic ranks.

3.3 Hierarchical Attention Branch Network

In this paper, we propose Hierarchical Attention Branch Network (H-ABN) that hierarchically applies ABN to the feature maps extracted by CNN according to the hierarchical labels given to the plankton images. Figure 2 shows an overview of the proposed method. The proposed method first extracts feature maps from plankton images using CNN. In this paper, we empirically use ResNet [10] as a feature extractor. Next, the feature maps extracted by CNN are input to H-ABN to classify plankton images. H-ABN consists of multiple attention and perception branches. The number of attention branches is determined by the number of ranks in the taxonomic ranks to be considered. Each attention branch performs class classification for the labels of each taxonomic rank and generates an attention map. Note that the attention branch of the proposed method differs from the original ABN in the following two points. In the proposed method, the attention map is multiplied by the feature map and input to the attention branch one layer below. The features extracted in the upper attention branch are added to the features extracted in the lower attention branch. This is because the features used in the hierarchical classification of plankton images are expected to be effective in the classification of the lower layer as well. The classification

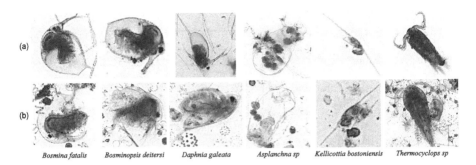

Bosmina fatalis   Bosminopsis deitersi   Daphnia galeata   Asplanchna sp   Kellicottia bostoniensis   Thermocyclops sp

Fig. 3. Examples of plankton images in our dataset: (a) DB1 and (b) DB2, where images of the same *species* are presented.

Table 2. Configuration of our dataset used in the experiments, where all *species* in DB2 are included in DB1.

DB	Train	Val	Test	# of *species*	# of sites
DB1	15,886	2,961	3,799	76	26
DB2	—	—	13,174	44	6

is performed sequentially from the highest attention branch, and finally the classification of the target label is performed in the perception branch. H-ABN takes into account not only the shape of the plankton but also the hierarchical structure of the labels. The features used in the classification of the upper ranks, which are less biased, can be applied to the feature maps of the lower ranks as an attention map, reducing the degradation of the classification accuracy due to label bias. H-ABN is trained using the sum of the cross-entropy losses computed for each branch as the overall loss.

4   Plankton Image Dataset

This section describes the plankton image dataset with labels based on taxonomic ranks used in the experiments. The dataset consists of zooplankton images collected from 32 lakes and marshes in Japan between 2006 and 2022. The plankton community images were obtained by scanning samples with an upright fluorescence microscope (OLYMPUS BX63) at a magnification of 40x. We define a boundary box for each plankton using the Computer Vision Annotation Tool (CVAT)[2] and annotated each plankton with a label of its five taxonomic ranks (*order*, *class*, *family*, *genus*, and *species*). Each plankton was cropped based on the bounding box to obtain 35,820 plankton images. For evaluating the classification accuracy, we divide the dataset into DB1, which consists of plankton images collected at 26 sites, and DB2, which consists of plankton images collected at the other 6 sites, as shown in Table 2. The number of taxonomic labels

[2] https://github.com/opencv/cvat.

in DB1 is 3 for *order*, 7 for *class*, 28 for *family*, 45 for *genus*, and 76 for *species*, while those in DB2 are 3 for *order*, 7 for *class*, 20 for *family*, 28 for *genus*, and 44 for *species*. Note that all 44 plankton *species* in DB2 are included in the 76 *species* in DB1. Figure 3 shows examples of plankton images in DB1 and DB2. As shown in Fig. 3 (a), DB1 contains clear images with little background debris. On the other hand, as shown in Fig. 3 (b), DB2 contains images with a lot of background debris and images partially overlapped with other plankton. Furthermore, the shape of the plankton differs depending on the environment, even if they are the same type of plankton, since the sampling sites are different. The generalizability of the plankton image classification method can be evaluated by training with DB1 and testing with DB2. The dataset in this paper will be available to the public under a research-use license.

5   Experiments and Discussion

This section describes experiments using our dataset to demonstrate the effectiveness of the proposed method in plankton image classification.

In this experiment, we evaluate the fundamental performance using DB1 and the generalizability using DB2, as shown in Table 2. We use 15,886 images of DB1 for training and 3,799 images of DB1 for validation. The plankton image is padded to be square, resized to 224×224 pixels, enhanced by histogram equalization, and used as input for each method. Random flip, random rotation, color jitter, random erasing [21], cutmix [22] are used as data augmentation in training. Random erasing masks rectangular regions of random position and size in the image with black color. The ratio of the masked area to the entire image is 0.002 to 0.2, and the aspect ratio is 0.3 to 3. Cutmix swaps a rectangular region of random position and size between two images and weights the labels in proportion to the size of the rectangular region for each label. The probability of cutmix is set to 0.5 and the parameters α and β are set to 1. In this experiment, we use ResNet-50 pre-trained on ImageNet as the feature extractor of the proposed method. In the proposed method, the perception branch of H-ABN is fixed to *species* and the attention branches of H-ABN are varied from it class to *genus*. Nesterov Accelerated Gradient (NAG) [15] is used as the optimizer, the initial learning rate is 0.001, the batch size is 64, and the number of epochs is 200. We compare the classification accuracy of the proposed method with ResNet-50 [10], ABN [6], and Marginalization Classifier (MC) [4] to demonstrate the effectiveness of the proposed method. MC is an image classification method using hierarchical labels that performs classification in the upper layers based on the predicted probability of each class in the lowest layer estimated by CNN. Experiments on the ETH Entomological Collection dataset have demonstrated that classification accuracy is improved when the hierarchical structure of labels is taken into account. In this experiment, the two ranks (*genus* and *species*) with empirically highest accuracy are used in MC. We use the accuracy, which is the percentage of correct classifications, and the F1-score, which is the harmonic mean of precision and recall, as the evaluation metrics. Note that we use only

Table 3. Results of the experiments using DB1, where the values in bold indicate the highest values of accuracy [%] and F1 score [%] at each rank.

Method	Class Acc. [%] F1 [%]	Order Acc. [%] F1 [%]	Family Acc. [%] F1 [%]	Genus Acc. [%] F1 [%]	Species Acc. [%] F1 [%]
ResNet-50 [10]	99.3	98.6	94.2	93.1	90.5
	99.2	95.3	83.2	79.1	74.9
ABN [6]	99.5	98.8	94.2	92.9	90.5
	99.5	98.1	85.2	80.0	76.6
MC [4]	99.5	98.6	93.9	93.0	90.5
	99.5	94.5	80.8	78.5	74.4
Proposed (G,S)	**99.6**	98.8	94.5	93.6	91.2
	99.6	96.6	**83.1**	79.4	77.5
Proposed (F,G,S)	99.4	98.7	94.2	93.0	90.4
	99.3	97.7	86.1	83.1	**79.2**
Proposed (O,F,G,S)	99.5	**98.9**	**94.9**	**94.1**	**91.8**
	99.5	**97.8**	83.0	80.1	77.8
Proposed (C,O,F,G,S)	99.5	98.8	94.5	93.4	90.8
	99.5	96.9	84.1	80.0	76.9

accuracy for evaluating the results for DB2, since each method uses a model for 76 classifications to perform 44 classifications on DB2.

Table 3 shows the experimental results for each method for DB1. Focusing on the accuracy of *species*, all the methods exceed 90%. Focusing on the F1-score, the proposed methods have a higher F1-score than the conventional methods. In particular, the proposed method with four levels of labels (*order*, *family*, *genus*, and *species*) achieves the highest accuracy. When plankton from the same sampling sites are included in the training and test, all methods can classify plankton with high accuracy.

Table 4 shows the experimental results of each method for DB2. The accuracy of DB2 is lower than that of DB1. The classification accuracy is decreased due to changes in the plankton shape depending on the environment at the sampling site and the large amount of debris in the sample. Focusing on conventional methods, MC is more accurate than ResNet-50 and ABN, since MC classifies images using a hierarchical structure of labels. The proposed method has the highest classification accuracy when all labels in the five ranks are used, since H-ABN takes into account the shape of the plankton step by step from *class* to *species*.

Figure 4 shows examples of plankton images misclassified by the proposed method. Figure 4 (a) shows the misclassified plankton image, the estimated label and the ground-truth label, and Fig. 4 (b) shows the plankton image corresponding to the estimated label of (a). The proposed method correctly classifies up to *genus* and incorrectly in *species* since the global shape is the same. These plankton images are misclassified even by experts since the species differ due to differences in the length of the plankton beard and the shape of the organ.

Table 4. Results of the experiments using DB2, where the values in bold indicate the highest values of accuracy [%] at each rank.

Method	Class Acc. [%]	Order Acc. [%]	Family Acc. [%]	Genus Acc. [%]	Species Acc. [%]
ResNet-50 [10]	88.4	82.2	74.2	64.3	59.1
ABN [6]	88.4	82.5	73.2	64.8	59.5
MC [4]	88.5	83.1	74.8	68.4	63.0
Proposed (G,S)	88.8	84.0	75.8	65.6	60.2
Proposed (F,G,S)	90.3	84.8	77.5	68.6	61.9
Proposed (O,F,G,S)	92.6	86.4	79.0	69.9	64.0
Proposed (C,O,F,G,S)	**93.4**	**88.8**	**80.7**	**71.6**	**65.4**

Hierarchical image classification by H-ABN allows us to fully take into account the shape of the plankton. On the other hand, it is not always possible to distinguish local structural differences, so we are planning to develop a mechanism that can take into account detailed differences in plankton shape.

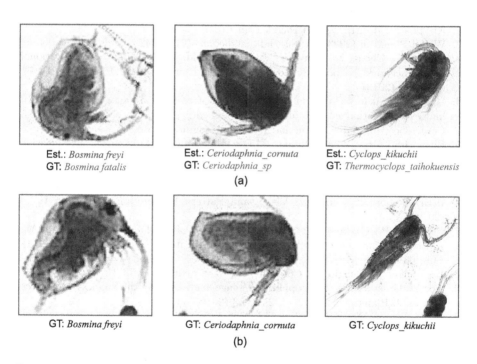

Est.: *Bosmina freyi*
GT: *Bosmina fatalis*

Est.: *Ceriodaphnia_cornuta*
GT: *Ceriodaphnia_sp*

Est.: *Cyclops_kikuchii*
GT: *Thermocyclops_taihokuensis*

(a)

GT: *Bosmina freyi*

GT: *Ceriodaphnia_cornuta*

GT: *Cyclops_kikuchii*

(b)

Fig. 4. Examples of plankton images misclassified by the proposed method: (a) misclassified plankton image, estimated label, and ground-truth label and (b) plankton image corresponding to the label estimated in (a).

6   Conclusion

We proposed the plankton image classification method using Hierarchical Attention Branch Network (H-ABN) to take into account the taxonomic ranks of the plankton. We also constructed a plankton image dataset by annotating labels based on the taxonomic ranks to samples collected in Japanese lakes and marshes to classify plankton images according to the taxonomic ranks, We demonstrated the effectiveness of the proposed method in plankton image classification through performance evaluation experiments using the constructed plankton image dataset. In the future, we plan to investigate a classification method that focuses on the fine structure of plankton and an automatic plankton detection method from plankton community images.

Acknowledgments. We thank Ryotaro Yoshida for his contribution to this study. This work was supported by ERCA ERTDF Program Grant Number JPMEERF20214003.

References

1. Kaggle (2015). https://www.kaggle.com/c/datasciencebowl
2. WHOI-Plankton (2023). https://hdl.handle.net/1912/7342
3. Cheng, K., Cheng, X., Wang, Y., Bi, H., Benfield, M.C.: Enhanced convolutional neural network for plankton identification and enumeration. PLoS One **14**(7), e0219570 (2019)
4. Dhall, A., Makarova, A., Ganea, O., Pavllo, D., Greeff, M., Krause, A.: Hierarchical image classification using entailment cone embeddings. In: Proceedings of the IEEE Conference Computer Vision and Pattern Recognition, pp. 836–837 (2020)
5. Ellen, J.S., Graff, C.A., Ohman, M.D.: Improving plankton image classification using context metadata. Limnol. Oceanogr. Methods **17**(8), 439–461 (2019)
6. Fukui, H., Hirakawa, T., Yamashita, T., Fujiyoshi, H.: Attention branch network: learning of a attention mechanism for visual explanation. In: Proceedings of the IEEE Conference Computer Vision and Pattern Recognition, pp. 10705–10714 (2019)
7. González, P., Castaño, A., Peacock, E.E., Díez, J., Del Coz, J.J., Sosik, H.M.: Automatic plankton quantification using deep features. J. Plankton Res. **41**(4), 449–463 (2019)
8. Goodfellow, I., Bengio, Y., Courville, A.: Deep Learning. MIT Press (2016)
9. Gorsky, G., et al.: Digital zooplankton image analysis using the ZooScan integrated system. J. Plankton Res. **32**(3), 285–303 (2010)
10. He, K., Zhang, X., Ren, S., Sun, J.: Deep residual learning for image recognition. In: Proceedings of the IEEE Conference Computer Vision and Pattern Recognition, pp. 770–778 (2016)
11. Kyathanahally, S.P., et al.: Deep learning classification of lake zooplankton. Front. Microbiol. **12**, 3226–3238 (2021)
12. Lumini, A., Nanni, L.: Deep learning and transfer learning features for plankton classification. Eco. Inform. **51**, 33–43 (2019)
13. Lumini, A., Nanni, L., Maguolo, G.: Deep learning for plankton and coral classification. Appl. Comput. Inform. **19**(3/4), 265–283 (2023). https://doi.org/10.1016/j.aci.2019.11.004

14. Luo, J.Y., et al.: Automated plankton image analysis using convolutional neural networks. Limnol. Oceanogr. Methods **16**(12), 814–827 (2018)
15. Nesterov, Y.: A method of solving a convex programming problem with convergence rate $O(1/k2)$. Soviet Mathematics Doklady **27**(2), 372–376 (1983)
16. Silva, N.L., Marcolin, C.R., Schwamborn, R.: Using image analysis to assess the contributions of plankton and particles to tropical coastal ecosystems. Estuar. Coast. Shelf Sci. **219**, 252–261 (2019)
17. Sosik, H.M., Olson, R.J.: Automated taxonomic classification of phytoplankton sampled with imaging-in-flow cytometry. Limnol. Oceanogr. Methods **5**(6), 204–216 (2007)
18. Suthers, I., Rissik, D., Richardson, A.: Plankton: A Guide to Their Ecology and Monitoring for Water Quality. CSIRO (2019)
19. Yang, L., Luo, P., Loy, C.C., Tang, X.: A large-scale car dataset for fine-grained categorization and verification. In: Proceedings of the IEEE Conference Computer Vision and Pattern Recognition, pp. 3973–3981 (2015)
20. Zheng, H., Wang, R., Yu, Z., Wang, N., Gu, Z., Zheng, B.: Automatic plankton image classification combining multiple view features via multiple kernel learning. BMC Bioinform. **18**(16), 1–18 (2017)
21. Zhong, Z., Zheng, L., Kang, G., Li, S., Yang, Y.: Random erasing data augmentation. Proc. AAAI Conf. Artif. Intell. **34**(7), 13001–13008 (2020)
22. Zhou, B., Khosla, A., Lapedriza, A., Oliva, A., Torralba, A.: CutMix: regularization strategy to train strong classifiers with localizable features. In: Proceedings of the IEEE Conference Computer Vision and Pattern Recognition, pp. 6023–6032 (2019)

Author Index

H. Lu et al. (Eds.): ACPR 2023, LNCS 14407, pp. 421–425, 2023.
https://doi.org/10.1007/978-3-031-47637-2

Printed in the United States
by Baker & Taylor Publisher Services